THREE PEOPLES, ONE KING

THREE PEOPLES

ONE KING

*Loyalists, Indians,
and Slaves in the
Revolutionary South,
1775–1782*

JIM PIECUCH

THE UNIVERSITY OF SOUTH CAROLINA PRESS

© 2008 James Piecuch

Published by the University of South Carolina Press
Columbia, South Carolina 29208

www.sc.edu/uscpress

Manufactured in the United States of America

17 16 15 14 13 12 11 10 09 08   10 9 8 7 6 5 4 3 2 1

Library of Congress Cataloging-in-Publication Data

Piecuch, Jim.
Three peoples, one king : loyalists, Indians, and slaves in the revolutionary South,
1775-1782 / Jim Piecuch.
    p. cm.
    Includes bibliographical references and index.
    ISBN 978-1-57003-737-5 (cloth : alk. paper)
1. Southern States—History—Revolution, 1775–1783. 2. South Carolina—History—
Revolution, 1775–1783. 3. Georgia—History—Revolution, 1775–1783. 4. United
States—History—Revolution, 1775–1783—British forces. 5. American loyalists—
Southern States. 6. Indians of North America—Southern States—History—18th
century. 7. Slaves—Southern States—History—18th century. I. Title.
    E230.5.S7P54 2008
    973.3′140975—dc22

                                        2008006203

To all those courageous Americans—white, red, and black—who gave their lives during the Revolution in the hope of creating a different future for America within the British Empire

CONTENTS

ILLUSTRATIONS

Maps

PREFACE

Certain terms used in this book require a brief explanation. When referring to those American colonists who supported the British, I have used the term "Loyalists" throughout the text, forgoing use of the synonym "Tories," which had a derogatory connotation in the Revolutionary era. When quoting from sources, however, I left the terms "Tory" and "Tories" unaltered. I have used the terms "Whigs," "rebels," and "Americans" interchangeably when referring to those colonists who supported the Revolution. To maintain consistency with the documentary sources, I have used the term "Indians" rather than "Native Americans." The terms "blacks," "slaves," and "African Americans" are used interchangeably. In those rare instances involving blacks who were not slaves, I have indicated their free status. Charleston, South Carolina, was spelled "Charles Town," "Charlestown," and "Charleston" during the 1770s and 1780s; I have left the original spelling intact in quotations but used "Charleston" uniformly in the text.

In manuscript collections in which each page is numbered, such as the Cornwallis Papers, I have given only the number of the first page of the cited document in the endnotes. The information or quotation from that document may appear on a subsequent page or pages. To reduce the length of the endnotes, I have employed several abbreviations for sources and archives. A list of these abbreviations precedes the notes.

ACKNOWLEDGMENTS

The completion of a work of this magnitude requires the assistance of many people. I would like to thank Professor James Axtell of the College of William & Mary for his guidance and support, along with Professors James Whittenburg and Ronald Schechter of William & Mary and Eliga Gould of the University of New Hampshire for their advice.

I am grateful to the David Library of the American Revolution, the Institute of Southern Studies at the University of South Carolina, and the William L. Clements Library for providing fellowship support, and to the College of William & Mary for providing several research grants. Many archivists and librarians also provided valuable assistance, and although space does not permit me to list them all, Sam Fore and Henry Fulmer of the South Caroliniana Library, John Dann and the staff of the Clements Library, Kathy Ludwig and the staff of the David Library, Linda Baier of the Harriet C. Irving Library at the University of New Brunswick, and the staffs at the Library of Congress, the Georgia Historical Society, and the Earl Gregg Swem Library at the College of William & Mary merit special thanks.

Anne Yehl also deserves thanks for an outstanding job in assisting me with research.

In conclusion I want to express my gratitude to my wife, Lori, and son, Joey, for their patience and support, and to my Siberian huskies, Shyleea and Max, who knew that a long run in the woods can be the best remedy for writer's block.

Introduction

ON THE MORNING OF DECEMBER 14, 1782, the weak winter sun revealed dozens of British ships clogging the waters of Charleston harbor in South Carolina, waiting for the shift of the tide that would carry them over the bar and out into the Atlantic. Throngs of people, blacks as well as whites, crowded the decks, the murmurs of thousands of voices drowning out the sounds of water lapping against wooden hulls, of masts and spars creaking in the wind. The passengers discussed with sadness the events that had led them to this point, and the uncertain future that lay ahead.

Hundreds of miles to the west, in towns scattered throughout the wilderness between the Appalachians and the Mississippi River, thousands of Native Americans also pondered their past and their future. Like their black and white counterparts aboard the evacuation fleet, they had committed themselves to supporting the royal cause in the American Revolution. That cause was now irretrievably lost. Yet all of those who had fought for it—black, red, and white Americans; British and German soldiers—had made great efforts on behalf of King George III. The proof of their commitment could be found in the thousands of graves that seeded the soil of South Carolina, Georgia, and East and West Florida, from the Atlantic Ocean to the Mississippi, from the Gulf of Mexico to the Ohio River. It could be found in the ashes of burned Indian towns, in the bloody scars left by whips across the backs of slaves who had fled to the British, in the once-prosperous farms and plantations lying desolate after having been confiscated by the victorious American rebels.

In that gloomy December, white Loyalists, African Americans, and Native Americans all wondered how things had gone so very wrong, how the hopes they had entertained for their future within the British Empire, which had dimmed and flared so many times during the past seven and one-half years, had finally been extinguished. Had they themselves failed to do enough? Did the British government fail them? Or were there other reasons for the distressing outcome of the war? Whatever conclusion they reached, one thing was certain: this was not the fate that anyone among them had envisioned in 1775.

British officials had certainly not expected such an outcome either. From the start of the American Revolution, King George III and his ministers believed that the support of the numerous southern Loyalists, Indians, and slaves would enable the army to restore royal authority in Georgia and South Carolina with relative ease. Yet, despite a promising start when British forces finally launched a campaign in the South at the end of 1778, the effort eventually failed. In the aftermath of defeat, British leaders devoted little effort to an analysis of the reasons for the failure of their southern operations, focusing instead on blaming their political opponents, or avoiding blame themselves, for the lost war.

Historians, however, have since sought to explain why the British failed to regain control of South Carolina and Georgia. Most attribute the British defeat to a fundamental error in planning the southern campaign: officials in London "grossly exaggerated the extent of loyalism in the South."[1] Don Higginbotham wrote that the decision to undertake the southern campaign was made because the ministry "mistakenly thought great Tory strength lay slumbering in the South."[2] He blamed the royal governors for "disseminating false information" in this regard, thus creating the "illusion" of numerous Loyalists in the South.[3] The eminent British historian Sir John Fortescue stated that the British based their military plans for the southern colonies "on the presumed support of a section of the inhabitants. Of all the foundations whereon to build the conduct of a campaign this is the loosest, the most treacherous, the fullest of peril and delusion." It was not surprising, Fortescue declared, that the campaign met "with the invariable consequence of failure and disaster. . . . The mere fact that the British Ministry rested its hopes on the co-operation of the American loyalists was sufficient to distract its councils and vitiate its plans."[4] Piers Mackesy likewise wrote that the "real miscalculation" made by British officials in their planning "was the strength and vitality of the loyalists."[5] Elsewhere he asserted that British planning was handicapped by advice from "biased and out-of-touch loyalists" who convinced the king's ministers that large numbers of Loyalists stood ready to assist British troops.[6] Continuing in the same vein, David K. Wilson insisted that British strategy in the South was based "on the erroneous premise that the majority of the population in the southern colonies was loyal to the king" and criticized British leaders for clinging to this idea "notwithstanding the accumulation of considerable evidence to the contrary."[7] Those who have written on the southern campaign for a popular audience generally share these opinions.[8]

Only a few historians believe that British officials had been fairly accurate in their appraisal of Loyalist strength in the South. John Shy insisted that the British assessment of the numbers of southern Loyalists was at least partially correct, writing that "British estimates of American attitudes were frequently in error, but seldom were they completely mistaken."[9] John Richard Alden went a step further, describing southern Loyalists as "numerous, vigorous and dangerous," and noting that Loyalists comprised a large proportion of the population in both South Carolina and Georgia.[10]

Those who concede that British officials were generally correct in believing that Loyalists were relatively numerous in the South nonetheless argue that southern Loyalists failed to come forward and actively assist the British.[11] Some of these historians attribute this lack of Loyalist support to flaws in British policy, as well as to the Loyalists' essentially passive nature. In his study of the Loyalists' role in British planning, Paul H. Smith found that British officials had no consistent policy regarding the employment of Loyalists in support of the army. "The capacity of the Loyalists to affect the outcome of the war, their real ability to thwart the aims of the Revolution, was directly tied to their projected role in British plans to end the rebellion," he wrote. "Since they were almost entirely dependent upon British military decisions, their part can be understood only in terms of British efforts to organize them. For this reason it is fruitless to attempt to assess their contribution in terms of their strength, concentration, attitudes, and military capacity, without examining British plans for their mobilization."[12]

Smith described the British attitude toward Loyalists as one of "ambivalence," with the ministers "eager to use them and unwilling to make the concessions and detailed preparations required to weld them into an efficient force." He concluded that "the Loyalists never occupied a fixed, well-understood place in British strategy. Plans to use them were in the main *ad hoc* responses to constantly changing conditions."[13] In addition, Smith stated that British leaders never fully understood the Loyalists, whom he described as "conservative, cautious, abhorring violence. . . . The Loyalist's virtues were military weaknesses. He was generally uncertain of his position, and was disinclined to commit himself boldly. He was more likely to hesitate than to volunteer, to watch on the sidelines than to fight openly."[14] This has become the prevailing view among historians. With regard to South Carolina, Wallace Brown declared that Loyalists there "are exceptionally open to the charge of timidity and equivocation."[15] Ann Gorman Condon wrote that "American historians have been inclined to dismiss [Loyalists] as weak and unimaginative hangers-on, as lackeys of the Crown."[16]

Such criticism of the southern Loyalists, which originated during the Revolution and continues to pervade the secondary literature, has proved to be an obstacle to an accurate assessment of Loyalist contributions to the British effort to regain control of the southern provinces. Denunciations of the Loyalists came from both British and American writers. Lt. Gen. Charles, Earl Cornwallis, commander of the British southern department, described loyal South Carolinians in November 1780 as "dastardly and pusillanimous."[17] Cornwallis's complaints earned him the sympathy of a French observer, the marquis de Chastellux, who wrote that it was the British general's sad fate "to conduct, rather than command, a numerous band of traitors and robbers, which English policy decorated with the name of *Loyalists*. This rabble preceded the troops in plunder, taking special care never to follow them in danger. Their progress was marked by fire, devastation, and outrages of every kind."[18] The views expressed by Cornwallis and Chastellux demonstrate a paradox in opinions of the Loyalists. On one hand, Loyalists are criticized as passive, while on the other, they are assailed as brutal, vengeance-driven purveyors of death and destruction.

The earliest American historians of the Revolution in the South, writing in the heat of anti-British sentiment that persisted well into the nineteenth century, established this portrait of Loyalists as venal, bloodthirsty traitors to the glorious American cause.[19] By the 1850s this had become the standard historical account. In 1851 Joseph Johnson blamed the Loyalists for both the viciousness of the war in South Carolina and the harsh measures the Whigs applied against the Loyalists. "They caused the horrors of a civil war, by which the country was desolated; and with it, the vindictive or retaliatory acts, the banishment, sequestration, and the destruction of life and property, on both sides," Johnson asserted.[20] Those who joined the loyal militia in the South Carolina backcountry in 1780 "were the most profligate and corrupt men in the country," M. A. Moore declared in 1859.[21]

Attacks on the Loyalists also became a staple in fictional works. The nineteenth-century writer William Gilmore Simms published a series of historical novels based on events in Revolutionary South Carolina, many of which first appeared in serial form in magazines and have been frequently reprinted. "Simms never treated the Loyalists with either sympathy or admiration," one historian noted in polite understatement.[22] In his novel *Joscelyn,* for example, Simms describes Loyalist leader Thomas Brown as a drunkard, "a savage, a brute, in many respects, ferocious and cruel." Simms portrays Moses Kirkland, another prominent Loyalist, as an incompetent coward.[23] Loyalist partisans practice "lust, and murder, and spoliation" in Simms's *The Scout.*[24] Similar themes pervade the rest of Simms's Revolutionary novels, such as *Eutaw.*[25]

The trend of depicting the Revolution in the South as a clear-cut conflict between good and evil, the former personified by the American rebels and the latter by their opponents, continued with the work of Lyman C. Draper, who has been described as a "hero-worshiper and patriot" and "a maker of heroes."[26] Draper's account of the Battle of King's Mountain glorified the brutal overmountain men who butchered Patrick Ferguson and his Loyalist detachment.[27] Later historians have given these early histories far more weight than they deserve, either accepting them at face value or insufficiently questioning their overall accuracy.

Canadian historian Thomas Raddall identified an important reason why Loyalists have seldom received fair treatment in accounts of the Revolution. He observed that for Americans, the struggle for independence "was an epic story to be written in epic fashion, with scant regard for the other side of the argument, indeed with scant regard for the truth where the truth diminished in any way the glory of their achievement." Raddall asserted that as a result, while the rebels' cause was "fundamentally just," historians have ignored the often less-than-heroic means the rebels employed in order to succeed, along with "the persecutions, the confiscations and banishment they inflicted upon their fellow-Americans."[28]

Thus the violent nature of the Revolution in the South has often been over-looked, except when acts of cruelty can be attributed to the British or Loyalists. Participants in the Revolution and later historians have ignored, downplayed, or attempted to justify the brutality with which Americans treated their enemies, for such viciousness contradicted the very ideals for which the rebels fought. As Charles Royster observed, American revolutionaries "agreed that the future of American liberty depended first on winning the war and second on how the war was won. Liberty could survive, many Americans believed, only if the people showed themselves to be worthy defenders of it."[29] The rebels soon learned, how-ever, that winning the war often required measures that contrasted sharply with the ideals of their cause. Rather than recognize their willingness to sacrifice prin-ciple in the name of necessity, most revolutionaries found it easier to blame the British and Loyalists for initiating acts of cruelty, leaving the Americans no choice but to retaliate in kind. Historians too chose this more palatable course.

Higginbotham, in one example of this practice, wrote that "brutality and sav-agery . . . had no appeal for the Americans in 1775." He described the revolutionar-ies' goal as "organized resistance carried out with restraint," while noting "the absence of British suppression and American vengeance." Noting that the conflict in the South was exceptional for its high level of violence, Higginbotham blamed this on the Loyalists. He described them as "for the most part angry, bitter men" who "wanted a course of harsh retribution" against their former oppressors. The "bloodthirsty loyalists" drove the Americans "into open defiance," while influenc-ing Banastre Tarleton, Patrick Ferguson, Lord Rawdon, and other British officers "most exposed to tory opinions" to embrace harsh, coercive policies.[30]

Some writers concede that the Whigs were occasionally guilty of acts of vio-lence and cruelty but continue to insist that the British and Loyalists behaved much worse. Cynthia A. Kierner wrote that "scholars and contemporaries agree that the Whigs were less ruthless than their opponents. . . . Tories and British regulars terrorized the backcountry's civilian population, murdering, plundering, taking prisoners, and causing chaos in many communities."[31] Walter Edgar argued that British occupation policy in the South depended on cruelty for its success: "From Charles, Lord Cornwallis, to the humblest Tory militiaman, the occupying forces believed that fear and brutality would cow the populace." Edgar blamed the British for the atrocities committed by both sides, stating that they "were initiated by British regulars or their Tory allies. Patriot militia bands responded in kind, and the violence escalated into a fury that laid waste to entire communities."[32]

Few historians have challenged this view. Fortescue described the rebel mili-tia's "intimidation of loyalists" as a form of "terrorism" that "soon degenerated into indiscriminate robbery and violence," leading to Loyalist retaliation and "in Carolina, a civil war of unsurpassed ferocity."[33] Martha Condray Searcy was even more emphatic in placing responsibility for the violence in the South on the Whigs. "The rebels began the violence," she wrote, referring to the outbreak of the Revolution in Georgia, and added that no evidence indicates that Georgia Loyalists retaliated in kind.[34]

Two other obstacles to an accurate assessment of the numerical strength of the southern Loyalists, their contribution to the royal cause, and the soundness of British plans based on the expectation of Loyalist support are the difficulty in gauging the Loyalists' numbers and the fact that the allegiance of many southerners frequently shifted from one side to another. Statistical evidence of Loyalist strength in the South derives from the claims submitted to the British government after the war by Loyalists seeking compensation for their losses. These data indicate that loyalism was more common in South Carolina and Georgia than in any other colony except New York, but claims were filed by only a small fraction of Loyalists, making any evidence derived from the claims incomplete.[35]

People in the southern colonies supported the British cause for a variety of reasons, some of which had more to do with local conditions than with attitudes toward imperial governance.[36] Other colonists were neutral or not firmly committed to either side, so that in addition to the contest between staunch Loyalists and Whigs, the Revolution in the South was "a struggle for the allegiance of the rank-and-file of the colonies' white population."[37] In a study of political allegiance in Revolutionary Georgia, Leslie Hall concluded that many people adhered to whichever side was best able to provide them with land or protect their claims to the land they owned.[38] Rachel Klein, explaining the rebels' success in controlling the South Carolina interior, wrote that "the whigs more consistently represented the broad class interests of rising backcountry slaveowners."[39] While these assertions are undoubtedly true so far as neutral southerners and lukewarm Whigs and Loyalists are concerned, they overlook those whose loyalism arose from a commitment to political principles, and which led them to sacrifice their land and economic prospects rather than forsake their allegiance to Great Britain.

Given the preponderance of opinion, is it possible to come to any other conclusion than the prevailing one that British policy in the South was fundamentally flawed, based on chimerical predictions of Loyalist support provided by biased Loyalists and royal officials? Or that the few southern Loyalists were either passive or brutal, and thus of little use to the British? In fact, a careful study of the documentary evidence leads to very different conclusions. Casting aside the unsubstantiated reminiscences that constituted many of the early histories of the Revolution in the South, and carefully analyzing contemporary accounts from both British and American sources, reveals that British officials were indeed correct in believing that large numbers of Loyalists inhabited Georgia and South Carolina, and that they would contribute greatly to the effort to restore royal authority in those provinces.

The best evidence for this can be found by comparing British assessments of Loyalist strength in the South with those made by their American opponents. When compared, the reports are virtually interchangeable. Biased and out of touch the Loyalist exiles and royal officials may have been; yet Americans in the South held identical opinions in regard to the numbers and military potential of the Loyalists, as well as of the possible dangers that would arise if Indians and slaves assisted the king's forces. American generals Robert Howe, Benjamin Lincoln, and Nathanael Greene and civil officials such as South Carolina governor John Rutledge did not share the Loyalists' biases, and they were certainly not out of touch: they were on the scene and in close contact with the inhabitants of the southern provinces.

This suggests that British officials based their plans to regain control of the Deep South colonies on accurate information, and the evidence further demonstrates that when British troops arrived in the South, large numbers of Loyalists came forward to assist them. Some Loyalists did hesitate to openly support the British, not from a "passive" nature but from fear instilled by years of persecution at the hands of the rebels. The unremitting campaign of Whig cruelty, which far surpassed the brutality attributed to the Loyalists, also eventually drove many loyal Americans to abandon their allegiance to Britain in order to escape continued suffering. The British failed to restore royal authority in Georgia and South Carolina, not because Loyalists were too few, too passive, or too cruel, but because the rebels relentlessly murdered, imprisoned, abused, and intimidated those who supported the king's government. Many British officers recognized this situation and sympathized with the Loyalists' plight. "The richest loyalist runs the risk of becoming a beggar" if left unprotected by the British army, a Hessian officer noted in 1778.[40]

Like the Loyalists, Indians constituted one of the pillars on which British hopes for the reconquest of the southern provinces rested. Also like the Loyalists, the Indians have been criticized for providing inadequate support to the British and for committing acts of cruelty that drove many white southerners into the rebel camp. As James H. O'Donnell III noted, "the general theme that the Indian was an utter villain" arose during the Revolution and "would continue to distort historical accounts."[41] Peter Marshall believed that "a strong case can be made for the view that the horror aroused by Indian participation in military campaigns far exceeded the assistance thus secured by either side."[42] Edward J. Cashin asserted that the British should have avoided using Indians altogether. "The decision to use Indians was a major miscalculation by the British high command," he wrote, adding that the policy insured that land-hungry backcountry settlers, most of whom were "Indian haters," would support the rebels.[43]

Cashin based his opinion on the erroneous assumption that if British officials had not called upon the Indians for support, the latter would have remained idle spectators to the Anglo-American conflict. Indians recognized that they had a great stake in the outcome of the Revolution, and they would have participated regardless of what British ministers in London decided. "The logic of nearly two hundred years of abrasive contact with colonizing Europeans compelled the choice" most Indians made to support Britain, Gary Nash observed, since it was the colonists "who most threatened Indian autonomy," whereas for more than a decade the British government had attempted to halt the influx of settlers onto Indian land.[44]

British officials did make several errors in their plans to use Indians against the rebels. First, the ministers assumed that the Indians would act only when instructed to do so by British Indian agents, overlooking the fact that the Indians were independent allies who preferred to fight the colonists on their own terms, which did not always coincide with British plans. Second, British leaders tended to think of the southern tribes as a single entity, overlooking the divisions between the four southern Indian nations, some of which had been aggravated by Britain's own Indian agents in order to provide security for the colonists by promoting animosity among the Indians. Furthermore, all of the major southern Indian nations, except the Chickasaws, were riven by internal dissension that made unified action by even a single nation difficult to achieve. Third, British officials failed to realize the animosity that existed between the Indians and back-country whites, regardless of whether the latter were Loyalists or Whigs. This produced the paradox of committed Loyalists alternately fighting the rebels and joining with their white opponents against their erstwhile Indian allies. Despite these flaws in British policy, southern Indians did contribute significantly to the British effort in the South; even when they remained inactive, the Indians constituted a potential threat that rebel leaders could not ignore, and the mere rumor of an Indian attack frequently diverted Whig militia and regular troops that would otherwise have been employed against the British and Loyalists. Responding to the Indian menace in the same manner as they dealt with the Loyalists, the Whigs unleashed a torrent of brutality to suppress their Indian enemies and intimidate them into withdrawing from the conflict.

The role of Britain's third group of supporters in the South, African American slaves, was overlooked for nearly two centuries. Most historians followed the path of David Ramsay, the South Carolina rebel who wrote in his influential history of the Revolution that slaves were "so well satisfied with their condition, that several have been known to reject proffered freedom . . . emancipation does not appear to be the wish of the generality of them."[45] Ramsay could not have helped personally observing the flight of thousands of slaves to the British; he and those who wrote afterward evidently preferred to write histories that would please themselves and their patriotic readers rather than face the unpleasant fact that for most African Americans, it was the British, not the Whigs, who provided the opportunity to gain liberty. As Nash noted, "the American Revolution represents the largest slave uprising" in American history. "Discovering the power of the revolutionary ideology of protest, slaves found the greatest opportunities for applying it by fleeing to the very forces against which Americans directed their ideological barbs."[46] Nash added that this uprising "was carried on individually rather than collectively for the most part, because circumstances favored individualized struggles for freedom."⁴⁷ The war "gave slaves new leverage to challenge both the institution of chattel bondage and the allied structures of white supremacy." Divisions in the planter class between Whigs and Loyalists shattered the white unity on which the slave system depended, and these divisions allowed slaves to seize opportunities to alter their status that arose amid the wartime chaos.⁴⁸

Driven by their desire for freedom, African Americans refused to remain idle during the struggle. "Whatever the schemes of patriot and tory leaders during 1775, local slave leaders . . . were attentive and active participants rather than ignorant and passive objects," Peter H. Wood wrote. "Black activists sought to capitalize on the white struggle in their plans for freedom fully as much as white factions tried to implicate half a million blacks in their political designs."⁴⁹ Most slaves, hoping to escape bondage amid the tumult of war, naturally looked to the British. Many slaves had heard of the Somerset case, tried in England in 1772, in which James Somerset, a slave brought to Britain in 1769, sued for his freedom. Although Chief Justice Lord Mansfield was reluctant to issue a decision that would emancipate the fourteen thousand slaves then in England, he eventually ordered Somerset released. Mansfield's ruling effectively abolished slavery in Great Britain.⁵⁰ Some American slaves had concluded that they would be free if they could somehow get to England. The slaves had not forgotten this when the war began. Even if the British army did not offer them outright emancipation, slaves were "accustomed to sorting out degrees of exploitation. If their goal was freedom, the British offered the quickest route to it, almost the only route, in fact, in the South."⁵¹

Although British leaders recognized that slaves were likely to assist them in their efforts to suppress the rebellion and discussed various means of employing them, the ministry never settled on a policy for the use of slaves. This is hardly surprising, since royal officials recognized that any tampering with the institution of slavery risked doing more harm than good to the king's cause. The status and wealth of many southern colonists were inextricably linked to slave ownership.⁵² Furthermore, the constant danger of slave revolt filled white southerners with "a chilling fear which even the rhythmic tedium of daily life could never entirely smother." Few white inhabitants of Georgia or South Carolina, whatever their political opinions, could contemplate any change in the slave system unaccompanied by violent upheaval. "A successful insurrection loomed as total destruction, as the irretrievable loss of all that white men had won in America." It would be a "social revolution" that was "wholly destructive" of southern white society.⁵³ The Whigs, in fact, capitalized on rumors that the British government planned to arm slaves; they did it to motivate their supporters and to try to bring Loyalists into the rebel camp. "The latent distrust of the slave seems to have been deliberately exploited by Southern patriots as a means of arousing animosity toward the British and of coercing those who were lukewarm or timid about breaking with England," Benjamin Quarles wrote; "such propaganda was effective in stilling any inclination to make a warrior of the Negro."[54]

The British government's failure to establish an official policy concerning slaves meant that, as Ira Berlin observed, "the British proved to be unreliable liberators . . . as they feared identification as the slaves' friend would drive slaveholding Loyalists into the Patriot camp." When forced to deal with large numbers of runaway slaves, "British commanders wavered," which "made it impossible for fugitives to predict whether they would be greeted as freed people or slaves, treated as allies or spoils of war." Yet, if this inconsistency prevented many slaves from fleeing to the British, southern slaves clearly understood that they could not expect any opportunity for freedom from the Whigs.[55]

The limited use that the British made of slaves antagonized many rebels and alienated some Loyalists, although not all southern whites embraced the institution of slavery. In the backcountry, where loyalism was strongest, "white frontiersmen with little sympathy for the nabobs of the tidewater sometimes sheltered such black men and women" who had run away from their masters, "employing them with no questions asked."[56] Nevertheless, Sylvia R. Frey went so far as to assert that in 1780 "the South Carolina pacification program broke down primarily because of British attempts to use slaves as weapons against their masters."[57] This is a considerable overstatement, since British officials tried to disrupt the system of slavery as little as possible. Although the British often employed rebel-owned slaves in noncombat roles with the army, many others, whether owned by Whigs or Loyalists, were returned to their plantations. In the end, British reluctance to draw on the support of African Americans to the fullest possible extent hurt the royal cause by depriving the British of a valuable resource. Already outraged at the limited use the British had made of slaves, the Whigs' animosity could not have been made much worse, and any dissatisfaction arising among white Loyalists from the creation of large units of black troops would have been more than offset by the accession of strength to the British army. Even in a restricted role, African Americans made significant contributions to the British effort to regain the southern provinces, and their potential had not come close to being fully realized.

As was the case with Loyalists and Indians, the rebels responded ruthlessly to the threat from their slaves. Again, historians have tended to overlook this aspect of the Revolution in the South. Wood attributed this to a desire on the part of most Americans to preserve the idea that the Revolution, a noble cause, was fought and won by noble Americans in a noble manner. "After all," Wood wrote, "the Revolutionary Era remains the most closely guarded treasure in our national mythology. Adding too much realistic detail about the situation of African Americans at the moment when the colonies were declaring their independence might well, in the words of James Baldwin, 'reveal more about America to Americans than Americans wish to know.'"[58]

Had British leaders chosen to arm large numbers of slaves, they might have faced much difficulty in coordinating the actions of Indians and blacks because they would have had to overcome the effects of their own previous colonial policies. William S. Willis observed that "the Colonial Southeast was the only place where Indians, Whites, and Negroes met in large numbers." Since the colonists constituted "a frightened and dominant White minority [that] faced two exploited colored majorities," colonial officials "willfully helped create ... antagonism between Indians and Negroes in order to preserve themselves and their privileges" from the danger of combined Indian-slave opposition.[59] The methods used to promote animosity between slaves and Indians included laws prohibiting blacks from entering Indian lands and hiring Indians to capture runaway slaves. These policies were partially effective, although J. Leitch Wright noted that the policy "failed as often as it succeeded ... Africans and Indians intermingled, learned each others' language, intermarried, and at times made common cause against whites."[60]

Unifying white Loyalists, Indians, and slaves in a common effort to aid the British army in retaking Georgia and South Carolina would certainly have been a difficult, but not impossible, task. The British belief that these three diverse peoples would be the means by which royal authority would be restored in the southern colonies can be likened metaphorically to a rope in which each of the three groups was a strand; once braided together, this rope would be strong enough to bind South Carolina and Georgia to the British Empire. British officials correctly expected considerable Loyalist support; however, they failed to realize the divisions within the Indian nations, as well as the utter lack of harmony among Loyalists, Indians, and slaves, which complicated any attempt to bring them to act in concert. In addition, neither Indians nor slaves were so pliable as to act only when and if the British government demanded their assistance. The Indian nations pursued their own interests as allies rather than as subjects of King George, while African Americans challenged British hesitance to employ them by fleeing in large numbers to the British army and offering their support. Frustrated at their inability to direct the Indians and fearful of the consequences of arming slaves, British officials relied primarily on the Loyalists; made little effort to encourage cooperation between Loyalists, Indians, and slaves; and thus deprived themselves of the full strength that would have accrued to them by fully mobilizing and unifying their diverse supporters. This enabled the rebels to suppress the Loyalists and Indians separately, while only a fraction of the vast potential of southern slaves to support the British was brought to bear against the Whigs. As a result, Britain's southern strategy, although sound in conception, failed because the ministers formed no detailed plan for its execution. Yet, in spite of this impediment, Loyalists, Indians, and slaves contributed far more to the British effort to retake South Carolina and Georgia than has been previously recognized. What is striking about their role in the southern provinces is not that they contributed so little but that, in the face of unremitting, brutal opposition, they contributed so much.

The geographic scope of most histories of the Revolution in the South encompasses Georgia, the Carolinas, and Virginia. This study shifts the regional focus to South Carolina, Georgia, East Florida, and West Florida, which permits a more coherent analysis of the roles of Loyalists, Indians, and slaves. The Floridas were the homeland of three of the Indian nations allied to the British, served as refuges for southern Loyalists and slaves seeking to escape the Whigs, and functioned as bases from which British regulars, Loyalists, and Indians operated against the frontiers of Georgia and South Carolina. While the recapture of North Carolina and Virginia constituted key elements in the British southern strategy, the British made no sustained effort to mobilize their supporters in Virginia, while their efforts to do so in North Carolina were brief except in the vicinity of Wilmington.

This regional study of the American Revolution is undertaken from the perspective of the British and their supporters. As such, it seeks to correct the exaggerated tales of untarnished American valor and the unmitigated perfidy of those who adhered to the royal cause. The result is an often unflattering portrayal of the Whigs, while Loyalist, Indian, and slave supporters of the British appear in a more favorable light than is usual. An objective analysis of the sources permits no other interpretation. As Nash stated, "for many of the people of North America the struggle for life, liberty, and the pursuit of happiness in the 1770s and 1780s was carried on by fighting with the British and against those American patriots upon whom our patriotic celebrations have always exclusively focused."[61] Those peoples—white, red, and black—who supported King George III do not deserve to be ignored or unjustly criticized by historians solely because they pursued a different dream for America's future.

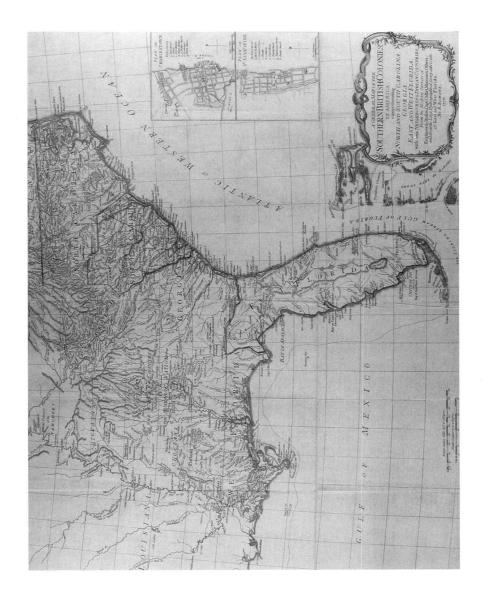

ONE

Revolution Comes
to the Deep South

BETWEEN 1763 AND 1775 the dispute between Great Britain and several of the North American colonies over the issue of taxation grew increasingly bitter. American Whigs refused to concede that the British Parliament had the authority to tax the provinces, while British officials believed that parliamentary sovereignty was the foundation on which the empire rested and would not consider surrendering that authority to the colonists.

The colonies of the Deep South responded to the imperial crisis in different ways. South Carolina's political leaders, the wealthy planters of the lowcountry, embraced Whig principles and took a prominent role in the colonial resistance to British policy. Although they did not speak for all of the province's inhabitants, they were powerful enough to align the colony with their neighbors to the north in the revolutionary movement. Georgians, kept in check by their skillful and popular royal governor, Sir James Wright, and fearful that opposition to Parliament's authority might cause them to forfeit British protection from their powerful Indian neighbors, hesitated to commit themselves fully to the Whig cause. Finally, pressured by South Carolina's Whigs and incited by its own small but vocal rebel party, Georgia became the last of the thirteen colonies to join the American resistance in 1776. In the provinces of East and West Florida, Whigs were few; most inhabitants showed little interest in the disputes of the 1760s and 1770s, and both provinces remained loyal to Britain when hostilities began in 1775.

SOUTH CAROLINA

South Carolina was one of the wealthiest provinces in North America. Charleston, the fourth-largest town in the American colonies, was the provincial capital as well as a leading commercial center. On the vast plantations in the coastal region known as the lowcountry, enslaved African Americans produced large crops of rice and indigo for export, enriching the aristocratic planters who dominated the economic and political life of the colony. Protective of their power and privileges, the planters actively opposed British policies that appeared to threaten their rights.[1]

When Parliament passed the Stamp Act in 1765, imposing a tax on newspapers, customs documents, and legal papers, South Carolina planters as well as many Charleston artisans believed that the law encroached on their right to be taxed only by their own provincial assembly, and they prepared to resist any attempt to enforce the act. With the law scheduled to take effect on November 1, protests began in October. Opponents of the stamp tax burned an effigy of the stamp distributor, broke several windows at his house, and eventually forced him to resign. They also conducted a mock funeral for "liberty." Yet, compared to their counterparts in many other colonies, South Carolinians' resistance to the Stamp Act was relatively restrained; they did not engage in the kind of destruction practiced, for example, in Boston. Tensions ended when Parliament responded to the protests by repealing the act in early 1766.[2]

Parliament's imposition of the Townshend Revenue Acts in 1767 again strained the province's relationship with Britain. The taxes on imported glass, lead, paint, paper, and tea were seen as another attempt to raise money from the colonists without their consent. Charleston's artisans, who were most affected by the acts, expressed immediate dissatisfaction and soon pressured the planters and merchants, who had initially shown little concern about the new taxes, to join them in opposing the law. Representatives of all three groups agreed to halt the importation of British goods until the acts were repealed.[3] The opponents of British policy, who styled themselves "Whigs," employed harsh methods to enforce the nonimportation agreement. Adopting the motto "Sign or Die," the Whigs threatened violence to anyone who showed reluctance to subscribe to the pact.[4] In most cases, however, the coercion was economic: "associators denied nonsubscribers the use of their wharves and refused to purchase their rice, indigo, or other plantation products."[5] Yet, many prominent merchants refused to cooperate, so that British exports to South Carolina dropped by no more than 50 percent. Merchants who had agreed to nonimportation, seeing their competitors profiting by ignoring the agreement, sometimes resumed the purchase of British goods. Parliament repealed the Townshend duties in April 1770, except for the tax on tea.[6]

While lowcountry Carolinians denounced British policies they considered oppressive, their counterparts in the province's interior or backcountry raised similar complaints about the treatment they received at the hands of the lowcountry planters who governed them. "The planters of South Carolina . . . were unwilling to grant representation to the upcountry, and its House of Commons was an exclusively eastern body."[7] The Commons House of Assembly ignored the desire of backcountry residents for representation, local courts, and other institutions to establish order and secure their rights. When an outburst of violent crime struck the backcountry in 1767, many of the inhabitants joined together to demand that the provincial government address their grievances. Known as "Regulators," these people meted out punishment to criminals while pressuring officials to grant them the right to vote, provide courts and jails, and institute other legal reforms. By 1769, when the movement came to an end, the Regulators had achieved many of their demands. Provincial officials created four judicial districts in the backcountry, each with its own sheriff, court, and jail, and established two parishes whose inhabitants could elect representatives to the assembly. Nevertheless, backcountry representation in the assembly remained disproportionately small until the eve of the Revolution, when the provincial congress, in an effort to increase backcountry support for the Whigs, allocated about one-third of its seats to representatives from the region.[8]

Shortly after Regulator unrest had subsided, the assembly voted in December 1769 to send a contribution of fifteen hundred pounds sterling (nearly two hundred thousand dollars in 2002 value) to the Society of the Gentlemen Supporters of the Bill of Rights, an organization devoted to assisting British political radical John Wilkes in his opposition to the government. Wilkes was popular among South Carolina Whigs; Charleston's artisans had earlier formed a "John Wilkes Club."[9] Lt. Gov. William Bull and the council were aghast, not only because they opposed the payment but also because it had been made without their consent. The council therefore refused to permit the assembly to recover the funds from the 1770 tax receipts. To force the council's hand, the assembly refused to pass a tax bill that did not cover the expense of the donation to Wilkes. Bull and the council found this unacceptable, and a deadlock ensued. When Gov. Lord Charles Montagu arrived in September 1771, he too resisted the assembly's efforts to include the Wilkes funds in a tax bill and eventually dissolved the house. Both sides remained intransigent, as the dispute evolved into a debate over the relative powers of the assembly and the council. "No annual tax bill was passed in South Carolina after 1769 and no legislation at all after February 1771. For all practical purposes royal government in South Carolina broke down."[10]

The breakdown of legal government enabled the Whig committees to take effective control of affairs in Charleston. They were therefore ideally situated to take advantage of the next crisis in the imperial relationship—the passage of the Tea Act in 1773. Parliament's intention had been to assist the financially troubled East India Company by allowing it to sell tea directly to the colonists at a lower cost; the act actually reduced the tax on tea. To the Whigs, however, the act appeared to be a ploy by the British government to deceive them into abandoning their opposition to British taxation by purchasing taxed tea, something they had avoided since the repeal of the Townshend Acts. When a shipment of tea arrived in Charleston on December 1, a crowd gathered to protest. The merchants to whom it was consigned, fearing the wrath of the mob, refused to accept it. Before a confrontation could develop, Lieutenant Governor Bull confiscated the tea for nonpayment of the tax and stored it in town. This action defused the protests in Charleston.[11]

In Boston opponents of the Tea Act had dumped a large quantity of tea into the harbor in mid-December. Parliament responded to the news by passing the

Coercive Acts, which closed the port of Boston and placed Massachusetts under military government. South Carolina's Whigs believed that the Coercive Acts foreshadowed a British attack on the people's liberty throughout the colonies, and they joined their eleven northern neighbors in sending representatives to the Continental Congress in Philadelphia.[12]

When the delegates returned, the Whigs called for the election of a provincial congress, as the assembly was still moribund as a result of the Wilkes fund dispute. The congress adopted a nonimportation agreement, chose delegates to attend the Second Continental Congress, and began preparations to resist the British with force. In the spring of 1775 reports of fighting between British troops and Americans at Lexington and Concord and rumors that British officials planned to incite slave revolts and unleash Indian attacks on South Carolina radicalized the Whigs. They used coercion to enforce nonimportation and make people sign the Continental Association declaring their opposition to British policy. The recently arrived royal governor, Lord William Campbell, found the Whigs in control of the militia and himself powerless to assert any authority. Fearing for his safety, he took refuge aboard a British warship in Charleston harbor on September 15, 1775. Royal authority no longer existed in the province.[13]

Because lowcountry planters dominated the assembly and nearly all of them were Whigs, the transition from royal government to Whig control was relatively smooth. This made it virtually impossible for Loyalists to retain a voice in provincial affairs.[14] One of the few who expressed an opinion displeasing to the Whigs quickly felt their wrath. On August 12, 1774, the Reverend Mr. John Bullman, assistant rector at St. Michael's Church, preached a sermon in which he urged the people to keep their proper station, do their duty, and not usurp the authority of others. His advice "afforded the Demagogues a handle to work up such resentment in the minds of the People" that Bullman was immediately labeled an enemy of liberty. The vestry of St. Michael's forbade him to officiate at future services. Although seventy-four church members later signed a petition requesting that Bullman be reinstated, the vestry refused. The humiliated minister returned to England in the spring of 1775.[15] His fate was a harbinger of what awaited South Carolina's Loyalists when they dared to challenge the Whigs.

The rebels had other concerns besides an occasional critic. They worried about the political attitude of their neighbors in Georgia, who in their opinion did not exhibit sufficient zeal for the revolutionary cause. The Georgians showed little desire to cooperate in nonimportation, leading angry South Carolinians to declare that the province should "be amputated from the rest of their brethren, as a rotten part that might spread a dangerous infection."[16]

Loyalist clerics and wavering Georgians were minor problems compared to other dangers the Whigs faced. From the beginning of the dispute with Britain, South Carolina's large slave population had complicated the political situation. In 1775 slaves outnumbered the province's white population by 104,000 to

70,000. With nearly two-thirds of whites living in the backcountry and more than 90 percent of slaves in the lowcountry, the fear of slave insurrection was pervasive among lowcountry whites.[17] To keep their laborers subservient, the planters established a system of rigid control that constituted "the most rigorous deprivation of freedom to exist in institutionalized form anywhere in the English continental colonies."[18] Thus, much of the restraint that the Whigs demonstrated during the Stamp Act protests was the result of whites' concern that any tumults might provoke unrest among the slaves. The fear was well founded, as some "disorderly negroes," emulating white opponents of the stamp tax, marched through Charleston in January 1766 shouting "Liberty." The march threw Charleston residents into an uproar; provincial officials called out the militia and sent emissaries across the colony looking for signs of slave rebellion.[19]

As relations with Britain worsened, the actions of a black Methodist preacher named David Margate made clear to whites that the threat from their slaves might be magnified by the conflict. Margate had been trained in England and sent to America by the countess of Huntingdon to convert slaves to Christianity. In late 1774 or early 1775 he preached a sermon in Charleston on the delivery of the Israelites from bondage in Egypt, declaring that "God will deliver his own People from Slavery." Whites recognized the incendiary nature of this message, and some of Margate's white supporters had to rush him out of town before he was lynched.[20] Taken to Georgia, he was promptly sent back to England by other sympathetic whites.[21]

Fear of slave rebellion was also widespread among backcountry settlers. Many backcountry residents hoped to one day become slave owners themselves; while they were hostile toward the lowcountry aristocracy, they "were not hostile to slavery."[22] One of the Regulators' complaints had been that whenever they managed to "save a little Money . . . Wherewith to purchase Slaves," robbers learned of it and stole the funds.[23] The number of slaves in the backcountry grew steadily in the years before the Revolution, reaching about six thousand by 1770.[24]

Rev. Charles Woodmason, an Anglican missionary, recognized the fear of slave revolt in the backcountry as he traveled through the region in the 1760s, and he used it to strengthen his argument for religious tolerance. Woodmason pointed out the threat that arose from "an *Internal* Enemy," the province's numerous slaves. "Over these We ought to keep a very watchful Eye," he advised, "lest they surprize us in an Hour when We are not aware, and begin our Friendships towards each other in one Common Death."[25] In promoting the establishment of schools in the backcountry, Woodmason tried to tap into this fear to dampen the inhabitants' desire for slaves. He expressed the hope that education "may prove a Means of lessening the Number of Negroes that are now employ'd as family Servants and therefrom by Degrees freeing this Land from an Internal Enemy that may one day be the total Ruin of it."[26]

Woodmason also found backcountry inhabitants to be extremely hostile to the Indians and likewise appealed to this sentiment to advance his agenda. "There is an External Enemy near at Hand, which tho' not formidable either to our Religion or Liberties, still is to be guarded against," he told a Presbyterian audience in urging them not to discriminate against people of other denominations. "These are our *Indian* Neighbours. Common Prudence, and our Common Security, requires that We should live like Brethren in Unity, be it only to guard against any Dangers to our Lives and Properties as may arise from that Quarter."[27] He also demonstrated the value of education by contrasting white society with that of the Indians, asserting that among the latter, "for want of due Instruction, the most Savage Dispositions and detestable Practises contrary to the Principles of Humanity as well as of Religion, are transmitted down from one Wretched Generation of Creatures to another."[28] Woodmason may not have actually held such opinions, but he was clearly aware that appeals of this nature would be effective in winning support from the backcountry settlers. The Whigs would employ the same tactic a few years later in an attempt to convince these same people to support the rebellion.

GEORGIA

Georgia, the most recently founded and weakest of the thirteen rebel provinces, was the last to join the revolutionary movement. During the first years of the dispute between Britain and the colonies, Georgia's royal governor James Wright, who had held his office since 1760 and whose political skill and dedication to his province's welfare made him one of the most capable provincial governors in the British Empire, succeeded in checking the more radical elements in Georgia. It was not until the summer of 1775 that the Whigs finally wrested authority from him and dragged the province into revolution.[29]

The Stamp Act brought the first challenge to Wright's popularity and leadership skills in 1765. Most Georgians opposed the act, believing that it infringed on their liberty. Various protests took place in Savannah, while some opponents of the act organized themselves as "Sons of Liberty." Wright thwarted the effort of an extralegal meeting of the assembly to send delegates to the Stamp Act Congress in New York, although when the representatives met officially in December, they dispatched a petition to London demanding the act's repeal. Believing himself bound to enforce the law, Wright closed the port of Savannah until ships could be legally cleared through customs using stamped documents, a clever maneuver that soon led Savannah's merchants to petition for enforcement of the act so that their trade could resume. With the help of the provincial rangers, merchants, and ships' officers, Wright then intimidated the opposition and put the Stamp Act into effect.[30] Despite his success in upholding the law, Wright realized that the Whigs had seriously threatened his authority and expressed "the greatest Mortification to see the Reins of Government nearly hoisted out of my Hands, His Majesties authority Insulted, and the Civil power obstructed."[31]

The governor had won the battle over the Stamp Act, but his victory made Whigs more determined to challenge him on other issues. In 1767 the assembly refused to provide supplies for British troops in the province as required by the Quartering Act. The representatives also challenged the status of the Provincial Council, claiming that it could not properly be considered the upper house of the legislature nor act in that capacity. Wright stood firm on both issues and eventually triumphed. In January 1768 the assembly abandoned their challenge to the council; they conceded to Wright on the Quartering Act three months later, although Gen. Thomas Gage withdrew the troops in August. However, the representatives blamed Wright for causing both disputes. Wright replied with a scathing critique of the assembly.[32]

The legislators renewed the battle in December 1768, when in spite of Wright's admonitions, members adopted an address to the king protesting the Townshend Acts. In response, Wright immediately dissolved the assembly. Most Georgians, however, paid little heed to either the Townshend Acts or the assembly's opposition to them until September 1769, when protest meetings were held in Savannah, at which participants voted to adopt a nonimportation agreement. Upon learning that the councillor Jonathan Bryan had presided at one of the meetings, Wright suspended him from the council. The governor also worked quietly to convince people not to sign the agreement, and this, along with the lack of any means to enforce nonimportation, resulted in the complete failure of the agreement. Even criticism from South Carolina's Whigs and their threat to suspend trade with Georgia failed to prod Georgians to further action.[33]

Wright battled the assembly again when in April 1771 the members chose Noble Wimberly Jones as their Speaker. Because Jones had been a vocal opponent of British policy, Wright refused to accept Jones's election, whereupon the assembly chose Archibald Bulloch instead and then passed a resolution declaring that the governor had violated their privileges. Wright dissolved the assembly, reported the situation to London, and received orders to disapprove whomever the assembly chose to be Speaker at their next session. The governor then left for England, leaving Lt. Gov. James Habersham to deal with the matter. Three times at its next meeting the assembly elected Jones as Speaker. They eventually replaced him with Bulloch at Habersham's insistence, only to provoke another dispute with the lieutenant governor over editing the assembly's records to remove references to Jones's election. Habersham dissolved the assembly, but the dispute began anew when that body reconvened the next year. The quarrel paralyzed the provincial government, so that no taxes were assessed or collected for two years.[34]

In February 1773 Wright returned to Savannah as Sir James, the king having bestowed a baronetcy upon him for his services as governor. Wright soon regained much of his former popularity when he procured a large land cession from the

Creek Indians. The governor toured the new lands, laying out towns, while the provincial government's land office received a deluge of claims from eager settlers. Unfortunately for Wright, the goodwill engendered by the Creek land cession, which had diverted Georgians' attention from the revolutionary movement, did not last long. When Creeks who did not approve of the cession attacked the province's frontier in late 1773 and early 1774, many Georgians hoped that Wright would use the attacks as a pretext to extort more land from the Indians. When Wright and Indian superintendent John Stuart instead brought a peaceful end to the dispute in October 1774, backcountry inhabitants denounced the governor, believing that he had sacrificed their interests for the Indians' benefit. The Whigs capitalized on this to win many new adherents to their cause.[35]

Overshadowed by the threat of war with the Creeks, the Tea Act had gone virtually unnoticed in Georgia. However, when the British government responded to the Boston Tea Party by passing the Coercive Acts, Whigs seized the opportunity to renew their protests against imperial policy. At a meeting in Savannah on July 27, 1774, Whig leaders resolved, despite some opposition, to raise money to aid the Bostonians. A subsequent meeting on August 10, held in spite of Wright's proclamation declaring the gathering illegal, approved resolutions condemning the Coercive Acts and supporting American rights. Those attending also decided not to send delegates to the Continental Congress that would soon convene in Philadelphia.[36]

This somewhat restrained protest resulted in part from serious divisions among the Whigs. The assembly was dominated by representatives from Christ Church Parish, many of whom were also leaders in the Whig movement. Many had strong ties to Wright and other royal officials; while they opposed British policy, they hoped to achieve reform within the existing system "with as little accompanying disturbance as possible." They especially wished to avoid having the assembly's power pass into the hands of extralegal meetings and congresses. The inhabitants of St. John's Parish, who were descended from New England immigrants and advocated a more radical resistance to British policy, challenged the conservatives' authority. The Christ Church conservatives, therefore, blocked the St. John's representatives' attempt to send a delegation to Philadelphia.[37]

Wright worked to counteract the effects of the August meeting by promoting dissenting views. In the weeks after the meeting, petitions circulated throughout Georgia expressing opposition to the Whigs' proceedings. The petitioners noted that the people whose opinions differed from those of the Whigs had been denied admission, that the meeting's purpose had been misrepresented, and that attendees who disagreed with the Whigs had been ignored. Seven of these petitions, with 633 signatures, still survive as an indication of Loyalist strength in the province, although many signers later joined the Whigs.[38]

After several months of quiet, Whig agitation resumed in December when St. John's Parish adopted the Continental Association and demanded that Georgia send representatives to the Second Continental Congress. Fearful that the radicals might gain control of the opposition movement, many conservative Whigs agreed to convene a provincial congress in January 1775. Wright tried to thwart the Whigs by calling the assembly to meet on the same day, hoping that since many members of the assembly had planned to attend the congress, the extralegal meeting might not take place. The representatives duly appeared when the assembly met. Wright delivered an address that "was a sincere attempt to . . . discourage revolutionary activities." The members listened politely; they then ignored two petitions with 260 signatures denouncing the colonial radicals and went on to vote their approval of the actions of the Continental Congress. Wright then dismissed the members before they could take further action in support of the rebels.[39]

Free now to join their fellow Whigs, many assembly members took their seats in the provincial congress. Representatives adopted the Continental Association and chose three delegates to attend the Continental Congress, but those elected declined to go because not all of Georgia's parishes had been represented at the congress. In a further demonstration of the Whigs' lack of support, only St. John's and St. Andrew's parishes put the Continental Association into effect, causing angry inhabitants of the former to cut off trade with the rest of Georgia and attempt, unsuccessfully, to secede and join South Carolina.[40]

News of the fighting at Lexington and Concord finally swung the political balance in favor of the Whigs. Reports of the incident reached Savannah on May 10, and that night rebels broke into the town's powder magazine and carried off the stores. Georgia Whigs attracted new supporters by pointing out that British troops had attacked the colonists and spreading rumors that British officials planned to incite Indian wars and slave insurrections. Another provincial congress, which convened in Savannah on July 4, assumed control of Georgia's affairs and committed the province to the Whig cause.[41] Later that month Wright wrote that "the friends of government are falling off daily because they get no support." Although his own commitment to king and country did not waver, the governor had no power to enforce his authority and could only watch as rebellion raged about him.[42]

Despite their initial enthusiasm, the Whigs faced many difficulties. Georgia's white population numbered about twenty-five thousand in 1775, barely equal to the number of slaves in the province, and whites were bitterly divided among themselves. This, along with the presence of the Creeks on Georgia's western frontier and the proximity of East Florida, would make it hard for the rebels to protect themselves against a serious British effort to reassert royal authority in the province. The Whigs had joined the revolution, but they would not find it easy to make their rebellion succeed.[43]

East Florida

The provinces of East and West Florida were established in 1763 from territory that Spain ceded to Britain at the end of the Seven Years' War. Both colonies were left open to settlement under the terms of the Proclamation of 1763, which halted the western expansion of existing colonies at the Appalachians. East Florida's boundaries were the St. Mary's River to the north and the Apalachicola River to the west. Settlement was concentrated along the Atlantic coast for approximately fifty miles north and south of the capital, St. Augustine. There were several large plantations along the St. John's and St. Mary's rivers, and another plantation south of the capital at New Smyrna, where some one thousand indentured servants from Minorca and southern Europe labored. The province grew slowly: its non-Indian population was only about three thousand in 1775, half of whom were African American slaves.[44] Most slaves had been imported from Georgia, South Carolina, or directly from Africa to meet the demand for labor on the newly established plantations.[45]

Shortly after the Spanish cession, Gov. James Grant arrived with a few settlers along with some troops to garrison the fort at St. Augustine. Land grants attracted immigrants, who established plantations along the rivers. Trade with the Indians developed, and soon East Florida was exporting furs, lumber, turpentine, rice, indigo, and a variety of other goods.[46]

The Stamp Act aroused no opposition in East Florida. The handful of settlers complied with its terms, although Governor Grant reported that all of the inhabitants rejoiced when the act was repealed early in 1766. While British taxation was clearly unpopular, East Florida depended on a parliamentary subsidy to finance its government and defense, so the inhabitants had little grounds to protest the payment of taxes. Nor was there an assembly to provide a forum for complaints against imperial policy; the province's free white population was too small to require the creation of a legislature, and none was elected until 1781.[47]

East Floridians continued to show little sympathy for the Revolutionary cause in subsequent years. In part this was because a majority of the free white settlers were government contractors, artisans who supplied the army, or former soldiers. Scots were numerous and in all of the colonies displayed a staunch loyalty to the Crown throughout the Revolution. The province's weakness relative to the Indians, and its vulnerability to a Spanish attack, also helped strengthen loyalism there. So too did the strong leadership of Gov. Patrick Tonyn, a former army officer who arrived in 1774. Grant had left East Florida in 1771, and in the interim Lt. Gov. John Moultrie had administered the province. Tonyn had seen extensive military service in Europe and brought his military habits to his new post. Even though his uncompromising attitude alienated some East Floridians, Tonyn scrupulously enforced parliamentary legislation in the province and tolerated no opposition. During the Tea Act controversy, Tonyn had matters so firmly under control that he informed British officials that all the tea destined for the southern colonies should have been sent to St. Augustine, where the duty would have been paid, and the tea could then have been shipped to the other American provinces without incident.[48]

When the war began, Tonyn, acting on Lord Dartmouth's instructions, issued a proclamation offering Loyalist refugees land grants exempt from quitrents for ten years and protection. Large numbers of Loyalists, mostly from Georgia and the Carolinas, found the offer enticing, especially as Whig persecution increased. Small farmers constituted the majority of immigrants, although planters with their slaves, traders, and ministers came as well. The influx of Loyalists insured that the province would remain firmly pro-British. After Parliament prohibited the rebel colonies from trading with the rest of the empire, the British West Indies, along with the army and navy, looked to East Florida to meet their demand for food and other goods, sparking rapid economic growth and making it relatively easy for most Loyalist immigrants to support themselves.[49]

WEST FLORIDA

West Florida extended westward from the Apalachicola River to the Mississippi, with its northern boundary, adjusted in 1764, set just above the thirty-second parallel. The British government appointed George Johnstone governor and established the provincial capital at Pensacola. Two former French settlements, at Mobile and Natchez, were the only other significant population centers. In the 1760s West Florida developed more slowly than its eastern counterpart. British merchants in West Florida quickly opened a highly profitable trade with Spanish Louisiana, which continued until the early years of the Revolution. Growth accelerated in the 1770s as settlers became aware of the great fertility of the Mississippi valley soil, although disease and the hot climate led to the deaths of many immigrants. The capital and the lands along the Mississippi were home to the majority of the province's inhabitants, who numbered about twenty-five hundred whites and six hundred slaves in 1774.[50]

The Stamp Act triggered protests from West Florida's inhabitants, who were still struggling to establish themselves and did not need an additional financial burden. Many of them refused to accept their land grants in order to avoid paying the stamp duty. Determined to enforce the law, Governor Johnstone threatened to award the land to others if the tax were not paid. Angry settlers and Johnstone's political opponents, who saw the unrest as an opportunity to stir up animosity against the governor, subjected Johnstone to "a torrent of abuse." Lt. Gov. Montfort Browne circulated a petition calling for Johnstone's removal, but no organized groups arose to oppose the Stamp Act.[51] Quiet returned to the province after the act's repeal in 1766, and the inhabitants virtually ignored the Townshend Acts and other subsequent parliamentary legislation that produced strong resistance elsewhere in America.[52]

West Floridians elected their first assembly in 1766, and Johnstone enjoyed good relations with the representatives, although he frequently quarreled with the military officers in the province over the proper limitations of the civil and military spheres.

The governor also had problems dealing with the Indians. The Mortar, a leader of the Upper Creeks, criticized the British for failing to prevent whites from settling on Indian land and accused the governor of fomenting war between his people and the Choctaws. Angered when the Creeks killed two whites, Johnstone advocated an attack on that nation with the help of the Chickasaws, Choctaws, and Cherokees. British officials, however, insisted that every effort be made to accommodate the Indians. Johnstone's declining popularity in the province and his aggressive Indian policy led to his recall in 1767. Lieutenant Governor Browne became acting governor until he too was recalled as the result of complaints. Elias Durnford then assumed the office of lieutenant governor until the arrival of Peter Chester in August 1770.[53]

Chester's arrival coincided with an influx of settlers from the older colonies, who were attracted by the rich potential of the Mississippi valley lands. The governor encouraged immigration with generous land grants. In dealing with the assembly, Chester strove to uphold the royal prerogative and his own authority as governor. This resulted in conflicts, which ended when he dissolved the assembly in 1772. The legislature did not convene again for six years.[54]

Chester took advantage of the disturbances in the provinces along the Atlantic coast to induce settlers to come to West Florida. He offered generous land grants to newcomers, as well as the right to cut timber on royal lands without charge, provided it was shipped to the West Indies. Among the immigrants attracted by the governor's generosity were members of the Company of Military Adventurers and their families. These Connecticut residents, over one hundred families numbering some seven hundred people altogether, began arriving in Pensacola in March 1774. Chester granted land to qualifying veterans of the Seven Years' War and advised the rest to occupy land as squatters until royal approval arrived for their grants. The settlers were later joined by others fleeing New England because of their Loyalist sentiments.[55]

In October 1774 the Continental Congress appealed to West Floridians to join the American resistance, sending a letter explaining its actions and criticizing British policy. The letter, addressed to Speaker of the Assembly Edmund Rush Wegg, accomplished nothing. Wegg was also the province's attorney general, and he turned the letter over to Governor Chester, who in turn refused to make its contents public.[56]

Some West Floridians, however, did support the American rebels. The most notable, James Willing of the Natchez district, tried to win over other inhabitants, apparently with some success, but he eventually left for Pennsylvania. Those with Whig sentiments, if not already outnumbered by Loyalist neighbors, were soon overwhelmed by the influx of Loyalist refugees. At the outbreak of war, Chester issued a proclamation publicizing Dartmouth's offer to grant land to loyal refugees; by April 1776 large numbers of Loyalists were arriving in the province, most of them from South Carolina and Georgia. Virginians and

Pennsylvanians also traveled to West Florida by boat down the Ohio River to the Mississippi. Between 1775 and 1781 the provincial council granted lands to between 1,312 and 1,643 refugees, although these figures do not reflect the total number of refugees who came to the province.[57]

THE NATIVE PEOPLES OF THE SOUTH

Five Indian nations occupied the lands south of the Ohio River and west of the line of white settlement, all of whom would play a role in the Revolutionary struggle. Three of these nations, Catawbas, Cherokees, and Creeks, lived adjacent to rebel colonies. American leaders would enlist the Catawbas in their service and work to keep the Cherokees and Creeks neutral. The Choctaws and Chickasaws, who lived farther west, were generally ignored by the rebels until late in the war. The British, on the other hand, while dismissing any possibility of winning Catawba support from the outset, made great efforts to maintain the loyalty of the four larger nations. The Cherokees and Creeks, by their proximity to the rebellious southern colonies, were a potentially valuable asset to the royal cause. Although more distant, the Choctaws and Chickasaws could contribute to the defense of the Floridas and could possibly be employed against the frontiers of the rebel provinces as well. Together the Cherokees, Creeks, Choctaws, and Chickasaws possessed a total of about fourteen thousand fighting men.[58] This was a powerful resource for the British if the Crown's Indian agents could unify the nations and coordinate their actions with those of regular troops and Loyalists.

The Catawbas were the smallest of the southern tribes. Their towns, centered along the Catawba River, lay wholly within the boundaries of North and South Carolina. They had assisted the British and colonists during the imperial wars with France and Spain, which had enabled them to procure favorable trade terms and abundant presents from their allies. However, the expansion of white settlements in the Carolina interior eventually led to conflict and violent confrontations. By the mid-1750s one Catawba leader recognized that "the White people were now seated all round them and by that means had them entirely in their power." With the Catawba population plummeting below five hundred after a 1759 smallpox outbreak, the tribe concluded that accommodation of the whites offered their only hope of survival. After being granted a reservation in 1763 at their own request, they subsisted by pursuing runaway slaves and renting their land and selling handicrafts to the colonists.[59] Their weakness had rendered them, in the words of one observer, "inoffensive, insignificant people."[60]

The Cherokees, residing in what is now northwestern South Carolina, western North Carolina and Virginia, and eastern Tennessee, shared the longest border with the colonies of any southern Indian nation. They had been subjected to increasing pressure from expansionist whites in the years before the Revolution. In 1759 they had gone to war against the colonists, only to see their towns destroyed, which forced them to make peace in 1761. Afterward the

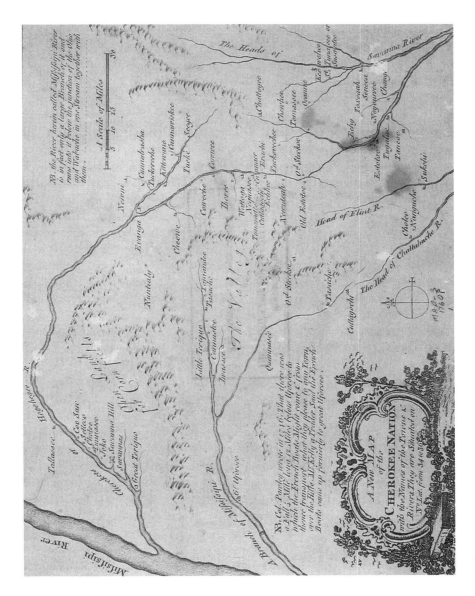

Cherokees sought "stability in their relationship with whites," which led their leaders to cede land in order to maintain peace. Some Cherokees, unwilling to accept the loss of land, challenged those who favored conciliatory policies. This internal conflict shattered Cherokee unity in March 1775, when settlers from North Carolina led by Richard Henderson purchased a vast tract of land west of the Appalachians for £10,000 ($1.3 million) in trade goods.[61] The treaty, signed at Sycamore Shoals on the Watauga River, enraged Dragging Canoe, the son of Attakulla Kulla, who did not share his father's willingness to accommodate the colonists. Dragging Canoe walked out of the negotiations, denounced the transaction, and pledged to resist with force any further white encroachment on Cherokee territory.[62]

At the start of the Revolution, the Cherokee population was estimated at between twelve and fourteen thousand, of whom some three thousand were capable of bearing arms.[63] British officials classified the Cherokees into "four divisions" according to the locations of their towns. The Overhill Cherokees lived along the Little Tennessee and Tellico rivers, the Valley and Middle divisions were located in the Blue Ridge Mountains, and the Lower Towns were situated along the border with South Carolina.[64]

The Creeks inhabited an area comprising western Georgia and much of present-day Alabama and Florida. Whites referred to those living along the Coosa, Tallapoosa, and Alabama rivers as Upper Creeks and designated others whose towns were located near the Chattahoochee and Flint rivers as Lower Creeks. This distinction vastly oversimplified the divisions within the Creek nation, which was in fact a conglomeration of native peoples. "One might refer to the Creek 'confederation,' but it would be more meaningful to employ 'confederation of confederations,'" explained J. Leitch Wright Jr.[65] These Indians did not consider themselves Creeks, the name given to them by whites, but instead "identified with their families and towns more than with any larger political organization." Their primary loyalty was to their clan, which was determined by matrilineal descent, and their secondary loyalty was to their town. This made efforts by either the British or the American rebels to deal with the Creeks exceedingly difficult, since authority among the Creeks was so decentralized.[66] When the Revolution broke out, Creek allegiances were often determined by ethnicity. "In general, pure Muskogees supported Britain, and those in the opposing moiety," with the exception of the Seminoles, "looked to the United States and Spain." The non-Muskogees, who had inferior status in Creek society, may have seen an opportunity to challenge Muskogee dominance by supporting the opposite side in the conflict.[67]

Spanish influence among the Creeks further complicated British relations with these Indians. Some Lower Creeks "preserved a strong attachment to the Spanish" after the Seven Years' War, and Spanish officials who hoped someday to regain the Floridas did their best to maintain communication with them.

Spanish vessels occasionally visited the Florida coast to transport friendly Creeks to and from Havana, where the Indians were welcomed and given presents.[68]

Creeks who inhabited East Florida, known as Seminoles, were developing an identity as a separate nation in the eighteenth century, although they remained at least nominally part of the Creek confederation during the Revolutionary era. The leader of this Creek faction, Ahaya of Cuscowilla, known to the whites as Cowkeeper, lived in the area of present-day Gainesville. An ally of the British since 1740, Cowkeeper remained a staunch friend of Great Britain throughout the Revolution. Governor Tonyn, finding the Seminoles well disposed to the British and realizing that East Floridians could ill afford hostilities with their Indian neighbors, worked to maintain good relations with Cowkeeper's people.[69]

By the 1760s African Americans had begun to establish a presence in Creek territory. Most were the slaves of whites involved in the Indian trade, who ignored laws forbidding traders to bring slaves into the Indian nations. The Creeks saw and often adopted the traders' racial attitudes. A few Creeks even acquired slaves of their own. Other blacks among the Creeks were runaways who had been adopted into the nation. These people were often accorded a relatively low status among the Creeks, unless they married Indians or remained long enough to win full acceptance. For the most part, however, the Creeks cooperated with their white neighbors in maintaining the slave system. Under the terms of a 1763 treaty with Georgia, South Carolina, North Carolina, and Virginia, the Creeks received a bounty of £5 ($650) in goods for every runaway slave they returned. The colonists' generosity arose from their desire to prevent interaction between slaves and Indians; in 1768 Governor Wright of Georgia noted the danger that might arise if Indians armed fugitive slaves to assist them in the event of war with the whites. To further promote the colonists' objective, a 1774 treaty between Georgia and the Creeks required the Indians to hand over to white officials any slave they found in their territory and increased the bounty to £50 ($6,500) in goods for each slave the Creeks returned.[70]

The Choctaws, whose territory encompassed southern Mississippi and western Alabama, were also a divided people.[71] After their emergence as a nation sometime in the seventeenth century, they remained split into the Western, Eastern, and Sixtowns groups. This structure "preserved ethnic, geographic, political, and cultural differences." These differences contributed to a Choctaw civil war, fought from 1747 to 1750, and even in the 1760s many Choctaws identified primarily with their ethnic group rather than with the larger Choctaw nation. Some went so far as to consider the other divisions of the tribe to be separate nations altogether. Each division maintained its own clan organization and political organization.[72] Authority was divided among civil leaders, war leaders, and clan leaders.[73]

The Choctaws had been allies of the French until 1763 and during the Seven Years' War had fought against the pro-British Chickasaws, with whom they had been frequently at war since the 1730s. After the cession of West Florida to Britain, they encountered difficulties in adjusting to the new relationship with the British. Although the British negotiated an end to the war with the Chickasaws, British inability to supply the Choctaws with adequate trade goods in the 1760s and early 1770s complicated the relationship. When the British demanded a land cession from the Choctaws at the Mobile Congress of 1765, the Indians reluctantly complied in exchange for trade goods, but the transaction placed further strain on the Choctaw-British relationship.[74]

So too did the behavior of traders who flocked to the nation. Charles Stuart, the Choctaws' agent, estimated in 1770 that rum comprised 80 percent of the sales that traders made to the nation.[75] Governor Chester worried in 1771 that the "great abuses and impositions" of the "licentious" traders might provoke a war.[76] The Choctaws also fought a war against their traditional enemies, the Creeks. British officials encouraged this conflict, which had begun with "a series of revenge killings" between the two nations. A trader and British agent to the Chickasaws, James Colbert, at the behest of Governor Johnstone, "persuaded the Choctaws to reply to the last killing not with another murder but with numerous war parties." The Creeks responded in kind, and the war escalated; by 1771 the death toll had reached an estimated three hundred people in each nation. The war continued until the outbreak of the Revolution.[77]

The Chickasaws inhabited what is now northern Mississippi and western Tennessee. In 1731 a French observer had estimated their population at 3,000, plus an additional 250–300 Natchez Indians who lived among them. Their numbers had dropped to approximately 1,600 by the end of the Seven Years' War but had increased to about 2,300, including 450 warriors, at the outbreak of the Revolution. Their performance in the many wars of the eighteenth century earned them a reputation as "the most warlike people on the Mississippi," and many visitors to their country praised their courage and fighting spirit.[78]

The Chickasaws had maintained the best relations with Great Britain of any southern nation during the years before 1763. Unlike their neighbors, the Chickasaws never accepted French domination and maintained a trading relationship with the British. Royal officials considered the Chickasaws as long-time allies; they failed to recognize that Chickasaw support for Britain had been a tactic to maintain independence from French control. Whatever the previous reasons for the Chickasaws' pro-British stance, royal officials worked to cement the relationship after the French had been driven from North America. Both Johnstone and John Stuart used the Proclamation of 1763 to assuage Chickasaw fears that whites would encroach on their territory. The presence of the agent James Colbert, who had been living with the tribe since 1729 and was the father of six sons by Chickasaw women, helped reinforce ties. Whites living among the Chickasaws introduced slavery to the nation by the 1750s. Colbert alone owned 150 slaves.[79]

Chickasaw-British relations were not wholly pacific, however. Indian leaders complained that traders took unfair advantage of them and that immigrants to West Florida passed without permission through Chickasaw territory, in some cases occupying Chickasaw lands. Stuart and Johnstone attempted to halt such practices but lacked the means to end them completely.[80]

Relations between the Chickasaws and the other southern tribes were generally good after the end of the Seven Years' War. The Chickasaws and Choctaws made a peace agreement, which still held at the outbreak of the Revolution, thereby insuring that two of Britain's tribal allies would have no obstacles to collaboration. Some Chickasaws who had moved eastward to the Tennessee River valley did anger the Cherokees, who attempted to drive them out in 1769. After the Chickasaws "soundly defeated" the Cherokee party, both nations coexisted without further conflict.[81]

JOHN STUART AND BRITISH INDIAN POLICY

The British government's policy toward Indians in the fifteen years before the Revolution greatly influenced how the southern nations responded to the conflict and also affected many colonists' attitudes toward Great Britain. Beginning in 1761 British officials began to develop "an imperial policy for the wilderness . . . which was in sharp conflict with both the aspirations of landless frontiersmen and the vested interests of many business groups involved in land speculation." The most important element of this policy, the Proclamation of 1763, prohibited colonial governors from granting lands or permitting settlement in areas where such expansion might encroach on Indian territory.[82]

Responsibility for managing British relations with all of the Indian nations south of the Ohio River and east of the Mississippi lay with John Stuart, superintendent of Indian affairs for the southern department. Born in Scotland, Stuart had immigrated to South Carolina, where he secured appointments to various local offices and briefly served in the provincial assembly. Beginning in the late 1750s Stuart developed a strong friendship with Cherokee leader Attakulla Kulla, who urged provincial authorities to appoint Stuart as agent to the tribe after the Cherokee War ended in 1761. Stuart received the appointment in 1762 on the recommendation of South Carolina governor Thomas Boone.[83] Stuart's diplomatic skills and concern for the Indians' welfare earned him "great prestige" among the southern Indian nations, although many colonists "detested him because he tried to maintain the Indian boundaries."[84]

The tensions between Stuart and the colonists arose from differing views of "what form the greatly expanded British empire would take" in the aftermath of France's expulsion from North America. While provincial land speculators, politicians, and Indian traders wished to be allowed to pursue their own interests in dealing with the Indians, Stuart and his superiors in London believed that "only centralized frontier government based on British-Indian alliances could ensure peace and prosperity." To accomplish this, British leaders recognized that trade abuses and encroachment on Indian land, the major sources of conflict between whites and Indians, would have to be halted.[85]

Stuart "targeted whites, rather than Indians, as the chief threat to peace" and promptly set out to establish "fair and stable trade relations" to end the economic exploitation of the southern nations.[86] The Indians were particularly vulnerable to unscrupulous traders, since by the mid-eighteenth century they had become "almost completely dependent on trade for their livelihood." Indians traded deerskins for cooking utensils, muskets, ammunition, rum, and other commodities brought into their nations by white traders, who increased their profits by inflating prices, falsifying weights and measures, and plying their Indian clients with rum to induce them to accept one-sided bargains.[87] The superintendent urged the British government to take control of the Indian trade, license traders, restrict the sale of rum, and fix prices for trade goods to prevent abuses. Officials from the Indian department would enforce these regulations. With support from Indian leaders, the London government, Governors Wright and Johnstone, and Gen. Thomas Gage, the commander in chief in North America, Stuart put most of his plan into effect beginning in 1766, despite opposition from many colonists. Stuart and his deputies found it impossible to halt all of the abuses in the Indian trade, but they managed to limit traders' exploitation of the Indians.[88]

Stuart also succeeded in checking the colonists' expansion into Indian lands during the 1760s. The Proclamation of 1763 gave the superintendent the necessary authority to prevent settlers from encroaching on Indian territory and insured that royal officials in the provinces would support him, whether or not they agreed with the terms of the proclamation. Settlers, however, soon chose to ignore the law, and by 1770 Virginians and North Carolinians had begun settling in the Watauga, Nolichucky, and Holston river valleys west of the Appalachians. This was Cherokee land, but the settlers disregarded both Cherokee protests and the orders of provincial governors. The squatters tried to legitimize their actions through the Sycamore Shoals treaty, which was repudiated by Stuart and Gov. Josiah Martin of North Carolina.[89]

With the cooperation of Governor Wright, Georgians did manage to win the British government's approval for their acquisition of a large tract of Indian land in the interior of that province. Claimed by both the Cherokees and Creeks, the former nation agreed to cede the land to the colonists as payment for debts owed to traders. Creek leaders accepted the cession with some reluctance, and the transaction was concluded in 1773. Georgia thus acquired more than 1.6 million acres of land.[90]

Stuart opposed the cession but agreed to manage the negotiations. He believed that using debt owed to traders as leverage to wrest land from the Indians undermined imperial authority. He informed Wright that many Creeks had repudiated their leaders' decision to cede the land and that relations with that nation might become hostile. His prediction proved true when Creek parties attacked the Georgia frontier in December 1773 and then ambushed a militia force sent to chastise them. In response, other Georgians encountered one party of Creeks and killed their leader, Big Elk, along with all of the men, women, and children in the Indian camp. Fearing a full-scale Indian war, Georgia's leaders asked General Gage to send troops and, in conjunction with the other southern provinces, imposed an embargo on trade with the Creeks. The embargo helped avert war and eventually brought the Creek dissidents to accept the cession, although tensions remained high on the frontier.[91]

With the dispute between Britain and the colonies moving rapidly toward armed confrontation, the colonists' actions continued to inflame the Indians and push them into the arms of the British. During the Creek crisis an Indian leader who came to Augusta in March 1774 to discuss peace was "treacherously slain" by a colonist named Thomas Fee. When Fee was arrested in South Carolina on Wright's orders, a mob who applauded the murderer's actions freed Fee from the jail at Ninety Six.[92] Another Georgian, the planter and prominent rebel Jonathan Bryan, deceived the Creeks into leasing him a vast quantity of land. Uncertain of what they had signed, the Creeks presented the document to Stuart and Wright in Savannah. Upon examination, Stuart found that seven or eight Indians had granted Bryan a ninety-nine-year lease to all their hunting grounds in East Florida. The Creeks "were much surprised and Offended at it, they severely reprimanded the Indians who had signed the Deed & who hapened to be present." The signers replied that they thought they had granted Bryan only permission to build a house and keep a few cattle nearby on their land. "The Indians insisted that the Deed should be cancelled, and those who had signed tore away their Marks & Seals from it." However, when the Creeks left Savannah, Bryan "intercepted about 20 . . . and having made them Drunk prevailed upon them to execute a new Deed."[93] David Taitt, Stuart's agent to the Creeks, feared that Bryan's actions "will certainly be the Cause of an Indian War." He promised to meet with Creek leaders and convince them to oppose any land cession.[94] Although Bryan continued his efforts to persuade the Creeks to uphold the agreement they had signed, Taitt assured Stuart that the Indians would ignore Bryan's demands.[95]

Bryan's clumsy attempt to defraud the Creeks and the murder of the Creek leader helped strengthen Stuart's position with that nation at a time when it appeared that the British government might call on the Indians for assistance against the rebels. By late December 1774 General Gage warned Stuart that some Americans had been telling the Iroquois that the king had abandoned the Indians. "I mention it to you," Gage wrote, "lest the like Methods should be attempted to debauch the Southern Nations." Gage urged Stuart to "keep all the Indians firm in their Love and Attachment to the King and in a Temper to be always ready to Act in his Service."[96]

This was Stuart's intention, but he found his situation further complicated when Wright and Tonyn suddenly decided that the time was right to make their own attempt to acquire Indian land. In December 1774 Tonyn informed Stuart that the Creeks appeared willing to sell more of their territory, and if so, he would "consider a Proper Time to fix for a Congress to Treat for it."[97] A month later Wright wrote the superintendent, reporting that the Creeks were willing to cede land. The governor had bypassed Stuart and written directly to his deputy, David Taitt, with instructions "to see whether *they* [the Creeks] will offer or propose it as we think it will be a good Exchange."[98] Well aware that "the Indians can have no such powerfull motive of quarelling with us as our insatiable avidity for land," Stuart took steps to check Tonyn's and Wright's "Inclination to be tampering with the Creeks for more Land." He informed the East Florida governor that the Indian boundaries could not be changed without royal approval and suggested that Tonyn's energy would be better spent on improving relations with the Seminoles.[99] Stuart then procured Gage's support to insist that Wright abandon his own plan to acquire Creek land.[100]

Stuart's adept handling of Indian relations, and the colonists' own behavior, insured that the southern Indian nations were well disposed toward Britain at the outbreak of the Revolution. Nevertheless, the superintendent would have to overcome some obstacles of his own creation to employ Indians effectively against the rebels if and when that measure became necessary. First, if the British government intended to use slaves as well as Indians against the Whigs, they would have to overcome the effects of their own policy of sowing discord between the two races. Stuart had spent a decade trying to "prevent the Indian country [from] becoming an asylum for negroes"[101] and had personally emphasized the importance of "breaking that Intercourse between the Negroes & Savages which might have been attended with very troublesome Consequences."[102] This work might now have to be undone. Second, Stuart now found it necessary to bring the Creek-Choctaw war to an end, after he had already rebuffed overtures from both nations to help them negotiate peace. The war he had encouraged to protect the colonists from the Indians now became an obstacle to any effort to employ the Indians against the colonists.[103] On October 24, 1775, Stuart instructed his brother Henry to be ready to bring the Creeks and Choctaws to the negotiating table as soon as Gage approved the measure. However, it was not until October 1776 that John Stuart finally met with leaders from both nations and brought the war to an end.[104]

Even with all of the southern Indian nations committed to support the king, there were drawbacks to employing them against the rebels. Not only would the Indians prove less tractable than Stuart and officials in London hoped, but also their method of waging war, which emphasized sporadic raids by small parties, was not compatible with the sustained type of military campaigns that the British planned to subdue the Whigs. Furthermore, when Indians went to war, it meant that they were unable to hunt and plant. Since they could not provide for their own subsistence, they naturally expected their white allies to provide the food and goods needed for their survival.[105] The Indians' dependence on agriculture also made them vulnerable to their enemies; "whenever whites destroyed Indian granaries and cut down their corn the effect was devastating. Survivors fled to the woods, where they starved."[106]

When war between the British and American rebels broke out in April 1775, the ministry in London had not sent Stuart any orders to employ the Indians, but in response to the warning Gage had sent him in December, Stuart took precautions to "guard against any Attempt . . . to debauch the Indians" in his department. He promised to do his best to keep the southern Indians firmly attached to the king and ready to act when called upon.[107] The Chickasaws and Choctaws, Stuart informed Gage, were all "in the most freindly Disposition towards us," and the Cherokees and Creeks likewise adhered to the British.[108] Two months later Stuart confirmed that the southern tribes were still well disposed, but he warned that the Creeks and Cherokees lacked arms and ammunition, which he urgently wished to provide them "at this very critical conjuncture."[109]

No matter how hard the Whigs might try to win over the southern Indians or at least keep them neutral, they could never overcome the advantages the British held at the start of the conflict. The British government already had an organization in place with agents and commissaries who often lived among the nations to which they were assigned; they were better able to supply the Indians with arms and trade goods; and most important, Stuart had consistently opposed the colonists' attempts to illegally purchase or settle on Indian lands.[110] In 1775 "the primary pressure on the southern Indians was the colonial desire for land, a desire which seemed to the natives an insatiable lust." Thus, the southern Indian nations had good reason to involve themselves in the conflict and naturally leaned toward the British, who "represented a source of protection" against the encroaching settlers.[111] Furthermore, in the 1770s most of the Indian nations were in the midst of a cultural and spiritual revival that brought unprecedented unity and manifested itself in part in a movement to prevent further loss of territory to the colonists.[112] To the Indians, the war was merely "a continuation of the struggle about Indian land and who was to get it."[113] The Creeks, Choctaws, Cherokees, and Chickasaws were prepared, if necessary, to fight alongside the British to insure that they retained their land.

TWO

The British Government and Its Supporters React to the Revolution

As ROYAL AUTHORITY COLLAPSED in South Carolina and Georgia at the beginning of 1775, the Whigs moved rapidly to consolidate their control of both provinces. Rebel officials, with the aid of mobs, persecuted Loyalists and enacted harsh measures to prevent slave insurrections. They adopted a milder approach to the Indians, attempting to win their support or at least to neutralize them through diplomacy and gifts.

The British government, unwilling to abandon the southern provinces, considered various means to regain control of them. The ministry sifted through numerous proposals and eventually decided to send troops to reestablish royal authority with the aid of Loyalists. However, British forces arrived too late. The Whigs resorted to force and defeated the South Carolina Loyalists, and then they repulsed the British expedition that attempted to capture Charleston. Shortly afterward the Cherokees ignored the advice of British Indian agents, attacked the rebels, and suffered an overwhelming defeat. By the end of 1776 both the king's supporters and his troops were beaten and demoralized, although East and West Florida still remained securely under British control.

ORIGINS OF THE SOUTHERN STRATEGY

Responsibility for the planning and conduct of military operations against the American rebels lay with King George III's ministers. Lord North, the chief minister, felt himself ill-suited to lead the British war effort. "Upon military matters I speak ignorantly, and therefore without effect," he confessed to the king.[1] Although he participated in planning operations during 1775, in subsequent years North would be only peripherally involved in determining the conduct of the American war. North's failure to provide leadership left management of military affairs in the hands of the secretary of state for the American department, Lord Dartmouth, and from November 1775 Lord George Germain. Although Germain's contentious personality often made it difficult for him to cooperate with his fellow ministers, his consistent support for a tough American policy, skill in parliamentary debate, and abilities as an administrator and strategist convinced North and the king that Germain was well qualified to direct the war.[2]

King George III shared Germain's opinion that the government must take a firm stance on the American issue. "The colonies must either submit or triumph," he asserted; "we must not retreat." He enjoyed a good relationship with Germain, and while he left the details of managing the war to his ministers, he followed the situation closely, "often offering advice more sensible and realistic than that of his senior officers."[3]

Royal officials considered New England the center of the rebellion and focused their initial efforts on defeating the rebels there in the belief that once this had been accomplished, the other provinces would quickly submit to British authority. Yet, at the same time, reports from the southern colonies indicated that Loyalist sentiment in that region was strong. A steady stream of correspondence from America and from Loyalist exiles in England described the great opportunities waiting to be reaped in the South should British troops be sent there to cooperate with the Loyalists. This led the ministers to consider a variety of plans for regaining control of the southern provinces.[4]

Alexander Innes, Gov. William Campbell's secretary, informed Dartmouth in May 1775 that there were numerous Loyalists in South Carolina, but he warned that without military assistance they were rapidly losing hope. "The King's Friends in this Province (who are not a few if they durst appear) are in the lowest state of despondency," Innes wrote, "expecting every moment to be drove from their Occupations, and Homes, and plundered of all they have earned."[5] Less than a month later Innes reported that many Charleston Loyalists were signing the rebel association from "dread of the terrible consequences both to their persons and properties that may follow a refusal," which was to be expected, since they had been left "without *Leader, Countenance* or *Protection.*"[6]

While some Loyalists in Charleston succumbed to Whig intimidation, Governor Campbell found that the situation in the backcountry appeared more promising. "The intolerable tyranny and oppression" practiced by the rebels "has already given offence to the moderate of their own party and has stirred up such a spirit in the back part of this country, which is very populous, that I hope it will be attended with the best effects," he informed Dartmouth in July. Campbell added that representatives from the Camden and Ninety Six districts had visited him, bringing news that Loyalists in those areas numbered "some thousands." The governor instructed these emissaries to tell the people "to persevere" and pledged that he would provide them with "both protection and reward as soon as it is in my power."[7]

Confined aboard a "poor solitary worm eaten Sloop" in Charleston harbor after the rebels forced him to flee his home, Campbell waited impatiently for Gage and Adm. Samuel Graves to answer his requests for military support. He complained to Dartmouth in August "of the ill consequences that has attended the total neglect of this Province," asserting that South Carolina's Loyalists had become "so abandon'd to despair" that it was almost impossible for him to convince them that support from the British government was coming.[8] Yet the situation, Campbell noted, was not entirely hopeless. On August 19 militia colonel Thomas Fletchall had written the governor that "a departure from the Laws and Principles of the Constitution of government is Not so universal as has been represented." At a muster six days earlier the members of Fletchall's backcountry regiment had drawn up a "Memorial of Loyalty," and only two men had refused to sign it. Fletchall estimated that four thousand men in his district "would Appear in Arms for the King" if called upon.[9] Loyalist leader Moses Kirkland, who had made his way to Charleston from the backcountry, also confirmed in mid-September that four thousand men could be recruited "for the service of government whenever a force appears on this coast." According to Kirkland, these men needed only arms and "a few experienced officers" to effectively cooperate with British troops.[10]

From Georgia, Sir James Wright sent similar reports to Dartmouth. "There are still many friends to government here," he wrote on June 9, "but they begin to think they are left to fall a sacrifice to the resentment of the people for want of proper support and protection, and for their own safety and other prudential reasons are falling off and lessening every day."[11] Later that month Wright told Campbell that "without any *protection or support*" from the army or navy, Georgia was "at last likely to be drawn in" to the rebellion.[12] Yet, Wright still considered most Georgians loyal, informing Dartmouth that although a majority of Georgians had signed the rebel association, "great numbers have been intimidated to sign."[13] The governor's implication was clear: most Georgians would return to their allegiance if they received assistance from the government.

A few dissenters challenged these reports. One writer stated that most Charleston residents were Whigs and that "it is dangerous for the friends of government (who are very few in number) to speak or write their sentiments."[14] Another, allegedly a deserter from the British army, believed that royal authority could not be restored in South Carolina; the king's troops "can do nothing in this country," he asserted.[15]

Such accounts, buried amid a flood of letters from governors, lesser officials, and Loyalist exiles testifying to the strength of southern loyalism, had no effect on the ministry. The weight of evidence convinced the ministers that if the Loyalists received support from a small military force, they could reestablish royal authority in the southern provinces. Campbell's and Wright's reports made an operation of this sort urgent, since Loyalist morale appeared to be collapsing in the face of Whig persecution, and loyalism might wither beyond recovery if assistance did not come quickly.

Many people believed that an effort to regain control of South Carolina and Georgia would benefit from the support of Indians as well as Loyalists. Several army officers urged the ministry to employ Indians to assist in crushing the rebellion. General Gage wrote Dartmouth in June 1775 suggesting that "we must not be tender of calling upon the Savages," because the rebels were using New England Indians to aid in the siege of Boston. From Nova Scotia, Gen. James Grant wrote that same month that "a few scalps taken by Indians . . . would operate more upon the minds of these deluded distracted People than any other Loss they can sustain."[16] Patrick Tonyn, one of the most persistent advocates of using Indians against the rebels, asserted that "the Americans are a thousand times more in dread of the Savages than of any European troops."[17] Ironically, John Stuart "could see no advantage to using the Indians until it could be done in such a way as to damage the American cause materially," and in 1775 he worked to keep the Indians at peace until they could be used in a manner he thought proper.[18]

While Dartmouth had been reluctant to order British agents to employ the Indians, his successor Germain recognized the Indians' potential value, believing that in addition to their actual military contributions they would "strike terror" among the rebels.[19] Yet, like Stuart, he realized that the government would have to proceed cautiously in this regard. Germain wrote Tonyn praising the governor and Stuart for their successful efforts to keep the southern nations' allegiance, while recommending restraint in employing Indians against the rebels. Germain pointed out that "the making those Savages Parties in the present unhappy Dispute, is a measure of a very delicate Nature, and perhaps ought not to be pressed forward, but in proportion as it may be necessary to counteract any Steps of the like Tendency, which may be taken by the Rebels."[20]

A major reason for Germain's reluctance to authorize the use of Indians was his fear that the ministry's opponents in Parliament, who sympathized with the American rebels, would take advantage of the issue to turn public opinion against the war. Germain's deputy, William Knox, warned that this might happen and was soon proved correct.[21] In the House of Lords, opposition peers denounced the idea of using Indians against the rebels. Lord Shelburne described proposals to do so as "barbarous" and "cowardly," while the Duke of Richmond assailed the notion of inciting "those assassins to stab your enemy in the back."[22] The opposition in the House of Commons also vociferously criticized any plan to use Indians against the rebels.[23]

If determining the role of Indians in the war was, as Germain put it, "very delicate," the question of whether or not to seek aid from slaves was even more vexatious. From the beginning of the conflict a surprising number of Britons advocated arming slaves and granting them freedom as a reward for their assistance. This idea, although horrifying to most Americans, seemed reasonable to many in Great Britain, where attitudes toward slavery had been gradually changing.

In the years before the Revolution, comments by Britons concerning American slaves demonstrated their inability "to recognize that in the colonies the revolutionary new division of men arising from racial slavery was not simply one of temporal condition." For example, the bishop of London had referred to blacks as "truly a Part of our own Nation," while the authors of a 1771 geography book recommended that slaves who behaved well should be freed and allowed to become planters, which would unite them to the whites by "bands of friendship, and by mutual good offices."[24] These ideas reflected the growing strength of the emancipation movement in Britain. By the 1760s many Britons had come to regard slavery as a moral wrong and thought that blacks laboring in the colonies should be treated as subjects rather than property. As the likelihood of war increased, some abolitionists saw an opportunity to weaken the rebellious Americans by striking a blow against slavery. "Proclame Freedom to their Negroes, then how long would they be a people?" Sir William Draper asked in 1774. "They would soon cry out for pardon, and *render unto* Caesar *the things which are* Caesar's."[25]

Others who advised the ministry to arm slaves did so simply because they believed it to be an expedient way to defeat the rebels. Some members of Parliament proposed to strike at the economy of the southern provinces by emancipating the slaves, but the House of Commons rejected the proposal.[26] Opposition leader Edmund Burke argued that "declaring a general enfranchisement" of slaves would not have much effect. He naively suggested that to counter a British threat to emancipate the slaves, the Americans might act first to grant slaves their freedom and arm them to fight the king's troops.[27]

The ministry's supporters in Parliament rejected such arguments. On October 26, 1775, William Lyttelton, a former governor of South Carolina, told the House of Commons that the southern colonies were the weak link in the rebel chain because of "the number of negroes in them" and suggested that "if a few regiments were sent there, the negroes would rise, and embrue their hands in the blood of their masters." Lyttelton did not shrink from this violence, asserting "that the colonies ought to be conquered and then to have mercy shown them."[28] Most members of Parliament, however, sided with former West Florida governor George Johnstone, who pronounced the scheme "too black and horrid to be adopted."[29] Lyttelton's motion to arm slaves failed by a vote of 278 to 108.[30] Ralph Izard, a South Carolinian who was then in London, denounced Lyttelton for "encouraging the Negroes . . . to drench themselves in the blood of their masters."[31]

British army officers had fewer qualms regarding the arming of slaves. Shortly before giving up his command, Gage endorsed the idea, telling Lord Barrington, the secretary for the army, in June 1775 that "things are now come to that Crisis, that we must avail ourselves of every resource, even to raise the Negros, in our cause."[32] Gen. John Burgoyne advised King George that Indians should be employed in support of the army and that "arms should be provided for the Negro slaves to overawe the southern colonies."[33] Burgoyne even suggested that the northern Indians could be used to transport arms southward for the slaves.[34]

In addition, various officers assigned slaves a prominent part in several plans that they submitted to Germain for retaking the southern provinces. One suggestion, devised by Captain Dalrymple of the 20th Regiment, called for the creation of a corps of two thousand Irish Catholic volunteers, who would be dispatched to the Chesapeake to assist Virginia's governor, Lord Dunmore. To this force, Dalrymple recommended, Dunmore "should add the bravest & most ingenious of the black Slaves whom He may find all over the Bay of Chesapeake." Dalrymple described these blacks as "full of Intelligence, Fidelity & Courage as will be found upon Enquiry." He believed that the combined black and Catholic force could raid along the shores of Chesapeake Bay or even capture Philadelphia if the opportunity arose.[35]

A variation of this plan recommended that the expedition to the Carolinas then preparing to sail under the command of Gen. Charles, Earl Cornwallis should be sent instead to Chesapeake Bay. The troops could capture Baltimore, the writer asserted, and augment their numbers by adding five thousand indentured servants and convicts, along with "the Bravest and most Ingenious of the Black Slaves." This force could destroy supplies and ironworks along the shores of the bay, bribing other slaves to destroy facilities farther inland. After achieving its objectives in the Chesapeake, "the Army of Troops, Convicts, Blacks &c may carry the war into Pennsilvania" and still be available "to Subdue the Carolinas in Winter."[36]

Yet another proposal, from an officer who had served in the West Indies in earlier wars, asked Germain "to judge, of what Service a Regt of Stout Active Negro's will be, Commanded by White Officers." The writer did not envision this regiment as a combat unit; instead, its members would "Contribute to ease the Soldier, from many dutys both discouraging and prejudicial to the healths of those" needed to actually fight the rebels. Another benefit of such a unit, the writer noted, was that upon its going ashore in any of the southern colonies, "not a Slave in ten, but would desert to Such a Corps, a Circumstance I am well assured much more dreaded; & of more fatall Consequences to the Rebells then the loss of a Battle." He added that many planters in the West Indies had "Expressed their Surprise . . . that Government have made no application to the west India Collonies, for a Body of their Negros on this Occasion." These planters, the writer noted, said that Jamaica alone could easily furnish one thousand slaves for such a regiment, and if the ministry approved the plan, the slave unit could be ready for action by April 1776.[37]

The same writer sent a more detailed proposal to Lord North, listing the number of slaves each West Indies province could contribute to the proposed regiment, which was to consist of two battalions of seven hundred men each, with white commissioned and noncommissioned officers drawn from existing regiments. The black troops were to be armed and equipped in the same manner as other British soldiers, and "every Negro of the Sd Regt who Shall distinguish himself during the war, shall receive his Freedom, & if he is rendred Unfitt for Service a Small pension of £4 [$525] a year during Life." The government would either reimburse the owners for the slaves provided to the army or replace them with "other Negros taken from the Rebells."[38]

As some of the writers indicated to the ministers, precedent existed for employing slaves to assist in military operations. British forces had made considerable use of slaves in the Caribbean during the Seven Years' War, while free blacks performed militia duty in the West Indies. In Jamaica unclaimed runaway slaves labored in royal service to support army garrisons under the provisions of a 1757 law, carrying supplies, mounting artillery, and cleaning barracks. An officer in Dominica wrote that without the assistance of slaves he did not have enough troops to perform all of the duties at his post.[39]

Thus, as these reports indicated, many West Indian planters were surprised that "the government did not ask them to supply slaves for military service in North America. . . . Some of the large planters in Jamaica were willing to provide a thousand slaves for military service on the mainland." Their willingness to do so arose in part from their desire to help suppress the rebellion, as well as from their fears that the unstable conditions created by the Revolution increased their danger from both the rebels and their own slaves.[40]

Several other prominent Britons and Loyalists, including the writer Samuel Johnson and former South Carolina attorney general Sir Egerton Leigh, urged the use of slaves in some capacity, while others, such as Thomas Day, ridiculed the "American patriot, signing resolutions of independency with the one hand, and with the other brandishing a whip over his affrighted slaves."[41] The ministry, however, refused to go further than the tacit permission that Dartmouth had given Lord Dunmore in July to use the black troops the latter had already raised.[42]

Domestic opposition to the arming of slaves contributed to the ministry's hesitance in the matter. Several British "Gentlemen, Merchants, and Traders" petitioned King George III in October 1775 to express their horror at the idea of arming slaves, urging him to reject any such proposal.[43] Memorials from London and Bristol protesting a policy of harsh coercion in America included denunciations of promoting "insurrections of negroes" as "improper," while the *Annual Register* criticized proposals to arm slaves as undermining both the social system and property rights.[44] A British traveler in America, having heard rumors that the ministry planned to arm slaves, predicted "that such action would put an end to all quarreling between American patriots and Tories, for 'in that case friends and foes alike will be all one.'"[45] The duke of Manchester declared that it would be difficult to bring the Americans to accept a peace agreement after the government had enraged them by "giving orders to arm the Indian tribes against them; and encouraging the black slaves to rise and cut the throats of their masters."[46]

As the duke had correctly observed, the question of whether to employ Indians and slaves against the rebels was linked to the larger issue of how the war was to be fought. Sharp divisions existed between those civil and military officials who advocated a harsh policy of subjugation and others who favored applying just enough force to bring the Americans to their senses in order to promote reconcili-ation.[47] Realizing that if they "raised the Negroes or placed greater emphasis on the Indians . . . the task of reconciliation would have been far harder," moderates preferred to rely on British troops and Loyalists to defeat the rebellion. Because a harmonious restoration of the imperial relationship was the ministers' primary goal, they settled on an attractive option.[48]

Lord William Campbell had reported that the mere presence of so many slaves made South Carolina vulnerable. "I leave it to any person of common sense to conceive what defence they can make in a country where their slaves are five to one," he wrote.[49] Sir James Murray also noted that while a small military force "can make but little impression on the Continent of America," it appeared likely that a minimal number of troops could "overawe the southern colonies on account of their Negroes."[50] The ministers decided that slaves could provide passive assistance by tying down a large percentage of rebel troops to guard against insurrection, easing the task of the king's soldiers and yet avoiding the complications that arming slaves would create. Therefore, "British military lead-ers and Crown officials seized upon the idea of intimidating independence-minded white southerners with the threat of a slave rising without, however, actually inciting one."[51]

Lord North then set to work reassuring Parliament, the British public, and Loyalist slave owners that the ministry had not originated the idea of using slaves and Indians against the rebels. In the House of Commons on November 20, 1775, he stated that "there never was any idea of raising or employing the negroes or the Indians, until the Americans themselves had first applied to them."[52]

The ministry's failure to take full advantage of slave support proved an immense benefit to the rebels. Southern Whigs recognized that the large slave population in the region made them particularly vulnerable, but they also understood that any British effort to arm the slaves would alienate many Loyalists. While attending the Continental Congress in Philadelphia, Georgia delegates Archibald Bulloch and John Houstoun told John Adams "that if 1000 regular Troops should land in Georgia and their commander be provided with Arms and Cloaths enough, and proclaim Freedom to all the Negroes who would join his Camp, 20,000 Negroes would join it from the two Provinces [Georgia and South Carolina] in a fortnight." In the Georgians' opinion, only the fact that many Loyalists owned slaves would prevent British officials from taking such a step. "They say," Adams wrote, "their only Security is this, that all the Kings Friends and Tools of Government have large Plantations and Property in Negroes. So that the Slaves of the Tories would be lost as well as those of the Whiggs."[53]

Most Whigs did not share Bulloch's and Houstoun's confidence that the min-istry would not arm slaves, so when rumors that such a policy had been adopted reached the southern provinces, an uproar ensued. Governor Wright reported in late May 1775 that a report "that administration have it in view . . . to liberate the slaves and encourage them to attack their masters, have thrown the people in Carolina and this province into a ferment." Although Wright considered the information "absurd and improbable," he noted that it "had an exceeding bad effect and I am afraid will involve us all in the utmost distress."[54] The rumors received apparent confirmation when Whig Arthur Lee wrote from London to an acquaintance in South Carolina declaring that "the ministry had in agitation not only bringing down the Indians on the inhabitants of this province but also to encourage an insurrection of their slaves." The rebels circulated tales that Governor Campbell had brought fourteen thousand stand of arms for the slaves' use. (A stand of arms consisted of a musket, a bayonet, and a cartridge box.) Campbell informed Dartmouth that it was impossible to describe "the flame that this occasioned amongst all ranks and degrees; the cruelty and savage barbarity of the scheme was the conversation of all companies and no one dared contradict" the reports.[55]

One of the infuriated Whigs, Thomas Lynch of South Carolina, wrote in horror that the British government "calls in Savages to ravage our frontiers—to massacre our defenceless women—and children—offers every incitement to our Slaves to rebel—and murder their masters." These actions, Lynch said, strengthened the rebels' will to fight but had little other effect, as he saw only "our Indians keeping the peace, against all acts—used to detach them from us, by lies—calumnies—and interest. Our Slaves remaining faithful—against the promise—even of liberty."[56]

Henry Laurens, one of the most moderate rebels, declared that "the discoveries which have lately been made of a Settled plan to involve us in all the horrible Scenes of foreign & domestic Butcheries (not War) have not tended to lull us into Security—While Men of War & Troops are to attack us in front the Indians are to make inroads on our backs—Tories & Negro Slaves to rise in our Bowels." Like Lynch, he observed that the news had made Whigs more determined to resist. If Britain intended "to manumit & Set free those Africans whom She Captivated, made Slaves, & Sold to us, the people are also ready to anticipate the pious work—they are ready to fight against her Soldiers, against false Brethren, against Indians" rather than submit, Laurens declared.[57]

Thus, the decision not to arm slaves deprived the ministry of one of its potentially most powerful weapons against the rebels and yet brought the government no advantage. The rumors that British officials planned to instigate slave rebellions did as much damage to the royal cause as the actual arming of slaves would have done, without the offsetting benefit of strengthening the army with black troops. The ministry preferred to rely primarily on the Loyalists, supplemented by Indian support when necessary, and would persevere in this policy throughout the war.

THE LOYALISTS: RESISTANCE AND DEFEAT

With royal government no longer functioning in South Carolina, the Whigs moved quickly to consolidate power. Their Council of Safety, chosen by the rebel congress to act in an executive capacity to manage provincial affairs, had as its primary goal the suppression of Loyalists. The council unleashed a campaign of persecution targeting virtually anyone who did not endorse the rebel position. Georgia's Whigs, hampered by opposition from Governor Wright and the strong Loyalist element in that province, moved more slowly. Prodded by their counterparts in South Carolina and eager to strengthen their own authority, rebels in Georgia eventually bludgeoned the Loyalists there into submission. From the royal governors to small farmers, almost everyone in those provinces who supported the British or preferred to remain neutral suffered; "harassment was directed almost as vigorously at the least powerful of Loyalists, the wives and children," as it was against men who opposed the Whigs.[58]

The earliest indication of how far the Whigs in South Carolina were prepared to go to punish Loyalists came in April 1775, when some rebels considered capturing Governor Campbell as a hostage to exchange for Loyalists whom they had identified as particularly dangerous. When the Whigs learned that Moses Kirkland, a prominent backcountry Loyalist, had reached safety aboard the British warship *Tamar* with Campbell's help, the rebel Arthur Middleton proposed "*that the Gov.* by whose Assistance he escaped, should be taken into Custody & offered in Exchange for K." Cooler Whigs rejected the idea, but Middleton warned that it was possible that the governor "may yet be nab'd, if he does not take care of himself."[59]

However, the Whigs continued to show restraint until the summer of 1775, when rumors that British officials planned to incite Indian attacks and slave insurrections provided a pretext for the rebels to raise troops and take action against Charleston's Loyalists. The Whigs then informed royal officials that they were "Hostages, & must Suffer whatever might be inflicted, on any of the Americans." The newly raised rebel forces helped to intimidate Loyalists and the wavering and checked the "dangerous Spirit of resistance, to the recently usurped authority." Yet, one Loyalist observed that even these units "were not without Symptoms of discontent & Sedition."[60]

In the Whigs' opinion, the best way to deal with such discontent was to employ violence against anyone who refused to sign the Continental Association or otherwise challenged rebel authority. Several rebels forced their way into the bedroom of Dr. Alexander Garden, who was severely ill, to demand that the prominent Charleston physician and suspected Loyalist sign the association. Too sick to read the document, Garden signed with the stipulation that he would renounce it if its contents were at variance with his allegiance to Great Britain. After recovering, Garden decided that he should probably not have signed it.[61]

Garden's treatment was mild compared to the fate of others. On June 9 the rebels took Laughlin Martin and James Dealy, the former a man "of Some Credit in Town," into custody. The "two impudent fellows . . . had not only refused to Subscribe the Association but threatned vengeance against the whole Country by exciting an Insurrection." An impromptu court sentenced the two men to be tarred and feathered, after which they were "put into a Cart & driven up & down the Broad Street—instantly after that degrading punishment was over they were put on board a Vessel in order to be banished hence for ever."[62] The brutal punishment "did much to cow loyalists in the capital."[63]

George Walker, the gunner at Fort Johnson, was another who made the mistake of holding political opinions contrary to those of the Whigs. On August 12, when a ship captain invited him to join in a toast of "damnation" to George III, Walker delivered a scathing reply.[64] As punishment for this "insolent speech," the rebel mob seized Walker, tarred and feathered him, and then carted him from one "Tory House" to another.[65] At each stop Walker was forced "to drink damnation" to the inhabitants.[66] Loyalists visited by the mob and their prisoner included Alexander Innes, James Simpson, and William Wragg. At Fenwick Bull's home the crowd threw a sack of feathers onto Bull's balcony and asked him to keep it until it was his turn to be tarred and feathered. Eventually the rebels released Walker at the home of another Loyalist, Dr. George Milligen.[67] Having twice refused to sign the association, the doctor replaced Walker as the target of the crowd's wrath. The throng surrounded Milligen "like so many hissing snakes," so that he drew his sword to defend himself. He eventually reached safety inside his house but left for England later that month.[68] Reflecting the Whigs' amusement at the Loyalists' distress, Arthur Middleton joked that while he knew of no "pressing necessity" for Milligen's departure, it was probable that the doctor "had an unconquerable Dislike to the mode of Cloathing lately adopted," a reference to the tarring and feathering of Walker. To prevent other loyal inhabitants from escaping to British vessels, the Council of Safety took steps to prevent the Loyalists from using their boats to travel within the harbor.[69]

On August 2 another Whig mob confronted Thomas Brown, a recent immigrant from Yorkshire, at New Richmond in the backcountry. Brown's refusal to sign the Whig association sparked a struggle in which Brown wounded one of his attackers and then held off others with his sword until he was struck in the head from behind by a musket. The Whigs then tied Brown to a tree, tarred his legs, and applied burning wood to his feet, which caused him to lose two toes. They also partially scalped him and carted him through several settlements before leaving the battered Loyalist in Augusta, Georgia. This brutality forced Brown to sign the association, but he soon recanted.[70]

Even members of the clergy were not exempt from Whig intimidation. "Our Committee has shut up all the ports the Courts & the *Church*," Middleton wrote, "the last for a Sermon preach'd in it by Mr. Smith which they did not like."[71] The Anglican rector of Prince George Parish in Georgetown, the Reverend James Stuart, was "violently assaulted by a Savage Mob" because of his loyalism. When he appealed to local officials, "the very Judge applauded the Brutality of the Banditti" who had attacked him "and then encouraged the Aggressors . . . to insult him in their Court of Justice."[72]

The various mob actions terrified most Charleston Loyalists. "The people were in such a humour that I believe there was scarce a non-subscriber who did not tremble," Whig printer Peter Timothy observed.[73] Hoping to capitalize on the fearful atmosphere they had created, the Whigs decided to stage a public display of power to intimidate the wavering inhabitants of Charleston into signing the association.

On July 22 the Council of Safety convened to hear the cases of twenty-four men, including several high-ranking provincial officials, who had refused to sign. The Whigs expected that their inquiry, backed by the implied threat of violence, would force many prominent Loyalists to recant and that others would follow their example. Those appearing before the committee included Chief Justice Thomas Knox Gordon, Attorney General James Simpson, four judges, and some lesser officials. However, only three of the men signed the association. The majority instead shared the views of Judge William Gregory, who declared himself "ever a faithfull Subject & He has taken two Oaths of Allegiance [to the king] and will never break them." Simpson was the most vocal in denouncing the rebel association, insisting that he could not "subscribe it without Perjury and Perfidy."[74]

Disappointed with the unexpectedly poor results of their proceedings, after a few days of deliberation the Whig committee decided that the reasons the Loyalists had given for refusing to cooperate in the rebels' measures were unsatisfactory. The nonsubscribers were ordered to surrender their weapons, barred from leaving Charleston, and forbidden to interact with Whigs.[75]

The committee made an exception for William Wragg, confining him to his plantation outside of town, from whence he wrote to Henry Laurens to explain his refusal to take the rebel oath and to protest the injustice of the Whigs' proceedings. "Can Liberty be worth contending for or ever preserved, when the first principles, & the essential foundations of it are violated?" Wragg asked. "I have seen Sentence; & am still at a Loss to know my Offence." Wragg added that he would remain on his plantation as the Council of Safety had ordered, but he chided Laurens and the Whigs for their fears of "the formidable power of twenty Gentlemen, whose Age, Disposition, & the Education of most of them" hardly qualified them as dangerous conspirators.[76] Laurens agreed that the Whigs had been too harsh in their treatment of Loyalists and urged his colleagues to act with moderation in hopes that kind treatment might induce most to change their views. "Our Cause is good, it does not Stand in need, like Mahomet's Religion, of Sword & Fire to bring Men into it," Laurens wrote.[77]

In fact, the rebel leaders recognized that they had not succeeded in eradicating loyalism in Charleston. Despite a summer of vigorous persecution, the Council of Safety worried in late September that "there are more [Loyalists] within this Metropolis than without it in proportion to numbers."[78]

The Loyalists outside the town also had to be dealt with. Recognizing that it would be more difficult to impose their will on the inhabitants of the vast backcountry region than it was in Charleston, Whig leaders first opted for an attempt at persuading Loyalists to join them. In April the Committee of Intelligence composed the first of four letters it circulated throughout South Carolina in the spring and summer of 1775. These letters denounced Britain's American policy, warned that the British planned to use force to snuff out American liberty, and urged unified resistance against such measures. While it is impossible to determine the effect of the letters, Governor Campbell believed that they did hurt the royal cause.[79]

Campbell, who maintained a clandestine correspondence with backcountry Loyalists with the assistance of the Charleston merchant Andrew MacKenzie, felt frustrated at his inability to aid the king's supporters.[80] The governor could do little other than to inform Thomas Fletchall, the acknowledged leader of the backcountry Loyalists, that he "was without power to protect, or assist you." Campbell could only reassure Fletchall and his followers that the government would eventually take steps to aid them. Meanwhile, he advised Fletchall to keep the peace, cultivate loyalism among the people, and "by every means avoid giving offence, or doing the smallest injury to any of your Fellow Subjects, and rest satisfied at present."[81]

The Whigs believed that if they could convert Fletchall to their cause, it might defuse the impending crisis in the backcountry. On July 14 Henry Laurens wrote to the Loyalist leader, reviewing the rebels' reasons for resisting British authority and appealing for Fletchall's support on the basis of racial solidarity. With the province "alarmed by threats of Invasions by the British Soldiery, of instigated Insurrections by our Negroes, of inroads by the Neighbouring Tribes of Indians & of what is far more to be dreaded the practices & insidious acts of false Brethren," it was urgent that everyone stand together for mutual protection, Laurens stated. He gave Fletchall an opportunity to dissociate himself from other Loyalist leaders, stating that he had heard accounts that Fletchall was friendly to the Whigs "but that you were deterred, partly by the malevolent artifices of Ministerial Hirelings" and by a fear of losing his militia commission. Laurens thus left open a door by which Fletchall could restore himself to the rebels' good graces.[82]

Fletchall replied on July 24, assuring the Council of Safety that while "many reports have been maliciously asserted against me," he could prove they were false. There was little of comfort in the remainder of his letter, however. Fletchall readily admitted that not a man in the militia regiments between the Savannah and Broad rivers had signed the Whig association but that many had instead signed a loyal resolution circulated by Joseph Robinson. Insisting that he had not compelled anyone to sign either document, Fletchall stated that while he did not concur with the Whigs' views, he was not "an enemy to my country." For the time being, he declared, "I am resolved, and do utterly refuse to take up arms against my king, until I find it my duty to do otherwise."[83]

Like Robinson, other Loyalists challenged the rebels by circulating resolutions declaring their allegiance to the king. People living along the Pacolet River composed a statement expressing their "utmost abhorrence and detestation" of "the dareing proceedings of those infatuated people, who call themelvs committee men, or Liberty boys." To counter such actions, the Loyalists promised to "embody at the shortest notice, to support the rights of the crown, as soon as called by any Legal Authority."[84]

The Loyalists soon got the opportunity to act on their pledge. While the Council of Safety sparred with Fletchall, they took more forceful steps to gain control of the backcountry by dispatching Maj. James Mayson with a company of rangers to seize Fort Charlotte on the Savannah River. The outnumbered militia garrison surrendered to the rebels without resistance on July 12. Mayson took the two pieces of artillery and other captured supplies to Ninety Six, leaving a few men to hold the fort. When the Loyalists learned of Mayson's action, Robert and Patrick Cunningham and Joseph Robinson assembled about two hundred men, who marched to Ninety Six on July 17, forced Mayson to surrender, carried off all the supplies taken from the fort except the two cannons, and then released their prisoners.[85]

The Loyalists' success against Mayson convinced the rebel colonel William Thomson that vigorous measures were needed if the Whigs were to gain control of the backcountry. Thomson informed the Council of Safety that Fletchall, Robert Cunningham, and Robinson had deceived the backcountry settlers into opposing the Whigs. If the three were Indians, Thomson wrote, he would consider himself justified to "Send the Councill of Safety their Scalps." However, Thomson believed that "the poor People by them deluded I think may yet be Brought Over by fair Means." He recommended that the Reverend William Tennent be sent to persuade them; "as they are Chiefly of his Religion, I think he would undeceive and Open the Eyes of many of them."[86]

The council decided to follow Thomson's advice and act against the Loyalist leaders while seeking to persuade the backcountry people to join the Whigs. The council ordered an inquiry "into the Conduct of Mr. Kirkland," which was purported to have "a very dark and suspicious aspect." Council member Arthur Middleton wanted Kirkland to receive "such punishment as his Crimes deserve; as the matter has been represented he has certainly been guilty both of Mutiny & Desertion."[87] A week later the council received the evidence it desired in the form of an affidavit allegedly proving Kirkland to be "a rebellious, seditious xxxx" and questioning the allegiance of the Indian trader Richard Pearis.[88] In addition, the council dispatched Tennent, the Reverend Oliver Hart, and William Henry Drayton to the backcountry "to cure this Evil." Henry Laurens hoped that "by proper applications all those people may be brought at least to promise absolute neutrality & many of them to join us."[89] To strengthen the hand of its emissaries, the council ordered Thomson to send rebel militia units on a sweep through the province. The council authorized its emissaries to call for assistance from the militia if they found it necessary.[90]

Drayton and Tennent set out together on August 2.[91] Their first report to the Council of Safety, written five days later, contained little good news. At Congaree

Store, in the midst of settlements of German immigrants, the Whigs summoned the people to a meeting. "To our great mortification not one German appeared but one or two of our friends," the men wrote. The people in the area were said to believe that if they took up arms against the king, they would lose their land. Conceding that their hopes of success were "but small in this quarter," Drayton and Tennent added that they had resorted to threats in order to force some of the Germans to listen to them. They asked Colonel Thomson to order a muster, "& we have declared if the Officers disobey, they shall be broke."[92]

In response to Thomson's threats, many people attended the August 9 meeting, although Tennent noted that a large number "had come a great way to oppose" the Whigs.[93] The rebel emissaries harangued them, however, until all but fifteen men agreed to sign the association. However, Drayton and Tennent's subsequent efforts were less successful. At an August 11 meeting on the Saluda River they convinced only one person to subscribe, while the next day not even one of one hundred people whom Drayton addressed at Evan McLaurin's home would sign.[94] Nevertheless, Drayton informed the Council of Safety that he believed that if these people were allowed to elect representatives to the provincial congress, they would recognize its authority. However, he also warned that unless Moses Kirkland was prevented from returning to the backcountry, "our progress will have been in vain."[95] In reply, the council authorized Drayton to "spare no expence to secure & have him brought" to Charleston.[96]

Meanwhile, Hart had traveled to the forks between the Broad and Saluda rivers after conferring with Drayton and Tennent on August 7. There he gave a sermon on the political situation, which his audience "heard with Attention." He later learned that "one opposer was convinced and sharply reproved one who quarreled with the Sermon."[97] This small victory marked the limits of Hart's success. The next day Hart stayed at the home of the Reverend Philip Mulkey and was disappointed to learn that his host "rather sides with ministerial Measures." Hart probed others for their sentiments, finding to his chagrin that "People, in general, are certainly (as they say) for the King; ie, for the Minister, & his Measures; one Man, with whom we conversed, fairly trembled through Madness." On August 11 Hart discussed affairs with more of Mulkey's neighbors and "found them so fixd on the Side of the Ministry, that no Argument on the contrary Side, seemed to have any Weight with them." That evening Hart preached to between twenty and thirty people with no better result. One Loyalist said that he "wishd 1000 Bostonians might be killed in Battle. . . . On the Whole they appear to be obstinate and irritated to an Extreme." After the sermon Hart spoke with Fletchall, who said that while he did not wish to fight his countrymen, he nonetheless disapproved of the Whigs' measures "and complain'd of sundry Threats which He says are given out against Himself, and the Inhabitants of the Frontiers." Several people who listened to the discussion "seem'd almost universally, by Words & Actions to applaud every Thing" that Fletchall said. Hart concluded that "there appears but little Reason, as yet, to hope that these People will be brought to have a suitable Regard to ye Interests of America."[98]

Hart spent a few more days in the area but made no progress. On August 13 he noted that "there is the greatest Appearance of a civil War" unless God intervened to prevent it. The next day he attended a meeting, where Joseph Robinson "Read a ministerial Piece" that Hart thought was "well calculated to fix the Minds of all disaffected Persons. With Sorrow I saw Marks of Approbation set almost on every Countenance." At that point Hart evidently began to fear that the Loyalists might seize him or his papers; he began writing his diary entries in code and did not stop doing so until September 5, when he was on his way home from his unsuccessful mission.[99]

Tennent, who had joined Hart, was also frustrated. "The Pamphlet sent up by the Governor has done much damage here. It is at present their Gospel," he wrote in reference to the "ministerial Piece" that Hart had denounced. "It seems as though nothing could be done here."[100] Like Hart, Tennent feared that the Loyalists in the area were so strong "that they are nearly ripe to shew themselves and make no Scruple to threaten the whole province with Devastation in a short time." Tennent had also heard rumors that three thousand Cherokee warriors were to join them and that British troops would also arrive soon. "In short," the frustrated minister wrote, the Loyalists "are preparing a great Dish of Blood for you and expect . . . to bear down all before them." The situation had "all the Appearance of an hellish Plott," Tennent declared.[101]

Drayton's arrival spurred a new effort to convert Fletchall, although the latter, abetted by Robinson and Thomas Brown, remained obstinate. Unwilling to give up, Drayton and Tennent focused their efforts on the weak-willed colonel at an August 23 meeting from which Brown, Robinson, and other Loyalist leaders were absent. The two Whigs convinced Fletchall to muster his regiment and allow Drayton and Tennent to address the men. When Brown later learned what Fletchall had done, he tried to dissuade the colonel and nearly came to blows with Drayton in the process. Fletchall refused to change his mind, however, and the meeting went ahead as scheduled the next day.[102]

The event fell far short of the Whigs' expectations. Only 270 of about 1,500 men in Fletchall's regiment attended, the rest having taken the advice of their officers and remained at home. Drayton's harangue provoked a swift challenge from Moses Kirkland, and their confrontation nearly provoked "a terrible riot." Fletchall and others had to intervene to prevent Kirkland from striking Drayton. After calm had been restored, Tennent spoke, after which Brown made a rebuttal. At the close of the meeting, about 70 men signed the association, most of whom had already signed it at other meetings. Drayton and Tennent then turned their attention to other regions but failed to make significant inroads among the Loyalists.[103] Members of the Council of Safety were not surprised at the poor results. "As I expected you have not hitherto made many Proselytes, &

I am sory to prophecy that you will not meet with much more success," Middleton wrote Drayton on August 22.[104]

Thomas Brown reported the failure of the Whig emissaries to Governor Campbell on October 18. "Every Artifice Fraud & Misrepresentation were practiced to impose upon the People," Brown wrote, but the Loyalist leaders had prepared the people for "these Incendiaries," so that Drayton and his colleagues won few converts.[105] Campbell accurately summed up the outcome of the Whigs' mission in a report to the ministry. Having been sent "to poison the Minds of these People," they "succeeded so badly, that they have been under a Necessity . . . to effect by Force what they could not accomplish by Threats, Bribes, or Persuasion."[106]

Drayton had in fact concluded that since persuasion had not had much effect, stronger measures were needed to sway the Loyalists. On August 21 he advised the Council of Safety to apply economic pressure against its opponents. If the Loyalists were "debarred all communication with Charles Town & all trade with the Country Stores, they will be much chagrined," he stated.[107] The council adopted this recommendation, which created consternation among the Loyalists. Moses Kirkland reported that "Thousands of poor People" were "much distressed" because they were "not allowed the Liberty to pass over any Ferry, nor deal in any Store, nor have their Corn ground at any Mill; they are not allowed to purchase Salt to eat with their Provisions, their Estates are threatned to be taken from them." If this were not enough to make them sign the rebel association, Kirkland said, behind these measures lay the further threat that "their Lives next are to be taken by Sword." Kirkland's own life was endangered: the Whigs had offered a reward for his execution or capture; his plantation had been plundered; and he had been forced to employ "Life Guards, to escort me from place to place." He decided to leave the province and sail to Boston, where he hoped to convince Gage to send troops to aid the Loyalists.[108]

Kirkland's assessment of Whig intentions was correct; Drayton was already planning to use force against the Loyalists. Responding to the Council of Safety's fear that Kirkland's arrest might provoke an uprising, Drayton said that such would not be the case if the other Loyalist leaders were taken at the same time. Noting that when Thomson's militia had marched through Loyalist areas, "the King's men . . . were terrified," Drayton intended "to march into the heart of Fletchall's quarters with about 800 men and 6 pieces of cannon," expecting the show of force to be enough to overcome the Loyalists without bloodshed.[109] Thomson announced his readiness to give Drayton "all the Military aid in my power, whenever he shall think proper to demand it."[110]

Seeking a pretext to use force against the Loyalists, Drayton found it when he learned in late August that Kirkland and his followers were "actually in Arms to attack Augusta & Fort Charlotte." As soon as he had confirmation that Kirkland's troops were moving, Drayton told the Council of Safety that he would consider himself "fully authorized . . . to proceed to every extremity that may have a tendency to suppress those Men who oppose the authority of Congress."[111] Drayton then gathered militia from Thomson's and Andrew Williamson's regiments at a camp near Ninety Six. By mid-September the rebels numbered some 1,100 men. The show of force thwarted Kirkland's plan; Drayton then sent parties to capture or kill Kirkland, Brown, and Robert Cunningham. All three escaped, however, and Brown and Cunningham assembled 200 Loyalists to oppose Drayton. Fletchall soon arrived with an additional 250 men and assumed command, over the objection of some of the more militant Loyalists.[112]

Rather than risk defeat, Drayton appealed to Fletchall to negotiate. Had Brown and Cunningham accompanied him to the negotiations, Fletchall may have been more resolute, but both feared that the Whigs might seize them, so Fletchall went with six other men. Preferring to avoid conflict and aware that his men were short of ammunition, Fletchall and the Whigs signed the Treaty of Ninety Six on September 16.[113] Both sides agreed that the "misunderstandings" between them should not be allowed to develop "into quarrels and bloodshed." The Loyalists then declared that they did not oppose the proceedings of the rebel congress, nor did they plan to aid British troops, but rather wanted only "to abide in their usual peace and tranquility." They promised to turn over to the rebels anyone who spoke against the Whig authorities, and in exchange Drayton promised that the Loyalists would not be molested so long as they remained peaceful.[114] "I am persuaded Fletchall & his people will be true, & I make no doubt but that the affair is now crushed," Drayton exulted. Yet, Drayton feared the attachment of the backcountry people to Governor Campbell and wrote that "our Safety is utterly precarious while the Governor is at liberty." Drayton advised the council to "make Hostages of the Governor & the officers" of the Crown or else his success might be undone.[115]

Some Loyalists believed that Drayton had taken unfair advantage of Fletchall and therefore did not consider themselves bound by the treaty. Brown stated that Fletchall had been "struck with terror" upon watching the maneuvers of the Whig militia. Brown and Cunningham considered making a surprise attack on the Whigs with their eight hundred men during the negotiations but decided against it. They undoubtedly wished they had carried out their plan when Fletchall returned with the treaty. Upon learning its "shameful disgraceful" terms, many of the men were "seized with Rage & Indignation" and swore "that they would never abide by them."[116] Cunningham told Drayton that the latter had dishonorably taken advantage of people "half scared out of their senses at the sight of liberty caps and sound of cannon." Cunningham stated that he would not abide by the agreement, which he pronounced as "false and disgraceful from beginning to ending."[117]

Brown and Cunningham met afterward to discuss a course of action. Since they were short of ammunition, they decided to dismiss their troops until they received further instructions from Campbell. Brown then went to Charleston to meet with the governor. Kirkland had already managed to reach Charleston in disguise and get aboard the *Tamar,* where Campbell had taken refuge after the Whigs discovered that he had been discussing plans with backcountry Loyalists to cooperate with British troops. With Kirkland out of reach, the Council of Safety ordered Drayton to capture Robinson, Cunningham, and Brown or to drive them from the province. Brown was arrested but quickly released.[118]

Robinson had observed the rebels' military preparations at Ninety Six and heard that they intended to "burn and destroy the Houses and property of all Persons who refused to join them" as soon as they had enough troops. Robinson went to Charleston to seek advice from Governor Campbell, who advised him "to levy Forces and March against the Rebels." Robinson assembled two thousand men, but Fletchall had signed the treaty with Drayton before these reinforcements arrived. Learning that Campbell had fled Charleston and finding himself "without further Orders, Money or Military Stores," Robinson sent his followers home with instructions "not to suffer any false pretenses of the Rebel Party to deceive them, or to efface their principles of Loyalty, until we should enjoy a more favorable opportunity."[119]

Largely through Drayton's aggressive efforts, the Whigs had temporarily succeeded in neutralizing the backcountry Loyalists. Alexander Innes complained to Patrick Tonyn that if the Loyalists had been assisted by "any decent force" of troops, they might have accomplished much. "By what infatuation or neglect these unhappy provinces to the southward have been so totally abandoned, for such a space, I cannot imagine," Innes lamented.[120]

Peace in the backcountry did not last long, however. At the end of October two Whig actions provoked the Loyalist uprising that the rebel leaders had tried to forestall. First, the Whigs arrested Robert Cunningham, brought him to Charleston, and on November 1 ordered him imprisoned for refusing to recant. Cunningham's brother Patrick promptly organized a force in hopes of freeing Robert. Second, because the Cherokees were complaining of the stoppage in trade, the Council of Safety hoped to placate them and prevent an Indian war by dispatching a wagon with one thousand pounds of gunpowder and some lead for the Cherokees' winter hunt. When Patrick Cunningham learned of the shipment, he and Loyalist Richard Pearis spread word that the Whigs were supplying munitions to the Cherokees for use against the Loyalists. With 150 enraged followers, Cunningham overpowered the escorting rebel troops and captured the wagon.[121]

Whig colonel Andrew Williamson immediately summoned his militia to recover the ammunition. By November 18 nearly nineteen hundred rebels had taken position in a makeshift fort near Ninety Six. The Loyalists gathered about two thousand militiamen and surrounded the fort. Skirmishing continued until November 21, with small losses on both sides. That night the Loyalists sent in a demand for surrender, and representatives of the two sides met to negotiate the next day.[122] A treaty that was soon arranged allowed the rebel militia to leave the fort, whereupon it was to be destroyed. They would then return home unmolested, and the Loyalists would march across the Saluda River. Each side would release its prisoners, and neither side would engage in hostilities until the "differences between the people" were adjusted. This was to be done by referring the matter to Governor Campbell and the Council of Safety for arbitration—actually a moot point since there was no possibility that the rebel council would even consider Campbell's views. Any reinforcements coming to the assistance of either party "also shall be bound by this cessation," the treaty stated.[123]

The Loyalists upheld their part of the agreement, but Colonels Thomson and Richard Richardson, commanding other units of rebel militia, decided that "the Cessation of Arms was not binding on us." They proceeded to assemble men but encountered much opposition and had to resort to drafts to fill their ranks. In the Orangeburg and Congaree areas, the men drafted by Thomson "seem'd very insolent . . . & in fact did as much as to declare themselves Kings Men." There were similar problems with some of Richardson's conscripts. Thomson believed that some of these Loyalists had actually "murdered people in the Woods who had been our Associates." He decided to apply the coercive elements of the militia law to quell the resistance.[124]

Richardson began his campaign in late November with fifteen hundred men. The Whigs had an immense advantage because the Loyalists had just disbanded under the terms of the treaty and thought themselves protected by it. As Richardson marched through the backcountry arresting Loyalist leaders, other Whig parties swelled his force to double its original size. Some Loyalists tried to embody and resist but could not collect more than four hundred men, too few to challenge the large rebel force. Leaderless and intimidated, most of the Loyalists pledged neutrality to avoid further persecution.[125] Richardson sent six captured Loyalist officers to Charleston at the beginning of December, asking the Council of Safety not to set them free "as they are Look'd Upon as Active and pernitious men."[126] Two weeks later he sent down nine more captives, including Fletchall and Pearis.[127]

Many Loyalists fled to Cherokee territory, where Richardson's Whig militia caught up with them on December 21. After surrounding the Loyalist camp, Richardson ordered an attack. Patrick Cunningham managed to escape, but about 130 Loyalists were captured and 5 or 6 killed. Richardson wrote that it was "happy the men were Restrain'd or Every man had died," implying that the dead Loyalists may have been executed rather than killed in combat.[128]

A few Loyalists eluded the Whigs. Joseph Robinson, upon learning that the rebels had offered a reward for killing him, fled to the Cherokees and then made his way through Creek territory before finally reaching East Florida in 1777.[129] Capt. James Phillips and his company of loyal militia escaped the rebels with the assistance of Alexander Chesney, a nineteen-year-old who lived on the Pacolet River near Grindall Shoals. Chesney led Phillips and his men to his family's farm and then found another Loyalist to guide them to North Carolina, from whence they made their way to St. Augustine through Indian lands. Phillips's company formed part of the South Carolina Royalist Battalion later created in East Florida. "I piloted all the loyalists who came in my way," Chesney wrote. When the Whigs learned of Chesney's activities, they arrested him and ransacked his father's home. After a week's imprisonment they released him, offering him a choice of joining the rebel army or undergoing trial for aiding Loyalists. He chose the former "to save my father's family from threat."[130]

Chesney, Robinson, and other Loyalists were fortunate to escape the full fury of the Whigs. All of the Loyalist leaders whom the Whigs judged to be most influential and therefore most dangerous were subjected to harassment, imprisonment, and other forms of persecution. A total of 136 Loyalist prisoners had been sent to Charleston.[131] After two months' imprisonment, 33 of the captives, including Fletchall, Pearis, and Robert Cunningham, announced their willingness to "Settle Peace" with the Whigs. In a petition to the Council of Safety, they expressed regret that they had been at odds with their countrymen and their wish to see unity restored in the province.[132] Richardson urged the council to release Cunningham and any others who were repentant, so long as they pledged their property as security for their future good behavior.[133]

Release from prison did not bring an end to the Loyalists' troubles. Pearis endured nine months of captivity only to return home to find "his House burnt, his Property destroyed and his Family drove off." Pearis rejoined his family and learned that the Whigs who burned his home had also beaten and abused his daughters. He stayed with his family for a time "but was so harrassed that he was obliged to fly" to Charleston, where he obtained protection from the rebel governor John Rutledge.[134] Evan McLaurin, a merchant and militia leader who had managed to avoid capture, likewise could not escape persecution. The Whigs seized £400 ($52,500) worth of deerskins he had shipped to Charleston, and harassment at home ruined his business.[135]

The Whigs exulted in their victory. The Council of Safety embraced Richardson's and Thomson's sophistry and approved their decision to ignore the terms of the treaty between Williamson and the Loyalists.[136] Henry Laurens expressed joy at the speed with which the rebels had managed to suppress the king's supporters. They had "obliged many hundreds of the Insurgents to Surrender their Arms, took about 150 prisoners of the most troublesome ringleaders & drove out of the Country Such as would not Surrender."[137] With the most active Loyalists either gone from the province or in prison, Laurens stated that "the common people whom they had deluded are convinced of their mistake & in general declare their willingness to join their Brethren" in defense of their rights.[138]

Governor Campbell expressed great disappointment at the Loyalists' defeat. He had hoped that the backcountry people would remain united and prevent the Whigs from gaining complete control of the province until British troops arrived.[139] He attributed their decision to sign a treaty with the rebels to "want

of a leader of either consequence or knowledge enough to direct their enter-
prises." The unscrupulous Whigs then "broke every article of it and are I am
told determined to extirpate the whole body" of Loyalists.[140]

Although the rebels did not go as far as Campbell had feared, they did take
advantage of the disorganization of the Loyalists resulting from the imprisonment and exile of their leaders. The Whigs seized this opportunity to appoint
reliable men to command the backcountry militia. With the rebels in control of
the militia, "the loyalists stood no chance. They could not organize a counter-
force, for they were disarmed, atomized, and terrorized."[141] Yet, rebel leaders
realized that they had by no means eradicated loyalism in the backcountry. In
1776 the Council of Safety had to send ammunition to the Whig militia in the
Ninety Six district "to keep the Tories in awe, who were plenty enough in that
section and continued to do more mischief."[142]

The Whigs continued to harass any Loyalist who challenged their authority.
On June 29, 1776, rebel troops arrested John Champneys for refusing to do duty
with the militia. He was imprisoned in Charleston with twenty-one other Loyalists and suffered through several days of "insults and bad usage." The prisoners
petitioned rebel leaders for permission to take an oath of neutrality; they were still
awaiting a reply when someone fired a bullet through the window of their room.
"This leaden messenger occasioned the conversion of six of the prisoners, who took
the oath of allegiance . . . the same day," Champneys wrote. Eventually most of the
prisoners swore an oath declaring that the British government had violated American rights, which earned four men their release. However, although Champneys
had taken the oath, he and five other prisoners were marched to the Cheraw jail.
Champneys remained in prison there until January 15, 1777, during which time his
six-year-old son died. The Whigs refused his pleas to be allowed to return home to
aid his family. Champneys was finally sent back to Charleston and released on
February 24 with orders to leave South Carolina within sixty days.[143]

In Georgia the rebels' position was more precarious, and in consequence they
acted with more restraint than did their neighbors to the north. South Carolina's
Whigs grew so frustrated with Georgia's reluctance to join the rebels that on February 5, 1775, they banned all trade between South Carolina and Georgia, on the
grounds that the latter's populace was "unworthy of the rights of freedom, and as
inimical to the liberties of their country." The Continental Congress took similar
steps in May 1775.[144]

In response to this prodding, Georgia Whigs moved to consolidate their control by striking at the Loyalists. On June 5 the rebels ordered William Tongue, a
loyal refugee from New York who had just arrived in Savannah, to leave the province within seven days or "abide by any consequences that may follow." Three
other Loyalists received a similar warning.[145] Having heard a report that the pilot
John Hopkins had drunk a toast damning America, a rebel mob seized him at his
Savannah home on the evening of July 25 and carried him to the town square.

From the *Universal Magazine* 64 (April 1779). Courtesy of South Caroliniana Library, University of South Carolina, Columbia

There Hopkins was tarred and feathered and then carted through the streets for three hours. The mob forced him to "drink 'Damnation to all Tories and Success to American Liberty'" and repeatedly threatened to hang him. He was finally released, and the crowd dispersed with threats to apply the same treatment to the Reverend Haddon Smith, rector of Christ Church, who had refused to observe a fast day declared by the Continental Congress.[146] Wright witnessed the abuse of Hopkins, which the governor described as "a horrid spectacle."[147] When Smith learned of the incident and the threats made against him, he fled to Tybee and from there sailed to England.[148]

Loyalists living outside Savannah also faced persecution. Mobs at Sunbury tarred and feathered James Watts, a ship's carpenter, for loyalism and attacked James Kitching, the collector of customs, on the night of August 1. The mob plundered Kitching's home when he refused to sign the association. Kitching then fled by boat to Tybee, where he found safety aboard a British warship after a twenty-hour journey.[149]

Such mob actions notwithstanding, Georgia rebels worried about their province's reluctance to commit itself to the Revolutionary movement. Peter Taarling told John Houstoun that Georgia's Whigs lacked "warlike spirit." Taarling wished that Georgians "had a 10th. part" of the enthusiasm displayed by northern rebels and could only hope that "a few months more, may rouse us."[150]

Loyal Georgians thought that the Whigs were aggressive enough. One Savannah resident noted that Loyalists in the province were in no condition to protect themselves. They were "not sufficiently supplied with ammunition, nor can they possibly collect together those who would readily join them, they being dispersed up and down the country."[151] Dr. Thomas Taylor, an English immigrant who arrived at Savannah in December 1775, noted that "in this province two out of three are friends to government, but as there is neither ships nor troops to protect them, they know it is in vain to oppose the current, as the Carolina people are all in arms."[152] When Taylor reached the backcountry town of Wrightsborough in early January 1776, he found that most people in the vicinity were also loyal to Britain. "Altho' this Province has acceded to the Resolutions of the Congress yet the Majority of the People are Friends to Government," he wrote. News of the defeat of the backcountry Loyalists in South Carolina had further demoralized the Georgia Loyalists, however. They had learned that their counterparts "have been lately dispersd" and that "about 150 have been taken Prisoners who after being cruelly used were sent down to Charles Town. The rest dare not return to their Habitations so that the Country around is pillagd & desolate."[153] This convinced most of the king's friends in the Georgia backcountry to remain passive and avoid offending the Whigs.

When a British naval squadron arrived off Savannah in mid-January to procure rice for the Boston garrison, frightened Whigs took prompt action to prevent any cooperation between Loyalists and the Royal Navy. Eminent Loyalists, including Governor Wright, were "bound up by a parole, not to aid or assist any of his Majesty's ships or troops," while less prominent inhabitants suspected of loyalism were disarmed.[154]

Some Georgians showed reluctance to resist the British. When the Council of Safety ordered a militia company from St. Matthew's Parish to march to Savannah's defense in January, all but one of the men refused to go. The Whigs accused two Loyalists, tavern keeper James Pace and planter John Hall, of telling the militiamen that they had no obligation to obey rebels. The council ordered both men arrested.[155]

When fighting between the British ships and Georgians onshore broke out on March 3, many Loyalists took advantage of the confusion to flee to the British. The rebels "were inflamed" by the battle, and "particularly at our own People who had treacherously Joined the Enemy against us."[156] Governor Wright, who had already sought safety aboard a British warship, asked the naval commander to stay to protect the Loyalists, but that officer had orders to return to Boston. Wright, fearing for his own safety, had no choice but to abandon the province.[157]

The last vestige of British authority now vanished in Georgia "as a result of the battle and the flight of Governor Wright." The Whigs triumphed, "not because a majority of the Georgians were willing" to openly rebel, "but because a highly organized and determined minority" had overthrown royal government.[158] Wright would later state that with the help of the Loyalists he had "Checked the Spirit & Attempts of the Factions, & kept Georgia out of the Rebellion, & Prevented them from Sending Delegates to Congress for near twelve Months." He insisted that it was only the lack of troops and the efforts of South Carolina rebels in "Spiriting up the ill affected in Georgia, & giving them assistance" that led to the downfall of royal government in his province.[159]

Many Loyalists decided to follow the governor's example and escape while they still had an opportunity to do so. The merchant William Moss, expecting to be arrested or assaulted, had fled from Savannah to his plantation upriver when the British ships arrived. From there he sailed in his schooner to join the British, took several other refugees aboard, and went on to St. Augustine. John Lightenstone (or Lichtenstein), operator of a scout boat for the provincial government, fled his house at Yamacraw when the rebels came looking for him. He hid in a field until his slaves could safely get him to his boat and row him to the British flagship. Other Loyalists joined him; all were eventually taken to Halifax, Nova Scotia, leaving their families and possessions behind.[160]

Whig leader Lachlan McIntosh considered the skirmishes with the British fleet and its subsequent withdrawal to be a major victory. He hoped it would convince many Loyalists to join the rebels, but he still worried that the Loyalists "may prevail" in carrying out "their own Sinister Ends" of opposing the Whigs.[161] To insure that this did not happen, the rebels launched new attacks on the Loyalists. On June 26 the Council of Safety proscribed forty-three Georgians deemed a threat to American liberty. Some of the named Loyalists fled to East Florida, but most remained in the province and managed to escape harassment. The council took more aggressive action against the Reverend John J. Zubly. Zubly had staunchly defended American rights in articulate sermons and pamphlets since the Stamp Act crisis and had represented Georgia in the Continental Congress until his opposition to independence led him to resign. Despite his peaceable demeanor and prior contributions to the Whig cause, the council declared the minister a danger to public safety and ordered his arrest.[162]

Local Whig leaders also took steps to control or punish Loyalists. In September the rebel committee in St. Andrew's Parish decided that Loyalists could no longer be allowed to go at large. The Whigs asserted that the Loyalists showed "an Inveterate hatred, & malice against the cause of America . . . which threaten our own safety." The Loyalists were charged with various crimes, including the refusal to pay fines imposed on them by the assembly and "Rejoicing on every Prospect of the success of our Enemies whether Civilized (if they may be so called) or Savages." The committee ordered that twenty-nine men be taken immediately into custody until they took the oath of allegiance to the state or gave adequate security for their good behavior.[163]

The twenty-nine Loyalists marked for arrest were all men, but women did not escape persecution. "At the outbreak of the war, Loyalist women expected that 'their Sex and the Humanity of a civilized People' would protect them from 'disrespectfull Indignities.' Most of them soon learned otherwise." The Whigs "consigned female loyalists to much the same fate as their male relatives." Women whose husbands had fled were particularly vulnerable, and rebels frequently plundered their property. Loyal women were "verbally abused, imprisoned, and threatened with bodily harm even when they had not taken an active role in opposing the rebel cause." Women who directly aided the British, usually by helping prisoners or gathering intelligence, often suffered physical abuse as well.[164]

When possible, most Loyalist refugees brought their families with them; however, this did not protect them from other hardships. About 180 Loyalists fled to Amelia Island, where they spent the summer of 1776 suffering from heat, hunger, and insects. One refugee, Jeremy Wright, watched his property burning on the mainland after Whigs torched the buildings. Refugees traveling overland to East Florida could not escape the Whigs' wrath either. After the rebels plundered his Ogeechee River plantation in September 1776, James Shivers gathered his family and movable possessions and set out for East Florida. On the way he was attacked by Whigs, who carried off eight slaves and seventy-five head of cattle. He received two hundred acres of land from Governor Tonyn, however, which enabled him to establish a farm.[165]

Tonyn did everything in his power to fulfill his promise to make East Florida "an asylum to the friends of the Constitution." To facilitate settling the refugees, Tonyn procured Dartmouth's assent to suspend all restrictions on the sale and granting of provincial lands. Tonyn then issued a proclamation announcing the availability of land, which circulated in South Carolina and Georgia, encouraging further immigration.[166] Many refugees, however, found it difficult to obtain land because large tracts had been granted earlier to absentees who had never come to Florida. On November 1, 1776, forty-nine Loyalists from Georgia petitioned Tonyn, explaining their difficulty in acquiring small tracts of farmland. The governor referred the matter to London, and in March 1777 the government declared that all granted lands that had not been settled or developed for three or more years reverted to the Crown. This enabled Tonyn to divide the large parcels and provide land to the petitioners and other refugees.[167]

Tonyn also personally intervened to allow Loyalists to sell provisions and livestock that were badly needed in the province. Some refugees had brought these items to East Florida, and Loyalists in the rebellious provinces also managed to ship grain to St. Augustine. Unfortunately, royal officials there confiscated most of these goods in accordance with the British embargo on trade with the thirteen colonies. Tonyn issued licenses allowing Loyalists to circumvent the embargo, which alleviated the financial distress of the refugees while meeting the province's need for provisions.[168]

Fearing a Whig attack on East Florida, Tonyn decided to create a battalion of militia to defend the province. On August 20, 1776, he addressed the inhabitants of St. Augustine and urged them to serve. To his satisfaction, "the whole joyfully consented," and Tonyn appointed Lt. Gov. John Moultrie as colonel of the unit. Tonyn expected to raise four companies in St. Augustine, two from settlers along the St. John's River and four companies of blacks.[169]

The rebels had already launched attacks along the northern border of East Florida. In May 1776 the Georgia Council of Safety ordered Capt. William McIntosh to clear Loyalists from their plantations along the St. Mary's River. McIntosh attacked five plantations, captured four Loyalists, and destroyed buildings and crops. Tonyn had learned of the impending raid and ordered troops to the St. Mary's, but they arrived too late to prevent the damage. During a skirmish with the retreating rebels, three of the four Loyalist prisoners managed to escape. The Whigs struck again in early July, plundering plantations, carrying off some fifty slaves, and seizing a few Loyalists. A month later another raid destroyed a fort built by Charles Wright on the St. Mary's; the Whigs then plundered and burned the plantations between that river and the St. John's. The elderly Wright and twenty-four of his slaves "died of exposure and malnutrition" as a result of the upheaval. East Floridians in the area fled south seeking safety.[170]

Southern Whigs and Continental army commander Gen. Charles Lee decided to follow up the raids with an invasion of East Florida to eliminate the threat posed by the British presence there. In August, Lee assembled a force of Georgians, South Carolinians, and Virginians and began his march.[171] Rebel patrols eventually reached the St. John's River, devastating the property of the few remaining Loyalists along the way. However, the main force got no farther than Sunbury, Georgia, before sickness and lack of supplies halted its advance. The rebels then abandoned the effort.[172]

Tonyn then seized the initiative by launching retaliatory raids into Georgia. Despite his years of service in the regular army, "Tonyn adapted with startling ease to the type of warfare he was required to wage." He authorized Thomas Brown to organize refugees from the southern provinces into a ranger unit to defend East Florida and when possible to undertake operations against the

Whigs in Georgia.[173] In October the Loyalists counterattacked, burning plantations in Georgia at Beard's Bluff and in the area south of the Altamaha River without encountering serious opposition.[174]

The Loyalists had made a valiant effort to uphold royal authority, particularly in South Carolina. They had resisted persuasion, persecution, and economic coercion and held their own against rebel armed force. Only when the Whigs reneged on a peace agreement to surprise and disarm them and arrested their leaders did resistance in South Carolina finally collapse. Loyalists in Georgia had enabled Wright to remain in office longer than any other governor in the thirteen colonies, while East and West Floridians stood firm in their allegiance to the Crown. Despite several reverses, most Loyalists did not abandon their principles; they only awaited the right opportunity to rally again under the king's standard.

SOUTHERN INDIANS: A MIXED RESPONSE

All of the southern Indians carefully observed the developing conflict between Great Britain and the colonies. John Stuart expected the Catawbas to side with the Whigs but planned to restrain the other nations until British troops were available to cooperate with them. The rebels pursued an almost identical policy, inviting the Catawbas to join them while working to keep the neighboring Cherokees and Creeks neutral. However, neither Stuart nor the Whig agents could ultimately control the Indians. Seeing an opportunity to strike at the land-hungry colonists, the Cherokees ignored Stuart's admonitions and attacked the southern frontier in the summer of 1776. The assault failed; the Cherokees suffered a disastrous defeat that rendered them incapable of assisting the British for some time and convinced most Creeks to remain aloof from the conflict.

There was never any question regarding the Catawbas' alignment. On July 25, 1775, the South Carolina Council of Safety thanked Joseph Kershaw, the Whigs' representative to that nation, for sending assurances that "those People are hearty in our Interest" and willing to provide men to serve with the rebels.[175] Two Catawba leaders visited Charleston in August to inquire into the political situation. The Whigs explained that they were engaged in a quarrel with other white men and that they "expected their [Catawba] warriors would join ours."[176] Catawba interests and rebel interests, the Whigs asserted, were "just the same."[177] William Henry Drayton, always belligerent, warned the Catawbas that they faced dire consequences if they waged war against the South Carolinians.[178]

Any fears Drayton had that the Catawbas might ally with the British were unfounded. John Stuart made no attempt to court them, recognizing that those Indians had been "practised upon and seduced by the Inhabitants with whom they live." By autumn the Catawbas had begun to assist the rebels; forty of them went to the lowcountry to track down fugitive Loyalists and slaves.[179] Kershaw appointed Samuel Boykin as captain of the Catawba auxiliaries. Boykin and thirty-four Indians took the field in February 1776, again to capture runaway slaves.[180] In June, Boykin gathered about fifty Catawbas to help defend Charleston against the impending British attack. The Indians were promised "Colony pay."[181] These Catawbas comprised part of the defensive force at the northern end of Sullivan's Island.[182]

The Whigs could manage the Catawbas easily enough, but they knew that Stuart's influence with the other Indian nations would have to be countered. They decided to strike directly at the superintendent by circulating rumors that Stuart had received orders to lead Indian attacks and incite slave insurrections in South Carolina.[183] As the rebel leaders intended, Stuart quickly found himself facing the "Fury of a merciless and ungovernable Mob."[184] At the end of May 1775 he fled Charleston for the comparative safety of Savannah. Not content with having driven Stuart from South Carolina, Whig leaders in Charleston circulated handbills in Beaufort and Savannah repeating the allegation that the superintendent planned to order Indian attacks on the frontier. This, along with emissaries from South Carolina who proclaimed Stuart's villainy, inflamed the Georgians as well.[185]

Stuart met with some of Georgia's Whig leaders and tried to convince them that "no steps had ever been taken to interest the Indians in the Dispute between Great Brittain and the Colonies, but at the same time I told them that I had constantly considered it as my principal Duty to Dispose the Indians to confide in His Majesty's Justice and Protection, and to act for His Service if required." This statement did not reassure the rebels, who warned Stuart that it was dangerous for him to remain in Savannah. He then escaped in a canoe to a British warship, barely escaping the boatloads of armed and angry men who pursued him. Stuart then sailed to St. Augustine, where he found refuge but no respite from the Whigs' slanderous assaults. He learned that the rebels continued to spread "the Greatest falsehoods . . . in order to inflame the people against me."[186]

In what was undoubtedly a ruse intended to lure Stuart back to South Carolina so that the Whigs could place him in custody, the Committee of Intelligence wrote to the superintendent suggesting that he could demonstrate his good intentions by returning to Charleston, where the provincial congress would happily vindicate him if he could prove his innocence. Meanwhile, the committee declared, his property "stands as a Security for the good Behaviour of the Indians in the Southern Department."[187] Stuart, knowing the risks involved if he returned to Charleston, replied that he had no intention of inciting an Indian war. He added that it was ironic that his property was held as security for the Indians' good behavior, since their actions depended not on his instructions but "upon the Conduct of the inhabitants of the Provinces."[188]

Not content with having driven Stuart to East Florida and threatening to seize his property, the Whigs proceeded to take punitive measures against his wife and married daughter. On February 3, 1776, the provincial congress ordered that the two women be confined to their home in Charleston "as hostages for his [Stuart's] good behavior." Two days later the congress allowed Stuart's daughter to leave Charleston with her husband, on condition that she not leave the province, and permitted Mrs. Stuart to leave her house if accompanied by an officer. However, Stuart's wife could not receive visitors without written permission from rebel officials.[189] Henry Laurens believed that the measure was effective, writing that "nothing but Mr. Stuarts family has for Some time past been a barrier against the massacre & butchery of hundreds of Innocent families in Georgia and Carolina."[190] Stuart took a dimmer view of the matter, writing that his wife had been detained, "insulted and threatened."[191] Despite rebel precautions, Mrs. Stuart eventually escaped, and her son-in-law was immediately jailed "on suspicion of aiding and assisting her."[192]

With Stuart gone, the Whigs focused their attention on Alexander Cameron, his deputy to the Cherokees. Like Stuart, Cameron fled to avoid capture. On July 14 Cameron's friend and Whig colonel Andrew Williamson reported that Cameron had "gone to the Cherokee Nation" and that "at this Time there is a good deal of Confusion" in the backcountry "on Acct. of the expected Danger from the Cherokees." Williamson promised to quiet these fears, as he had received assurances from Cameron that the latter had no intention of ordering the Indians to attack the province.[193]

The Whigs then tried to convince Cameron to join them. When that failed, they resorted as usual to threats and violence. On July 23 the Council of Safety asked Williamson to offer Cameron a position as the Whigs' agent to the Cherokees, with the same salary he received from the British.[194] William Henry Drayton wrote Cameron that the rebels "look upon you as an object dangerous to our welfare" and would not be satisfied until Cameron had moved a sufficient distance from the Cherokees to be unable to exercise his duties as Stuart's representative. Drayton suggested St. Augustine or Pensacola as acceptable destinations. In case Cameron misunderstood the nature of the request, Drayton noted that it "carries all the force of a command."[195]

Replying to Drayton's threats in mid-October, Cameron politely stated that he could not comply with Whig demands. He also said that he found it strange that he was "threatened with condign punishment" when all his efforts had been directed "to cultivate peace and friendship between the Indians" and the South Carolinians.[196]

The Whigs did not even wait for Cameron's reply before sending their militia to seize him. Col. William Thomson set out with some troops in late July to find the agent and learned on July 31 that Cameron was at Oconee Creek with a dozen white men and several Indians. Thomson immediately marched to surprise his quarry, but on entering the town of Seneca he was ambushed by a party he estimated at thirty whites and thirty Cherokees. After driving off the defenders, Thomson burnt the village and six thousand bushels of corn. He then ordered other Whig units to burn nearby Cherokee towns. Captured whites informed

Thomson that Cameron was about thirty miles away, with "about one hundred and fifty white men and Indians."[197]

Cameron finally reached safety in the Cherokee town of Keowee in mid-August. He noted that the Cherokees were "very cross about the usage their father [Stuart] met with in Charles Town, and me at Long Canes being obliged to leave our houses. That they see plainly that the white people mean a war with them," a conclusion that was not surprising after Thomson's attack on Seneca. The Cherokees, Cameron believed, preferred war sooner rather than later and "are to a man resolved to stand for the great King and his warriors." He wanted ammunition for them and wanted to know Stuart's whereabouts. Despite the uncertain situation, Cameron took comfort in the Cherokees' loyalty both to him and to the king. They were "the most faithful Indians on the main," he wrote. The rebels intercepted this letter, which helped convince them that quick action was essential to forestall a Cherokee attack.[198]

Ominous reports of Cherokee intentions had been coming from the backcountry throughout the summer. Robert Goudey swore a deposition at Ninety Six on July 10 that earlier in the day Man Killer of Keowee, a Cherokee, told him that "Some Few Days ago, a Certain John Vann told the Indians in the Cherokee Nation that they must fall upon the White people on This Side Savannah River and kill them (Meaning the people of South Carolina)" but that the Georgians were not to be molested. According to Man Killer, the Cherokees had replied that "they Could not go to War, that they had no Ammunition."[199]

On August 20 the Reverend William Tennent informed Henry Laurens that the Loyalists were preparing to strike and that he had heard that "Cameron is among the over hill Cherokees and will soon join them with 3,000 gun men."[200] In a subsequent letter Tennent asserted that the Loyalists were too few to challenge the Whigs alone and that "their Dependance is upon the Savages to join their Army. & that the rest of the Inhabitants will be forced to join them, to save their Families from a Massacre."[201] Jonathan Clark of the Ninety Six district told Drayton that John Garwick, a friend of Cameron, had warned Clark that when British troops arrived in South Carolina, Clark should "remove from the frontiers." Garwick added that three weeks earlier Cameron had met with four hundred Cherokees and urged them to support the king's troops, and that the Indians, after being assured that Cameron would supply them with ammunition, signified with gunshots and war whoops their willingness to attack the colonists.[202]

Other accounts, however, contradicted these reports, leaving the Whigs uncertain as to how they should proceed. "Our Cherokee Indians according to advices which we have just received . . . are well disposed towards us," Henry Laurens wrote on August 20. He added that the Cherokees "pathetically lament the Scarcity of Gunn Powder & Bullets" but thought that "it would not be consistent with Sound policy if we were just now to Supply them with those articles."[203]

With the affairs of the British Indian department apparently in disarray, rebel leaders saw an opportunity to keep the Indians peaceful by assuming management of Indian affairs. In early August, South Carolina Whigs learned that Congress had created three Indian departments, divided geographically, and allocated ten thousand dollars to the southern department for presents and other expenses. South Carolina appointed George Galphin, an Indian trader with a Creek wife and several mixed-race children, to act as one of three agents to the Creeks. Andrew Williamson, the backcountry militia colonel, was named one of three representatives to the Cherokees.[204]

William Henry Drayton, still in the backcountry after his failed mission to convert Loyalists, took it upon himself to deal with the Cherokees as well. In September he met with some Cherokee leaders at the Congarees and attempted to explain the political situation. Drayton said that the Whigs were in part fighting to preserve the deerskin trade. He asserted that since the British abused fellow white men, the Indians should not expect better treatment.[205]

Yet, while Whig leaders courted the Cherokees, other whites undermined their efforts. In late September four Georgians murdered a Cherokee man and wounded two others "in cold blood." Although rebel officials claimed that the assault was "a contrivance by our Enemies to set those barbarians upon us," the crime increased their fears of an Indian attack.[206] Colonel Thomson sent some of his Whig militia to apprehend the culprits in order to conciliate the Cherokees.[207]

To further placate the Cherokees, in October the Whigs finally relented and agreed to provide them with gunpowder and lead. When the Loyalists seized the wagon carrying munitions, the rebels sent an emissary to the Cherokees with a promise that the ammunition would be sent as soon as the Whigs had recaptured it.[208]

While the Whigs attempted to gain the Indians' goodwill, Stuart and his deputies, whose activities had not been disrupted to the extent the rebels believed, continued to exercise their influence with the southern nations. As he had repeatedly told the Whigs, Stuart's goal was to keep the Indians neutral. He informed David Taitt, his representative to the Creeks, that in spite of the persecution he had suffered, he was "so far inclined to retaliate good for evil, that I wish to maintain peace." Stuart told Taitt to avoid any statements that might incite the Creeks to war and instead to try "to preserve peace, and attach the Indians to his Majesty's interest." Taitt's most important duty, Stuart declared, was "to frustrate the machinations of Mr. Galphin and his associates."[209] Stuart also sent talks to the Creeks and Cherokees in which he emphasized his desire that the Indians remain at peace. The "difference between the people in England and the white people in America . . . does not concern you," he told the Cherokees; "they will decide it between themselves." Stuart promised to do his best to provide supplies to both nations and urged them to follow the advice of his agents.[210]

Cameron worked particularly hard to keep the Cherokees neutral because of his own aversion to an Indian war. In November he told Stuart that if the Indians attacked the colonists, "the Issue of it would be terrible, as they could not be restrained from Committing the most inhuman barbarities on Women and Children." Cameron added that he thought himself unable to lead the Indians "against Friends, Neighbours and fellow Subjects . . . altho the behaviour of the people would almost justify me in doing it."[211]

In September, Gage finally sent Stuart instructions "to make [the Indians] take arms against His Majesty's enemies" if an opportunity arose.[212] Stuart, however, was reluctant to do so until the ministry confirmed the orders. The superintendent replied only that he would work to keep the Indians firmly attached to the king. He also advised his brother and deputy Henry Stuart to go among the Upper Creeks, try to obtain their commitment to assist the British, and then consult with Taitt as to how the Indians could be used to distress the rebels. After that, Henry Stuart was to visit the Cherokees and urge them to expel rebel agents and traders from their nation. John Stuart understood that it was more important to eliminate rebel influence and secure the Indians' allegiance than to launch a premature war.[213]

When Stuart learned in December that fighting had broken out between Loyalists and rebels in the South Carolina backcountry, he ordered Cameron to bring the Cherokees to aid the Loyalists but not to launch indiscriminate attacks on the frontier. Stuart's plan was foiled because Cameron did not receive the letter until six months later.[214] Many Loyalists, however, did take refuge among the Cherokees after their defeat. Whig colonel Richard Richardson believed that those Loyalists had actually "gone to bring the Indians Down" to attack the rebels. If so, Richardson declared, "it Cou'd not be in a better time," since the Whig militia was assembled and ready.[215]

The expected Indian attack did not come, but many Whigs believed that war was imminent. News reached Charleston on February 22, 1776, that the Cherokees had scalped two whites and "danced the War Dance." Other reports alleged that Stuart was in Boston discussing plans with British officers for an attack on the southern colonies. "Lord Dartmouth's Indian Engines will probably now begin their pious play of Butchering Women & Children," Henry Laurens wrote.[216] Some Whigs, however, believed that an Indian war would benefit them by uniting the backcountry people. Pierce Butler declared that "if the Indians are prevail'd on to attack us," the men in the frontier districts would unite to protect their homes.[217]

The Cherokees were, in fact, considering war. The militant faction in the nation saw conflict among the whites as an opportunity to strike back against those who had taken their land. Dragging Canoe, the militant leader, visited Henry Stuart at Mobile during the spring of 1776 to announce his support for the British. Henry Stuart provided Dragging Canoe with a large quantity of ammunition, which the latter brought to the Cherokee town of Chota. There

Stuart and Cameron conferred with leaders from all parts of the nation. The British agents urged the Cherokees to remain at peace, but they could not sway Dragging Canoe or other militants, who paid more attention to the Shawnee and Mohawk emissaries who favored war. Nor could accommodationist Cherokee leaders such as Oconostota or Attakulla Kulla dissuade Dragging Canoe. Stuart gave up his effort to argue for peace, contenting himself with obtaining a promise from the militants that they would not cross the Indian boundary or kill women, children, or Loyalists when they went to war.[218]

The Cherokees began their attacks on July 1, targeting frontier settlements from Georgia to Virginia and catching the Whigs by surprise.[219] Rebel leaders had been lulled to some degree; "the Cherokees had amused us by the most flattering Talks, full of assurances of friendship," Henry Laurens wrote. Then, "very suddenly, without any pretence to Provocation those treacherous Devils in various Parties headed by White Men" struck the frontiers, killing an estimated sixty South Carolinians.[220]

The attacks threw the South Carolina backcountry into confusion. "The whole country was flying," one Whig reported, "some to make forts, others as low as Orangeburgh." Officers tried to muster the militia, "but the panic was so great" that few men turned out at first.[221] The Cherokees "spread great desolation all along the frontiers" of the province, a Whig wrote; "Plantations lie desolate, and hopeful crops are going to ruin."[222] In North Carolina, William Sharpe wrote that people for fifty miles along the frontier in Rowan and Tryon counties had abandoned their homes and taken refuge in garrisons, and that four men and six children had been killed and a militia officer mortally wounded. "About thirty houses burned and plantations destroyed hundreds of fields loaded with A plentiful harvest laid waste and destroyed, many Cattle killed and horses taken away," he reported.[223]

As Henry Laurens had observed, many of the initial Cherokee attacks were conducted jointly by Indians and white Loyalists. On July 15 the Whigs repulsed an attack on a militia camp, after which the Indians fled and thirteen whites were captured. By July 19, however, reports began to arrive that "the white people in general had quitted the Indians" after an estimated 88 Cherokees and 102 whites made an unsuccessful attack on Lindley's Fort. Some whites who abandoned the Cherokees turned themselves in to rebel militia officers and were imprisoned at Ninety Six.[224]

Many Whigs believed that, before the attacks, the Cherokees and Loyalists had devised signals so that the Indians could identify and spare Loyalists. The Cherokees were said to have "observed sacredly" these signs, except in a few instances.[225] It is possible that some Loyalists received warnings from friends who had escaped to the Indians, but there is scant evidence that most Loyalists had advance notice of the Cherokee attack. One person who insisted that there had been collusion, the Reverend James Creswell, asserted that the Loyalists in the Ninety Six district "were really elated with the prospect" of Cherokee intervention. He accused Loyalist militiamen of failing to appear at musters in the weeks preceding the attack, which he considered proof that the Loyalists had made a secret compact "to assist the savages to ruin the country." Yet, Creswell also wrote that the Cherokees "killed the disaffected in common, without distinction of party," which, he said, caused many Loyalists to abandon their plans to cooperate with the Indians.[226]

Fulfilling Pierce Butler's prediction, the Cherokee attacks promoted unity among most backcountry inhabitants, regardless of their political principles. Loyalist Alexander Chesney "marched against the Indians, to which I had no objection," and seemed proud of the fact that he "helped destroy 32 of their towns."[227] Robert Cunningham "would not at first believe that the British Administration were so wicked as to Instigate the Savages to War against us." When he realized it was true, Cunningham and other Loyalists imprisoned in Charleston offered to serve against the Cherokees, and the Council of Safety released them from confinement.[228] Cunningham and Richard Pearis reported to Andrew Williamson's camp as volunteers. Although suspicious of Pearis, Williamson was certain of Cunningham's reliability. Even so, Williamson decided that "it would be improper to confer any public trust" on Cunningham because the backcountry people were "so much exasperated" by the sight of Loyalists, some "painted as Indians," cooperating with the Cherokees.[229]

Most backcountry Loyalists did not see any contradiction between their support for royal authority and serving against the Cherokees. The Indians' presence blocked settlers' access to new lands and thus to potential economic advancement, and conflict between whites and Indians was endemic to the frontier. Neither Governor Campbell nor Stuart's agents had given the backcountry Loyalists any indication that the king's supporters and the Cherokees were now allies in a common cause. Without such instructions, the Loyalists followed their usual behavior and acted to protect their homes and families from the Indian threat. As a result, the king's white supporters who assisted the Whigs found themselves pitted against other Loyalists and their erstwhile Indian allies, so that Britain's supporters ended up weakening each other while simultaneously strengthening the Whig position in the backcountry.

Other Loyalists who had been victims of Whig persecution took advantage of the confusion that resulted from the Cherokee attacks to escape to Indian territory. David Fanning of Raebern's Creek, South Carolina, had first fled to the Cherokees in late 1775 when the Whigs subdued the backcountry Loyalists. Captured in January 1776, Fanning was briefly imprisoned and then was jailed a second time on suspicion of conspiring to assist the Cherokees. Amid the chaos caused by the Indian attacks, Fanning escaped to his home, where he found that "a number of my friends had already gone to the Indians, and more disposed so for to do." Fanning assembled twenty-five men and joined a Cherokee party of over two hundred warriors on Reedy River. After finding that Whig posts in the area were too strong to be attacked, Fanning left the Indians and went to North Carolina.[230] Other Loyalists as well took the opportunity to escape to the Cherokees; at least fifteen were later captured in the rebel offensive against the Cherokee towns.[231]

By July 22 the Whigs had recovered from the first shock of the Cherokee attack, and Williamson had assembled seven hundred militiamen to punish the "treachery and faithless behavior" of that nation.[232] Some Catawbas joined the Whig forces and served as scouts during the invasion of Cherokee territory.[233] Williamson began his advance on July 31. In the early morning hours of August 1, a large party of Cherokees ambushed the militia but were driven off. The rebels found one Indian dead and three seriously wounded on the field; their own losses were three killed and fourteen wounded. Williamson resumed his march and over the next several days burned many towns. On August 12 some Cherokees ambushed a Whig detachment commanded by Andrew Pickens. The encircled rebels managed to fight off their attackers and claimed to have killed or wounded eighty-three Indians. The militia then continued their march, burning towns and crops while most of the Cherokees fled to the mountains.[234] "I have now burnt down every town, and destroyed all the corn, from the Cherokee line to the middle settlements," Williamson reported on August 22. He spared only the town of Little Chota, which was on land claimed by the Creeks.[235]

Other Whig parties encountered few Indians and carried out their work of destruction with little opposition. Lt. William Lenoir of North Carolina served in a fifty-man militia unit that set out on August 17 to invade the Cherokee lands. After uniting with other militia units, the force grew to thirty-five hundred. Lenoir did not see any Cherokees until September 6, when a party of militia encountered five Indians. The next day twenty Cherokees attacked Lenoir's detachment, which had separated from the larger unit and numbered one thousand men. One North Carolinian was wounded before the Indians withdrew. The Cherokees killed one man on September 12 after a Whig party had killed and scalped a Cherokee woman.[236] The expedition reached the Cherokees' Valley towns on September 19 and on that day and the next killed eight Indians and took several prisoners while destroying the towns and cornfields. Two militiamen were killed by Indians on September 22, and on the same day John Roberson "killed an old Indian prisoner & was put under Guard Tyed for it." Two days later a detachment brought in two white prisoners with their Indian wives and mixed-blood children, plus four blacks and "some other prisoners." The party had also taken between seventy and eighty horses, some cattle, and a quantity of deerskins. The plunder was sold the next day at high prices; the captured Indians and blacks were probably sold as well.[237]

The North Carolinians met Williamson's militia at the town of Hiwassee on September 26 after both forces had destroyed every Indian town within their reach. The combined force completed its work of destruction, which in addition to the burned towns and provisions, claimed the lives of an estimated two thousand

Cherokee men, women, and children. South Carolina reported a loss of ninety-nine men killed in the campaign; the casualties of the other southern states were lower. It had been a small price to pay to break Cherokee power.[238]

Some militia units continued to launch raids against the Cherokees until late in the year. Brig. Gen. Griffith Rutherford of North Carolina sent nearly one hundred men on a march deep into Cherokee territory in mid-October. They killed and scalped a few Indians, captured three others, and burned a small town of twenty-five houses. At an abandoned Cherokee camp the Whigs found an "Abundance of plunder, of Horses And Other Goods, to the Amount of Seven Hundred Pounds." When the raiders returned, they sold their plunder and divided the proceeds. The fate of the three captives, however, caused a dispute between Capt. William Moore, who wanted to keep the women and boy as prisoners until they could be properly questioned, and the other officers and men, who "Swore Bloodily that if they were not Sold for Slaves upon the Spot, they would kill and Scalp them Immediately." Moore relented to save the Indians' lives, and they were sold. Eager to procure more slaves and plunder, Moore's troops announced that they were "Very Desirous" to undertake another expedition against the Cherokees.[239]

The Whigs had to limit their actions against the Cherokees in order to end the war quickly and avoid the risk of being assailed on two fronts should British forces return to the South. Rebel officials therefore halted the militia raids. When a Captain Robinson of the Watauga settlement sought permission in mid-November to invade the Overhill Cherokee lands to get horses, he received a stern refusal from William Christian, who ordered that no one be permitted to enter Cherokee territory.[240]

The rebels' victory over the Cherokees had far-reaching consequences. Devastated by the Whig counteroffensive, the Cherokees sued for peace. Only Dragging Canoe remained intransigent, taking his followers farther west rather than surrender.[241] By making skillful use of the fact that some Loyalists had fought alongside the Cherokees, the Whigs also managed "to score a propaganda victory . . . by tapping deep-seated anti-tribal fears among the backcountry farmers." The rebels manipulated the Indian issue so well that they emerged from the Cherokee war "as the opponents of alliance with the Cherokees, even though they had themselves courted the tribe."[242] Drayton articulated the new Whig position, declaring that "the public would have received an essential piece of service" if the whites who had aided the Cherokees had "been all instantly hanged." In addition, he believed that the war provided an opportunity to eliminate the Cherokees once and for all. Drayton advised militia officers to "cut up every Indian corn-field, and burn every Indian town" and suggested "that every Indian taken shall be the slave and property of the taker; that the nation be extirpated, and the lands become the property of the public."[243]

The timing of the Cherokee attack, which had begun just three days after the British attacked Charleston, provided more propaganda for the Whigs, since it

appeared to confirm their allegations that the British government had instigated the Indian war. Henry Laurens thought that the Cherokees "probably
acted in a concerted Plan with the Ships & Troops,"[244] while the Reverend Creswell wrote that it was "quite evident that the savages were made acquainted
with the designs of the British fleet against Charlestown, and that there was a
concerted scheme between them against our country."[245]

Another consequence of the Cherokees' defeat was that it made the Creeks
reluctant to assist the British. When the rebels launched their counterattack,
Charles Lee stated that one of their objectives was "striking a necessary terror
into the minds of the other Nations."[246] Henry Laurens likewise hoped that a
Whig victory would make other southern Indians "simple Spectators of our
contest" with Britain.[247] The results of the war met these expectations; Stuart
failed to convince the Creeks to assist the Cherokees and later reported that "all
the Southern Tribes are greatly dispirited, by the unopposed successes of the
Rebells, and no appearance of any Support from Government." Whig Indian
agent George Galphin contributed to Creek inactivity by circulating reports of
the devastation inflicted on the Cherokees.[248]

Whig leaders had been working to undermine Stuart's influence with the
Creeks since the summer of 1775, although they remained more wary of that
nation than of the Cherokees. Thus, the South Carolina Council of Safety
advised the Georgians to reject Creek demands for gunpowder, warning that
complying might "be putting Arms into their Hands, which they might be
influenced to use against the Colonies." Instead, the South Carolinians suggested giving some Creek leaders a small quantity of powder, which might be
enough to satisfy them.[249] Galphin, however, warned the council that unless
they could supply the Creeks, the Indians would think that the Whigs had lied
to them about their friendly intentions, as Stuart's agents had told the Creeks
that the rebels were deceiving them. Galphin noted that "about half the uper
Towns" of the Creeks were aligned with the British because of the Whigs'
inability to provide supplies and were using "all there Interest to bringe the rest
of the nation to there way of thinking," albeit without success.[250] This report
convinced members of the council to promise Galphin that they would provide
the Creeks with clothing and ammunition. However, two months later the
council informed Galphin that they were unable to deliver the two thousand
pounds of gunpowder he had requested for the Indians.[251]

The Georgians also took steps to maintain peace with the Creeks. Upon learning in January 1776 of "some disturbances that have lately happened between an
Indian and some white people," the Council of Safety ordered Whig committees in
the frontier counties to arrest any whites who disturbed "Indian amity with this
Province."[252] This failed to satisfy Galphin, who worried in early February that the
disruption of trade made war with the Creeks imminent. Aware that "it is the
Trade with them that keeps them in our Intrest," Galphin warned that action was

necessary to counter Stuart's efforts to unite the southern nations against the rebels. The combined strength of the Indians, Galphin wrote, was "ten or twelve thousand Gun men, but as long as we can keep the Creeks our Friends they will be a Barrier between us & all the other Indians." However, "if the trade is stop'd from here they will all go to Florida, & then we may Expect an Indian War, when Thirty or forty stragling Indians made the Greatest part of Georgia run, what must the whole Nation do," he asked.[253] In reply, the council sent Galphin one thousand pounds of gunpowder for the Creeks and pledged to procure blankets and more gunpowder. They also promised to seek assistance from the Continental Congress.[254]

Galphin's worries appeared chimerical when about seventy Creeks who were in Savannah fought alongside the Whigs in the March battle against the British. Afterward, Stukychee of the Cussitas allegedly declared that "he & his people would now join & assist" the Americans.[255] Hoping to capitalize on this sentiment, the Georgia Council of Safety considered providing the Creeks with cattle in exchange "for their good offices."[256] In May, because "several accounts received respecting the Indians are very unfavorable," the council continued its efforts to keep peace by repeating its orders to backcountry militia officers to do everything possible "to prevent the murder of any Indians."[257] At the same time, the Whigs took precautions by assigning sixty mounted men to guard their western border "from the insults of Indians who are likely to be troublesome."[258]

Georgians' fears of a Creek attack increased in the spring and summer. Lt. Col. Samuel Elbert of the Georgia Continentals warned Charles Lee that information from St. Augustine indicated that a joint British-Creek invasion was probable. "The Savages are too Much inclin'd [to use] the Hatchet against us," Elbert wrote.[259] The Council of Safety pleaded with Lee for assistance in July, shortly after the Cherokees had begun their attacks. "To the west . . . are the most numerous tribes of Indians now in North America, viz.: the Creeks, Cherokees, Choctaws, and a number of small tribes, in the whole at least 15,000 gun men," the council reminded Lee. "All of these nations have been much tampered with by the emissaries of Government, and without the utmost exertions of prudence on our side, it is feared may be brought to act against us."[260]

Lee used the southern Whigs' fear of the Creeks to convince them to support his plan to invade East Florida. He told Gov. John Rutledge of South Carolina that the conquest of East Florida would "make a most salutary impression on the minds of the Creeks—which is an object of the highest consideration." Lee asked Rutledge to provide some South Carolina troops to the expedition.[261] After receiving Lee's proposal, the Georgia Council of Safety agreed with the general that the occupation of East Florida would, "from principles of dread, attach the Indians to our interest" and cut off British communication with the Indian nations.[262] "I heartily wish the settlements" in East Florida "were entirely broke up," Lachlan McIntosh wrote, endorsing Lee's plan. "It would detach the Creek Indians from their [British] Interest."[263]

Many Georgia rebels, however, preferred to wage war against the Creeks rather than invade East Florida. Having seen the ease with which the Cherokees had been defeated, the Georgians hoped to similarly destroy the Creeks and seize their land. They pressured their own government and Lee to attack the Creeks, but Whig officials refused to approve a measure that might devastate Georgia.[264] War with the Creeks appeared likely enough without seeking a confrontation; in October an ominous report reached Savannah that representatives from the Creeks, Cherokees, Choctaws, and Chickasaws were meeting with Stuart at Pensacola to decide whether to launch "a general War" on the rebels. According to the informant, five hundred Creeks in Florida were ready to attack Georgia.[265]

As Whig relations with the Creeks worsened, Stuart's prospects for retaining that nation's allegiance correspondingly improved. In September 1776 Galphin's nephew, David Holmes, partially undermined Galphin's work by joining the British. Stuart promptly employed Holmes to work with the Creeks to take advantage of the latter's influence with them.[266] Patrick Tonyn also labored to keep the Creeks attached to the British interest, despite Germain's instructions to refrain from "indiscriminate use of Indians against the rebels."[267] The governor defused a potential crisis in the summer of 1776, when twenty-two Creeks raided East Floridians living along Indian River. Insisting that the settlers were "much more alarmed than hurt," Tonyn rejected proposals to retaliate. Instead, he summoned the Indians who were in the vicinity of St. Augustine, "said what was proper," and secured their promise to identify the offenders. He also asked David Taitt to inform Creek leaders that "such violences ought to be punished."[268]

The best way to maintain good relations with the Creeks, Tonyn believed, was to use them in conjunction with backcountry Loyalists to harass the rebels. The governor blamed Stuart for moving too slowly to bring the Indians into action, complaining to Gen. Henry Clinton that Stuart needed "a strong Spur" to get him to act.[269] Tonyn also expressed his "fear" to Germain that "it is the intention of the Government not to employ the Indians," adding that such a policy would be a mistake. The Indians, Tonyn asserted, were "ready to join the British troops." The governor added that he was "well informed the back country of the two Carolinas wished greatly for the Indians to cooperate with them, for His Majesty's service, but were in great dread of the Indians making an indiscriminate attack." However, Tonyn believed that "it would be easy to conduct the Indians discriminately" by appointing proper guides for them and designating locations where they could rendezvous with the Loyalists.[270]

Pressure from Tonyn and others finally convinced Germain in October 1776 to approve the use of Indians. Germain advised William Howe, the British army's new commander in chief in America, that if the general decided to undertake "a Southern Expedition" during the upcoming winter, an "Indian war" might facilitate his operations.[271] Several weeks later Germain emphasized the "great Importance of engaging the Southern Indians in Our Interest" in another letter to Howe. Stuart would be awaiting Howe's orders to employ the Indians "in seconding any Operations you may think fit to direct" in the South, Germain noted.[272] Howe had already decided to use Indians, albeit only in a defensive role. He had ordered Stuart on August 25 "to engage the Indians for the defence of the Florida's" as soon as possible.[273]

Some Creeks had already begun to assist the British. About twenty Creeks and some Loyalists attacked rebel troops near Fort Barrington in Georgia in October, killing four, destroying several plantations in the vicinity, and sending the inhabitants and militia fleeing. Two months later another Creek party raided a rebel post at Beard's Bluff; they then killed four Whigs when the garrison emerged to pursue the attackers. Most of the rebels then deserted the post.[274]

Other Creek leaders also appeared ready to join the war. Tonyn and Thomas Brown managed to convince Cowkeeper to commit the Seminoles to assist in the defense of East Florida, while Emestisiguo of the Upper Creeks informed Stuart in November 1776 that his people would attack the Americans if the northern nations would cooperate with them. At the end of the month several hundred Creeks gathered to resist a rumored rebel attack on the Lower Creeks, but the report proved false.[275]

Stuart had to consider defensive strategy as well as offensive maneuvers. Both he and Governor Chester recognized the importance of protecting West Florida as the base from which the Indians would be supplied.[276] Stuart also understood that the Indians would have to bear most of the burden of West Florida's defense, since the white population was small. In August 1776 he informed Germain that there were about "four hundred good white men, traders and packhorsemen" who lived among the Indians and "might be embodied" for use "in carrying on any service jointly with the Indians." Stuart added that such men, "acquainted with the manner and language of the Indians[,] . . . might, I conceive, be very useful and tend to prevent the disorders and excesses which bodies of Indians, not conducted by white men might probably commit."[277] Howe, who had heard rumors that the rebels planned to attack West Florida, agreed. He instructed Stuart to prepare the Indians to defend the province and to "appoint proper persons to accompany and lead" them.[278]

Stuart assigned the Chickasaws to guard the trails that passed through the upper Tombigbee valley in case the rebels attempted to march overland against the British posts on the Gulf of Mexico. He provided them with arms and ammunition; but when the superintendent asked them in late 1776 to guard the Mississippi and Tennessee river approaches to West Florida, the Chickasaws refused, claiming that such duty would interfere with their winter hunt.[279]

PHANTOM SLAVE INSURRECTIONS, REAL REPRESSION

When reports that British officials planned to arm slaves and incite insurrections reached South Carolina and Georgia, rebel leaders immediately took steps to prevent their slaves from assisting the British. The Whigs put the militia on guard, searched for signs of slave rebellion, and took harsh action against any blacks who appeared dangerous. Slave laws were rigorously enforced, so that "black people—free and slave—found that regulations which had gone unenforced for years were given new life."[280]

Upon hearing the first rumors of the alleged British plan, Charles Pinckney, commander of Charleston's Whig militia, informed the Loyalist lieutenant governor William Bull that he had information of "some bad designs in the negroes." At Pinckney's request, Bull issued an order increasing the strength of militia patrols in the town.[281] One company during the day and two at night patrolled Charleston to guard against slave insurrection.[282] Whig Josiah Smith wrote that the militia's primary duty was "to guard against any hostile attempts that might be made by our domesticks."[283] He also noted that the provincial congress's decision to create three regiments of troops was intended to keep slaves "in awe," as well as to resist a possible British attack.[284]

Because rebel authorities in South Carolina knew that in the event of such an attack many slaves would flee to the British at the first opportunity, they carefully studied how to prevent slaves in the lowcountry from reaching the king's forces. A committee charged with planning the colony's defense proposed a drastic measure: if the British approached the coast, "All the negroes between the sea, and a line drawn from North Edisto Inlet to Tugaloo, thence along the river to Stono, thence to Dorchester, thence to Goose Creek bridge, thence to the mouth of Back river, thence to Cain Hoy, and thence to the sea, should be removed" to safer locations. The militia would then constantly patrol these boundaries to prevent any communication between the slaves and the British.[285] This plan would have deprived the province's most productive plantations of their laborers for as long as the British were in the vicinity of Charleston, and perhaps indefinitely if the British managed to occupy the town. Even so, South Carolina's Whigs preferred to let their plantations lie idle rather than risk the loss of their slaves. Such a massive relocation of people, however, would have been nearly impossible to carry out, and the confusion that would have resulted might actually have created opportunities for slaves to escape. Therefore, no systematic evacuation of slaves was ever attempted.

Some Whigs hoped that persuasion would suffice to prevent their slaves from fleeing to the British. In an effort to ensure that they remained at home, Henry Laurens summoned all the slaves on his brother's plantation to a meeting, at which he advised them "to behave with great circumspection" and "set before them, the great risque of exposing themselves to the treachery of pretended freinds & false witnesses if they associated with any Negroes out of your family or mine." Laurens said that the slaves "were sensibly affected" by his speech, "& with many thanks promised to follow my advice."[286]

Most rebels considered such mild measures insufficient to prevent a slave uprising. The Charleston press fueled white anxiety by frequently publishing material "calculated to incite the fears of the People." At the same time, reports that Governor Campbell had brought arms for them reached many slaves, encouraging some to "impertinent behaviour."[287] In late May or early June a schooner sailing from Charleston into the Carolina interior "was robbed by Some Negroes, they took Nothing else but Powder," adding further credence to reports that a slave revolt was imminent.[288]

Whig leaders responded to the threat by beginning criminal proceedings against blacks suspected of rebellious tendencies. "Trials of Several Negroes Suspected & charged of plotting an Insurrection have been conducted this Week," Henry Laurens wrote on June 18; "Jerry the pilot is among the most Criminal—two or three White people are Committed to prison upon Strong Negro Evidence." Laurens expected even more plots to be revealed, as the Reverend Oliver Hart had reported that one of his slaves and another owned by Joshua Ward "could make very ample discoveries." The Whigs immediately took the two slaves into custody so that they could be interrogated.[289]

A few days later the investigators reported that there was "very little foundation" to the rumors of an impending slave rebellion; "however one or two Negroes are to be Severely flogged & banished." The Whigs conceded that they had not found any substantial evidence of their guilt but thought it best to make an example of them. Two whites suspected of plotting with the slaves were released for lack of evidence. These findings did not reduce white apprehensions, however, and the militia was "kept on Duty Night & Day" as rumors of slave revolts continued to circulate.[290]

By early July the fears of insurrection began to abate. Henry Laurens declared on July 2, "I am sure we have nothing to fear from within."[291] Another Whig, Gabriel Manigault, concluded that the tales of impending slave revolts had no validity. "We have been alarmed by idle reports that the Negros intended to rise, which on examination proved to be of less consequence than was expected," he informed his son on July 8; "however a Strick watch has been Kept for fear of the worst."[292]

This air of assurance evaporated a few days later when the Council of Safety received a letter from St. Bartholomew's Parish, dated July 5, which claimed that Whigs there had discovered "that Several of the Slaves in the neighborhood, were exciting & endeavouring to bring abt. a General Insurrection." Local officials had arrested "such as were said to be the Principal leaders of their Infernal designs" and put them on trial. Several of the slaves were sentenced to receive "Exemplary punishmts," including the hanging of one suspect. The testimony of the accused slaves also revealed the instigator of the alleged insurrection: John Burnet, a Scot who "hath been a long time preaching to the . . . Negroes . . . In the Woods—and other Places." One of the accused slaves testified that another suspect had informed him that Burnet told his black listeners that "the old King had reced a Book from our Lord by which he was to Alter the World (meaning to set the Negroes free)" but had died and gone to hell for failing to follow his divine instructions. However, "the Young King, meaning our Present One, came up with the Book, & was about to alter the World, & set the Negroes Free." On the basis of this hearsay evidence, officials in St. Bartholomew's Parish arrested Burnet and sent him to Charleston for further interrogation.[293]

After examining Burnet, the Council of Safety found him guilty only of excessive enthusiasm for converting slaves to Christianity, which had led him to preach without obtaining permission from the slaves' owners. Burnet "denied having any Knowledge of the pretended Book," so the council released him on his promise not to return to St. Bartholomew's Parish. He then left for Georgia.[294] Despite Burnet's acquittal, rumors of slave rebellions continued to circulate and gain credence. Even Henry Laurens, who had dismissed the accounts a few weeks earlier, was now certain that "insurrections of our Negroes attended by the most horrible butcheries of Innocent Women & Children" were part of the ministry's "dark Hellish plots for Subjugating the Colonies."[295]

The Council of Safety believed that Thomas Jeremiah, known to the Whigs as "Jerry," intended to take a leading role in the ministry's supposed plot; he was the man Laurens described as the worst among the suspected black conspirators arrested in mid-June. Jeremiah, a free black whose skills as a harbor pilot had enabled him to amass considerable wealth, apparently angered the Whigs simply because he was a successful black man in a slave society. Laurens considered him "a forward fellow, puffed up by prosperity, ruined by Luxury & debauchery & grown to an amazing pitch of vanity & ambition."[296] During the interrogation of the black prisoners, one slave claimed that Jeremiah had asked him to bring some guns to a runaway slave named Dewar, "to be placed in Negro's Hands to fight against the Inhabitants of this Province, and that He Jeremiah was to have the chief Command of the said Negroes." Jeremiah also allegedly stated that he had enough powder but "wanted more Arms." A second slave said that when he had asked Jeremiah what he should do if war came, Jeremiah told him to "join the Soldiers; that the War was come to help the poor Negroes."[297]

On August 11 the Whigs put Jeremiah on trial, found him guilty of plotting an insurrection, and sentenced him "to be hanged and afterwards burned." Governor Campbell, who did not think that the legal proceedings deserved to be called a trial, protested to the presiding judge, pointing out "the weakness of the evidence" against Jeremiah. Campbell's intervention "raised such a clamour among the people as is incredible," the governor wrote, "and they openly and loudly declared that if I granted the man a pardon they would hang him at my door."[298] Campbell then asked Henry Laurens for assistance in preventing Jeremiah's execution, noting that one of the slaves who had testified for the prosecution had since retracted his testimony.[299] Laurens answered that he had brought the issues Campbell had raised before the Council of Safety and that "they utterly refused to take them under Consideration." Laurens added that he understood that Jeremiah had received a fair trial and justified the Whigs' threats of violence if he were to be released. "In the Calamitous Situation of this Colony under the threats of Insurrections, strong proofs of which the people are possessed of, no wonder they are alarmed at the Sound of Pardon to a Man circumstanced in all respects as Jerry is," he wrote.[300] Alexander Innes renewed the correspondence with Laurens the following day in hopes of obtaining a reprieve for Jeremiah, but without success.[301] Some rebels sneered at the governor's endeavors to save the condemned man; Peter Timothy told William Henry Drayton that "more force was exerted for his being saved, than there would have been for you."[302]

Privately, Laurens pronounced himself "fully Satisfied that Jerry was guilty of a design & attempt to encourage our Negroes to Rebellion & joining the King's Troops if any had been sent here." The "uncommon pains taken to Save his Life" by Campbell and Innes led the Whigs to suspect their motives; Laurens wrote that their efforts on the black man's behalf "had filled the minds of many people with great Jealousies against certain Crown Officers."[303] The governor believed that the rebels suspected Loyalists of involvement in the alleged plot to promote slave insurrections and sought an opportunity to punish them for it. "Happy it was for the friends of government in this country that the wretched creatures who were doomed to death could not be prevailed upon to accuse any white person though repeatedly told it was the only chance they had for life," Campbell wrote. "I am convinced if any had been accused they must have fallen a sacrifice to the fury of the mob."[304]

In a letter to Dartmouth, Campbell expressed his horror at Jeremiah's execution. "I could not save him My Lord! the very reflection Harrows my Soul!" the governor lamented. His only consolation was that he had done all in his power to save Jeremiah's life.[305] Campbell called the Whigs "a set of barbarians who are worse than the most cruel savages any history has described."[306]

Campbell's horror at the execution and compassion for the victim were shared by many in Britain when the news arrived there. Supporters of the government used the judicial murder of Jeremiah to justify taking a hard line against the rebels, whom they portrayed as savages. The pamphleteer John Lind included the incident in a tract designed "to demonstrate how American patriots were using terror to establish a regime which neither the British constitution nor English common law could ever legitimate."[307] The earl of Sandwich, speaking for the ministry in the House of Lords, declared that the rebels "have put an innocent free negro to death, attended with every circumstance of cruelty and baseness." He recounted how "a mock tribunal" had allowed the perjury of a slave to convict Jeremiah, even though provincial law did not allow a slave to testify against a free person. This affair proved the need for a harsh policy to suppress the rebels. "After such outrages, lenity would be culpable," the earl stated.[308] In a vain attempt to undo the damage Jeremiah's execution had done to the rebel cause, John Laurens, at his father's request, published a justification for the Whigs' actions in a London newspaper.[309]

Had the ministry wished to arm slaves, or at least to offer freedom to those willing to serve in the king's forces, the death of Jeremiah and the accompanying
outrage would have provided an excellent opportunity to justify the decision. If
the ministers had asserted that such measures were necessary to allow blacks to
protect themselves from rebel cruelty, it would have been difficult for opponents to
counter that argument. However, there is no evidence that Jeremiah's execution
caused the ministers to reconsider their policy in regard to slaves.

If the ministers still refused to give blacks a more active part in subduing the
southern rebels, slaves at least fulfilled their assigned role by keeping the Whig
militia occupied. The large number of slaves in South Carolina complicated efforts
to keep the rebel militia in service, for with most white men away from home, the
possibility of a slave insurrection increased. In September 1775 militia colonel Stephen Bull reported that he had been forced to send some of the men from Prince
William Parish home because "there were the fewest white men in proportion to
the Domestics" there. Bull observed that this was a common problem. "As to the
Argument of their domestics being left without white Men," he wrote, "they certainly are in the predicament with every other Parish or District on Field or Muster days; and you certainly will allow that when they [militia] are in a body they are
more safe and ready to march to . . . any other part where an Insurrection may be
apprehended."[310] However, Bull worried that "should a sudden Insurrection of our
Domestics happen," the militia lacked sufficient gunpowder "to make the least
defence."[311] Joseph Glover reported that in Colleton County "the Patrol Service
(which is one of the Materialist in the lower districts)" occupied so much of the
men's time that officers were unable to conduct any training.[312]

The decision by Virginia governor John Murray, Earl of Dunmore, to arm
slaves to suppress the rebellion in that province sparked another uproar in South
Carolina. Dunmore believed that his plan would deprive rebel planters of their
labor force, keep them at home to guard against slave uprisings instead of serving in the rebel forces, and most importantly, provide both soldiers and laborers
for the British army. This latter benefit appeared to be easily realized, as word of
Dunmore's proclamation of freedom to any slave who would join him, spread
verbally by the slaves and circulated by Loyalists, brought three hundred slaves
to the governor within a week of its issuance. The proclamation also "undoubtedly had an indirect effect on thousands of additional slaves," even if they did
not join the British, by "quickening their hopes for freedom."[313] It clearly linked
the British with emancipation in the minds of slaves across the South.

Dunmore's actions threatened to undermine the entire social and economic
structure of the southern provinces and also had the potential to provide enough
black troops to defeat the rebels. One Whig, writing from Philadelphia but
evidently familiar with southern slavery, described rebel views on the issue with
great insight. "Hell itself could not have vomitted any thing more black than his
[Dunmore's] design of emancipating our slaves," he declared, "and unless he is

cut off before he is reinforced, we know not how far the contagion may spread. The flame runs like wild fire through the slaves, who are more than two for one white in the Southern Colonies. The subject of their nocturnal revels, instead of music and dancing, is now turned upon their liberty. I know not whence these troubles may lead us. If our friends in England are not able to oblige the ministry to give way, we are lost; and already gone too far to retract with safety."[314]

South Carolinian Edward Rutledge, who several weeks earlier had urged the Continental Congress to discharge all blacks serving in the rebel army, asserted that Dunmore's actions would "more effectually work an eternal separation between Great Britain and the Colonies,—than any other expedient, which could possibly have been thought of." After the colonists saw "our Slaves emancipated for the express purpose of massacreing their Masters," Rutledge thought that they would no longer consider reconciliation with the mother country.[315]

Like their counterparts in Virginia who sought freedom with Dunmore, many South Carolina slaves escaped from their masters and made their way to Charleston, hoping to get aboard British warships stationed in the harbor. Some did reach the ships and began cooperating with Royal Navy sailors in nighttime raids along the province's coast. In early December, Whig leaders learned that nearly 500 black fugitives were camped on Sullivan's Island awaiting an opportunity to board the British vessels.[316] On December 9 Gen. William Moultrie ordered Maj. Charles Cotesworth Pinckney to take 150 men to the island "to surprize, seize, and apprehend" the slaves. The plan was frustrated, however, when Pinckney failed to locate a ford that would allow him to cross to the island.[317] The Whigs made a second attempt on December 18; in keeping with their policy of encouraging animosity between blacks and Indians, the Whigs sent 54 Catawbas to participate in the attack. Their early-morning assault killed an estimated 50 blacks and captured several more along with a few British sailors. Almost 20 blacks escaped and were picked up by boats from the British warships.[318] The Council of Safety hoped that the attack "will serve to humble our Negroes in general."[319]

Angered at the British naval officers for providing refuge to fugitive slaves, the Whigs repudiated an agreement by which they sold provisions to the navy in exchange for the officers' pledge not to take supplies by force. Fenwick Bull, a Whig who had gone aboard a warship on December 10 to discuss the British seizure of a merchant vessel, accused Capt. John Tollemache of harboring runaway slaves. Tollemache replied that the blacks "came as free men, and demanded protection; that he could have had five-hundred who had offered." He refused a demand to return the slaves, asserting that the Americans were rebels and that he had orders to distress them in any way possible.[320] The rebels believed that Tollemache's ship, the *Scorpion,* carried off between thirty and forty slaves when it left the harbor shortly afterward.[321] One of these was "a valuable black Pilot," whom the captain took "by way of Reprisal & for worse purposes perhaps."[322] Another was John Marrant, who had been "pressed on board" because the British "were told I could play on music." Marrant served as a musician in the Royal Navy until the end of the war.[323] When the other ships departed, each also had several blacks on board. Henry Laurens considered the British "robberies" of slaves "sufficient to alarm every Man in the Colony."[324]

In the spring of 1776 South Carolina Whigs began to suspect that a British attack somewhere in the South was imminent. They immediately took steps to prevent slaves from fleeing to the British by passing a law mandating the death penalty for any slave who tried to join the king's armed forces. Two slaves who stole a schooner in a vain attempt to reach British warships scouting Charleston's defenses were ordered hanged on April 27 to demonstrate that the law would be strictly enforced.[325] Undeterred, five of William Moultrie's slaves who worked as crewmen on a barge used the vessel to reach a British ship in May. Whigs believed that the British naval officers had "obtained ample means of information" from the fugitives.[326]

The rebels feared that if a British attack did come, the necessity of concentrating the militia to defend Charleston would make it difficult to control the large slave population in the lowcountry. "The Militia near the Sea Coast You Know Consists of Overseers, if they are kept from their business, little is to be expected in the Planting way," Pierce Butler stated. "Besides it is surely improper to leave numbers of Negroes without a White Man. By all Accts. at this time there is Scarce an Overseer on any of the Plantations from Purysburg to Combahee."[327] Affairs on Ralph Izard's plantation were in the "utmost distraction" in late March because five of the six overseers had been away on militia duty.[328] Gen. Charles Lee was aware of these problems but decided that concentrating all available troops to hold Charleston would ultimately prove to be the best means of keeping the slaves in check. It was important, Lee wrote, to convince slaves that the Whigs held real power, as "the opinion which the slave will entertain of our superiority or inferiority will naturally keep pace with our maintaining or giving ground."[329]

Lee's assessment was correct; the rebels succeeded in defeating a British attack on Charleston at the end of June without their slaves creating any disruption. When the opportunity offered, however, slaves continued to escape to British naval vessels that frequently patrolled the South Carolina coast. In early August the frigate *Active* landed a party of forty whites and twenty armed blacks on Bull's Island, where they took some cattle and "augmented their black Guard by stealing Six more Negroes." While Henry Laurens took comfort in the fact that none of his slaves had escaped to the British, he realized that he had been fortunate in that regard, for "many hundreds of that Colour have been stolen & decoyed by the Servants of King George the third—Captains of British Ships of War & Noble Lords have busied themselves in such inglorious pilferage to the disgrace of their Master & disgrace of their Cause."[330] Later, when Laurens suspected that one of his disgruntled slaves might try to escape to a British vessel, he ordered his overseer to secure the man in irons.[331]

After their initial outrage at reports that the British government planned to incite slave insurrections, Georgia rebels appeared to have worried far less about such an event than did their counterparts in South Carolina. It was not until January 1776, when British warships arrived at Savannah to procure rice for the garrison at Boston, that the Whigs in Georgia acted to prevent their slaves from revolting or fleeing to the British. The Council of Safety then sent the militia "to Strip the Negroe Houses" on both the Georgia and South Carolina sides of the Savannah River of "Arms and Ammunition." Whig troops searched the homes of overseers as well as slaves; all of the muskets and ammunition found were confiscated, although overseers were each allowed to keep one musket and thirteen rounds of ammunition. If the slaves did revolt and defeat their overseers, Whig officials did not want them to gain access to a significant supply of arms.[332]

Many slaves did attempt to reach the British ships, which angered rebels, who complained that naval officers were "encouraging our slaves to desert to them."[333] If this were not infuriating enough, some slaves added to the Whigs' frustration during a battle that erupted in March when the rebels tried to prevent the British from seizing several rice-laden vessels. British troops on Hutchinson's Island had retreated under a barrage of rebel musket fire, abandoning two pieces of artillery. Before the Whigs could secure these trophies, slaves belonging to John Graham, the Loyalist lieutenant governor, recovered the cannons and returned them to the British.[334]

Col. Stephen Bull, who had taken some of his South Carolina militia to reinforce the Georgians, believed that vigorous action had to be taken to halt the flight of slaves to the British and punish those who had taken refuge on Tybee Island while waiting to board Royal Navy vessels. Bull learned in mid-March that between 40 and 50 slaves belonging to South Carolinian Arthur Middleton, along with over 150 others, were at Tybee.[335] Bull urged the South Carolina Council of Safety to approve harsh measures against the runaways. If the British were permitted to carry off the slaves, Bull stated, it "will only enable an enemy to fight us with our own money or property"—money if the slaves were sold and the funds applied to the war effort, property if the slaves were armed.[336]

Bull proposed to solve the problem with the aid of seventy Creek warriors who were then at Savannah.[337] He suggested that the Indians raid Tybee and execute all the slaves who could not be recaptured; their owners could be compensated at public expense. The Creeks were the ideal people to conduct the raid and kill resisting slaves, Bull asserted, because the destruction of the refugees not only might "deter other negroes from deserting" but also "will establish a hatred or aversion between the Indians and negroes." A Creek leader had assured Bull of his willingness to lead a party in an attack on the fugitive slaves; however, Bull lacked the authority to order the measure and doubted whether the Georgia Council of Safety was resolute enough to approve his plan. He therefore sought authorization from South Carolina officials, while urging them to keep the matter "a profound secret" so that the slaves would not learn of the attack and flee or obtain arms from the British and ambush the Creeks.[338] Bull, who made up in astuteness what he lacked in morality, easily recognized the advantages of inflaming the hostility of two potential enemies toward one another at the outset of the conflict in order to spare the rebels the difficulty of opposing both.

On March 16 the South Carolina Council of Safety informed Bull that his plan was "an awful business notwithstanding it has the sanction of Law to put even fugitive & Rebellious Slaves to death, the prospect is horrible." The council advised Bull that it was up to the Georgians "to give that encouragement which is necessary to induce proper Persons to seize & if nothing else will do to destroy all those Rebellious Negroes upon Tybee Island or wherever they may be found." Indians could be used if the Georgians thought proper, but white men should lead them if possible. The owners of any slaves killed in the raid should be reimbursed by the public, and South Carolina officials were willing to share the cost with Georgia. The council also told Bull to blame the violence on the British: "to those Royal Miscreants who are carrying on an inglorious picaroon Warr let every inglorious unavoidable act of necessity which we may be driven to commit for our self preservation, be imputed."[339] Southern Whigs would resort to this device throughout the war, committing the most brutal acts of violence and then claiming that their enemies had left them no alternative.

The Georgia militia, dressed and painted like Indians, and some thirty Creeks attacked Tybee Island on March 25. They killed one of six British marines who were on the island at the time, wounded several others, and burned three houses. The rebels also captured a handful of white Loyalists and about a dozen slaves.[340] Evidently they killed many fugitive slaves, since the British claimed that both whites and Indians in the attacking party practiced "the most savage barbarity" and that in this regard the whites had behaved worse than the Indians.[341]

After the British left Georgia, some slaves continued to escape to British vessels whenever they appeared on the coast, while others made the trek overland to the Floridas. Georgia's Council of Safety noted in July that "negroes are daily inveigled and carried away from their plantations" by British warships.[342] In September, George Aaron, overseer at Henry Laurens's plantation at New Hope, Georgia, fled with five of Laurens's slaves and a sixth belonging to William McIntosh.[343] Laurens later learned that his slaves had gone to St. Augustine, and he complained that they "had been actually Stolen." He wrote that "the Man who had perpetrated that act of villainy had returned with a party in order to carry off as many more as he could take" and that he failed only because Laurens had already moved the remaining slaves elsewhere.[344] It is not clear whether Aaron took the slaves forcibly for his own benefit or they voluntarily accompanied him. Since Aaron would have found it almost impossible to manage six reluctant companions, in all likelihood the men agreed to escape together; perhaps he deceived the slaves with promises of liberty in Florida, only to sell them back into bondage after they arrived.

Georgia's rebel leaders worried that Loyalists in East Florida would arm the runaway slaves and employ them against their former masters, which led the Council of Safety to advocate an invasion of East Florida in the summer of 1776.[345] Governor Tonyn, however, lacked the resources to supply the fugitives; in October he wrote that "there are a number of Runaway Negros from Georgia, whom I relieved the Captains of the Navy of, to whom they fled for protection," but he added that he needed government assistance to support the slaves and white Loyalist refugees who had come to the province.[346]

Tonyn willingly armed blacks to defend his province. When he created a militia battalion in August 1776, he informed Germain that "we shall be able to raise four black Companies." Tonyn planned to maintain discipline in those units by assigning "double or treble" the number of white officers in comparison to the amount of officers in white companies.[347] Slaves served in the provincial militia throughout the war; others, perhaps free blacks or those who had escaped from rebel masters, joined Thomas Brown's Florida Rangers, which at one time included about 150 black soldiers.[348] Like their governor, "white Floridians assumed not only that slaves should be impressed to labor on fortifications but also that if need be they should be armed and employed as ordinary soldiers." Several planters along the St. Mary's River and on the coastal islands, areas particularly vulnerable to rebel raids, probably armed and trained their slaves to defend their estates.[349] Slaves also helped defend the province by providing intelligence of rebel movements. When 70 Whig militiamen from Georgia marched southward to attack a fort at Germyn Wright's plantation on the St. Mary's River, a slave warned Wright of their approach, so that the rebels found the defenders prepared for them and had to retreat.[350]

Unlike their neighbors in East Florida, the Loyalist planters of West Florida were not threatened by the Whigs and thus preferred to maintain the status quo in regard to slavery. The most serious danger West Floridians faced in 1776 was, in fact, a possible slave insurrection. On June 24 three neighbors called on the planter William Dunbar of Natchez and told him that they had discovered a slave conspiracy centered at his plantation. They named three of Dunbar's slaves and a fourth owned by another planter as the ringleaders. "Of what avail is kindness & good usage when rewarded by such ingratitude?" a shocked Dunbar asked himself. He summoned one of the accused slaves, who "seemed to know nothing of the matter" even when confronted by his accusers. Later that day, while the slave was in a boat "with his arms pinioned," he threw himself into the Mississippi and drowned. Dunbar attributed the suicide to the slave's feeling of guilt that "his intended Diabolical plan" had been discovered. The other three accused conspirators were tried on July 1, found guilty, and hanged the next day. Several other slaves suspected of involvement received milder punishments.[351]

West Florida was the only southern province where slaves had not been directly affected by the Revolution. In Georgia and South Carolina numerous slaves had sought freedom with the British, an eventuality that the ministry had apparently failed to consider when formulating its southern strategy. The slaves' actions had prompted British officers to grant blacks what protection they could provide, while royal governors Dunmore and Tonyn had, on their own initiative, armed blacks. Yet, in spite of these clear indications that slaves would not remain passive and that both civil and military officials were willing to employ blacks against the rebels, the ministry refused to alter its policy to take full advantage of slave assistance.

Royal Relief Fails

In the autumn of 1775 the ministry began preparations for an expedition to relieve the Loyalists in the southern provinces. Acting in response to the information he had received from southern governors, in early September Lord Dartmouth suggested a southern expedition to Gen. William Howe. Lord North, who hoped to mollify those Britons who demanded vigorous action by winning a victory with minimal effort, put the plan before the king on October 15. The next day the king approved the diversion of five regiments from Ireland, originally intended to reinforce Boston, for a winter campaign with the objective of retaking North Carolina.[352]

Dartmouth informed Howe of the plan, going so far as to suggest that "the Appearance of a respectable Force" in the South might "have the effect to restore Order and Government" in both Carolinas, Georgia, and Virginia.[353] The determination of where to attack first would be left to the officer in command of the expedition; Howe was to appoint a general and send him with some troops from Boston to the Cape Fear River to meet the fleet from Britain, which was assembling at Cork in Ireland.[354] Despite his insistence that Howe undertake the southern expedition, Dartmouth harbored doubts as to whether the army would find the Loyalist support on which its success depended. He told Howe that if the army found "no appearance of a disposition in the inhabitants of the southern colonies to join the King's Army, I fear little more will be effected than the gaining of some respectable post to the southward, where the officers and servants of government may find protection."[355]

Howe was reluctant to make the move, writing Dartmouth that he thought it better "to leave the southern provinces in the fullest persuasion of their security until the rebels have been defeated on the side of New York."[356] Yet, despite his objections, Howe complied with Dartmouth's orders and dispatched Gen. Henry Clinton from Boston with between twelve and fifteen hundred troops on January 20, 1776. Clinton doubted whether he could succeed because he believed that the southern governors had exaggerated the prospects of defeating the rebels. He noted that "governors are sanguine, the malady is catching, and ministers sometimes infected."[357]

Loyalists disagreed with Clinton, believing that the opportunity was ripe to regain control of the southern provinces. John Pownall informed Howe in

September "that a very considerable part of the People" in South Carolina "have shewn a Disposition to resist" the Whigs, and he urged the general to aid them.[358] One South Carolinian lamented "the inattention of Government, to this important Colony" in the two years preceding the British expedition. A province "in the habit of Alarm, upon every appearance of ill-humour in the most trifling Tribe of Indians on its Western frontier" was certainly vulnerable to a regular force, he maintained.[359]

En route southward, Clinton met others who echoed that opinion. At New York, Clinton conferred with former North Carolina governor William Tryon, whose assertion that the Scotch Highlanders in that province would eagerly support the British dispelled some of Clinton's pessimism. A mid-February conference with Lord Dunmore in Hampton Roads further raised Clinton's hopes for success. However, when the fleet reached Cape Fear at the end of the month, Clinton found that the Highlanders had risen prematurely and been defeated by the rebels at Moore's Creek Bridge. Furthermore, he did not meet the expedition from Ireland, which should have joined him there. Clinton thus had to formulate a new plan.[360]

While awaiting the Cork fleet, Clinton conferred with Lord William Campbell, who had arrived aboard the frigate HMS *Syren*. Campbell told Clinton that the Loyalists in South Carolina, "overflowing with zeal," had been "precipitate in showing themselves," and as a result they had been "overpowered, disarmed, and many imprisoned" by the Whigs. The general considered this report and the news of Moore's Creek Bridge "gloomy forebodings" of what lay ahead, although the southern governors "were not dispirited."[361] Clinton proceeded to formulate two plans that might replace the North Carolina operation. The first was to establish a post on the Chesapeake near Norfolk, Virginia, where the bay, Atlantic Ocean, and Dismal Swamp created a virtual island where Loyalists who joined the troops would have considerable security. The second contemplated an attack on Savannah and a march into the Georgia interior to open communication with the Loyalists in the South Carolina backcountry. Further delays in the arrival of the Cork fleet led Clinton to abandon both plans.[362]

Meanwhile, Tonyn submitted an even more ambitious scheme for Clinton's consideration. The governor proposed to take 150 regulars from the St. Augustine garrison, augmented by 30 rangers, 100 Loyalists, and 300 Indians, and march into Georgia. Tonyn believed that his force would gather more Loyalists and Indians as they marched and could capture Savannah and allow Governor Wright to resume his post. Thomas Brown would provide additional support by returning to the Georgia and South Carolina backcountry, where he expected to recruit 2,000 or 3,000 Loyalists. Uniting this force with the Cherokees, Brown intended to secure the backcountry and then march to the coast to join the other British units. Rather than lose time waiting for Clinton's reply, Tonyn dispatched Brown to the backcountry and informed the general of the plan. Clinton replied only that he had not yet decided where he would attack.[363]

Tonyn, impatient to strike the rebels, continued to press the general to adopt his plan and requested "full powers to carry it on with spirit and effect."[364]

Clinton did not authorize Tonyn to act, but the governor's idea may have influenced the general's thinking as he contemplated a third plan of his own. Like Tonyn's proposal, this plan was intended to take advantage of Loyalist and Indian support. Clinton believed that he could dispatch several hundred troops to Pensacola, from which location they would advance up the Alabama River and across Indian territory to the Georgia and Carolina backcountry. There they would unite with Indians and Loyalists to take control of the interior of those provinces. Clinton intended to insure continued Loyalist support by providing schools, courts, and political representation to the backcountry inhabitants. The plan was barely feasible, given the distances the troops would have to traverse through the wilderness; Clinton abandoned the idea when he learned that there were not enough boats at Pensacola to transport troops upriver.[365]

The first ships of the Cork fleet, which had been expected to sail on December 1, 1775, finally began straggling into Cape Fear in late April. The ministry's decision to increase the force to seven regiments, and a lack of naval escort, postponed the fleet's departure until February 10. Then foul weather dispersed the ships and caused further delay. When the entire force had assembled, Clinton consulted with Gen. Charles, Earl Cornwallis and Adm. Sir Peter Parker, the respective commanders of the land and naval forces, about how to proceed. Clinton argued that the delay had ruined any chance of assisting the Loyalists, since he had orders to rejoin Howe shortly and could not leave enough troops to protect them if they turned out as expected.[366]

Better than anyone else in the ministry or the army's high command, Clinton understood the problems that the Loyalists faced. Most British leaders believed that once regular troops had defeated the Whigs in a province, the Loyalists would be able to maintain control with little or no support from the army. Clinton, however, recognized that the rebels would not accept defeat so easily but would turn on the Loyalists once the army left. In that case, he declared, "all the friends of government will be sacrificed" in one province after another. Only sustained support from the army would enable the Loyalists to retain control of a province when it had been recaptured.[367] Clinton believed that "to bring those poor people forward" without providing adequate support "would have only exposed them to the resentment and malice of their enemies, and multiplied our difficulties by putting the rebels so much the more on their guard."[368]

Despite his reluctance to undertake an attack that in his opinion would harm the Loyalists more than help them, Clinton allowed Parker to convince him that Charleston was weakly defended and could be easily captured. Parker's insistence on attacking Charleston reflected the views of both Dartmouth and Germain; in November 1775 both had suggested the town as a promising objective should operations in North Carolina appear unfeasible. Dartmouth had gone so far as to instruct Governor Campbell to send emissaries to the backcountry to organize the Loyalists and lead them to the coast to meet the expedition. Clinton doubted that the town could be taken but convinced himself that the establishment of a post on Sullivan's Island at the entrance to the harbor would at least demonstrate to the Loyalists the government's intention to support them and provide a base for a future attack on Charleston.[369]

By February, South Carolina rebels expected a British attack and prepared to meet it, impressing every available slave to build fortifications to protect Charleston.[370] Whig leaders particularly feared that the arrival of the British would ignite a Loyalist uprising. Pierce Butler doubted the reliability of backcountry militiamen who had come to reinforce Charleston. "The real Sentiments of a great part of them I believe we are ignorant of," he noted.[371] Gen. Charles Lee, believing that the British would attempt to establish themselves on the mainland and summon the Loyalists to join them, posted troops to prevent Clinton's soldiers from coming ashore.[372] Other Whigs sought to intimidate Loyalists from aiding the British by launching another wave of persecution. "Supported by Military force, every appearance of Discontent or dissention, received immediate punishment," wrote one observer. Troops were quartered in the homes of suspected Loyalists, where they plundered and vandalized the contents. When the British fleet finally appeared, Whig militiamen began to make examples, "in terrorem, of such as discovered any disinclination to Act, or refused a Test-Oath, which was then tendered. The Crown officers, and all such as were more immediately suspected of disaffection, were put into close confinement, and their Papers Plate &c Seized."[373]

The Whigs had good cause for their fears, since many Loyalists hoped to escape to the British when the fleet arrived at Charleston. Several men deserted from rebel units and managed to reach a Royal Navy frigate that appeared off Charleston bar in May to sound the channel.[374] Other Loyalists coerced into serving with the Whig forces tried unsuccessfully to reach the British when Clinton's forces landed on Long Island. Alexander Chesney, posted across the channel from the British camp, tried with some friends to make a crossing "but failed for want of a boat."[375]

Parker's fleet, guided by black pilots, arrived off Charleston harbor on June 1. The presence of one pilot, Sampson, particularly angered many Whigs, who accused him of having convinced the British to attack the town. Clinton landed his troops on Long Island, north of Sullivan's Island, where the rebels were building a fort. People with the expedition had informed Clinton that the water between the islands was only eighteen inches deep at low tide, which would allow British troops to cross to Sullivan's Island and attack the fort by land while the navy assaulted it by sea. Unfortunately, on examination the channel proved to be seven feet deep, so the troops stood idle while Parker's warships attacked the fort on June 28. Parker, also acting on faulty intelligence, kept his ships too far from the fort for their fire to be effective, while the Whigs pummeled the Royal Navy. After the defeat, Clinton and Parker had no choice but to rejoin Howe, who was preparing to attack New York.[376]

The repulse of the British inspired the Whigs and left the Loyalists dispirited. In South Carolina "the success of the 28 June made some Converts" to the rebel cause.[377] Georgia's Whigs were "much Elated" at the news, Lachlan McIntosh wrote, while "the Torys now amongst us are ha[rdly worth] our Notice unless it is with pity & Contempt."[378]

Germain's deputy William Knox lamented these effects. "The worst consequence of this failure will be the shewing the rebels where their strength lies and how they may foil us again," he wrote. Yet, Knox found some reason for hope. "Loyalist support had been proven no mere chimera but a force of considerable potential which needed only to be encouraged, supported, and unleashed at the right opportunity," he concluded.[379] His views reflected prevailing British sentiment. The failure at Charleston "in no way dampened Britain's optimistic view of the temper of the region."[380] The expedition had not succeeded in aiding the Loyalists, but the Loyalists had not been given a chance to come forward and cooperate with the king's troops. They would have to wait several years for another opportunity.

Another effect of the Charleston operation, which went unnoticed in London, resulted from the timing of the attack. Although Clinton and Parker's schedule had been determined primarily by the delays in the arrival of the fleet from Cork, the attack on Charleston took place only three days before the Cherokees attacked the southern frontier. This coincidence convinced many in the South that there had indeed been collusion between the British and Cherokees and that the ministry was determined to employ Indians against the colonists.

In some respects the failure at Charleston worked to Britain's advantage. Had Clinton and Parker succeeded in taking the town or establishing a post elsewhere along the South Carolina coast, the British position would have acted as a magnet for Whig troops, who would have cut off any Loyalist access to it. The post would not have been tenable without supplies brought by sea, so that any delays or difficulties in the delivery of provisions or ammunition might have forced the garrison to surrender. Furthermore, the presence of British troops in the region would undoubtedly have caused the Whigs to make even greater efforts to suppress the Loyalists than they otherwise did, which may have demoralized and neutralized the king's supporters by the time the British were ready to undertake another campaign in the South. Taking these possibilities into account, outright failure in 1776 probably proved more advantageous for the British than a limited success.

Although the Whigs had suppressed the Loyalists and slaves, defeated the Cherokees, and kept most of the Creeks neutral, they did not consider themselves secure. Upon replacing Charles Lee as commander of the southern department in September 1776, Maj. Gen. Robert Howe noted that South Carolina and Georgia still had "innate foes of more colours than one, to guard against, & more numerous than those who are willing to oppose them." He expressed particular concern for Georgia, which if retaken by the British, "would immediately bring to their aid, the Creek nation, & other potent tribes of Indians." The presence of British troops there, Howe wrote, "would be a strong temptation for our slaves to elope, & a secure asylum for them when they do."[381] Howe worried that Loyalists in South Carolina might "spirit up & join" with the blacks, "whose great number & alarming temper make it necessary to guard against the worst." He believed that in Georgia "one third of the inhabitants are enemies to America, & only wait for an opportunity, to plunge a dagger, into its vitals," while slaves there were even "more ready to revolt" than those in South Carolina.[382] The Whigs' victories had won them nothing more than a respite; the king's supporters remained a potent foe.

"New Method of Macarony Making": Whigs tarring and feathering a Loyalist. Several southern Loyalists were treated in a similar manner. Courtesy of Library of Congress, Prints and Photographs Division, British Cartoon Print Collection, LC-USZ62-45386

"The Tory's Day of Judgment": A Whig mob inflicting punishment on Loyalists, a common occurrence in the colonies during the Revolution. From John Trumbull, *M'Fingal: A Modern Epic Poem* . . . (1795). Courtesy of Library of Congress, Rare Books and Special Collections Division, LC-USZ62-7708

Frederick North, Baron North, British prime minister during the American Revolution. From Benson J. Lossing, *The Pictorial Field-book of the Revolution* (1851, 1852). Courtesy of Rare Books and Special Collections, Thomas Cooper Library, University of South Carolina

Lord George Germain, secretary of state for the American department. Courtesy of Library of Congress, Prints and Photographs Division, LC-USZ62-45237

Sir William Howe, commander in chief of the British in America. Courtesy of Library of Congress, Prints and Photographs Division, LC-USZ62-3616

Hopothle Mico, or Tallassee King, 1790. Portrait by John Trumbull. Courtesy of Charles Allen Munn Collection, Fordham University Library, Bronx, N.Y.

William Legge, Earl of Dartmouth, the British secretary of state who resigned his office rather than prosecute the war in America. From Benson J. Lossing, *The Pictorial Field-book of the Revolution* (1851, 1852). Courtesy of Rare Books and Special Collections, Thomas Cooper Library, University of South Carolina

Captain Redhead of the Catawba Indians. Courtesy of South Caroliniana Library, University of South Carolina, Columbia

Overleaf: View of Charleston on June 29, 1776, one day after British forces failed in an attempt to take the town. Courtesy of South Caroliniana Library, University of South Carolina, Columbia

Sir Henry Clinton, who led the unsuccessful expedition against Charleston in 1776 and became commander in chief of the British forces in 1778. Courtesy of Library of Congress, Prints and Photographs Division, LC-USZ62-45188

Admiral Marriot Arbuthnot, who commanded the British fleet that helped to capture Charleston, South Carolina, in May 1780. From Benson J. Lossing, *The Pictorial Field-book of the Revolution* (1851, 1852). Courtesy of Rare Books and Special Collections, Thomas Cooper Library, University of South Carolina

The Siege of Charleston, which was surrendered to the British army on May 12, 1780. Courtesy of South Caroliniana Library, University of South Carolina, Columbia

Charleston in 1780 during the British occupation. From Benson J. Lossing, *The Pictorial Field-book of the Revolution* (1851, 1852). Courtesy of Rare Books and Special Collections, Thomas Cooper Library, University of South Carolina

Charles, Lord Cornwallis, who assumed command in the South after the British captured Charleston. Courtesy of South Caroliniana Library, University of South Carolina, Columbia

Defeat of the Loyalists at King's Mountain, October 7, 1780. Courtesy of South Caroliniana Library, University of South Carolina, Columbia

Death of Patrick Ferguson at King's Mountain. Courtesy of South Caroliniana Library, University of South Carolina, Columbia

British cartoon, published in 1780, criticizing the government for its use of Indian allies against the rebels. Courtesy of Library of Congress, Prints and Photographs Division, British Cartoon Prints Collection, LC-USZ62-34860

Lt. Col. Banastre Tarleton, an aggressive, effective cavalry commander until his defeat at Cowpens in January 1781. Courtesy of South Caroliniana Library, University of South Carolina, Columbia

The disastrous British defeat at Cowpens, January 17, 1781. Courtesy of South Caroliniana Library, University of South Carolina, Columbia

Lt. Col. Francis, Lord Rawdon, whose illness forced forced him to return to England in the summer of 1781. Courtesy of South Caroliniana Library, University of South Carolina, Columbia

Battle of Eutaw Springs, September 8, 1781, where the British won a tactical victory but then left Loyalists in the interior of South Carolina to fend for themselves. Courtesy of South Caroliniana Library, University of South Carolina, Columbia

Reception of the American Loyalists in Great Britain, 1815. Engraving by Henry Moses after a painting by Benjamin West. Frontispiece to John Eardley-Wilmot, *Historical View of the Commission Enquiring into the Losses, Services, and Claims of the American Loyalists at the Close of the War between Great Britain and Her Colonies in 1783 . . .* (1815)

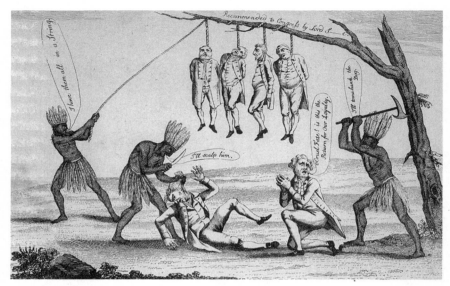

"The Savages Let Loose." In this British cartoon American rebels depicted as Indians celebrate their victory in the War for Independence by abusing Loyalists. Courtesy of Library of Congress, Prints and Photographs Division, British Cartoon Print Collection, LC-USZ62-5256

THREE

Whigs Ascendant

AFTER THE CLINTON-PARKER EXPEDITION's failure to capture Charleston, British strategy in the South focused on defending the Floridas from rebel attack and on maintaining good relations with the southern Indians until the time when their assistance might be required. Yet, Governor Tonyn, Loyalists, and Indians waged their own war against the Whigs outside the bounds of Gen. William Howe's plans. Shortages of provisions in East Florida led Tonyn to frequently send Loyalist and Indian raiders to capture cattle in Georgia, sparking sporadic warfare along the border between the two provinces. Responding to this threat, the Whigs repeatedly invaded East Florida, while in 1778 rebels from Pennsylvania descended the Mississippi River to attack West Florida.

Having secured control of South Carolina and Georgia, the Whigs labored to maintain the upper hand against both their internal and external enemies. They continued to persecute Loyalists and banished those who persisted in opposition. Rebel officials also strove to keep the Indians neutral in hopes of avoiding another attack on the frontier. Slaves endured continued repression, although many managed to escape to the Floridas.

However, Lord George Germain had not forgotten the southern provinces and urged General Howe to undertake a winter campaign in the region. Howe agreed in November 1776 that "South Carolina and Georgia must be the Objects for Winter," but he claimed that he needed fifteen thousand reinforcements before he could begin operations there.[1] Germain told him that it was impossible to send that many troops, so Howe abandoned the plan.[2] After studying an August 1777 memorial from Governors Wright and Campbell, which stressed the importance of retaking South Carolina and Georgia and the relative ease with which that task could be accomplished, Germain again advised Howe to undertake a southern campaign. "If Sir Wm Howe would carry any part of his army into the Southern Provinces this winter I should have no doubt of his success," Germain told his deputy.[3] Howe demurred, insisting that operations in the South were impossible unless he received additional soldiers.[4] Governor Tonyn also prodded Howe to attack Georgia, asserting that the conquest of that province would open a line of communication to the "back Settlements of the Southern provinces, where there are many well affected to His Majesty," but this advice failed to sway the general.[5]

SUPPRESSING THE LOYALISTS

By 1777 Whig attitudes toward the Loyalists had so hardened that even a moderate such as Henry Laurens saw no middle ground in the dispute. "A Man who is not a friend to the American Cause certainly holds principles, if he holds any, which are injurious to America," Laurens informed a Loyalist acquaintance. If such a person refused to bear arms against the British, "that Man may, without any torture of construction or expression, be deem'd an Enemy to the American Cause."[6]

To ferret out such enemies, South Carolina required its inhabitants to take an oath of allegiance to the state and to Congress. This was the basis of a process by which "the southern rebels systematically began to isolate and expose" Loyalists, although many of the king's supporters "adopted various subterfuges in order to evade the requirement or, to the same end, attempted to avoid having any contact with the local authorities administering the oaths."[7] The oath not only forced many Loyalists to reveal their beliefs, but it also served "to compromise people in the eyes of the British and to deter them from fighting for the British. A man who swore loyalty to Congress and his state would be a documented rebel if he fell into British hands. Worse still, if he served the British and then fell back into American hands, he would be a documented traitor."[8]

Those who refused to renounce their loyalty to Britain and take the oath to the rebel government were to be banished from South Carolina. Under the terms of the banishment act passed by the legislature in early 1777, Loyalists "were expected to remove themselves and their families from the state within sixty days or as soon thereafter as they could settle their business affairs and secure passage."[9] George Harland Hartley, organist at St. Michael's church in Charleston, was banished and lost an annual income of £450 ($59,000) from his various musical performances along with nearly two thousand acres of land. His wife accompanied him, as did his mother-in-law, Janet Cummings. Although Mrs. Cummings had not been banished, she chose to leave because her loyalty to Britain "exposed her to many insults from the mobs."[10]

Many other Loyalists left the state voluntarily to escape persecution, without waiting to be officially expelled. Despite continuous harassment from the Whigs, the Reverend James Stuart remained in his pulpit at Georgetown, where Loyalists were numerous, until December 1777. By then he had concluded that "there was no Law, Justice, or Protection for Loyal or even neutral Men." Believing that his life was endangered, Stuart fled to the West Indies.[11]

Evan McLaurin, one of the leaders of the backcountry Loyalists, likewise decided that it was too dangerous to remain in South Carolina and fled to East Florida. Traveling in disguise on the Santee River, McLaurin was discovered, pursued, and nearly captured by the rebels. He lost his canoe, weapons, and clothing but eventually reached St. Augustine. There McLaurin was commissioned as a major in the South Carolina Royalists, a provincial battalion commanded by fellow refugee Joseph Robinson. The influx of Loyalists soon increased the strength of the unit to three hundred men.[12]

Another prominent backcountry Loyalist, Richard Pearis, also feared for his life, despite Governor Rutledge's promise of protection. Pearis fled Charleston for the backcountry, where in August he organized four hundred Loyalists in the area between the Broad and Saluda rivers and prepared to march to Florida. The Whigs learned of Pearis's activities and sent Andrew Williamson's militia to prevent the Loyalists' escape. Rather than risk an armed confrontation, nearly all of Pearis's followers gave up on the plan and remained at home. Six of his supporters escaped with Pearis to Pensacola, where John Stuart appointed him captain of a loyal unit forming there.[13]

David Fanning had hoped to accompany Pearis to Florida but was thwarted by the Whigs. He had returned to South Carolina on March 10, 1777, but the Whigs arrested him the next day. Fanning managed to escape and return home, where he was "obliged to secrete myself in the woods, and was supplied with provisions by some Quakers and other Loyalists in the neighbourhood." Learning of Pearis's plan to lead a group of Loyalists to West Florida, Fanning gathered some of his associates with the intention of joining Pearis but was captured when a member of his party betrayed the plan to the Whigs. Fanning was tried for treason, was acquitted, and then failed in an attempt to escape to East Florida. After living in the woods for three months with another Loyalist named Samuel Brown, Fanning returned home, where he was repeatedly arrested and imprisoned. Each time he was released or managed to escape; yet, by the end of December 1778 he was back in rebel custody, in irons in the jail at Ninety Six.[14]

One Loyalist experienced even greater suffering than Fanning did. William Fortune refused to renounce his allegiance to the king in 1777 and as a result was imprisoned eight times, had his home repeatedly plundered, and finally fled to the woods. He emerged only for brief meetings with his wife, who supplied him with food. Fortune did not leave his forest refuge until British forces occupied South Carolina in 1780.[15]

Some Loyalists had enlisted in the state's Continental regiments, either to avoid persecution or because the Whigs had compelled them to do so by threatening them and their families. These men frequently attempted to desert or to subvert their comrades, and when they were identified, they suffered harsh punishment. Pvt. James Orange, captured after deserting, "repeatedly damned the Continental Congress saying he was good English Blood & would support the cause of Great Britain to his last." Orange received two hundred lashes as his penalty. Four other deserters later "found in arms against the United States" were executed in 1777, as were three other soldiers convicted of treason and encouraging desertion.[16]

A few Whigs considered their government's policies unduly harsh. Gabriel Manigault saw many of his acquaintances expelled from South Carolina, and he noted that banishment "is exceeding hard on them."[17] William Hasell Gibbes, an assembly member from Johns Island and member of the council, felt obligated despite his fervor for the Revolution to defend "the rights of others who differed from me in this respect." Gibbes argued that the state's Loyalists should be left unmolested, "provided their behavior was peaceable and that they didn't interfere with us or thwart our Opposition to British Government." His colleagues, however, ignored his advice.[18]

The principal reason why most rebels refused to show lenience to Loyalists was that the tough policies produced the desired effect: many of the king's supporters gradually lost their resolve and began to incline toward the rebels. In February 1777 Christopher Gadsden wrote, "we grow more and more united. Numbers of the Theorists join us Daily, as they begin to be convinced we are of the safest side."[19] Public displays of support for the rebel cause also influenced the Loyalists. After watching a June 28, 1777, celebration marking the anniversary of the repulse of the British attack on Charleston, a French visitor noted that the festivities fired the enthusiasm of the rebels while weakening the Loyalists' commitment. "Even the followers of the Royalists and many who are indifferent to the common cause," he wrote, "see the example set by the others at these affairs and are gradually educated around to their beliefs."[20]

The banishment, flight, conversion, and execution of numerous Loyalists failed to satisfy the Whigs, so in the spring of 1778 the assembly passed another act to accelerate the political cleansing of South Carolina. The new law required all males sixteen and older to swear allegiance to the state. Anyone who refused would forfeit the right to vote and to conduct business and legal transactions. Those who left the state rather than take the oath were subject to the death penalty if they returned. Dozens of Loyalists in the lowcountry promptly sold whatever property they could and sailed for Britain or the West Indies.[21] Edward Rutledge boasted that South Carolina had "sent forth Cargoes" of Loyalists into exile, which he described as "a small punishment, tho' apparently severe, for the many Injuries, they have, and the irreparable ones they would have brought on the virtuous part of our Community."[22]

Fleeing Loyalists experienced persecution right up to the moment of their departure. While a vessel "full to the *brim* with *Tories*" prepared to sail from Charleston, a rebel mob "assembled with Pitch, Tar and other Combustibles, to burn her at the Wharf." The ship was saved when some of those aboard cut the mooring lines and it drifted away from the dock.[23]

Loyalists with good connections among the Whigs, or who had valuable skills, often managed to avoid penalties. Dr. Alexander Garden refused to take the rebel oath and sought assistance from his friend Henry Laurens, who advised Garden to obtain a certificate from a magistrate that would satisfy state authorities. Garden then swore a declaration that he would always promote the best interests of South Carolina, which the Whigs accepted as satisfactory. "Garden was not troubled again and was allowed to go freely about his business."[24] The only physician in Beaufort, Loyalist James Fraser, was never asked to take the oath because the townspeople could not afford to lose his services.[25]

Many backcountry Loyalists, forced to choose between pledging allegiance to the Whigs or suffering under the new legal sanctions, came up with their own solution to the dilemma. Early in the spring Loyalists began assembling near Ninety Six with the intention of marching to East Florida. By late March leaders Benjamin Gregory and John Murphy had gathered about four hundred men, all of whom were mounted. A second party canceled plans to join Gregory and Murphy when rebel militia learned of their intentions. The Loyalists set out for the Savannah River, moving rapidly.[26]

At first the Whigs dismissed the Loyalists as "no more than a Plundering Party" and sent out a few militia, who searched for them without success.[27] However, when they realized the strength of the party, rebel leaders panicked. "The back Country is all up in Arms; The Tories . . . have risen, and as if informed by the same spirit and moved by the same spring, have put themselves in motion at one and the same time throughout all parts of the State," Gov. Rawlins Lowndes wrote. The Loyalists split into several parties as they moved, "plundering robbing and terrifying the Inhabitants" and picking up reinforcements on their route. On April 3 they crossed the Savannah River into Georgia, which put "that Country in a very great Consternation." Lowndes estimated that the Loyalists' numbers had increased to six hundred men by the time they entered Georgia.[28] He sent the South Carolina militia in pursuit, but they accomplished nothing more than to kill and capture a few stragglers.[29]

Continental commander Robert Howe also attempted to intercept the Loyalists. On April 6 he ordered Col. Samuel Elbert of the Georgia Continentals to gather as many troops as possible "to prevent the Insurgents, now embodied & marching to East Florida, from joining the forces of that province." Elbert was to treat the Loyalists "as Enemies to the united States" and use every means "consistent with the rules of war" to defeat them.[30] Not only did Elbert fail to halt the Loyalists, which Howe blamed on the lack of cavalry, but the refugees "Hoisted the British Kings standard, as they passed" through Georgia.[31] The impunity with which the Loyalists moved through Georgia and their summons to join them attracted as many as two hundred Georgians, including a party led by Col. John Thomas, and several rebel deserters.[32]

The Loyalists' successful march to East Florida convinced many Whigs that the maneuver was part of a larger British plan to attack the southern states. Georgia governor John Houstoun believed that the incursion presaged "the total Reduction" of Georgia.[33] William Moultrie agreed and predicted that an invasion was imminent. Rumors circulated of a simultaneous advance by Loyalists and Indians from West Florida and Loyalists and British regulars from East Florida.[34] Joseph Clay expressed concern at "the very great additional Strength" the British were "daily receiving from the great Defection" in the South Carolina backcountry.[35]

He warned Henry Laurens that the influx of Loyalists was making the British in East Florida "so formidable" that they might soon overrun Georgia.[36] Howe also expected "serious Consequences" to follow the Loyalists' junction with the British. Considering the weakness of the southern states and the "Disaffection among the People & that this Infection is still more prevalent in the Back parts of So Carolina," Howe thought it wise "to prepare for the worst."[37]

Howe's assessment of Loyalist strength was accurate, and only the vigilance of the Whigs prevented more of the king's supporters from reaching Florida. Along the Pee Dee River more Loyalists from North and South Carolina had assembled in the spring, but rebel militia from North Carolina attacked them. A battle ensued, and several men were killed on each side, including a Whig colonel.[38] This battle and constant militia patrols ended the Loyalist exodus. A few refugees who had slipped through the cordon informed Thomas Brown in April that other South Carolina Loyalists "thought proper to postpone their insurrection to a more favourable opportunity, as the rebels upon receiving intelligence of the March of Murphy and Gregory's party had embodied themselves in every district." Because the Loyalists were poorly armed, they could not overcome the Whigs without the element of surprise. The refugees also brought Brown a message from Robert Cunningham, "that 2,500 Men between the forks of Saluda and Broadriver" were prepared to assist Brown "whenever orders are sent for that purpose." An additional thirty-eight hundred men at the Congarees, along the Pee Dee and Enoree rivers and near the North Carolina border, were also reported as ready to aid the British.[39]

Some of these Loyalists did attempt to get to Florida; in succeeding weeks "several other large parties of the disaffected attempted to cross Savannah river," but the South Carolina militia prevented them from entering Georgia.[40] Ten Loyalists returned to Georgia in June with a proclamation from Tonyn offering pardon and ten dollars bounty to anyone who came to East Florida with their arms. These men announced that they expected to raise a thousand Loyalists in the Carolina backcountry, but the openness of their activities brought them to the Whigs' attention while they were still in Georgia. Some rebel militia, with the aid of more than twenty Creeks sent by Galphin, caught up with the Loyalists and their handful of recruits, killing and capturing several.[41]

The Loyalist exodus from the backcountry led Whig officials in Charleston to again administer the state loyalty oath to the town's inhabitants. Many people, however, stayed at home when the oath was administered rather than swear allegiance to the rebels.[42] Other Loyalists chose to leave the state rather than take the oath; "two Vessels full of Tories" left Charleston in early May.[43]

Hoping that some Loyalists could be won over to the Whig cause by generous treatment, Governor Lowndes and the council issued a proclamation on June 5 extending the time limit for taking the oath to the state by five days. News of this action caused "unspeakable Uneasiness" among Charleston Whigs, who held a public meeting to express their opposition to the measure. They denounced both

Lowndes and Christopher Gadsden, who had written the proclamation.[44] The mob threatened the governor, insisted that they would not allow the proclamation to be published, and intimidated printers into complying with their demands.[45] They also forbade that "any Magistrate administer the oath, to any of the recanting Tories." Fresh efforts were made to intimidate Loyalists, leading John Lewis Gervais to conclude that "the Tories will have no peace in this quarter." Gervais opposed the governor's policy, declaring that "experience teaches us, they [Loyalists] will never be our Friend longer than we are Successfull, in adversity they will remain our Ennemies, let them take what Oath they please."[46]

The response to the proclamation astonished Lowndes, who defended his action as "the best Policy, and peculiarly adapted to our Circumstances." He refused to withdraw the proclamation, despite "Intimations that the People were in such a ferment that fatal Consequences were to be apprehended" if he failed to do so. Some Loyalists did take advantage of the extended opportunity to take the Whig oath, "but the menaces of the populace have detered many, and frustrated the best plan that could be devised for Conciliating Peace and Union amongst us," Lowndes noted.[47] Charleston's Whigs were so blinded by their hatred of Loyalists that they refused to recognize that reconciliation might be more advantageous to their cause than continued hostility would be.

Still in a frenzy of rage against Loyalists, the rebels turned their wrath on Joshua Brown and two other Quaker ministers who had come from Pennsylvania to visit congregations in the South. The pacifist Quakers were imprisoned at Ninety Six for refusing to take the Whig oath. Convinced that the men were harmless, Henry Laurens asked Gervais to intercede and obtain their release.[48]

Unlike the peaceful Quakers, some Loyalists responded to the Whigs' aggressive behavior with violence. In the vicinity of Orangeburg, a group of Loyalists "cut off the Ears of one Prichard a Magistrate, and another Man," beat a Whig militia captain, and burned the house of an assemblyman. These acts "have thrown all that part of the Country into a general Panick, and so intimidated the Inhabitants that those well affected, are deterred from taking any steps for their own Security least . . . they should bring upon themselves the resentment of these banditti," Lowndes wrote. He sent one hundred regular troops to Orangeburg to reinforce the local militia, ordering the officers "to settle the point of Law, on the spot" if they captured the perpetrators of those acts.[49]

Backcountry Loyalists sent the Whigs a symbolic message by electing some of their leaders to the state legislature. Voters in the Little River district elected Robert Cunningham to the senate and two other Loyalists, Jacob Bowman and Henry O'Neall, to the house of representatives. O'Neall took his seat, along with the required oaths to the state. Cunningham and Bowman, however, chose not to attend the legislature.[50]

Despite such acts of resistance, loyalism continued to wane in response to the apparent decline in British fortunes and to relentless persecution. Gervais noted that the news that France had entered the war on the American side "gave great Satisfaction to all (except Tories)" in South Carolina, "& even some of those wished to recant."[51] Edward Rutledge boasted to John Adams that the French alliance had "worked wonders in the Minds of Men . . . you would still be amazed to see, what a Conversion has taken place in the political Opinion of Numbers; from the multitude of Disaffected, we have had whole Hosts of Patriots . . . who mean to be firm Friends to our good old Cause." Rutledge nevertheless doubted the sincerity of many of these converts, observing that their newfound Whig principles would last only "until they shall think it for their Interest to be otherwise."[52] By October many other Loyalists had also taken the rebel oath, though not in response to the French alliance. A Whig noted that "the uniform ruin that has attended all those who professed themselves friends to the British Tyrant, has cured many of their Toryism."[53] When the military outlook and rebel persuasion failed to sway the Loyalists, persecution, as always, proved the best antidote to loyalism.

Whig officials in Georgia moved more cautiously against Loyalists in that state, in part because factional divisions between moderates and radicals paralyzed the rebel government and also because there were so many Loyalists in the state. The merchant Joseph Clay complained that the state's leadership problems "arose in a great measure from so large a Number of the principal People being either Tories" or having withdrawn from politics to avoid becoming entangled in factional quarrels.[54] John Adam Treutlen wrote that "our small friends, the Tories, within our Bowels, are so very numerous & have such ties of Consanguinity, that all our Efforts against these Enemies of American Freedom have hitherto been languid and ineffectual." He suggested that the rebels might have to "take the treatment of these Men into their own hands" to suppress the Loyalists.[55]

In September 1777 Georgia finally took steps to punish the Loyalists when the assembly passed "An Act for the Expulsion of the Internal Enemies of this State." The law was intended to halt the activities of Loyalists in undermining the state's defense and sought to link the Loyalists to the Indian menace. Declaring that by providing information to the British in St. Augustine the Loyalists made it possible for the Indians to raid "our frontier settlements . . . sacrificing, in the most barbarous manner, numbers of our worthy citizens," the Whigs hoped to win popular support for the new law and to inflame Georgians against the Loyalists.[56]

The act established twelve-member committees in each county and authorized them to tender an oath of allegiance to Georgia and the United States to all white males age twenty-one or over. Anyone summoned by the committee had to bring along "two or more undoubted friends to American independence" to vouch for that individual's Whig principles. Those who failed to satisfy the committee would "be deemed enemies" and would have to leave Georgia within forty days. They would also forfeit half of their property to the state but could sell the remaining half and keep the proceeds. The penalty for failing to appear before the committee or refusing to accept its verdict was imprisonment without bail until the offender was forcibly removed from the state. If someone who was declared an enemy returned to Georgia without permission or was "found in arms" with the British, "upon conviction thereof, they shall suffer death."[57] The committee at Midway promptly summoned twelve accused Loyalists; three refused to appear and gave notice that they would leave Georgia within the allotted forty days. Eight who did appear failed to satisfy the committee and were banished.[58] The law proved effective, for only the most committed Loyalists were willing to endure such harsh punishments. The threat of death served as a powerful discouragement against taking up arms for the king so long as the Whigs held power.

Many Whigs, however, still worried that the Loyalists remained dangerous. "That there are many Disaffected" in Georgia "is past any Doubt—but I believe no greater proportion than in any other State," Clay noted in October 1777. "Fear from the very exposed situation of this State has operated very powerfully on many well Affected Citizens."[59] In response to these concerns, the assembly in March 1778 passed another law, which declared 117 people guilty of treason and banished them, leaving their property liable to seizure and sale to benefit the state.[60] Those banished included two ministers, William Ronaldson of Queensborough and former Whig John Zubly. The latter eloquently defended his loyalism in an essay entitled *To the Grand Jury,* and yet his legal arguments failed to overcome rebel wrath. In addition to banishing him, the Whigs destroyed his home and threw his books into the Savannah River. He fled to South Carolina, where he managed to avoid persecution from that state's Whigs.[61] John Jamieson of St. Paul's Parish had escaped the notice of the rebel committee in 1777, but while visiting Savannah in January 1778 the local Whigs charged him with loyalism. He refused to take "their detestable and absurd oath," whereupon the rebels seized half his property and banished him from the state. Before he could leave, the 1778 act went into effect, and the Whigs confiscated the remaining half of his property.[62]

Whig repression succeeded in checking any efforts by Georgia Loyalists to openly oppose the state government, but the rebels faced a more serious threat from the refugees in East Florida. Legal sanctions and persecution had driven thousands of Loyalists to seek safety there. Some 350 South Carolinians arrived in April 1776, many of them Germans from the Dutch Fork, Orangeburg, and Saxe-Gotha regions. In June another 500 refugees entered the province. Most were South Carolinians from Ninety Six district, but others were Georgians, and a few had made the long journey from North Carolina.[63]

Governor Tonyn quickly put some of the immigrants to good use. He gave Thomas Brown a commission as lieutenant colonel and instructed him to recruit rangers from among the refugees who had escaped to Indian territory. The governor initially planned to use this force to gather cattle in Georgia to alleviate East Florida's food shortage. Brown increased his force with recruits from the Loyalists entering East Florida, creating the battalion known as the Florida

Rangers. Tonyn employed this unit to implement his desire to carry the war to the rebels.[64]

In February 1777 Tonyn dispatched Brown with his Rangers and some Indians to seize cattle in Georgia. Gen. Augustine Prevost, commander of the East Florida garrison, provided 160 regulars to support them; British lieutenant colonel Lewis Fuser commanded the combined force. On February 17 Brown, with 20 rangers and 50 Creeks and Seminoles, attacked Fort McIntosh. The garrison of 70 rebels surrendered the next day after 4 intrepid rangers stopped a relief column of 300 men four miles from the fort. Fuser's troops arrived in time for the surrender, and Fuser's rudeness toward the Loyalists and Indians angered Brown, who warned Tonyn that such treatment might cause the Indians to withdraw their support. Fuser advanced to the Altamaha River, skirmished with a rebel force there, and decided to return to St. Augustine. Brown's Rangers brought two thousand head of cattle back with them.[65]

The raid convinced Georgia Whigs that it was necessary to invade East Florida to halt such depredations. Ignoring the objections of Continental commander Robert Howe, the Georgians sent an invasion force overland toward St. Augustine while a second detachment traveled south by sea. The land force faced sporadic resistance from small parties of Indians but reached the St. Mary's River on May 12, the day they had been scheduled to rendezvous with the invasion flotilla. On the night of May 14 some Indians captured about one hundred of the rebels' horses, provoking a skirmish the next day in which two Indians were killed, scalped, and mutilated by the Georgians.[66]

The American commander Col. John Baker then moved his camp to a safer location at Thomas Creek. On the morning of May 17 Brown, with about two hundred Loyalists and Indians, attacked Baker's slightly smaller force. The rebels retreated—directly into about one hundred British troops advancing to assist Brown. The stunned Americans fled into a swamp, leaving behind three dead and thirty-one prisoners. This victory ruined the rebels' prospects for a successful invasion.[67]

The seaborne invasion force finally reached Amelia Island on May 18, well behind schedule. The following day some of the island's Loyalist inhabitants attacked a Whig detachment, killing an officer and wounding two men. In retaliation, Colonel Elbert ordered his rebel troops to burn all the houses and kill all the livestock on the island. Having learned of Baker's defeat, Elbert decided that it was too dangerous to put his troops ashore on the mainland to march southward. He then found that his boats were unable to pass through the channel between Amelia Island and the mainland and were too unseaworthy to risk venturing into the Atlantic. On May 26 he decided to return to Georgia.[68]

After the invaders withdrew, Brown's Rangers, with Creek assistance, renewed their raids into Georgia during the summer and fall of 1777. They attacked a party of twenty-two rebel troops in August, killed fourteen, and then retreated.[69] Joseph

Clay lamented in late September that the raiders had "for some Months past been continually making incursions into our State" and that "not the smallest Check has ever been given to these People," other than one incident in which Continental troops drove off a party of rangers in a skirmish on the Altamaha River. Clay could not understand how a force that "never exceeded 150 including Indians" could operate with impunity in southern Georgia. This situation, Clay wrote, "is very much complained of by the Inhabitants & with great reason that they cannot be protected from such an inferior force."[70]

Brown struck again on March 13, 1778, capturing Fort Barrington on the Altamaha River. Swimming across the river to achieve surprise, Brown, one hundred rangers, and ten Creeks stormed the fort at dawn. They killed two rebels and took twenty-three prisoners along with some artillery; their own casualties amounted only to one killed and four wounded. "Fort Barrington was a great Obstruction to our Foraging, [and] as that difficulty is now removed," it would be easier to procure cattle, Brown reported.[71]

These successes led Tonyn to conclude that British strength in East Florida was sufficient to conquer Georgia and possibly South Carolina as well. He pointed out to William Howe the "numberless inconveniences from acting always on the defensive" and offered an alternate plan. "With this [St. Augustine] Garrison the Rangers and Indians, the province of Georgia may be taken in possession, which will give a fair opportunity to the Loyalists in South Carolina to show themselves," Tonyn wrote. Should the Loyalists in the latter state be as numerous as reported, "I should apprehend that province would soon be compelled to subjection," the governor stated.[72]

Tonyn never got the opportunity to test his plan because once again the Whigs responded to the menace by invading East Florida. Unless that province were conquered, Clay asserted, "we can have no Security," since the Loyalist inhabitants of the Georgia and South Carolina backcountry "are continually backwards & Forwards giving them every information."[73] Frustrated by the attacks of Brown's Rangers and "the Acts & Treachery of some among our-selves," John Houstoun agreed that an invasion was the only way to protect Georgia.[74] John Faucheraud Grimké, a major in the South Carolina Continen-tals, justified an invasion as necessary to prevent the British from uniting with Loyalist refugees such as the eight hundred who had recently marched to Flor-ida. He had heard rumors that Prevost intended to attack Sunbury as a diver-sion while other British troops would "March into the Middle Settlements of Georgia to be joined there by . . . 1000 or 1200 disaffected Insurgents from the back parts of So. Carolina, No. Carolina & Georgia."[75]

Christopher Gadsden argued that the large number of slaves in South Carolina made it necessary for the Americans to occupy East Florida. Free white laborers, Gadsden stated, could not compete with slaves who were hired out by their mas-ters, which he denounced as an "excessively impolitick" practice. The whites thus impoverished, along with "the Scum of all the States from Pennsylvania hitherward . . . will naturally flock to Augustine as an asylum and no doubt Britain will give them every Political Encouragement," he wrote. These desperate people would then harass both Georgia and South Carolina; the only way to prevent this was to deprive them of refuge in St. Augustine.[76] Gadsden was unique among southern Whigs in believing that because slavery denied poor whites economic opportunity, it drove some people into becoming Loyalists out of sheer necessity.

Gen. Robert Howe opposed the invasion of East Florida, believing that concentrating the regulars and militia for such an operation would leave Georgia vulnerable to attack from another direction. While conceding that the "daily Incursions from the Partizans of Saint Augustine . . . Aided, abetted and Encouraged by some of the Inhabitants" of Georgia and South Carolina, constituted a serious problem, he insisted that invading East Florida would not halt their operations. The rangers' knowledge of the country would enable them to plague Georgia even if they lost their Florida base.[77] The best plan, Howe advised the Georgians, would be to secure their southern frontier by establishing strong posts along their southern boundary and keeping scouting parties operating between the St. Mary's and St. John's rivers, "by which means the terror & alarm the Enemy delight to spread would be retorted upon them."[78]

Civil officials dismissed the general's objections, and Howe reluctantly began to organize the invasion force. Even before the troops set out, the army was troubled by dissension in the ranks. Loyalists who had sought relief from persecution by enlisting in Continental regiments saw the march into Florida as an opportunity to escape the rebels and join the British. The boldest of these men attempted to persuade their comrades to accompany them. Shortly before the army marched, a Sergeant Alcock of the 4th Georgia Battalion was charged with mutiny and "endeavouring to Enveigle Continentl. Soldiers to desert with him to the Enemy." The accusation, however, could not be proved, as no one could be found to testify against Alcock.[79] The Fourth Georgia, which included several British deserters, caused problems for Howe throughout the campaign.[80]

The Alcock incident was merely a prelude to the similar troubles Howe encountered when his army finally reached Fort Tonyn on the St. Mary's River. Three Continental privates were charged with mutiny on May 13, and the next day a Sergeant Tyrrell of the Fourth Georgia was tried on charges of mutiny and encouraging others to desert. Tyrrell was found guilty and on May 21 was executed in front of the whole army. Howe hoped that this punishment "may have a proper Effect upon the Minds of the Soldiers."[81]

Howe's optimism did not last twenty-four hours, for the next day James Lister, a deserter, was captured and accused of spying, sedition, and urging soldiers to desert. Lister, who may have earlier deserted from the British army, had taken fifteen of his comrades from the Fourth Georgia with him when he deserted. Three of the men soon returned of their own accord, another was killed, and ten were captured by a detachment sent in pursuit. Also taken was one private of the First Georgia.[82] One of Howe's officers stated that Lister's party intended to go to St. Augustine and that if they had succeeded, it "might by the Example have proved prejudicial to us."[83]

A court-martial sentenced Lister and eight other deserters to be executed. Howe had by now concluded that only harsh punishment could prevent an exodus of Loyalist sympathizers and other disgruntled soldiers from the ranks. Although the general later partially relented and pardoned three of the men, this time the executions had the desired effect. The Continental units experienced no further problems with desertion or attempted mutiny during the six weeks they remained in East Florida.[84] The Loyalists' efforts to escape to the British and induce others to follow, while disruptive to Howe's army, did little to impede the campaign as a whole, and in the end many sacrificed their lives without materially assisting the royal cause.

Howe succeeded in halting desertion among his regulars, but militiamen deserted frequently once they entered East Florida. In early June thirty Georgians went "off to the Enemy in a body," and individuals deserted often as well. Desertions were also "daily & frequent" from South Carolina militia units.[85] Like many of the Georgians, "some Carolinians had invaded Florida to escape from the Whigs."[86] When Whig officers decided in early July to abandon the campaign and withdraw to Georgia, a dozen men took advantage of their last opportunity to reach the British and deserted.[87]

While Loyalists in Whig units struggled to reach the British, their counterparts in the king's service labored to halt the invading army. Reports reaching American officers indicated that Brown's Rangers numbered 150 men, supported by 150 Indians, while 350 South Carolina Loyalists were said to be ten miles north of the St. John's River on May 21. An informant told the rebels that both Brown's troops and the South Carolinians "were extremely discontented with their Change of Situation & had expressed a wish to Return."[88] Prisoners taken by the Americans on June 23 provided a different account, stating that although the Loyalist soldiers "had been very discontented & that some of them had threatened to return to Carolina & throw themselves upon the Mercy of their Country," they had since been "Reconciled."[89]

The Loyalists showed few signs of demoralization in their encounters with the Whigs. Brown first attempted to threaten the invaders by dispatching seventy-five rangers and some Indians to unite with another party of Loyalists and strike the Whigs' rear, but the plan failed when some of the rangers deserted and informed the rebels. Whig troops then attacked and dispersed the party, capturing its commander, Capt. James Moore, and executing him. This forced Brown to burn Fort Tonyn on the St. Mary's River and retreat. Brown had more success on June 30. Pursued by about one hundred mounted Georgians, the rangers turned on the Whigs and, with the help of some regulars, drove off their enemies. At least nine rebels were killed in the encounter.[90]

This skirmish proved to be the only significant fighting of the campaign. Gen. Augustine Prevost had been "under very little apprehension of the enemy being able to effect any thing of consequence," and his prediction proved accurate.[91] The Whig leaders fell to arguing among themselves. Georgia governor John Houstoun and Andrew Williamson, commanding the South Carolinians, refused to take orders from Howe; the officer commanding the naval squadron wanted to retreat; and Howe could not impose a plan that satisfied everyone. On July 14 the Whigs began to withdraw. With them went about fifteen South Carolina Loyalists who had deserted on July 1.[92]

Forced back on the defensive, Howe contemplated yet another invasion of East Florida. He advised Congress that the capture of St. Augustine would end the raids on Georgia and "entirely crush the Spirit of Insurgency and defection too prevalent in the back parts" of that state and South Carolina.[93] Meanwhile, Howe prepared for a British attack, which he expected to coincide with "the rising of a number of Insurgents" in the two states.[94] Such a blow, he warned, would prove "fatal" to Georgia.[95] Congress approved Howe's proposed invasion, but subsequent British actions forestalled the plan.[96]

Once the rebels had left Florida, Brown's Rangers resumed their raids into Georgia. "We are again very much infested with Tonyns Banditti Stealing our Horses & Negros & doing us all the Mischief they can," Joseph Clay wrote on September 9. A few weeks later he complained that "the Floridians & Indians by their Robberies & Murders keep us in a continual State of Alarm."[97]

The rebels had not been content to target East Florida; they had decided to strike at West Florida as well. Aware of the potential danger, in January 1777 Gen. William Howe had ordered John Stuart to organize West Florida's growing number of Loyalists into companies and arm them to assist in defending the province. Stuart had promptly formed four companies designated the "Loyal Refugees."[98]

Despite considerable support in Congress for an invasion of West Florida, Henry Laurens had managed to have the proposal shelved for 1777. Laurens believed that the invasion would have dire consequences for the Whigs. Loyalists who had fled to that province had already demonstrated their antipathy to the revolution, Laurens noted, and "from Such Men we could expect neither assistance nor Secrecy, on the contrary they would join with numerous tribes of Indians who had not been thought of in the Scheme of attack." Furthermore, Stuart's agents could use the invasion to convince the Creeks that the rebels harbored aggressive intentions toward the interior of the continent and thus incite that nation to strike directly against South Carolina and Georgia.[99]

The next year, however, Congress had decided to carry out the scheme and dispatched about one hundred men under Capt. James Willing, the former Natchez resident, to travel down the Ohio and Mississippi rivers to strike at West Florida. Willing's party landed at Natchez on February 19, 1778, catching the inhabitants completely by surprise. Willing declared all the people in the area prisoners, paroled them, and claimed the region for the United States. Four days later some of Willing's troops landed at Manchac, where they again paroled all of the inhabitants.[100]

Willing's invasion raised the possibility that a significant number of settlers in the Natchez region would join the rebels, threatening British control of the Mississippi valley. William Dunbar believed that "perhaps one half of the Inhabitants were in the American Interest."[101] Another Loyalist stated that about one hundred Natchez settlers enlisted with Willing.[102] When Willing's men arrived at Manchac, the merchant John Fitzpatrick noted that "Several" of the inhabitants joined the rebels.[103] Governor Chester responded to the threat by sending John McGillivray to raise a provincial force at Mobile, which the governor hoped "might be the nucleus of a permanent military establishment in West Florida."[104]

Meanwhile, Natchez Loyalists took matters into their own hands. They petitioned the governor, declaring that they would break their paroles and resist the rebels if reinforced by one hundred regular troops, but they added that they would not act if the only assistance they received came from provincial troops or Indians.[105] A pair of Loyalists who had fled to New Orleans likewise worked to thwart the rebels. Robert Ross and John Campbell planted a spy in the home of Oliver Pollock, a merchant who procured supplies from the Spanish for the Whigs' use. Ross and Campbell were discovered plotting to prevent the shipment of supplies upriver to Fort Pitt and were banished from Louisiana. However, to avoid antagonizing the British, Louisiana governor Bernardo de Galvez halted the shipment.[106]

Willing had brought Loyalist Anthony Hutchins as a prisoner to New Orleans, where he was released on parole. In an effort to sow dissension among the rebels, Hutchins convinced several of Willing's men that their officers had cheated them out of their rightful share of plundered Loyalist property. He offered a one-thousand-dollar reward if they would capture Pollock and five hundred dollars each for Willing and his second in command. However, Hutchins abandoned his plan to seize the rebel leaders when he learned that some of Willing's men were returning to Natchez.[107]

Hutchins rushed back to Natchez, where he raised a party of about thirty Loyalists. In a well-executed ambush, Hutchins's men defeated an equal number of Willing's troops at White Cliffs on April 16, killing five rebels and capturing the survivors. Other Loyalists at Manchac, led by Adam Chrystie, united with a small force of provincial troops under Richard Pearis and attacked the rebels there. The fifteen Loyalists defeated and dispersed forty Whigs, killing several and taking the rest prisoner. They then withdrew because other rebel parties were in the area; Christie could not risk battle while encumbered with so many captives.[108] The inhabitants of Natchez renounced the pledge of neutrality they had given to Willing, restated their allegiance to Britain, and made a pact to "form ourselves into a garrison . . . and turn out as universally as necessary, to protect ourselves and the settlement."[109] Willing and the rest of his force remained in New Orleans, so that aside from plundering, Willing's chief accomplishment had been to strengthen Loyalist sentiment in West Florida.[110]

John Stuart raised four companies of Loyalist cavalry, each numbering about fifty men, in response to the Willing raid. These troops were "constantly employed in the service & defence of this Province," with two companies posted at Manchac and one at Natchez to scout along the Mississippi, while the fourth had some of its troops at Pensacola and the rest among the Cherokees. The troops "behaved with great Spirit, and resolution," Stuart reported.[111]

The Loyalists, despite a lack of direct assistance, had contributed much to the British cause. Those who had marched to East Florida had thrown the Whigs into a panic and provided needed reinforcements to that province. Brown's Rangers had harassed Georgia and helped thwart the 1778 invasion of East Florida, weakening the Whigs and increasing their vulnerability to the coming British invasion. In West Florida the Loyalists had overcome surprise and initial defeat to regain control of the Mississippi valley. Had it not been for the Loyalists' efforts, the strategic situation in the South at the end of 1778 would have been far less favorable to the British.

Neutralizing the Indians

John Stuart faced two major problems as he worked to obtain assistance from the Indians in 1777 and 1778. First, the repercussions of the Cherokee defeat temporarily took that nation out of the strategic equation and continued to have an effect on the other southern nations. Second, George Galphin's efforts to keep the Creeks neutral exacerbated the divisions in that nation, forcing Stuart to struggle to maintain the Creeks' allegiance. Nevertheless, Stuart managed to obtain some aid from the Indians, which helped the British defeat Whig attempts to invade the Floridas and kept pressure on the Georgia frontier.

With their food supplies destroyed, the Cherokees sent messages to the Whigs asking for peace. In early 1777 Andrew Williamson brought a "large deputation from the lower middle & valley settlements" who had "humbly" come to "sue for Peace."[112] Whig leaders agreed to meet with the Cherokees at DeWitt's Corner, South Carolina, on May 7. There, South Carolina representatives Williamson, Leroy Hammond, William Henry Drayton, and Daniel Horry along with Georgians Jonathan Bryan, Jonathan Cochran, and William Glascock conferred with six hundred Cherokees, many of whom had come in hopes of receiving presents. On May 20 the parties signed a treaty by which the Cherokees gave up almost all of their land in South Carolina except a small parcel in the western part of the state.[113] The Indians also agreed to release any prisoners they still held, white or black, and to return all horses they had taken. The treaty terms attempted to drive a wedge between the Cherokees and the British by requiring that any whites "who instigated or endeavoured to instigate the Cherokees to the late war or encouraged or aided them" and were still among them be turned over to the rebels. Anyone else, white or Indian, who attempted to instigate the Cherokees to further warfare, along with any traders unlicensed by American authorities, were likewise to be seized and brought to the rebels. If the Cherokees scrupulously adhered to these terms, all contact between the nation and the British would cease. For their part, the governments of South Carolina and Georgia promised to open trade with the Cherokees and to pay a reward for each runaway slave the Indians captured and returned to state officials.[114]

After reaching agreement with South Carolina and Georgia, the Cherokees faced additional negotiations with representatives of Virginia and North Carolina. Virginia governor Patrick Henry favored conciliation and instructed his state's delegates to agree to a new boundary "in the best manner you can for the Interest of the frontier Inhabitants, so that you at the same time do strict justice to the Indians."[115] However, the negotiations nearly collapsed when on July 2 an "evil minded" white person murdered a Cherokee man named Big Bullet. The Whigs apologized and promised to apprehend the killer. Cherokee leader Oconostota likewise pledged that the crime "shall not spoil the good Talks." He warned the rebel agents, however, that the British would use the murder to influence the Indians. "Cameron and Stuart will hear of this accident, they will laugh and be pleased at it," he said. "I shall tell my own people not to mind Camerons & Stewarts Talks." After a sham investigation, the Whigs professed to be unable to find the murderer and compensated the Cherokees with gifts.[116]

When negotiations resumed, Cherokee leaders Old Tassel and the Raven spoke for their nation. Both men affirmed their desire for peace and shifted blame for the war on the British agents who kept them "in blindness." They did, however, protest that the whites had acted as though "they only wanted our land" and had encroached on Cherokee territory, so that now the whites had "scarcely given us room to turn round." When the rebels argued that the encroachments were legal because of the treaty the Cherokees had signed with Colonel Henderson, the Raven insisted that "fear only made us agree to a settlement at all, but we expected Government would again remedy us." The rebels then blamed the trouble on the British, asserting that the king had granted the lands in question to the settlers but that Stuart and Cameron had lied about it in order to goad the Cherokees into a war against the rebels.[117]

This falsehood set the tone for the negotiations; the rebel commissioners had no desire to listen to the Indians' grievances, wanting instead only to impose the harshest possible terms on the Cherokees. Eventually the Indians submitted to rebel demands, although the Americans' intransigence had aroused their suspicions. "It seems misterious to me why you should ask so much land so near me," Old Tassel said. "I am sensible that if we give up these lands they will bring you more a great deal than hundreds of pounds. It spoils our hunting ground; but always remains good to you to raise families and stocks on, when the goods we receive of you are rotten and gone to nothing."[118] The treaty, signed on July 20, ceded vast tracts of Cherokee land to Virginia and North Carolina, required the Indians to return any prisoners they held, and barred whites from trespassing on the remaining Cherokee land. The Cherokees would be paid for returning runaway slaves. Unlike the treaty with South Carolina and Georgia, this agreement contained no provisions for seizing or barring British emissaries. Under the terms of the two treaties, the Cherokees surrendered over five million acres of land to the rebels.[119]

Whig leaders continued to pursue a tough policy toward the Cherokees after the treaties had been signed. When South Carolina sent commissioners to mark the new boundaries between that state and the Cherokees, Indians whose towns were in the lands just ceded asked permission to remain in their homes. The governor refused their request. In spite of such disappointments, most Cherokees remained "very pacific."[120]

The 1777 treaties with the Cherokees did not put a complete end to hostilities with that nation, however. Dragging Canoe, the most militant Cherokee leader, initially appeared willing to make peace. In reply to a talk the Whigs had sent him in April, he claimed that he had come to "see clear, that Cameron and Stewart have been telling me lies." The British agents, he said, had "told us that all that the Virginians wanted was to get our Land and kill us." Dragging Canoe said that he now realized that the white settlers were "the greatest friends we ever had." However, rather than attend the negotiations, Dragging Canoe said that he was going to confront the British agents about their lies.[121] The Cherokee leader, in fact, was just as skilled in duplicity as the Whig agents were; he used the time he had gained to lead many of the Overhill Cherokees, along with the more militant members of other groups, to the Tennessee River valley, where they established new towns. Dragging Canoe's faction, which came to be known as the Chickamaugas after a creek in their new homeland, had about one thousand fighting men. Their leader denounced the treaties that the other Cherokees had signed and pressed the British for arms so he could continue to fight the frontier settlers.[122] "Repeated attacks were made by the Indians upon the settlements" west of the Appalachians in the summer of 1778, which frequently forced the inhabitants to take shelter in nearby forts until the militia finally drove Dragging Canoe's Cherokees away.[123]

The defeat and dislocation of the Cherokees, along with the large land cessions they had been forced to make as the price for peace, did not escape the notice of the Creeks. Stuart informed Germain in January 1777 "that the fate of the Cherokee nation had damped" the Creeks' enthusiasm. Two hundred Cherokees, "entirely naked and destitute of everything," had joined Stuart at Pensacola after traveling through Creek territory, where the sight of their forlorn condition demoralized the Creeks.[124] In March, Stuart noted that some Lower Creeks had met with Galphin, whose reminders of "the success of the rebels, operated strongly on the minds of those savages." After returning to their towns, the Indians who had met with Galphin "began to form a party and to debauch the minds of many."[125]

The effects had not faded by June. "The distressed situation of the Cherokees has been beyond description," Stuart wrote. "Driven from their habitations and wandering about destitute of clothes and provisions, many of them perished." Their defeat had also affected the Choctaws and Chickasaws, Stuart noted after conferring with leaders of those two nations. "The fate of the Cherokees is constantly before the eyes of the other Indian nations and damps their spirits."[126]

This situation greatly complicated Stuart's situation, since he had received orders from Gen. William Howe to organize the southern Indians under the command of Loyalist refugees and send them to attack the rebels. Howe believed that the Loyalists' ability to distinguish between loyal and rebel inhabitants would enable them to target their opponents when operating against the backcountry settlements.[127]

Before he could carry out these orders, Stuart had to reverse the effects of the Cherokees' defeat. He instructed Alexander Cameron "to take every Opportunity of inculcating into the Cherokee Indians that they themselves are Principals in this War; that the Defence of them & their Land is one of the greatest Causes of it." Cameron should also remind them that they had gone to war "to do themselves Justice by the Recovery of their Lands" and "to discountenance in them every Idea of their being engaged in a War merely upon our Acct. the reverse being so far true that they began it contrary to your Advice & Opinion."[128]

It would take some time before Stuart's agents could raise the Indians' morale. Meanwhile, the Whigs seized the opportunity to increase their influence with the Creeks. In December 1776 Lachlan McIntosh sent a message to the Creeks in which he declared that the Georgians and the Creeks "are, and should be one People." McIntosh asserted that the British planned to take all the land belonging to both whites and Indians and to enslave Creeks and Georgians alike. The Cherokees, McIntosh said, had believed British lies, gone to war, and been driven from their country. He advised the Creeks to send their leaders to Savannah to meet with the Georgia officials; should they refuse, McIntosh would not be able to restrain his men "from going up to your towns & drive you out of your Country as the Carolinians have drove . . . the Cherokees."[129] Whatever benefit McIntosh hoped to obtain from this message was undone a few days later when, in response to a Creek raid that killed several rebel soldiers, the Whigs seized six Creeks who had been visiting the settlements and imprisoned them in Savannah.[130]

George Galphin, who had far more influence with the Creeks than McIntosh did, stepped in and summoned the Creeks to a meeting at his home at Silver Bluff, across the Savannah River from Augusta. On June 17, 1777, Galphin met with more than four hundred Lower Creeks and threatened that they would suffer a worse fate than that of the Cherokees if they waged war against the Whigs. Intimidated, the Creeks replied that they wanted peace and claimed that they had been misled by Stuart's agents.[131] Galphin reported that the Creeks "all went back well

pleasd" and that only three Creek towns opposed the Americans. Their opposition, he said, "is owing to the bad. people we have on the frontier of Georgia that
kild. Severall of their people Last winter." Galphin feared that some Georgians
wished to provoke a war with the Creeks, so he tried to keep the Indians away
from the settlements from fear that the Georgians would kill them.[132]

In the autumn Galphin traveled to the Ogeechee River for another meeting
with some 350 Creeks. Galphin spent seven weeks with them, from early November into late December, and although he complained of the "fataging time I had of
it among a parsile of Drunken Indians," he was able to report that he had again
"Sent them all home well pleased." He provided the Indians with enough goods to
load eighty horses. While conceding that the British still had some supporters
among the Creeks, he predicted that "by the Spring we Shall have a good footing
in that nattion." Galphin repeated his warning that the Georgians were the biggest
obstacle to peace, noting that whites in the Ceded Lands, the territory acquired in
the 1773 Indian cession, had killed five Indians before the Creeks retaliated by killing a Georgian and that the whites frequently stole the Indians' horses. If the
Georgians were not restrained, "it will not be in my power to keep pease Long,"
Galphin declared.[133]

Galphin's ability to influence the Creeks troubled British officials, who relied on
that nation's support to help defend East Florida and maintain pressure on Georgia.[134] Elias Durnford, an engineer officer at Pensacola, complained that the Creeks
"are much divided, so that it is not certain what part they may take as Golphin by
promises and his Interest keeps up a party in that nation."[135] Stuart at first tried to
downplay the effects of Galphin's diplomacy, asserting that at Galphin's May conference only "about 200 [Creeks] of little Consequence went" and that "the rest of
the Nation was extremely offended" by their meeting with Galphin.[136] However,
the results of Galphin's "tampering" struck home in late September, when Alexander McGillivray, one of Stuart's agents, discovered that the Oakfuskee Creeks were
"determined to murder Mr. Taitt, Mr. Cameron," and an interpreter.[137] McGillivray's warning saved Taitt and Cameron, but the Oakfuskees plundered them
and other British traders, and in early October a Cussita attempt to murder William McIntosh was thwarted by other Creeks. Two weeks later the Cussitas sent a
message informing Stuart that they had learned that the Upper Creeks planned to
remain neutral and that they intended to do the same. Stuart responded by halting
trade with those in the Creek towns who had harassed his agents and traders.[138]

Stuart admitted to Germain that Galphin had succeeded in dividing the
Creeks so that they would not provide as much support as expected.[139] Irritated
at that nation's lack of assistance, Germain expressed regret that they "do not
manifest that disposition to act in favor of Government, which we had been
taught to expect." The minister, who was losing confidence in Stuart, advised
General Howe to "frustrate the designs of the Agents employed by the Rebels,
& secure the future Affection of the Savages."[140]

In addition to Galphin's Creek adherents, a pro-Spanish faction in the nation undermined British efforts to maintain their influence. In 1777 the Creek leader Tunape and a large number of other Indians visited Havana, where they asked the Spaniards to open trade with them. Spanish officials expressed their regret at being unable to comply but offered to provide specific items requested by Tunape.[141]

Despite these difficulties, Stuart managed to convince some Creeks to operate against the rebels. In late March, Creek parties struck in western Georgia, where they killed three men at Clark's Fort.[142] Lachlan McIntosh warned Gov. Button Gwinnett that there were too few mounted troops to guard the frontiers and that as a result the Indians had been "very troublesome, & kill'd several people in different parts of the State within this Six Mos. past. we are under great apprehension this summer of a Genl. war with the Indians," instigated by the British.[143]

While Galphin was still meeting with the Creeks in the summer, a party of Cowetas stole several horses and then ambushed a rebel force that pursued them, killing twenty. The Cowetas also attacked a fort on the Ogeechee River and killed two rebels. The Whigs abandoned the fort, and the Indians burned it. Another group of Creeks attacked Capt. Thomas Dooly and twenty Continental recruits on July 22. Dooly and three other whites were killed; the rest of the Whigs fled. On July 31 a Creek party killed a woman and four children near the Ogeechee, "the only documented exception in the South" to the Indians' policy of striking only armed opponents. Stuart claimed that Samuel Dilkes, whose wife and children were the victims, had repeatedly abused the Indians and that personal revenge motivated the Creeks in this instance.[144]

These sporadic attacks helped the British by inciting the Georgians' rage against the Indians; white hatred of the Creeks was the most convincing argument Stuart could use to keep the Indians' allegiance. After the summer conference, Galphin had escorted Handsome Fellow and nine other Creek leaders to Charleston to consult with state officials. On their return journey, Thomas Dooly's troops with some other Whigs seized the ten Creeks and, ignoring Galphin's protests, imprisoned them at Augusta. The Indians were eventually released and escorted home by some Georgia Continentals. Galphin mollified them by claiming that Stuart had sent out the Creek party to kill Dooly in hopes of provoking a war.[145] John Lewis Gervais complained that "a few Georgia people have put us at the Eve of a War," just when peace with the Creeks seemed assured.[146] "It is impossible to say what will happen when the Handsome Fellow gets Home," John Rutledge wrote, echoing Gervais's concern; "I fear a Creek War will soon take place."[147]

Whig relations with the Creeks remained tenuous into the autumn. Although a few Creeks occasionally killed settlers on the Georgia frontier, news that the prorebel Creek faction had driven Stuart's agents out of their territory and plundered British traders led Gervais to assert that the Creeks "have at last declared in our favour."[148] However, while the incident had the potential to seriously disrupt Creek relations with the British, the Georgians continued to provoke the Creeks with aggressive actions. "I am afraid the people in the Ceded Land. will undo all we are Doing," Galphin wrote, noting that the Georgians had sent two surveyors onto Indian land to mark out plots. When the Creeks learned of this, Galphin warned, "it will make our Enemies words. true that we want to take all there Land." He urged Georgia officials to restrain their citizens in order to prevent war.[149]

Georgia's assembly, blinded to potential danger by their desire for land, instead considered launching a war against the Creeks. Robert Howe labored to dissuade them, insisting that Georgia lacked the strength to go to war with the Creeks. He also warned them that they would be unlikely to receive aid from the neighboring states, who were working hard to keep the Creeks neutral.[150] The Georgians finally abandoned the scheme, although Joseph Clay wrote that "'twas with the greatest difficulty we cou'd prevent our Assembly Resolving . . . to break out with the Creeks which if had taken place we must have been broke up as a State at once."[151] He found the push for a Creek war especially disturbing because it came "at that very time these People . . . were giving us the most convincing Proofs of their Pacific disposition towards us—by driving Stuart's Deputies out of their Towns & burn'd their Houses."[152]

Stuart spent the early months of 1778 attempting simultaneously to punish the Creeks for their hostile actions against his agents and to reestablish good relations with them. The cessation of trade led Upper Creek leaders to come to Pensacola to meet with the superintendent. Since they had not participated in the plundering, Stuart told them to carry out their winter hunt. Shortly afterward six hundred Lower Creeks arrived to make amends. Stuart avoided blaming the Indians as a group; instead he criticized those Indians who had "misbehaved," while praising those who had not for their faithfulness. The guilty individuals apologized and asked that the traders be allowed to return. Stuart consented, providing that the rebellious Creeks first permitted his deputies to go back among them. The Oak-fuskees did not go to Pensacola but sent Alexander McGillivray there with a message of apology and expressed their willingness to accept an agent, so long as it was not David Taitt, "who was obnoxious to them." Stuart instructed McGillivray to bring their leaders to Pensacola for further discussion.[153]

By spring Stuart had managed to bring most of the Creeks back into the British fold. In March he reported that "at the most pressing solicitation of the Upper & Lower Creeks, Messrs Tait and Mackintosh are returned to their Nations, guarded by strong partys of Indians, who are determined to protect them at the risk of their lives." With his agents back among the Creeks and the trade reopened, except to the pro-American towns, Stuart predicted "that every thing in that Nation will be brought into its proper Channel in a very short time."[154] The "leading chiefs of all the towns in the rebel interest" traveled to Pensacola in late April "to make their peace." Stuart believed that only a lack of direct support from British troops made the Indians hesitant to exert themselves more fully against the Whigs.[155]

Stuart's progress did not satisfy Patrick Tonyn, who planned to use the Creeks and Brown's Rangers to launch a major offensive against Georgia. Conducting his own diplomacy without consulting Stuart, Tonyn had succeeded in keeping the Seminoles and other Creeks living near East Florida "well disposed."[156] A French visitor estimated that there were only four hundred Indian warriors in the province but noted that "the English are humoring them and lavishing attention on them."[157] Tonyn wished to keep the Creeks satisfied until he received approval for his attack on Georgia. Again bypassing Stuart, he had written directly to William Howe to point out "the necessity of employing [the Indians] in some shape." The governor sought Howe's permission to invade Georgia using the East Florida garrison, Brown's Rangers, and the Indians. With such a force, Tonyn stated, "Georgia may be taken in possession, which will give a fair opportunity to the loyalists in South Carolina to show themselves . . . and if they prove as numerous as hath been given out, I should apprehend that province would soon be compelled to subjection and to own their allegiance to the King." Howe, less optimistic than Tonyn, did not approve the proposal.[158]

Equally frustrating for the governor was the news that Stuart had met with the Creeks and urged them to remain at peace. Tonyn complained to Howe that as a result of Stuart's work, "the object, formed by the rebels, is attained, to make the Indians neutral." Tonyn had expected hundreds of Indians to come to St. Augustine to assist the rangers in Tonyn's alternate plan of launching extensive raids in Georgia, but after Stuart's meeting only one hundred had arrived.[159] Stuart did promise that the Seminoles were ready to provide one thousand men to assist Prevost's forces whenever they were needed, but this failed to satisfy the governor.[160]

Tonyn had to abandon his strategy when the Whigs invaded East Florida. The Creeks' contribution to the province's defense was minimal. The Upper Creeks had planned "to harass and plunder the back settlements" of Georgia while many militiamen were away with the invasion force, but "the rebel party" among the Creeks threatened "to fall upon the [British] traders in the nation and the inhabitants of [West Florida] as soon as the others should turn out." The pro-British Creeks "entirely quenched the flame which was kindling by the rebel gang" but were too busy doing so to make the intended raids on Georgia.[161] About twenty Creeks who were in East Florida joined a much larger number of Seminoles to cooperate with Brown's Rangers; they frequently scouted the American camp at Fort Tonyn, and on June 1 they caught and scalped a Georgian soldier who had been traveling alone.[162]

The Whig invasion force also included some Indians, although neither their numbers nor their nation were recorded. Several of them were members of "a Party of Indians and Soldiers" who brought nine deserters "and the Scalp of a Tenth" back to the American lines.[163] These Indians may have been Creeks from the pro-American towns or Catawbas who accompanied Andrew Williamson's militia from South Carolina.

General Prevost complained that the Indians had provided little help during the invasion, noting that "they did not appear to be very forward to assist." He attributed the poor response to the Indians' belief that if the rebels conquered East Florida, it "would only be the prelude to their [Indians'] destruction" if they actively aided the British. Once the invasion had failed, Prevost observed, the Indians "then came very readily to offer their Services and to receive the presents which their good will and friendship merited in their opinion." Despite his dissatisfaction with the Indians, Prevost asked Gen. Henry Clinton to send more presents for them because "their friendship to us in great part depends upon it." Prevost believed that their support would be more reliable if British forces in the province could demonstrate a clear superiority over the rebels.[164]

After the abortive Whig invasion of East Florida, persistent rumors that a Creek attack on Georgia was imminent circulated in that province and South Carolina. Andrew Williamson ordered his militia to prepare for action after receiving a message from Galphin on August 9 that "the Creeks mean to immediately attack the frontier of Georgia."[165] Rawlins Lowndes, who had received a similar warning from Galphin "of a Storm Brewing up in the Creek Nation," worried that "our wild expedition to Florida and impotant taunts, will have a bad influence on our Indian Affairs." Lowndes complained that between the Indians and "our own disaffected Inhabitants," he was constantly occupied trying "to Counter-act their Plots and watch their movements."[166] On August 20 John Houstoun heard a report that eight Creek towns had declared war on the rebels and that Indians had killed twenty-four people on the Ceded Lands during the previous week. Like Lowndes, Houstoun blamed the failure of the Florida expedition for the Creek attacks. That nation, he said, "look'd on with eager Expectation and . . . were determined as usual to take the strongest Side." The rebels' lack of success, in his opinion, had convinced many Creeks that the British now had the upper hand.[167]

Galphin, however, did not expect a full-scale war with the Creeks, although he had warned that some Creek factions were preparing to strike. He believed that the Whigs still had "rather a majority of the whole Nation in our interest" and reported that pro-American Creeks had assured him "that they will make reprisals at Pensacola & Mobille for whatever mischief the hostile Indians may do on our frontiers."[168] Rebel officials soon received information indicating that the Creek threat had been exaggerated, but many Whigs were infuriated by the possibility of Indian attacks. "No terms should be kept with the perfidious Race," John Wells Jr. wrote. "Fire & sword are the only arguments that can avail with them."[169]

Galphin continued to assure rebel officials that the Creeks were under control, but scattered Indian raids across the backcountry in October raised new fears among the Whigs. Williamson again called out his militia in the middle of the month to defend the frontier, while Lowndes expressed concern that Stuart's "powerful Influence . . . operates strongly" among the Creeks.[170] Even Galphin began to lose hope of maintaining peace. "Stuart at Last has prevailed upon his frinds to Come against our frontier," the agent wrote on October 26. Galphin was trying to use other Creeks to discourage the pro-British faction from attacking but again blamed the Georgians on the Ceded Lands for creating the problem. He asserted that "had it not been for the Imprudence of Some of our one people it woud not been in Stuarts power and all his presents to have Set the Creeks upon us." Galphin pointed out that all the Creek attacks thus far had targeted settlers in the Ceded Lands, while settlements that had not shown hostility to the Creeks had not been molested. Nevertheless, Galphin urged a tough response to the raids, writing that some Creeks "will be allways a picking at us till they get a good Drubing we Can never put up with the Insultes we have recd from them without Leting them no we are there masters."[171]

The South Carolina Assembly considered the Creek problem in November and concluded that another effort should be made to negotiate peace with that nation, even if it was necessary to pay the Indians in order to prevent hostilities. However, if negotiations proved unsuccessful, the legislators decided, the Whigs should follow Galphin's advice and "carry the War into the Creek country."[172]

Augustine Prevost had no intention of allowing the Whigs to crush the Creeks. Reports reaching St. Augustine in October indicated that "the Southern Colonies of Carolina & Georgia were collecting a large Force on their Frontiers in order to attack the Creek & Cherokee Indians." Wishing to prevent a defeat that might deprive the British of further Indian support, Prevost decided "to effect a diversion both in the lower Settlements and the Centrical part of Georgia." To accomplish this, he dispatched Lt. Col. Lewis Fuser with 240 men and a galley to threaten the rebel fort at Sunbury, while the general's brother, Lt. Col. James Mark Prevost, led a joint land and naval force consisting of a regular battalion and 400 Loyalists to the Altamaha River. Lieutenant Colonel Prevost's troops "proceeded with so much secrecy and Expedition" that they reached "the heart of the Settlements of the Province of Georgia before the Rebels were apprised of his Arrival." This force drove the Georgians from several posts, killed Brig. Gen. William Screven in a skirmish, and captured 40 men and over 2,000 head of cattle. Fuser, however, retreated prematurely from Sunbury, which forced James Prevost to fall back as well. Prevost was accompanied by "a number of famillies attached to Governement."[173] Although General Prevost had been wrongly informed of rebel intentions, the foray demonstrated his commitment to assisting Britain's Indian allies.

Despite his difficulties with the Creeks, Stuart expressed great satisfaction with the behavior of the other nations. In May and June of 1777 he met with twenty-eight hundred Choctaws and Chickasaws at Mobile, where he "admonished them in the strongest manner to unite with the other Nations in the District, in making their mutual Defence a common Cause and forming a Confederacy to support the King's Cause." The Chickasaws declared their willingness to shed "their last Blood in His Majesty's Cause," a statement that "was received with applause and seconded by the principal Chactaw Chiefs." Stuart believed that the Indians were sincere and could be relied on to act when needed.[174]

If Choctaw assistance were required, Stuart worried that it might be hampered because of problems with alcohol consumption in that nation. "Excessive drinking was decimating" the Choctaws in 1777 as British traders inundated their towns with rum. Choctaw leaders asked Stuart to stem the flow; the superintendent promptly contacted Governor Chester to demand that restrictions be placed on the sale of rum to the Choctaws.[175] However, traders still managed to get rum to the Indians, so in February 1778 Stuart assigned Richard Pearis's company of Loyalists to put a stop to the practice.[176]

That same month Stuart reported that the Choctaws and Chickasaws were "perfectly well disposed" and that the five hundred Cherokee refugees at Pensacola, "notwithstanding the severe Chastisement which they lately received, are ready to act when called upon."[177] Chester, however, remained uneasy with the fact that West Florida's defense rested mainly in the hands of the Indians. He told Germain that he doubted the Indians' reliability because "many of them seem to be actuated solely by motives of self interest and will receive presents from anybody who will give them."[178]

The Chickasaws, who had the responsibility of disrupting rebel shipping on the Mississippi River, had been effective in harassing any vessels that passed. Spanish boats were not exempt from this interference, which led Governor Galvez to protest to Chester. "Not a boat has come down from Illinois, and not a trapper's boat, without being fired upon" by the Chickasaws, Galvez complained. In February 1778 he sent an envoy, Jacinto Panis, to Pensacola to demand that Chester end the harassment. In addition to negotiating with Chester, Panis had orders to obtain intelligence that might be useful in the event of war between Spain and Britain. Although Chester told Panis that he had no jurisdiction over the Indians, the governor ordered Stuart to inform the Chickasaws that Spanish vessels must be allowed to travel the Mississippi unmolested. Chester also protested that the Spaniards had been meddling with the Choctaws, inviting some of them to New Orleans and giving them presents. The negotiations ended without Chester and Panis coming to any agreement on Indian issues.[179]

Chester's fears that the defense of West Florida could not be entrusted to Indians appeared to be realized when Willing's expedition sailed down the Mississippi in the spring of 1778. Willing's vessels passed unnoticed because the Indians had left their observation posts. Stuart had posted a party of Choctaws under the command of one of his agents to watch traffic on the river, but they had returned home, and the Indians who were supposed to relieve them had not yet reached their station.[180] Willing's men tried to capture Henry Stuart, the superintendent's brother and deputy, who was at Manchac with a few Indians, but Stuart received warning of the rebels' approach and escaped to Spanish territory.[181] With Whig troops seemingly in control of the Natchez region, Loyalists worried about the effect it might have on the Indians. Anthony Hutchins wrote that he was "convinced that almost the smallest matter would turn the Chactaw and other Indians against us, who were ever ready to join the strongest side, and who are much caress'd by the Spaniards in the name of their antient friends the French."[182]

In response to the raid, John Stuart immediately instructed his agents to assemble as many Choctaws and Chickasaws as they could, put them under the command of white men, and "march to the assistance of the inhabitants."[183] Some Chickasaws took post to watch the Mississippi from the mouth of the Ohio to a point below Chickasaw Bluffs to look for rebel reinforcements, while others accompanied British troops and loyal militia attempting to drive out Willing's men.[184] Choctaw war leader Franchimastabe rushed with 155 men to Natchez, where they spent a month guarding the fort in the event that Willing returned. Farquhar Bethune, one of Stuart's agents, praised the "regularity and discretion" the Indians displayed while at Natchez, which he said were cause for "universal satisfaction." When the Indians left, Franchimastabe told the settlers that his people would stand ready to assist if the rebels returned. He also threatened that if the inhabitants desired "to take the rebels by the hand or enter into any treaty with them," the Choctaws would "treat you as our enemies."[185]

The rapid Indian response to the Willing raid did not satisfy Chester, who complained to Germain that despite "the great Expense which it has cost the Government for Presents, Provisions, etc.—to attach these Savages . . . they cannot when called forth be depended upon."[186] Germain shared Chester's anger and chastised Stuart for the "most unpardonable negligence in the officers you had appointed" in allowing Willing to reach West Florida undetected. It was bad enough that the Indians had not seen the rebels coming, Germain declared, but it was even worse that there were no Indians on hand to oppose the rebels' landing or to assist the Loyalists in defending the province. The money spent on the Indian department, Germain stated, should surely have been sufficient to engage the Indians to keep "a constant watch" on the Mississippi and have parties ready "of sufficient strength to defeat a much more formidable detachment than that which has been suffered to do so much mischief."[187]

Germain felt especially bitter over the lack of Indian assistance because he had just been forced to make a considerable effort in Parliament to defend their use against the rebels. In late 1777 Lord Chatham had denounced in the House of Lords the "bloody, barbarous, and ferocious" aspects of Indian warfare against the colonists,[188] while opposition members in the House of Commons also criticized Germain for employing Indians against the rebels. Lord Suffolk, however, defended the practice on the grounds that it was legitimate for the government "to use all the means that God and nature have put into our hands."[189] Led by Edmund Burke, the opposition renewed its protests against the ministry's Indian policy in February 1778. Burke called for a halt to the government's use of Indians, while Germain argued that "the Indians would not have remained idle spectators . . . it amounted to a clear undisputed proposition, that either they would have served against us, or that we must have employed them."[190] Burke's motion was defeated by a vote of 223 to 137.[191]

African Americans: Marking Time

Although the Whigs in Georgia and South Carolina rigidly enforced the slave codes and remained vigilant to prevent blacks from escaping to the British, enough slaves attempted to reach East Florida or go aboard British warships plying coastal waters that they caused significant problems for the rebels. Henry Laurens told Ralph Izard in June 1777 that "your Negroes are continually deserting the plantations" and going to Charleston, "where I have no doubt many of them would have embark'd in Men of War and other Vessels" had Laurens not been able to recover them. Laurens attributed the slaves' flight to two causes: "the Tyranny and Villainy of Overseers and Sometimes to . . . their own vicious Designs," that is, a desire to find freedom with the British.[192] Unwilling to tolerate such behavior, Charleston officials in August ordered the execution of a slave who had taken three women and two children with him and was "endeavouring to go on board the Men of War."[193] Yet, not all slaves who reached British warships were satisfied with the conditions they found, for a month earlier nine of them whom "the Men of War took are returned."[194] These slaves had probably been taken against their will, and the British officers, realizing that, allowed them to leave.

While fugitive slaves in South Carolina usually went to the coast seeking refuge with the Royal Navy, Georgia slaves fled overland to East Florida.[195] Other runaways concealed themselves in the swamps and forests to await a favorable opportunity to join the British. Before leaving Providence, Rhode Island, to act as agent for a merchant firm in the South, Elkanah Watson was warned of the danger he might face with "the negroes in some of the Southern States in partial insurrection." He undertook the journey anyway and soon found that the menace was real. "We had been cautioned to be on our guard against the attacks of runaway negroes, in the passage of swamps near Wingan Bay" in South Carolina, Watson wrote. While crossing a swamp in November 1777, "fourteen naked negroes armed with poles, presented themselves in the attitude of hostility, across the road." Watson and a companion drew their pistols and charged the blacks, who dropped the poles and fled into the woods.[196]

When found by their masters, such fugitives faced severe consequences. In February 1778 Pennsylvanian Ebenezer Hazard witnessed the recapture of a runaway slave near Pocotaligo, South Carolina. While another slave bound the runaway, the master watched from horseback, gun in hand. "The poor Negroe's looks, arising from terrible apprehensions of future punishment, were such as I think must have affected a savage," Hazard wrote, and yet the master showed no trace of sympathy.[197] After several fugitives belonging to Henry Laurens and other planters were recovered, John Lewis Gervais told Laurens that he would sell one of them as punishment and give the others "a Severe Correction at the Work house."[198]

Even if most slaves remained on their plantations, their insubordinate behavior increased, to the consternation of their masters. In June 1777 a black driver, March, "was very Saucy" when a white overseer accused him of stealing rice. The overseer "laid hold of him, but the Negro proved to be the Strongest & threw him." Other slaves refused to obey the man's orders to help him subdue March, so the overseer left. He returned shortly afterward to find that March had cut off part of his own left hand; March then attacked the overseer with a knife. Only then did the other slaves intervene. March was sent to Savannah to be treated and then lodged in the workhouse.[199]

Despite Whig reluctance to alter the slaves' situation, the vulnerability of the southern states to British attack led the rebels to use slaves in their traditional role as laborers to assist white troops. When rumors of a possible British invasion circulated in South Carolina in late 1777, William Henry Drayton asked the council "for all the labouring Negroes belonging to those who had been banished by the abjuration Act," as well as slaves owned by other prominent Loyalists not covered by the act, to work on Charleston's fortifications. The council granted the request, and Drayton assigned the slaves to dig a channel connecting the Ashley and Cooper rivers, which would serve as an obstacle to protect the land approaches to the town.[200]

Robert Howe asked Georgia authorities to provide three hundred slaves "to act as Pioneers" for the army invading East Florida in 1778. The assembly reduced the number to two hundred, but only fifty-six reported to camp.[201] They were assigned to clear roads and perform other forms of heavy labor. One black was killed in a skirmish.[202] There is no evidence that any of the slaves tried to escape; perhaps the executions of white deserters intimidated them from making the attempt.

One South Carolina Whig believed that slaves should not only assist the army as pioneers and laborers but also serve as combat soldiers. Henry Laurens's son John, an aide to George Washington in Pennsylvania, wrote to his father on January 14, 1778, requesting "a number of your able bodied men Slaves" to be trained as soldiers. The younger Laurens asserted that his plan would both provide badly needed troops and "advance those who are unjustly deprived of the Rights of Mankind to a State which would be a proper Gradation between abject Slavery and perfect Liberty."[203]

In his reply Henry Laurens tried to convince his son to reflect on his proposal before pursuing it further. "More time will be required for me to consider the propriety of your scheme for raising a black Regiment, than you seem to have taken for concerting the project," the elder Laurens wrote, because "a Work of this importance must be entered upon with Caution & great circumspection."[204] The elder Laurens cautiously probed his colleagues in Congress to learn their opinions of the plan but found no supporters. He warned John that slaves might not wish to exchange the "comfortable" conditions of bondage for service far from home, "where Loss of Life & Loss of Limbs must be expected by every one every day."[205]

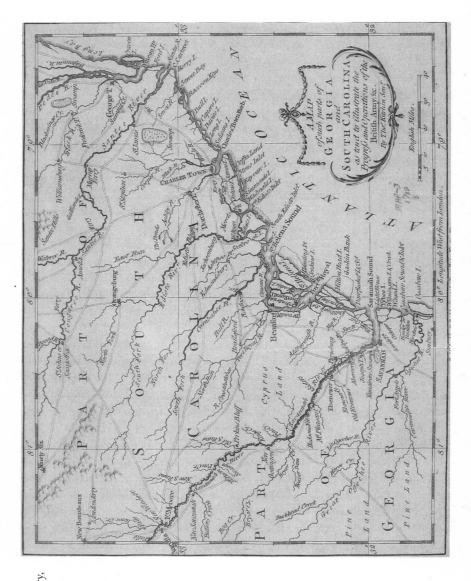

1780 map. Courtesy of South Caroliniana Library, University of South Carolina, Columbia

John Laurens conceded that he had "that monster popular Prejudice" against him, but he insisted that his proposal was for the public good. He countered his father's objections by arguing that most slaves would welcome "being rescued from a State of perpetual humiliation." Furthermore, slavery had conditioned blacks to accept subordination, hard work, and deprivation, making them well qualified to be soldiers.[206]

These arguments failed to convince Henry Laurens, who wrote that "the more I think of & the more I have consulted on, your scheme, the less I approve of it."[207] This reproach caused John to ask his father's forgiveness "for the trouble which I have given you on this excentric Scheme."[208]

Although the Whigs' attitude toward slaves remained largely unchanged, a growing number of Loyalists began to recognize that blacks were reliable allies. At the end of June 1778 Louisa Susannah Wells, along with thirteen other banished Loyalists, boarded the ship *Providence* bound for England. Earlier in the year a ship carrying another group of exiles had run aground while leaving Charleston harbor. The passengers on the *Providence* suspected that the white pilot "had been bribed to run that unfortunate vessel on the Shoals." The Loyalists on the grounded ship had to remain in South Carolina for several months, and the people aboard the *Providence* wanted to avoid a similar fate. "For this reason," Wells wrote, "we chose a Negro Pilot" named Bluff, paying him one hundred dollars in rebel currency in addition to his master's fee. In an effort to reassure the Loyalists without making the risky statements that had led to Thomas Jeremiah's death, Bluff cautiously told them that "he was a true friend to British Manufactures," which, Wells said, "was as much Loyalty as he durst own." Bluff got the Loyalists safely out of the harbor.[209] In West Florida the inhabitants also turned to blacks for assistance, and several served on board the naval vessels assigned to defend the province's rivers.[210]

Britain's supporters in the South had suffered greatly in 1777 and 1778. Loyalists had been relentlessly persecuted, and many of them were banished or voluntarily fled the southern provinces. The Cherokees were forced to make peace, and the Whigs sowed dissension among the Creeks that limited their contributions to the British. Except for a few hardy individuals who escaped to the Floridas or took refuge in swamps, slaves had to accept their lot until new opportunities for freedom appeared. Nevertheless, the king's supporters had enjoyed some success. Hundreds of Loyalists had reached East Florida, joined provincial units, and carried the war back to the Georgians. They had thwarted an attack on West Florida and the rebels' annual invasions of East Florida, and in the latter case caused the Whigs to squander manpower and resources without achieving anything worthwhile. Stuart had brought the Chickasaws and Choctaws into action to defend West Florida, eliminated much of Galphin's influence with the Creeks, and helped keep Cherokee resistance alive among the Chickamauga faction. Loyalists, Indians, and slaves awaited only the arrival of British troops to step forward once again and challenge the rebels. That day was nearly at hand.

FOUR

The British Return

WHEN FRANCE ENTERED THE WAR on the American side in March 1778, British officials were forced to rethink their strategy for subduing the colonies. The ministry could not expect its armed forces to undertake large-scale offensive operations against the rebels, since forces had to be diverted to deal with France as well as possible Spanish intervention. George III and his ministers decided to withdraw some of the troops who had been fighting the rebels and redeploy them in preparation for operations against France and Spain.[1]

The British government also reshuffled the army's command and made a final effort to negotiate peace with the Americans. In February 1778 William Howe resigned and Henry Clinton succeeded him as commander in chief in America. Clinton, along with Lord Carlisle, William Eden, and George Johnstone, were appointed commissioners to discuss peace terms with the rebels in the hope that an agreement could be reached before British forces had to face a war against both France and the colonies. The British offer was generous—"everything a colonial heart could desire." If the Americans renounced independence and agreed to make a voluntary contribution to the cost of defending the empire, the British government would give up its authority to tax them.[2] Should the offer be rejected, it would at least quiet those in Parliament who demanded negotiations with the Americans. The commissioners informed Germain in July that the rebels refused to accept the terms and that only force could end the rebellion.[3]

Germain, who had been skeptical of negotiations from the outset, had advised Clinton in early 1778 that after the summer campaign ended in the North, the army should undertake a southern offensive in October.[4] As it became apparent that the peace commissioners could not sway the rebels, Germain reminded Clinton that "the Recovery of South Carolina and Georgia in the Winter, or even the latter Province, if the Other requires a greater Force than can be spared, is an Object of so much Importance."[5]

In accordance with these instructions, Clinton dispatched an expedition to Georgia in November 1778. British troops easily captured Savannah and temporarily occupied most of the Georgia backcountry. However, the rapid reaction of numerically superior Whig forces drove the British to retreat to the environs of Savannah. Although Gen. Augustine Prevost thwarted the rebels' plan to attack the town by launching his own offensive into South Carolina, Prevost's army was too weak to accomplish anything of lasting importance. The British withdrew to Savannah, where they were besieged in the autumn by a French fleet and a combined Franco-American army. British regulars, assisted by Loyalists, Indians, and armed slaves, made a staunch defense that routed the French and rebels. With Savannah secure, Clinton prepared to launch the second phase of the southern campaign, an attack on Charleston.

RESURRECTING THE SOUTHERN STRATEGY

While the Whigs held control of the southern provinces, Loyalist exiles sent a steady stream of proposals to British officials urging the recovery of those colonies. All of the plans relied primarily on the support of Loyalists; most also counted on additional assistance from slaves or Indians. Germain's deputy, William Knox, who had lived in Georgia and still owned property there, "served as the most direct channel of influence" between southern Loyalists and the ministry. Knox favored an offensive in the South and advised Germain that operations there would be greatly facilitated by the aid of Loyalists and Indians.[6]

In August 1777 Governors William Campbell and James Wright and their lieutenant governors, William Bull and John Graham, sent Germain a memorial urging a prompt offensive in the South to relieve the Loyalists. Had such an attack been made the previous winter, the authors believed, "a great number of the inhabitants" would have seized "the opportunity of showing their loyalty." In the intervening months it was certain that "many who were then well-disposed to government have from various motives since changed their sentiments or are under necessity of seeming to have done so." Even so, there were still enough Loyalists to help the army restore British authority in Georgia and South Carolina. The writers recommended shifting the focus of the war southward before the "friends of government . . . despairing of relief," submitted to the rebels or left for the Floridas.[7]

Former South Carolina attorney general James Simpson offered his own plan, a proposal for an attack on Charleston, which he sent to Germain in September 1778. Simpson asserted that the conquest of that town would lead to the occupation of most of South Carolina. Afterward, he suggested, Loyalist refugees from the northern colonies could be resettled in South Carolina. There, "when joined to the well affected," they "would prove much superiour, to any Malcontents, who might remain amongst them."[8]

The following month Moses Kirkland sent Clinton a detailed proposal for a southern campaign. Kirkland, who was in New York after having fled South Carolina in 1775, proposed that a force of regulars, Loyalists, and Indians advance into Georgia from East Florida while troops from New York attacked Savannah by sea. After taking Savannah, the united army could march to Augusta and open a line of communication with the backcountry of both Carolinas, "and the Friends of Government will flock from all parts to that Post to join his Majesty's Troops." John Stuart could assemble the Chickasaws and Choctaws, link up with the Cherokees, and march to the Long Canes district of South Carolina to meet the troops and Loyalists. To prevent the rebels from reinforcing Georgia and the Carolinas, Kirkland suggested that the Overhill Cherokees and Shawnees attack the overmountain settlements and the Virginia frontier. This accomplished, a second expedition from New York could seize Charleston.[9]

Kirkland sent a revised version of this plan to the peace commissioners a week later. The most significant alteration was that he assigned slaves a role. Although a slave owner himself, Kirkland proposed to incite a slave insurrection. The labor of slaves provided the crops that allowed the rebels to finance their war effort, he noted. "But the instant that The Kings Troops are put in motion in those Colonies, these poor Slaves would be ready to rise upon their Rebel Masters, and be a great means of compelling them to seek refuge in the interior Provinces." Apparently Kirkland intended to restore the slaves to their laborer status once they had ousted their masters, for he made no mention of what was to be done with them afterward and yet noted that once the rebels were gone, Britain would benefit from the produce of the southern colonies.[10]

Continuing to press for a southern campaign, Patrick Tonyn believed that the rebels were on the verge of collapse and that a blow in the South would prove fatal to them. "I am certain the four southern provinces are incapable of making any very formidable resistance, they are not prepared for a Scene of war," he wrote. A British attack, Tonyn predicted, "will operate to effect a quick surrender."[11]

The peace commissioners, having failed to attain their original objective, turned their attention to subduing the rebellion and also favored a southern campaign. On September 21, 1778, George Johnstone told William Smith, a prominent New York Loyalist, that he desired "a Winter Expedition to reduce S. Carolina with the Help of the Indians and Negroes."[12] The commissioners believed that "a footing gained and kept to the Southward by assistance of a few troops, back settlers, and Negroes, will show the Southern Colonys their danger."[13] The British would then have an opportunity to try the long-desired experiment of restoring civil government in Georgia, which they hoped would put the Loyalists "in a Condition to defend their Persons and their Propertys, & to turn against the Ennemys of Peace the Edge of Criminal Law."[14]

Some of the proposals for southern operations seemed so fantastic as to be unworthy of serious consideration. When Wright suggested an attack using eleven thousand troops supported by Indians, Germain dismissed the scheme as useless.[15] Nevertheless, Germain recognized the importance of offensive action in the southern colonies and devoted much effort during the winter of 1777–78 to formulating plans for operations there. With the assistance of Knox, Germain devised a plan that began with the recapture of Savannah. A combined force of British troops, southern Loyalists, and Indians would next attack Charleston. Success there, Germain believed, would insure British control of Georgia and South Carolina and lead to the quick recovery of North Carolina and Virginia.[16]

When it became apparent that France would enter the war as the rebels' ally, Germain issued new orders to Clinton that set the stage for the southern campaign. The king, Germain wrote, had decided that "the War must be prosecuted upon a different Plan from That upon which it has hitherto been carried on." Clinton's most important assignments for the upcoming campaign were to bring Washington's army to battle and to raid the New England coast. Germain expected these operations to be finished by October, and at that time, "it is the King's intention that an Attack should be made upon the Southern Colonies, with a View to the Conquest & Possession of Georgia & South Carolina," Germain explained. "The various accounts we receive from those Provinces concur in representing the distress of the Inhabitants, and their general disposition to return to their Allegiance." Arms would be provided to enable Clinton "to raise & embody the well affected Inhabitants." Germain advised Clinton to attack Georgia as soon as possible, with troops from New York joining the forces in East Florida and the Indians in a three-pronged attack. Once Georgia was secured, Germain believed, backcountry Loyalists would be able to reach the army there and invade the interior of South Carolina in conjunction with another expedition from New York aimed at taking Charleston. These maneuvers would lead to the rapid submission of South Carolina.[17]

With their military manpower already strained before French intervention, British officials agreed that Loyalist assistance was essential if the government were to retake and hold several provinces with the limited number of regular troops that could be spared to operate in the South. However, there was some disagreement concerning the actual strength of the Loyalists and the manner in which they should be used. George III and his ministers shared the belief that there were large numbers of Loyalists in the southern provinces.[18] One army officer told Gen. Jeffery Amherst, who had accepted overall command of the British army in 1778, that Americans who supported the king must "disguise their Sentiments, and never will venture to declare for Britain 'till they see a prospect of being placed in Security against their Enemies." If the British were to succeed, they had to adopt the same harsh measures that the Whigs had used against the Loyalists. The latter must be put "in possession of the Government and of the Sword. Disarm or expel our Opponents . . . Reward Our Friends by the possession of Forfeited Lands, and punish our irreclaimable Enemies agreable to the Forms of Civil Justice."[19]

Some officers doubted that the Loyalists were numerous enough to accomplish such a task. Charles Stuart, son of the earl of Bute, wrote his father that southern governors had been blinded by the "pretended affection of the people" and failed to see "the political state of the Country, and their own vanity flatter'd by promises of personal attachment induced them not only to listen to the artful and cunning insinuations of even the leaders of fashion, but to declare their Colonies submissive subjects of the Crown."[20] Capt. Frederick Mackenzie of the 23rd Regiment, reflecting the views of many army officers, expressed the same opinion even more bluntly. "Nothing can be done to the Southward of Pensylvania," he declared.[21]

Disagreements also arose over the use of Indians and slaves. Although Clinton supported the general plan, he was reluctant to employ Indians to assist his troops. In a discussion with William Smith on May 28, 1779, he expressed "his Dislike of the Savages and their unmanageableness."[22] Other officers also disliked relying on blacks and Indians. Alexander Innes, the inspector general of provincial troops and former aide to South Carolina governor Campbell, complained to Clinton that Loyalist regiments in New York included "Negroes, Mulattoes, Indians, Sailors and Rebel Prisoners . . . to the disgrace and ruin of the provincial service."[23]

Germain had no qualms about using Indians against the rebels, but he hesitated to endorse arming slaves. In March 1778 he cautiously advised Clinton that the army might somehow divide the South Carolina backcountry from the lowcountry, which would leave the large slaveholding planters with the choice of submitting to British authority or having either to give up their slaves or to have their slaves abandon them.[24] Beyond that the minister was unwilling to proceed. One reason for his reluctance to assign a large role to slaves in the southern campaign was the continued denunciation of such a policy by members of the opposition in Parliament. During debates on the conduct of the war in 1778, Edmund Burke warned of "the horrible consequences that might ensue from constituting 100,000 fierce barbarian slaves, to be both the judges and executioners of their masters."[25]

Ironically, British officials showed less hesitation to employ blacks on a large scale to bolster the defenses of the West Indies. Slaves built and repaired fortifications on the various islands, repaired naval vessels in ports, and performed other tasks to support the regular troops, while free blacks and mulattoes served in some of the island militias and enlisted in the navy. Jamaica also raised a regular regiment of free blacks, although Germain refused to grant the unit official status. Nevertheless, the island's assembly authorized the regiment in April 1782, with the support of the king. A second battalion was quickly raised, and in November recruiters went to Charleston to enlist a third battalion. Gen. Edward Mathew, commanding at St. Lucia, procured slaves from Charleston and elsewhere to serve in his command.[26] Perhaps Britons found using blacks to fight the French less distasteful than employing them against the Americans.

Necessity was another factor that led to the arming of West Indian blacks, and the needs of the West Indies were a major reason for undertaking the southern campaign. The war had halted the trade between the islands and the rebel provinces, depriving the West Indies of their traditional source of provisions. The recapture of the southern colonies could provide needed supplies from the mainland. Germain reminded Clinton in August 1778 that the West Indies were suffering from shortages of provisions and lumber, which could be obtained from the southern provinces once Clinton had subdued them.[27]

South Carolina and Georgia were also economically valuable in their own right. The government was hard-pressed to raise the funds necessary to finance the war, and the prospect of revenue from the profitable crops raised in the South made the conquest of that region particularly appealing to Germain.[28] One Loyalist reported that the annual prewar trade of the two provinces had amounted to £630,000 ($82.75 million) and "in the present State of Things" might now be worth considerably more. The possession of the southern colonies would thus relieve the strain on Britain's finances while depriving the rebels of valuable resources.[29] Charles Jenkinson of the Treasury Department, realizing that Britain might lose some of the colonies, believed that it was wiser to sacrifice New England than the southern provinces with their abundant crops of rice and indigo.[30]

Given the power of these arguments, Germain's instructions, and his own inclinations, Clinton dispatched an expedition from New York in November 1778 to capture Savannah. He placed Lt. Col. Archibald Campbell, a Scot with extensive military experience, in command of the troops. Anticipating success, the peace commissioners provided Campbell with a commission as civil governor of Georgia and the authority to restore that province to the king's peace if a significant percentage of the inhabitants declared their allegiance to Britain. In a burst of optimism, the commissioners also gave Campbell a commission as governor of South Carolina in the event that he was able to regain control of that province as well.[31]

Germain expected the southern Loyalists to turn out in large numbers when Campbell arrived in Georgia, and his optimism was shared by Loyalists in New York. "Our late Accounts from that Quarter give us every Reason to expect the Troops will be joined by very considerable Numbers of the Inhabitants of the back parts of the Carolinas, when they find Georgia will be an Assylum for them," Germain told Clinton in early December.[32] Charles Inglis believed that if southern Loyalists received "any Rational Support," they would "take a much more active Part hereafter than they done hitherto. They have severely felt the Iron Hand of Oppression and Persecution" and now realized that they might "lose every Thing unless the King prevails." Inglis hoped that enough Loyalist volunteers would come forward to require all of the five thousand stand of spare arms that Campbell carried with him.[33] Another New York Loyalist, Daniel Coxe, expected a large number of Georgians to join Campbell, in which case "the three Southern Colonies of Georgia & the two Carolinas must be completely subjected this Winter."[34] William Franklin, Benjamin Franklin's Loyalist son and former New Jersey governor, predicted that if Campbell's "Blow is properly follow'd up . . . it will soon be all over with Congressional Power in the Southern Colonies."[35] Clinton, who was more cautious, sent Alexander Innes to accompany the expedition to Georgia, with orders to learn "the Situation of the Country and disposition of the Inhabitants" and carry the information directly to London.[36]

Campbell's rapid success convinced British leaders that the southern strategy was sound. Support for the ministry's policy in America had been wavering in

Parliament and among the British public since the 1777 defeat at Saratoga, but the easy capture of Savannah in December 1778 and the successful defense of the town the following autumn indicated that further success was probable in the southern colonies.[37] One Briton wrote in the spring of 1779 that as a result of the recent victories in the West Indies and Georgia, "it is the general prevailing Opinion here that peace will take place in the course of this year."[38] Even opposition writers in London began to think that the fortunes of war had swung in Britain's favor. Some of the most vocal antiwar newspapers conceded that Campbell had achieved an impressive victory. One opposition paper, while still urging the government to grant the colonies independence, nevertheless proposed that only twelve provinces be given up and that Georgia be retained.[39]

When Gen. Augustine Prevost crossed the Savannah River in the spring of 1779 and marched to Charleston without encountering substantial opposition, it further confirmed the belief that South Carolina could easily be retaken. Germain told Clinton that Prevost's campaign, along with "the information I have of the state of South Carolina and the disposition of the majority of the inhabitants," made him optimistic that Prevost "will find *means to effect the reduction of Charleston,* and that the province will be speedily restored to the King's obedience."[40] The news that Prevost had withdrawn to Georgia (his invasion of South Carolina had been a feint to disrupt rebel operations) did not dampen Germain's enthusiasm. Seven weeks later the minister urged Clinton to attack Charleston, observing again that Prevost's almost uncontested advance and retreat presented "indubitable proof of the indisposition of the inhabitants to support the rebel government." An offensive by Clinton's troops in South Carolina, Germain declared, would almost certainly "be attended with the recovery of the whole of that province; and probably North Carolina would soon follow," allowing Clinton to restore both colonies to the king's peace.[41]

The ministry's supporters responded to the capture of Savannah with their own plans and demands to attack South Carolina. In the summer of 1779 Richard Oswald, whose connections gave him a great deal of influence in the government, composed a memorandum in which he asserted that the "partial dismemberment of America" was the only plan likely to succeed in bringing the rebellion to a successful end. "That prospect is now in a good train," he observed, "by the Recovery of Georgia. And if we succeed in South Carolina, we may hope that the Spirit of the Rebellion will So far Subside, as that the Outstanding Colonies to the Northward will find it their Interest to listen to terms of Amnesty." Oswald considered South Carolina vulnerable due to the weak American forces there, the difficulty of sending reinforcements from the North, and because "the nature of the great Estates & Valueable property in Slaves, renders an obstinate Resistance more dangerous and alarming to Individuals." He urged that Prevost's army be reinforced so that it would be strong enough to capture Charleston, after which the rest of South Carolina would have to submit.

Oswald predicted that this would likely be followed by the recovery of North Carolina, Virginia, and Maryland.[42]

Several weeks later Oswald elaborated on his plans for South Carolina in a supplementary memo. He now warned that the capture of Charleston would be difficult. "The place is . . . much stronger than most people imagine," and the rebel leaders there "are violently Inimical" to Britain, he wrote. Oswald insisted, however, that success would be worth the effort. After royal authority had been reestablished, the people would reconcile themselves to British rule, so that "the recovery of this single province may be supposed to be opening a way to Settling peace, in some shape, over the whole Continent." Any delay in making this effort, Oswald believed, could be fatal; the rebels in South Carolina would use the time to improve their defenses, so that "it may never again be in our power to make any, or at least so successful an Impression upon them, as we can do now."[43] Oswald apparently envisioned the recapture of the southern provinces as a strictly military operation, for he made no mention of any role for Loyalists, Indians, or slaves in the undertaking.

Leading Whigs feared that the British success in Georgia foreshadowed worse consequences to come. At the very least, Henry Laurens expected Campbell's troops to strip Georgia of its crops, livestock, and slaves and then to withdraw to St. Augustine. However, Laurens thought it more likely that with aid from "Auxiliary forces of Savages and disaffected Persons," the British would hold their position.[44]

Clinton remained cautious, the optimism of Britons and the fears of Whigs notwithstanding. He recognized that the loss of Georgia had caused the rebels "no small Consternation, and to apprehend Consequences in a country where besides Indians blacks ye Govt. has many friends."[45] However, the general wavered in his determination to follow up on Campbell's victory. "Our Successes to the Southward, Suggest an attempt against Charles town," he wrote Germain in April 1779. Clinton then went on to state that he did not want to risk sending reinforcements southward when he did not know the location of the French fleet. Furthermore, he had "as yet received no assurances of any favorable temper in the province of South Carolina to encourage me to an undertaking where we must expect much difficulty." If he sent only a small force to South Carolina, "it might induce a Number of persons to declare for us, whom we might afterwards be obliged to abandon; and thus might destroy a party, on whom we may depend if Circumstances will permit a more Solid attempt in a proper Season." He concluded that it would be better to wait until October before attacking Charleston.[46]

Germain also wanted more information regarding the number of Loyalists in South Carolina and dispatched James Simpson to Savannah to inquire into the matter. Simpson had the "Knowledge of the Country & People" necessary "to detect and prevent Imposition" by those who might supply incorrect information, Germain noted. Simpson had orders to report the results of his investigation to Clinton to help the general plan his next moves in the South.[47]

After reaching the Georgia capital, Simpson encountered many acquaintances, most of whom had come to the town under flags of truce seeking "Negroes and other property which had been carried away" during Prevost's raid on Charleston. Some of these people sought out Simpson "to inquire after Connections and Relations they had in Europe." In these conversations Simpson carefully probed for useful information. He learned that while "there are still too many amongst them who will use all their influence to prevent a restoration of the public tranquility," many South Carolinians were tired of the war and its disruptions. Simpson told Germain that many Loyalists had fled the province, that others "had found means to make their Peace" with the Whigs after years of "almost unremitting persecution," but that many still hoped that British forces would come to their relief. Simpson warned Germain that although significant numbers of Loyalists were willing to aid the British, many would hesitate until they had absolute assurance that the army would protect them.[48]

Simpson's report satisfied Germain that the time had come to follow up the victory in Georgia with an attack on South Carolina. The initial test had demonstrated that the southern strategy had been soundly conceived. Its ultimate success now depended on whether it could be equally well executed.

The Invasion of Georgia and the Loyalist Response

Clinton launched the southern campaign in November 1778, when he sent Archibald Campbell with some twenty-five hundred troops from New York with orders to attack Georgia. To support Campbell's force, Clinton instructed Augustine Prevost to advance into Georgia from East Florida. The fleet from New York reached Tybee Island on December 23.[49] Campbell was optimistic; he believed that with additional troops from New York and "a Re-inforcement of 6000 Loyalists from the back Countries, in Conjunction with the Indian Tribes who were attached to Government," he could occupy both Georgia and South Carolina.[50] Campbell informed Patrick Tonyn and Prevost that after taking Savannah, he planned "to move . . . as far up the Country as the Strength and Disposition of the Enemy will admit" to unite with the backcountry Loyalists. He asked the two East Florida officials to notify John Stuart of the plan so that the Indians would "make a Diversion in my favour along the Back Woods of Georgia."[51]

On the night of December 25, Campbell sent a company of light infantry ashore to "pick up some of the Inhabitants" who could provide intelligence of the strength and position of the rebel forces. The troops returned the next morning with "a White Overseer and a Black named Peter." The two told Campbell that Savannah was defended by twelve hundred Continentals and six hundred militia with ten pieces of artillery; three galleys guarded the river approaches to the town. Campbell therefore decided to land at Girardeau's plantation and try to capture the town in a surprise attack.[52]

Campbell's troops went ashore on December 29 and quickly drove off the small American force at the plantation. By early afternoon the British army was arrayed opposite the strong American defenses a half-mile south of Savannah. While Campbell pondered his plan of attack, a "confidential Slave from Sir James Wright's Plantation" came to him with information. Campbell, after questioning the man, "found that he could lead the Troops without Artillery through the Swamp upon the Enemy's Right."[53]

Almost nothing is known about this slave, whose name was either Quash or Quamino Dolly. He apparently came to Campbell on his own initiative, perhaps out of loyalty to his former owner, Governor Wright, or from a desire to obtain his freedom by assisting the British. Whatever the slave's motives, Campbell did not hesitate to adopt the man's advice as soon as he determined that his information was accurate. The slave guided a part of Campbell's force through the swamp into the rear of the rebel lines, taking Gen. Robert Howe's troops completely by surprise. The maneuver, which Campbell supported with a frontal attack, routed the Whigs. About 100 Americans were killed and 450 captured; the remainder fled. British casualties numbered only 26. The slave's assistance had proven valuable indeed. Campbell's victorious troops then marched to Savannah and occupied the town.[54]

Meanwhile, Prevost had begun his northward advance, entering Georgia on November 20 with about seven hundred British and Loyalist troops. A second force of over four hundred men moved by sea to Sunbury, capturing the town and its rebel defenders on January 10, 1779.[55] The threat from the Creeks greatly facilitated Prevost's march. Gov. John Houstoun wrote that Georgia's defenses along its southern border had been "particularly weaken'd . . . by drawing off the Troops and Volunteers, to the Westward, in opposition to the Indians."[56] In addition, Andrew Williamson had taken six hundred South Carolina militia into Creek territory to check the anticipated attack, and thus this force was too distant to come to Georgia's aid.[57] The remaining militia in southern Georgia made "extraordinary Exertions" to assist the planters in removing their slaves, rather than resisting Prevost's advance.[58]

As both the ministers and military commanders had expected, slaves and Indians had, directly and indirectly, contributed to the initial British success in Georgia. Those aspects of the southern strategy were working, and if the Loyalists came forward, it augured well for British prospects of regaining control of the southern provinces.

Some Loyalists began turning out as soon as they heard reports that British forces were en route to Georgia. In late 1778 a group of Loyalists assembled under a Captain Coleman south of Broad River in South Carolina. The Whigs moved to disperse them, but Coleman attacked first, routing the rebels and killing four. By the time the Whigs had regrouped, Coleman was in Georgia on his way to join the British. The frustrated Whigs contented themselves with burning the homes of several of Coleman's men.[59]

Christopher Friedrich Triebner, the Lutheran minister and teacher in the German settlement at Ebenezer, made his way to Savannah the day after its capture and later guided Campbell's troops to his hometown. On January 2, in a sermon "against Rebellion and Licentiousness," Triebner urged his congregation to submit to the king's authority.[60] Campbell appointed him as a magistrate, and the minister soon found himself busy administering the oath of allegiance to many of Ebenezer's inhabitants.[61]

On January 4, 1779, Campbell and Adm. Hyde Parker issued a proclamation calling upon Loyalists and any other "well-disposed Inhabitants" to unite under the king's standard. The two officers promised all who joined them "the most ample Protection in their Persons, Families and Effects."[62] The rebels resorted to intimidation in an effort to prevent people from responding to the summons, which prompted Campbell to issue another proclamation on January 8. Angered that "skulking Parties . . . under Colour of the Night, have the Audacity to rob, and otherways ill treat those true and faithful Subjects of His Majesty," Campbell threatened severe punishment to "such wicked and destructive Enemies." He also offered rewards of ten guineas (the equivalent of nearly fourteen hundred dollars in 2002) for every rebel civil or military officer taken prisoner and two guineas for ordinary rebels.[63]

Despite this harassment, many Georgians took the British oath. On January 9 Campbell organized "several Companies of Militia to patrole the Country" between Cherokee Hill and Ebenezer.[64] Others guarded the crossing of the Savannah River at Hudson's Ferry; several acted as scouts and spies to keep Campbell informed of rebel movements.[65] Thomas Manson, an Augusta Loyalist, took advantage of the confusion created by the British invasion "to make his Escape from the Repeated Insults he received from the Populace on Account of his Suspected Loyalty to the British Government." He traveled seventy miles through woods and byways to reach Savannah, where he joined a company of Loyalist volunteers.[66] A British deserter reported on January 12 that two hundred Loyalists had already offered their services to Campbell.[67] "The inhabitants of this province are coming in daily here in great numbers wishing to give up their arms and take the oath of allegiance to the King," a Hessian soldier wrote a few days later.[68] Dr. Thomas Taylor observed that "people have flocked to the different British posts, have freely taken the oaths of allegiance, and many have joined the King's army, Thomas Fleming with 100 horsemen, Henry Sharp with some 200 horse and foot, and many others."[69] On January 19 Thomas Robinson asserted that "there is not a Rebbel in Arms in the Govemt, all that New them selves to be gilty Run to South Carolina, and the Rest Com in, Give up their Arms, many of which tuk up Arms in Govmt Sarvis."[70]

When Prevost arrived in Savannah, he brought with him 250 Georgians and South Carolinians who had tried to join the British but "were pursued by the rebels and driven into the wilderness," where "they had to nourish themselves six days with roots and herbs until General *Prevost* rescued them." The British planned to train these men "to be regular soldiers."[71]

An exuberant Archibald Campbell informed Germain on January 19 that he knew of only two men who had refused to accept the terms of his proclamation of pardon, and these had "hurried off to the Rebels."[72] "I have got the Country in arms against the Congress," Campbell boasted to peace commissioner William Eden. He asked Eden to press the ministry to "hurry out a Proper Governour for this Province, with every necessary arrangement for the Reestablishment of Legal Government. Its effects at this Juncture, whilst the minds of the People in the neighbouring Provinces are worn out by persecutions, extortions, & apprehensions; must operate more powerfully than twenty thousand troops."[73]

When Germain received Campbell's reports, he was ecstatic, praising the colonel and predicting that "you will be joined by very considerable Numbers, upon your Arrival at Augusta; and be able to form such a Force there, as you may without Hazard, penetrate into" South Carolina.[74] In March, Germain informed Georgian exiles in England who were receiving government pensions that their payments would cease and ordered them to return to the province. The government provided funds for their passage. Recent exiles who had applied for assistance were also given travel allowances and told to return.[75] Most welcomed the opportunity to do so. Exiled Georgian S. H. Jenkins discussed the news with other southern Loyalists living in London; all were "confident that Government will keep possession of Georgia at all events.—God grant it may be so!" Jenkins wrote.[76]

Savannah's capture elevated the spirits of New York Loyalists, who greeted the official announcement with joy. Rumors abounded that Campbell, reinforced by Indians and Loyalists, was already marching on Charleston.[77]

As Loyalist morale increased, southern Whigs grew pessimistic, since they feared that the loss of Savannah, combined with Loyalist assistance to the British, might prove devastating to the rebel cause. When news of Savannah's capture reached the backcountry on December 29, 1778, George Galphin wrote that it immediately "DisCoreged the Inhabitents the most of them Says. thy will Lay Down there armes & the rest is Coming in" to South Carolina.[78] One rebel warned his commander on January 7, 1779, that Campbell's troops were "encamped at one Blyths who from his knowledge of the swamp on this [South Carolina] side may probably Introduce a party of the Enemy into our neighbourhood—He being a man long suspected of dissaffection to our great & glorious Cause."[79] Three days later militia colonel Stephen Bull complained that exchanged British officers had, while in rebel custody, "been Allowed to go at large and had an Opportunity of Conversing & Enquiring from some Tories & Disaffected," from whom they had probably learned much about the defenses in southeastern South Carolina.[80]

Maj. Gen. Benjamin Lincoln, who had replaced Howe as commander of the southern department on January 3, received several reports that large numbers of backcountry Loyalists intended to join the British.[81] "I have been told, that many of the disaffected mean to join the Enemy, if they can get an opportunity," Andrew Williamson wrote on February 1, "but I have taken every Precaution in my Power to Guard against their wicked Intentions, by Keeping Spies amongst them whom I can depend upon to inform me of their proceedings." Williamson noted that the Loyalists had not yet begun to organize, and he believed that "we shall be able to Keep them Quiet, especially if we can prevent the Enemy Crossing the Savannah—In Case of such an Event I Scarce make a doubt of their being joined by Numbers of the Tories."[82] William Moultrie shared Williamson's concern, telling Lincoln that if the British established a post at Augusta, "they would encrease by the disaffected and posibly by the Indians."[83] Joseph Clay estimated the number of Loyalists who had joined Campbell "from Florida the back parts of this state [South Carolina] & of the Georgians" at between "2 & 3000."[84]

Henry Clinton was perhaps the only person with an interest in the southern campaign who viewed the situation with calm detachment. Although satisfied with the results in Georgia, he hesitated to approve any hasty movement northward. "I have as yet received no assurances of any favourable temper in the province of South Carolina to encourage me to an undertaking where we must expect so much difficulty," he informed Germain on April 4.[85]

The general's caution cooled some of Germain's enthusiasm. Germain continued to emphasize the importance of recovering South Carolina in his correspondence with Clinton but agreed that the "Assistance of the Loyal Inhabitants is essential to the Success of all Operations" there. Germain also conceded that "it is equally necessary, to avoid being deceived in our Expectations from them."[86]

Campbell, meanwhile, prepared to follow up his initial success by organizing a temporary government at Savannah and then advancing into the Georgia backcountry. Acting in his capacity as governor of Georgia, he created a board of police on January 13 to function as a temporary civil authority. He appointed Louis Johnston as superintendent, along with two assistants.[87] The board operated until Governor Wright resumed his office and the province's prewar civil government was reestablished.[88]

With his political task completed and Prevost on hand to manage military matters in the capital, Campbell prepared to march to Augusta. Sometime after the capture of Savannah, he had dispatched Col. James (or John) Boyd to the backcountry. A South Carolina refugee who had accompanied Campbell to Georgia from New York, Boyd had promised to recruit several hundred Loyalists in his home region to reinforce Campbell's small army.[89]

Campbell was eager to get to Augusta because he had learned "that Colonel Boyd with a large Body of Loyalists meant to join me." Reports indicated that Boyd had recruited about one thousand men. "Many Loyalists" also came from Augusta to urge Campbell to come to the assistance of the king's supporters there.[90] They assured the British commander that "the very sight of The King's troops in that quarter, would be the means of collecting a considerable number of loyal Subjects . . . that would be willing to accompany the King's troops wherever the Service required." Campbell also expected to meet a large force of Indians at Augusta.[91]

On January 24 Campbell left Ebenezer with nine hundred men, intending "to clear that part of the Province of Rebels, and to protect such Inhabitants as chose to return to the allegeance of The King." At various places along his route, Campbell met numerous people "who promised to form into Companys and give every Assistance possible to promote The King's Service." These people took the oath of allegiance and received arms and ammunition from the British.[92] Enough Loyalists came forward at Briar Creek to enable Campbell to organize a militia force there.[93]

As the British continued their advance, Campbell learned that the Whigs planned to execute three brothers who had recently joined the British and had been captured in a skirmish with rebel militia. To alert the Whigs that he would not tolerate such practices, Campbell sent a detachment within sight of the rebel camp to prepare for the hanging of two rebel leaders "notorious for their cruel Treatment of the Loyalists of Georgia." At the same time, Campbell dispatched an officer to the Whigs with an offer to exchange prisoners and a threat to hang six men if the rebels executed their three captives. The Whigs quickly agreed to exchange their prisoners for three men of equal rank.[94]

Whig troops were unable to offer serious resistance to the British. South Carolina could not assist the Georgians because its militia had to remain in Ninety Six district "to keep the Tories and Indians in subjection."[95] Gen. Samuel Elbert commanded the troops who were supposed to oppose Campbell, but Elbert thought himself too weak to make a stand and retreated into South Carolina. Although Lincoln believed that Elbert had acted wisely, he lamented the dangers that might ensue. Should the British pursue Elbert, Lincoln warned, "it is easy to see that many ill consequences will result from such a measure; our supplies will be affected, the Indians uncontrouled, and the Tories have an opportunity to triumph over & distress the good inhabitants of these States."[96] To prevent such problems, Lincoln reinforced Elbert with Williamson's militia and eight hundred North Carolinians under Gen. John Ashe. "If the enemy are suffered there to roam at pleasure, in their arms our disaffected inhabitants will find an asylum, and the Indians, who are too much disposed to mischief, will have at hand stimulators thereto, & supporters therein; hereby our enemies will augment their force and greatly weaken and distress us," Lincoln predicted.[97]

Subsequent events showed that Lincoln's fears were well founded. Elbert soon reported "that the disaffected people are collecting" in the backcountry.[98] Joseph Kershaw informed Lincoln that some Loyalists had "Actualy rose and attempted to possess themselves of a quantity of Powder" kept in a fort on Broad River. He predicted "that if a speedy stop is not put to them they may soon become formidable."[99]

On January 31 British troops entered Augusta, where they "found but a few families, and some of these had but the female part at home." However, over the next several days large numbers of people came into town and took the oath to George III. Campbell organized them into a militia, appointing as officers men who were "most agreeable to the generality of the Inhabitants."[100] Eventually fourteen hundred men who "had joined us with their Arms; and took the Oath of Allegiance" were embodied in twenty companies.[101] One of Campbell's officers complained that the Georgians "could not be brought to any regularity; therefore no real, substancial Services from them could be depended on" for some time.[102] Campbell actually considered many of his new Georgian militiamen a liability, telling Clinton that "it was our misfortune at this period to be encumbered with some irregulars from the upper country under the denomination of *crackers* . . . whose motions were too voluntary to be under restraint" and who were prone to pillage when sent on scouting expeditions. When the Whigs assembled a large force north of the Savannah River, "the crackers . . . found many excuses for going home to their plantations" in spite of Campbell's entreaties.[103]

Campbell tried to accommodate these unusual supporters and began to fortify the town, intending to establish a post there to support the backcountry Loyalists. He told one American, who forwarded the information to the Whigs, that he had taken command of the Georgia expedition on condition that the country was to be held and that to abandon it would "falsify his honour to the People and deceive them."[104]

A steady stream of visitors came to Augusta with information and supplies. Loyalist scouts brought Campbell regular reports of rebel activities. An emissary from Wilkes County brought a letter from the inhabitants "offering to surrender several stockaded Forts on the Frontiers of Georgia" fifty miles from Augusta. Campbell immediately dispatched eighty men to take the forts and to find Boyd's Loyalists. The officers took with them a letter from Campbell promising that he would protect the frontier people from Indian attack. All but one of the forts were taken without resistance; the troops captured that one by storm.[105] Loyalists from nearby Wrightsborough brought provisions for the British troops. In addition, Campbell met an Indian leader "who came from his Nation to receive and give a Talk." After the British gave their visitor a generous quantity of presents, he returned home.[106]

In accordance with orders from General Prevost, four days after setting out for Augusta, Campbell had dispatched Thomas Brown and the Florida Rangers to secure Burke County. Brown's force, which included Daniel McGirt's independent Loyalist rangers, numbered 400 men and was reinforced by 200 Georgians under Col. John Thomas. These men attacked 250 rebels who occupied the Burke County jail, but they were repulsed. Having been joined by three more parties of Loyalists, Brown renewed the attack but was driven off a second time.[107]

By February 12, notwithstanding the promises he had made to the Loyalists, Campbell decided to withdraw from Augusta. The anticipated Creek reinforcements had not arrived, provisions were scarce in the area, and he was unsure if Boyd's Loyalists were coming to join him. With large numbers of rebels gathering across the Savannah River, Campbell also worried that he was too distant from Prevost's forces and might be cut off. After waiting two days longer for Boyd and the Creeks, the British troops began their return march.[108] The rebels followed, but McGirt's Loyalists acted as a rear guard, "way-laying the roads" and keeping the pursuers away from the main British column.[109]

On the way to Savannah, Campbell received a letter from Prevost approving the withdrawal. Prevost believed that insufficient Loyalist support, rather than the combination of factors Campbell had noted, made it necessary to abandon Augusta. "I always thought that our being able to keep our Post at Augusta depended on the single circumstance of the Back-Country People's Joining heartily in the cause," Prevost wrote, "as without that we *must be certain of finding great difficulty if not impossibility in preserving a communication to such a distance.*"[110] In a letter to Clinton, Prevost again expressed disappointment at the lack of support in the backcountry, but he attributed it to the fact that "the rebels were already in arms and in possession of all the passes," which prevented the Loyalists from "communicating with the King's troops." Prevost expected greater success in the future, noting that a majority of the backcountry inhabitants "(even by accounts of rebels) are loyal in their inclinations."[111]

Meanwhile, Boyd, with the aid of Zachariah Gibbes, had enlisted about 600 men and united with a smaller band of North Carolinians. The combined force of between 700 and 800 men made its way across western South Carolina to join Campbell at Augusta. After entering Georgia, Boyd defeated a smaller rebel force in a skirmish. Whig militia under Andrew Pickens took up the pursuit of the Loyalists. Unaware that Campbell had left Augusta or that his own force was being pursued, Boyd continued his march. On February 14 he halted his men for a rest along Kettle Creek, where Pickens with several hundred Whigs attacked them. Although taken by surprise, Boyd fought valiantly until he was mortally wounded. Many of the Loyalists, however, had not been able to reorganize after the initial attack and eventually retreated. Pickens, satisfied with what he called "the severest check and chastisement the Tories ever received in Georgia or South Carolina," paroled most of his prisoners.[112] Campbell later reported that 270 of Boyd's men finally reached the British.[113]

The disaster at Kettle Creek had severe repercussions for the British. Afterward most Loyalists in "the upper Savannah River region were fearful of showing their true colors for over a year, until the British capture of Charleston in 1780."[114]

Whig leaders recognized that Pickens's victory would have a devastating effect on the Loyalists. Andrew Williamson felt "great pleasure" at the news.[115] Benjamin Lincoln told John Rutledge that "the repulse the tories have met with from Colo. Pickins, must brighten up our affairs in the upper part of the country. It will give peace and quiet to our friends there, open our communication with the Indians, and convince the unfriendly that real support cannot be found but in the arms and affections of their brethren."[116] Lincoln, however, still feared that the British intended to make "this part of the country . . . the seat of war for the ensuing campaign." Lincoln believed that the British "must be encouraged to make the attempt from the small resistance they met with in the conquest of so much of Georgia, the expected support from the Indians and disaffected in the back parts of these States, and from the little risque, they suppose, they should run in holding the possession."[117]

With Campbell's force gone from Augusta and Boyd's followers routed, the Whigs moved troops into Georgia to block any new British effort to seize control of the backcountry. As Williamson explained, the rebels' objective "was to prevent the Enemy crossing Savanna River, and keep open our Communication with the Indians, being well convinc'd" that if the British army managed to enter South Carolina, "their Strength wou'd soon become formidable, by the Numbers of disaffected Persons who wou'd immediately flock to their Standard." If the British tried to invade South Carolina, Whig leaders wanted to force them to attack in the lowcountry, where there were fewer Loyalists. This would make it "easier to repel them from thence, than from the back Country where the greater Part of the Inhabitants would join with, and support them."[118]

The Whigs moved quickly to eliminate the scattered remnants of Boyd's force and to punish the Loyalists who had come forward while Campbell was at Augusta. One party of Loyalists who escaped from Kettle Creek was captured by a rebel force under Capt. Absalom Beddell. The Whigs immediately hanged seven of their prisoners.[119] Capt. William Few, leading a group of rebels that one Loyalist described as a "villainous tribe of plunderers," launched a ruthless campaign to suppress the Loyalists. He began "ravaging the country for 30 miles above Augusta, without regard to age or sex, the widow or the orphans cries. Not satisfied with rapine, they have dragged forth the peaceable inhabitants to war, and, worse than the heathen savages of the wilderness, murdered, in cool blood, a Mr. — who refused to join them in their infamy," an Augusta resident wrote.[120]

Many people who had declared their loyalty only a few weeks earlier changed their allegiance again after Campbell's departure.[121] Whig officer John Dooly reported on February 16 "that a number of People that has Taken the oath of alegence to the King" now wished to join the rebels, and that some had already done so and fought alongside Dooly's troops in two skirmishes. Most of these men claimed that "thay ware forced to Take the oath and there is a Good Many Good Men may be Got in if thay Can be pardond." Dooly asked his superior, Colonel Elbert, how to handle such cases, although he did not hesitate to express his own opinion that it was better to get these men into the Whig ranks than to drive them back into the arms of the British. He asked Elbert to reply quickly, "as the poor people Seems much Confused at this Time about one party Robing and plundering the other."[122]

Whig leaders quarreled among themselves over how to treat those who had taken the oath to Great Britain. Some residents of Augusta "had openly cheered the arrival of British troops," and many rebels disliked the fact that these men were still among them. Whig hard-liners wanted Georgia officials to punish suspected Loyalists and believed that Gov. John Wereat "coddled Tories." When Wereat and the council released Joseph Maddock, a Quaker who had been imprisoned for sheltering Boyd, and then asked South Carolina officials to release three other Georgians confined in Charleston for loyalism, the more radical rebels became enraged.[123] A group of Whig officers in Burke County chose a moderate course and decided to issue a proclamation allowing anyone who had taken the British oath, with the exception of nine men considered particularly obnoxious, to repudiate their loyalism and receive pardon. Those who failed to comply would forfeit their property and "be deemed as Enemies & dealt with accordingly."[124]

Captured Loyalists suffered particularly harsh treatment. Georgia's civil officials claimed jurisdiction over a Loyalist prisoner of war named Fleming and wanted him imprisoned "untill they could have an opportunity of Punishing him for his Treachery," although they finally agreed to his exchange.[125] Andrew Williamson convened a court in April to try twelve Loyalist prisoners for various offenses. Two confessed to having been "with the Indians in arms" against the Whigs; nine others admitted either having served with the British forces or considering themselves to be British subjects. The court ordered all eleven to be held in close confinement. The twelfth prisoner testified that the British had forced him to take an oath to the king and was released.[126]

Reports of the cruel treatment of Loyalist prisoners led Augustine Prevost to send a protest to Lincoln. Prevost had heard that "many of the Prisoners taken from us are treated with a severity by no means justifyable." Loyalist captives, whether taken in battle or while "attempting to join the standard of their lawful Sovereign, ought to be consider'd as Prisoners of war," Prevost stated. If the Whigs insisted on trying Loyalists "by new-made Laws," he declared, "you cannot but be sensible that a prior Right intitles Great Britain to consider every American as a Subject, and consequently things may be brought to a point . . . that will be productive of dreadful consequences." Prevost warned Lincoln that his treatment of captured rebels would be determined by the manner in which the Whigs treated Loyalist prisoners.[127]

Whig officials in South Carolina, believing that harsh punishment would be most effective in frightening the state's Loyalists into quiescence, treated those who had joined the British with extreme cruelty. Gov. John Rutledge gathered a force of twenty-seven hundred militia "to crush any Insurgents in our back Country, if the people should still continue so infatuated as to attempt to rise."[128] The assembly passed an "Act to Prevent Persons Withdrawing from the Defense of the State to Join Its Enemies," which authorized Rutledge to punish anyone who had joined the British and did not surrender within forty days; the penalty was death and the confiscation of the offender's property.[129]

The Whigs held about 150 Loyalist prisoners, including 20 of Boyd's men, at Williamson's plantation. Rutledge ordered them to be brought to Ninety Six for trial in hopes "that a speedy Example of the most principal Offenders may have a good Effect, to prevent further Insurrection" in that heavily Loyalist district.[130] The trials began on March 22 and lasted until April 12. Half of the prisoners were released, and the court found the remainder guilty of treason. About 50 were reprieved on the grounds that they had either been deceived into joining the British or had lacked "proper information on the nature of our contest with Great Britain." The remaining prisoners were sentenced to death.[131]

To intimidate the numerous Loyalists in the vicinity of Orangeburg, Rutledge then ordered the prisoners moved to that town. The condemned men joined other prisoners in what must have been an extremely overcrowded blockhouse. On April 19 Continental colonel John Christian Senf reported that there were 43 prisoners of war and "132 criminals"—apparently Loyalists, since they included 11 officers—at Orangeburg.[132] Four days later a free black prisoner was hanged, and 5 other Loyalists were sent to Ninety Six "to be there executed."[133] Lt. Col. James Prevost attempted to intervene, arguing that the men should be treated as prisoners of war and exchanged, and hinting that the British would retaliate if the men were hanged. This failed to sway the Whigs, who carried out the execution of the 5 prisoners. The rest of those sentenced to death, however, were reprieved.[134]

Those hanged at Ninety Six were not the only victims of Whig vengeance. On March 17 William Tweed and Andrew Groundwater were hanged in Charleston after being captured while attempting to join the British. Tweed had been under suspicion since February 20, when his Charleston house burned down; the rebels believed that he had deliberately set the fire in an attempt to burn the town.[135] The destruction of Boyd's party and the wave of executions that followed undoubtedly deterred many Loyalists from trying to reach the British army.

After leaving Augusta, the British made a brief stand at Briar Creek, where on March 3 they inflicted a crushing defeat on the rebel force that had followed their retreat. James Prevost, who had assumed command of the detachment when Campbell returned to Savannah, feinted against the front of the American position while part of his force made a roundabout march and struck the rebel rear. Routed by the surprise attack, the Whigs suffered between four and five hundred casualties, while the British lost only sixteen men.[136] Prevost, however, made no attempt to remain in the backcountry, so the Loyalists there remained unsupported.

While British troops held positions to protect Savannah, the area outside their lines became a battleground on which Loyalists and Whigs contended for control. Col. John Thomas took 150 loyal militiamen to Burke Country to strike a Whig party in early March, but the rebels defeated Thomas's advance guard, captured other Loyalists in the area, and then withdrew before Thomas could catch them.[137]

Later in the month a combined force of Georgia and South Carolina Whig militia encountered a Loyalist unit and fought a two-hour battle by moonlight. Each side had about 200 men, but the rebels finally drove off their opponents after killing Loyalist major Spurgin and a few of his men.[138] Other Loyalists took advantage of the South Carolina militia's absence to raid on the north side of the Savannah River. Gattoes, a fugitive slave, guided the raiders to Black Swamp and the home of his former master, a Mr. Cowper. On the night of March 25 the Loyalists attacked the house and captured several prisoners, including Cowper and two American officers. One of Cowper's slaves summoned nearby rebel troops, but by the time they arrived, the Loyalists had gone.[139]

Such raids worried rebel leaders, who feared that South Carolina was vulnerable to a British invasion. Governor Rutledge labored to assemble a large militia force at Orangeburg, where the men would be in a position to move either to the defense of Charleston or to attack the British in Georgia. Loyalist and neutral sentiment slowed the formation of Rutledge's force; one thousand men had arrived by mid-April, but two hundred others deserted on the march.[140] Lincoln feared that he might have to withdraw his troops from the north bank of the Savannah River unless he received reinforcements from the North. He believed that Congress had underestimated British strength in the South by considering only the number of British regulars there. That was an error, Lincoln asserted, since it ignored the many Loyalists aiding the king's army. He noted that "there is not that union of sentiment among the inhabitants of this State I expected to find;—in the back parts of the country especially there are many disaffected people both in this State and North Carolina, who will be ready to join the enemy the first favorable opportunity, and give every aid to the savages in their power."[141] Lincoln noted that the South Carolina militia lacked the strength to simultaneously support the Continentals, guard the frontier against the Indians, and protect the area "about Orangeburgh, Broad & Saluda rivers, from those more unfriendly men, *the Tories.*"[142]

Lincoln's fears, although well justified, were premature. The British preferred to consolidate their control of Georgia before undertaking operations in South Carolina. Campbell appointed Maj. James Wright Jr., son of the former governor, to command the provincial battalion that the British intended to raise, but few men enlisted. The Georgia Loyalists, as the unit was designated, remained understrength throughout the war.[143] Given the effects of Boyd's defeat at Kettle Creek and the fact that their position at Savannah isolated the British from their supporters in the backcountry, the lack of recruits is hardly surprising.

The British had more success in civil affairs. Campbell had received permission to return to Britain once the situation in Georgia was stabilized, and before leaving he appointed James Prevost as lieutenant governor. Campbell believed that placing the general's younger brother in that office would facilitate cooperation between the civil and military authorities. James Prevost assumed his duties on March 4. He called on Georgians to assist the British, invited Loyalists from other southern provinces to settle in Georgia, and announced that rebel plunderers would be punished.[144] Prevost's tenure was brief; Germain ordered Governor Wright to return to the province at the beginning of March. Wright had instructions to resume his position as governor and call for the election of an assembly as soon as possible, so that the inhabitants of other provinces should "see it is not the Intention of His Majesty & Parliament to govern America by Military Law; but, on the contrary, to allow them all the Benefits of a local Legislature, & their former Civil Constitution."[145]

Wright arrived in Georgia in July, along with Lt. Gov. John Graham and Chief Justice Anthony Stokes, but decided to delay the assembly elections. He was unsure if there were enough Loyalists to justify convening the assembly and advised Germain that the province should remain under military rule until he had time to assess the situation. Germain disagreed, telling William Knox that he doubted Wright's capacity to govern Georgia. Like Germain, most royal officials and Loyalists in the province favored restoring civil government, believing that its success would convince many rebels to return to their allegiance.[146] Wright, however, continued to resist, arguing that continued rebel incursions to within a few miles of Savannah "left the province so much exposed and disconcerted me to that degree" that he postponed issuing writs for elections until March 1780.[147]

The governor correctly understood that the most pressing question in the spring of 1779 was not how Georgia should be governed but whether it could be held. In April, Lincoln crossed the Savannah River with five thousand troops and marched toward the capital and its outnumbered garrison. Realizing the danger of waiting for Lincoln's blow to fall, Augustine Prevost rapidly assembled his troops, entered South Carolina, and drove directly toward Charleston. The move, as Prevost had intended, forced Lincoln to cancel his plans and hurry back to defend the town.[148]

Prevost's invasion force included many Loyalists, including seventy under Daniel McGirt.[149] Supported by Indians, McGirt's force operated as raiders independently of the army. On May 3 William Moultrie reported that McGirt's "parties of horse and Indians, are ravaging the country in a barbarous manner, killing people and burning a number of houses as they go on."[150] In June some of McGirt's men stopped at a plantation owned by Eliza Wilkinson's family. They behaved better than the wild tales that preceded them had led Wilkinson to expect. "To tell the truth, they behaved to us more like friends than enemies," she wrote. Still, her opinion of them was not high. "Nothing but the hope of raising themselves on the ruin of others, has induced them to engage in the war against us," she declared. "I fear *principle* governs very few. *Interest* reigns predominant."[151]

Many South Carolina Loyalists took advantage of Prevost's invasion to join the British. Robert Ballingall reached the army in early May and served until he was captured by the rebels at the end of the month. The Whigs confined him in "a loathsome crowded Gaol" until October, when he was paroled due to ill health.[152]

Another Loyalist who joined Prevost, Jeremiah Savage, was also caught and imprisoned. Thomas Fenwicke, a planter on Johns Island, informed the British of the location of a Whig militia camp; Prevost's troops then attacked and virtually annihilated the rebels there. Several other Loyalists made their way to the British army, although one group in the Camden area who planned to capture a powder magazine was discovered, and several of them were jailed.[153] Prevost had expected a better response from the Loyalists and complained that "very few and those of little influence joined the King's standard." The problem, he asserted, was the same one that Campbell had encountered in the backcountry—not a lack of Loyalists, but their fear of persecution. He noted that "the most zealous" Loyalists were afraid to act because they faced punishments "so severe and awful."[154]

Prevost's invasion had upset Lincoln's plans, frightened the Whigs, and enabled some Loyalists to join the British. However, as Lincoln's army rushed toward Charleston, the British general had to withdraw from the vicinity of the town. By the end of June the British were back in Savannah, except for a detachment that Prevost left to hold Beaufort.[155]

While the two armies maneuvered across the South Carolina lowcountry, the civil war between Whigs and Loyalists flared up anew in Georgia. In late May and early June, Benjamin Few led 150 Richmond County Whigs against Loyalists gathering in lower Burke County. Few dispersed "some parties of the Enemy that was there Embodiing against us," capturing several of their leaders. The rebel militia also defeated a small party of Florida Rangers in a skirmish, capturing three. Few believed that these successes would keep the Loyalists in check. "I Don't think Any number in that Country will Again Attempt to take Up Arms Against us," he wrote, "as many of them seem Convinced of their Error and have again promised their Allegeance to the United States."[156]

McGirt made a foray into western Georgia during the summer but was defeated by rebel militia under Col. John Twiggs. A short time later part of McGirt's force suffered another defeat while harassing Whigs along the Ogeechee River. Thomas Brown's Rangers, who with some Indians had been raiding in the area, retreated after learning of McGirt's defeat.[157]

Small victories such as these accomplished little, as bands of Loyalists, often including Indians, continued to strike at Georgia's rebels. John Wereat feared that "the concerted Invasions of the Enemy's Irregulars and Indians, who are at this time making different inroads upon us," might cause large numbers of Whigs to leave the province. Wereat warned Lincoln that the British "will aim at a total subduction of Georgia this Fall," which if successful, would create "a very dangerous situation" in South Carolina. "The great defection of the upper parts of that Country is well known—a circumstance on which the Enemy found the most sanguine hopes," Wereat wrote. Once the British were established at Augusta, Wereat believed that "the greatest part of the Inhabitants" of Georgia, "worn out with fruitless opposition and actuated by the fear of loosing their *all,* would make terms for themselves." Once they had done so, they would proceed naturally "from one step of infamy to another," so that "we have not the least doubt of their joining the Enemy." The proximity of Augusta to the Indians, he pointed out, would also make possession of the town of great benefit to the British. He asked Lincoln to send Continental troops to Georgia to prevent such a disaster.[158]

In the meantime, Wereat sought to prevent defections by punishing Georgians who had joined the British. After learning that three such men had been captured and were confined aboard prison ships at Charleston, Wereat asked Lincoln to send them to Georgia to stand trial. One of the three, James Lambert, had especially angered the Whigs; "having been a Member of the House of Assembly & a Captain of Militia," he was charged "with Deserting with his whole Company to the Enemy." His two companions were accused of "crimes of a like nature."[159] The Georgia militia contributed by plundering suspected Loyalists, "under an idea of what they call distressing of our Enemies." Lincoln asked Lachlan McIntosh to put an end to such behavior because it was alienating many Georgians and driving some to seek safety with the British.[160]

Loyalists in South Carolina proved equally difficult to subdue; some escaped to Georgia, and others harassed the Whigs when the opportunity arose. In June, Andrew Cumming and twenty-three others made their way to Ebenezer, where they joined the New Jersey Volunteers. When Lieutenant Colonel Prevost learned of Cumming's feat, he sent the South Carolinian back across the Savannah "to Pilote some Loyalists to Georgia who were much distressed by the Rebells." With five men, Cumming returned to South Carolina, but he found on arriving at Orangeburg that the Whigs had learned of his presence and were searching for him. Deciding to return to Georgia, Cumming and his small band eluded pursuit and burned three wagons loaded with rebel supplies.[161] Another group of Loyalists, described as "Two Companys of Out Lyers," frequently sallied from their refuge in a swamp near Saltketcher's to distress the Whigs.[162]

On September 1 the comte d'Estaing arrived in Georgia with a French fleet and army, and Lincoln immediately marched American forces to Savannah to unite with his ally. Large numbers of "His Majesty's well-affected subjects" fled to the town as the French and Americans approached, increasing a population already swollen by refugees from the backcountry. Others who had sworn allegiance to the British after the capture of Savannah, expecting the British to be defeated, joined Lincoln's army.[163] As the rebels approached Savannah, they wreaked vengeance on the Loyalists, taking "prisoners, negroes, and horses." During the siege of the town, both French and American soldiers "plundered the country in the most shameful manner," according to Loyalist accounts. They carried off "provisions and stock . . . robbed poor people of their bedding and clothes," and pillaged the homes of absent Loyalists.[164]

The Loyalists fought back with vigor throughout the siege. They had a powerful incentive to do so, since John Glen, the Whig chief justice of Georgia, had

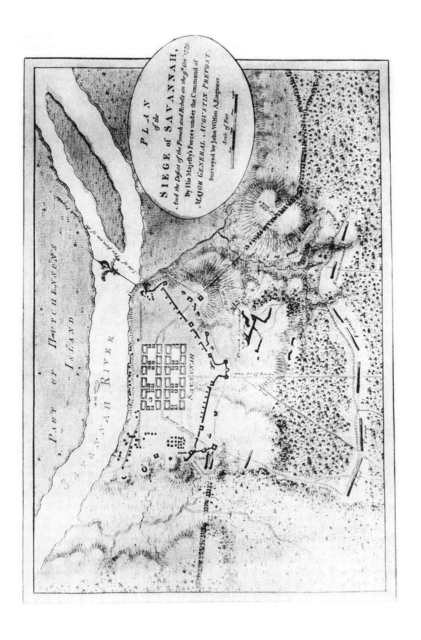

From J. F. W. DesBarres, *Atlantic Neptune* (1774–82)

declared that the French and rebels would show no leniency when they captured Savannah. "It was not now a time to use gentle & moderate measures, but
to make reprisals and to retaliate," Glen told a Loyalist prisoner.[165]

In addition to the 350 Georgians who served in the militia defending the
town, Loyalist spies kept General Prevost informed of the situation in the enemy
camp. Three South Carolinians crossed the Savannah River with Lincoln's army
and then hurried off to inform Prevost of the Americans' numbers and position.[166] Some of the soldiers in the rebel army were also Loyalists, and they
provided Prevost with a steady flow of information. A French officer complained
that Loyalists serving with the Whig militia "continually betrayed us" by giving
the British "the most exact account of all our operations."[167]

Other Loyalists operated in the rear of the French and American lines. Rebel
troops captured five white men and three blacks who had been stealing horses
twenty-five miles above Midway; some of the prisoners were from the Florida
Rangers. Three other Loyalists were taken at Midway, and an American officer
reported that there were "Several villains about us, that has taken to the Swamps."
These men also stole horses from the rebels at "every opportunity."[168]

French and American troops attempted to storm the British defenses on
October 9 and were repulsed, suffering heavy losses. The South Carolina Royalists distinguished themselves by holding their ground against a furious assault.[169]
The *Royal Georgia Gazette* praised the spirit displayed by both regular troops
and militia in the town's defense, while Anthony Stokes declared that the "conduct of the Militia and Volunteers, who went into the lines to defend the town,
would do honour to veteran troops."[170] Governor Wright asserted that the
French and Americans had been "defeated by the persevering Resolution &
Bravery of the Loyalists."[171] In his report to Germain, Prevost included the
Georgia militia with the regular units of the garrison as deserving praise for
their service during the siege. Three militiamen were killed and one wounded in
the campaign; four soldiers of the Georgia Loyalists also died in action.[172]

After their attack failed, the French sailed to the West Indies, and Lincoln
withdrew his troops to South Carolina. Frustrated by the defeat, rebel troops
"exacted reprisals throughout Georgia" before crossing the Savannah River.[173]

Loyalists in South Carolina seized the opportunity offered by the British victory to escape to Savannah. Moses Buffington, an ensign in the South Carolina
Royalists, wrote his father that several of their acquaintances had recently made
their way to Georgia and that more were said to be on their way. These refugees
launched frequent raids into South Carolina, often with unfortunate consequences. Conrad Besinger, a deserter from the South Carolina Continentals,
was captured on Bull Island in November wearing a British uniform. The Whigs
sentenced him to hang. In January 1780 rebel militia captured ten South Carolina Loyalists who had been raiding in the state.[174]

Georgia Loyalists also renewed their raids in the backcountry after the enemy armies had left. Daniel McGirt's troops killed several Whig militia officers in a foray from Savannah in October. The rebels managed to disperse one Loyalist raiding party in early December but failed to capture any of them.[175] Shortly afterward a rebel officer complained of the trouble caused by "these stragling Parties which are always coming from Midway settlement."[176] Later in the month the Whigs dispersed another group of Loyalist raiders, capturing two. Both prisoners were killed while attempting to escape from jail in Augusta.[177]

If circumstances seemed to be improving for Loyalists in Georgia and South Carolina, their counterparts in West Florida found their situation deteriorating. In the aftermath of the Willing raid, many settlers along the Mississippi decided that Britain could no longer protect them and moved across the river to Spanish territory, where they took an oath of allegiance to Spain. John Fitzpatrick observed in July that "more or less of the Men are daily deserting to our Neighbours the Spaniards. The Number the Spaniards have now in their Service is 96."[178]

This depletion of Loyalist strength weakened the province at an inopportune time. Spain declared war on Britain on June 21, 1779, but Gen. John Campbell, commanding at Pensacola, did not learn of the declaration until September 8. By that time Galvez, who had received notice of hostilities earlier, had already invaded West Florida on August 27. At Baton Rouge, which surrendered to the Spaniards on September 21, 150 Loyalists participated in the unsuccessful effort to defend that post. The terms of capitulation required the British to surrender the fort at Natchez to the Spaniards as well. This greatly angered the people there; they had been prepared to resist a Spanish attack. By the time Galvez completed his conquest of the Mississippi River settlements, some 500 Loyalists had taken up arms to defend their homes. All were allowed to return home and remain undisturbed providing they took an oath of allegiance to the king of Spain.[179]

Governor Chester and General Campbell quarreled about how to meet the Spanish threat. Campbell believed that West Floridians were "in general, self-interested and without public spirit."[180] He complained to Clinton of "the little prospect I have of reinforcement or aid from either inhabitants or Indians in case of Pensacola or Mobile being attacked." The people "seem averse and backward to military duty," Campbell wrote.[181] Campbell wanted Chester to convene the assembly to pass a militia law, which would facilitate future assistance from the loyal inhabitants. Chester, however, did not want to deal with the fractious representatives and refused to summon them. In September forty-nine residents of Pensacola asked the governor and council to allow them to embody as a temporary militia, while in October fifty-eight people in the province's interior requested permission to build a fort on the Tombigbee River and organize a company to patrol their district. Chester and the council approved both petitions. The governor later created two troops of Loyalist dragoons to guard the province's shrunken boundaries.[182]

THE INDIAN CONTRIBUTION

British officials relied on the Indians to provide crucial assistance when the king's troops finally launched the southern campaign in late 1778. Germain and Clinton expected John Stuart to bring a large number of Indians to cooperate with Archibald Campbell's invasion force, which would enable the British to regain control of the Georgia backcountry and perhaps much of South Carolina as well. However, the failure of the Indians to rendezvous with Campbell's troops, resulting primarily from problems in communication, caused British leaders to question the Indians' reliability. Later in the campaign, the Indians would provide valuable assistance to the British, although never at the levels that Germain had expected. Nevertheless, the Indians aided the British cause simply by constituting a potential threat that the Whigs could not ignore.

On December 2, 1778, Germain wrote to Stuart explaining the plan to seize Savannah and march into the backcountry. Germain ordered Stuart "to exert your utmost influence with the Indians of your department to supply a constant succession of parties to act as the commander of the King's troops in Georgia shall direct." Stuart, Germain said, should accompany the first party to Augusta and establish his headquarters there.[183] Stuart had not received these instructions by the time Campbell arrived in Georgia—in fact, it was not until December 12 that the superintendent received Germain's dispatches dated July 1 and August 5. These letters indicated that an attack in the South had been planned, but they did not say when. Stuart assured Germain that he had informed the Indians that troops were on the way and that "it has greatly contributed to secure their affections to the King's interest."[184]

Meanwhile, Campbell had taken Savannah and marched to Augusta, where he did not find the large number of Indians that Germain had promised would join him. Campbell did not realize that the Indians, albeit indirectly, had already contributed to the success of his operations. Continental commander Robert Howe noted that Georgia's defenses had been "rendered very weak" because he had been forced to detach "a considerable number of the Regular Troops to the westward, to prevent the Ravages of the Indians." This reduced the force available to defend Savannah against Campbell's attack.[185] After replacing Howe, Benjamin Lincoln chose to divert Andrew Williamson's South Carolina militia to guard against Indian attack, rather than use the troops to oppose Campbell's advance to Augusta. "When we consider that in the back parts of your Country and the State of Georgia there are a number of disaffected people and that they are stimulating the indians to acts of hostility," Lincoln told Williamson, it was necessary to employ the militia to protect the frontier.[186]

Waiting at Augusta for Creek reinforcements, Campbell began to wonder if the Indians really intended to support the British and that, if not, it would be better to keep them neutral. He wrote to George Galphin in late January asking for help "in . . . restricting the Indians to a State of Neutrality." Although Galphin's reply seemed satisfactory, Campbell heard reports that the Whig agent could not be trusted, so he sent a Loyalist spy to make inquiries about Galphin. The spy soon reported that Galphin "was one of the most violent Rebels in America" and that despite the assurances he had given Campbell, "he was actually sending a natural Son of his with two Carolina Men to raise the Indians against us." British troops intercepted the three emissaries and found letters to the Creeks "full of every Encouragement that could incite them to War." That same day ninety of Galphin's slaves escaped to the British. Campbell sent the slaves to Savannah as security for Galphin's future good behavior.[187]

The failure of the Creeks to join Campbell contributed to his decision to leave the backcountry. Shortly after leaving Augusta, he sought to reassure the Creeks by sending them a message asserting that he had not left "from Fear of the Rebels."[188] He told them that although he was disappointed that they had not met him, he would send troops to meet them as soon as he learned that they were coming to join him. Meanwhile, they were not to harm any frontier inhabitants who supported the king.[189]

Although the Indians had not joined with the troops as expected, as soon as Stuart learned of the plan he had moved quickly to send the Creeks to aid Campbell. Patrick Tonyn had sent Stuart the details of Campbell's proposed operations, but the letter did not reach Pensacola until the end of January. On February 1 Stuart dispatched David Taitt to the Upper Creek towns to assemble the Indians and proceed to Augusta. Creek leaders promised to provide one thousand men by March 9, long after Campbell had left the backcountry. Taitt asked Campbell to send troops to meet this party before setting out on the scheduled day with only eighty Indians. The number increased to four hundred, along with several Loyalists, by the time Taitt reached the Ogeechee River. The party waited several days for British troops to arrive, only to learn from a Loyalist that the Whigs had discovered their presence and that at least four hundred rebel militia were moving to attack them.[190]

To elude the Whigs, the Creeks divided into at least three parties. Taitt sent one group of Indians and Loyalists to operate in South Carolina, where they destroyed an abandoned fort. Intimidated by the growing numbers of rebel militia, many Indians soon returned to their towns, while others made their way to Savannah. On March 29 the Whigs caught and attacked one party of about 70 Creeks, killing 6 Indians and 2 Loyalists and capturing 3 Indians and 3 Loyalists. The rebels scalped the dead Indians and marched with the scalps displayed on a pole. Eventually about 120 Creeks reached Savannah; over the next several weeks other parties arrived and increased the number to 300.[191] Whig Joseph Habersham described these operations against the Indians as "a very providential Circumstance, more especially as the Indians were given to understand by the Enemy that they wou'd meet with no Opposition in joining them." According to Habersham, the Indians complained that "they have been deceived, and are returning in great wrath." He hoped that this experience would convince other Indians not to assist the British.[192]

Dissatisfied with the Indians' efforts, Augustine Prevost admonished Taitt, telling the agent that he would "expect more punctuality from the Indian Promises than formerly, it being their Interest to act in Concert with the King's Troops." Despite his disappointment, Prevost told Taitt that he still believed that the Indians could "render essential Service if they suffer themselves to be guided" by white men. The general added that he had instructed Loyalists in the interior of Georgia "to give all assistance to the Indians."[193] Governor Wright shared Prevost's disappointment at the Indians' seemingly lukewarm support and expressed doubts about their commitment to the British cause.[194] After receiving Prevost's and Campbell's reports, Germain stated that he "was surprised to find the Indians not mentioned" but realized that their delay in responding resulted from the difficulties in communication.[195] He believed that the presence of troops in Georgia would convince the Indians of "His Majesty's ability to crush his Enemies," which would prompt them to ignore the rebels and commit fully to supporting the British.[196]

One reason for the Indians' hesitant response to British calls for aid was Stuart's incapacity. Gen. John Campbell warned Clinton on February 10 that the Indian superintendent was "in the last stage of consumption" and that his death might lead to "great confusion" in Indian affairs.[197] Stuart died on March 21, and his brother Charles, along with Alexander Cameron, assumed temporary management of the department, so British relations with the Indians underwent no significant change.[198] Germain termed Stuart's death "a Misfortune" but noted that "his long Ill-State of Health had disabled him from discharging the active Duties of his Office." Now that Spain had entered the war, Germain decided to divide the Indian department to deal with that nation in the Mississippi valley and the American rebels along the Atlantic coast. Germain therefore assigned Cameron to superintend the Choctaws and Chickasaws in West Florida, while Thomas Brown assumed control of Cherokee and Creek affairs. The minister also determined that the superintendents' duties were "at present, merely Military" and placed them directly under Clinton's command.[199]

Lincoln, unaware that Stuart's illness provided an opportunity for the Whigs to increase their influence with the Indians, luckily chose the same time to make a new diplomatic effort aimed at detaching the Indians from their alliance with the British. In late January he urged Williamson to arrange a meeting with Indian leaders, because "it is much easier to keep them in our interest, than to reduce them to terms of reason and a good brotherhood after the hatchet is taken up."[200] The general advised Governor Lowndes to do everything possible to provide supplies for the Indians, and he also solicited Galphin's help "to keep the Indians friendly."[201] Williamson agreed to make an effort at negotiations, since the Whigs could not afford an Indian attack on the frontiers. If that occurred, he warned, it would be impossible to keep the militia "from going Home to protect their families."[202]

Williamson and Galphin met with Cherokee leaders at Fort Rutledge in March and received assurances that the Cherokees would remain at peace. Lincoln expressed satisfaction at the successful negotiations, telling Galphin that he was "quite satisfied with the measures you adopted."[203] The Chickamauga faction of the Cherokees, however, still refused to participate in discussions with the Whigs. Instead, they attacked the overmountain settlers along the North Carolina and Virginia frontiers. The overmountain militia in return destroyed eleven Chickamauga towns, forcing the Indians to move to new areas. Nevertheless, the Chickamaugas continued to raid the frontier, often in conjunction with some of the more militant Upper Creeks.[204]

Those Creeks who had joined the British in Savannah launched frequent raids into South Carolina and the Whig-controlled areas of Georgia, further disconcerting the rebels. A detachment of Georgia militia pursued one Indian raiding party into South Carolina, bringing on a skirmish in which a rebel major named Ross suffered a mortal wound.[205] On April 22 at least thirty Creeks and Loyalists, the latter "painted & disguised as Indians," crossed the Savannah River and burned the house of a Whig officer named Hartstone.[206] Whigs worried that the party, and the fifty other Indians reported to be at Abercorn, "will do a great deal of mischief." William Moultrie asked Governor Rutledge to send down some Catawbas who "would be of infinite service" against the Creeks.[207]

Even the Catawbas' commitment to the Whigs had been called into question, however, as Creek raids fed new rumors of a full-scale Indian attack in the backcountry. Joseph Kershaw visited the Catawba nation to investigate reports that some Catawbas had left their lands and joined the British. He found that all but four of the men were present, and the Catawbas were able to account for the whereabouts of the missing men.[208] This did little to mollify Lincoln, who grew increasingly worried that a Creek attack was imminent. "I always supposed it would be in the enemy's plan to bring down, if possible, the Indians on our frontiers," Lincoln told Galphin.[209] "I am of opinion that the principal design of the enemy in bringing out the Indians, is to divert us from the general object, to terrify and keep at home the militia," the general explained to Williamson. Without the support of the militia, Lincoln knew that his own army would have a difficult time resisting an attack from British regulars.[210]

The anticipated attack came at the end of April, not in the backcountry but from lower Georgia as Prevost began a drive toward Charleston. At least one hundred Creeks accompanied the British troops; Prevost employed them, along with Loyalist irregulars, as scouts in advance of his main force. One Indian and two Loyalist scouts were wounded in an encounter with the Whigs at the Saltketcher River; in another skirmish, Indians pursued and scalped some retreating rebels.[211]

Such incidents helped Prevost by inducing rebel militiamen to leave the ranks. "The terror excited by the Indians, who wore their war dresses, and wantonly displayed the instruments of torture, with which they were accustomed to aggravate the sufferings of their prisoners, created the most appalling dismay," one rebel declared. "Whigs, of unquestionable patriotism" serving in the militia left their units and rushed home to protect their families from Indian "depredations."[212]

Creek attacks on the frontier further hindered Whig leaders' efforts to assemble as many militiamen as possible to oppose Prevost. On May 8 Williamson informed Lincoln that most of Andrew Pickens's men had "gone home on Accot of the Indians having made some Incursions on the frontier and killed & Scalped some Persons" in the area. Williamson thought that the Indian danger was less serious than reported and promised to send five hundred men to assist the army "as soon as the Inhabitants are made Sensible, that the numbers of Indians sd. to be coming down is much exaggerated."[213]

In response to reports that "the Enemy's Indians are ravaging the Country," John Rutledge "wrote pressingly, for the Catawba Indians to come down, as a Match for those of the Enemy."[214] The Catawbas promptly dispatched ninety men to assist the Whigs.[215]

The Creeks who accompanied Prevost's troops seized a considerable number of slaves in South Carolina and took many of them to Savannah. They refused Governor Wright's advice to sell the slaves, although several Creeks traded their plundered slaves for horses. Others took slaves to East Florida, where some Seminole Creeks eagerly exchanged cattle for them. The Creeks' demand for slaves grew sufficiently large to induce some whites to bring plundered slaves into the nation to trade for horses and cattle.[216] David Tait blamed the "Georgia Volunteers" for the Indians' sudden desire to plunder slaves. During the invasion of South Carolina, Tait said, these Loyalist troops had "set a bad example to the Indians, who cannot now be restrained from taking Negroes."[217]

With Prevost's troops back in Georgia, exhausted Whig militiamen used the possibility of Indian attack as an excuse to demand that they be allowed to return home. At the beginning of July, Williamson told Moultrie that it was "impossible to keep his men in the field any longer." Williamson's militia, Moultrie wrote, "have played the old stale game of Cameron's being in the Cherokees, with a number of white men and Indians, ready to fall on their part of the country." Moultrie conceded that the militia would have to be permitted to leave as soon as Governor Rutledge gave his approval.[218]

Although many Creeks had been active with Prevost and on the frontier, rebel leaders remained uncertain about the intentions of the nation as a whole. Galphin believed that the Creeks preferred neutrality. At the end of May, Lincoln received a talk from that nation, accompanied by "Beads and White Wing, emblems of their peaceable intentions." Lincoln advised John Rutledge to send a talk in reply to "confirm them in their present good disposition," and he suggested that the address might be more effective if delivered jointly by himself and the governor.[219]

At Augusta, however, Lachlan McIntosh saw indications in August that "the Enemy mean to Harass us upon every Side by the Savages & themselves untill they get the whole state into their possession, & make an Irruption into Carolina from this quarter." Most of the militia who had not joined the British, McIntosh wrote, remained "penned up in Little Forts to Secure their Familys from the Savages, to whom they are exposed, & harass them Continualy."[220] A few days later a Whig officer reported that "a number of Indians" had crossed the Savannah River into South Carolina, frightening local residents.[221] The same officer reported on August 19 that another "party of painted Villains" had entered South Carolina.[222] This group of "twenty Painted White Men & Eighty Indians" burned a house and killed and scalped a Whig militiaman. The raiders also carried off "Most of the Negroes from One of Mr. Cowpers Plantations," although rebel lieutenant James Moore believed that the Loyalist Cowper, who was in Savannah, may have sent the party expressly to recover his slaves. Moore noted that "the Men are so much Alarm'd at the Indians coming Over (On Account of their families) that Should they make another Attempt & Succeed most every Man will Move their Women & Children & many themselves I am Afraid."[223] The whites accompanying the Indians were undoubtedly Loyalist refugees who wore Indian costume to avoid recognition and thus protect their families from Whig retaliation.

The Creeks continued to make "excursions across the Savannah" as far south as Purysburgh, doing "mischief in the predatory way."[224] Whig leaders admitted that they lacked the strength to prevent these raids, which John Wereat believed presaged a new British attack on the backcountry. Should Prevost retake Augusta, Wereat warned, the "great defection of the upper parts" of South Carolina would bring an accession of Loyalists into the British ranks, and "the Enemy will find not the least difficulty, whenever they have a mind, of bringing the Savages upon the Frontiers of Carolina."[225]

To bolster Whig strength in the region, Lincoln dispatched five hundred Virginia soldiers to Augusta. He also tried to restrain the Georgians, who had recently killed some friendly Creeks. Lincoln urged state officials to do everything possible to mollify the Indians to prevent them from assisting the British.[226]

The Creeks might have provided even more assistance to the British had a smallpox epidemic not struck their towns in the autumn. Brought south by the Maryland Loyalists sent to reinforce Pensacola and passed on to Indian visitors in the town, the disease killed many Creeks and incapacitated others. Those who were uninfected fled to the woods to avoid contracting the disease, further reducing the number of Creeks that Brown could employ.[227]

Those Cherokees who had not signed the 1777 treaty moved southward in August and launched their own attacks on the South Carolina frontier.[228] Williamson marched against them with the militia, and a detachment under Andrew

Pickens captured "The Terrapin a Principal Headman of the Outlying Cherokees," who had led the raiding parties. Williamson's militia burned eight Cherokee towns and destroyed at least fifty thousand bushels of corn. Several Cherokee leaders came to Williamson on August 28 and "pleaded hard to save their Corn and Houses." Williamson replied that "their bad Conduct had obliged me to come into their Country with an Army, I was resolved to Carry destruction through their Towns & Settlemts." Unless the Cherokee raiders returned to "the Settled Towns in the Nation and Resided among their Countrymen," Williamson said he would disregard their pleas. The Indians accepted the ultimatum. Williamson hoped that the blow would "Secure the peace and quiet of our frontiers" by intimidating the Creeks as well as the Cherokees.[229]

Just when Indian raids began to place a strain on the Whigs, Governor Wright learned that Prevost had jeopardized future cooperation by insulting Creek leaders at an early August meeting in Savannah. After their talks with the general, the angry Creeks announced their intention to "return home immediately," while some declared that "they had been very ill treated." Wright asked Alexander McGillivray to find out what had transpired at the conference. Suspecting that a lack of activity was the root of the problem, Wright suggested that the Indians "might be of service" if they joined a group of regulars and militia guarding Hudson's Ferry on the Savannah River, or "if they can't remain inactive, they might amuse themselves, by going over the River into Carolina."[230] Wright later spoke to the Creeks himself and learned that they were eager "to go on any duty or Service that might be required of them."[231]

Prevost, ignorant of the effects that Indian raids had on the Whigs, remained unhappy with the level of Indian support. "Instead of the great assistance expected from the numerous tribes of allied Indians . . . not above eighty Creeks have attended the army or appeared in any force anywhere" in the South since the capture of Savannah, he told Germain.[232] David Taitt disputed this obvious understatement of Creek numbers, asserting that the Creeks had been quite effective, given the difficult circumstances under which they had to operate.[233]

Prevost soon moderated his views. Having learned that Alexander Cameron was leading a large number of Indians to attack the frontier, he was preparing "to make some movements in favour of the Indians" when the arrival of the French fleet at Savannah forced him to cancel his plans.[234] An estimated eighty Cherokees and Creeks were in town when the siege began; the Cherokees were assigned to guard Hutchinson's Island, where a large number of civilians had taken refuge, while the Creeks served in the defensive lines.[235] Henry Laurens hoped that a French and American victory at Savannah might prove fatal to the British alliance with the Indians by bringing "disgrace" on the British "in the Eyes of their Savage Connections who will probably take part against them in their Disaster."[236]

Laurens's optimism was misplaced, for not only did the British defeat their attackers, but also many Indians came to the aid of the king's troops, although they were too far away to reach Savannah before the siege ended. Two hundred Cherokees arrived in the town on January 6, 1780, bringing four hundred horses. Later that month one hundred Creeks reached Savannah unmolested by the rebels.[237]

In addition to the French and American attack on Savannah, the British faced another threat in the South in 1779 as Spain prepared to enter the war. While still neutral, the Spanish sought to gain influence with the Choctaws by lavishing presents on them in an attempt to undermine their support for the British. James Colbert, agent to the Chickasaws, visited the Sixtowns Choctaws in November and found nearly every man wearing medals and coats provided by Spanish agents. Colbert questioned the Choctaw leaders, who assured him of their continued loyalty to Britain. The British subsequently increased the quantity of their own gifts, but many Choctaws from the Sixtowns faction shifted their allegiance to Spain.[238]

Germain had underestimated the effects of Spanish influence with the Indians; instead he had ordered the commander in West Florida, Gen. John Campbell, to undertake an offensive against Louisiana as soon as Spain entered the war. The minister believed that with the aid of the West Florida militia and "a Number of faithful Indians," Campbell could easily capture New Orleans.[239] However, the Spanish struck first, invading West Florida on August 27 with a force that included 160 Indians from Louisiana.[240]

The timing of the attack was unfortunate for the British, since a party of Creeks had arrived at Pensacola ten days earlier. Campbell had provided them with arms and ammunition, and the Indians had gone to Savannah. Their appearance impressed Philipp Waldeck, a German chaplain, who described them as "most wonderfully developed, large and strong." They would have been a valuable reinforcement for West Florida's defense had Campbell realized that an attack was imminent.[241] Shortly after the Creeks left, a group of Choctaws arrived. Waldeck described them as "braver in war" than the Creeks but physically less impressive. He noted that there was no Choctaw interpreter in Pensacola, so that a Creek had to handle the task. Campbell supplied the Choctaws with the arms and ammunition they requested, although his officers angered the Indians by telling them "in rather rough fashion that they must control their people so that they cause no damage."[242] The Choctaws were still at Pensacola on September 14 when Campbell, ignorant of the Spanish invasion, secured their promise to provide two hundred men for an attack on New Orleans.[243]

News of the Spanish attack forced Campbell to adopt a more genial attitude toward the Indians, many of whom had gone to Pensacola after learning that war had broken out in the Mississippi valley. British officials "clearly see that in the present situation, it is more necessary to flatter them [Indians] so as to keep them friendly," Waldeck wrote, noting that the newly arrived Indians had demanded gifts. "And if it is not to our advantage, still we must give them presents so that they will not take up arms against us. On the other hand the Spaniards do all they can to draw these savages away from us."[244] The Spanish efforts achieved some success when a considerable number of Sixtowns Choctaws later joined Galvez's force and fought alongside the Spaniards at Mobile.[245]

After the fall of Mobile, some Loyalists decided that it was unsafe to remain in West Florida, and during their emigration they developed a new respect for Indians. William Lee hired a trader to guide his family to Georgia through Creek territory. At one point during their journey they spent seventeen days with the Creeks, finding them to be "a very sensible and intelligent people." Lee quickly came to admire the Indians' social equality. He concluded that "they are the most happy people in the world" and were not to "be pitied, but rather to be envied."[246]

The Creeks' hospitality to Loyalist refugees showed their continued commitment to the British, but the Spanish did not relent in their efforts to win Creek and Choctaw support. Galvez received some Choctaw leaders in New Orleans, one of whom alarmed Cameron by later declaring that "whoever gives us the most will be the most regarded."[247] Lt. Col. Lewis Fuser, commander of the St. Augustine garrison, learned in October that "the Indians recd from the Spaniards presents of great value" and that Spanish agents had invited some chiefs to Havana, "with promises to send them soon back with three ships loaded with goods for them." If the report were true, Fuser wrote, it meant that the Spaniards planned to reestablish a post in Florida from which location they could "be at hand to indispose the Indians against us."[248]

AFRICAN AMERICANS IN ARMS

The arrival of British troops in Georgia at the end of 1778 provided slaves with the chance to seek freedom by escaping to the king's forces. Many slaves had awaited this opportunity since the start of the war and quickly took advantage of it. Some, such as the slave who enabled Archibald Campbell to capture Savannah with ease, made significant contributions to the British cause. Others, although their individual efforts were less spectacular, also provided valuable support to the British. Their actions demonstrated that slave assistance could be a powerful asset in the ministry's effort to regain control of the southern colonies. However, British leaders still did not adopt a coherent policy for the use of slaves, and it was left to British military and civil officials to determine what role blacks would take in southern operations.

Southern Whigs knew that many of their slaves would flee if the British established themselves in the region. When reports arrived that Clinton had dispatched an expedition to Georgia, the planters began to worry. "If the Ennemy unfortunately got possession of Savannah, there will be an absolute necessity in my Opinion to withdraw the hands from those plantations," John Lewis Gervais informed Henry Laurens.[249] Indian agent George Galphin, who lived far up the Savannah River, thought that if the British invaded, he would "be obligd to Send of most of my negros toward the Congerees."[250]

The Whigs' fears were well founded because large numbers of slaves from both Georgia and South Carolina escaped in the weeks following the British capture of Savannah. On January 20 South Carolinian Nathaniel Hall complained that "thirteen of my Negroes have run away, and are gone over to the Enemy." Two other slaves he owned in Georgia had been taken by the British, while another two had been "carried off by an Overseer of Lord Wm. Campbell," evidently a Loyalist who had taken the slaves with him when he went to join the British.[251] The owner of a plantation in Georgia noted on February 5 that "near 50 Negroes" had run away.[252] Georgian Samuel Stiles wrote that "when Col: Prevoe came to Georgia the first time two of our most Valuable Carpenters named Sampson and Sam went to Mcgerts Scouting party," while a carpenter named Jack, his wife Cumba, and a "Yellow boy" named Swan joined Campbell immediately after the capture of Savannah. Stiles, who had fled to South Carolina, could account for only three of his slaves.[253] Oliver Hart observed in mid-February that since the British had arrived in Georgia, "Negroes in abundance" had joined them, including "some Hundreds" who had escaped from South Carolina. "Negroes are a very precarious Tenure, any where near the Environs of Georgia," Hart stated.[254]

Many Georgia planters sent their slaves to South Carolina to prevent them from falling into British hands.[255] They also carried off Loyalists' slaves when they could. Campbell tried to prevent this. Shortly after taking Savannah, he learned that Whigs were "carrying off a large Body of Negroes to Purisburgh . . . which belonged to the Loyalists of Georgia." Campbell rushed troops to Zubly's Ferry to interrupt the movement, but they arrived too late. Seeing many of the slaves on the South Carolina side of the river, Campbell devised a stratagem to recover some of them. A "Confidential Mulatto" with a musket went to the riverbank "with a Number of Negroes . . . to call out to the Rebels for God's Sake to send over the Boats and save his Master's Slaves from falling into the hands of the King's Troops." When the rebels crossed the river, the mulatto fired his musket as a signal to British troops concealed in the trees. Those troops emerged, seized the boats, and crossed the river; they returned with eighty-three blacks.[256]

Campbell did not explain the reasons for his actions. Undoubtedly he hoped to recover slaves belonging to Georgia Loyalists and at the same time to deprive the Whigs of a valuable resource. However, the fact that he had many blacks with his troops and used them to execute a complex ruse showed that he considered slaves to be important military auxiliaries. Faced with the dilemma of whether to treat slaves as property or as allies, and without clear directions from his superiors, Campbell, like other British officers in the South, tried to do both.

Unrestrained by such ambiguities, many Whigs tried to recover slaves, either by theft or through official channels. In early February a South Carolina militia captain and his men, who were supposed to be guarding Hudson's Ferry, crossed into Georgia during the night, captured "a number of negroes," and then "immediately deserted their post, and returned home with their booty."[257] Benjamin

Lincoln received numerous requests from slave owners who wanted flags of truce so they could go to Savannah and demand that British officials return their human property. Although Lincoln provided the flags, he warned one applicant that previous attempts to recover slaves had "proved fruitless," noting that many people had already given up the effort.[258]

The experience of an unidentified American officer who accompanied two women, Mrs. Heyward and Mrs. Pelot, to Savannah in an effort to regain their slaves provides important insight into why British officers refused to return fugitives. When the trio approached the town by boat, a British patrol vessel met them and took them to Commodore John Henry, commander of the naval squadron in Georgia. The American officer told Henry the purpose of their visit, which provoked the latter into a tirade on the issue of slavery. The women's "idea of recovering Negroes was treated as Chimerical, especially those that deserted" to the British, the officer reported. Henry insisted that such slaves "were free, they were the Kings, he cloathed, fed, & employed them—we cannot answer to return them, there was an idea of Cruelty in delivering of them up to enraged Mistresses who no doubt wd. correct them Severely." The officer attempted to argue, but Henry would not listen; "he honestly confessed they had & wd. receive every thing that deserted from us." Henry added that he detested plundering by Loyalists who seized and sold slaves because it ran counter to "the idea of freedom which they endeavour to propagate among the Slaves." The American officer complained to Lincoln that Henry had been adamant to the point of rudeness.[259]

After getting a glimpse of southern slavery, Loyalists in provincial units from the northern colonies expressed sympathy for the slaves. In a letter to his wife, Lt. Col. Stephen Delancey of New York described his horror at the treatment of slaves and the anger toward slave owners that it inspired. "The Negro's and Negro Women are inhumanly treated, are two-thirds naked, and are very disgusting to the Eye and another Sense," he observed. He could not accept "the great Cruelty made Use of to the poor ignorant Wretches" and in consequence had developed a revulsion toward white masters. "These circumstances of Cruelty to these People render the Persons who exercise it disagreable, nay odious to me," Delancey wrote. "When a Set of People can sit down enjoying all the Luxuries of Life without feeling the least Sensation or Compunction for the Sufferings of those poor Wretches . . . I must conclude them Obdurate, Selfish, and Unfeeling to the greatest Degree imaginable."[260]

The statements of Henry and Delancey indicate that many royal military officers in the South felt genuine compassion for slaves and that efforts to take slaves from the rebels and to prevent the return of blacks who had fled to the British often arose from humanitarian motives. Of course, not all British officers were so generous. One, in a statement that reflected widespread opinion in the army, pronounced several slaves taken in South Carolina to be "all a Prize & my property."[261] This officer arranged to have a Loyalist merchant in Savannah sell the slaves for him and asked the merchant to provide the same service for several other officers.[262]

Slaves may not have been aware that British officers harbored such sentiments; yet, they understood that their chances for freedom were far greater if they reached the king's forces than if they remained with their Whig owners. Thus, the exodus of slaves to the British army continued throughout the winter and spring of 1779. David George, owned by George Galphin, had learned to read and became a preacher at Silver Bluff. This marked him as particularly dangerous to the Whigs, so when British troops marched into the Georgia backcountry, rebel officials imprisoned George and his wife. Campbell's troops liberated George and sent him to Savannah, where his wife supported them by working as a laundress for British officers. While their situation could hardly have been comfortable, George preferred it to slavery and sent his wife and children into hiding when the Americans approached Savannah in the fall of 1779.[263]

Large numbers of South Carolina Whigs living along the lower Savannah River and near the coast abandoned their plantations because of the proximity of the British, taking their slaves with them. Edward Rutledge believed that removing slaves, "in whose Fidelity" the planters could "place very little dependence," was the only way to prevent mass escapes unless rebel authorities could adequately protect the plantations.[264] William Moultrie agreed, noting that "a great number of negroes" living along the Savannah River escaped to the British in Georgia "in spite of our care." Moultrie planned to cross the river, recover some of the runaways, and then attack the British post at Abercorn, which acted as a magnet for both slaves and American deserters. The attack, made in early April, failed and cost the rebels two galleys.[265] The British repaired both vessels and added them to their fleet. Because of a shortage of seamen, Commodore Hyde Parker assigned twelve blacks to each galley with orders that they be considered as "Ordinary Seamen," as were the white crew members.[266] Thus, in an ironic twist, blacks became crewmen aboard vessels originally sent to recapture fugitive slaves.

The flight of so many slaves raised South Carolinians' fears of an insurrection. In Charleston on the night of March 4, "the town was alarmed by the Ringing of the Bells in St Michaels Church Steeple." Several men climbed the steeple, where they "found a Negro man—pretending to be fast asleep, and apparently drunk." Most Charleston residents believed that the bells were "intended as a Signal for the Perpetration of some diabolical Plan—it may be for burning the Town—or Perhaps something worse."[267]

Whenever British forces raided rebel-held territory, they took large numbers of slaves. Although Americans uniformly insisted that the slaves had been stolen, undoubtedly many blacks accompanied the British voluntarily. When British troops landed at Beaufort in February, Gen. Stephen Bull wrote that "they have carried off above 300 negroes belonging to different people."[268] The rebels frequently accused McGirt's Loyalists, a unit that included several blacks, of stealing slaves.[269] In early March a rebel Captain McCoy "lost a number of his negroes" to McGirt's rangers.[270]

Slaves' desire for freedom did not always prove beneficial to the British. During the night of February 11, while at Augusta, Archibald Campbell prepared to cross the Savannah River and attack a rebel post. Before he could begin the operation, "a very great Noise and scattered Firing" erupted at the point where the crossing was to take place. Four escaping slaves had been spotted by rebel sentries and the whole camp aroused. The slaves reached British lines, but Campbell believed he had lost the element of surprise and canceled the intended attack.[271]

To deal with the large number of slaves who had joined the British, voluntarily or otherwise, Campbell appointed five men to serve as commissioners of claims. Campbell gave the commissioners responsibility for managing "all the property, real and personal," of both rebels and absent Loyalists who were not represented by local attorneys. He instructed the commissioners to appoint overseers to supervise the plantations, slaves, and livestock of such persons, as well as to prosecute anyone who stole slaves or livestock from plantations under the commission's management.[272] The commissioners began their work on March 15. They observed "that a number of negroes and other effects, the property of persons in actual rebellion against his Majesty; as also of others now absent from this province, have been seized and detained under various pretences, by persons who have no authority for the Same." The commissioners ordered "all persons having possession of negroes or other effects, as above described," to report to their office, where the commissioners would assume control of the slaves and determine what was to be done with them.[273] Eventually 250 of these slaves were formed into a pioneer corps for the army.[274]

Slaves accused of criminal behavior fell under the jurisdiction of Savannah's temporary civil authority, the board of police. When an overseer, Joseph Weatherly, was murdered in February 1779, the board suspected that two slaves, Charles and Sandy, had committed the crime. The members questioned several other slaves in their investigation, and the slaves' testimony, although often conflicting, strongly indicated that the suspects were indeed guilty. However, the board did not find the "direct proof" it sought and asked Maj. Archibald McArthur, the army commandant in Savannah, if the suspects should be released or confined until they could be brought to trial. There are no records of McArthur's response or the ultimate disposition of the case.[275]

The board also took steps to restore Georgia's plantation economy by assuring that many slaves continued to work as agricultural laborers. During its brief period of operation, the board appointed sixteen overseers for plantations owned by absentee Loyalists. The board granted the overseers wages of forty pounds (fifty-two hundred dollars) per year from public funds.[276]

Some slaves who had fled to the British or had been forcibly taken from Whig masters became dissatisfied and returned to their owners. One such slave, owned by the rebel official John Walton, grew tired "of the hardships of being away from his family & connections." He turned himself in to the Whigs at Augusta, where he gave Gen. John Ashe a fairly detailed account of British troop movements.[277] Between March 1779 and early 1782, when rebel forces surrounded Savannah and made it virtually impossible to leave the town, hundreds of dissatisfied slaves left to seek freedom elsewhere. Many were believed to have gone to East Florida or South Carolina, while others fled to the Georgia backcountry. Some went to or remained in Savannah, where they passed as free. Two slaves who escaped from John Williamson in June 1781 wore military clothing. "*Hercules,* a black fellow, about 22 years old, wears a soldier's uniform, red and buff. *Jacob,* about 19 years old, stout made, wears a Hessian uniform," Williamson stated in an advertisement.[278] He did not explain how the two men obtained their uniforms, although it is most probable that they were issued from army stores. Hercules and Jacob may have served with the army before being restored to their master and then, unwilling to return to their former bondage, escaped.

If some slaves found that the British provided fewer opportunities for freedom and independence than they had expected, most knew that they could expect no change in their condition from the Whigs. When Campbell's troops captured Savannah, John Laurens had immediately used the emergency to renew his proposal to arm slaves for rebel service. In February 1779 Laurens told his father that only Spanish intervention "or the adoption of my black project" could save Georgia, and he asked for the elder Laurens's support for an effort "to transform the timid Slave into a firm defender of Liberty and render him worthy to enjoy it himself."[279] Henry Laurens dropped his earlier opposition in response to the crisis in the South and, in turn, solicited backing from George Washington, assuring the general that "had we Arms for 3000. such black Men as I could select in Carolina I should have no doubt of success in driving the British out of Georgia & subduing East Florida before the end of July."[280]

Alexander Hamilton, who had become friends with John Laurens while both served on Washington's staff, lent his support to the proposal. Writing to John Jay on March 14, Hamilton stated that the plan to arm South Carolina's slaves was "the most rational, that can be adopted, and promises very important advantages." Hamilton worried that if the rebels did not arm slaves, "the enemy probably will; and that the best way to counteract the temptations they will hold out will be to offer them ourselves. An essential part of the plan is to give them freedom with their muskets." As an incentive to adopt this plan, Hamilton suggested that South Carolina whites "may be excused from the draft on condition of furnishing the black battalions." However, Hamilton realized "that this project will have to combat much opposition from prejudice and self-interest."[281]

A week later a congressional committee appointed to examine the situation in the South made its recommendation on the Laurens plan. Observing that lengthy service in the field would deplete the numbers of the South Carolina militia and serve as a "temptation to Negro Slaves to rise in Rebellion or at least to desert to & strengthen the hands of the Enemy," the committee first urged Virginia and North Carolina to send assistance to their southern neighbor. Next, the committee recommended that the governments of Georgia and South Carolina consider arming blacks to serve either in existing Continental battalions or in separate units commanded by white officers. Congress would reimburse the slave owners for the cost of those slaves who enlisted.[282]

On March 29 Congress approved the committee's proposal and recommended to South Carolina and Georgia that those states arm three thousand slaves for their defense. Benjamin Lincoln endorsed the plan, telling Gov. John Rutledge that if South Carolina "would so far comply with the recommendation of Congress as to raise two Battalions of Blacks," the militia could be relieved from their near-constant duty.[283]

Although John Laurens traveled to Charleston to press the assembly to adopt Congress's recommendation, South Carolinians refused to give it serious consideration. Henry Laurens warned his son that "the pride . . . of too many of our fellow Citizens" and "the avarice of others would impel them to revolt from the proposition."[284] One of the handful of representatives who supported enlisting black troops, David Ramsay, noted that the proposal was "received with horror by the planters, who figured to themselves terrible consequences."[285] Christopher Gadsden, the unofficial spokesman for Charleston's artisans, also denounced the measure. "We are much disgusted here at the Congress recommending us to arm our Slaves, it was received with great resentment, as a very dangerous and impolitic Step," he wrote.[286]

Despite John Laurens's strenuous efforts to gain support, the assembly rejected the plan by an overwhelming margin when it was finally brought to a vote. Charles Cotesworth Pinckney suggested an alternative: offering slaves, along with land and cattle, as a bounty to British and Hessian officers to induce them to desert to the rebels. Lincoln ignored the idea.[287] "Prejudice and private interest will be antagonists too powerful for public spirit," Hamilton consoled Laurens. Hamilton declared that a lack of virtue in the southern states "has fitted their inhabitants for the chain, and . . . the only condition they sincerely desire is that it may be a golden one."[288]

Had South Carolinians chosen to arm slaves when Congress first recommended doing so, they might have been in a better position to defend their state when Prevost's army invaded at the end of April. Instead, the British received another large influx of fugitive slaves as they marched to Charleston, while other slaves fled to Whig-controlled areas. Many of Edward Telfair's slaves escaped when the British entered South Carolina, some of them going to Dorchester and others to Charleston. They were taken up by other Whigs, who refused to return them until Lincoln ordered it. On May 8 Capt. James Moncrief and a party of British cavalry came upon several slaves whom the rebels had set to work felling trees to delay the British. With no apparent difficulty, Moncrief immediately employed them to undo the destruction.[289]

As the British army advanced, South Carolinians struggled to maintain control over their slaves. Eliza Lucas Pinckney told her son that the British had plundered and burned his house and that his slaves were gone. She did not know "whether they went voluntarily with the Enemy or were taken by force." The British visited another Pinckney plantation, Belmont, "and distroyed every thing in the house but took none of the Negroes." Mrs. Pinckney and a neighbor, who also had an estate in the Belmont area, had sent slave emissaries there with instructions that all the slaves should join their masters at Santee, but none came. The Pinckneys had more slaves at Beach Hill and ordered them to remain there, as the place was deemed safe from the British. Eliza Pinckney had doubts, however. "I know not what to do in regard to the Beach Hill and Belmont Negroes unless I could hire a white man to go and fetch them away," she wrote in frustration, "or whether it would be best to remove them without if they chuse to come away for they all do now what they please every where." She added that masters on other plantations in the path of the British had ordered their slaves to leave and met outright refusal. Even if her slaves were not seized by the British, she conceded that they might "choose to go to them, and in that case I fear we should not be able to prevent it."[290]

Hoping to save his family and slaves from Prevost's troops, Thomas Tudor Tucker sent his sister, in company with another family, into the state's interior. They had not traveled far when "the Negroes grew insolent & deserted them." Of the slaves who had remained at home with him, Tucker lost "one valuable Fellow who thought proper to look out for a new Master."[291] The presence of the king's army gave slaves unprecedented control over their own destiny. Masters could do little to enforce obedience, for any attempt at coercion was likely to send an angry slave fleeing to the British.

American officers shared the planters' concern over the loss of their slaves. Moultrie, who was attempting to delay Prevost's advance, informed Lincoln that the British had several vessels collecting slaves along the rivers. He urged his commander to "over take them and prevent them carrying away the negroes."[292] Whig officers also diverted militia who might otherwise have opposed the British to keep slaves in check. One unit ranged "to Willtown, Pon Pon, and other places; where they heard the negroes were very unruly, and doing great mischief . . . in order to quell them," Eliza Wilkinson wrote. She worried about her family's slaves; a Loyalist riding ahead of Daniel McGirt's rangers told her that McGirt would take the slaves from their plantation when he arrived. Some of McGirt's troops reached Wilkinson's plantation on June 3. Although they did not carry off any slaves, the detachment included "several armed negroes . . . who threatened and abused us greatly," she complained.[293] The entire slavery-based social order appeared to be crumbling.

In an effort to curb the flight of slaves and Loyalists to the British, John Rutledge ordered some of them to be executed. According to the Loyalist John
Wells, in 1779 the governor had taken "the lives of his fellow creatures without
a trial or hearing, as their complexions were a few shades darker than his own."[294]
This was probably the same incident that rebel soldier James Fergus described in
his journal. On May 12 Fergus recorded that "four men, two white and a mulatto
and Negro, were taken outside the lines and brought in supposed to be deserting to the enemy. The governor, coming by at the time, was asked what should
be done with them. He said, 'Hang them up to the beam of the gate,' by which
they were standing. This was immediately done."[295]

Not all slaves aided the British, however. The first news of Prevost's invasion
to reach the rebels was brought by slaves who remained loyal to their Whig
masters.[296] A "sensible faithfull Negro" provided Moultrie with a detailed
description of the British army's encampment near Charleston on May 15.[297]
The efforts of one runaway slave to aid the British were undone by another slave
in an unusual incident that occurred on May 25. Learning from "a Negroe
wench who went to them" that Whig officer Morton Wilkinson was nearby
with thirty troops, British officers sent a detachment of sixty men to surprise the
rebels. When the British reached the house of a Mrs. Ladson, two miles from
Wilkinson's, one of the Ladson slaves told them that they were four miles from
their destination and that Wilkinson and his soldiers had gone to Charleston.
The false report deceived the British, who "through out great threats against the
Wench." The slave then informed Wilkinson of his encounter with Prevost's
troops. Even though the slave had saved him from death or capture, Wilkinson
concluded from this affair that "our domesticks are so treacherous" that the
British "never want for information."[298]

When Prevost withdrew from the vicinity of Charleston, large numbers of
slaves followed his army, but many fell behind the retreating troops and were
retaken by the Whigs. "About three hundred negroes have been taken from the
enemy," Lincoln wrote on May 17. He ordered the quartermaster general to com-
pile a list of the slaves' names and owners so that their masters could reclaim
them.[299] An American officer posted on the Ashepoo River reported to Lincoln on
June 25 that British boats were "carrying Negroes and other plunder to Georgia."[300] Another Whig, who observed the passage of a British column the same
day, noted that "Large droves of Negroes march by."[301] Other blacks remained in
South Carolina with Loyalist detachments. After a skirmish, American troops
captured "four whites and three blacks" near Eliza Wilkinson's plantation. Another
man, described by Wilkinson as "one of the enemy's Negroes," was caught trying
to elude rebel guards and was beaten so badly that Wilkinson "could not help
shedding tears." Sickened by the cruelty, she intervened to halt the beating. She
later permitted the man to escape, fearing that if British troops returned and
"should find the Negro in such a bloody condition, they would use us very ill."[302]

After Prevost returned to Georgia, both sides resumed raiding and seized slaves from one another at every opportunity. In July a party of rebel militia skirmished with a British detachment and recaptured about fifty slaves.[303] When the British evacuated Beaufort in September, rebel officer John Barnwell rushed troops to Port Royal Island and "savd about two hundred slaves, whom I have sent of to Return to their respective Owners."[304] Whig militia also crossed the Savannah River to steal slaves from Georgia. In early August, Lincoln learned that a group of militiamen had plundered slaves there and were en route to Augusta with their booty. The general criticized the act as "a mode of conduct unjust, impolitic, and if not corrected, will destroy every idea of military discipline." Lincoln asked Gen. Lachlan McIntosh to find the slaves and send them to the quartermaster general "to be disposed of." The officers who had led the raid, Lincoln asserted, were "apeing the enemy in a practice which we reprobate in the strongest terms." At least the British, Lincoln conceded, had made amends "by returning the Slaves belonging to the estates of deceased persons, to widows, minors and Orphans." He feared that rebel plundering might jeopardize this arrangement.[305]

The number of slaves stolen by the rebels was small compared to the thousands more removed from South Carolina by Prevost's army and who continued to flee to the British. This presented a serious problem for Governor Wright. Having resumed his office, Wright's first inclination was to insure that Loyalist slave owners retain control of their bondspeople. Before leaving England, he and other exiles had asked Germain to order British naval officers not to transport out of Georgia slaves who fled to their ships. They asked the minister to require the navy to turn over the slaves to their owners' attorneys. The Loyalists feared that without such a policy, they would never be able to recover fugitive slaves.[306] Wright apparently failed to understand the slaves' desire for freedom. After returning to Georgia, he noted with pride that "many of his Negroes . . . on their hearing of the Province being retaken and of his Return, made their Escape from the Persons who had bought them, and went back to him."[307] Some indeed may have returned because of their attachment to Wright, but it is probable that others came seeking freedom rather than a resumption of their bondage.

In July 1779 the merchants James Graham and Basil Cowper forced Wright and the council to reconsider the slaves' situation when they submitted a petition requesting permission to use slaves as payment for debts owed to Britons. The petitioners noted that "great Numbers of Negroe Slaves have come in of themselves, and are brought into this Province from So Carolina by his Majesty's Army, Indians and others." These slaves had been formerly owned by debtors of the petitioners and other British merchants and, in Graham's and Cowper's opinion, constituted "the only resource left for securing part of their just debts." Therefore, the petitioners asked that "such property may be delivered up or secured for the payment of British debts."[308]

After extensive deliberation, the governor and the council made what they believed to be the best possible decision, given the complexity of the situation. They agreed that the constant influx of slaves into the town "seems to be a growing Evil" that required prompt action, but the cases of individual slaves were so different that no single solution could apply. Slaves belonging to Georgia Loyalists or to widows and orphans would be restored to their owners, the council decided, while those owned by loyal South Carolinians would be held in trust for them. Slaves taken by the army fell outside the bounds of civil authority, and the council left their disposition to General Prevost. Slaves who had fled from rebel masters would be supervised by commissioners, whom the council would appoint, until such time as appropriate laws might be passed to clarify their situation. All slaves not returned to Loyalist owners would be hired out or employed on public works projects. In addition, a building would be designated for the detention of "all such Negroes as may prove unruly or Abscond."[309]

The problem of Indians claiming slaves proved even more difficult to solve. Wright told the council that "he considers the Indians being thus possest of Negroes is attended with very serious and dangerous Consequences." The governor had met with Creek leaders and offered to purchase the slaves, but the Indians refused to sell, asserting that Prevost had promised that they could keep any plunder they took during the invasion of South Carolina. Seeing British troops "Seize upon all the Negroes they Could get," the Indians stated that they only "did the same" and planned to bring the slaves back to their nation. Wright and the council agreed that they had no authority to interfere with the Creeks in this regard.[310]

These decisions were compromises designed to accommodate the slaves to some extent without alienating either Loyalist slave owners or Indian allies. They also solved the practical problem of how to obtain some services from the runaways, who had to be clothed and fed at government expense. After receiving Wright's reports, Germain approved of his handling of the situation. Germain did, however, remind the governor to treat fugitive slaves well in order to encourage others to take refuge with the British.[311]

Slaves soon proved their value to the British when a French fleet and army arrived in Georgia in September. The enemy's unexpected appearance forced Prevost to make every exertion to put Savannah in a defensible condition. He brought in slaves from plantations outside the town to work alongside other blacks attached to the army and British troops; the fortifications were completed with a swiftness that astonished French officers.[312]

Benjamin Lincoln brought his army to join the French in an attack on Savannah, and many of the Americans saw the operations in Georgia as an opportunity to recover fugitive slaves. One Whig officer reported that he had retaken seven of his slaves since arriving in Georgia and hoped to find more when Savannah was captured.[313] South Carolina officials tried to convince the French to turn over a former slave named Sampson, who had been taken prisoner when French warships captured a Royal Navy vessel off the Georgia coast. After learning of the seizure, Charleston printer Peter Timothy wrote Lincoln on September 25 that "there was on board a Negro who (tho' I am averse to sanguinary Punishments) it would, in my Opinion, be highly exemplary to hang up at a Yard-Arm." Timothy declared that Sampson, a former harbor pilot, had "voluntarily remained with the Enemy, doing them many essential Services to the Injury of the States." These included piloting Sir Peter Parker's fleet into Charleston harbor in 1776, piloting Archibald Campbell's expedition to Savannah, and having piloted British naval vessels that had raided rebel shipping along the southern coast. Timothy insisted that Sampson's "Treachery and Ingratitude merit Punishment, and there are others to whom he should be made an Example of Terror."[314] John Rutledge described Sampson as "very useful" to the enemy, "& hurtful to Us." The governor asked Lincoln "to get this Fellow secured, & sent hither, in safe Custody, that he may receive the Punishment due to his Crimes."[315] Lincoln did not act on the matter, despite further prodding from Rutledge. The general had already been at odds with Estaing and probably wished to avoid provoking another dispute.[316]

While the rebels plotted to recapture and punish slaves, Prevost decided to arm some of the blacks in Savannah to strengthen his vastly outnumbered army. When Loyalist William Hanscomb volunteered his services, Prevost ordered him to raise a company of black pioneers. These men were later armed to defend the town.[317] Rev. John Zubly noted that "during the siege 8, or more of my slaves were constantly in arms."[318] One black soldier, Scipio Handley, was a former South Carolina slave who, fearing that his life was endangered by his support for the British, had fled Charleston in 1775 with Lord William Campbell. After Savannah was retaken, Handley voluntarily went to Georgia from Barbados; when the French and rebels arrived in September, he vowed to do all he could to help defend Savannah, for he expected no mercy if he fell into the rebels' hands. During the siege, Handley "was Employed at the Armoury Shop, Running grape shot and Carrying them out to the Redoubts and Batteries." While engaged in this duty he was severely wounded by a musket ball in the leg.[319]

An estimated two hundred armed blacks participated in Savannah's defense; some of them, along with the Cherokees, guarded Hutchinson's Island, where many people went to escape the bombardment. Prevost's decision to arm slaves provoked protests from some Georgians who thought the step "unjustified under any circumstances." A writer in the *Royal Georgia Gazette* excused Prevost's actions as a response to the presence of black troops with the French army, and after the siege another writer conceded that the black soldiers had generally behaved well.[320]

Blacks also contributed to the defense in other ways. Two slaves reached Savannah on September 21 with news that Lincoln's troops had united with the French and that the combined army was very strong. The Loyalist Elizabeth Lichtenstein Johnston recalled that when shells fell in the town's streets, black children would rush to smother the fuses with sand and then bring the shells, along with any solid shot they could find, to the British artillerists, who were short of ammunition. For this hazardous service, the children received seven-pence for every cannonball and shell they turned in.[321]

The most important service blacks provided was guiding reinforcements to Savannah, without which Prevost could not have withstood the siege. Prevost had left Lt. Col. John Maitland of the 71st Regiment with about eight hundred troops at Beaufort when the main British army withdrew from South Carolina. Although the Americans captured a messenger sent to summon Maitland to Prevost's assistance, Maitland learned of the situation and marched to Savannah. The French and Americans were aware that Maitland might make such a move, so Estaing ordered French warships to guard the Savannah River and prevent Maitland's detachment from crossing. However, twenty miles from the town, when it seemed to Maitland that a crossing was impossible, the British encountered several black fishermen who told them of a passage through the creeks and swamps. This enabled the troops to elude the French blockade and safely reach Savannah.[322]

According to a French account, Maitland brought many blacks to Savannah along with the British soldiers. One of Maitland's officers, Francis Rush Clark, stated that when the British crossed the Savannah River, they left their sick troops, women, and black baggage handlers on the South Carolina side under the protection of British naval vessels. Clark did not indicate whether these were the only blacks with Maitland's force or if there were others who accompanied the troops across the river.[323]

Those left on the north side of the Savannah River were fortunate because the heavy French and American bombardment killed and wounded dozens of people in the town, the majority of whom were blacks.[324] Both races shared the struggle to survive the artillery fire. Anthony Stokes, a Mrs. Cooper, and several African Americans waited out one night's cannonade in a cellar so packed with rum and supplies that Stokes "could hardly creep in." On a subsequent night, a shell set fire to the house where Stokes had taken up residence. He and two of his slaves escaped, but eight other slaves perished. Stokes then moved to a more distant house, which was "crowded, both inside and out, with a number of whites and negroes."[325]

The town's defenders and inhabitants withstood the bombardment and repulsed a Franco-American assault on the town, after which the attackers began a withdrawal. Prevost then sent some black troops outside the lines to harass the enemy. On October 16 a British naval officer observed "our armed negroes skirmishing with the Rebels the whole afternoon."[326] This action occurred "on Mr. McGillivray's plantation," where the blacks and Whigs fought for control of several buildings. The buildings changed hands several times until a shortage of ammunition "obliged the blacks to retreat in the evening with the loss of one killed and three or four wounded, the enemy's loss is not known," another Briton reported.[327] Two days later the naval officer wrote that "the armed negroes brought in two Rebel Dragoons and eight horses, and killed two rebels who were in a foraging party."[328]

French black troops and American slaves took advantage of the confusion following the attack on Savannah to reach the British. During Estaing's withdrawal, his black soldiers became insubordinate and began deserting to the British, forcing officers to station guards around their camp. In November, Philip Porcher, a South Carolina merchant and planter, confirmed that he lost 157 of his own slaves, along with 7 belonging to other masters, to the British.[329]

Once the French and Americans had departed, many white Georgians decided that it was unwise to keep black troops under arms. On October 23 eighteen residents of Savannah and Christ Church Parish complained to the council that "a Number of Slaves appear in Arms and behave with Great Insolence, Joined by some white persons." The signers warned of "the dreadful Evils that must arise, if such Proceedings are not checked" and asked that "all Slaves may be immediately disarmed" and their white companions forbidden to trouble anyone. The council referred the matter to General Prevost.[330] In addition, several prominent Loyalists wrote to Germain urging him not to adopt a policy of arming slaves to fight the rebels. They had already lost many slaves and feared that if the British formed black military units, large numbers of slaves would leave their plantations in hopes of earning their freedom by serving in the army.[331]

Prevost ignored the complaints and kept armed blacks in the field. Whig colonel Francis Marion learned in December that "several small parties of Negroes" were crossing the Savannah River and "pillaging" on the South Carolina side. He tried to intercept them with mounted patrols but failed to catch anyone.[332] At the end of January 1780 a rebel officer sent to procure information on British forces in Georgia reported that "some Armed Negroes & 200 Indians was incampt before Savanna." The British garrison, the officer added, "had no fresh provisions but what the Negroes plunder" from South Carolina.[333] Rebel officer Daniel Horry reported in mid-February 1780 that in addition to the black raiding parties, the garrison of Savannah included "four hundred Negroes Armed."[334] Prevost also utilized "Black Pioneer Companies" to continue strengthening Savannah's defenses after the siege.[335]

Like Prevost, officials in the Floridas also made increasing use of armed blacks in 1779. An account of the regulars and militia available to defend East Florida that year indicated that more than one-seventh of the troops were black.[336] Governor Tonyn, however, found that the fourfold increase in the province's black population since the start of the war presented great difficulties. Loyalist slave owners demanded the return of their slaves, and Tonyn sought Germain's advice as to how to resolve the situation.[337]

In West Florida blacks began to assume a military role as the Spanish threat increased. Shortly after Gen. John Campbell assumed command in the province, he asked Clinton to send him "a company of Negroes" to strengthen his force.[338] Apparently he was referring to the pioneer units at New York. When Spain declared war on Britain, Adam Chrystie armed and uniformed his own unit of twenty-two blacks to help defend the province.[339] After learning of the Spanish declaration in early September, Campbell told Lt. Col. Alexander Dickson that he had authorized an officer to join Dickson at Baton Rouge "with as many men as he can collect—/Regular Inhabitants Indians and even Negroes/" to attack the Spanish.[340] Campbell clearly intended to utilize every available man, regardless of race, against the Spaniards. Galvez's offensive forestalled Campbell's planned maneuver, but Dickson did employ armed blacks in his unsuccessful defense of Baton Rouge.[341]

The first stage of Britain's southern campaign had been generally successful. Many Loyalists had come forward to support the British, although the defeat of Boyd's party at Kettle Creek and the abandonment of those who had declared their allegiance to the king at Augusta, leaving them vulnerable to Whig retribution, prevented many Loyalists from openly committing to the British. The Indians had disappointed British officials by providing far less support than expected; yet, despite Spanish tampering, most of the nations remained committed to their alliance with the king. Perhaps the greatest cause for optimism had been the number of slaves who had come to the British and the many contributions they had made of information, labor, and military service. Their assistance augured well for future operations, had either Germain or Clinton been bold enough to arm slaves in large numbers.

The siege of Savannah had clearly demonstrated the potential of Loyalists, Indians, and blacks working in cooperation with British troops. Together, these disparate allies had withstood a vastly superior force and preserved Georgia as a base for the next phase of the campaign. Their victory inspired Britons and Loyalists alike; Gen. Charles Grey, back in England after serving in the northern campaigns, wrote that "it is the first time I have seen day light in this business."[342] The campaign indicated that Britain's supporters in the South, if employed together and in a coordinated manner, might provide the decisive force needed to regain control of the region. Unfortunately for their cause, British officials in London, New York, and Georgia all celebrated the victory but overlooked the significance of how it had been won.

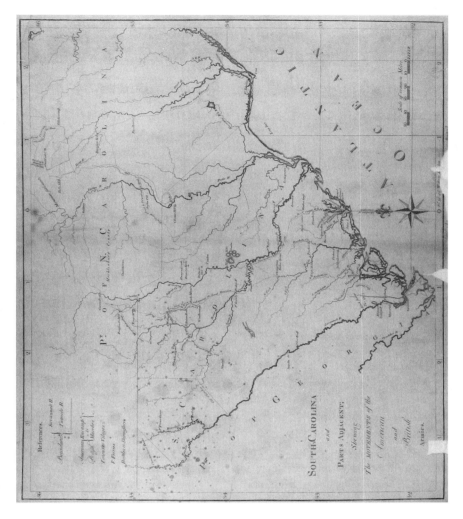

Map published in Trenton, N.J., 1785.
Courtesy of South Caroliniana Library,
University of South Carolina, Columbia

FIVE

The Reconquest of South Carolina

As soon as Henry Clinton received word that Savannah remained in British hands and Estaing's fleet had left the American coast, he immediately launched the long-awaited second phase of the southern campaign, the attack on Charleston. Ever since Archibald Campbell's expedition had taken Savannah, Germain had pressed Clinton to move against South Carolina. Prevost's raid to the gates of Charleston had increased Germain's confidence that Clinton could easily take the town. "The feeble Resistance Major Genl. Prevost met with in his March and Retreat through so great a part of South Carolina is an indubitable proof of the Indisposition of the Inhabitants to support the Rebel Government," he told the general.[1]

Clinton had intended to dispatch troops to attack South Carolina in early October 1779, believing that this would give him the winter and spring to follow up on any victory he might win. A rumored French attack on Jamaica, however, forced Clinton to postpone his plan, and the French and American attack on Savannah caused another delay. In late December, Clinton sailed at last from New York with about nine thousand troops. Bad weather scattered the fleet, and the first vessels did not reach Savannah until the end of January 1780. British troops landed in South Carolina in mid-February, advancing cautiously toward Charleston, which they surrounded and captured on May 12 after a lengthy siege. At a cost of fewer than three hundred casualties, Clinton had captured the most important town in the South along with over five thousand American soldiers.[2]

Southern Whigs had been aware that South Carolina was the next British objective and realized that its loss might prove disastrous. As early as February 1779 John Rutledge warned Benjamin Lincoln that all accounts indicated that "this Country will be the Seat of War, and the Enemy, from the disaffection of our People . . . expect a Conquest."[3] A congressional committee informed Lincoln that if the British occupied South Carolina, they would "act on a very different plan from what they formerly have; i.e. to settle the Country as they Conquer it, by securing all those whom they may suppose dangerous and to give the Noted Tories a Considerable command."[4] David Ramsay noted that Charleston "binds three States to the authority of Congress. If the enemy possess themselves of this town, there will be no living for honest whigs to the southward of the Santee."[5]

British hopes and Whig fears appeared to be realized after Charleston's surrender. As British columns advanced into the backcountry without opposition, thousands of South Carolinians swore allegiance to George III. Clinton took steps to organize the Loyalists into a militia before leaving the province in early June, and the new commander in the South, Gen. Charles, Earl Cornwallis, prepared to advance into North Carolina. Meanwhile, Congress appointed Gen. Horatio Gates, the hero of Saratoga, to take command of American forces in the southern department. Gates promptly chose to assume the offensive and marched his army into South Carolina, where Cornwallis inflicted a crushing defeat on the rebels at Camden on August 16.[6] Although Gates's campaign ended in disaster, his approach invigorated the demoralized Whigs, who repudiated their oaths to Britain and rallied to partisan leaders Thomas Sumter and Francis Marion. These Whig bands resorted to their usual tactic of attacking Loyalists, complicating British efforts to organize their supporters and establish firm control in both Georgia and South Carolina.

Deciding that the occupation of North Carolina would be the best way to secure South Carolina, Cornwallis advanced to Charlotte in September. British major Patrick Ferguson, inspector general of the loyal militia, marched into western North Carolina to protect Cornwallis's flank. On October 7 the Whigs attacked Ferguson at King's Mountain, killing or capturing his entire force. Ferguson's death in the battle, along with the deaths of so many Loyalists and the rebels' brutal treatment of the prisoners, deprived the Loyalists of a respected leader and shattered their morale. While many Loyalists continued to assist the British, violent Whig persecution, combined with Cornwallis's neglect, seriously undermined their subsequent effectiveness.

Cornwallis also chose not to use Indians, depriving himself of another valuable source of support, although the Creeks, Choctaws, and Cherokees all contributed to the defense of British posts in Georgia and West Florida. Thousands of slaves who came to the British were employed in various capacities; yet, once again Cornwallis devised no policy to take full advantage of their assistance. The ministry's strategy had called for a combined effort of British troops and Loyalists, supported directly by Indians and indirectly by slaves, to subdue the rebels. However, Cornwallis, determined to win in the South with British regulars alone, ignored the plan, thus depriving himself of the support on which success had been predicated.

Mobilizing the Loyalists

Clinton did not call on the Loyalists for aid when his army landed in South Carolina. He did not want to "expose them to the malevolence of their enemies before I was fully certain of success," he wrote.[7] Therefore, he "avoided . . . every measure which might excite the loyal inhabitants to rise in favour of government, and thus bring danger and trouble upon themselves, at a time when the King's army, being employed in the reduction of Charles town, could not assist or second their struggles."[8]

Nevertheless many Americans joined regular British units during and after the operations against Charleston. Some of these recruits were rebel deserters; others were Loyalists. On March 27 the 71st Regiment requested ammunition for ten men who had "Joind from the Rebels since our Last Return"; two more rebel deserters enlisted by April 28. Another man joined the 71st by May 9, and three others joined the 42nd Regiment; records do not indicate whether these were rebel deserters or Loyalist volunteers. Seven Loyalists, all of whom were without muskets, enlisted in the South Carolina Royalists on June 6.[9] Some of these men had been in hiding for several years to escape Whig persecution. Because the records do not cover all of the units in South Carolina at the time and the information contained in them is limited, it is impossible to know how many men the regular regiments enlisted. For example, on May 23 and June 21 officers requested a total of eighty-four muskets for the Royal North Carolina Volunteers, a unit composed of loyal refugees from that province. However, there is no mention of whether these were arms for new recruits or replacement weapons for the veterans.[10] It is likely that some of the arms were replacements and others were for recruits. Incomplete as they are, the records show a small but significant number of American enlistments in both British and provincial units in South Carolina.

Other South Carolinians returned to their allegiance when they encountered Clinton's advancing army. Twenty-five inhabitants of Edisto Island came aboard a British vessel to ask for protection on February 14; they were promptly dispatched to collect horses for the army. Clinton, however, soon announced that he did not wish to grant protections unless the applicants demonstrated genuine proof of their loyalty.[11]

Many Loyalists were eager to take up arms with the British regardless of Clinton's hesitance. Thomas Harvy and Moses Eastan wrote to Clinton on March 18 on behalf of loyal South Carolinians who were "willing and Ready to Ade and asist In the Behalf of his magistye to Defeet the Reabls." Whig cavalry had been sent to arrest Harvy, Eastan, and their comrades and to confine them in Charleston, but the Loyalists escaped and hid in the woods. They asked for troops to assist them, promising that soon they would require only ammunition to be able to protect themselves.[12]

In Ninety Six district a Colonel Moore assembled 150 men and attacked a log house where the Whigs kept a supply of ammunition, but the Loyalists were driven off.[13] William Moultrie, learning of another uprising in Colleton district, ordered the militia there "to disperse the disaffected that are in Arms."[14] The Whig commander, Col. William Skirving, failed to do so because three of his four companies joined the Loyalists.[15] From Camden, Joseph Kershaw warned Lincoln that the Loyalists there were gathering strength. "We are much threatned here by the disaffected," he reported.[16] A representative from North Carolina arrived at the British lines on April 19 and informed the officers that many of the inhabitants were "dissatisfied with the oppression of the rebels." He offered the assistance of "several thousand armed men."[17]

Loyalists gave passive support to the British by refusing to turn out when Whig officials summoned the militia, while others took a more active role in procuring intelligence. Hessian captain Johann Ewald obtained information about rebel positions on March 29 from a Loyalist whose son was serving in Lincoln's army. Asked to explain this paradox, the man told Ewald that the Whigs had forced his son to enlist by threatening the family with banishment and the confiscation of their property. Elias Ball, a Loyalist who had accompanied a British foraging party and managed to avoid capture when Whig cavalry surprised the detachment on May 5, rushed to inform Lt. Col. Banastre Tarleton of the incident. Ball told Tarleton that the rebels had gone to Lenud's Ferry, where the British officer overtook them with his dragoons. Tarleton's attack caught the Whigs by surprise, inflicted over one hundred casualties, and recovered the seventeen British prisoners.[18]

Although initial indications of Loyalist support augured well for British prospects in both South and North Carolina, the situation in Georgia showed that Loyalists remained vulnerable to rebel harassment without troops to assist them. Clinton had planned to have a detachment from his army march from Savannah into the backcountry to create a diversion while the main British force attacked Charleston, but he later ordered the troops to Charleston to assist in the siege. Governor Wright warned the general that the change in plan would leave Georgia vulnerable to rebel incursions, and within a few weeks this prediction proved correct.[19] "I have received petitions from the very much distressed and loyal inhabitants who have been drove from their settlements in St. George's Parish and downwards to St. Phillips . . . for assistance & protection" as the result of Whig raids, the governor informed Clinton on April 6. Wright appealed to Clinton for aid, warning that Georgia "will be broke up and totally ruined if something is not speedily done."[20]

Clinton remained focused on Charleston. With the town's surrender imminent, he decided that the time was right to call South Carolina Loyalists to action. On May 3 James Simpson, acting as Clinton's secretary, relayed the general's orders to Richard Pearis and other Loyalists with the army to go "amongst the Inhabitants of the interior parts of the province in whose loyalty . . . there is much reason to confide," inform them of the army's plans, and summon them to its assistance. The emissaries were to give the Loyalists "the Strongest Assurances of Effectual Countenance, Protection and Support"; inform them that British regulars would soon march into the backcountry, and have the Loyalists gather arms and provisions so that they would be ready to join the troops when the latter arrived. Once they had gathered sufficient strength, the Loyalists were also to seize prominent Whigs. Should rebel forces block their route of march to join the British troops, the Loyalists were to fight their way through such opposition, but they were not to undertake any other aggressive action until they had united with the army and been properly organized.[21]

Charleston surrendered shortly after the emissaries left for the backcountry. In the aftermath of victory, events demonstrated that British expectations of Loyalist support in South Carolina had been sound. Two hundred inhabitants of Charleston signed a congratulatory address to Clinton and Adm. Marriot Arbuthnot.[22] Clinton issued a handbill and proclamation to the inhabitants, "well calculated to induce them to return to their allegiance."[23] In the former, the commander in chief asked for "the helping hand of every man . . . to re-establish peace and good government." Clinton promised in return "to avoid giving them any trouble but what is necessary to secure them peace, liberty, and prosperity."[24] On May 22 Clinton sought to assure the Loyalists that he would protect them; he threatened punishment for anyone who continued to oppose British authority or who harassed the Loyalists. Noting that generous offers of pardon and protection had been made to the rebels, Clinton warned that any "attempt to hinder or intimidate, the King's faithful and loyal subjects" would "be treated with that severity so criminal and hardened an obstinacy will deserve" and that the offenders' property would be confiscated. The general again promised Loyalists that the army would guarantee their security.[25] A subsequent proclamation, issued jointly by Clinton and Arbuthnot on June 1, offered former rebels "a full and free pardon . . . for the treasonable offences" they had committed, except the murder of Loyalists.[26] Clinton and Arbuthnot also pledged that henceforth South Carolinians were to be taxed only by their own assembly, not by Parliament, thereby removing the original cause of the dispute with Britain.[27]

The combined effect of the victory at Charleston and the proclamations produced immediate results. "A general revolution of sentiment seemed to take place, and the cause of Great Britain appeared to triumph over that of the American Congress," Tarleton wrote.[28] Only two days after the surrender, a German soldier with Clinton's army stated that "from what we learn of the disposition of the Inhabitants if the war is prosecuted with vigor in these Southern Colonies Rebellion will suffer a severe Shock in the Course of this Summer."[29] On May 24 twenty-five Loyalists, armed and mounted, arrived in Charleston after a ride of one hundred miles from the Orangeburg district to request ammunition "to secure themselves against the rebels' depredations."[30] They told Clinton that the district contained "a great many more friends to government . . . ready to shew their loyalty by their services against the Rebels by whom they have been persecuted."[31] Others followed them; by May 25 Clinton noted that fifteen hundred armed men had come in to offer their assistance. In addition, some of the most prominent leaders of the rebellion had submitted; these included former governor Rawlins Lowndes, Charles Pinckney, Henry Middleton, and Daniel Horry.[32] "From every Information I receive, and Numbers of the most violent Rebels hourly coming in to offer their Services, I have the strongest Reason to believe the general Disposition of the People to be not only friendly to Government, but forward to take up Arms in its Support," Clinton wrote to Cornwallis on May 29.[33] Several days later Clinton made a similar report to Germain. "With the greatest pleasure," Clinton announced, he was able to say that "the inhabitants from every quarter repair to . . . this garrison to declare their allegiance to the King, and to offer their services, in arms, in support of his government." Those who came in often "brought prisoners, their former oppressors or leaders; and I may venture to assert that there are few men in South Carolina, who are not either our prisoners, or in arms with us."[34]

Confirmation of this opinion came from many other sources. "Since Charleston has been in our possession, more than 2,000 men have come from the country who have voluntarily offered their services to His Britannic Majesty," Hessian major Wilhelm von Wilmowsky wrote on June 4.[35] Some of these people were from the backcountry, but almost 1,600 lowcountry inhabitants took the British oath in the immediate aftermath of Charleston's surrender. In addition, between June 17, 1780, and July 31, 1781, a total of 1,866 people appeared before Crown officials in Charleston to swear allegiance to Great Britain.[36]

James Simpson, who at Clinton's request had made inquiries to determine the strength of loyalism in Charleston, at first provided a more cautious assessment. "Loyalists who have always adhered to the King's Government are not so numerous as I expected," Simpson reported. However, he did find many Loyalists along with numerous Whigs who had decided to switch their allegiance. Simpson warned Clinton that the Loyalists "are clamorous for retributive Justice" and that this would create disruption in the province "until those People whose persecuting spirit hath caused such calamities to their fellow subjects shall receive the punishment their Iniquities deserve." Although the situation in town was not as good as Simpson had hoped, he believed that once British authority had been reestablished, most people would support it.[37] By July 1 Simpson believed that this prediction had been confirmed. Some zealous Charleston Loyalists organized militia companies and arrested between 100 and 150 town residents for alleged parole violations.[38]

Reports from the backcountry were equally encouraging. On May 30 Maj. John André, Clinton's aide, told Patrick Ferguson that there was "no reason to doubt that the inhabitants" of the backcountry "are very well disposed to take an active Part" in support of the British.[39] Lt. Col. Nisbet Balfour, commanding a British column marching from Charleston to Ninety Six, sent Cornwallis favorable reports of the loyalty of the people he encountered, particularly in the Orangeburg district, where 294 Loyalists organized themselves into an association for defense.[40] "As to the Militia arming to defend the country, I have not the smallest doubt of it," Balfour declared.[41] From Friday's Ferry on the Congaree River, Alexander Innes, now commanding the South Carolina Royalists, informed Cornwallis that "the general disposition of the Country" was "as favourable as Your Lordship can wish." Innes had to intervene to prevent some Loyalists from avenging themselves against Whigs who had viciously persecuted them in the past.[42]

When he learned of Charleston's surrender, David Fanning abandoned his neutrality and joined Robert Cunningham in organizing a group of backcountry Loyalists. Fanning traveled one hundred miles through the region, distributing Clinton's proclamations to the inhabitants with considerable effect. "We now found ourselves growing strong, and numbers flocking daily to us," he wrote. Fanning and Cunningham took their party to Whitehall, the home of Gen. Andrew Williamson, where they found that the Whig leader and his militiamen had submitted to a small party under Richard Pearis. The Loyalists occupied the fort there, taking fourteen swivel guns and the garrison's arms.[43] Joseph Robinson of the South Carolina Royalists also returned to the backcountry to announce that relief was finally at hand. He praised his former friends and neighbors for persevering in their loyalism "notwithstanding all the Vicissitudes, all the exertions of Cruelty, and all the institutions jesuitically calculated to alienate the minds of the people from their Duty to their Sovereign."[44]

Robert Gray, a Loyalist from the Cheraw district, wrote that after the British had occupied posts in the interior of South Carolina, the "conquest of the Province was complete." He estimated that Loyalists were "in a number about one third of the whole" in the province but comprised half of the population in Ninety Six district, while the people of Orangeburg district were "almost unanimous" in their loyalty and "readily took up arms to maintain the British government." Many Whigs took the British oath, some enrolling in the militia, "because they believed the war to be at an end in the Southern provinces & partly to ingratiate themselves with the conquerors, they also fondly hoped that they would enjoy a respite from the Calamities of war."[45]

"Appearances in this Province are certainly very favourable," Cornwallis informed Clinton on June 2. "I shall most earnestly endeavour to regulate the Government of S. Carolina to act towards the Inhabitants, & to establish such kind of Force as I think most likely to conduce to the essential Good" of the king's service. Cornwallis added "that in a business of such infinite Importance, Regulations must not be too hastily made, nor Professions too easily accepted."[46]

The repercussions of Clinton's victory also extended to North Carolina, where Loyalists inspired by the capture of Charleston began to assemble with the intention of joining the British army. Some eleven hundred Loyalists gathered in Lincoln County on June 15 but were defeated by the rebels after "a warm and obstinate Fight." Another group of Loyalists, also estimated at eleven hundred, embodied on June 25 at the forks of the Yadkin River, eluded rebel militia, and marched for South Carolina.[47]

The reports from South Carolina had a significant effect across the Atlantic as well. Since early 1780 Britons had waited impatiently for news of Clinton's

operations, while the British press announced that the rebellion was near collapse and that the battle for Charleston was to be the "Armageddon" of the
American war, bringing "instant victory" if Clinton succeeded.[48] Public morale
badly needed a boost. "We are much in want of some Success to keep up the
Spirits of the Empire," a young British employee of a merchant house in New
York wrote in March.[49] When news that Clinton had captured Charleston
reached Britain, "the street celebrations . . . were exuberant and wild." The victory appeared to validate the ministry's American policy, stifling criticism and
inspiring Lord North to seek new parliamentary elections in hope of further
strengthening his position.[50] Clinton instantly became, according to one
observer, "the most *popular* man in England."[51]

King George III and Germain shared in the exuberance when they read
Clinton's dispatches. Now that the Loyalists were assured "of effectual & permanent Protection," Germain told Clinton, they "will not hesitate to avow their
Loyalty and arm themselves for the Defence of their Country."[52] Satisfied that
South Carolina was securely in British hands, Germain in July ordered all South
Carolinians who were in England and receiving financial support from the government to return to the province. Germain's belief that all of the southern
colonies would soon return to their allegiance was widely shared by British
political leaders and much of the public in the summer and fall of 1780.[53]

The assessments of the situation in South Carolina made by officials in London, Loyalists, and army officers might be dismissed as mere wishful thinking if
they were not confirmed by the Whigs. Writing from Camden on May 24, South
Carolina governor John Rutledge declared that if the British sent troops into the
backcountry, "the disaffected will certainly flock to them, & those who are not
disaffected will either abscond, if they can," or be taken prisoner and put on
parole.[54] William Seymour, a sergeant in the Delaware Continentals, heard reports
while his unit was encamped in North Carolina that the British were overrunning
South Carolina and "obliging the inhabitants, as they came along, to take the oath
of allegiance to the King. In this, indeed, they had not much difficulty, for most
part of them" joined the British.[55] "Vast numbers flocked in and submitted; some
through fear, some through willingness, and others, perhaps, through a hope that
all things would settle down and war cease," Whig James Collins remembered.[56]
Tarleton Brown, a South Carolina militia captain, described the gloom that over-
came the rebels: "The country now seemed to be almost in complete subjugation
to the British." Yet, had they not been "aided and abetted by those unprincipled
and bloodthirsty tools [Loyalists] . . . the enemy would never have gained a solid
foothold upon our shores."[57] North Carolina governor Abner Nash told Thomas
Jefferson that British troops posted at Cheraw Hill were gathering "a considerable
Number of new recruits from amongst the Inhabitants."[58]

As promising as the situation appeared for the British, affairs in South Carolina
required careful management because those who had professed their loyalty did so

for a variety of reasons, and therefore many could be easily alienated. Some observers recognized this fact. "The greater part of the rural population of this part of America are, I believe, favorably inclined toward peace, *for they gain nothing by this war,*" Hessian captain Johann Hinrichs stated. "The safe rule, according to which one can always ascertain whether a man is a loyalist or a rebel, is to find out whether he profits more in his private interests, his mode of life, his way of doing things, etc., when he is on our side or on that of the enemy." Hinrichs believed that exceptions to this rule were rare and that only a "small number" of Loyalists acted from "love and faithfulness to God and their lawful King."[59] Robert Biddulph believed that a large portion of Charleston's inhabitants accepted British rule only because circumstances forced them to do so. "The Peace of this Country is fully established," he wrote, "but there is such a fund of Hatred and Animosity in the Hearts of the People, as Time only can extinguish."[60]

In the wake of their disastrous defeat, even ardent rebels had little choice but to reconcile themselves to the new situation.[61] William Moultrie explained that demoralized Whigs now sought nothing more than a return to prewar normalcy: "The people quite harassed out and tired of war; their capital fallen, and their army prisoners, no place of safety for them to fly to with their families and property; the British troops in possession of their whole country, and no prospect of relief from the neighboring states; in this situation they thought all further resistance was useless, they therefore readily accepted of the pleasing offers, in hopes they would have been suffered to remain peaceably and quietly at home with their families, and to have gone on with their business undisturbed, as before."[62]

Whig James Collins found the situation to be more complex than Moultrie described it, asserting that some rebels remained "determined to fight it out to the last let the consequence be what it might," while others were ready to "give up all for lost" when circumstances appeared unfavorable. Collins also classified Loyalists as those who "were Tories from principle," others who "believed it impossible for the cause of liberty to succeed," and those who "were Tories entirely through fear." He identified another group who had no principles of their own but "pretended friendship to all . . . not knowing into whose hands they might fall." These people, Collins wrote, sometimes acted as British informers once the king's troops had taken control of the province.[63]

Either unaware of the complex and conflicting motives that had led people to take the oath of allegiance or believing that he could satisfy everyone, Clinton on June 3 issued another proclamation, which later caused the British some difficulty in the province. With rebel forces in South Carolina virtually nonexistent, Clinton saw no reason to keep large numbers of captured Whigs bound by paroles, the pledges they had given not to take up arms again until exchanged. Clinton's proclamation released from parole everyone except those captured in the operations against Charleston. He considered this "a prudent measure," believing that it would prevent "inveterate rebels" from subverting British authority under the protection of parole. Better, Clinton thought, that all of the inhabitants declare their principles so that they could be identified and dealt with.[64] He therefore announced that "it is become unnecessary that such paroles be any longer observed." As of June 20 all those on parole were to consider themselves "restored to all the rights and duties belonging to citizens" and would be expected "to take an active part in settling and securing His Majesty's government."[65] Clinton believed that he was making a magnanimous gesture that would promote reconciliation, although the Whigs soon came to view the proclamation's terms in a different light.

Before departing for New York at the beginning of June, Clinton established a board of police in Charleston to handle civil matters, but he did not fully restore civil government in South Carolina. Although he had promised "the restoration of civil government" in his May 22 proclamation and had brought former North Carolina governor Josiah Martin on the expedition with the intention of appointing him temporary civil governor, Clinton decided that the situation did not yet justify reestablishing civilian rule.[66] He worried that civil officials would interfere with military policy and also repeat the practice of their counterparts in Georgia by punishing some former Whig leaders, thus hampering reconciliation.[67]

Clinton's refusal to restore civil government angered many officials, including Germain, Admiral Arbuthnot, and several South Carolina Loyalists. Arbuthnot insisted that the province's inhabitants would "continue obstinate from the dread of remaining under Military Law" but would readily submit to British rule under civil authority.[68] Lt. Gov. William Bull believed that the restoration of civil rule would "establish the public Tranquility on a lasting Foundation," while James Simpson asserted that reconstituted civil authority would demonstrate "the superiour Advantages and Security" of British government and win over former rebels.[69] On July 4 Germain told Clinton that "the Re-establishmt of the Constitution . . . cannot fail to have sufficient Influence on the wavering and indifferent among the Inhabitants of Charles Town, to fix them in their Submission to legal Government."[70] Some Whigs feared the effects that the restoration of civil rule in South Carolina would have on their cause; Alexander Hamilton declared that it would "conciliate the greatest part of the people" and "prepare the minds of their neighbours to yield an early submission."[71] Yet, Clinton continually found reasons to delay action, so that in the end, civil rule was never restored in South Carolina and an important opportunity to consolidate control was lost.[72]

With civil government a distant prospect, the town's military commandant, Brig. Gen. James Paterson, and the board of police headed by Simpson as intendant general shared authority in civil matters. In addition to Simpson, Clinton had appointed Robert William Powell to the board to represent Charleston's merchants, Alexander Wright to speak for the planters, and Lt. Col. Alexander Innes as military representative. Two other prominent Loyalists, William Bull and Sir Egerton Leigh, also served on the board after their arrival in South Carolina in February 1781, with Bull replacing Simpson as intendant general.

The board functioned primarily as a court to settle lawsuits involving debt and other civil matters.[73] Bull described the board's work as "business of a very complicated and often a delicate nature," since its decisions had to convince South Carolinians that justice was impartially administered.[74] He and Simpson believed that the board succeeded in this regard.[75]

As commander in the South, Cornwallis supervised both the board of police and the commandant as well as the field army. Clinton had left Cornwallis broad discretion in the exercise of his authority, specifying only that the earl should make the defense of Charleston and control of South Carolina his first priority, and then, if circumstances permitted, advance into North Carolina if it could be done without jeopardizing the security of South Carolina.[76]

Cornwallis took prompt steps to assure that those South Carolinians whose private interests outweighed political principles would be drawn back into the royal fold. Loyalist exiles "had their property, or what remained of it, restored." However, the "havoc made by the Americans" when they controlled the province "often defeated this intention." Cornwallis also promoted trade, suspending the Prohibitory Act, which had banned commerce between the rebellious provinces and the rest of the empire, thereby "allowing merchants to convey to Charles town a variety of manufactures which had been long wanted throughout all the southern provinces, and permitting them to receive payment in the produce of the country."[77] The earl, considering trade to be a privilege "exclusively enjoyed" by loyal subjects, prohibited rebels from participating in it, which served as a powerful incentive for many people to take the British oath.[78] Large numbers of South Carolinians, from interest or loyalism, found employment in the army's civil departments. The army quartermaster's department alone employed 225 civilians.[79]

Believing that lenience would best win the support of the people, Cornwallis adopted a surprisingly generous policy. He "attempted to conciliate the minds of the wavering and unsteady, by promises and employments." He ordered the army to avoid plundering or otherwise abusing the province's inhabitants so as not to alienate anyone.[80] However, the earl believed that Clinton's proclamations had been too generous in granting protection to "some of the most violent rebels and persecutors."[81] He also saw the danger of allowing disaffected people to serve in the militia, and he ordered his subordinates to exclude from the militia all those "who are not sufficiently loyal."[82]

Some Loyalists expressed dissatisfaction with Cornwallis's leniency, worrying that former rebels who declared loyalty without altering their real opinions might endanger the British position in South Carolina. Samuel Carne saw no evidence that "having been steadily Loyal avails more than those Enjoy who shed their fellow Subjects blood, & are since admitted." He wrote, "Allmost all who Apply are made good Subjects . . . God grant we may never find them otherways."[83] These fears proved well founded, as the earl's lenient policy created two serious problems. First, many of those whom he had pardoned without investigating their principles remained ardent rebels and secretly continued to support the rebellion. Second, Cornwallis's generosity toward former rebels "produced not the intended effect: It did not reconcile the enemies, but discouraged the friends." Loyalists "reflected on their own losses and sufferings" at the hands of the Whigs, and they angrily watched as Cornwallis restored their former persecutors, unpunished, to equality with the most steadfast supporters of the British.[84]

Rallying the genuine Loyalists and organizing them into a militia capable of holding South Carolina if and when the British army advanced northward was the linchpin of British strategy in the South. To accomplish this task, on May 22 Clinton had appointed Maj. Patrick Ferguson of the 71st Regiment to act as inspector of militia in the southern department. Clinton ordered Ferguson, "without loss of time, to form into Corps all the Young or unmarried Men of the Provinces of Georgia and the two Carolina's" to serve under Cornwallis's orders. The men were to be formed into companies of fifty to one hundred men that, when possible, were to be consolidated into battalions; otherwise the companies would serve independently. Ferguson was to allow the men of each company to elect their commanding officer and to enforce discipline "with great Caution, so as not to disgust the Men, Or mortify unnecessarily their Love of Freedom." Additional measures were intended "to Procure the general & hearty Concurrence of the Loyal Inhabitants" and included limited terms of service (a maximum of six months on duty out of twelve) and assurance that militiamen would not be "drawn into the regular Service without their Consent."[85]

Creating an effective militia in a region that had been under Whig control for five years was a daunting task. "The severity of the Rebel government has so terrified and totally subdued the minds of the people, that it is very difficult to rouse them to any exertions," Cornwallis later observed.[86] As determined as Ferguson was, he could not personally organize every unit; officers at some of the British posts had to assist in their districts. Even with such aid, Ferguson's task required "the greatest attention to a multitude of details. The area involved was immense, the problems staggering, and the time limited." Qualified officers had to be found, the men's loyalty vetted, and those enrolled given arms and training.[87]

The internal politics of the British army severely complicated Ferguson's efforts to organize an effective militia. During the siege of Charleston, Clinton had learned that the ministry had denied his request to resign his command, which angered Cornwallis, who had expected to replace Clinton as commander in chief. With his ambition thwarted, Cornwallis took out his frustration on Clinton, refusing to participate further in planning operations and requesting a separate command. Clinton obliged, but soon the officer corps became factionalized over the issue, and Clinton blamed Cornwallis for fomenting this unrest.[88] Because Ferguson had been appointed by Clinton, Cornwallis automatically distrusted his inspector of militia. Lt. Col. Nisbet Balfour, a protégé of Cornwallis, disliked Ferguson and perhaps desired the militia command for himself. On May 22 Balfour had visited Clinton and told the commander in chief that "it was *generally* reported that Ferguson was violent tempered and treated his men with harshness" and that he should not be given command of the militia. Clinton replied that he had heard no such reports and gave no credence to rumors. He attributed Balfour's remarks to the "infernal party" divisions prevailing in the army.[89]

Clinton had not left Charleston when Cornwallis and Balfour began plotting to replace his militia plan with one of their own, despite the earl's dislike of administrative work. Cornwallis preferred to seek victory on the battlefield, rather than devote his energy to organizational tasks that took a long time to produce tangible results. "Probably the chief reason" for his failure to fully mobilize Loyalist support in South Carolina was "his distaste for the matter, which admitted of no soldierly approach."[90] Intent on advancing his own career, Cornwallis undoubtedly undertook the effort to create his own plan for a loyal militia so that he, rather than Clinton, could claim credit in the event of success.

Meanwhile, Ferguson accompanied Balfour to the interior of the province, where the erstwhile inspector of militia received orders from Cornwallis on June 2 "to take no steps whatsoever in the militia business" until receiving further instructions; Ferguson promised to "pay the utmost implicit Obedience" to the order.[91] This left Balfour free to begin organizing the militia. "I have employ'd a faithfull person near Orangeburgh, who assures me of the loyalty of that district, and propose, empowering him, to raise an association to take up arms, and keep the peace untill the militia is formed, which I think there is no doubt of effecting," Balfour informed Cornwallis on June 6. He assured the earl, "As to the Militia arming to defend the country, I have not the smallest doubt of it," and he noted that "Ferguson remains perfectly quiet, since he rec. your letters" but still appeared eager to organize a militia upon the original plan formulated by Clinton. Altogether, Balfour felt satisfied with the progress of the militia, although he observed that it was difficult to find "men of property, and consequence" to serve as officers.[92]

Cornwallis recognized the importance of giving commissions to "locally prominent persons" whose influence would help convince others to actively support the British. Unfortunately, most leading South Carolinians who had not fled the province or been banished had cast their lot with the Whigs. Cornwallis therefore chose men such as James Cary of Camden district to command the militia. An attorney and planter who had immigrated to South Carolina in 1764, Cary did not have great influence, but he was well known in the district. Although he had taken the Whig oath, he had never participated actively in the rebellion. Cornwallis found Cary's loyalty beyond question, but Cary's performance as a militia colonel was poor.[93]

Robert Ballingall proved to be one of the better militia officers Cornwallis appointed. When the British army arrived in South Carolina, rebel officials imprisoned Ballingall. He was released when Charleston surrendered, and on July 20 Cornwallis gave him command of the militia south and west of Charleston, an area expanded in September to include all of St. George's, St. James, Goose Creek, and St. Andrew's parishes, along with James Island. While many other militia officers soon came to be scorned by British commanders, Ballingall retained the favor of both Cornwallis, who acknowledged his success "in raising & training the Militia," and Gen. Alexander Leslie, who praised Ballingall's "honor, Integrity, and good sense."[94]

Despite the lack of qualified officers and Ferguson's enforced idleness, militia matters had "a promising appearance" in late June. The volunteers "equalled the wishes of their leaders, both as to numbers and professions of loyalty."[95] Cornwallis informed Clinton on July 14 that the organization of the militia in "the lower districts" of the province was "in great forwardness."[96] This was particularly true in Charleston, where twenty-seven residents petitioned Cornwallis on behalf of the inhabitants for "permission to embody, arm and uniform themselves in a volunteer company" to assist in suppressing "the most cruel and unnatural rebellion that ever disgraced the historick page."[97]

Many Loyalists took action without waiting for the arrival of British troops. A British detachment marching through St. Matthew's Parish met twenty of these men on June 5; they had with them a notable prisoner, former Georgia governor John Wereat. The next day rebels arrived "from all quarters" to submit, and on June 10 an entire company of armed militia joined the British.[98] When troops reached Ninety Six on June 22, they found that local Loyalists had already arrested over forty rebels and confined them in the jail. Dr. Uzal Johnson, a New Jersey Loyalist, observed that the "friends to Government . . . who have just now got the opportunity to retaliate gladly embrace it." He thought this response understandable, given that many Loyalists had been "obliged to hide in Swamps & Caves to keep from Prison themselves."[99]

Despite this promising start, problems quickly arose with the militia, one of which was a shortage of arms, "the most serious" that the British experienced during the war. The problem resulted partly from the army's failure to send adequate supplies of muskets to the South, as well as from British officers' indiscriminate distribution of weapons, which often placed muskets in the hands of men who then joined Whig partisan units. Thus, when Col. Ambrose Mills went to Camden on October 1 to procure muskets for his 180 militiamen, he found himself competing with two other militia units and a provincial regiment for "less than 200 old French muskets." Mills received only sixty-one of them.[100] The shortage became so severe by January 1781 that Balfour informed Clinton that the army was "much distres'd from their being no small Arms in Store, which must be very disadvantageous to the Militia & provincial Establishments & if not soon supplied will preclude the raising any more Levies of the latter in this district."[101] Three months later Balfour again found it necessary to "request in the strongest Manner a further Quantity of small Arm's" for the militia and new recruits in South Carolina and Georgia.[102] Arms were essential because the

Whigs had long ago disarmed suspected Loyalists. From October to December 1780 British officers issued over seven hundred muskets for the militia in Georgetown, Orangeburg, Ninety Six, Beaufort County, and Colleton County. Some of these were replacements for damaged or poor-quality weapons.[103] One officer noted that Ballingall complained "loudly of the last Arms & Powder sent to the Country being very bad."[104] With insufficient and poor-quality muskets, the militia's effectiveness was badly impaired.

Some officers also expressed doubts about the sincerity of pledges of loyalty made by former Whigs. Evan McLaurin of the South Carolina Royalists wrote from Ninety Six that he was well aware of "the temper the People hereabout are in at present," and he declared that "[Andrew] Williamson is the only man of all those formerly active against us; on whom we could firmly depend" if rebel fortunes improved. McLaurin was particularly worried about dissatisfaction among the inhabitants of the Long Canes settlements, where unrest simmered after British troops seized the people's horses.[105]

Such actions alienated both Loyalists and former Whigs, while the attitude of many British officers undermined the commitment and morale of many militiamen. Robert Gray reported that "the abuses of the Army in taking the peoples Horses, Cattle & provisions in many cases without paying for them . . . disgusted the inhabitants." Gray also noted that "almost every British officer regarded with contempt and indifference the establishment of a militia among a people differing so much in customs & manners from themselves" and made no effort to conceal this opinion. This damaged the spirit of men who, after years of persecution, lacked the confidence necessary for military success and needed encouragement, not derision, from British officers.[106]

Nevertheless, the organization of the militia continued to go well and gained impetus in mid-June when Cornwallis, satisfied that Ferguson had been sufficiently chastised, allowed him to assume his assigned duties.[107] Unlike his arrogant counterparts, Ferguson "cultivated a familiarity with loyalists unusual among British officers." He spent much time conversing "with the country people on the state of [political] affairs. . . . He was as indefatigable in training them to his way of thinking, as he was in instructing them in military exercises." His behavior "went far to secure the respect and obedience" of those he encountered.[108] On June 27 Balfour reported that he and Ferguson had organized militia battalions at Ninety Six, Orangeburg, and adjacent areas with a combined strength of five thousand men.[109] When Ferguson left Ninety Six on June 23 with forty provincials to begin operations against Whig partisans, more Loyalists came "flocking to him from all parts of the Country."[110] Affairs appeared equally good in the Camden area, where Lt. Col. Francis, Lord Rawdon, noted that the militia were "not only well disposed, but very zealous."[111]

By the end of June, Cornwallis informed Clinton that he felt satisfied with the progress the militia had made so far. For administrative convenience, Cornwallis kept the militia districts that the Whigs had drawn.[112] "As the different Districts submitted I with all the Dispatch in my Power formed them into Militia & appointed Field Officers according to the old Divisions of the Province," he reported. "I invested these Field Officers with Civil as well as Military Power, as the most effectual means of preserving Order and reestablishing The King's Authority in this Country." The earl created two classes of militia. Men over forty years old "and of certain Property, Family or Service" were to remain at home to maintain order except "in Case of an Insurrection or an actual Invasion of the Province." Those younger than forty would serve on terms almost identical to those Clinton had formulated. Cornwallis declared that the militia was "composed of Men, either of undoubted Attachment to the Cause of Great Britain, or whose Behaviour has always been moderate." To prevent prominent former Whigs whose loyalty was doubtful from adversely influencing others, Cornwallis placed them on parole and sent them to the sea islands; anyone else believed to be "notoriously disaffected" had been disarmed, ordered to remain at home on parole, and told that they could provide the army with supplies, wagons, and horses in lieu of militia service.[113]

Although Loyalist support had met British expectations and the organization of the loyal militia was off to a promising start, three factors combined to prevent the Loyalists from realizing their potential as an effective force. First, many Whigs continued to resist and resorted to their old tactics of harassing and brutalizing the Loyalists, which in conjunction with defeats inflicted on the loyal militia by these rebel partisans, intimidated the Loyalists and demoralized the militia. Second, after witnessing the initially poor performance of the militia and the treachery of some Whig-infiltrated units, most British officers lost all confidence in the militia and simply stopped employing it, thus depriving its members of the experience they would have gained from serving alongside regular troops. Third, the approach of Gen. Horatio Gates with an American army in July renewed the hopes of many rebels, causing them to break their oaths of loyalty and rejoin the fight; this greatly increased the pressure on the loyal militia at a time when its members were still inadequately trained and equipped.

Whigs who gathered in the Carolina swamps and forests to plan resistance recognized the importance of targeting the Loyalists. In the northeastern part of the province, partisan leader Francis Marion understood that any delay in striking the Loyalists could prove fatal to the rebel cause. Given time to organize and gain experience and cohesion, the loyal militia might soon become formidable. This, above all, was what Marion hoped to prevent. Whigs in northwestern South Carolina adopted a similar strategy. In early June about one hundred rebels under Cols. Edward Lacey and William Bratton attacked a party of Loyalists commanded by Col. Charles Coleman at Mobley's Meeting House near Winnsboro, killing a few and dispersing the remainder.[114]

The loyal militia suffered a worse defeat on July 12. Cornwallis dispatched Capt. Christian Huck of Tarleton's British Legion and thirty-five dragoons to operate against Whig partisans near the North Carolina border. Huck brought sixty mounted militiamen with him, and another three hundred joined him during his march. Rebel partisans launched a surprise predawn attack on the detachment, inflicting about ninety casualties, mostly among the militia. After the battle, the Whigs executed one of their Loyalist prisoners, a militia major named Ferguson, because some rebels alleged that he had murdered a young man without provocation.[115] A few weeks later Tarleton found that people in the lowcountry were still "*scar'd,*" and yet some militiamen turned out when he summoned them.[116]

Events in North Carolina compounded the demoralizing effects of Huck's defeat. Continued Whig persecution led hundreds of Loyalists there to ignore Cornwallis's instructions to remain quiet until the British army moved north. Instead, eight hundred men took up arms, although they were quickly beaten by the rebels. The survivors reached the British post at Cheraw, and from there reports of their defeat "diffused universal consternation amongst the inhabitants of South Carolina."[117]

Other events involving the loyal militia inflicted short-term damage to the British position in South Carolina and produced long-term harm to the relationship between the British army and the Loyalists. In the vicinity of the Enoree and Tyger rivers, Col. Mathew Floyd had organized a militia battalion, which the British supplied with arms and ammunition. The man who had commanded the rebel militia of that district, John Lisle, who was noted "for his violent persecution of the Loyalists," had fled the province but was later captured. Taking advantage of the terms offered in Clinton's June 3 proclamation, Lisle pledged allegiance to Britain and was permitted to return to his home, where he became Floyd's second in command. Shortly after Huck's defeat, he seized Floyd and led the entire battalion to join the rebels. This incident, Tarleton stated, "ruined all confidence between the regulars and the militia."[118]

A second instance of treachery worsened the problem. As British troops concentrated at Camden in August to meet Gates's advancing army, Maj. Archibald McArthur of the 71st Regiment ordered Col. Ambrose Mills of the militia to escort over one hundred sick soldiers to Georgetown. After the detachment had marched beyond supporting distance from the British regulars, Whig partisans attacked them. Some of the militiamen mutinied and took their own officers prisoner, including Mills, Robert Gray, and Col. James Cassells.[119] The rebels transported the captives to North Carolina, where they "were put into a dungeon loaded with Irons & treated in the most barbarous manner."[120] Mills later escaped, and although Cornwallis blamed him for failing to properly screen his recruits, the earl still considered the colonel "a very good man," who had simply been too credulous regarding people's professions of loyalty.[121] The incident confirmed the belief of many British officers that they had erred "in placing confidence in the inhabitants of the country when acting apart from the army."[122]

Cornwallis had already reached the same conclusion. "The want of subordination and confidence of our militia in themselves, will make a considerable regular force always necessary for the defence" of South Carolina, the earl told Clinton in mid-July. "It is needless to attempt to take any considerable number of the . . . militia with us when we advance"; since Cornwallis expected to be joined by many North Carolina Loyalists, he decided it was unwise to bring along "too many useless mouths."[123]

Efforts to turn the loyal militia into an effective force were further hampered by the approach of Gen. Horatio Gates and his Continental army in late July. Gates's march toward South Carolina emboldened the Whigs, provoking new outbursts of rebellion. Gray recalled that Gates's advance "seemed to be a signal for a general revolt in the disaffected parts of the back Country."[124] Many people used Clinton's June 3 proclamation, which had released them from parole, as a pretext to claim that they could legitimately abjure their oaths of allegiance.[125] Rumors that relief was coming "gave a turn to the minds of the inhabitants of the southern provinces." Rebels who had reconciled themselves to defeat now plotted a resurgence; "hostilities were already begun in many places, and every thing seemed to menace a revolution."[126] Cornwallis feared that Gates's arrival "shall shake the Confidence & consequently the fidelity of our Friends."[127] He later told Clinton that Gates's advance "very much intimidated our friends, encouraged our enemies, and determined the wavering against us."[128] In Balfour's opinion, the effect was even worse and undermined his confidence in the Loyalists. "In vain we expected, loyalty and attachment from the inhabitants," he wrote, but "the moment [Gates] came near," they "revolted and joined him." Balfour concluded that there was no difference between Loyalists and rebels—"they are the same stuff as compose all americans," he declared.[129]

Gates did all he could to encourage South Carolinians who had joined the British to return to the Whig fold. On July 29 he wrote to rebel militia officers asking them to assure the Whigs that his army was marching to their aid and offering pardon to all those who "from the Necessity of protecting their persons and property have been obliged to profess a temporary acquiescence under the British Government." The following week Gates issued a proclamation containing his offer of amnesty. The promise of military assistance and pardon induced many who had taken British protection to join the rebels. So too did Gates's orders that he would not honor the paroles of American prisoners unless they had been taken in arms. Any man who had simply given his parole when British forces arrived in his district was to be considered liable for service in the Whig militia, and those who refused would be punished.[130] By encouraging people to violate their oaths and paroles, Gates subjected them to great risk if they fell into British hands. British officers believed that those who broke their oaths or paroles had to be punished to prevent other South Carolinians from defecting, and thus Gates's actions inflamed the already volatile situation and fed the spiral of violence in the South.

Col. Thomas Sumter, who raised his own force of rebel partisans and had recently made unsuccessful attacks against British posts at Rocky Mount and Hanging Rock west of Camden, encouraged Gates to seek support from Americans who had taken British protection. He assured Gates's aide that "the Chief of the Militia Downwards are our friends Ready to do their Duty." Although conceding that many of those friends "are in arms against us," and admitting that two who had been captured by the British after switching sides had been hanged at Rocky Mount, Sumter insisted that many South Carolinians were eager "for an opportunity to Join the army."[131] After his attack at Hanging Rock, Sumter reported, "Both British and Tories are pannick struck," and he expressed his belief that fifteen hundred men could march across South Carolina "with ease."[132]

Gates's call to arms had the desired effect. John Lloyd estimated that "at least 7/8's of the People returned to their allegiance" before Gates advanced into South Carolina. However, when the inhabitants were summoned to assist the British in repelling the invasion, "great numbers, notwithstanding their professed contrition, and avowed loyalty, left the British, for the American standard, under which, they have since done, and continue to do infinite mischief."[133]

Yet, even during this period many Loyalists provided valuable service to Cornwallis. As Gates's troops marched through North Carolina, they were harassed by Loyalists who seemed to have "surrounded them on all sides."[134] Whig officer Charles Porterfield reported that the people in the vicinity of Cedar Creek had "gone with the Brittish, with all their baggage & Cattle."[135] At Jenning's Branch, Richard Caswell with the North Carolina militia worried that he would not be able to keep his advance a secret because Loyalists, "which are Numerous in proportion to the Inhabitants of this part of the Country," would inform the British of his movements.[136] Caswell's fears were well founded, for Loyalists kept Lord Rawdon, the British commander at Camden, fully informed of rebel movements.[137] On August 5 Caswell learned that "a Considerable Number of Tories were Collecting" with Rawdon's army with the intention of attacking his North Carolinians.[138]

Other Loyalists created problems in the rear of the American army. From Drowning Creek, Continental officer Matthew Ramsey wrote that he was plagued by Loyalist partisans operating from swamps and who launched raids intended to prevent supplies from reaching Gates's army. The Loyalists had recently attacked a rebel party and rescued twenty Loyalist prisoners; with only fifty men in his command, Ramsey did not dare to challenge them.[139]

One bold Loyalist, a Camden resident, rode directly into Gates's camp, where he feigned surprise at finding the American army. The man conversed with Gates, provided some accurate but incomplete information about the British at Camden, and then departed with a promise to return with additional intelligence. Col. Otho Holland Williams and other rebel officers suspected that the man was a spy and urged Gates to detain him, but the general refused. The mysterious visitor never returned, which confirmed Williams's suspicions.[140]

In addition to the contributions of individuals and partisans, the loyal militia also played a role in the Camden campaign. As Tarleton marched his troops from Charleston to Camden in early August, Col. John Coming Ball joined them with twenty-five militiamen, who served as guides and rode ahead to procure intelligence; this enabled Tarleton to reach his destination without interference from the various Whig parties operating in the area. The Camden district militia was less successful—Sumter attacked forty men guarding Wateree Ferry on August 15, killing seven and capturing the rest, including their commander, Colonel Cary. In other operations Sumter captured more Loyalists, one hundred British regulars, and forty supply wagons bound for Camden. Tarleton recovered all the prisoners, wagons, and supplies three days later when he crushed Sumter's partisans at Fishing Creek.[141]

Cornwallis relied on the militia, with a small contingent of provincials and British convalescents, to hold the town of Camden when he marched to attack Gates on the night of August 15. Another three hundred militiamen accompanied the British army. The earl placed these men in reserve on his left. During the battle, the Continental troops made a bayonet charge against this flank, causing Rawdon to bring up the militia and other reserves to hold the line.[142] The American attack was checked, and the militia evidently performed adequately, for while they were not singled out for particular praise after the battle, neither did they receive any criticism.

Cornwallis's troops routed the rebels, and as the scattered Continentals and militiamen fled northward, emboldened Loyalists pursued and captured significant numbers of them. Because many of the fugitives had thrown away their weapons in their flight, they were often unable to resist.[143] "Those who escaped the Dangers of the Field knew not where to find protection," Otho Williams wrote. "The Wounded found no relief from the Inhabitants who were immediately in arms against us, and many of our Fugitive Officers and men were disarm'd by those faithless Vallains." He added that other Loyalists had stolen horses and seized supplies during the retreat, while "some of those desperate Rascals have been daring enough to fire upon parties of our Regular Troops."[144] Many of those who captured fleeing rebels and American supplies were committed adherents to the British cause, but in other cases, "news of this immense British victory caused many armed men to change their loyalties on the spot."[145] Williams complained that many of the men who captured Gates's soldiers had previously "flatter'd us with promises of joining us against the Enemy."[146] Those who regretted having broken their oaths seized the opportunity to ingratiate themselves with the British by bringing rebel prisoners into Cornwallis's camp.

The victory at Camden produced a new surge of Loyalist sentiment in South Carolina, undoing much of the earlier damage caused by defeat, defection, and Gates's advance. Many inhabitants enlisted in provincial units, including the British Legion, the New York Volunteers, and the American Volunteers. With the

Continental army again removed as a threat, other Loyalists abandoned their reluctance to serve with the militia. By late August over four thousand men had been enrolled in seven battalions in the backcountry, of which fifteen hundred could be brought into action on short notice. Other battalions, although weaker, had been formed elsewhere in South Carolina.[147] Cornwallis believed that in the wake of his victory, "the internal commotions and insurrections in the province will now subside." He decided to teach those who had broken their oaths a lesson by inflicting "exemplary punishment on some of the most guilty, in hopes to deter others in future from sporting with allegiance and oaths."[148]

Yet, in spite of the great victory at Camden and Tarleton's destruction of Sumter's force on August 18, the rebels managed to derive some benefits from the campaign. Robert Gray, recently exchanged and working to organize the militia in the Cheraw district, pronounced his task "impossible," because "at least three fourths of the inhabitants" in the region "had taken active parts" in rebellion when Gates had approached. Even among the Loyalists, "many had their nearest connections among the rebel refugees and could not be trusted," Gray observed. He did find many reliable Loyalists "on Black and Lynch's creek" and along the Little Pee Dee River. These, however, could not assemble, because doing so "exposed their families and property to the resentment of the rebels from Cape Fear who have been indefatigable in persecuting them upon every occasion." Once the Cape Fear River became the northern boundary of British control, Gray believed, these Loyalists could be relied on. Until then, he suggested that a force of mounted regulars, supported by militia drawn from other parts of South Carolina and the North Carolina provincials, could maintain "the publick peace."[149]

Some British and Loyalist officers concluded that it would be wiser to abandon plans to rely on the militia and instead recruit men for provincial units. Evan McLaurin asked Cornwallis for permission to create a new South Carolina provincial battalion, a plan that won the endorsement of Alexander Innes. The latter told Cornwallis that McLaurin "had a superior plan to any man of this part of the province." Innes said that he disagreed with those who believed that forming provincial units would be "detrimental to the Militia." He considered "every man inlisted to serve in a provincial Corps . . . a usefull soldier gain'd to the King's Service," whereas he was "well convinced the Militia on their present plan will ever prove a useless disorderly, destructive banditti." According to Innes, men who were of little value in the militia became "different men in a regular provincial Corps." As proof, he noted that of the thirty-five men he had enlisted in the South Carolina Royalists since June, "no Men cou'd behave with greater spirit," while "their late associates" in the militia "behave in so dastardly and cowardly a manner."[150]

Tarleton agreed that loyal South Carolinians would be more useful in provincial corps than as militia, although he preferred incorporating them into existing units rather than organizing new regiments. In veteran units experienced officers could train and lead the recruits, depleted units could be brought to full strength, and "considerable service" might be derived from the recruits, Tarleton believed.[151] Cornwallis thought the idea was worthwhile, and he urged Lt. Col. George Turnbull, commander of the New York Volunteers, to incorporate three companies of South Carolinians into his unit. However, Turnbull demurred, believing that the South Carolinians were too unruly.[152]

By September, Cornwallis also concluded that provincials should replace the militia. He informed Clinton that "as I have found the Militia to fail so totally when put to the Trial . . . I am determined to try Provincial Corps alone" in the future.[153] The earl authorized the Loyalist major John Harrison to recruit five hundred men in the region between the Pee Dee and Wateree rivers and form them into a provincial battalion. Cornwallis thought it "extremely probable" that this plan would succeed.[154] Later he authorized Robert Cunningham to enlist a second provincial battalion. Harrison's efforts failed, and while Cunningham appeared "more likely to succeed," Cornwallis put a stop to the formation of Cunningham's corps "on finding that all the principal officers of the militia of Ninety-Six were entering into it, by which means I should have been totally deprived of the use of that militia."[155] Two weeks later Cornwallis's frustration with the militia caused him to reverse himself and order Cunningham to renew the effort to recruit a provincial corps. In October, acting on his own initiative, Lt. Col. John Harris Cruger, commanding at Ninety Six, authorized Moses Kirkland to enlist at least four hundred men to serve as provincials for a year.[156]

While the militia's performance had not been stellar, it had not been as poor as Cornwallis described it. Capt. James Dunlap of the Queen's Rangers led fourteen provincials and sixty mounted militiamen against what he believed was a small Whig party on July 14, only to encounter several hundred rebels. In a charge, Dunlap's men scattered the Whigs, killing and wounding about thirty. However, when the rebels regrouped and counterattacked, the same militiamen who moments earlier had performed so well fled without resisting.[157]

Patrick Ferguson conceded that the militia had not always met his expectations, but he was certain that with time and training, an effective militia could be established. He stated in late July that the militia was "Daily gaining confidence & Discipline."[158] Shortly afterward he explained to Rawdon that "the Men have been so little accustom'd to Military restraints, & become so soon home Sick, that it is almost impossible to assemble any Number of them on a sudden call of danger, or to keep them many days together." Ferguson lectured them about their poor behavior, which prompted them to draw up and sign a resolution pledging to serve faithfully in the future.[159] On August 29 Ferguson asked Cornwallis "to observe that the Different bodys of Militia East of broad river that have behaved so ill with the Army, were form'd in a hurry, without the assistance of any officers of the Army to establish order & Discipline, employ'd immediately on Service, & no Scrutiny made into the Loyalty of the Officers or

Men." As a result, many rebels were permitted to enroll and then immediately joined the Whigs when Gates's army approached. It was "to be expected that a Mungrill Mob without any regularity or even organization, without fidelity without officers, without any previous preparation employd against the Enemy, would bring the name of Militia into discredit," Ferguson wrote.[160]

Although Ferguson's arguments did not alter Cornwallis's opinion, the earl had no choice but to continue relying on the militia to secure South Carolina. With most of the army at Camden preparing to invade North Carolina and recruitment of the new provincial battalion progressing slowly, Cornwallis had to depend on the militia and garrisons of provincials at Ninety Six and Augusta to defend the backcountry. The security of the northeastern part of the province between Camden and Georgetown was left to the militia alone, with regulars conducting occasional forays to support them.

Along the Little Pee Dee River, where Loyalists were numerous, Maj. Micajah Ganey assembled two hundred militiamen in late August to attack Francis Marion, whose Whig partisans were operating in the vicinity. Outnumbered four to one, Marion relied on surprise and attacked a detachment of Ganey's militia on September 4. The Whigs routed and pursued the forty-five Loyalists, only to be driven off when they encountered Ganey's main force. After checking his pursuers with an ambush, Marion escaped. His victory encouraged over one hundred men to join him, but news that Ganey's militia had reassembled and was to be reinforced by other militia units and British troops from the small garrison at Georgetown forced the Whigs to withdraw into North Carolina.[161]

Shortly after the skirmish, one of Marion's officers resorted to the kind of terror that had proven so effective at suppressing loyalism. Capt. Maurice Murphy and several rebels visited the home of a man named Blackman. Finding that Blackman favored the royal cause, they gave him 150 lashes with a bullwhip. When Blackman still refused to recant, Murphy released him. Murphy's uncle, Gideon Gibson, rebuked his nephew for permitting such cruelty, whereupon Murphy shot Gibson dead.[162] Loyalists in the area suffered "terrors & great distress" as small parties of rebels assailed them at every opportunity.[163]

Marion soon returned to South Carolina. On September 28 he attacked a post on the Black Mingo River held by forty-seven Loyalists commanded by Col. John Coming Ball. The Loyalists retreated after a brief exchange of fire in which they suffered a loss of three killed and thirteen captured; the prisoners were "men of family & fortune," and Marion hoped that their loss "may be a Check to the militia taking arms against us." Marion planned to attack another Loyalist detachment at Black River Church; however, Cornwallis dispatched Maj. James Wemyss with British troops to quell the uprising, causing so many of Marion's men to return to their homes that the partisan leader had to retreat once again. Nevertheless, Marion declared that "the Toreys are so Affrighted with my little Excursions, that many is moving off to Georgia with their Effects," while others had taken refuge in the swamps.[164] British officers confirmed this. "There are hourly people coming in from Peedee, giving dreadful accounts of the depredations committing there by the Rebels," Robert England wrote.[165] Wemyss noted that in the vicinity of Georgetown, "the whole Country is in Confusion & uproar, all the friends of Government have been plundered of their Negroes" and other property.[166] Three days later Wemyss reported that the rebels "continue to hunt out, & plunder every friend of Government. . . . The people here are exceedingly alarmed."[167]

Assisted by fifty militiamen, Wemyss and his regulars chastised the Whigs, sending the armed bands fleeing and burning about fifty houses owned by men who had broken their oaths to serve with the rebels. He believed that if two hundred regulars were left on the Pee Dee, they could secure the region against Marion with the aid of the Georgetown and Cheraw militias.[168] Turnbull disagreed, asserting that if "Wemyss cou'd not Establish a Militia when he was there with a Force," a detachment in the vicinity could not rely on militia support. "Depend upon it Militia Will never do any good Without Regular Troops," Turnbull declared.[169] Balfour advised sending the militia from Orangeburg, which he considered the most reliable, to secure the Pee Dee region.[170]

In the backcountry Whigs also repeatedly harassed the Loyalists. On August 17 two hundred Georgians, South Carolinians, and overmountain men assembled to attack an equal number of loyal militiamen at Musgrove's Mill. Reinforced the next evening by two hundred South Carolina provincials under Alexander Innes and another one hundred militia, the Loyalists attacked the rebels, who were posted on a wooded ridge. Innes was wounded, and his troops were forced to retreat after suffering heavy casualties.[171]

Despite frequent Whig incursions, Ferguson's work with the militia in Ninety Six district had begun to pay dividends; "his intensive training of some of his Tory companies had turned them into competent soldiers" and earned him the respect of the men.[172] On September 12 he led one hundred militiamen and forty provincials to strike three hundred rebels from the overmountain region under Joseph McDowell. Ferguson caught up with the rebels later that day, and the militia fought well in an attack that routed the larger Whig force. The victory had immediate repercussions; two days later many people in the area came in to take the oath of allegiance to Britain.[173]

Unable to gain the upper hand in the backcountry against the provincials and militia, the Whigs terrorized individual Loyalists whenever the opportunity arose. On September 9 a rebel party captured John Hutchison and Gardiner Williams of Jackson's Creek. Williams had participated in the defense of Rocky Mount, while Hutchison had been specifically targeted because "he had been very Active with Us in his duty Since the Surrender of Charlestown," Loyalist colonel John Phillips believed. Phillips begged Cornwallis to arrange Hutchison's exchange, fearing that the rebels "will do him Every Injury in their power" and perhaps even hang him.[174]

Gov. John Rutledge encouraged the harsh treatment of Loyalists. In a proclamation issued on September 27, he offered pardon to South Carolinians who
had taken the British oath, provided they joined the Whigs within thirty days
and agreed to serve six months in the militia. Those who held British commissions or had signed congratulatory addresses to the British commanders were
not eligible, however. Rutledge threatened all who refused his offer with banishment and confiscation of their property.[175] A few days later Rutledge instructed
Sumter to deal sternly with the Loyalists. "It will be expedient to apprehend &
secure every Subject of the State, who holds any office or Commission under his
Britannick Majesty," Rutledge wrote; "you are not, on any Account whatever to
put any Prisoners whom you take that owe Allejiance to the State of So. Carolina . . . on Parole, but have them properly confined to be tried, as soon as Courts
of Law can be held, for so capital an Offence as taking Part with the Enemy."
Rutledge did offer to forgive those "compelled to do Duty, as Militia-Men," if
they proved that they were actually Whigs and had not committed "atrocious"
acts while in British service.[176] The governor justified his policy by accusing the
British of having committed atrocities against South Carolina's Whigs.[177]

When Cornwallis advanced northward at the beginning of September, he
assigned two tasks to the militia. The majority were to guard key posts in the
army's absence and to protect the army's supply line between Camden and
Charlotte.[178] A Whig prisoner who escaped from Camden reported that the
town's garrison consisted of five hundred militiamen, and those men not cur-
rently on duty "were all ordered into Camden" to serve for three months.[179]
Other accounts indicated that there were between three hundred and six hundred Loyalists at the Waxhaws and about five hundred at Fishing Creek, most
of them newly enlisted provincials.[180] The backcountry militia had a more active
role: Ferguson was to lead them into western North Carolina to protect the
army's left flank. The earl had some doubts about the militia's ability to carry
out this task. He told Clinton that while Ferguson believed that his men were
reliable, "I am sorry to say that his own experience, as well as that of every other
officer, is totally against him."[181] However, Cornwallis also believed that the
militia might perform better if used offensively; "if ever those people will fight
it is when they attack & not when they are attacked," he told Balfour.[182]

Unfazed by Cornwallis's skepticism, Ferguson set out with 500 militia and
about 100 provincials in early September. Learning that a Whig force was
nearby, Ferguson, with 40 provincials and 100 militia, attacked and routed the
220 rebels on September 11.[183] They collected recruits as they marched, so that
the force numbered 800 when it reached Gilbert Town, North Carolina, on
September 23. There 500 people took the British oath.[184] "The Tories were flocking to his standard from every quarter," one Whig stated.[185]

This marked the zenith for the loyal militia, and collapse swiftly followed.
The threat that Ferguson posed to the overmountain settlements aroused the

inhabitants, hundreds of whom turned out to attack the Loyalists. Joined by other rebels from the Carolinas, they moved to attack Ferguson's detachment. Ferguson learned of their approach and withdrew, maneuvering until he reached King's Mountain, just south of the North Carolina border and twenty-five miles west of Charlotte, where Cornwallis lay with the main army. He dispatched messengers to the earl requesting support, but none came. Instead, on October 7 the rebels surrounded King's Mountain and attacked the Loyalists. In a battle lasting less than an hour, the Whigs killed Ferguson and 150 of his men and captured the remainder.[186]

The defeat in itself was enough to shake the Loyalists' confidence, but the cruelty with which the Whigs treated their enemies shattered Loyalist morale. On their march to King's Mountain, the rebels had begun to display their savagery by attacking four unarmed Loyalists, "butchering two young men" and leaving two elderly men "most barbarously maim'd."[187] During the battle the rebels had refused to cease fire when the Loyalists tried to surrender; they shot down two men who were waving white flags and wantonly increased the Loyalists' casualties. When they withdrew from King's Mountain with their prisoners after the battle, the over-mountain men left over 160 badly wounded Loyalists untreated on the field.[188]

The families of loyal militiamen who lived near the battlefield were the first to witness this carnage. The day after the battle, "the wives and children of the poor Tories came in, in great numbers," wrote Whig soldier James Collins. "Their husbands, fathers, and brothers, lay dead in heaps, while others lay wounded or dying; a melancholy sight indeed!" Collins "could not help turning away from the scene . . . with horror, and . . . could not refrain from shedding tears."[189] As reports of the slaughter circulated, many Loyalists feared that it was too dangerous to provide further support to the British. Most of the men in David Fanning's small detachment of loyal militia on the western frontier of South Carolina deserted after learning of Ferguson's defeat.[190] Rawdon noted that the disaster had "so dispirited" the Loyalists in Ninety Six district that Cruger suspected they "had determined to submit as soon as the Rebels" arrived in the backcountry.[191]

The rebels' treatment of the prisoners further demonstrated the risks Loyalists faced if they openly supported the king. On October 14 twelve Whig officers formed a tribunal "to try the Militia Prisoners Particularly those who had the most Influence in the country." Thirty men were condemned to death for alleged crimes, and the executions began in the evening. Nine men, including Lt. Col. Ambrose Mills, "fell a Sacrafice to their infamous Mock jury," a Loyalist prisoner declared. The remaining twenty-one were reprieved.[192] The pleas of relatives failed to save the lives of their loved ones. Another prisoner stated that "words can scarce describe the melancholy scene" that transpired when the two daughters of one victim learned of their father's death; they "swoon'd away and continued in fits all night." This prisoner also reported that "Mrs. Mills with a young child in her arms sat out all night in the rain with her husband's corps[e]."[193]

The next day, perhaps fearing that they too might soon be executed, about one hundred prisoners made their escape during a lengthy march. Three more tried to escape on October 17; two succeeded, while the third was wounded in the attempt. The wounded man was executed the following morning.[194] Given the conditions of the march, it was not surprising that many men risked their lives trying to escape. "Many of our Prisoners were so wearied out that many of them were obliged to give out on the road," two officers of the New Jersey Volunteers later stated; "they then roll'd them down in the mud—and many of them they left there were trod to death and many of them cut to pieces."[195] The Whigs denied the wounded medical treatment until November 1, nearly a month after the battle, when Dr. Uzal Johnson finally received permission to treat the injured captives. He was bandaging a man named Catchum when Whig colonel Benjamin Cleveland came on the scene and rebuked Johnson, saying that Catchum "was a Damnd Villain & deserved the Gallows." The infuriated Cleveland then "struck me over the Head with his Sword, and levild me, he repeated his stroke & cut my Hand," Johnson wrote.[196]

Such treatment inspired further attempts to escape, so that eventually about six hundred of the captives succeeded in fleeing their confinement.[197] Among them was Lt. Anthony Allaire, who escaped with two other prisoners on the night of November 5 and reached safety at Williams's Fort after a seventeen-day journey, during which Loyalists provided the fugitives with food, shelter, and guides.[198] Alexander Chesney, a militia lieutenant who had served with Ferguson throughout the summer and fall, also escaped. The Whigs had offered to parole Chesney if he would drill their militia in Ferguson's manner and threatened him with death when he refused. After reaching his home with aid from Loyalist families, "I was obliged to conceal myself in a cave dug in the branch of a creek" with two Loyalist cousins, Chesney wrote, since the Whigs controlled the area. When Maj. Jonathan Frost tried to assemble the remaining Loyalist militia in the district, the rebels appeared at the rendezvous and captured Chesney and several others. Frost pursued the rebels with other Loyalists, hoping to free the prisoners, but he was killed in the unsuccessful effort.[199]

The escape of so many prisoners actually benefited the rebels, as the returned captives spread word of the harsh fate awaiting any Loyalists who fell into Whig hands. These reports, as much as the defeat at King's Mountain, discouraged many Loyalists from assisting the British.[200] Accounts of the prisoners' sufferings circulated widely; the *Royal Georgia Gazette* published a detailed description of the rebels' "base and infamous proceedings."[201] Tarleton observed "the depression and fear" that such reports "communicated to the loyalists upon the borders, and to the southward."[202] The loyalists' demoralization was also evident to American officers. "Many of the Tories seem disposed to return to their Allegiance, and would submit to any Terms which might be offered to obtain a Pardon," Gen. William Smallwood informed Horatio Gates in late October.

Smallwood believed that a proclamation offering amnesty to Loyalists "would effectually draw at this Crisis numbers from the British Interest."[203]

Cornwallis, angered by the reports of abuse and recognizing that Whig cruelty to prisoners undermined Loyalist morale, threatened to retaliate. He told Smallwood that "the cruelty exercised on the Prisoners taken under Major Ferguson is shocking to Humanity; and the hanging poor old Colonel Mills, who was always a fair, and open Enemy to your Cause, was an act of the most Savage barbarity." The earl added that he had heard that a Captain Oates of the loyal militia "was lately put to Death without any Crime being laid to his Charge." Cornwallis demanded that Smallwood put an end to "these most cruel Murders." Otherwise, the earl declared, it would be necessary for him, "in justice to the suffering Loyalists, to retaliate on the unfortunate Persons now in my power." Anticipating that the Whigs would blame him for initiating the violence toward prisoners, Cornwallis asserted that he had never permitted any rebels to be executed, with the exception of two or three who had enrolled in the loyal militia and then joined the Whigs.[204] The earl later made another protest to Gates, stating that "the officers and men taken at King's Mountain, were treated with an inhumanity Scarce credible" and that he therefore felt himself "under the disagreeable necessity of making some retaliation for the unhappy men who were so cruelly and unjustly put to death."[205]

The Whigs ignored Cornwallis's complaints. Although Gates privately disapproved of the harsh treatment of the King's Mountain prisoners, he expressed "astonishment, at Lord Cornwallis's finding fault with a cruelty, he and his Officers are continually practicing."[206] John Rutledge had no sympathy at all for the Loyalist captives. He described the men Cleveland had executed as some "of the most noted horse Thieves & Tories," implying that their fate had been well deserved. The governor insisted, without a shred of proof, that the British "have hanged many more of our People," and he remarked that "his Lordship has mistaken the Side on which the Cruelty lies."[207]

The treatment of the prisoners taken at King's Mountain became the norm for captured Loyalists. Robert Gray noted that a militia prisoner was usually considered "a State prisoner . . . who deserved a halter" rather than a prisoner of war, "& therefore" the Whigs "treated him with the greatest cruelty." If not "assassinated" immediately after capture, loyal militiamen were usually confined "without friends, money, credit, or perhaps hopes of exchange." As a result of such treatment and the murders committed by rebel partisans, the Loyalists "became dejected & timid," Gray noted. Many joined the Whigs because it was the only way a man could "go to sleep without danger of having his throat cut before morning." Gray believed that if the Whigs had treated captured Loyalists as prisoners of war, which was how the British treated rebel militiamen, "many more would have sided with the royal Standard."[208]

In addition to driving many Loyalists into inactivity or even into the rebel ranks, the defeat at King's Mountain had other important consequences for the

British. Ferguson's death deprived Cornwallis of the officer most capable of making the militia an effective force. One British soldier stated that Ferguson possessed great intelligence and military skill and that Ferguson's death "frustrated a well concerted scheme for strengthening our army, by the co-operation of the well affected inhabitants, whom he had undertaken to discipline and prepare for active service."[209] Gray considered the loss of Ferguson a catastrophe for the Loyalist cause. "Had Major Fergusson lived, the Militia would have been completely formed," Gray wrote. "He possessed all the talents & ambition necessary to accomplish that purpose . . . the want of a man of his genius was soon severely felt."[210] Ferguson's defeat also forced Cornwallis to abandon the invasion of North Carolina and retreat from Charlotte.[211] The army's withdrawal compounded the dispiriting effects of King's Mountain on the Loyalists while bolstering rebel morale.[212]

Georgia Loyalists too came under increasing rebel pressure in the autumn of 1780; they had in fact enjoyed little respite from harassment except for a brief period during the late spring and summer. In February, Governor Wright had informed Clinton that Whig parties continued to raid with impunity. Partisans struck in areas nominally under British control, capturing Loyalists and carrying off hundreds of slaves. One group routed a Loyalist detachment and killed its commander, while others penetrated within fourteen miles of Savannah.[213]

The arrival of Clinton's army in South Carolina failed to stop these incursions, despite the presence of the garrison at Savannah and 104 men of the Georgia provincials at Abercorn. After an April raid in which the Whigs burned barns and rice and carried off many slaves, Augustine Prevost proposed forming Daniel McGirt's irregulars into a corps of provincial cavalry, believing that they were ideally qualified to conduct partisan warfare, but Clinton ignored the suggestion.[214] As late as May 20 Wright reported that rebel parties from South Carolina were still "plundering, killing, and carrying off the inhabitants within 5 or 6 miles" of Savannah.[215] Nevertheless, Wright managed to hold elections for the provincial assembly in April. Whig control of the backcountry prevented some parishes from sending representatives, so that only fifteen members attended the opening session on May 9. Wright assured them that the tumults of recent years would vanish under beneficent British rule. The assembly passed an act barring 151 named rebels from holding civil or military office, and as a gesture of loyalty that body enacted a duty on exports to be paid to the British treasury. However, the province's ravaged condition left it unable even to support itself. Parliament provided an annual subsidy of £3,000 ($390,000), which proved insufficient to meet Georgia's expenses.[216]

After the capture of Charleston, Clinton ordered Thomas Brown to occupy Augusta with his Rangers and secure the backcountry. Brown reached the town about June 8, having advanced part of the way on the South Carolina side of the Savannah River. On his march, Brown accepted the surrender of hundreds of Georgia and South Carolina Whigs and paroled them. Many other Georgians traveled to Augusta and surrendered to Brown there. The inhabitants of the town and surrounding area then petitioned Governor Wright, asking that he restore the king's peace in the district.[217]

Brown organized the Augusta Loyalists into a militia under Col. James Grierson, while Cols. Matthew Lyle and Thomas Waters assumed command of the militia in St. George's Parish and the Ceded Lands, respectively. By mid-August, Governor Wright described the situation in the backcountry as "peaceable and quiet," and he rejected Balfour's proposal to send British troops to the Ceded Lands to disarm former rebels.[218] Brown, however, did not share the governor's confidence; he worried that "unless a considerable number of the most obnoxious" Whigs in the Ceded Lands "are removed, the loyalists in the neighbouring parishes will not be able to live in peace."[219]

Events soon demonstrated the accuracy of Brown's assessment. Elijah Clarke, whose Georgia Whigs had been operating farther north, attacked Augusta on September 14. By threatening Georgians who had taken the British oath with death if they refused to join him, he assembled about six hundred men and struck so swiftly that Brown did not have time to call out the loyal militia. Brown, his Rangers, and several hundred Indians took position in and around a stone house and withstood a siege until September 18, when Cruger approached with a relief force. Cruger had left the militia to hold Ninety Six and marched to Brown's aid as soon as he learned of the rebel attack. The Whigs retreated upon learning that Cruger was nearby; Cruger's troops captured many of the fugitives, and the loyal militia captured sixty-eight. Forty-five of the latter group took the oath to Britain and were released, while a few prominent rebels were sent to prison in Charleston. Brown hanged thirteen prisoners found to have previously taken British protection, and Cruger's troops marched to the Ceded Lands, where they burned the homes and carried off the cattle of some of the men who had joined Clarke. Governor Wright, having earlier recommended that "an Army . . . march without Loss of time into the Ceded Lands . . . to lay Waste and Destroy the whole Territory," approved of the destruction. The inhabitants, Wright declared, "have by their late conduct forfeited every claim to any favour or protection."[220] When Cruger returned to Ninety Six, he left "between 2 & 300 Georgia Militia on the Ceded Lands" to stamp out the last vestiges of rebellion. Cruger considered them "very equal to the task, & exceedingly well inclined."[221]

After Clarke's defeat, Lt. Gov. John Graham traveled to Wilkes County to assess the relative strength of the Loyalists and Whigs there. Of 723 male inhabitants, he found 255 (35 percent) to be committed Loyalists. Fifty-seven men were neutral, and the remainder were rebels.[222]

Overall responsibility for securing Georgia and East Florida rested with Lt. Col. Alured Clarke, who replaced General Prevost when the latter returned to England shortly after the fall of Charleston. Before assuming command at Savannah, Clarke visited St. Augustine to inspect the defenses there. He found the fortifications adequate but the garrison too small to withstand a powerful attacking force. Governor Tonyn assured him, however, that at least 150 inhabitants could be counted on to join in defending the town.[223]

In West Florida the Loyalists' fortunes continued to decline as Bernardo de Galvez pressed his offensive. Recognizing the danger, Gen. John Campbell tried to bolster the province's defenses by authorizing Adam Chrystie to form two troops of light dragoons. However, Chrystie had barely begun recruiting when the Spaniards attacked Mobile in late February. Militia from the surrounding settlements evaded the Spanish besiegers and reinforced the garrison. Their arrival raised the defenders' morale but failed to prevent Galvez from capturing the town on March 14. Seventy militiamen and twenty-eight provincial dragoons from the Royal Foresters who had participated in Mobile's defense were among the prisoners. Other militiamen accompanied Campbell and a force of British regulars and Indians that marched from Pensacola to assist the defenders, but Mobile surrendered before the relief force arrived. Campbell then withdrew, and a detachment of the Royal Foresters that he left behind to protect the settlers and collect cattle was surprised and captured by the Spaniards shortly afterward.[224]

The Indians' Role

Britain's Indian allies made few significant contributions to operations in Georgia and South Carolina in 1780. This resulted largely from Cornwallis's reluctance to employ them, although many British officers expressed a desire for Indian assistance against Whig raiders in the backcountry. The Creeks and Choctaws, however, played an important role in the defense of West Florida and could have been even more valuable had Maj. Gen. John Campbell adopted a wiser policy toward them.

Once they learned of the impending British attack on Charleston, Whig leaders feared that Indian cooperation in the backcountry might doom their efforts to hold the South Carolina capital. Benjamin Lincoln worried that rebels on the frontier might provoke an Indian war, so on January 18, 1780, he instructed George Galphin to make sure that the settlers did not attack the Indians and told the Indian agent to prevent the Georgians from committing "barbarities" against the Creeks, as they had done in the past.[225] In March, Lincoln received encouraging news from Andrew Williamson that the Spanish attack in West Florida had drawn the attention of the Choctaws, Chickasaws, and Creeks in that direction. Those Creeks in the vicinity of the Georgia and South Carolina backcountry, Williamson believed, "are in our Interest except a few Restless fellows. . . . On the whole I believe we have little to fear from that Quarter."[226]

Williamson's assessment regarding West Florida was generally correct, but he underestimated the Creeks' commitment to the British and failed to consider the Cherokees. There were about three hundred Cherokees at Savannah, "holding themselves in readiness" to serve with Clinton's army, when the British fleet arrived there.[227] Had Clinton followed his original plan to send troops from Savannah into the backcountry, the Cherokees were to have accompanied the British detachment. However, when Clinton ordered those troops to Charleston instead, their commander, Gen. James Paterson, decided to leave the Indians in Georgia.[228] A few Indians chose to go with the British anyway; Uzal Johnson noted that one evening during the march, "two Indian Captains John & James" visited his battalion's camp. The Loyalists seemed amused by their guests and "smoak'd tobacco & drank grog with those Devils Incarnate."[229]

Many British officers shared Johnson's low opinion of the Indians. According to a German officer, Paterson had chosen to leave the Indians in Savannah "because of their barbarity."[230] Hessian captain Johann Hinrichs, having encountered only one Indian since arriving at Savannah, had no personal knowledge of them and apparently based his views on talk he heard in camp. "As soldiers, they are anything but dangerous to one accustomed to balls, lead, and hand-to-hand combat," Hinrichs asserted. "Hiding in bushes and behind trees, waiting to take a shot at someone, and upon meeting with the slightest resistance taking flight with amazing agility, but showing up at another place just as quickly—these are their principal military virtues." Such tactics did not impress Hinrichs, who declared that Indians "cost many times more than real soldiers and do more harm than good."[231]

Bored with enforced idleness and in "great dread of the small pox" that had broken out in coastal Georgia, the Indians at the beginning of March told Augustine Prevost that they wished to leave Savannah and return to their homes. Prevost told Clinton that the Indians could not be prevented from leaving "if we wish them to remain our friends." He added that their departure would not affect his ability to defend Savannah, because the Indians "are not people to be employed in the diffence of a place; they can not suffer the appearance of being shut up." He also advised Clinton that messages should be sent to halt other Indian parties en route to the town.[232] Clinton agreed with Prevost's suggestions and instructed his subordinate to retain the Indians' "goodwill & let them understand they are to be called upon shortly."[233] In mid-March the Indians left Savannah after promising to return when summoned.[234] On their homeward journey, one group of Indians was attacked by a Whig party that "kill'd four men and one woman and took one man two boys and a girl prisoners."[235]

Governor Wright appreciated the Indians more than most army officers did and expressed displeasure at their departure. Believing that Clinton's cancellation of the march into the backcountry left Savannah vulnerable to attacks from rebels based in Georgia's interior, Wright urged Clinton to pay closer attention to Indian relations. British officers might consider the Indians "useless in the field," the governor wrote, but if the Cherokees left Savannah "in disgust, and the Creeks being stop't and sent home again, most like may be disgusted also," they might decide to cast their lot with the Whigs. If so, Wright warned, the Indians "would harrass the King's Troops . . . & receive the Rebels amongst them," and in that case, "we could never subdue the rebellion."[236] In his reply, Clinton ignored Wright's comments about the Indians and assured the governor that the rebels would be too occupied in South Carolina to menace Georgia.[237]

Clinton did, in fact, hope that the Indians would cooperate with his forces; at the start of the campaign he had told Thomas Brown that "it was not his intention to expose the Indians unreasonably by incursions into the different provinces in rebellion but to reserve their services for some more decisive blow" when they could receive assistance from British troops.[238] Later, Clinton asked Alexander Innes to bring "an old sachem and Creek young warriors with you" from Savannah to visit the army's camp at Charleston. "I wish them to see our army," Clinton wrote, but he reminded Innes to keep the Indians under control on the march northward. Brown, Clinton added, was to remain in Georgia and keep the Indians there "in good humour." When Charleston fell, Clinton promised to immediately send Brown orders on how to employ the Indians.[239] In late April a Lower Creek chief, accompanied by Loyalist William McIntosh, finally arrived at the British lines outside Charleston and met Clinton. Johann Ewald wrote that the chief, "Ravening Wolf," had been sent "by several Indian tribes" to learn whether the British were strong enough "that it was worth the trouble for these nations to venture further into an alliance" with them.[240] The rebels had told the Creeks that the British army "was in very bad condition in order to get his nation away from supporting the English." Clinton therefore ordered that the chief be given a tour of the British camp and siege lines.[241] The general regretted that no Cherokee leaders had come; "it would have been of consequence," he stated, perhaps believing that the sight of a powerful British army would encourage them to cooperate more actively in the future.[242]

After Charleston surrendered, Clinton ordered Brown to march into the backcountry and take post at Augusta. Brown welcomed the opportunity, since it would place him nearer to the Cherokees and Creeks; he estimated that 360 of the latter were actively assisting the British on the frontier and believed that the pro-Whig Creek faction could now be convinced to align themselves with the British. He appointed Charles Shaw to act as his representative in Savannah to promote cooperation with Lieutenant Colonel Clarke.[243]

Once he had established himself at Augusta, Brown informed Cornwallis that he had dispatched messengers to the Creeks and Cherokees with orders to end hostilities against the inhabitants of Georgia and South Carolina. Brown asked the earl for permission to demolish Fort Rutledge, which had been a source of irritation to the Cherokees because it was located on their land. He also told Cornwallis that he had promised the Indians that all settlers illegally residing on Indian land would be removed.[244] Brown intended to remedy Whig injustices to the Creeks and Cherokees by enforcing the Indian boundary, regardless of how frontier settlers might react.

In addition, Brown proposed an ambitious plan to attack the overmountain settlements. Wishing to prevent the Creeks and Cherokees "from seeking satisfaction for any losses they may have sustained" at the hands of Georgians and South Carolinians, Brown suggested, "I should order the indians to drive the Virginia & Nth. Carolina Banditti who have forcible possession of their lands at Wattoga, Caen Tuck, & c—I mean Henderson's settlement as it is generally called."[245]

Brown discussed these matters with Balfour, who endorsed the destruction of Fort Rutledge in a letter to Cornwallis. Balfour believed that dismantling the fort would allow the Indians to move freely on the frontier, where there were many rebels, and that "the nearer the Indians are brought to these gentry the better." With regard to the proposed attack on the overmountain settlements, Balfour elaborated on Brown's earlier arguments but did not offer his own opinion. The overmountain settlers were "a sett of Banditti, who have settled by force upon the lands of the Creeks & Cherokees," Balfour explained, and "had been allways complained of by the indians, as a grievous encroachment." Brown had told Balfour that the British had promised to resolve that problem at the first opportunity, and that if they did not take action now, the Indians would be disappointed. Brown therefore planned "to warne the people, to leave, these lands in a certain time, and in case of non compliance to take the consequences."[246]

On June 28 Brown repeated his request to move against Watauga, telling Cornwallis that the Cherokees, who with the Creeks were sending a delegation to Augusta, would press the issue when they arrived. "At this juncture it perhaps will be more politic to secure the affections of our indian allies than to employ them on such services where there is a difficulty of discriminating between friends & foes," Brown suggested. There would be no such problem at Watauga, because all the settlements there were "the asylum of plunderers & robbers" committed to the rebel cause. Brown also asked for money to assist almost seven hundred Indian families who were in a "distressed miserable condition."[247]

Before answering Brown, Cornwallis ordered Balfour to "explain to Col. Brown in the most positive Manner, that I wish to keep the Indians in good humour, but on no Account whatever to bring them forward or employ them."[248] The earl finally found time to reply to Brown on July 17 with a letter that must have shocked its recipient. "I will in a few words tell you my Ideas & wishes in regard to the Indians," the earl bluntly announced. They were to be "kept in good humour by civil treatment & a proper distribution of such presents as are sent from England for that purpose, but I would on no Account employ them in any operations of War." Although he approved the destruction of Fort Rutledge, Cornwallis dismissed the Cherokees' complaints about the overmountain settlers as "too intricate for us to enter upon" at present; he advised Brown to placate them with a promise to rectify the matter in the future. Nor would Cornwallis provide funds for the Indian department; Brown would have to make do with whatever presents had been allocated by the government. Since he did not intend "to make any Military Use of the Indians," the earl declared, he could not "think myself justifyed in suffering the Publick to be put to any considerable Expence about them." In any case, he felt that there was no need for charity, stating, "If their Houses have been destroy'd, the Rebuilding an Indian Hut is no very expensive Affair, and I dare say they will get their usual Crops of Corn this Year." Cornwallis closed his harsh letter by citing a report from General Campbell in Pensacola that the Creeks there "staid only as long as they could extort presents," feasted on British provisions, and left just at the time Campbell thought a Spanish attack was imminent.[249]

In an uncharacteristically rude manner, Cornwallis had made it clear that he considered the king's Indian allies to be barely worth the expense required to maintain their allegiance. Although his decision undoubtedly saved the British treasury a few thousand pounds, Cornwallis's shortsighted refusal to adopt Brown's proposal to attack the overmountain settlements had serious consequences. Had he dispatched Brown to lead the Creeks and Cherokees against the Whigs there, Cornwallis would have removed a dangerous threat to his subsequent operations. Under Brown's skillful leadership, a series of determined raids, even if unsuccessful in dislodging the settlers, would have prevented the overmountain men from harassing the frontiers of Georgia and South Carolina; more importantly, the Wataugans would not have been able to act against Patrick Ferguson's detachment in the autumn, which had such fatal consequences for the British and Loyalists. As Isaac Shelby, who commanded some of the overmountain militia at King's Mountain, later noted, reports that "these Indians were preparing for a formidable attack upon us" at the time he marched against Ferguson made him "unwilling that we should take away the whole disposable force of our counties." The threatened Cherokee attack thus reduced the size of the force Shelby employed against Ferguson; an actual attack might have kept all of the overmountain rebels at home.[250]

Cornwallis had several reasons for choosing to keep the Indians idle. In Britain the opposition in Parliament had again assailed the ministry for its Indian policy in the spring of 1780. Members especially criticized the Indian department's heavy expenditures. Lord Shelburne accused John Stuart of having reaped enormous personal profit from contracts to supply goods to the southern nations, without any substantial return to the government in the form of Indian assistance. This forced Germain, who was concerned with spiraling costs in the Indian department, to order officials in America to reduce expenses.[251] Cornwallis also believed that Indians could contribute little to his military operations. He may have been influenced in this regard by James Simpson, with whom he had worked closely in Charleston. Simpson made it widely known that in his opinion and that of many other southern Loyalists, the Indians "are not wanted. . . . With the Troops they are of no Use. To let them loose they would injure Friends as well as Foes."[252] In addition, Cornwallis recognized that assigning the Indians an active role might alienate many backcountry inhabitants, both Loyalists and former Whigs who had taken the oath to Britain. Acting on Cornwallis's instructions, Ferguson

issued a proclamation when he entered North Carolina in September. This procla-
mation was designed to reassure the inhabitants by denying rebel claims that the
British planned to use Indians against them, pointing out instead that "the only
Indians employ'd since the Invasion of Carolina are those of Catawbaw by the
Rebels."253

If Cornwallis did not wish to use the pro-British Indians, neither did he want
the Catawbas to aid the Whigs. Lord Rawdon, arriving at the Waxhaws settlements on June 11, noted that people there feared that "they shall be troubled by
the Catawba Indians." Rawdon reported that the Catawbas had "retired into
North Carolina with their families" and movable property after hearing reports
that the British troops were accompanied by a party of Cherokees. To prevent
the Catawbas from raiding, Rawdon told local Loyalists to inform them that if
they returned and behaved well, they would receive protection, but if they
molested the Loyalists, "their settlement shall be utterly destroyed."254

Despite Rawdon's threats, Thomas Sumter used Catawba territory as the
base where he organized his partisans in the summer of 1780. In addition to
supplying Sumter's men with food, the Catawbas contributed many volunteers
to the rebel force. According to one estimate, two hundred Catawbas served
with Sumter in his attacks against British posts at Rocky Mount and Hanging
Rock. Some served with Sumter throughout the southern campaign, and others
joined William R. Davie's partisan unit.255

Cornwallis thus deprived the British of Indian assistance while the Catawbas
continued to aid the Whigs, and it was not long before South Carolina and Georgia felt the effects of the earl's policy. In August, Evan McLaurin informed Balfour
that "a Body of about 300 mountaineers from Wataga" were plundering the South
Carolina frontier—the same men against whom Brown had intended to employ
the Indians. McLaurin warned that the Wataugans "will be a Thorn to us" unless
the British built a fort near their settlements, which would provide a secure base
from which the Indians could harass them. This, McLaurin believed, would keep
the Wataugans home "for fear of exposing their families to the Indians." If such a
step were not taken, "we shall not have either a quiet or an honest back Country,"
McLaurin declared. "The Indians God knows are good for Little but still they are
a Bugbear & then would ly between the Province & the Overhill Settlements so as
to interrupt the Intercourse between them."256

The vulnerability of the frontier posts became painfully evident on September
14, when Elijah Clarke attacked Augusta with six hundred men. The rebels opened
their assault by striking the camp of several hundred Cherokees and Creeks outside the town; the Indians had come to confer with Brown. The surprise attack
drove off the Indians before Brown arrived with his troops to assist them, but the
rangers and Indians managed to recapture and occupy a stone house. The next day
fifty Cherokees crossed the Savannah River to reinforce Brown's besieged force.
The Indians and provincials held out until troops from Ninety Six relieved them

on September 17. Joining the soldiers and militia in pursuit of the fleeing Whigs, the Indians seized and reportedly scalped several of Clarke's men. Cruger praised the Indians' performance in his report to Cornwallis.[257]

The sudden attack on Augusta and the Indians' valorous performance in the defense of that post convinced Balfour that it was necessary to use Indians to protect the frontier. "I own the best mode, of at once stopping all these kind of expeditions, appears to me to be, the employing the Indians, to clear certain districts, where these people retreat to, & resort," he advised Cornwallis. Balfour noted that Andrew Williamson, who had taken protection and was now providing the British with advice, agreed that allowing the Indians to attack rebel partisans, within "certain boundarys . . . would certainly effect the purpose." Balfour urged Cornwallis to act quickly, before the backcountry revolt "gains head, and becomes perhaps too powerful for any of our posts."[258] Cornwallis chose not to act, depriving himself of an excellent opportunity to convince the backcountry Loyalists to cooperate with the Indians, since the latter's contribution to the defense of Augusta was widely known.

British success in South Carolina had failed to secure the frontiers of that province or Georgia but placed the rebels at too great a distance to threaten East Florida. Yet, Governor Tonyn carefully watched the progress of the Spanish offensive in West Florida. With many troops having been transferred from his province to Georgia, Tonyn relied more than ever on Indians to defend St. Augustine. In July 1780 Germain gave the governor direct authority over the Seminoles, who remained steadfast despite British inability to provide them with adequate supplies and the efforts of Spanish agents to win their allegiance.[259]

British officials in West Florida were in even greater need of Indian assistance as Galvez continued his offensive by attacking Mobile in February. Hundreds of Choctaws had been camped near Mobile until early in the year, "but official stinginess and their own boredom drove them home," so that only eighteen were present when the Spanish arrived.[260] The British also had problems with the Creeks. In January, Governor Chester had made an unauthorized grant of Creek lands "to himself and others his Favorites and Dependents," which provoked the Creeks to plunder some of the province's inhabitants. Furthermore, Campbell's low opinion of Alexander Cameron hampered coordination between the army and the Indian department. Campbell considered the superintendent "no wise qualified . . . to act but in a subordinate Degree" and asserted that Cameron was "lost, bewildered . . . and unequal to the Task" assigned him.[261]

Despite this turmoil, the Indian agents responded quickly to the Spanish attack. Charles Stuart ordered Farquhar Bethune to bring as many Choctaws as possible to relieve Mobile; six hundred Indians were en route when they learned of the town's surrender, whereupon most returned home. Bethune brought the remaining two hundred to Pensacola. Stuart had remained at Mobile, was captured by the Spaniards, and died of an illness soon afterward. Cameron blamed Campbell for the loss of Mobile, complaining that the general's habit of summoning the

Indians every time a Spanish attack was rumored and then dismissing them when the threat failed to materialize had alienated the Indians to a point where they would soon refuse to assist the British at all.[262]

Cameron's assessment of the potentially harmful effects of Campbell's policy was correct, although the superintendent underestimated the Indians' tolerance. The Choctaws who went to Pensacola participated in Campbell's unsuccessful effort to relieve Mobile, covering the flanks of the British column and roving ahead to gather intelligence.[263] When Campbell withdrew after learning of Mobile's surrender, he left fifty Choctaws to keep watch and send warning if the Spaniards marched to Pensacola. Again, however, Campbell grew tired of the expense for provisions and presents and dismissed the Indians, thus depriving himself of information on Spanish activity around Mobile.[264]

In late March, believing that Galvez intended to attack Pensacola, Campbell again called upon the Indians for aid. By early April, at the same time that Germain was frantically composing orders for Campbell to unite the Chickasaws, Cherokees, and Creeks to defend what remained of West Florida, nearly sixteen hundred Creeks and Choctaws had arrived in the town. Germain distrusted the Choctaws, whom he suspected harbored pro-Spanish sympathies.[265] Some officers shared Germain's suspicions. "We can trust the Creeks a bit more than the Choctaws," Philipp Waldeck wrote, because the latter "tend to favor the Spanish." Nevertheless, the Choctaws' martial appearance impressed him. "What a wonderful regiment could be made of them," Waldeck stated. "But would they accept discipline? Discipline is something about which they know nothing. Even the chief does not control them."[266]

Campbell expressed his appreciation for the Indians' support at a meeting with Creek leaders on April 12 and promised them presents, but he could not restrain himself from criticizing the Creeks for killing some livestock. The Creek leader replied that his people had come to fight the Spaniards, not to get presents. He declared that his people had killed livestock "in youthful exuberance" rather than from hunger. Apparently aware that his remarks had upset the Creeks, Campbell said nothing about the Indians' behavior at a meeting the next day with the Choctaws. Campbell's patience must have been severely strained by May 1, when Waldeck noted that the Indians were committing "all sorts of excesses. They get drunk and then are unmanageable. Today they even attacked our own outpost."[267] Cameron had hoped to keep the Indians active by sending them to harass the Spaniards around Mobile, but Campbell disapproved, fearing that they would commit "indiscriminate murder." With nothing to do, the Indians "sold most of their provisions for rum . . . and when very drunk they were very insolent and obstreperous," and yet Campbell, needing their aid against the Spanish, chose to ignore their behavior.[268]

If the Indians created problems for Campbell, they created greater difficulty for Galvez, who realized that they represented a serious obstacle to an attack on

Pensacola. In an effort to remove the advantage that the Indians provided the British, Galvez wrote to Campbell in April suggesting that neither side employ them. Reviewing what he considered the brutal aspects of Indian warfare, Galvez argued that in the interest of humanity the Indians should not be allowed to take part in the conflict. Campbell replied that Indians in British service always acted "under proper leaders" who prevented the cruelties that Galvez described. He rejected the Spaniard's proposal as "insulting and injurious to reason and common sense." Galvez's proposal convinced Campbell that the Indians were indeed an asset to the British.[269] Reluctantly, Campbell conceded that the Indians' presence had prevented Galvez from launching his attack.[270]

Cameron agreed, telling General Clinton that British retention of Pensacola "is entirely owing to the great numbers of Indians that speedily repaired hither to our assistance." The superintendent remained dissatisfied with Campbell's treatment of the Indians; he complained to Germain that Campbell "thinks they are to be used like slaves or a people void of natural sense."[271] As Cameron noted, the Indians' role in protecting Pensacola certainly had not improved the general's opinion of them. The general sent Germain a litany of his grievances, which included the "unbounded waste" in the Indian department and the need to civilize "these barbarians" by teaching them English concepts of property ownership and settling them in English-style towns.[272]

Continued disagreements between Cameron and Campbell threatened to paralyze the Indian department. When Cameron asked the general to enlist fifty white men to lead the Indians in battle, Campbell allowed Cameron only four and soon afterward decided that the expense was unnecessary and told Cameron to dismiss them. Campbell also was parsimonious when Cameron requested presents for the Indians, disgusting the superintendent and his deputies, who believed that gifts were essential to keep the Indians' allegiance. Cameron's request that one hundred Indians be placed on duty as scouts was refused; Campbell further advised the superintendent not to receive Creek visitors but to send them to Thomas Brown at Augusta, since Brown was the Creeks' agent. Cameron believed that Campbell's actions jeopardized the British-Indian alliance.[273]

While Campbell and Cameron feuded, many Indians left Pensacola and others listened to the importunities of Spanish agents. The Upper Creeks at Pensacola had begun "to grow sickly" by mid-June and decided to return home, promising that they would be "relieved by fresh parties from different parts of the Nation." Charles Shaw ordered Alexander McGillivray to accompany the Creeks to their towns to counter growing Spanish influence. According to Shaw, the Spaniards had gained a foothold in two towns whose inhabitants had been "in the Rebel interest" and "seduced a few of them to Visit Governor Galvez at Mobile, who has promised to load them with Presents and Rum." One of George Galphin's sons too was urging the Creeks to visit the Spanish governor.

Shaw advised Brown to invite "the Chiefs that may lean toward the Spanish interest to visit him at Augusta," where Brown's influence might "fix them firmly in His Majestys interest."[274]

Growing Spanish influence among the Choctaws also troubled British officials. In the fall Campbell informed Clinton of reports indicating that the Choctaws were "in the greatest torment, tumult, and confusion, from the contest between the British and Spanish parties." Campbell believed that the British would maintain the Choctaws' loyalty but conceded that "our success is far from being clear and certain."[275]

Campbell remained the most serious obstacle to the maintenance of good relations between Britain and the Indians. On August 26 a party of Choctaws arrived in Pensacola to report that they had met with Galvez and "received presents . . . but were dissatisfied with them." Believing that the Choctaws intended to auction their allegiance to the highest bidder, British officials told them that because they had gone to the Spaniards, they would receive nothing. When the Choctaws apologized and pledged to support the British, they were given presents. Then, to demonstrate their sincerity, the Choctaws killed and scalped three Spanish soldiers they encountered east of Mobile. The Choctaws brought the scalps to Pensacola "but received no reward, and for their cruelty . . . were treated with contempt."[276]

The Spaniards had been part of a truce party en route to Pensacola, and their deaths prompted Galvez to send Campbell a letter of protest, in which he threatened to allow Spain's Indian allies to retaliate in kind. Campbell in turn reprimanded Mingo Pouscouche, the Choctaw leader. Angered by what he considered a ridiculous consideration for the Spanish enemy, Pouscouche replied that in the future his followers would kill any Spaniard they encountered, regardless of age or sex. In the autumn Choctaw parties attacked the Spanish near Mobile and brought three scalps and a captured family to Pensacola in a defiant display of their independence. Having learned a lesson, Campbell refrained from comment and obtained the family's release in exchange for presents.[277]

Farther west, beyond the reach of interference from Campbell or Cornwallis, the Chickasaws guarded the Mississippi River and blocked rebel plans to expand in that direction. They frequently seized rebel vessels trading with New Orleans, boarding the boats and "knocking the crew on the head."[278] When Virginia soldiers constructed Fort Jefferson below the mouth of the Ohio River on Chickasaw territory in April 1780 and settlers built homes nearby, the Chickasaws refused to tolerate the incursion. Led by James Colbert, they drove the settlers into the fort, burned the houses, and harassed the garrison. With their supplies cut off, the defenders faced surrender before the arrival of a relief force saved them. The Chickasaw reaction, however, convinced Virginia officials that the post was untenable; it was abandoned in June 1781. The Chickasaws also rebuffed Spanish efforts to undermine their attachment to Britain.[279]

THE DIVERSE EXPERIENCES OF AFRICAN AMERICANS

The arrival of Clinton's army in South Carolina gave slaves there the opportunity, which they had long awaited, to seek freedom with the British troops. Thousands of slaves, sometimes with the encouragement of British officers, escaped to the army. Many did find freedom, although they still spent their days at hard labor, while others found themselves back in bondage under new masters. Despite such disappointments, African Americans contributed consistently and significantly to the British army's success.

Realizing that fugitive slaves would strengthen the British in their operations against Charleston, Whig John Laurens sought to preempt this by renewing his efforts to arm South Carolina's slaves. He received considerable support from Benjamin Lincoln, who reminded state officials that the British army's successful use of black troops at the siege of Savannah proved that slaves could fight effectively. That argument failed to sway the governor and the council, although they agreed to assign slaves to work on Charleston's fortifications. Lincoln then demanded a reinforcement of two thousand militia for the defense of Charleston and said that if the state could not provide them, an equal number of blacks should be armed instead. Governor Rutledge ignored the request.[280] At the end of February a frustrated Lincoln insisted that Rutledge immediately reinforce his army with "Black Volunteers" or else the general would withdraw the Continental troops from Charleston.[281] Officials refused to bend to Lincoln's threat, correctly assuming that he would not carry it out. As the siege progressed, it became increasingly difficult to procure slaves to work on the defenses; one observer noted that "the few Negroes remaining in Town are obliged to be pressed daily, & kept under guard, as the masters as well as the Slaves, were unwilling they should work."[282]

The Whigs did permit a handful of blacks to serve aboard the state's armed row galley *Revenge* because a shortage of white seamen left them no other option.[283] In addition, a German officer recorded that his detachment was ambushed four miles from Charleston on March 30 by three hundred rebel "light infantry and Negroes." If he was correct, the blacks were not part of an official unit. More likely, he mistook black laborers and officers' servants with the Whigs for soldiers, although there is a slight possibility that a rebel officer may have armed some slaves on his own initiative.[284]

While the Whigs risked the success of their cause rather than tamper with the institution of slavery, large numbers of slaves threw off their bondage. To them, "the arrival of the British army was a liberating moment."[285] One of Clinton's officers, Lt. Col. James Webster, sent patrols into the countryside to post "placards encouraging Negroes to come into the English lines."[286] Most slaves could not read these notices, but that was not necessary. "Great hordes of Negroes followed the army partially for want of food and partially to escape from their masters," one observer noted.[287] Clinton's aide, Maj. John André, wrote on March 4 that five hundred blankets were needed for blacks who had come to the army.[288] Slave women as well as men fled to the king's troops. Fifteen of fifty-three runaways on John Ball's plantation were women. One, a slave named Charlotte, escaped on May 10, was returned to Ball, and soon escaped again with fourteen other slaves. Many slave women took their children with them. More than one-third of the slaves evacuated from Savannah in 1782 were women, and nearly one-fourth were children.[289]

Some slaves who came to Clinton's army brought prisoners with them. At the end of February three blacks arrived with a British deserter; they had ignored the soldier's efforts to persuade them to bring him to Charleston. The deserter's commanding officer, Maj. James Wemyss, permitted the blacks to testify at the man's court-martial.[290] An astute black man helped the British capture two Whig officials, council member Edward Rutledge and the marquis de Malmedy, a French officer in American service, on May 3. Rutledge, Malmedy, and two other men had fled Charleston by boat but encountered British troops when they came ashore. Rutledge and Malmedy eluded the soldiers and then met the slave, whom they asked to lead them past the troops. Instead the man took them to the British lines, whereupon the enraged Malmedy drew his sword and attacked the guide, who defended himself with a knife. The altercation, in which both men were wounded, attracted British soldiers, who seized the two Whigs.[291]

Not all blacks went to the British voluntarily; officers repeatedly sent out detachments to gather slaves to assist the army. Many of these slaves had been left behind by their masters, sometimes under the supervision of wives and children but often without any white supervision.[292] The army's seizure of slaves aroused the enmity of white South Carolinians, who, a Hessian officer wrote, "hated us because we carried off their Negroes and livestock."[293] Loyalists as well as Whigs resented the loss of their slaves, especially when their attempts to recover them failed.[294]

British officers remained uncertain of how to deal with the large number of fugitives flocking to them. Slaves represented a large and valuable pool of laborers for the army and simultaneously diminished the rebels' labor resources. However, far more slaves came to the army than it could possibly employ, and all of the fugitives, whether employed or not, needed to be fed and clothed. Clinton also worried that any attempt on his part to fundamentally change the slave system would alienate white Loyalists and make it harder to reconcile former rebels.[295]

Before the army left New York, the British had given some consideration to how they should handle the slave issue once they had control of Charleston. An unnamed official suggested that Clinton "publish a Proclamation relative to Negroes; ordering all such as may come in, to give their Names, together with their Masters Names, and former places of Abode" to the newly appointed civil officials, who would then designate a person to enroll the blacks and provide them with certificates proving that they had voluntarily offered their services.

Those blacks who did not have such certificates, except for slaves whose masters resided in Charleston, "must be imprisoned; this will prevent the bad effects found at New York, and put it in the Generals power to make the proper use of them in labouring for the different departments."[296] The author intended that the British should make use of African American volunteers but avoid the difficulties that would ensue if large numbers of slaves fled to the army and then remained in Charleston, or followed the troops, without employment. Having numerous unidentified and unregulated slaves in the vicinity of the army, the author believed, would create problems both for the army and for civilians and could impede the pacification of South Carolina.

Patrick Ferguson submitted his own proposal for using the slaves to fortify key posts, which would enable a limited number of regulars, supported by loyal militia, to maintain control in South Carolina and Georgia. Ferguson suggested that blacks already with the army, along with others seized from rebel owners, could construct the fortifications. These slaves could be "allow'd rebel lands to Cultivate for their Subsistance & half their time for that Purpose" and could spend their remaining time fortifying the posts at little expense to the British.[297]

Clinton had already devised a plan before he received Ferguson's suggestions. On February 13 the general appointed Lt. Col. James Moncrief and two civilians, George Hay and James Fraser, to act as commissaries of captures. Their duty was to gather "Negroes, Cattle, Rice, Forage, and other Articles serviceable to the Army" from abandoned plantations and distribute them for "the use, Convenience & benefit of the Troops."[298] In little more than a month the commissaries reported that they had taken up 317 blacks and assigned them to various military departments. Seventy were employed by the quartermaster general, 96 with the engineers, 35 with the commissary general, 60 with the artillery, 6 with the provost marshal, and 5 in the hospital. The commissaries retained the other 45 to assist in gathering supplies.[299]

In early April, Clinton issued additional orders stating that "Negroes will also be Wanting and as their employment will save the Troops much Toyl & Fatigue— The General orders whenever they may be taken from the Enemy they be sent immediately" to one of the commissaries of captures. These slaves would then be apportioned "to each Corps as soon as there shall be enough Collected for the Publick Service."[300] By April 28 the number of blacks assigned to the Royal Artillery as carpenters, collar makers, and laborers had increased to 154.[301]

As Clinton intended, black labor freed hundreds of British troops from fatiguing duties and allowed them to participate in the siege operations. He had brought two companies of black pioneers from Savannah and assigned them to repair roads and bridges.[302] The slaves who joined the army in South Carolina helped British soldiers and sailors carry supplies forward as the army advanced. When the British crossed the Ashley River at the end of March, "Negroes moved the cannons, munitions, and provisions" to the new position.[303] Blacks also fortified the many positions the army occupied during Clinton's cautious approach to Charleston. On April 9, 134 African Americans used a specially designed cart to haul four British gunboats and two flatboats overland from the Ashley to the Cooper River. Other blacks accompanied British and Hessian foraging parties, helping to round up cattle and bring them to the army's camps. After Charleston's surrender, Clinton assigned black workers the task of dismantling the British siege works outside the town, and within ten days they completed the bulk of the work.[304]

The British corps that marched from Savannah to Charleston also employed blacks in various capacities, such as driving cattle and sheep collected from rebel plantations, but they were kept under strict supervision.[305] All African Americans with the detachment were required to carry passes and "March regularly with the Baggage of their Several Battalions."[306] The troops were prohibited from allowing refugee slaves to join them; orders stated that "every Negroe Vagabond & Stragler is Positively forbid to follow the Army under pain of the most severe and Immediate punishment."[307]

As important as slaves' labor was to British success in the Charleston campaign, the information that blacks provided was of even greater value, even if it was sometimes inaccurate. An escaped slave who left Charleston in mid-February gave British officers a fairly precise estimate of rebel strength but mistakenly reported that the Whigs planned to attack the detachment marching north from Savannah. Another slave who reached the British a few days later brought an accurate report of Lincoln's position. As the siege progressed, escaping through the American defensive lines became extremely dangerous, and yet blacks continued to make the effort. Duncan, the slave of a Charleston artisan, fled from the town and gave Major André a detailed report on the situation of the rebel army and the quantity of provisions in the town. Several blacks reached British lines on April 3 with news that reinforcements from North Carolina had recently arrived in Charleston; they also provided information on Whig casualties. On May 3 five slaves arrived with a report that supply shortages had reduced the defenders to half rations.[308]

Some information from slaves enabled the British to surprise and defeat various Whig detachments. A black man informed Maj. Gen. Johann Christoph Von Huyn on the night of March 22 that five rebels were lurking less than a mile away. Von Huyn promptly dispatched a patrol to the place his informant had indicated. The Hessians captured four of the five Americans, who had been sent to seize a sentry in order to obtain information.[309]

While marching to attempt a night attack on Whig cavalry posted at Monck's Corner, Banastre Tarleton's troops captured a slave whose information enabled Tarleton to win a crushing victory on April 13. The prisoner, Thomas Johnston, was carrying a military dispatch for the rebels; from the information it contained, along with Johnston's report, which Tarleton "purchased for a few dollars," the British commander obtained complete information of the American position. Tarleton put this knowledge to good use in an assault that surprised and routed the rebels. He then sent a detachment forward to capture a second American post at Biggin's Bridge. The British captured one hundred prisoners, four hundred horses, and fifty wagons loaded with supplies.[310] The following night "two Negroes came in" to Patrick Ferguson's camp at Monck's Corner with information that twenty rebel cavalrymen were concealed in a nearby swamp. Capt. Abraham Depeyster and twenty men found and attacked the Whigs, killing two and capturing one man and five horses.[311]

British officers recognized that blacks' ability to travel between the lines with relative ease could be a problem if some slaves were acting as spies for the rebels. On March 14 Captain Hinrichs warned Cornwallis that "it was very easy, especially for Negroes," to pass between British outposts. Cornwallis promptly tightened security around the army's camps.[312] Two slaves accused of being rebel spies were tried by a British court-martial on March 24. Twelve days earlier a black man had told Hessian guards on James Island that three Whigs were coming that night to spy on the British army. Following their informant's directions, the Hessians found a boat and two slaves named Fortune and May. Shortly afterward the troops captured two Charleston residents, John Witta and William Sterling. The whites insisted that they had come to the island to check on their families, but a Hessian standing guard at Sterling's house testified that a second black informant had warned him that he was in danger of being captured or killed by the two Whigs. Sterling and Witta were probably imprisoned, while Fortune and May won acquittal by testifying that "they were obliged by order of their Master to row [the whites] over, which they did, or they would have been severely beat."[313] British officers' willingness to allow blacks to testify at courts-martial, in their own defense or against whites, indicates a growing respect for slaves, who had demonstrated their intelligence and reliability by consistently providing the army with sound information.

Blacks also assisted the British in other ways. In February "a captured Negro boy" acted as a guide for Lieutenant Colonel Webster's detachment on its march to Stono Ferry.[314] Hessian captain Johann Ewald noted that the boy "spoke such a poor dialect that he was extremely hard to understand." When Ewald's troops received orders on February 19 to form three parties and "collect information about the enemy and to hunt up Negroes and livestock," each party had a black guide, but again problems arose because the troops could not understand the slaves' dialect. However, during their excursion the troops found a household slave "who agreed quite sensibly to tell the truth about everything." Ewald brought the slave to Gen. Alexander Leslie, who found him "to be a great treasure" when he provided detailed information on American strength and positions.[315]

In addition, slaves fulfilled the role that Germain had originally envisioned for them by reducing the number of men available to defend Charleston. When Gov. John Rutledge ordered Col. Benjamin Garden to send reinforcements to the town at the beginning of March, he instructed Garden to retain half of his militia "for keeping the Negroes in Order."[316]

While blacks' contributions to the success of the British campaign earned them the respect of many army officers, their plight as slaves won them sympathy as well. During and after the siege of Charleston, Clinton's troops had an opportunity to observe the conditions of slavery, and often they did not like what they saw. Sgt. Roger Lamb of the Royal Welsh Fusiliers was amazed to find "almost every white man, in this boasted land of liberty, keeping a great number of slaves!" Lamb believed that South Carolinians would be targeted for divine punishment because they promoted "that abominable and notorious traffic, the slave trade. How any people pretending, as the Americans do, to the profession of christianity, can dare to drive on an horrible traffic in the blood of their fellow creatures . . . is a dreadful solecism, at which a Pagan may laugh." Lamb added that his revulsion at this "deplorable evil" was widespread in the army.[317]

German observers were particularly vociferous in their criticism of slavery. Carl Bauer of the Grenadier Battalion Platte found that slaves who worked as personal servants were "kept well" but that field slaves were treated "contrary to all humanity." He described them as naked, underfed, forced to dwell in "miserable huts," and subject to horrifying punishments. "For little faults they are hung up, tied by both hands, and whipped dreadfully on their bare backs," Bauer wrote. "In proportion to their crime an iron nail is sometimes tied to the whip." However, Bauer also believed that slaves were "as obstinate as undomesticated cattle."[318] Lt. Christian Bartholomai expressed "great sympathy" for the slaves' misery and "asked why the negroes on the land are treated so hard and miserably here." South Carolinians replied that they could "insure their safety from insurrection and destruction [only] by employing the whip and fear" and declared that blacks were lazy "and must always be driven to work with a whip."[319] Hessian units recruited at least forty-seven blacks in South Carolina, most of whom served as drummers. This was a more consequential contribution than it may appear, since the addition of a black drummer allowed a white soldier to return to the combat ranks. Other former slaves worked as servants, teamsters, and equipment porters. In general, German soldiers showed a "tolerant attitude" toward blacks.[320]

Not all of the king's soldiers looked as kindly on slaves. When the Queen's Rangers, a provincial unit, returned to New York after the Charleston campaign, the troops smuggled a slave man and woman aboard the ship. One of their officers, Stephen Jarvis, discovered the slaves, whereupon he sold them in New York and distributed the proceeds among everyone in his unit. When Lt. Col. John Graves Simcoe learned of the transaction, he convened a court of enquiry, which reprimanded Jarvis.[321]

Like the men of the Queen's Rangers, neither Clinton nor Cornwallis showed any particular sympathy for the slaves. After appointing the commissaries of captures, Clinton took no further action in regard to slaves until May 20, when he informed Cornwallis that he would leave orders to "prevent the Confusion that would arise from a further desertion of them to us." The commander in chief believed that blacks could best be employed "on abandoned Plantations, on which they may subsist." Until he could devise a better plan to deal with refugee slaves, Clinton authorized Cornwallis to "make such Arrangements as will discourage their joining us."[322] Clinton had no intention of issuing a southern version of his Phillipsburg Proclamation, which he had issued in New York on June 30, 1779. In that document Clinton announced that "any Negro the property of a Rebel, who may take refuge with any part of this army" would not be sold or given up to any claimant. Furthermore, he promised "every Negro who shall desert the Rebel Standard, full security to follow within these Lines any occupation which he may think proper."[323] Since slaves were far more numerous in South Carolina than in New York, Clinton probably thought that the army could not employ all those who might come in and preferred them to remain at home, where they would not complicate the army's movements or require management and subsistence.

Clinton did permit some of the fugitives to accompany the army to New York. He allowed each regiment to take along ten blacks to be employed as pioneers, as long as their masters had been in rebellion at the time the slaves fled to the army. Clinton also ordered that none of the former slaves were to be taken to New York without their consent. About five hundred South Carolina slaves sailed north with the army in early June.[324]

Before leaving Charleston, Clinton took further steps to deal with the slaves. On May 27 he issued a proclamation appointing Robert Power, William Carson, and Robert Ballingall as custodians of all fugitive slaves. The proclamation ordered everyone "who may have any slaves belonging to the Inhabitants of this Province in their custody or possession" to "forthwith deliver them" to the three commissioners. Clinton, however, did not explain what the commissioners were supposed to do with these slaves.[325] A week later Clinton sent Cornwallis and Paterson some suggestions for dealing with slaves. After conceding that the issue was so complex that "it is impossible to settle any thing positive," Clinton reminded the two generals that priority should be given to putting the province's lands back into productive cultivation. He recommended that slaves owned by Loyalists should be returned, on the masters' pledge that they would not be punished for fleeing. If masters broke their word and punished slaves, the slaves would be forfeited to the government. Clinton was more generous toward rebel-owned slaves. These, he said, "belong to the Public; and after serving it faithfully during the war are entitled to their Freedom." Until the war's end, these slaves would work in the various military and civil departments and be provided with "adequate Pay, Provision, and Cloathing." Clinton then offered an intriguing idea: "Why not settle the Negroes on Forfeited Lands after the war?"[326] In spite of his reluctance to deal directly with the difficult issue of emancipation, Clinton clearly recognized the value of slaves' services and showed a willingness to free at least some slaves and give them the means to support themselves once the rebels had been subdued.

Dissatisfied with these instructions, for reasons he did not express, Cornwallis asked the commander in chief for further directions. "All I can do about Negroes is already directed to be done," Clinton replied. "But Care must be taken that they are not ill treated—Something is now in Contemplation."[327]

Whatever else Clinton had in mind, he did not communicate it to Cornwallis, thus leaving the earl to devise his own policy. Determining the disposition of thousands of slaves was one of the most complex of the many problems Cornwallis faced. Tarleton described the difficulties involved in formulating a policy in a situation where Loyalist slave owners and freedom-seeking slaves were entirely at odds: "It is here necessary to observe, that all the negroes, men, women, and children, upon the approach of any detachment of the King's troops, thought themselves entirely absolved from all respect to their American masters, and entirely released from servitude: Influenced by this idea, they quitted the plantations, and followed the army; which behaviour caused neglect of cultivation, proved detrimental to the King's troops, and occasioned continual disputes about property of this description."[328]

Tarleton, whose father had amassed a fortune in the slave trade, was less sympathetic to slaves than many other British officers were, but he accurately pointed out the complexity of the issue. The southern army could not be fed unless slaves raised the necessary crops, and many slaves would not work on the plantations without white supervision. Keeping the slaves in bondage thus served one of the army's essential needs; yet, the British could not be expected to retain the loyalty of people who had come to them seeking freedom only to be returned to their plantations. It was a dilemma that British leaders never solved.

Cornwallis decided to instruct the board of police to appoint three commissioners of claims to settle questions of slave ownership and to manage the slaves who had taken refuge with the British. The board selected Carson and Ballingall, whom Clinton had appointed in May, along with Thomas Inglis. The trio set about returning some fugitives to Loyalist owners, while assigning others owned by Whigs still in rebellion to John Cruden, the commissioner of sequestered estates. Many more blacks were put to work on Charleston's fortifications or hired out to various departments of the army. Some eight hundred slaves were assigned to the engineer and ordnance departments.[329] Tarleton approved of Cornwallis's solution, noting that the commissioners soon "produced arrangements equally useful to the military and inhabitants."[330] James Simpson agreed. He pronounced the earl's plan "perfectly Satisfactory" but complained that as intendant of the board of police, he was still "almost pestered to Death with Vexatious Complaints about the Negroes."[331]

Cruden, a North Carolina Loyalist, had his share of problems as well. He held responsibility for some one hundred plantations that belonged to people in rebellion or absent from South Carolina. These properties were sequestered, which meant that Cruden held them in trust until the government determined whether or not they should be returned to their owners. Meanwhile, Cruden had to manage more than five thousand slaves assigned to put the lands into production to support the army. He had more slaves than he could usefully employ on the plantations, so he hired some out to various army departments and assigned one to carry messages to Cornwallis. Nevertheless, Cruden tried to induce more blacks to join the British by paying cash rewards to those "most forward in coming to the lines."[332]

Fugitives who found themselves assigned to plantation work or to menial tasks with the army often disliked their new status as much as their previous bondage and therefore rebelled or fled. In July, Nisbet Balfour had to send British regulars to suppress an insurrection on the sequestered plantation of Ralph Izard. Balfour ordered the troops to punish those responsible for the uprising.[333]

Slaves employed by the army departments were assigned separate living areas, received poor-quality rations in comparison to those of white troops, and lacked access to medical care. "Overworked and undernourished, they fell easy prey to disease."[334] The result, as a Briton attached to the army hospital observed, was that many blacks assigned to work there "have taken the first opportunity of Deserting from their Duty." Other slaves serving on British naval vessels fled when sent ashore to get supplies.[335]

Several of Henry Laurens's slaves had been taken by the British but deserted and returned home. These slaves disliked their overseer, and on their return they notified James Custer, Laurens's manager, that they would not serve under that individual again. Custer believed that he had no choice but to grant their request and promised that the slaves could choose the plantation at which they would work.[336] Laurens's literate slave Samuel Massey informed his master that more than fifteen slaves on one plantation had left "with the kings people," although one had since returned. Massey added that most of the slaves there "can hardly be purSwaided to Stay" but that those at another plantation "are all for Staying at home."[337] The ability to go to the British gave these slaves a great deal of leverage in negotiating the terms of their bondage.

Many blacks simply did not want to remain slaves or live in conditions similar to slavery, regardless of whether their masters were Loyalist or Whig, British or American. From the capture of Charleston until the American army surrounded the town and cut off all escape routes in the spring of 1782, large numbers of South Carolina slaves continued to escape white control in search of freedom. George Turnbull complained in September 1780 that work on the fortifications of Camden had been slowed by the slaves' frequent desertions.[338] The fugitives included field hands, artisans, and personal servants, some of the latter belonging to Loyalist officers. Most were men, although many women and children also escaped. Some mingled with free blacks, slaves, and refugees in Charleston; others sought passage to New York or went to rural areas. The risk of flight was so great that one man advertising thirty slaves for sale boasted that they had "never quitted the plantation or their work in the most alluring times."[339]

In an effort to stop blacks from fleeing, British officials made concessions to placate them. The board of police took the first step in June 1780, ruling in accordance with Clinton's orders that slaves who had escaped from Loyalist owners would be returned but not punished. As the army grew more dependent on black labor, Balfour went a step further, issuing an order on February 9, 1781, that no slave "attached to any of the publick departments" could be returned to an owner without the slave's "own, free consent." Instead, the government would compensate the owners of slaves who refused to return, paying them one shilling and sixpence per day for skilled workers and eightpence for laborers. The British army would also feed and clothe these slaves.[340] Even William Bull, who declared that blacks had become "ungovernable," recognized that they could no longer be treated with the harshness practiced before the Revolution. He personally pardoned two slaves sentenced to death for robbery and also suspended the death sentence of a free black convicted of burglary.[341]

Some of the slaves who left the state were carried off by their masters in the weeks following Charleston's surrender. Both John Lewis Gervais and Governor Rutledge attempted to send their slaves to North Carolina, but the evacuation was "Stoped . . . by the Tories" and the slaves sent "back to our respective plantations," Gervais stated.[342]

Among the reasons that Loyalists tried to prevent slaves from leaving the province was their desire to reclaim slaves previously confiscated by the Whigs, as well as to alleviate a shortage of labor on their own plantations. William Ancrum, manager of the Colleton estate at Wadboo, informed the family's heirs in Britain that a shortage of slaves hindered his efforts to make the plantation profitable. The problem, he said, arose "from the desertion of the Negroes, which they have been too much encouraged to, by the smallpox spreading among them & their being under little or no Subjection to the Overseers."[343] Besides smallpox, a "malignant Fever" broke out in July among blacks in and near Charleston. This disease, which James Simpson said did not appear to affect whites, killed blacks "in great numbers," further worsening the labor shortage.[344]

Other Loyalists simply wished to seize slaves for themselves. In Ninety Six district Evan McLaurin reported that there were not enough slaves to work on the sequestered estates because Loyalists who had acquired slaves belonging to abandoned rebel plantations "are encouraged to keep them by Persons now in Authority." He advised Balfour to issue a proclamation that would "enable us to discharge our Duty . . . without Irritating those *friends* who are as fond of Negroes as of the Laws—as the surest method of keeping the Negroes we have together—& of inducing the others to return." McLaurin also asked Balfour for money to purchase clothing and tools for the slaves, since most of them received no pay for their labor. Unless the slaves' basic needs were met, McLaurin declared, "they may be so neglected that they run away."[345]

While some Loyalists thought themselves entitled to take slaves from rebels as a reward for their fealty, many Whigs took the oath of allegiance to Britain solely in hopes of regaining their slaves. In May, British troops seized thirty-seven slaves owned by John Lloyd, a rebel who had been captured and later released. Although he considered himself "a capital Sufferer by the British," Lloyd took protection so that he could initiate legal proceedings "to get back some of my Negroes."[346] However, five months later Lloyd gave up all hope of recovering his slaves.[347]

In rare cases some South Carolinians preferred not to reclaim slaves for fear that service with the British army had ruined them. Charleston resident Peter Bounetheau owned a black man named William, who was "very expert in blowing the French Horn." Maj. Charles Cochran of the British Legion, having heard of William's talent, borrowed him "for the purpose of blowing a Horn on some particular occasion." However, Cochran did not return the slave as promised; instead, William accompanied the legion during its operations in the interior of the province, which culminated in Tarleton's victory at the Waxhaws on May 29. When Cochran returned to Charleston, he told Bounetheau that William "was so serviceable to the Legion that he positively could not spare him" and offered to provide another slave in exchange for him. Bounetheau demurred, asserting that William was worth much more than a field hand. Bounetheau then accepted Cochran's offer to purchase William for one hundred pounds sterling (thirteen thousand dollars), but Cochran left for England without paying. Bounetheau petitioned Cornwallis, requesting the promised payment and adding that he did not want William returned, "for as he has been now a long time engaged in a sphere widely different from that of a domestick Servant . . . Your Memorialist is apprehensive he may be rendered unserviceable in that line."[348]

Bounetheau's fears may have been justified, for many slaves turned against their masters. One enslaved man informed Rawdon in Camden that his master had been making suspicious excursions into the woods, which led to the capture of two rebel parties who had been stealing "Negroes & Horses belonging to the Army." The slave must have enjoyed the twist of fate that placed his master "in Gaol; & in Irons."[349]

Another slave, Boston King, left his master, found employment with the British army, and later wrote a memoir of his experiences. King's owner had hired him out to a man who abused him badly. On one occasion the man beat King so violently that he could not work for two weeks; later King "was beat and tortured most cruelly, and was laid up three weeks," which led King's owner to intervene to halt the abuse. Shortly after King recovered, his employer took him from Charleston to the country to avoid the approaching British army. Sometime after the town's surrender, another slave took a horse that King had borrowed from a white man. Since the horse's owner "was a very bad man, and knew not how [to] shew mercy," King did not dare confront him. "To escape his cruelty," King wrote, "I determined to go to Charles Town, and throw myself into the hands of the English. They received me readily, and I began to feel the happiness, liberty, of which I knew nothing before."[350]

King encountered many difficulties in his new life, including loneliness and a bout with smallpox. The disease raged among the black refugees, killing at least two thousand of them.[351] To prevent their troops from becoming infected, the British moved all of the infected blacks to an open area a mile from their camp. "We lay sometimes a whole day without any thing to eat or drink," King stated. However, he soon met a soldier from the New York Volunteers with whom he was acquainted, and the man provided King with supplies until he recovered. The British then transported King and two dozen other black convalescents by wagon to Camden, where they were assigned to the New York Volunteers. King proudly referred to the unit as "our regiment." When his benefactor was wounded in the battle of August 16, King repaid the soldier's earlier kindness by tending him for six weeks. King then became the servant of a captain in the regiment.[352]

One day King left camp to go fishing and returned to find his regiment gone and replaced by a few loyal militia. King was "greatly alarmed," but the militia commander, a Captain Lewes, assured him that he would soon rejoin his unit. Later, Lewes, hoping to gain a slave, asked King if he would accept him as his new master. After King refused, Lewes declared that he had "been long enough in the English service" and was "determined to leave them." The statement "roused my indignation," King wrote, and acting on principles of loyalism stronger than those of Lewes, the former slave "spoke some sharp things to him." Lewes threatened to put King in irons and whip him, so King decided to escape. The next day Lewes sent King with a boy to get about fifty horses that the captain had stolen from the British garrison at Rocky Mount. Lewes left after the pair brought him the horses, which gave King an opportunity to flee. He found his regiment the following day and informed his captain of Lewes's actions; the British dispatched a mounted force that recovered forty of the horses and burned Lewes's house. King remained with the New York Volunteers for another year.[353]

King's devoted service to the British and his courage in rebuking a white man indicated the extent to which the war had allowed blacks to challenge the boundaries of slavery. Another black or mulatto man who challenged these limits did so by leading his own band of Loyalist partisans against the Whigs in northeastern South Carolina. The conduct of the man, described only as "Gibson, a coloured man and his party of tories," according to the rebels, was "shocking to humanity." Among the alleged atrocities they attributed to Gibson were the murder of a militia colonel and several other Whigs and the burning of houses.[354] Perhaps Gibson's greatest offense in their eyes, though, was the fact that he was a black man who not only dared to use force against whites but also had gotten other whites to follow him in so doing.

The valor of men such as Gibson and King did nothing to change Cornwallis's poor opinion of blacks. The capture of twelve black soldiers, probably Continentals from the Maryland and Delaware regiments, at Camden on August 16 angered Balfour. He asked Cornwallis if it would "not be worth while, to convince *Blacke* that he must not fight against us—to sell them" into slavery.[355] Cornwallis approved the proposal.[356] The earl also tried to keep blacks with the army under strict control; on September 27 he repeated orders, issued at an unspecified earlier date, "for Marking all Negroes belonging to the Army, with the Number of the Regt. or the Initial Letters of the Department that Employs them," probably in the form of a cloth badge. Cornwallis instructed his officers to inform all blacks that the deputy provost marshal had orders "to take up, & flog out of the Encampment all those who are not Mark'd agreeable to Orders" and that those "found quitting the Line of March in search of plunder" would be executed immediately.[357]

The situation of blacks in Georgia and East Florida changed little during this time. Until the imminent surrender of Charleston forced the Whigs to abandon the lowcountry, rebels occasionally plundered slaves from loyal Georgians' plantations. In late March, for example, a Whig party attacked Governor Wright's farms south of the Ogeechee River and carried off "as many of the negroes as they could."[358] British officials may have attempted to counter such raids by arming slaves, although the evidence is sketchy. John Lewis Gervais heard a report that Whigs under Andrew Pickens "killed about 60 Negroes in Arms, & some white Men with them" in an April battle five miles from Savannah.[359] Wright did recognize the need to arm blacks to strengthen the weak forces defending Georgia; in the fall he convinced the assembly to pass legislation authorizing him "to order out Negroes to construct such fortifications and works as may be thought necessary for the security of the town or in any other parts of the province, also in case of necessity to arm and employ Negroes for our defence."[360] Unlike the Whigs, Georgia's Loyalists accepted the risk of altering the slave system for the sake of their own security.

After taking command in Savannah, Alured Clarke was plagued by slave owners from South Carolina seeking the return of their property. Former Whigs who had taken British protection, these people claimed that they were thus entitled to reclaim their slaves. The blacks objected, telling Clarke that their services "in the defence of Savannah, and on many other occasions," along with "the apprehensions they are under of being treated with cruelty in consequence of it," entitled them to remain with the British. Clarke referred the matter to Cornwallis, although he made his own sympathies clear. Whatever the merits of the masters' arguments, Clarke wrote, "an attention to Justice, and good faith, must plead strongly in behalf of the Negroes."[361]

British officers in West Florida, faced with an even greater threat, did not hesitate to use slaves to assist in the defense of Mobile. At the town's surrender on March 14, the Spanish counted fifty-five armed blacks among the prisoners.[362]

The capture of Charleston had laid the foundation for the reestablishment of British control in South Carolina and Georgia. The Loyalists' response had fulfilled

Germain's expectations, thousands of slaves had flocked to the king's troops, and the Indians had expressed willingness to attack the Whigs. Lincoln's army no longer existed, and the defeat of Gates and Sumter in August had removed much of the remaining rebel opposition. King George stood to retain at least two of his rebellious American provinces if Cornwallis capitalized on these advantages.

Unfortunately for the British cause, Cornwallis squandered many of these advantages. He refused to use the Indians, thus giving the growing Whig partisan forces free rein to operate against the backcountry Loyalists. He delayed the organization and training of the loyal militia because of his dislike of Ferguson; he then ignored Ferguson during the invasion of North Carolina, thus leaving the Loyalists to be slaughtered at King's Mountain. The defeat, along with constant Whig harassment, weakened Loyalist morale and reduced the militia's effectiveness. In addition, while the earl accepted the use of blacks in noncombat roles with the army, he showed no inclination to tap the potential of slaves to serve effectively as soldiers, even though they had demonstrated this ability during the siege of Savannah.

None of this boded well for Britain's ability to secure the southern provinces; nor did the Spanish attack on West Florida. Nevertheless, the foundation for success, albeit damaged, was still solid. The question was whether Cornwallis would repair and build on it or if his future actions would result in its destruction.

SIX

Precipice

DURING THE PERIOD FROM November 1780 to the end of June 1781, the outcome of the British effort to maintain control of South Carolina and Georgia hung in a precarious balance. Despite the demoralizing effects of Ferguson's defeat and the cruelties inflicted on the prisoners taken at King's Mountain and other Loyalists, many supporters of the British remained steadfast in their allegiance. The arrival of Gen. Nathanael Greene to replace Horatio Gates as commander of the American southern army, the destruction of a Loyalist party at Hammond's Store in late December, and Daniel Morgan's victory over Banastre Tarleton at Cowpens the following month inspired the Whigs. However, Morgan's and Greene's subsequent retreat across North Carolina with Cornwallis in close pursuit shifted the situation in favor of the British. Many Whigs and neutrals, believing the rebel cause to be lost, took British protection; meanwhile some dispirited Whig partisans left the field entirely or prepared to abandon the fight in South Carolina and withdraw northward to unite with Greene.

With Cornwallis and his army far to the north and the British and Loyalist troops in South Carolina and Georgia generally tied to fixed positions, some rebels took advantage of the opportunity to raid throughout the countryside. Lord Rawdon, who held the field command in Cornwallis's absence, skillfully employed detachments to keep the rebels in check, while the apparent successes of Cornwallis, first in driving Greene into Virginia and then defeating him at Guilford Court House, North Carolina, in mid-March, seemed to promise ultimate British success. Yet, continued rebel activity demonstrated that the Loyalists were still not secure and took a steady toll of the militia. The situation, though fluid, remained precarious for both of the contending parties—whichever side received significant assistance first was likely to gain the upper hand.

In late April the balance began to tilt in the Whigs' favor. Cornwallis had withdrawn his troops to Wilmington, North Carolina; the men were exhausted from endless marching, lack of supplies, and heavy losses at Guilford Court House. While the earl pondered his next move, Greene marched his army back to South Carolina. Cornwallis rejected the options of pursuing Greene on land or bringing his troops back to South Carolina by sea; instead, he chose to march into Virginia and unite his depleted command with British forces operating in the Chesapeake. Greene's return, Cornwallis's departure, and the realization that the lightning British march through North Carolina had been little more than a dazzling show, with no substantial benefit to the royal cause, revitalized the rebels. Greene threatened the key British position at Camden, while Whig raiders, inspired by the hope of victory, struck at the posts that guarded the town's communications with Charleston.

Rawdon fought back capably, defeating Greene at Hobkirk's Hill on April 26, but he was unable to prevent the Americans' escape with their army intact. The only way Rawdon could create a mobile force strong enough to pursue Greene and destroy the Continental army was by stripping the British posts of troops, which would then leave those positions vulnerable to partisan attacks. The army might then be cut off from supplies and reinforcements. Rawdon had no alternative but to abandon the interior of South Carolina and Georgia and try to defend a more compact position closer to the coast. Loyalists wishing to relocate within the shrunken boundaries of British-held territory had to accompany the troops in their retreat. Those who decided to remain at home would have to make their own peace with the rebels. Even John Harris Cruger's valiant defense of Ninety Six in June did not prevent the evacuation of the town, while Augusta fell to Whig forces. The loss of the backcountry cut off direct communication with the Indians, who had remained relatively inactive except in West Florida, where they fought stoutly in the unsuccessful defense of Pensacola. Blacks continued to support the British with labor and information but still constituted an underutilized resource. By the autumn of 1781 control of the southern backcountry, and with it the balance of power in the Deep South, had shifted decisively in favor of the Whigs.

LOYALIST PERSISTENCE

Despite the disaster at King's Mountain, the subsequent suffering of the prisoners, and the demoralizing effects of Cornwallis's retreat from Charlotte, many Loyalists persisted in supporting the royal cause. With the army in winter quarters at Winnsboro, British officers relied on the militia to secure most of South Carolina. Balfour assigned two militia regiments to guard the line of communication between Charleston and Camden in late October. Although he considered the units' combined strength of about four hundred men inadequate, he wrote, "but we must do the best we can With them."[1] Balfour doubted that these men were capable of performing strenuous duty, but he believed that they "will surely be enough to guard ferrys, which is the most easy of all services."[2]

In the northeastern part of the province, Francis Marion continued his efforts to destroy the loyal militia. He attacked a party of Loyalists near Georgetown in mid-October, killing a Lieutenant Evans and mortally wounding a Captain Garner, whom Marion described as "the most active persons against us & the head of all the torrys on the Lower part of Peedee." The Whigs then raided Georgetown, where Colonel James Cassells with seventy militiamen occupied a redoubt and refused to surrender. Marion withdrew after paroling several prisoners and noted with satisfaction that most of the Loyalists in the region had moved across the Santee River in search of greater security. However, Marion's gains were partially offset by the defection of one of his officers to the British; Col. John Ervin had assumed command of several Loyalists and was busily engaged burning the homes of Whigs.[3] Nevertheless, Marion's success attracted more followers, increasing his force from seventy to two hundred men within a month.[4]

Balfour responded by ordering Col. Samuel Tynes to embody his militia at the High Hills of Santee. Tynes assembled between 150 and 200 men and posted them at Tearcoat Swamp, where he felt so secure that he neglected to station guards around his camp. Marion's slightly smaller force attacked the Loyalists on the night of October 25, achieving complete surprise. The Loyalists fled without offering significant resistance. Tynes escaped but was captured shortly afterward. Six of his men were killed, 14 wounded, and 23 captured. The Whigs also seized 80 horses and a large quantity of arms. Many of the demoralized survivors joined Marion's force.[5]

British officers realized that immediate action had to be taken against Marion and the Whig bands who followed in his wake exacting vengeance. The cruelties of the latter so angered Balfour that he told the commander at George-town to look for "an Opportunity of retaliating, upon those Scoundrels, who hang our Friends so freely." Balfour hoped to capture some of these people "to make an immediate example of before their Eyes."[6] Cornwallis was just as angry and wrote to Clinton, "Colonel Marion had so wrought on the minds of the people, partly by the terror of his threats and cruelty of his punishments, and partly by the promise of plunder, that there was scarcely an inhabitant between the Santee and Pedee, that was not in arms against us." The earl ordered Tarleton to take his cavalry and suppress the rebels.[7]

Marion planned to greet Tarleton with a surprise attack but found the British too well posted. Tarleton moved through the area burning homes and crops; Marion noted that "he spares neither Whig nor Tory." The partisan leader had no choice but to retreat, since his men were "in great Dread of Tarleton's Horse" and many refused to turn out.[8]

Tarleton's presence had the opposite effect on the Loyalists. Although Cornwallis recalled him to deal with Sumter before Tarleton had an opportunity to bring Marion to battle, the British Legion commander found that his operations "had taken very desirable effect." At Singleton's Mills on November 12, the "militia flocked to Lieutenant-colonel Tarleton, and assured him of their friendly dispositions, which they durst not manifest before Marion's retreat."[9] Loyalists emerged from their refuges in the swamps and offered Tarleton their services. Unable to provide material assistance, he encouraged them to persevere. Colonel Tynes, who had recently escaped from rebel custody, began assembling his militia to cooperate with another British force in the area.[10]

After Tarleton withdrew, Marion planned another attack on Georgetown but was thwarted by the arrival of "two hundred Torrys under the Command of Captns. Barefield & James Lewis." The rebels and Loyalists skirmished, with some losses on each side. In one encounter, Barefield's men captured Marion's nephew, Gabriel Marion. A Loyalist killed the prisoner upon learning his identity. The next day some Whigs captured a Loyalist mulatto named Sweat and executed him, believing that he had killed Gabriel Marion.[11] However, the rebels soon left the area when they realized that no support from the Continental army was forthcoming. "Many of my people has Left me & gone over to the Enemy," Marion told Gates in late November, "for they think that we have no Army coming on & have been Deceived, as we hear nothing from You." Marion added that unless he received support from the army or other militia units, "the Enemy will have the Intire Command of the Country on the North of Pedee."[12]

The invigorated Loyalists acted to realize Marion's fears. Colonel Tynes and several of his officers joined a small British detachment, and Tynes promised to assemble 150 men to secure the High Hills of Santee. James Cassells promised to bring his militia back into action, while 300 militiamen from Orangeburg and Pee Dee took the field against the Whigs.[13] By the end of November, Tynes assured British officers that "he could keep matters quiet with his Militia" in the region.[14]

With Tarleton's help, the Loyalists in the northeastern part of the province had withstood the Whig attacks, but their counterparts in the backcountry faced severe pressure. Cornwallis took prompt steps after Ferguson's defeat to strengthen the militia in Ninety Six district, asserting that they needed "considerable Encouragement." He confided to Balfour that "should the Militia of this Country absolutely refuse to Serve, the Consequences would indeed be fatal." As an incentive, Cornwallis ordered that three months' back pay be given to those militiamen who "have been in Constant Service." He also sought a competent commander for them and considered appointing Robert Cunningham, "who by all Accounts is the most popular Man amongst them."[15] Since Cunningham had decided a few days earlier to abandon his attempt to recruit a provincial battalion, Cornwallis sought some way to take advantage of his influence with the people. In addition, Cornwallis believed that the militia would be more effective if it was supported by a force of provincial cavalry, and so he assigned James Dunlap to raise and command the unit.[16] The earl hoped that a revitalized force might be able to "strike some blow" at the Whigs to avenge the Loyalists "who have been everywhere seized and most cruelly treated."[17]

Moses Kirkland agreed, asserting, "Without giving the Rebells a Suden Check" the backcountry militiamen would not recover their confidence. Kirkland had 115 reliable men in his regiment, he reported, but confessed that they were still frightened and demoralized after King's Mountain.[18] Two days later, having received accounts that the rebels planned to attack Ninety Six district, Kirkland stated that most Loyalists "think it Needless making any resistance, and the Greater part incline to be hiding in Swamps," while others intended to make peace with the Whigs.[19]

These pessimistic assessments convinced Balfour that militia was useless. He suggested that if Cunningham would not attempt to raise a provincial corps, Evan McLaurin should be allowed to try. "The idea of militia, being of consequence, or use, as a military force—I own I have now totally given up," Balfour told Cornwallis. However, Balfour hoped that Cunningham might be able to make the militia more effective, just as Ballingall had done with his regiment. Balfour also urged Cornwallis to find a role for Robert Gray, who "seemes to me, by much the best Militia man I have seen" and "would yet make something" of the militia.[20]

While Cornwallis struggled to restore the militia's effectiveness, Sumter's partisans and smaller groups of Whigs took advantage of the situation by terrorizing the Loyalists.[21] Sumter's foray into Ninety Six district, Cornwallis wrote, resulted in "our friends terrified beyond expression either flying down the Country or submitting tamely to the insults & Cruelties of the enemy."[22] In the northwestern part of the province, a group of rebels led by William Kennedy, all of whom lived in the woods for fear that they would be captured if they remained at home, waged a brutal campaign against local Loyalists. Kennedy was reputed to be so violent that each time someone heard him fire his rifle, they would proclaim, *"there is one tory less."* In one encounter with his Loyalist opponents, Kennedy killed a fleeing man with a rifle shot at 140 yards. "More than half the party of tories were killed" in that skirmish and *"not one* taken prisoner—for that occured but seldom, the rifle usually saved us that trouble," a Whig observed. On another occasion Kennedy was one of a party that captured several Loyalists, among them a man accused of killing one of Kennedy's friends. Kennedy and his followers wished to hang the man, but an officer insisted that the Loyalist be given a trial first. The captive was sent under guard to a nearby rebel camp, only to find that Kennedy was one of his escorts. The Loyalist protested that Kennedy would kill him on the way, a prophecy that was fulfilled when the Loyalist allegedly tried to escape and Kennedy shot him down.[23]

The militia's inability to defeat the raiders cost them Cornwallis's sympathy, as it had Balfour's. "The Accounts I receive . . . of the Supineness and pusillanimity of our Militia takes off all my Compassion for their Sufferings," he wrote; "if they will allow themselves to be plundered & their families ruined by a Banditti, not a third of their numbers, there is no possibility of our protecting them."[24] He denounced the Loyalists as "dastardly and pusillanimous" in a letter to Gen. Alexander Leslie, who had brought a British detachment from Chesapeake Bay to reinforce the army in South Carolina.[25] The earl decided to accept Balfour's advice and authorized McLaurin to begin recruiting a provincial corps as a substitute for the militia.[26]

Meanwhile, Cornwallis dispatched Major Wemyss and 250 British regulars to drive Sumter from the backcountry. A rapid march enabled Wemyss to reach

Sumter's camp at Fishdam Ford undetected in the early morning hours of November 9. Wemyss ordered an immediate attack, which drove off the rebels, but they regrouped and began firing into the British from the darkness. Wemyss was wounded and, in the confusion that followed, his troops withdrew. Both sides claimed victory.[27] Sumter, however, resumed his attacks on Loyalists after the battle, creating "the utmost horror" in the backcountry, so that "all the loyal Subjects instead of thinking of self defence are running as fast as possible to Congarees."[28] The panic caused Cruger to join the list of officers who had lost confidence in the militia. "A few of the Inhabitants on Long Cane have been plunderd many more deserved it for their pusilanimous behaviour," he wrote, noting that "about forty to fifty rebels frighten'd the whole regiment, two or three Loyalists are kill'd, & many disarm'd. I think I shall never again look to the Militia for the least support."[29]

This forced Cornwallis to order Tarleton to suspend his operations against Marion and move against Sumter instead. Tarleton set about the task with his usual energy, pursuing the Whigs and catching them at Blackstock's on November 20. Another confused battle followed as the rebels attacked Tarleton's advance guard, other British troops counterattacked without orders, and Tarleton had to lead a cavalry charge to extricate his outnumbered infantry. The battle ended in a draw, but Sumter suffered a severe wound and withdrew afterward, so that calm was restored in the backcountry.[30]

Cornwallis hoped that Tarleton's success "will give our friends more Spirit," and his wish was granted.[31] Two days after the battle, Cunningham reported to Cornwallis's headquarters at Winnsboro "full of Zeal" and accepted a commission as brigadier general commanding the backcountry militia.[32] The earl had again reversed himself and decided that the militiamen in Ninety Six district were the only militia in the province "on which . . . we could place the smallest dependence," although they had been "so totally disheartened since the defeat of Ferguson that, of that whole district, we could with difficulty assemble 100."[33]

Cunningham made rapid strides in restoring the militia's morale. About 100 militiamen joined provincial troops in suppressing the Whigs in Long Canes district and remained behind to secure the area. In December, Cunningham's brigade mustered a greatly increased strength of 91 officers and 464 men, although many lacked arms. Among them were several veteran officers and men who had been captured by Sumter and escaped during the chaotic November battles. Cunningham's promotion did cost the militia one officer—Moses Kirkland, who felt that he had been slighted and refused to serve any longer.[34]

Cornwallis ordered Tarleton to position his troops near Ninety Six to prevent Whig interference with Cunningham's efforts.[35] The earl asked Cruger to send "as many of the Militia as possible" to serve with Tarleton. "If any body can put spirit into them he will," Cornwallis wrote.[36] The Loyalists soon felt confident enough to retaliate against the Whigs; "a strong Party of Tories" plundered rebel settlements along the Pacolet River in early December.[37]

Largely through Tarleton's efforts, the British had restored a degree of control in the backcountry as well as in northeastern South Carolina. However, Loyalists in the Camden area did not fare so well, despite the presence of a strong British post in the town. In early November the militia destroyed much of their remaining credibility with the British when twelve men allowed themselves to be overpowered by sixteen rebel prisoners, which created new suspicions of treachery among Cornwallis's officers. At the same time, Whig harassment grew so severe in the vicinity of Lynch's Creek and the Waxhaws that many Loyalists there prepared to move to Camden for greater security. Whig officers learned of the plan in early November and dispatched some mounted militia to seize the Loyalists' property and use it to supply American troops.[38] Rawdon showed little sympathy for the Loyalists' plight, sarcastically noting that "at least a dozen terrified Militia Men" had come to Camden, fleeing from a battalion of North Carolina provincials that one of Rawdon's officers had dispatched to drive off the rebels.[39]

Rawdon devised his own plan to make the Camden district Loyalists more effective by forming "a kind of Fencible Regiment," which would be more professional than the militia but not have to perform the long-term duty required of provincials.[40] He intended to form several companies of thirty men each, all volunteers, who would enlist for six months to serve within their home district. The men would be paid for their services, and Rawdon named Loyalists Isham Moore and Henry Richbourg as ideally qualified to command the unit.[41]

While Rawdon waited for Cornwallis's reply to this proposal, some parties of Loyalists marched to Lynch's and Cane creeks to intercept rebel supply wagons and gather provisions. William Smallwood dispatched Gen. Daniel Morgan with five hundred infantry and Col. William Washington's one hundred cavalry to protect rebel supplies and attack the Loyalists if possible. These troops forced the Loyalists to fall back, and Washington then moved against a strong force of militia at Col. Henry Rugeley's plantation north of Camden.[42]

Ignoring Rawdon's order to withdraw to Camden, on November 28 Rugeley placed his men in a fortified building and prepared to resist the Whigs, since reports indicated that they had no artillery. However, Washington mounted a pine log on a wheeled carriage and in the darkness deceived Rugeley into thinking that the contraption was a cannon. Washington then demanded Rugeley's surrender, and the Loyalist colonel reluctantly capitulated; he and over one hundred militiamen were taken prisoner.[43] Rugeley was perhaps more intimidated by the Whigs' threat to put all the defenders "to immediate death if they did not give up" than he was by the spurious cannon.[44]

Some rebel militia officers wished to exact vengeance against three of the prisoners taken at Rugeley's, whom they described as "Notorious Offenders." Fortunately for the captives, Continental officers intervened to prevent any abuse, asserting that the men were prisoners of war and could not be put on trial for treason.[45]

While the Loyalists in the area surrounding Camden suffered most from the Whigs, those living near the British army's main encampment at Winnsboro enjoyed more security because the rebels seldom ventured too close to so many regular troops. Local people "peaceably supplied" abundant food for men and horses, and the position was so secure that Cornwallis dispersed his sick soldiers to nearby plantations to recuperate.[46] The earl himself became ill, and Rawdon, who assumed temporary command of the army, received a steady flow of intelligence from Loyalists that enabled him to monitor rebel activities. One dependable spy, finding it too dangerous to go into the rebel camp because many people there knew him, sent his niece to obtain information. When rebel plunderers captured Loyalist David George and two wagons bound for the British army, George took the opportunity to observe the rebel army; after his release he sent the British a report of its strength and position.[47]

Cornwallis's army might not even have reached Winnsboro without Loyalist assistance. During the retreat from Charlotte, "only the exertions of the loyalist militia kept the army wagons moving." Yet, instead of appreciating the efforts of the men who wrestled heavily laden wagons through mud and across rain-swollen streams, British officers frequently abused the Loyalists. "In return for their exertions, the militia were maltreated, by abusive language, and even beaten by some officers in the quarter-master general's department," wrote Pennsylvania Loyalist and commissary of captures Charles Stedman. He reported that "several of them left the army" in response to such treatment and cast their lot with the rebels.[48]

Like his officers, Cornwallis refused to recognize the Loyalists' contributions. Instead, he maintained that they were not doing enough to help him, complaining that "the friends hereabouts are so timid & so stupid that I can get no intelligence."[49] He was exaggerating; David George provided him with another fairly accurate report of rebel strength, positions, and intentions on December 30, and other Loyalists sent a steady stream of information to headquarters.[50] Cornwallis also rejected a request to supply muskets to the militia. "I have lost so many Arms by the Militia that I am much afraid of trusting them," he wrote to explain his decision.[51]

Cornwallis's criticism notwithstanding, the Loyalists had begun to recover and to hold their own against the Whigs. Even Rugeley's defeat resulted from the colonel's determination to make a stand against a far superior force. The backcountry militia fought well in a battle on December 12 against Elijah Clarke's 400 rebels. Lt. Col. Isaac Allen led 150 provincials and 250 militia from Ninety Six, caught Clarke at Long Canes, and routed the Whigs. A month later Ballingall's militia dispersed rebel partisans who had been harassing British posts and Loyalists southwest of Charleston.[52]

John Rutledge, who received accurate intelligence from Whig sympathizers, calculated in early December that some 1,040 loyal militiamen were on duty at various posts in South Carolina, not including the militia in Charleston.[53] Rutledge worried that Cornwallis would consolidate his hold on the province by sending "every disaffected person, out of the State with his family, & apply his property to publick use."[54] Thomas Jefferson was similarly pessimistic. "Georgia and South Carolina are annihilated, at least to us," he told Maryland governor Thomas Sim Lee in mid-January.[55]

As Whigs began doubting their ability to regain the southern provinces, many Britons came to believe that the situation had finally shifted in their favor. Frederick Mackenzie, an officer in the New York garrison who had always doubted that the southern campaign could succeed, experienced a surge of optimism in December 1780. He and his fellow officers now had "the most sanguine hopes" that once Cornwallis took the offensive, the war would be brought to a quick end. "I do not see how the Rebellion can possibly exist much longer," Mackenzie stated.[56] George III was similarly hopeful. "The signal Successes which have attended the Progress of my Arms in the Provinces of Georgia and Carolina . . . will, I trust, have important consequences in bringing the War to a happy conclusion," he declared in an address to Parliament.[57]

The improvement in the British and Loyalists' situation was only temporary, however. On December 2 Maj. Gen. Nathanael Greene arrived in Charlotte to supersede Gates as commander of the Continental army in the South. Seeking a location where he could better supply his troops and simultaneously threaten the British, Greene marched into South Carolina with most of his troops and camped at the Cheraws. He then dispatched Lt. Col. Henry Lee's legion to cooperate with Marion. The remainder of his army, under Morgan, moved west to threaten Ninety Six.[58]

Greene found the provisions he sought at the Cheraws, but he received little support from local Whigs, who "were naturally very hesitant to leave their homes to join the army even for a short period of service" because of the large number of Loyalists in the area.[59] "The people are two thirds Tories," an American officer asserted.[60] Greene concluded that his army was in the midst of a predominantly Loyalist region.[61] "This is really carrying on a war in the enimy's Country," he informed Alexander Hamilton. "For you cannot establish the most inconsiderable Magazine or convey the smallest quantity of Stores from one part to another without being obligd to detach guards for their security."[62] Loyalists seized Greene's couriers so frequently that the general did not dare express himself fully in his correspondence, and they threatened a mill that Greene relied on to supply grain for his troops.[63] Rawdon had "so many persons watching Greene, that I think he cannot make any movement without my receiving early notice of it."[64]

The newfound aggressiveness of the Loyalists around Greene's army impressed Robert Gray. Previously, he noted, the approach of rebel troops would send Loyalists fleeing great distances or to the swamps to hide. As they recognized that they would have to rely on themselves rather than the British army for protection, however, they became bolder. Now the Loyalists "kept hovering round" the Whig camp "in small parties, picked up stragglers & fired upon them from every swamp." Near Georgetown and along the Pee Dee River, they "cut to pieces" small rebel detachments, "killed their sentries," and otherwise harassed the enemy.[65]

Elsewhere the Loyalists were equally active. The militia defeated a group of partisans at Long Canes in early December, and a few days later, when the Whigs attacked a camp of provincials and militia near Ninety Six, the king's troops rallied and routed the rebels. The militia pursued the fleeing Whigs for two miles, taking about 10 prisoners and capturing a large number of wagons and cattle. At least 30 rebels died in the battle.[66] Isaac Allen praised the militia's behavior, noting that they "have been with me in two excursions and behaved extremely well"; he told Cornwallis that he had "a good opinion of their Loyalty and Spirit."[67] In late January 1781 a Whig officer reported that many Loyalists "have embodied within 30 Miles of Head Quarters and for two days have been so troublesome" that Greene had to detach 200 troops to deal with them.[68] Rebel major Frederick Kimball wrote that in the Camden district, Loyalists frequently captured members of his militia, while Rawdon noted that on one occasion 60 loyal militiamen arrived at Camden and requested to be employed against the Whigs. Rawdon had 214 militiamen on duty at Camden on January 1, 1781, of whom 53 lacked arms.[69] In addition, Morgan's troops found that they had entered a Loyalist stronghold when they reached the Pacolet River. "With a few exceptions, the Men are all Tories & the Women all Whores," one of Greene's officers wrote.[70]

Greene realized that he had to do everything possible to sustain the Whigs and check the Loyalists; otherwise many of the rebels' lukewarm supporters would revert to neutrality or perhaps even take British protection.[71] "The enemy are now recruiting in all parts of this state," he wrote, "and the command of gold, aided by the public distress and loyal feeling, has been too successful in making one conquest the stepping-stone to another. At present they are in possession of all the fertile and populous parts of South Carolina."[72] Greene therefore instructed Marion to remain active so that "you may frighten the Tories by these movements to desert the British and lay down their arms."[73] Greene likewise told Morgan that the latter's main objective would be to inspire the rebels and annoy the enemy.[74] Later he advised Morgan that "the impudence of the tories who are collecting in different quarters" indicated that the "enemy and the tories both will try to bring you into disgrace if possible to prevent your influence upon the Militia especially the weak and wavering."[75]

Emboldened by the presence of Continental troops, Whigs moved quickly to suppress the Loyalists with yet another campaign of terror. When rebel militiamen approached the High Hills, all but twenty of Colonel Tynes's militiamen fled from their post. Abandoning his remaining troops, the "exceedingly frightened" Tynes took refuge in Camden.[76] A few miles south of the Enoree River, fifty rebels attacked twenty-five militiamen, seriously wounding four and capturing seven or eight.[77] The militiamen were unable to protect the Loyalists, and Greene's aide

Lewis Morris described the violence that ensued: "The tories, who after the defeat of Genl Gates had a full range, are chased from their homes, hunted thro' the woods and shot with as much indifference as you would a buck"; as a result, "they were daily returning to their allegiance and petitioning for protection.[78]

The carnage horrified Gen. Charles O'Hara, who had arrived in South Carolina in December 1780 with Leslie's reinforcements and witnessed the effects of the Whigs' brutality on the march to join Cornwallis. O'Hara wrote that the sights he saw "are beyond discription wretched, every Misery which the bloodiest cruel War ever produced, we have constantly before Us . . . the violence of the Passions of these People, are beyond every curb of Religion, and Humanity, they are unbounded, and every Hour exhibits, dreadfull, wanton Mischiefs, Murders, and Violences of every kind." O'Hara noted that many Loyalists had been forced to flee to the vicinity of Charleston or to Georgia in search of safety.[79] "Desolation and Ravage make rapid progress," Loyalist John Lloyd noted, "and notwithstanding every Military effort and attention, the Loyalists are frequently surprised, killed, taken, or plundered by the incursions of their Neighbours."[80] No one was exempt; on the night of December 4 some Whigs found two Loyalists ill with smallpox, "shot both the Sick Men in their Beds, tho' they were incapable of making the least defence; & afterwards murdered the old Man of the House in the same Manner."[81]

Like O'Hara, Cornwallis was stunned, not only by the Whigs' ruthlessness but also by their insistence that the British were responsible for the violence. "The accounts of the cruelty of those rascals is really shocking," he told Rawdon, "and if it is capable of aggravation their impudent accusation of us makes it the more provoking."[82] In response to a letter from Clinton in which the commander in chief informed the earl that George Washington had protested British acts of cruelty in the South, Cornwallis replied that although he had been "provoked by the horrid outrages and cruelties of the enemy in this district, I have always endeavoured to soften the horrors of war." Cornwallis noted that Gates and other rebel officers had acknowledged his humane treatment of captured and wounded Whig soldiers. This, he said, sharply contrasted with "the shocking tortures and inhuman Murders which are every day committed by the enemy, not only on those, who have taken part with us, but on many who refuse to join them."[83]

Robert Gray warned Cornwallis that if the Whigs were permitted to "continue this outrage it will be productive of the worst effects." The Loyalists, Gray declared, "will lose all confidence if they find themselves doomed to the halter when captives, whilst the rebels" received humane treatment when taken prisoner. Gray noted that one of his best officers, a Captain Oates, had been promptly hanged after the rebels captured him. "Several others have met with the same fate while others have been subjected to rigorous corporal punishments," Gray added.[84]

The earl responded by writing to Greene and threatening retaliation if the Whigs continued their ruthless behavior. "If Truth could be heard, the Feelings of Mankind would decide that in the Southern Provinces, the Rights of Humanity have been invaded by the Enemies of Great Britain," Cornwallis asserted. He pointed out that Whigs had altered some of his letters that they had intercepted to make it appear that he had endorsed a policy of brutality. This was untrue, Cornwallis declared, as "no man abhors Acts of Cruelty more than myself." However, he warned that if the rebels continued their savagery, he would respond in kind. "The proving to the suffering Loyalists that I am in earnest to protect them, & to retaliate on their inhuman Oppressors, is a duty which I owe to my Country," Cornwallis stated.[85] Greene did not respond.

Privately, Greene held both sides responsible for the situation. "There is nothing but murders and devastations in every quarter," he wrote.[86] "The whole country is in danger of being laid waste by the Whigs and Torrys, who pursue each other with as much relentless fury as beasts of prey," Greene observed while at the Cheraws. "People between this and the Santee are frequently murdered as they ride along the road." However, for several months Greene did nothing to halt the savagery, probably because it worked to his advantage. He had noted that some Loyalists "are now coming in, in many parts; being tired of such a wretched life."[87]

Greene's own troops soon demonstrated that they could match the militia in atrocious behavior. When Morgan began his westward movement, 250 Georgia Loyalists under Col. Thomas Waters had begun attacking Whigs in the vicinity of Fair Forest Creek.[88] According to some reports, the Loyalists planned to fortify a house near the creek and "establish there a Magazine of provisions," but they retreated on learning of Morgan's approach.[89] Morgan ordered William Washington to pursue Waters with his cavalry and some mounted militia. On December 27 Washington encountered the Loyalists at Hammond's Store. Although in a strong position atop a hill, the Loyalists broke and fled when Washington's cavalry charged them.[90] In the ensuing melee 150 Loyalists were killed or wounded—"hacked to death or badly mutilated"—and 40 captured, while the rebels did not suffer a single casualty.[91] The death toll was exceedingly high, given the fact that, as Morgan noted, the Loyalists scattered at the start of the engagement "without making any Resistance."[92] The reason for the large number of Loyalist dead was that the rebels murdered both fleeing men and those who tried to surrender. "Washingtons men had in remembrance Some of Mr. Tarltons former Acts and Acted accordingly," Capt. John Davidson of the Maryland troops wrote, referring to the alleged massacre of Continental troops at the Waxhaws.[93]

The day after the battle, the Whigs put one of the prisoners on trial. He was "found guilty of desertion to the enemy and piloting the Indians on our army, they making great havoc among them; upon which he was hanged on a tree the same day."[94] When or where this Indian attack occurred was not specified, but its description does not correspond to any known events at that time.

Sixty Loyalists managed to escape the slaughter and reached Fort William with news that Washington was in pursuit. The garrison then abandoned the post and fled to Ninety Six, which was only fifteen miles distant.[95]

Morgan believed that Washington's victory had been "fatal to the disaffected. They have not been able to embody since," he wrote on January 15.[96] Greene too recognized the importance of the battle. "Nothing could have afforded me more pleasure than the successful attack of Lt Coll Washington, upon the Tories," he told Morgan. "I hope it will be attended with a happy influence upon both Whig & tory, to the reclaiming of one, and encouragement of the other."[97]

Pondering how to capitalize on the victory, Morgan decided that it was essential to maintain his position. "To Retreat will be attended with the most fatal Consequences," he declared. "The Spirit which now begins to pervade the People, & call them into the Field will be destroyed—The Militia, who have already joined, will desert us, & it is not improbable, but a Regard to their own Safety will induce them to join the Enemy."[98] However, a few days later, with provisions growing scarce and hearing rumors that Tarleton was approaching, he decided to rejoin Greene and leave militia under Andrew Pickens and William Davidson to check the Loyalists. Morgan hoped that Tarleton would ignore the rebel militia and focus his attention on the Continentals.[99]

Cornwallis had indeed ordered Tarleton to pursue Morgan and drive the rebels from the backcountry. The earl planned to march northward with his own troops to prevent Morgan from reaching Greene's army. After the two forces cut off and destroyed Morgan's detachment, Cornwallis intended to deal with Greene.[100]

Loyalists greatly facilitated Tarleton's pursuit of Morgan. Capt. Alexander Chesney, who had been exchanged, arrived from Ninety Six about January 12 to guide the British troops. Tarleton sent Chesney to find Morgan's force, and when this was done, the British commander sent several Loyalists as spies into Morgan's camp.[101] Other valuable information came from a Whig militia colonel who had been captured by a "party of determined loyalists."[102] At least fifty Loyalists accompanied Tarleton's detachment, serving as guides and messengers. While the British regulars rested on the night of January 16, Loyalists searched for Morgan and brought Tarleton a steady stream of information. The next morning, when Tarleton encountered Morgan's troops deployed for battle in a field locally known as "the Cowpens," Loyalists familiar with the area provided him with a detailed description of the terrain.[103]

Believing that Cornwallis's troops must now be coming up behind the rebels, Tarleton promptly attacked. The British troops drove back Morgan's soldiers but broke ranks to pursue when they thought the Whigs were fleeing the field. However, Morgan rallied his men, counterattacked, and overwhelmed Tarleton's force. The survivors and their commander escaped and rejoined Cornwallis.[104]

Contrary to Tarleton's assumption, the earl had been nowhere near Cowpens. That was not the fault of the Loyalists; Cornwallis noted that "the great assiduity of Phillips and his Militia" and wagons provided by loyal civilians had enabled his army to begin its march on schedule.[105] Loyalist guides had also done an efficient job leading Leslie's reinforcements forward. Cornwallis, however, had delayed his march without informing his subordinate.[106]

Infuriated by news of Tarleton's defeat, Cornwallis decided to pursue Morgan in hopes of retaking the British prisoners. Morgan, who was already retreating as fast as his troops could march, linked up with Greene's force, and the combined American army fled across North Carolina and into Virginia with Cornwallis in hot pursuit. The earl left Balfour in command of South Carolina, with Rawdon to exercise actual control of the troops in the field.[107]

Unlike the defeat at King's Mountain, the Battle of Cowpens did not demoralize most Loyalists. Instead, Greene's rapid flight and Cornwallis's pursuit had the appearance of a British victory. Balfour noted that "the effects of Tarletons misfortunate action, were greatly counteracted & the country saw the decided superiority of our army—who in several skirmishes was successful to a great degree."[108] Loyalists therefore actively continued to support the British, while many Whigs believed that their cause in the South had been lost beyond retrieval and accepted royal authority.

Some Loyalists struck back at the Whigs on the night after the battle, killing Maj. James Dugan of the rebel militia, his brother, and two other men. Chesney gathered his own followers, who had scattered during the battle, and found Robert Cunningham encamped at Fair Forest. Despite Chesney's urgent appeals for action, "we could not prevail on General Cunningham to use any exertions to embody his brigade of Militia."[109]

This caused Balfour to consider reinforcing Ninety Six with more regulars, which would enable Cruger to operate more effectively against the rebels. Balfour believed that Cruger's "being able to detach two hundred men on an emergency effectualy gains the assistance of the Militia who without the aid of troops . . . are of no sort of use."[110]

The situation in the backcountry, however, was not as bad as Balfour feared. Some Loyalists did consider theirs to be a "hopeless cause" after the Battle of Cowpens and joined the rebels, but most persisted in the struggle.[111] A rebel militiaman declared that after that battle, "it was now almost Fire & Faggot Between Whig & Tory, who were contending for the ascendancy" in a conflict that raged until late May.[112]

To many Whigs, including some of the most prominent men in the province, it was their cause that appeared hopeless, and they took the oath to Britain. John Rutledge noted that the British "make a great Parade of Mr. [Arthur] Middleton, *'formerly Presidt of the Contl Congress,'* & old Mr. [Gabriel] Manigault having applied to be admitted as British Subjects, wch they have been—Indeed, I fear many will follow their Example."[113] On January 16, 1781, Balfour informed Germain that "many of the principal Inhabitants of the Province, & some who held the Chief Office under the late Rebel powers have reverted to their Loyalty & Declared their Allegiance to His Majesty's Government."[114] Between February 16 and April 9, 1781, a further 210 men swore allegiance to Britain.[115]

British officers took advantage of the promising situation to strengthen the militia and to create provincial cavalry units. Rawdon devised a new plan of "raising Militia Corps upon Pay, which I think will answer well."[116] In Charleston the militia impressed observers as being both smartly uniformed and "well disciplined."[117] Officers in Camden district were busily enlisting men for two troops of dragoons. Stephen Jarvis, a Connecticut Loyalist serving in the Queen's Rangers, used a generous enlistment bounty to recruit twenty-six men at Charleston. Maj. Thomas Fraser marched his South Carolina dragoons through Ninety Six district, enlisting several men who had previously served under Ferguson.[118]

At the beginning of February, Cornwallis sent Rawdon a warning from North Carolina that this respite would not last long. "Some Georgia refugees & other Banditti are assembling at Gilbertown, & Sumpter is again in the field," the earl wrote.[119] He was soon proved correct, as rebel partisans took advantage of the army's absence to launch a new campaign against Loyalists and British posts. Moses Kirkland reported on February 22 that the roads in the Congarees region were "so Infested with small parties of the Rebells" that he had to cancel his intended journey to join Cornwallis.[120] These were units from Sumter's command, which crossed the Congaree River a few days later to attack British supply lines and raise recruits. Sumter issued a proclamation promising pardon to Loyalists who joined him and threatening anyone who refused. "To give weight to these threats," Rawdon wrote, "several persons known to be friendly towards us, were inhumanly murdered; tho' unarmed, & remaining peaceably at their own houses. Either thro' fear or inclination, many joined the Enemy." Rawdon added that "the savage cruelty of the Enemy, who commit the most wanton murders in cold blood, upon the Friends of Government," made it nearly impossible to hire couriers "at any price."[121]

Dividing his forces into three detachments, Rawdon planned a concerted movement to trap Sumter. While these troops maneuvered, Sumter attacked and captured a wagon train. After the militia escort "laid down their arms," more of Sumter's men reached the scene; complaining that "they had not discharged their pieces," they opened fire and killed seven prisoners. British lieutenant colonel John Watson, commanding one of Rawdon's columns, captured six of Sumter's men shortly afterward and retaliated in kind. Watson believed that this was the only way to deal with the rebels after finding that so many people, "without arms, and taking side with neither contending party, but residing peaceably in their own houses, have been murdered."[122]

The capture of the wagon train marked the limit of Sumter's success. Sumter decided to send his booty down the Santee River by boat and ordered Loyalist Robert Livingston to pilot the little convoy. Livingston guided the boats directly under the guns of a riverside fort, enabling the British to recover the supplies and capture the rebel guards. The Whigs went on to attack a small post garrisoned by South Carolina provincials, only to be repulsed. Meanwhile, Rawdon's three columns converged on Sumter's force, but the commander of one British detachment disobeyed Rawdon's orders and changed his route of march, allowing the rebels to escape the trap. In his flight, Sumter encountered other British troops, and the Whigs were dispersed with a loss of eighteen killed. On March 6 other South Carolina provincials defeated Sumter yet again, killing ten rebels. By the end of the month Rawdon was able to report that he had put an end to Sumter's threat, while simultaneously quelling Marion's activities with a surprise attack that captured and destroyed the latter's base.[123]

During the campaign the Whigs had continued to abuse Loyalist prisoners, prompting Balfour to protest to Marion. Noting that he had received continuous reports of "the very ill treatment which such of the King's militia whose misfortune it is to be captured by you are daily receiving," Balfour declared that he had no choice but "to put in force retaliation of all severities imposed by any of your people on such prisoners of war; and for this purpose, I have directed the militia to be separated from the continental prisoners, that they may experience those hardships and ill usages in their full degree, which too many of ours labor under." Nevertheless, Balfour stated that he would gladly put an end to such policies as soon as he was assured that captured loyal militiamen were humanely treated.[124] Rawdon evidently did not bother waiting for dubious assurances; in March, Marion accused him of having "hanged three men of my Brigade for supposed Crimes" and vowed to retaliate against an equal number of British prisoners.[125]

Marion also responded to a complaint from Watson by indicating that he hoped the war could be fought according to civilized principles. Watson in turn asserted that if Marion personally adhered to the laws of war, he must be "ignorant of numberless transactions" carried out by the Whigs, such as the case of Thomas Wise of the loyal militia, who had been "whipped almost to death" after being captured. Another prisoner, Watson wrote, had handed over his pistol "and was instantly shot through the body with it" and then was "cut through the skull in five or six places with his own sword." He died two days later.[126]

Even Gen. William Moultrie, a prisoner since the fall of Charleston, was sufficiently disturbed by Whig cruelties to join in the protests. After Balfour convinced him that the rebels had murdered three Loyalists, Moultrie wrote Marion that such actions "cannot answer any good purpose" and urged him to halt "such unwarrantable practices," which disgraced the rebel cause.[127]

Although it was difficult for the British to identify the perpetrators of these crimes, Sumter and his troops were apparently greater offenders than Marion and his followers. Sumter believed that anyone who did not bear arms in the Whig cause should be considered an enemy and "treated as their baseness and perfidy authorize."[128]

The most brutal of the Whigs, however, were the overmountain men, as they again demonstrated by murdering a British officer. On March 23 Elijah Clarke with 180 rebels attacked a British and Loyalist force only half as large near Ninety Six. Many of the British and Loyalist troops were killed in the American charge; the remainder took refuge in nearby houses but soon surrendered. An estimated 30 British and Loyalist soldiers were killed and 40 captured, including their commander, James Dunlap.[129] Not content with this victory, some rebels "forced the Guard" escorting the prisoners and killed Dunlap. Andrew Pickens, the Whig partisan leader, described the crime as an "inhuman action." He dispatched a flag of truce to Ninety Six to inform Cruger of the murder, relating "with what horror and detestation American Officers looked on the act." Pickens offered a ten-thousand-dollar reward for the apprehension of the murderer, identified as "Cobb an over Mountain Man." Yet, at the same time Pickens tried to justify the crime as retribution for the "many barbarous massacres" of Whig prisoners taken by Loyalists.[130] Despite Pickens's obvious sincerity in repudiating Dunlap's murder, most Whigs seemed to have approved of the crime, as the lucrative reward never led to Cobb's capture. The apparent ease with which the murderers overpowered Dunlap's guards also hints at their possible collusion with the killer.

Although the Loyalists' determination and Rawdon's skillful operations against the partisans had checked the Whigs' ruthless onslaught, events took a sudden and decisive turn against the British at the end of April. After three months of marching and fighting, Cornwallis withdrew his depleted army to Wilmington, North Carolina. While the king's troops recuperated, Greene decided to ignore the British army and march his Continentals back to South Carolina. The fifty-two hundred British, German, and provincial troops in the province greatly outnumbered Greene's force, but the Whigs had two offsetting advantages. First, the partisans augmented Greene's force by several thousand men, and second, most of the British troops were tied to fixed posts to protect the communications between Charleston and the interior. The only way Rawdon could assemble enough troops to challenge Greene in the field was by weakening the numerous garrisons, which would then be easy prey to the partisans.[131]

Cornwallis proceeded to compound Rawdon's problems. Rather than follow Greene, the earl decided to march to Virginia and unite his troops with the larger British force in the Chesapeake. Recognizing that this move endangered royal control of South Carolina, Cornwallis was convinced that if he pursued Greene, he would still arrive too late to assist Rawdon, and he consoled himself by remarking that "if we are so unfortunate as to lose some of the Outposts and the Country of S. Carolina . . . Charleston is not in danger."[132] Capt. Johann Ewald believed that Cornwallis's decision would prove fatal to the Loyalists. "Why not operate out of one point and use all our force there to be the master of at least one province?" he asked. Ewald declared that the Loyalists had been "constantly deceived" and now would be made "miserable" by being left without protection; "yet we still want to find friends in this country!"[133]

Loyalists reacted in different ways to the news of Greene's approach. Some fled to British posts for refuge; others hid in the swamps and woods to escape the rebels. The South Carolina Royalists brushed aside Whig partisans and marched from Ninety Six to Camden to reinforce Rawdon.[134] Large numbers of militiamen likewise showed "great zeal and fidelity, in coming from considerable distances to offer their services" at Camden. Even so, the supply of provisions there was so limited that Rawdon was unable "to benefit by their assistance, excepting only those whose particular situation exposed them to suffer from the enemy, and who were on that account received within the post."[135] Loyalists also kept Rawdon fully informed of Greene's maneuvers.[136]

Greene immediately concluded that aggressive action was required to prevent the Loyalists from making a decisive contribution to the defense of South Carolina.[137] "More of the Inhabitants appear in the Kings interest than in ours," he informed Samuel Huntington, president of the Continental Congress. Greene added that the rebel militia "can do little more than keep Tories in subjection, and in many places not that."[138]

Greene decided to take a position near Camden, where he could hold the British garrison in place while the partisans moved to suppress the Loyalists and cut Rawdon's supply lines. In the northeastern part of the province, Marion, Henry Lee, and other Whigs attacked British posts, militia units, and individual Loyalists. Micajah Ganey assembled the loyal militia at Drowning Creek to oppose them, but Whigs under Col. Abel Kolb dispersed Ganey's men and hanged a Loyalist prisoner named Caleb Williams. Marion sent Col. Hugh Horry and 70 men to intercept a group of Loyalists attempting to link up with Watson's regulars, who were operating in the area; instead the Whigs encountered a foraging party and killed 2 British soldiers and captured 13 others, along with 2 Loyalists and 2 blacks. A few days later 40 Loyalists attacked Kolb's home, killing him and two other men in retaliation for the hanging of Williams.[139] Rawdon dispatched 150 Loyalist volunteers from Camden to relieve the pressure on Ganey and Watson by attacking the Waxhaws settlements. They burned buildings and killed several rebels and then eluded troops that Sumter sent to capture them. In reprisal, Sumter's men rampaged through Loyalist settlements at Mobley's Meeting House and Sandy Run, "burning and killing."[140] Rawdon showed his determination to punish such offenses by hanging "One Smith, for murdering a friend of Government."[141]

Amid this inconclusive fighting, Marion and Lee won a significant victory, capturing Fort Watson on the Santee River. The garrison of 130 British regulars and loyal militiamen held out for nearly a week, until the Whigs constructed a log tower that enabled them to fire into the fort.[142] Among those who surrendered on April 23 were 40 "principal torys" whose capture Lee hoped would demoralize other Loyalists.[143]

Whig operations in the backcountry also produced mixed results. When Andrew Pickens reached the Enoree River with his militia, he found Loyalist parties active in the area and said that if he had not arrived when he did, many disheartened rebels would have evacuated the area.[144] Pickens attempted to attack various detachments of the loyal militia in the region, but all of them managed to elude him and reach Ninety Six. He then planned an attack on Cunningham's militiamen, who were near the town, but two Whig parties blundered into each other and mistakenly opened fire, alerting Cunningham. The Loyalists then withdrew.[145]

Sumter had more success along the Broad River. On April 25 he reported that many Loyalists in the vicinity appeared ready to give up the struggle and were "hiding out until they Know what terms may be offered."[146] To force them to submit, he sent rebel militia "through the Tory Settlements in Both forks" of the river to "Disperce parties of Tories that are Lying out," although other Loyalists were "embodying West of Saluda River." He prepared to attack them, believing that the defeat of those Loyalists would "leave all the Back Country open and Secoure, quite to 96."[147]

Whig attacks extended even into the lowcountry, where the partisans enjoyed some success despite the proximity of the Charleston garrison. "The enemy in partys of two & three hundred have over run all the country to the southward" of Charleston, Balfour wrote.[148] He ordered British troops and the provincial cavalry to assemble at Dorchester, summon the militia, and then move against the rebels, but Whig colonel William Harden struck before this force was ready. Harden's party captured a Loyalist captain and 25 militiamen at Four Holes and a day later killed 4 Loyalists and captured 3. The rebels then moved against Fort Balfour at Pocotaligo. After capturing militia colonels Edward Fenwick and Nicholas Lechmere at a nearby house, Harden demanded the fort's surrender, threatening that he would give the defenders no quarter if they resisted. Col. Fletcher Kelsall of the militia, who commanded the fort, capitulated; the Whigs took about 100 prisoners. Other Loyalists in the area fled to the swamps. Robert Ballingall arrived shortly afterward with 130 regulars and 40 militia and forced Harden to withdraw.[149]

Greene's plan to suppress the Loyalists succeeded to a considerable extent. William R. Davie, the army's quartermaster general, noted that the Whigs had "overawed the Loyalists who were numerous" in the province.[150] As always, Whig brutality had its effect. "We are astounded to hear of the most terrible cruelties, that are perpetrated on those who will not be false to the King again," a Hessian officer wrote.[151] Balfour noted that the Whigs "have adopted the System of murdering every Militia Officer of ours as well as every man (although unarmed) who is known to be a loyalist. the terror this mode of conduct has struck you will easily suppose," he told Cornwallis, "some immediate stop must be put to it, or the consequences will be very fatal."[152]

Rawdon realized that if he did not take action, the partisans would sever his supply lines and force him to evacuate Camden, with devastating consequences for Loyalist morale. Balfour had already recommended that the British abandon their posts in the interior and consolidate their forces east of the Santee River. Deciding that it would be better to decisively defeat Greene, Rawdon left Camden in the hands of the militia and some armed blacks and marched out to attack the Continentals on April 25. His force included the South Carolina Royalists as well as many militiamen. Rawdon borrowed a favorite rebel tactic and positioned Loyalist riflemen on the flanks of his army as snipers to harass Greene's troops and pick off their officers. After a hard-fought battle, the British and Loyalists drove Greene's troops from their position on Hobkirk's Hill. When Watson's detachment arrived on May 7, Rawdon advanced again in an effort to inflict another defeat on the rebels, but Greene withdrew to avoid combat.[153]

With Greene's army still intact and British supply lines threatened by partisans, Rawdon felt he had no choice but to order the evacuation of Camden on May 9. His troops destroyed all the supplies they could not carry with them, leveled the fortifications, and "brought off not only the militia who had been with us at Camden, but also the well-affected neighbors on our route," with their families, slaves, and possessions.[154] Many of the Loyalist refugees went to Charleston, where "they built themselves huts, without the lines, which was called Rawdontown: many of these unfortunate women and children . . . died for want, in those miserable huts."[155]

The evacuation of Camden left the backcountry isolated, and Sumter quickly moved to strike the Loyalists there. Some of his troops attacked a Loyalist party at Bush River, killing three and capturing twelve. "The Tories are Very uneasee & Will Numbers of them Disert if oppertunity Serves," Sumter wrote, noting that sixteen Loyalists deserted from a British fort in one night. Others were "Coming in fast from the Country & Will in my oppinion Cheifly Give up if We Can hold our Ground a little longer."[156] When Sumter marched to the Congarees, he found that small Loyalist parties were "Troublesom in different parts of the Country" but that their operations were little more than a nuisance and more than offset by the number of men in the area who joined the Whigs.[157] Cunningham struck back later in the month, sending some of his militia on a raid north of Ninety Six. They destroyed Wofford's ironworks along with other buildings and killed several rebels.[158]

Although the Loyalists were "very troublesom over Peedee & Waccomaw" in early May, they lost any hope of direct British support when Balfour ordered the evacuation of Georgetown.[159] The garrison withdrew on May 23, which, Marion asserted, prevented the Loyalists "from destroying our friends."[160] Yet, some Loyalists continued to harass the Whigs around Georgetown, forcing Marion to dispatch troops in mid-June to suppress them.[161]

The actions of a few such bands of hardy Loyalists could not prevent the collapse of British control in the province. The surrender of the British post at

Orangeburg on May 11, of Fort Motte near the confluence of the Wateree and Congaree rivers on May 12, and of Fort Granby on the Congaree three days later smashed the British hold on the interior of South Carolina. One of Greene's aides calculated the total of prisoners taken at the three posts to be 10 British officers and 205 men, and 22 Loyalist officers and 375 men.[162] The loss of manpower left the British too weak even to attempt to regain control of the lost territory.

With British forces confined to the vicinity of Charleston, Greene took his army to attack Ninety Six while Whigs and Loyalists battled each other across much of the province. He could do nothing to stop the bloodshed, lamenting that "not a day passes but there are more or less who fall a sacrafice to this savage disposition. The Whigs seem determined to exterpate the Tories and the Tories the Whigs. Some thousands have fallen in this way in this quarter, and the evil rages with more violence than ever." Greene feared that if "those private massacres" were not ended soon, "this Country will be depopulated . . . as neither Whig nor Tory can live."[163] A Hessian officer reported that "mounted bands of rebels scour the whole neighborhood" on both sides of the Santee River, "drive the loyalists from their homes—which they destroy after carrying everything away—make all the roads insecure, and have murdered many people."[164]

Balfour also deplored the cruelty, but like his Hessian colleague, he found the Whigs to be chiefly responsible for it. "The enemy have uniformly murdred in cold blood, all our Militia whom they have been able to get at," he wrote, noting that the surviving Loyalists were terrified and did not dare turn out to support the British. Greene's march to Ninety Six, Balfour added, aroused his sympathy "for the miserable districts of Loyalists in the back country . . . those poorer people who are indeed our only friends."[165] Cornwallis showed no concern whatsoever for the Loyalists; he advised his subordinates to abandon both them and the backcountry. "The perpetual instances of the weakness and treachery of our friends in South Carolina, and the impossibility of getting any military assistance from them, makes the possession of any part of the country of very little use," he told Rawdon.[166] To insure adequate provisions for the Charleston garrison, Cornwallis suggested that Balfour might find it wise to "turn out of Town all parole Men & disaffected People, with their families & many Negroes, & to shut your Gates against many of the poor country people, & all Negroes."[167]

Instead, Rawdon and Balfour sought to bolster Loyalist morale by issuing a proclamation on May 24; in it they exhorted those in evacuated areas "to stand firm in their Duty and Principles" against "the insidious artifices" of the Whigs. They promised pardon to anyone who had "been forced to join the Enemy, as the only Means of preserving themselves and their Families from the savage Cruelty of the Rebel Militia." Loyalists who came to British posts were promised "every Support."[168]

Rawdon and Balfour meant what they said and took steps to assist and protect the Loyalists. Balfour, aided by generous donations from lowcountry

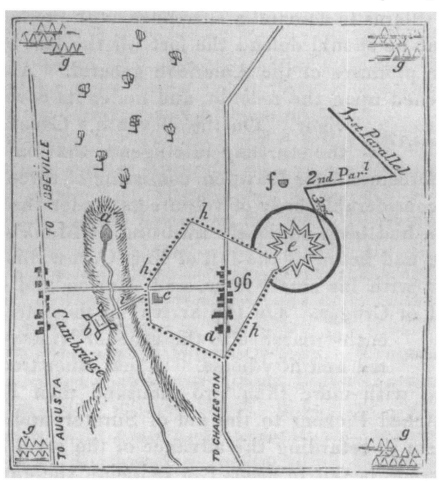

Plan of the Siege of Ninety-Six. From Benson J. Lossing, *The Pictorial Field-book of the Revolution* (1851, 1852). Courtesy of Rare Books and Special Collections, Thomas Cooper Library, University of South Carolina

Loyalists totaling nearly three thousand guineas (four hundred thousand dollars), created a force of provincial cavalry from the South Carolina Royalists and new volunteers to counter the rebels' raids. In May, Alexander Chesney, who had abandoned his backcountry home after the Battle of Cowpens, took three newly raised companies to Dorchester, where a soldier noted that the majority of people remained loyal. Chesney's troops were assigned to protect sequestered plantations that supplied Charleston. Balfour also ordered Loyalist Alexander Stewart to create an independent company on James Island.[169]

Even more important than these measures was the arrival at Charleston on June 3 of three British regiments with a combined strength of over three thousand rank and file. The reinforcement enabled Rawdon to take his own troops, along with the newly arrived grenadier and light infantry companies, and march to the relief of Ninety Six. Rawdon set out on June 7, and Balfour sent Loyalist messengers ahead of the troops to inform the garrison that relief was on the way.[170]

Greene's army had been skirmishing with Loyalists throughout its march to Ninety Six. After reaching the Wateree River, Otho Williams observed that "we are now farther advanc'd into South Carolina, and particularly that part which is most attach'd to the Kings interest."[171] On May 21 the American advance guard "killed about twelve Tories," while the main body of Continentals came upon a Loyalist encampment and killed another eleven men.[172] Greene also dispatched his light infantry and cavalry "to Surprise a party of tories," but the Loyalists withdrew before the Whigs arrived. Shortly after the cavalry set off in pursuit, another group of Loyalists mistook the rebel infantry for British troops and emerged from a swamp, "& being undeceived" captured a Whig soldier. One Loyalist was killed in the subsequent exchange of fire. Returning to the scene, Greene's cavalry killed four more Loyalists and captured six. The next day rebel troops "Surprised a party of Tories within sight of Ninety Six," killing four.[173]

After reaching Ninety Six and beginning siege operations, Greene and his officers found themselves in the midst of hostile territory. Williams asserted that "the Enemy have had such footing and influence in this Country that their Success in puting the Inhabitants together . . . has Exceeded even their own Expectations."[174] Greene wrote that while he was already aware that "a very large majority of the People from inclination were in the Enemys interest" in the province, he believed that in the backcountry "there are five for one against us. The Tories swarm around us and render it extreme difficult to get either forage or subsistance for our Troops."[175] As many as five hundred Loyalists were reported to be concealed in swamps and forests near the American lines. Greene tried to induce them to surrender by offering them pardon, but few accepted.[176] Civil war continued to rage across much of the backcountry. "The Daily deliberate murders committed by pretended whiggs and reputed Tories . . . are too numerous & too shocking to relate," Williams observed.[177]

Inside the fortifications, Cruger's 350 New York and New Jersey provincials, aided by 200 militia under Cunningham, resisted stoutly. Another hundred Loyalists—women, children, and the elderly—took refuge inside the stockade. Despite his inability to obtain any information from outside, Cruger steadfastly believed that Rawdon would come to his aid.[178]

As Rawdon marched to relieve Ninety Six, large numbers of Loyalists joined the British troops. "The Tories join fast," Henry Lee informed Greene.[179] Another Whig officer reported that people flocked to Rawdon when his troops reached Orangeburg. On June 18 the rebels captured "15 or 18 Arm'd Tories" who had been on their way to meet the British.[180] With Rawdon's army shielding them from the Continentals, other Loyalists assembled and attacked the Whigs, causing so many of Sumter's men to return home to protect their families that the corps temporarily became too weak to take the field.[181]

On June 17 a bold Loyalist rode among Greene's troops, pretending to be nothing more than a curious farmer until he reached a point opposite the gate in the stockade around Ninety Six, whereupon he raced toward it under a barrage of Whig gunfire. He brought Cruger a message that Rawdon was fast approaching. Realizing that he had no time to await the outcome of his siege, Greene launched a desperate attack the next day, which failed to breach the British fortifications and cost him 150 men. The rebels retreated, and Rawdon arrived on June 21. He tried to bring the Continentals to battle, but Greene took advantage of his head start to keep a safe distance from the British troops.[182]

Rawdon returned to Ninety Six, where an examination of its circumstances convinced him that the post had to be abandoned. "But that no proof of attention to our friends might be omitted," Rawdon explained, "I ordered the principal Inhabitants to be convened; & desired that they should state their wishes." He suggested that if the Loyalists were willing to defend the district against the Whigs, he would leave behind a small force of troops and occasionally send larger detachments to assist them. If the Loyalists preferred to leave the area, he promised to settle them on abandoned rebel plantations within the contracted sphere of British control. Many Loyalists chose to leave with the British to "be secure against the savage cruelty of the Rebel Militia." Once they had been resettled, the men promised Rawdon that they would "embody, & make incursions into the disaffected Settlements."[183]

More than eight hundred men who had served in the Ninety Six district militia were among those who evacuated the area. Other Loyalists joined the column as it made its way across the province, while some Loyalists sought safety in Georgia or among their Indian neighbors.[184] Before leaving, Loyalists in the Long Canes district burned several Whig-owned houses and drove off all the livestock they could not bring with them.[185]

Most Loyalists, however, chose to remain at home and make the best of their situation. An informant told Otho Williams that many people around Ninety Six were "averse to going to Cha: Town."[186] Whig colonel William Henderson noted that few Loyalists along the Pacolet River seemed willing to relocate closer to Charleston. After the evacuation of Ninety Six, Greene expressed satisfaction that the number of Loyalists who accompanied the British was far less than he had expected.[187] Yet, if many Loyalists did not persist in the fight, neither did they abandon their principles. When the Delaware Continentals marched through a settlement along the Broad River on June 24, William Seymour found that the inhabitants made no secret of the fact that they were "all Tories," although they made no effort to harass the rebels.[188]

Throughout the final campaigns in the South Carolina interior, the Whigs continued their relentless persecution of the Loyalists, and when possible, the latter retaliated in kind. After capturing Fort Motte, rebel troops prepared to hang the captured German militiamen from Orangeburg until Col. William Thomson intervened and ordered the men released. Near Camden the Whigs captured Capt. Francis Tidwell of the loyal militia and hanged him; to increase their enjoyment of the spectacle they did not tie Tidwell's hands. The rebels roared with laughter at Tidwell's vain struggle against the noose; when their entertainment ended with Tidwell's death, they left the body hanging for three days as a warning to other Loyalists. Several Loyalists captured in a skirmish near Georgetown were also hanged. Across the province, individually or in small groups, Loyalist prisoners suffered death at the hands of the Whigs.[189]

Levi Smith, an officer in the loyal militia, managed to survive his captivity and tell of the savagery that prisoners encountered. In a "grisly" narrative of his experiences in May and June, Smith recounted how after his capture he was stripped and "forced to run for a mile ahead of his mounted captors" in his underclothes. "When he collapsed, the rebels beat him with the flat sides of their swords." During his confinement he watched the Whigs hang an officer and two privates of the loyal militia for having collaborated with the British. A Whig officer accused Smith of burning a tavern and ordered him hanged, despite Smith's protestations of innocence. A rebel soldier, who feared that his brother in British captivity might be executed in retaliation, secured Francis Marion's intervention to spare Smith. Soon afterward the Whigs placed fourteen other prisoners in irons and sent them under militia guard to Greene's camp. The prisoners had not gone far when the militia commander ordered them shot. Thirteen died, and the fourteenth, Joseph Cooper, survived even though a rebel stabbed him in the throat with a sword to insure that he was dead. Cooper escaped from the murder scene after the militia left, dragging the corpse of his companion who was still chained to him. Sympathetic women found and freed Cooper, who eventually made his way to Charleston. The Whig militiamen returned to camp and boasted of their deed, frightening most of the remaining prisoners into joining the Whigs. Smith clung to his principles, however, and was later paroled by Greene. He too sought safety in Charleston.[190]

Rawdon and Balfour could do little to halt the persecution, although they were fully aware that rebel cruelty drove many Loyalists to take up arms with the Whigs. "I am well convinced, that numbers have joined the enemy merely to shield themselves from the atrocious barbarity of the rebel militia, which has been beyond what I have ever heard of among the most savage nations," Rawdon wrote.[191] Balfour renewed his threat to retaliate against the rebel militia prisoners in Charleston. Addressing the captives, Balfour declared that he had repeatedly protested to Whig leaders regarding "the outrages committed by the American Troops" and "the rigourous treatment, in many cases extending to Death, which the Loyal Militia, when made Prisoners, most invariably experience." Since

American officers had "wholly Neglected" his pleas, Balfour announced that he had no alternative but to use the prisoners he held "as Hostages for the good usage of all the Loyal Militia, who are or may be made Prisoners of War."[192] The prisoners answered that they were willing to accept the threatened punishments for the good of their cause, but a day later they sent a more moderate reply in which they expressed mortification at the treatment some captured Loyalists had received. However, they insisted that such cruelty was not sanctioned by American officers and attributed the violence to ignorance of the laws of war on the part of Whigs and Loyalists alike.[193]

Unlike the Whigs, many Loyalists held Greene responsible for the savagery. "The deliberate murders committed in cold blood, under your influence and direction in the Carolinas in the space of two months, exceed the number ever committed in any war recorded in the history of Europe," a writer in the *South Carolina Royal Gazette* asserted in an essay addressed to the American commander.[194]

Greene, in fact, had begun trying to halt the carnage, albeit with little success. In early June he learned that Col. Leroy Hammond's regiment of Whig militia was "murdering and plundering the Inhabitants not in arms in a most barbarous and cruel Manner" along the Saluda River. Greene assured the victimized people of his "detestation of such a practice" and promised to stop it.[195] He then ordered Andrew Pickens to take "proper Measures" to halt Hammond's depredations and suggested "capital punishment" for anyone guilty of plundering and murder. "The Idea of exterminating the Tories is not less barbarous than impolitick; and if persisted in, will keep this Country in the greatest confusion and distress," Greene stated. He urged Pickens to set an example by attempting to win over Loyalists to the rebel cause, even if it angered "the most worthless part of the Whigs."[196]

Greene's intentions were good, and yet he could not always control even his own Continental troops, let alone the militia. Henry Lee's legion contributed significantly to the carnage, despite Lee's own criticism of South Carolinians as worse than "the Goths and Vandals" in plundering and murder. The "bloodletting" practiced by the legion in retaliation for alleged British atrocities "blurred the distinction between policy in war and cruelty for its own sake."[197]

Faced with a choice of death or switching allegiance to the Whigs, most Loyalists opted for the latter, especially after the British evacuated the interior of South Carolina. By the end of June, Loyalist morale was on the verge of complete collapse, and British hopes of retaining control in the South were evaporating along with it.

The situation in Georgia was equally bad. Small Whig parties continually raided the backcountry; in November 1780 the provincial council complained of "the many cruel murders and depredations which are daily committed on His Majesty's peaceable and loyal subjects."[198] Governor Wright noted that rebel galleys were raiding along the coastal rivers, plundering property and slaves at every opportunity. Since the army had no troops to spare, he did his best to counter the attacks with militia.[199]

Whig activity intensified in January 1781 as the rebels attempted to interrupt the flow of supplies to Augusta by attacking vessels on the upper Savannah River. Thomas Brown dispatched a force of Rangers and militia to the South Carolina side of the river to drive off the Whigs, but the rebels ambushed the detachment. The militia fled, and the Rangers surrendered. The Whigs then executed the provincial officer and five other prisoners. One man escaped and informed Brown, who sent a larger force of forty Rangers, thirty Indians, and more militia to strike the rebels.[200] Brown followed with forty more Rangers and an equal number of militia and Indians, and they were later joined by another one hundred militiamen. This force camped at Wiggan's plantation, where about five hundred rebels assaulted the militia posted on Brown's left flank. The militia, "without returning a shot . . . fled into camp in the greatest disorder & confusion imaginable," but the Rangers and Indians still repulsed the rebel attack. Later the Whigs attacked again, and once more the militia fled, except for ten men. Again the Rangers and Indians restored the situation with a charge that dispersed the rebels. Five Indians and five Rangers were killed.[201] Brown then scoured the surrounding area, recovering many of the goods plundered from the supply ships and burning the houses where he found such items. He asked Balfour to assist him by sending the South Carolina militia to patrol the north bank of the Savannah, and Balfour promised to send what aid he could.[202]

Brown received a small reinforcement in late January when thirty Loyalists from the overmountain settlements made their way through Cherokee territory to Augusta, but this was not enough to enable him to halt Whig raids.[203] In mid-February, South Carolina rebels entered upper Georgia and "assassinated eleven people, some of them in their beds." Those murdered, Wright noted, "were such as had very early shown their loyalty and . . . had been most active and useful in reducing the rebellion."[204] Brown sent two parties of militia, each numbering one hundred men, under Col. James Grierson and Maj. Henry Williams, to find the rebels, but the raiders escaped, leaving only a few stragglers to be captured by the militia.[205]

The elusive rebels continued to launch attacks on Georgia throughout March and April, inflicting grievous losses on the Loyalists. Whigs murdered several people in the Ceded Lands, as well as thirty-five others in the environs of Augusta, where the garrison proved unable to protect the region's inhabitants.[206] The Quaker settlement at Wrightsborough, "known to be prosperous, largely pro-British, and unwilling to defend itself, became a favorite target." The rebels killed several of the pacific Quakers, killed or carried off two thousand cattle, and burned a plantation and grist mill.[207]

With some understatement, Wright reported in late April that the situation in Georgia had "taken a very unfavourable turn," as the Whigs continued to murder

"Pickt Men and such as they thought were most firm in their loyalty." The attacks, Wright observed, came without warning so that the militia had no time to assemble to protect the people. The "unheard of Cruelty of the rebels was so shocking that the generality of the people took to the Swamps for shelter against these worse than Savages, who say they will Murder every loyal Subject in the Province." Wright asked Cornwallis for troops to protect the Loyalists, remarking that if left undefended, they were "doomed to death and distruction," which was "poor encouragement for them to persevere in their loyalty."[208] Many loyal Georgians too hoped that Georgia's defenses could be strengthened; they told the governor that "our means of Defence have been considerably lessened by the cruel and wanton Murders of near one hundred Men, who have fallen a Sacrifice for their Loyalty." The land communication with Charleston had been severed, and rebel parties were "daily making Inroads to within a few Miles of Savannah," they observed. They suggested that Wright reinforce the militia at Ebenezer and raise two troops of provincial cavalry to improve the situation.[209]

The Whig raids were followed by a full-scale attack on Augusta in May. When Greene moved to besiege Ninety Six, he ordered Henry Lee's legion to unite with militia under Elijah Clarke and Andrew Pickens and drive the British from the Georgia backcountry. On May 21 Lee captured Fort Galphin and its garrison of loyal militia at Silver Bluff on the South Carolina side of the Savannah River; he then joined Pickens and Clarke, who had already surrounded Augusta. Brown, with his Rangers, militia, and several Cherokees, Creeks, and Chickasaws, gallantly defended the town until June 5, when rebel artillery emplaced in a tower overlooking Fort Cornwallis made further resistance hopeless. After Brown surrendered, Lee sent him to Savannah with an escort of Continentals to prevent the rebels from murdering their longtime nemesis. Brown's guards received so many threats en route that they feared for their own lives.[210]

Colonel Grierson was not so fortunate as Brown. Pickens had sent most of the Loyalist prisoners across the Savannah River for their own protection but confined Grierson in an Augusta dwelling. On June 6 a Whig rode up to the door of the house "and without dismounting Shot [Grierson] So that he Expired Soon after." The murderer rode away, and shortly afterward Henry Williams, who was also in the house, "was Shot at and badly Wounded in the Shoulder."[211]

Dr. Thomas Taylor, a Loyalist, believed that Grierson's murder could have been prevented and the killer caught. On the day of Grierson's death, Taylor endured "bitter curses" from the Whigs when he brought the colonel some water. Grierson told Taylor that "his Life was threatened & if not remov'd from the Place where he then was he was certain the Threat would be executed." Taylor passed this information to Brown, who in turn informed Lee. Lee did nothing. After the murder, rebel troops undertook what Taylor described as "a sham Pursuit ... for a few Minutes after the Murderer but he was permitted to escape." Taylor added that many other Loyalists shared Grierson's fate. "It would transcend Belief were I to recount the Murders committed by these Wretches upon the unhappy Tories all over the Country," he wrote. The barbarity of the rebels, Taylor asserted, was four times worse than anything Indians were capable of doing.[212] Grierson and Williams were not the only intended victims; Richard Pearis later wrote that he too "had been nearly assassinated by the Rebels" after his capture at Augusta.[213] Greene denounced the murder and offered an exorbitant reward of one hundred guineas (nearly fourteen thousand dollars) for the killer's capture. Not surprisingly, however, none of the many rebel witnesses revealed the identity of the criminal.[214]

The fall of Augusta sent hundreds of Loyalist refugees fleeing to Savannah, where Wright armed as many as he could and sent them to garrison the fortifications at Ebenezer. Other Loyalists hid in swamps, while a few continued to fight the Whigs.[215] On June 19 Elijah Clarke reported that he had to divert some of his militia to Wilkes County because "Outliers & Indjans" were "Burning Robing & Destroying" the Whigs there.[216]

The Loyalists' actions paled in comparison to the onslaught the Whigs unleashed once they had regained control of the interior of Georgia. William Lee, a Loyalist who had fled West Florida after the Spanish captured Mobile, had bought a farm in Richmond County, about one hundred miles from Savannah, and found himself in the midst of the rebels' campaign of vengeance. The Whigs "committed great depredations upon the Loyalists, by plundering their houses, and very frequently killing them," he wrote. Many people escaped to Savannah or Charleston, while "others sheltered themselves in the woods, and were many of them caught and killed, even when begging for life, upon their knees!" Reluctant to leave his pregnant wife, Lee remained peaceful and hoped that the rebels "would let me alone." The Whigs soon disabused him of that notion when a party called on him, carried off much of his property, and left after warning him that if he did not join them or leave the province within a day, they would kill him. Lee hid in the woods until his wife safely delivered their daughter; he then made his way to Savannah.[217]

East Floridians, despite fears of a possible Spanish attack, remained immune to the hardships encountered by Loyalists to their north and west. The province actually prospered, becoming self-sufficient in the production of both grain and cattle. East Florida produced more naval stores than there were ships available to export them, and Patrick Tonyn planned to build a town and fort on the St. Mary's River.[218]

While East Florida thrived, West Floridians faced the loss of the remainder of their province to Spanish conquerors. Gen. John Campbell knew that Bernardo de Galvez would move against Pensacola after seizing Mobile and did everything possible to strengthen his position. In addition to improving Pensacola's fortifications, Campbell bombarded British officials with pleas for assistance.[219] When aid failed to arrive, Campbell decided to disrupt Galvez's plans by attempting to recapture Mobile in January 1781. The Loyalist Royal Foresters participated in the campaign, which resulted in a failed assault on Mobile, after which the British force returned to Pensacola.[220]

Galvez arrived at Pensacola with a powerful force of Spanish and French troops and warships on March 9 and by the end of the month had begun siege operations. Hoping to create a diversion that might force Galvez to lift the siege or at least to detach part of the Franco-Spanish army, Campbell took steps to instigate a Loyalist uprising at Natchez. Three Natchez residents, John and Philip Alston and John Turner, wished to oust the Spaniards from the area and had sent an emissary to Campbell asking for his support. Although some people at Natchez believed that the three secretly planned to turn control of the district over to the Americans once the Spanish were defeated, Campbell authorized the trio to resist the Spanish and provided their emissary with commissions to raise a force among the Natchez inhabitants.[221]

Many people along the Mississippi had come to accept Spanish authority and were reluctant to participate in a rebellion, but the Alstons and Turner convinced two influential settlers, John Blommart and Jacob Winfree, to support the revolt. Blommart and Winfree helped to assemble some two hundred Loyalists and a few Indians to attack Spanish Fort Panmure at Natchez. The fighting began on April 22 and lasted until the Spanish commander surrendered his seventy-six troops on May 4.[222]

Meanwhile, Galvez had tightened his noose around Pensacola. Despite the efforts of the defenders, whose number included over forty of the Royal Foresters and about one hundred of the town's inhabitants serving as militia, Campbell surrendered on May 10.[223] When the victorious Loyalists at Natchez learned that Pensacola had fallen, they realized that they could not resist the large force that Galvez would undoubtedly bring against them and so surrendered to a small Spanish detachment that arrived at Natchez on June 22. The Spaniards treated the rebels with leniency. Galvez granted amnesty to most of them but imprisoned Blommart, Winfree, and other leaders. Blommart was tried and convicted of rebellion and had his property confiscated.[224]

With the entire province in Spanish hands, West Floridians had to choose whether to submit to Spanish authority or flee. Some took refuge with the Choctaws; a larger number made their way to Chickasaw territory, where they cooperated with the Indians in operations against the Americans and Spaniards along the Ohio and Mississippi rivers.[225]

West Florida Loyalists, although few in number, had fought hard to defend the province and suffered much as a result. As some later stated in a petition to Parliament, they had contributed funds to build fortifications, "formed themselves into volunteer companies for their defence," sortied to sea to attack rebel privateers, and "joined and did duty with his Majesty's troops . . . formed themselves into provincial corps, and were employed upon the most dangerous services, till the reduction of the province." Many "had their plantations plundered and burned" by James Willing's raiders; "others had their properties laid waste, and large stocks of cattle destroyed" during the fighting against the Spanish. Many lost property to the Spaniards as a penalty "for having contributed to the public defence," while those who fled the province after the Spanish conquest forfeited their lands.[226] Altogether, they paid a high price for their loyalty to king and country.

THE INDIANS REJOIN THE BATTLE

Despite being ignored by Cornwallis and alternately courted and mistreated by John Campbell, the southern Indians stood ready to assist the British when needed. Thomas Brown and Alexander Cameron had done an excellent job of assuaging the Indians' hurt feelings, which was fortunate because Cornwallis finally took the advice of his subordinates and called upon the Indians for aid in December 1780; Campbell also needed their help to defend Pensacola. The crisis in West Florida reduced the number of Indians available to serve in Georgia and South Carolina, since the Creeks divided their efforts between the two areas.

If Cornwallis had seen no value in using Indians during the summer and fall of 1780, John Rutledge remained aware of the threat they posed. When Daniel Morgan marched into the South Carolina backcountry in December, Rutledge advised him to send a "confidential person" to George Galphin, who, Rutledge said, still possessed great influence with the Creeks. Rutledge wanted Galphin to warn the Creeks that the Spanish were moving against the Floridas and that American forces with French aid would soon recover South Carolina and Georgia. Therefore, the Creeks should "get all the Goods they can from the British, but, by no Means . . . take up the Hatchet, or kill any of our People, for if they do so, as soon as the English are beat, We shall fall upon them." Rutledge hoped that this message would intimidate the Creeks, since reports indicated that a large number of them were with Brown at Augusta and intended "to act agst. our people." The governor suggested that if Morgan recaptured Ninety Six, he should then move against Augusta because the British "will hold their Influence over the Indians, whilst they keep that place."[227]

Aside from the fact that, unbeknownst to the governor, Galphin had died three weeks earlier, Rutledge's information was correct; Cornwallis had already authorized Brown to order the Indians to attack the overmountain settlements to prevent the inhabitants from reinforcing Greene. Brown informed the earl on December 17 that the Cherokees and many Upper Creeks "have chearfully agreed to attack the plunderers & banditti" in that region. Cherokee leaders promised Brown that they would move against the rebels immediately and continue to fight as long as they were supplied with arms and ammunition. Brown assigned "a proper number of whitemen & traders to head the different war parties," which would be under the overall command of Brown's deputies. Brown added that on the Ohio River some Cherokees had recently attacked rebel boats that were headed to New Orleans for supplies, "killed the guard," and sent the captured women and children to Augusta.[228]

Cornwallis had evidently made his decision with great reluctance, since it was not until December 29 that he told Balfour that the time had come to inform Clinton "of my having employed the Indians, as there will be a considerable expense attending it."[229] Cornwallis wrote to Clinton the same day, explaining that he had "directed Lieut.-Colonel Brown to encourage the Indians to attack" the overmountain settlements. "The good effects of this measure have already appeared," the earl noted. "A large body of the mountaineers marched lately to join the Rebels . . . but were soon obliged to return to oppose the incursions of the Indians." Cornwallis pointed out that if Brown's reports of their behavior were accurate, the Indians' "humanity is a striking contrast to the shocking barbarities committed by the mountaineers."[230] Cornwallis was pleased with the Indians' help, telling Rawdon that Brown "seems to have cut out work enough for the Back Mountain men with his Indian friends."[231]

The Indian attacks did succeed in preventing many militia units from joining Greene's army. In late December, Greene learned that the Cherokees had "murdered a number of Inhabitants on the frontiers of N. Carolina" and that the militia of that state had "marched against their lower towns."[232] Some Cherokee attacks struck South Carolina as well. "The Cherokees . . . have lately killed some people on the Frontiers of No. & So. Carolina, which has prevented, & will prevent, them from turning out," John Rutledge wrote.[233]

Although the Cherokee attacks deprived Greene of reinforcements, they resulted in another catastrophe for that nation. The Whigs received advance notice of the impending attack from Joseph Martin, Virginia's agent to the Cherokees, and state officials decided to launch a preemptive strike. Col. John Sevier assembled two hundred militiamen in December and marched against the Cherokee towns. After routing a Cherokee party in a battle in which sixteen Indians were killed, Sevier advanced to the Tennessee River and burned a Cherokee town. Joined by another four hundred men under Arthur Campbell, the rebels continued their march, burning Hiwassee Old Town and Tellico, killing a few Cherokees, and suffering a handful of casualties before returning home. Altogether, the Virginians destroyed at least ten Cherokee towns and several smaller villages totaling over one thousand dwellings, along with over fifty thousand bushels of corn. They reported killing twenty-nine Cherokee men and capturing seventeen prisoners, mostly women and children.[234]

By February 8 Campbell was able to inform Greene that the Cherokee threat to Virginia had ended. The militia had, Campbell boasted, "dealt out to them, not a few of the miseries that were designed for us. The Over Hill Country were chiefly made a Field of desolation, the Families dispersed in the Mountains to starve." Not surprisingly, Campbell reported that "the Cheifs were greatly humbled" and wished to make peace.[235] Greene replied that he welcomed the opportunity to make peace "on the most generous & liberal principles."[236] He promptly appointed commissioners to meet with the Chickasaws as well as the Cherokees and to arrange a settlement.[237]

Campbell's assessment proved to be overly optimistic. The Cherokees renewed their attacks in March but again paid a high price and achieved little. Once again their operations limited the reinforcements available to Greene. On March 10 a Maryland officer noted that some of Campbell's overmountain militiamen had recently joined Greene, "but the indians having lately done mischief in his country was not joined by many of his countrymen from the mountains indeed it has prevented a greater number of fine fellows from joining us."[238] In April, Greene found that his army was short of lead because supplies expected from North Carolina had been diverted for that state's militia to use against the Cherokees.[239] Campbell apologized on April 23 that he could not send the militia Greene had requested, since his county was "Pressed hard by the Indians." In Campbell's opinion, this was part of a deliberate "scheme of the British General . . . to employ some of our best Militia in opposing the Indians, in order to facilitate his operations in the low Country." Unless Greene could cut off the Cherokees' access to Brown at Augusta, Campbell warned, that nation would never keep the peace.[240] Indian attacks also prevented some South Carolina militia from joining Greene at the siege of Ninety Six. On May 24 Col. Robert Anderson said that he could not aid Greene because most of his men had been sent to the frontier in the wake of Indian attacks there.[241]

The Whigs responded with another invasion of Cherokee territory. Sevier burned fifteen Middle Cherokee towns in March, which convinced some Cherokee leaders to undertake peace negotiations.[242] Two months later other Cherokees announced their desire for peace to North Carolina officials and asserted that only a few of their people still wanted to assist the British. Some Whigs, however, thought it might be advantageous to ignore the peace offer and continue to attack the Cherokees in order to "make them cede lands."[243] Brown learned of the rebels' campaign from Indian refugees and denounced the savagery of the Whig militia. "Men, women and children thrown into flames, impaled alive or butchered in cold blood!" he recounted.[244] As usual, these draconian tactics had demonstrated their effectiveness by forcing the Cherokees to submit.

Brown received some Indian help in his operations against rebel partisans in January, but his messages of encouragement in the spring failed to convince the badly beaten Cherokees to continue fighting. He sought assistance from the Creeks, who could provide little support because most were engaged in the defense of West Florida. A few Creeks, Cherokees, and Chickasaws participated in the defense of Augusta and were taken prisoner when the garrison surrendered.[245]

Britain's Indian allies were not alone in their suffering during this period; the prorebel Catawbas also experienced hunger and the destruction of their homeland. In December 1780 "General" New River, the Catawba leader, visited

Greene's headquarters with a letter of introduction from Gates, which testified to that nation's loyalty to the Whigs. New River asked Greene for supplies because his people were in great want, and he complained that the Catawbas had been mistreated by whites in upper South Carolina. New River wanted Greene's permission to settle his people in the vicinity of Charlotte. Before Greene could consider the proposal, however, Cornwallis's advance into North Carolina forced the Continental army to retreat. Unwilling to face British wrath for their support of the rebels, the Catawbas accompanied Greene in his flight to Virginia. They returned to South Carolina a few months later, only to find that the British had burned their homes and carried off their livestock.[246]

In East Florida, Patrick Tonyn did all he could to maintain good relations with the Seminoles so that he could rely on their aid if the Spanish attacked the province. To discover Spanish intentions, Tonyn sent a Loyalist to Havana, ostensibly to discuss a prisoner exchange. The emissary learned that after the Spaniards captured Pensacola, "it is determined to attack this province, for which purpose preparations are making."[247] The governor wished to retain the Seminoles' goodwill by supplying them with provisions, but he lacked the funds to purchase them.[248] He had to apply repeatedly to Alured Clarke for bread, meat, and rum from government stores, along with the wine, coffee, and sugar that Cowkeeper, the Seminole leader, personally favored. "I have no fund whatsoever for Indian contingencies," Tonyn complained, despite the fact that Germain had made the governor responsible for relations with the Seminoles and that it was essential to give them "the usual hospitable and friendly reception."[249] Clarke, who was in St. Augustine, shared Tonyn's fear of Spanish attack and therefore agreed to provide the requested goods, but he noted that provisions were in such short supply that little could be spared "without manifest Risk to the security of the Garrison." Tonyn then appealed to Clinton for the supplies and funds required to preserve the Seminoles' allegiance.[250]

Clinton approved the expense for the Indians without complaint, particularly in West Florida; he told Campbell that "it is absolutely necessary to keep those people in good humor," regardless of the cost.[251] Yet, Campbell continued to deny the Indians presents and supplies "unless he calls them upon actual service," Alexander Cameron complained. Cameron noted that the Choctaws had been acting on their own initiative against the Spaniards, which prevented them from hunting, and therefore they believed that they were entitled to food, clothing, and presents. Campbell, however, denied Cameron's request for these items, telling the superintendent to purchase the goods with his own funds. Campbell, said Cameron, "does not understand anything of Indians."[252]

Despite Campbell's stubborn stinginess, the Choctaws continued to provide valuable service in the fight against the Spanish. Cameron proudly reported at the end of October that those Choctaws who had flirted with Galvez had come to Pensacola; turned over all their Spanish flags, commissions, and medals to

Cameron; and recommitted themselves to the British alliance. To demonstrate their sincerity, they harassed the Spanish around Mobile. The Choctaws were so effective, Cameron stated, that "not a Spaniard can venture out of sight of the fort but they knock up and carry off his scalp," forcing the Spanish to cross the bay to obtain fresh water.[253] After learning of the Choctaws' activities, Campbell sent eight Loyalists from the Royal Foresters to lead 130 Indians in an attack on one of the Spanish posts at Mobile. This party assaulted the fort on October 28, but the Loyalists fled when the Spaniards opened fire with cannons. The Choctaws showed more courage by advancing close to the fort, killing several Spanish soldiers, and burning nearby houses before retreating.[254]

In mid-November, Campbell learned that a Spanish attack was imminent and wrote to Cameron and Brown requesting that they immediately send as many Indians as possible to Pensacola. Explaining the strategy he intended to use against the Spaniards, Campbell told Brown that the Indians "have it still in their power, by frequent attacks & constant alarms, in short by continually harrassing & hanging on the enemy's rear, in case of siege, greatly to impede the operations, if not totally defeat & disconcert the designs of any force they can send against us."[255] When a hurricane devastated the Spanish invasion fleet, Campbell sent word to the agents to have the Indians return home. Campbell again asked for Creek help against a rumored Spanish attack in January 1781, and he again canceled the request when British officials promised to dispatch reinforcements from Jamaica. Campbell's actions angered the one thousand Creeks who were on their way to Pensacola when they learned they were no longer wanted.[256]

Rather than wait for the Spanish to attack Pensacola, Campbell decided to disrupt Galvez's plans by seizing Mobile. Over 400 Choctaws joined 160 British and German regulars, 200 Pennsylvania and Maryland provincials, and a handful of West Florida Loyalists in an assault on January 7, 1781. The attack broke the Spanish lines, but the commanding officer, Col. Johann von Hanxleden, was killed; other German and British officers were killed or wounded; and the ranking officer, a Maryland Loyalist, called off the assault. With the command system disrupted, no one signaled the Indians to join the attack; however, led by Cameron's deputies, John McIntosh and Farquhar Bethune, the Choctaws fired on the Spaniards from concealment, which covered the withdrawal of the regulars and provincials. Their fire drove back some of the defenders, who tried to reach a boat and escape, but the Choctaws pursued the Spaniards into the water and took at least forty scalps before breaking off the action. Ignoring the pleas of Choctaw leaders to renew the attack, the white officers decided to return to Pensacola. Some British officers later blamed the Choctaws for the failure of the expedition, although there was not a shred of evidence to support their allegation.[257]

The long-awaited Spanish attack on Pensacola finally materialized in March 1781, when Galvez arrived with a powerful fleet and four thousand troops; he would later be joined by an additional three thousand Spanish and French soldiers and a few Choctaws from the Sixtowns faction. Campbell could muster only fifteen hundred British, German, and provincial troops, along with some armed blacks, militiamen, and Choctaws and Creeks. One Spanish officer estimated the Indians' strength at one thousand, although the actual total was probably half that number. Yet, Campbell chose to conduct a passive defense with his own troops, relying on the Indians to oppose the Spanish advance.[258]

The knowledge that their security depended on the Indians made some Loyalists uneasy. James Bruce, the collector of customs at Pensacola, understood that if the Indians did not come to West Florida's defense, "the consequences to us will soon be fatal."[259] Yet, when the Indians arrived to aid in the town's defense, Bruce complained that the only alternatives to leaving Pensacola's non-combatants exposed to Spanish bombardment were to "trust our women & children etc. to the power of the merciless savages in the woods" or accept Galvez's offer to provide them with sanctuary during the siege.[260] While Bruce valued the military assistance of the Indians, he could not overcome fears of their alleged barbarism.

The Indians began proving their worth shortly after Spanish troops came ashore. On March 19 a group of Indians led by a British officer captured a Spanish boat, killing ten of the crew and bringing one survivor to Pensacola.[261] Three days later the Indians struck the Spanish camp in the evening, shooting "at the troops that were around the fires, killing three and wounding four of our soldiers," wrote Galvez, "not leaving us at peace until morning."[262] After a raid behind Spanish lines on March 25, Indians brought twenty-three captured horses and two scalps into Pensacola; two days later they drove off five boatloads of Spaniards attempting to land. On March 28 the Indians again attacked Galvez's troops, but they were driven off after some skirmishing in which four Indians were wounded. Galvez reported that three of his troops had been seriously wounded in the affair.[263]

Galvez advanced his army closer to Pensacola on March 30 and again met fierce Indian resistance. Soon after the Spanish began their march, "a large group of Indians emerged from their hide-outs in the woods, firing rapidly." Galvez brought up artillery and attacked, driving the Indians back.[264] Seeing an opportunity to defeat the Spaniards, Campbell dispatched some of his own troops and fifty armed blacks with artillery to reinforce the Indians. A four-hour battle ensued, after which the mixed British force withdrew. Spanish casualties were three killed and twenty-eight wounded, while British losses totaled one Indian killed and two Indians and one black wounded. The Indians returned to town with several trophies, including drums, scalps, and the head of a Spanish soldier. Choctaw leader Franchimastabe believed that the foray could have been more successful had Campbell given the Indians more substantial support.[265]

The near-constant Indian attacks delayed Galvez's operations and forced his troops to undertake additional work "to construct the entrenchment that was necessary for all camps because of the Indians."[266] As one Spanish officer noted, "being in the midst of woods and surrounded by savages who hid in the forest and insulted us at all hours, this operation was indispensable."[267] However, fortifications did not prevent the Indians from attacking the camps. They struck again on the night of April 5, wounding two soldiers and "disturbing the whole army" throughout the night.[268]

Skirmishing continued throughout the month, with the Indians continuing to play the major role for the British, receiving only occasional assistance from regular troops and armed blacks. Several groups of Indians made their way through Spanish lines to reinforce Pensacola, including a small Creek party that on its way to the town captured a Spanish boat and killed three crewmen.[269] Fifty Chickasaws attacked Galvez's camp before entering British lines on April 27 with "a great number of scalps, firelocks, and bayonets" as trophies.[270]

In a final, desperate effort to drive off the Spaniards, Campbell dispatched all of his Indian auxiliaries on May 7 with orders "to endeavour to get upon the rear of the enemy's encampment."[271] However, the warriors were unable to pass around the lines and instead attacked a Spanish outpost. A short skirmish ensued, in which the Indians were driven off; they returned to Pensacola with ten scalps and one prisoner. It was their last battle. On May 8 a Spanish artillery shell struck the powder magazine in the redoubt that anchored Campbell's defenses, virtually annihilating the defenders. Spanish troops seized the position, and Campbell opened surrender negotiations. The Indians did not wait to be taken prisoner; they simply disappeared into the forests outside the town and returned home.[272]

Although the Indians had borne most of the burden of Pensacola's defense, Campbell downplayed their contributions. When the Spanish landed, Campbell wrote, "no Indians could be got to oppose them"; yet, at the same time he observed that the Spanish force was too strong to attack with his own troops. Campbell described the Indians' attacks on the Spanish as producing "more noise than advantage." Overall, Campbell declared that the Indians were "of very little use," and during the siege he even suspected that they intended to betray the British. "I fear much they are secretly and underhand instigated and encouraged to this conduct in short there is no dependence on the present set of our savage auxiliaries," he asserted.[273] In subsequent reports Campbell continued to blame the Indians for his inability to hold Pensacola.[274]

Cameron defended the Indians against Campbell's criticism and instead blamed the general for the defeat. If Campbell had followed his advice, Cameron insisted, two thousand Indians, rather than five hundred, would have been on hand to defend Pensacola. Campbell's habit of repeatedly summoning and dismissing the Indians, along with his refusal to provide them with the goods they requested, convinced many of them that the general did not respect them or value their contributions.[275] Cameron expressed pride in the Indians' behavior during the siege. "The Indians in general . . . behaved with great spirit and attachment," he told Germain, "and had we but as many more of them . . . we would have driven the whole Spanish army into the sea. No men could behave better than they did."[276] Most of Galvez's officers probably would have agreed. In the entire campaign, a Spaniard wrote, the body of an Indian killed on the battlefield was "the only one dead or alive that we have been able to take during the siege."[277]

The loss of Pensacola, and the Whigs' capture of Augusta a month later, "signaled the end of effective functioning of the Southern Indian Department." St. Augustine, Charleston, and Savannah were the only remaining British posts in the South, and except for the Seminoles in East Florida, the Indians could not reach these places without undertaking a long and hazardous journey through rebel-controlled territory. No means existed by which the British could easily provide their allies with arms and supplies.[278] At the end of May the Indians were already "in the utmost distress for goods among them and particularly ammunition," Cameron reported.[279] Whether the British could derive further support from the Indians under such conditions, or even maintain the alliance, was an open question.

AFRICAN AMERICANS: STEADY SUPPORT

During the last months of 1780 and the first half of 1781, blacks continued to aid the British in a variety of ways, providing labor, intelligence of Whig movements, and sometimes armed assistance. The British withdrawal to Charleston and Savannah limited slaves' opportunities to join the king's troops. Some blacks were unhappy to find that fleeing to the British had not improved their condition, and they escaped again or rebelled. In general, however, most African Americans remained a reliable source of support to the British, although neither civil nor military officials had yet devised an official policy for dealing with the slave issue.

Information provided by slaves kept the British informed of rebel plans and often enabled British troops to defeat the Whigs. Slaves provided Cornwallis, Rawdon, Tarleton, and other officers with useful intelligence throughout the fall and winter of 1780. The British thwarted Francis Marion's plan to capture six British schooners that were transporting supplies on the Santee River when some blacks informed the British of Marion's intentions. In January 1781 a slave informed a detachment of the Queen's Rangers about the location of Col. Peter Horry's rebel partisans. The Queen's Rangers promptly marched to attack Horry, routed the Whigs' advanced guard, and then dispersed the main rebel force.[280]

Blacks ran great risks when they procured intelligence for the British, as the fate of one man captured in the vicinity of Greene's army made clear. "Yesterday the famous Majr. Gray, the infamous Spy, and Notorious Horse thief, lost His Mullatto Head. it is exhibited at Cherraw Hill as a terror to Tories," an American officer reported.[281]

Most slaves, however, continued to perform the more mundane tasks of laborers on fortifications and plantations. At Ninety Six slaves worked to strengthen the defenses, a process hampered during the winter of 1780–81 because, Isaac Allen noted, the "Poor naked Blacks can do but little [in] this cold weather."[282] When Greene began his siege of the post several months later, Cruger organized slaves into "a sort of labor battalion."[283] Their duties included improving the fortifications and, on at least one occasion, following the provincials in a sally against the American siege lines, where they gathered up the Whigs' entrenching tools after the troops drove off Greene's soldiers. After the rebels cut off the defenders' water supply, Cruger sent naked blacks on nightly forays to a stream outside the fortifications to get water for those besieged in the fort. This desperate measure enabled the defenders to hold out until Rawdon relieved them.[284]

In October 1780 Balfour ordered the commanding officer at Georgetown to fortify the town "by callg. in all the Negroes, you want" to construct defenses. When the work was completed, Capt. John Saunders returned the slaves to their masters.[285] Work on the defenses at Savannah proceeded "very fast" in November, since the governor and the council had ordered planters to provide four hundred slaves for the work.[286] At Augusta, Thomas Brown took advantage of a law passed by the Georgia Assembly in the spring of 1781 to impress slaves to strengthen the forts there. Some of these blacks remained in Fort Cornwallis during the subsequent siege, repairing damage inflicted by the attackers. One slave was killed during the battle, and the Whigs kept the remainder after Brown surrendered.[287]

As important as the slaves' efforts were in bolstering British defenses, blacks would have contributed much more had not a variety of factors limited their usefulness. Disease, Whig raids, the slaves' own opposition to performing plantation labor, and the continued failure to establish any kind of consistent policy toward blacks prevented the British from taking full advantage of their slave supporters.

Epidemic disease claimed the lives of numerous slaves and incapacitated others. An outbreak of smallpox at Camden in late 1780 killed many slaves, caused others to flee, and greatly delayed the construction of fortifications.[288] In February 1781 Loyalist William Burrows wrote that thirty slaves on his lowcountry plantation had died from smallpox and camp fever, and he worried that he was "in danger of losing several more."[289]

Rebel raiding parties carried off slaves whenever they could. Robert Muncreef, who had already found it "impossible to employ the Negroes to advantage" for want of a boat to carry products to Charleston, complained in February 1781 that his situation had grown even worse: his estate's "Stock is much exposed as well as the negroes to a sett of Plunderers who go about in parties & distress the different plantations exceedingly."[290] A month later Sampson Neyle reported that Whig raiders "took off 41 of my Negroes," although twenty-four escaped and returned to him.[291] "The rebels carried off above 160 of the best of my Negroes and many belonging to other loyal subjects" near the confluence of the Santee and Wateree rivers, William Bull lamented in June. These raids prevented the lowcountry plantations from producing an appreciable quantity of

crops in 1781, which forced John Cruden to purchase food for the slaves, overseers, and Loyalist refugees living on the sequestered estates.[292]

Slaves assigned to plantation labor often resented their situation, having
expected more than a simple change of masters when they fled to the British. This
dissatisfaction led to an insurrection on Johns Island in January 1781. Several
slaves, angered when a white overseer took corn they believed was theirs, attacked
him with farm tools. In the ensuing altercation, the overseer killed one slave and
injured two others before escaping. Balfour dispatched the loyal militia to restore
order. Seven of the slaves were tried for their part in the revolt; one was sentenced
to death, a second to branding, and the remaining five to severe whippings.[293]
Such punishments did nothing to improve relations between blacks and Loyalists
or to strengthen the slaves' attachment to the British cause. Unrest among plantation slaves persisted; in March, Bull noted that with so many white men having
left their plantations for military service, "all attention to the care of their Negroes
was relaxed, the slaves became ungovernable," and "the code of laws calculated for
the government of that class of people could not be carried into execution."[294]

Without guidance from London, civil and military officials did not consider
themselves authorized to establish a slave policy of their own. They continued to
devise solutions as problems arose, but these never seemed to fully satisfy either
slave owners or slaves. James Simpson told Germain in December 1780 that the
board of police in Charleston had been inundated with demands from Loyalists
that their slaves be returned. Some of the slaves in question had been seized by the
Whigs to penalize recalcitrant Loyalists; others had been taken by rebel raiders.
Simpson declared that the board "should have been glad to have been excused
interfering in a matter of so much moment if it could have been delayed." However, the Loyalists were "urgent and clamorous" and had evidence to back their
ownership claims, so the board finally relented and ordered all such slaves returned
to their owners. Simpson never explained the reasons for the board members' reservations, although they probably hesitated to return some slaves who were serving
with the army; they may also have been reluctant to alienate the slaves.[295]

Civil officials also encountered problems with ship captains and military
officers over the disposition of slaves. Many of the former carried off slaves when
they sailed from Charleston, a practice that the board of police tried to halt by
fining a captain who had concealed eight blacks aboard his Jamaica-bound vessel in March. Cruden criticized army officers for continually requisitioning
slaves from sequestered estates for duty with various military departments and
thus making it more difficult to make the plantations productive.[296]

Army officers could not agree among themselves on how to deal with blacks. In
November 1780, when Col. William Mills and his loyal Cheraws militia accompa-
nied Maj. James Wemyss in an expedition along the Black and Pee Dee rivers,
Wemyss ordered that "all the Captured Negroes were to be put under the Care of
Colonel Mills." According to a witness, "all the Negroes that were taken on that

Expedition were either Captured by the Troops or came in of their own Accord."
Wemyss ordered Mills to send the slaves "southward out of the reach of their Rebel
Masters."[297] Either Mills could not control the slaves or he used them to harass
suspected rebels. Balfour informed Cornwallis that Mills had "three hundred
negroes he is carrying across the country pillaging & robbing every plantation he
comes to," and he asked the earl to put a stop to the plundering.[298] Mills insisted
that Wemyss had given him 100 slaves as compensation for losses suffered at the
hands of the Whigs; he said that the other 160 slaves he had with him were intended
for Cruden's sequestered estates.[299] Cornwallis, however, declared Wemyss's action
"null & void," observing that while Mills's "sufferings may be great . . . He does
not deserve from us any distinguished favour."[300]

The large number of blacks with the army in the field also troubled Cornwallis.
On December 15, 1780, he informed Tarleton that "there were rather more black
attendants, both male and female, than I think you will like to see" with the British Legion's convalescents at Winnsboro.[301] In early January, Cornwallis repeated
his orders of September requiring blacks with the army to wear identification
badges. At the same time, however, he declared that he did not wish to inconve-
nience the troops by enforcing the restrictions "relative to Negroes" and asked only
that battalion commanders insure that all blacks with their units were placed
under the direction of officers who would be responsible for their conduct. The
officers must have complied slowly and reluctantly, because Cornwallis thought it
necessary to repeat the orders on January 24.[302]

When Gen. Alexander Leslie arrived in South Carolina to reinforce Cornwallis, his detachment included a large number of blacks, some of whom had
joined the British during their foray in the Chesapeake. These blacks accompanied Leslie's troops on their march to join Cornwallis and were joined by
other slaves along the way. The numerous blacks impeded Leslie's progress, so
on December 27 he issued orders that "All Blacks, or people found in the
Camp, not belonging to Offrs. or Deptmts." were to be immediately placed in
confinement.[303]

At Charleston army officers had fewer reservations about employing blacks and
hired many to work in the various departments. A list compiled in March 1781
showed 652 blacks employed by the army as laborers, artisans, teamsters, and
nurses. Others found work with the navy repairing and maintaining ships. Fifty-
six blacks were employed in the Royal Artillery Department in April 1781, 60 the
following month, and 74 in June. All were classified as laborers except a handful
who were listed as noncommissioned officers. Of these, there were two sergeants
in April and one in May and June; King Staniard held that rank each month. Two
blacks held the rank of corporal in April and May and four in June; Ned Garorie
(or Arorie) and a man named Washington held that rank throughout the period.[304]
Clearly, some British officers believed that a few blacks could be trusted in positions of responsibility.

Rumors reached Greene in February that the British had "ordered two Regts of Negroe's to be immediately embodied," but in fact British officials made little use of armed blacks despite the deteriorating military situation.[305] To hold Camden while he marched to attack Greene's army outside the town, Rawdon "had the redoubts all manned with Negroes & Tories," but this was only a temporary expediency. At Pensacola, John Campbell augmented his force with an estimated fifty black "foot soldiers."[306] When the town surrendered to the Spaniards, the articles of capitulation stipulated that all "free Negroes, mulattoes, and mestizos will be maintained in their status" and that all slaves who had worked on the British fortifications would be returned to their masters. Any blacks "who during the siege have been absent through fear" were to be returned to their owners when found.[307]

The assemblies in Georgia and East Florida both passed bills that allowed the governors to arm slaves. Georgia representatives authorized Wright to do so should an emergency arise; yet, even after the fall of Augusta no attempt was made to arm blacks.[308] The first assembly ever elected in East Florida convened in late March of 1781, and the next month they approved a slave code based on those of Georgia and South Carolina. Believing that the code's provisions for the trial of slaves were too oppressive, Tonyn and the council withheld their assent. Assembly members refused to conduct any further business until their version of the code was approved, although later they did agree to refer the matter to officials in London, who eventually ruled in favor of the assembly.[309]

In May representatives passed a militia law that permitted the provincial government to draft slaves to serve as either laborers or soldiers. Owners would be compensated one shilling per day for each drafted slave; Tonyn considered this a burdensome tax on slaveholders, since he calculated the actual value of a slave's labor at four or five shillings per day. Masters who refused a request to provide slaves would be fined fifty pounds (sixty-five hundred dollars). Slaves serving in the militia were to be whipped for minor breaches of discipline, whereas whites guilty of the same infractions would be fined. However, no racial distinctions were made for capital offenses, such as sleeping on duty. The law provided rewards in the form of clothing, medals, and money for slaves who demonstrated particular valor, but there was no promise of freedom in exchange for service.[310]

While British slave policy remained ambiguous, southern Whigs stubbornly clung to their belief that blacks were nothing more than property and deserved to be treated as such. When Daniel Morgan marched toward Ninety Six in December 1780, Governor Rutledge saw an opportunity to recover some of his slaves who were in the area. He suggested that if Morgan moved nearer the town, the slaves could be recaptured and sent to Charlotte.[311] After Morgan's victory at Cowpens, Rutledge again raised the issue. "I am in great Hopes," he wrote Morgan, that the general's success "will afford a good opportunity of bringing away my Negroes." Rutledge indicated that Andrew Pickens and other rebel militia officers would help Morgan recover the slaves, and he prodded the general to act "as soon as possible." If he did not regain his slaves quickly, Rut-ledge declared, it would be too late for them to plant a crop, and he would be unable to earn any profit from their labor for the year.[312]

At Cowpens the Whigs did capture about seventy blacks who had accompa-nied Tarleton's detachment. Pickens distributed eight slaves, five men and three women, as booty to some of his militiamen: three rebels received two slaves each for their services, and two others were each awarded a single slave.[313] Other blacks were captured in the days following the battle when Whig militia seized part of the British baggage train, including "horses, negroes, wagons and all other prop-erty" east of Broad River. A second band of militia captured twenty-seven blacks and twenty-two whites.[314] The former were undoubtedly returned to bondage as spoils of war.

Thomas Sumter took the use of slaves as booty a step further in May 1781, when he decided that slaves seized from Loyalist owners should be given as bounties to men who enlisted in South Carolina military units. Sumter considered this an ideal method of gaining recruits for his force, and Governor Rutledge concurred. Sumter set the value of a healthy adult slave at four hundred dollars and the worth of those over forty or under ten years of age at half that amount. A private would receive a bounty of one prime slave for a ten-month enlistment, while lieutenants would receive one and one-half slaves, captains two, majors three, and a colonel three and one-half.[315] Nathanael Greene approved the plan, observing that "it will have its advantages" so long as care was taken to insure that the slaves used as bounties had been owned by Loyalists.[316] He immediately authorized Sumter to take the blacks captured at Fort Granby "belonging to the Tories or disaffected" and apply them "to the fulfilling your contracts with the ten months Troops."[317] Francis Marion, however, feared that awarding slaves to recruits would promote plundering and increase the violence of the Loyalist-Whig conflict. He therefore refused to implement the policy in his brigade.[318]

In the eight months following the Battle of King's Mountain, the British posi-tion in the Deep South had deteriorated dramatically. Nathanael Greene's inva-sion of South Carolina, combined with partisan attacks on British supply lines, made it impossible for Lord Rawdon to hold the backcountry. Thomas Brown's surrender at Augusta similarly broke the British hold on the interior of Georgia. The Loyalists, who had persisted admirably in their support for the British despite defeat and violent persecution, either had to withdraw to the coast with the British or submit to the rebels. Not surprisingly, Loyalist morale underwent a precipitous decline in the wake of this disaster. The Indians' assistance had not been sufficient to affect the outcome of the contest, even though Cornwallis had eventually authorized their use. The Creeks and Choctaws fought well in a los-ing effort at Pensacola but were not available to take part in the battle against the Whigs. Alone, the Cherokees could do little more than distract the rebels.

In addition, the loss of both Augusta and Pensacola, which isolated the Indians from the British, raised doubts as to whether the Indians would remain participants in the struggle. Neither the ministry nor army officers were yet ready to arm slaves to meet the emergency; blacks continued as usual to perform dutifully in supporting roles. Rather than tamper with the institution of slavery, British civil and military officials looked to Cornwallis for a victory that would save the situation in the South. The earl too wanted to bring on a decisive battle and had marched to Virginia to seek it.

SEVEN

British Collapse

THE LAST EIGHTEEN MONTHS of the war in the South saw continued fighting between the king's supporters and their Whig opponents, but no reversal of the decline in British fortunes. On the contrary, the surrender of Cornwallis's army at Yorktown, Virginia, in October 1781 and Parliament's subsequent decision to end the American war insured that defeat was inevitable, no matter what efforts Loyalists, Indians, and slaves might make. Yet, in spite of their all-but-hopeless circumstances, all three groups stood firm in their allegiance to Britain until the very end.

Loyalist morale, which had plummeted in the spring of 1781 after British troops withdrew from the southern backcountry, recovered in the summer. In both Georgia and South Carolina, Loyalists within the British lines provided important service in the militia and emerged to launch punishing raids against the Whigs. Those Loyalists who had not withdrawn to Savannah or Charleston with the British also attacked the rebels when opportunity offered, challenging Whig control in both provinces and straining rebel resources. Only after the British government made clear that it would make no further effort against the Americans did Loyalist resistance begin to subside, and even then some Loyalists were willing to continue the fight, had British officials permitted them to do so.

Whig offers of pardon in combination with continued persecution and threats to confiscate Loyalists' property did induce some people to submit to the rebels. However, thousands preferred to leave their homes rather than sacrifice their principles when the British evacuated the southern provinces.

The loss of Pensacola and Augusta severed the lines of communication and trade between the British and their Indian allies. Nevertheless, the southern Indians persisted in their commitment to the alliance. Choctaws and Creeks traveled hundreds of miles across rebel-controlled territory, fighting when necessary, to pursue cooperation; the Chickasaws continued to fight the king's enemies to the west; and the Cherokees raided the Georgia and Carolina frontier. The great distance separating the British and Indians, however, along with the passive military policy adopted after Cornwallis's surrender, made effective British-Indian operations impossible. Thus, the Indians' efforts were wasted, serving only to bring down Whig retribution on the southern nations. Even worse, the ministry ignored the Indians' interest at the peace negotiations and ceded all of the land between the Appalachians and the Mississippi to the new United States, so that the Indians would be forced to seek accommodation with their vengeful enemies.

Those slaves who had committed themselves to the British rarely considered the question of changing allegiance; for them, the choice between returning to bondage under rebel masters or gambling on the possibility of freedom with the British was no choice at all. They continued to serve wherever royal officials assigned them. The dire military situation in late 1781 gave a few South Carolina slaves the chance to take a new role in the conflict. As members of a cavalry unit known as the "Black Dragoons," former slaves served in combat, providing an effective auxiliary force that horrified the Whigs. The Dragoons and thousands of other blacks left South Carolina and Georgia in the British evacuation, some to find freedom and others to continue in bondage.

THE LOYALISTS: DESTRUCTION, ACCOMMODATION, OR FLIGHT

As British officials struggled to salvage their position in South Carolina in the summer of 1781, they remained uncertain as to whether they could still rely on Loyalist support. Nisbet Balfour believed that it was possible to establish a defensive perimeter from Lord's Ferry on the Santee River to Orangeburg and from there south along the Saltketcher River to the Savannah River. "By this it is conceived that we may be able to cover the richer Parts of the Province & it is also proposed to place the Loyalists from the back Country upon the Lands of those, who have so often revolted against us," he wrote. However, Balfour questioned the reliability of the Loyalists, declaring that "the Efforts of our Friends" were "so Pusillanimous, that I fear that Country must be totally ruined & torn to pieces without one single advantage here after to be reaped from the boasted Loyalty" of the South Carolinians.[1] John Cruden did not think Balfour would gain the expected benefits from the plantations within the proposed zone of British control, declaring that Whig raids had already ruined the sequestered estates, while many overseers "and other persons employed . . . on These Estates have been murdered," and many others had fled to escape the Whigs' wrath.[2] James Simpson had lost confidence in the Loyalists and blamed them for the recent military reverses. The Loyalists' desire to avenge the wrongs they had suffered earlier, Simpson declared, had driven large numbers of South Carolinians, who might otherwise have accepted British rule, to take up arms with the Whigs.[3]

Yet, others found reason for optimism. William Bull told Germain at the beginning of July that "there is great reason to hope that the gloomy representations of the state of the province . . . will soon clear up and open a more pleasing prospect." Bull noted that many loyal and neutral South Carolinians had abandoned the rebels, so that Greene's army "begins now to melt away."[4] A few days later the *South Carolina Royal Gazette* published the names of 211 men who desired to take the oath to King George. They were instructed to report to the board of police on July

12 to "receive certificates" of their loyalty, which would entitle them to their full rights as British subjects.[5]

Whig observers found it difficult to assess the Loyalists' attitudes. In mid-July, Andrew Pickens had to dispatch some of his militia to check a mixed force of Loyalists and Indians that had been raiding in the Long Canes area, while some of his other troops sought another Loyalist force commanded by William Cunningham. Pickens also worried about the large number of Loyalists who were escaping to Indian territory, evidently to join the Creeks and Cherokees in attacking the rebels.[6] Less than a week later Pickens noted that some Loyalists had launched raids from Indian territory, and he expressed concern that "the Tories from Orangeburgh" might also launch attacks; however, he also stated that Loyalists in the Ninety Six area "are giving up very fast."[7] Gen. Isaac Huger did not think that the Orangeburg Loyalists posed much of a threat, reporting that they "are much displeased, several have sent to me saying they would come in" if Huger could assure their protection. Some of these people also provided Huger with useful information.[8] Henry Lee believed that if Greene offered the Loyalists full pardon, their resistance would evaporate. Greene agreed and ordered his subordinates to give Loyalists every incentive to join the Whigs, including pledges of protection and the right to keep their arms.[9]

Other rebel leaders did not notice any decrease in Loyalist resistance, despite the violence that the Whigs employed against their opponents. "Such scenes of desolation, bloodshed and deliberate murder I never was a witness to before!" Continental major William Pierce wrote. "Wherever you turn the weeping widow and fatherless child pour out their melancholy tales to wound the feelings of humanity. The two opposite principles of whiggism and toryism have set the people of this country to cutting each other's throats, and scarce a day passes but some poor deluded tory is put to death at his door."[10]

To retaliate against the Whigs for their cruelty, and also to send a message, aimed at those who had taken British protection, about the dangers of deserting to the rebels, the British hanged Col. Isaac Hayne of the Whig militia on August 4. Hayne had commanded a rebel party that captured Andrew Williamson near Charleston a month earlier; although Williamson had not taken an active role with the British, the very fact that he had taken the oath to George III made him a traitor in the eyes of most rebels. Balfour had sent a detachment of Loyalist cavalry in pursuit of Hayne, and these men had defeated the Whigs, killing ten or twelve; released Williamson; and captured Hayne. At his trial Hayne argued that he had taken the British oath only because the illness of his family placed him under duress and, furthermore, that the oath had become invalid after the Whigs regained control of the area in which he lived. Rejecting these arguments, Balfour, with Rawdon's concurrence, sent Hayne to the gallows.[11]

With unabashed hypocrisy, the rebels denounced the execution of Hayne as an "open violation of all the laws of humanity and justice."[12] Greene vowed to retaliate as soon as the Whigs captured a British officer of high rank.[13] In response to Greene's threat, Balfour asserted that any such action by Greene could not be justified, since Hayne's situation was far different from that of military prisoners of war. Therefore, Balfour warned, by retaliating, Greene would only provoke the British to retaliate in kind, and a cycle of vengeance might begin. Balfour also reminded Greene that British officers had shown great forbearance by refusing to retaliate in kind "when Lieut: Tulker of the Loyal Militia was publickly executed" and "when Colonel Grierson & Major Dunlap fell, without attempts to secure them, by the hand of Licensed & protected Murderers."[14] After learning that some members of Parliament had described Hayne's execution as murder, several South Carolina Loyalists wrote to King George expressing support for the decision to hang Hayne, enclosing a list of 299 South Carolina Loyalists murdered by the Whigs to show which side was guilty of greater cruelty.[15]

As Balfour had hoped, Hayne's execution did intimidate many men who had joined the Whigs after taking protection to return to the Loyalist fold. John Rutledge reported that Hayne's death "had the Effect wch the Enemy foresaw, & expected . . . indeed, a much greater Effect than you can conceive." Most of the "Protection Men" in Col. William Harden's regiment of Whig militia "again submitted themselves, to the British Government," reducing Harden's force to fewer than fifty. Fortunately for the rebels, Rutledge wrote, Greene's proclamation threatening retaliation had "removed the Apprehensions" of the remaining militiamen. However, if Greene did not keep his promise to execute a British officer, Rutledge warned, "our Militia will be dispirited, & fall off—Indeed you cannot suppose, if the British offer 'em Pardon, for having joined us, (wch. they do, if they will quit us,) that they will adhere to our Cause, if We refuse to support 'em, by Retaliation."[16]

Inspired by the defections from the Whig militia, the Loyalists continued to resist, complicating Greene's situation. In early August 60 men attacked a detachment of Henry Lee's legion near Orangeburg and freed 17 prisoners; accounts indicated that an increasing number of Loyalists were coming to the town to cooperate with Isaac Allen's battalion of New Jersey provincials. Another party of 150 Loyalists began attacking the rebels in the Drowning Creek–Pee Dee River area.[17] Greene complained in frustration that the southern war was far different from that in the North, where "most of the people are warm friends, here the greater part are inveterate enemies."[18] He told George Washington that the southern army was too weak to regain control of South Carolina, in part because the British had the aid of "near 1000 Militia Tories," who were "exceeding good marksmen."[19] Later, Greene revised his estimate and asserted that at least 2,000 Loyalists were serving in the militia in the fall of 1781.[20]

Greene decided that aggressive action might improve his circumstances, so in late August he left his encampment in the High Hills of Santee and advanced toward Charleston. At the same time the British army under Lt. Col. Alexander

Stewart, who had assumed command when illness forced Rawdon to return to England, marched to the Santee River. Learning of Greene's approach, Stewart fell back, but Greene caught up with the British and attacked them at Eutaw Springs on September 8. After a hard-fought battle in which both sides suffered heavy losses, Stewart held the field and forced Greene to retreat. The next day, however, Stewart withdrew and shortly afterward abandoned Orangeburg and other advanced posts to concentrate his forces around Charleston.[21]

Stewart's withdrawal allowed the Whigs to claim victory. Governor Rutledge therefore considered the time opportune to punish anyone who refused to commit to the Whig cause. "Every man who refuses serving when called upon must be deemed an enemy and taken prisoner and sent to the British . . . and must not be permitted to return," he ordered. "All their property must be taken . . . for the use of the State." Individuals holding British paroles but who had not been under the command of an American officer at the time such paroles were issued were to join the rebel militia or be classified as enemies and punished. Anyone entering the British lines without permission from Whig officials "must be treated as carrying intelligence to the enemy and suffer accordingly." Rutledge exempted no one. "Any woman who will go to town or in the enemy's post without leave, must not be permitted to return," he declared.[22] His punitive measures also included "the wives and families of all such men as are now with and adhere to the enemy." All of these people were to be forcibly removed from their homes and sent into the British lines. Although he was aware that this policy would cause much suffering, Rutledge asserted that the "blame can only be imputed" to their relatives who supported the British "and to the British commanders, whose conduct . . . justifies this step."[23] There was to be no middle ground in the final phase of the struggle.

Some Whigs believed that unnecessary cruelty toward Loyalists, particularly the seemingly endless murders, would prove counterproductive. If everyone who took the oath to Britain was "punished with death," Christopher Gadsden wrote, "the natural consequence will be, that they will . . . either withdraw with their effects from the Continent, or being driven to dispair will become our determined enemies."[24]

Rutledge partially relented in late September, deciding that an offer of pardon to Loyalists "would be well-timed at this juncture." He hoped that the offer would convince "many, to return to their allegiance and behave well, which would not only deprive the British of their services, but turn those services to our advantage." The governor excluded those who held royal commissions or had signed addresses congratulating Clinton and Cornwallis on their victories.[25] Loyalists who took an oath of allegiance to the Whigs and agreed to serve six months in the militia would be fully pardoned and preserve their property, and their wives and children would not be forced to go within the British lines.[26] Loyalists within the rebel lines who did not swear the rebel oath within thirty days, however, were nonetheless to be compelled to serve in the militia. Rutledge instructed Sumter that anyone who might "insist on their being British Subjects, & therefore, refuse to do Militia Duty, may take their choice, either of doing it, or going into the Enemy's Lines, & if they will not go, & refuse to do Duty, they must be tried, & fined."[27]

Henry Lee believed that neither pardon nor threats would induce the Loyalists to submit unless they were convinced that the Whigs held firm control in the state. "In a contention for the confidence of a people, alternately the subjects of each contending power, it is a matter of the highest consequence to preserve the appearance of superiority, if in reality inferior," Lee declared, "for such decisive weight has interest in the conclusions of the heart, that the man must believe he will ultimately receive protection from your arms before he can persuade himself to become your avowed assistant."[28]

Even without British support, however, Loyalists effectively challenged the rebels in many parts of South Carolina, making it impossible for the Whigs to maintain more than a semblance of control. One rebel officer wrote on September 20 that he had "been much alarmed by the Tories" who had recently raided along Lynch's Creek, "where they had made robberies and shed blood." The Whigs failed to locate that Loyalist band, so they set off in search of another two hundred Loyalists said to be "in full march to destroy or carry our stores at Black Mingo." These Loyalists proceeded as far as Waccamaw, did "a deal of mischief," and withdrew before the rebels arrived. Yet another party "came down Britton's neck, and carried off some horses," which forced the rebels to leave a detachment to guard "against the Tories" in the area.[29]

Along the border between North and South Carolina, other Loyalists continued to plague the rebels. "Upwards of 300 hovers" near Little River, Col. Peter Horry reported in late September, adding that they had recently driven off one militia unit sent to check them and put heavy pressure on others. Hector McNeil was said to have between one thousand and fifteen hundred men in the field in North Carolina.[30] A few days later Francis Marion informed Greene that the "Cheraw Regt is so Disturbed with the torrys I am affraid they will not come out" and that many rebel inhabitants had fled the area. McNeil, Marion added, had recently given the Whigs "a flogging, killed 11 and wounded & took 30."[31] On September 27 Marion sent more bad news; Loyalists in the Saltketcher region had also become "very troublesome."[32] Fortunately for the Whigs, the next day Horry announced that their militia had defeated McNeil's Loyalists and killed their commander, greatly reducing the Loyalist threat in the northeastern part of the state.[33]

If McNeil's defeat and death damaged the Loyalists' position, Cornwallis's surrender to a combined Franco-American force at Yorktown on October 19 devastated whatever hopes they retained that the British might yet regain control of the South. In London, Parliament responded to the news by voting, in January 1782, to halt offensive military operations against the colonists. Although George III remained determined to prosecute the war, the ministry's loss of support in Parliament led to Germain's resignation in February, and the next month Lord North also resigned. Lord Rockingham, the new chief minister, and the earl of Shelburne, secretary of state for the colonies, were both sympathetic to the Americans and opened peace negotiations.[34]

Inspired by Washington's success, Greene marched his army toward Charleston in mid-November. Loyalists informed the British of his approach, but the newly arrived commander of the southern district, Gen. Alexander Leslie, chose not to contest Greene's advance. Finding the morale of his soldiers poor, Leslie ordered the evacuation of the post at Dorchester, forty miles from Charleston, and also withdrew the troops and Loyalists from Wilmington, North Carolina.[35] The only opposition Greene encountered during his march came from Loyalists. "Twenty or thirty tories were killed wounded and taken in the different skirmishes," he wrote.[36]

While the disaster at Yorktown had demoralized the British, it galvanized the Loyalists into taking a more active role against their enemies without expecting the army to assist them. William Bull noted that the people in and around Charleston were "with great alacrity laying in large supplies of wood, grain etc. in order to avoid any distress which the want thereof may occasion to them or may weaken the necessary and obstinate defence of the town" and that they continued to show "a steady attachment to the British government and loyalty to the King."[37] On November 1, 150 Loyalists went to Charleston to obtain "clothes, blankets and arms." They also brought four wagons to carry the expected issue of ammunition, which they apparently intended to use against the rebels.[38]

At Orangeburg the Loyalists "kept Sumter pretty much within his pickets," and their leader, Henry Giessendanner, wrote to Leslie asking for aid to drive out the rebels.[39] Sumter sent an officer to arrest Giessendanner, but the Loyalist escaped. Efforts to get other Orangeburg Loyalists to accept Rutledge's offer of amnesty brought so few converts that Sumter declared in frustration, "Nothing but the sword will reclaim them!"[40] Greene found that "the Tories are getting troublesome and insolent," not only around Orangeburg but also "in the Forks of Edisto, and even up as high as the ridge towards Ninty Six." He suggested that Sumter and Pickens establish a post at Orangeburg to "check their insolence and prevent supplies from going to Charles Town," if Sumter thought that the state troops and militia were adequate for the task.[41] Yet another group of Loyalists was active at the forks of the Saluda River, endangering Whig forces there.[42]

In accordance with Greene's instructions, Sumter marched toward Orangeburg, skirmishing with Loyalists along his route, only to blunder into a powerful force of Loyalists who had launched an offensive from Charleston. The combined strength of the Loyalist parties was about five hundred men, under the command of Gen. Robert Cunningham. The Loyalists dispersed Sumter's advance guard, harassed the Whigs in the area for more than a week, and then separated. Cunningham withdrew toward Charleston with some of the troops, while William Cunningham with nearly one hundred men and Hezekiah Williams with two hundred set out on different routes for the backcountry, easily eluding rebel pursuit.[43]

William Cunningham's detachments defeated their Whig opponents on several occasions. They forced one rebel party to surrender at Tarra's Spring, after which Cunningham allegedly executed all but two of the prisoners. Cunningham later surrounded another rebel force in a house at Hayes's Station, forced them to surrender by setting the building on fire, and then executed three men who earlier had participated in whipping Cunningham's brother to death. Other Loyalists also identified and killed some of the prisoners who had committed cruelties against them or their families. In addition, Cunningham's troops burned mills, houses, and crops. Meanwhile, Williams's party captured a Whig post at Whitehall as well as a wagon train; among the teamsters and guards taken prisoner was Andrew Pickens's brother John. Williams later turned John Pickens over to some Cherokees, who allegedly burned him to death. Some Loyalists chose to go to Cherokee territory and to continue harassing the Whigs from there, but Cunningham and Williams returned to Charleston with most of their men in December, defeating some of Sumter's troops along the way.[44]

Cunningham's raid encouraged other Loyalists to strike at the rebels, and Whig leaders feared that Loyalist attacks would jeopardize the army's intended operations. Sumter reported that on November 22 Loyalists attacked a rebel foraging party near Orangeburg, killing four men, capturing four, and taking twelve horses.[45] "I am convinced you have No Idea of the Number of tories that is between this and Charlestown," Sumter wrote Greene from Orangeburg, "Which when Collected will be a Great Reinforcement to the enemy" unless something was done to defeat them or win them over to the rebels.[46] In addition to the numerous Loyalists outside British lines, Greene learned from a reliable informant that "there is in Charlestown not less than 1000 Tories who bear Arms."[47]

The Whigs' fears soon proved to be exaggerated. Leslie's refusal to provide the Loyalists with military assistance, combined with the rebels' ruthless retaliation for the havoc Cunningham had wrought, resulted in a collapse of Loyalist morale. Sumter's men scoured the woods and swamps around Orangeburg, killing or capturing several Loyalists. A few began to come into the rebel camp and surrender, while others fled west of the Edisto River. Greene and Sumter agreed that a combination of intimidation and offers of pardon would induce many Loyalists to submit, and this strategy had immediate effect.[48] As it became clear that no help could be expected from the British army, "the people disheartened by being unsupported, gradually made a submission to the enemy," a Loyalist officer wrote.[49]

On December 9 Sumter reported that "Considerable Numbers" of "the Outlying Tories, Who are much terified by So Many parties being out," had surrendered. He allowed most of them to return to their homes but worried that "from the Temper of the people," abetted by many militia officers, "Many of them Will be privately Injured."[50] Many Loyalists decided to take the risk, since it was no greater than the danger they faced if they continued to resist. More than two hundred had given up by December 19, and another fifty had been captured. Sumter noted that "there is Still a Great many lying out," but he believed that they would soon surrender. "The Number and Retchedness of the Women & Children Cant be Conceived," he observed, adding that it was "Utterly out of the power of Many to Move, or Subsist much longer where they are."[51]

Some of the afflicted Loyalists sought refuge within the British lines. Upon arriving in Charleston, Leslie found the Loyalists' distress so great that he said he would have "to get my heart Steeled" in order to be able to focus on his other responsibilities.[52] Their sufferings, Leslie declared, were "beyond belief." Yet, while he lamented his inability to provide the Loyalists with more than a fraction of the financial relief they required, he also questioned their military value.[53] He complained of the expense involved in supporting "the Several Regiments of militia from Camden, and Ninety Six,"[54] even though their 750 men comprised a significant percentage of his total force.[55] In addition, he informed Clinton that the South Carolina provincials "are mostly deserted"; only 120 men remained in early December.[56]

Leslie tried to reduce defections by issuing a proclamation assuring the Loyalists that his army was committed to their protection. He attempted to win back those who, "partly through Dread of the Cruelty of their Enemies, and partly from false Representations being made to them of the State of Publick Affairs," had cast their lot with the Whigs. At the same time he threatened to inflict "the severest Punishments" on anyone who had taken British protection and later took up arms against royal authority.[57] The proclamation had little effect, for less than two weeks after it was issued, Leslie noted that "people are daily quitting the town and great part of our militia are with the enemy . . . the whole of the country is against us but some helpless militia with a number of officers, women, children, Negroes etc."[58]

The Loyalists' fading morale and their frequent desertions came as welcome news to the Whigs, who gained confidence as they realized that their opponents "have lost their spirit & their hopes." Whig judge Aedenus Burke noted in late January 1782 that about one hundred Loyalists from Charleston and the backcountry districts had recently deserted to the Americans. "The Tories are turning arrant Rebels," he exulted.[59] Edward Rutledge believed that many people in Charleston were ready to surrender, asserting that "99 in 100 of them would come out if they thought they would be received."[60]

One factor encouraging the Loyalist exodus was the confiscation legislation passed by South Carolina's reconstituted assembly in early 1782. Designed both to raise revenue for the state government and to punish Loyalists, the confiscation act seized the property of those whom the assembly considered the most notorious Loyalists and assessed a 12 percent fee on the estates of lesser offenders. The law, clearly "legislation of revenge," also banished most of those whose estates were confiscated.[61] Those subject to confiscation or amercement included people who had signed congratulatory addresses to British officers, banished Loyalists who had returned to South Carolina after the capture of Charleston, men who held civil or military commissions under the British, "& some others who have been guilty of extraordinary Offences."[62]

Even some ardent Whigs considered the new law unduly harsh. Edward Rutledge favored limited confiscation and protested when the list of those subject to the act grew to "an amazing Length."[63] Although Burke believed that "the men who are the objects of it should never be received into the bosom of this Country," he opposed confiscation because it threatened the rights of all citizens to be secure in their property and would also create unnecessary hardship by bringing "many families & their children to beggary & ruin."[64] Arthur Middleton shared Burke's concern: "I cannot approve of the inhuman Sentence of visiting the Sins of the Fathers upon the guiltless women, Children. . . . It is a Doctrine suited only to the Climates of Despotism."[65]

If some Whigs disliked the confiscation act, they were nevertheless satisfied with its results. Only a few days after the legislative committee released its confiscation list, the information filtered into Charleston, where the names of 222 people subject to confiscation were eventually published in the *South Carolina Royal Gazette*.[66] In response, Whig officials began receiving "several broad Hints" from Loyalists in the town "wishing that we wd permit they would return to their *Countrymen*."[67] "The Confiscation Act began to work on them some time since," Burke noted in May, "and continues to sweat them considerably."[68] American major William Pierce believed that Burke had understated the Loyalists' reaction; Pierce declared that the confiscation act had "put the tories into a state of insanity, and all they want is the gibbet and halter to put an end to their existence."[69]

Loyalists denounced the confiscation act as yet another example of the Whigs' atrocious behavior. One writer called the law "an unprecedented injustice" that revealed the rebels' true motives: "the desire of power" and "a lust after the wealth of others."[70] William Bull stated that confiscation was "cruel to the loyalist" and added that members of the rebel assembly had vied with one another in promoting "an excess of severity" toward Loyalists.[71] Leslie too considered the confiscation laws unduly harsh and eventually sent British troops on forays to seize rebel-owned slaves with whom to compensate Loyalists for their confiscated property.[72]

Despite the threat of confiscation and the decline in British fortunes, many Loyalists still refused to submit to the Whigs. Leslie noted in late January 1782 that people came into Charleston every day seeking protection.[73] Having kept his militia in the field until the British army withdrew into the lines around the town, Robert Ballingall was one of those who abandoned their homes to seek safety with the British. The Whigs immediately took their vengeance; his "Plantation and House was plundered, his negroes & Effects carried off," and his property seized by state officials.[74]

Other Loyalists remained outside the lines and harassed the Whigs when opportunity offered. On January 2, 1782, near Governor Rutledge's plantation, Pennsylvania Continentals who had recently arrived to reinforce Greene realized that their ammunition wagons had fallen behind during the march. Because it was feared that "the Tories, who are very numerous, should take them," troops were sent back to escort the wagons to camp. That night Loyalist raiders fired on the guards but failed to capture the wagons.[75] A few days earlier a Pennsylvania officer noted that in a "German settlement" south of the Congaree River, where his regiment had camped, the inhabitants were, "like the greater part of this country, all Torys."[76] However, these Loyalists generally avoided combat with regular troops, focusing their attacks on individuals and small parties of militia. Their raids sparked vicious little battles in which neither side gave quarter.[77] In addition to the casualties they inflicted, these diehard Loyalists often forced Greene to divert troops from his main force. For example, the rebel general had to send a militia company to the Beaufort area in January "to protect and guard that part of the Country . . . from the ravages of the Tories."[78]

As usual, the Whigs responded to this harassment by unleashing a torrent of violence on any Loyalists they could find. The "inveterate hatred & spirit of Vengeance" the rebels displayed shocked Burke, although he attempted to justify it by claiming that it had been inspired by the earlier "cruelty of the British." He noted that South Carolina women "talk as familiarly of sheding blood & destroying the Tories as the men do" and observed that one member of the assembly "kept a tally of men he has killed on the barrel of his pistol, and the notches amount to twenty-five. I know another who has killed his fourteen, &c. &c."[79] Burke asserted that the Whigs were so consumed with vengeance that "you cd. not enter a Company that some do not talk of hanging many hundreds." If the laws against murder, theft, and house burning were enforced, he declared, "I may venture to affirm, there are not one thousand men in the Country who cd. escape the Gallows."[80]

Amid the carnage and chaos, many Loyalist units continued to serve and often performed well. The South Carolina Royalists comprised part of a force that inflicted a costly defeat on the rebels outside Charleston in January.[81] On February 24 Col. Benjamin Thompson, a New Hampshire Loyalist who commanded the British cavalry during his brief stay in South Carolina, emerged from the British lines to attack and rout Marion's brigade. Thompson praised the "spirit and intrepidity" that the militia demonstrated in the battle. "No men behaved with greater gallantry," he wrote.[82] John Cruden had formed his own Loyalist cavalry unit in October 1781 to protect the sequestered plantations. Before the troops were ready, Cruden realized that they would not be strong enough to resist Greene's army, so he instead financed the construction of galleys and assigned the erstwhile cavalrymen to these vessels. The troops and galleys succeeded in covering some of the plantations long enough for their produce to be shipped to Charleston. When

Leslie's army retired within the town's defenses, however, Cruden had to abandon the sequestered plantations that lay outside British lines.[83]

Encouraged by the performance of his Loyalist troops, Cruden then devised a plan to enlist seven hundred of the refugees in Charleston and form a corps of marines to raid along the coast. He presented the proposal to Balfour, who replied that he lacked the authority to approve the plan and suggested that Cruden seek permission from Clinton. Cruden wrote to Clinton on February 19, explaining that he would provide his marines with vessels, augment their numbers with "a few Companys of determined Negroes," and send them to raid the coastal inlets, capturing or destroying rebel privateers and merchant ships. He even offered to equip this corps at his own expense.[84]

An even more ambitious plan was proposed by the earl of Dunmore, former governor of Virginia, who arrived in Charleston in late December. During his stay in the town, Dunmore "endeavoured to procure the best information of the state of affairs." These inquiries convinced him that Loyalists were numerous enough to retake control of the southern colonies if properly led. Dunmore asked Germain for permission to recruit a Loyalist force separate from the regular military establishment, with which he would carry out this plan.[85] However, by that time both Clinton and Germain knew that they were about to be replaced and so took no action on the proposals. Their successors rejected both Cruden's and Dunmore's plans.[86]

By the spring of 1782 the Loyalists were ready to join in an offensive to retake the interior of South Carolina. "If ever our army take the field they will give a powerful assistance," Robert Gray wrote. "Ninety-Six & Orangeburg Districts would be recovered by their own inhabitants & they would not be easily dispossessed again."[87] However, when it became clear that the British had ruled out any further aggressive action, the Loyalists offered to take matters into their own hands.

On April 1 a rebel spy who had just left Charleston informed Greene that the Loyalists hoped to launch an attack against the rebels. "The refugees and most respectable inhabitants have had two or three meetings," the informant reported, "and addressed Gen. Leslie to request he would make use of 1200 of them as soldiers, and go out and attack the army you command."[88] Additional information reached Greene on April 11 that "the Refugees are pushing the General [Leslie] very hard" for permission to undertake an offensive. Greene initially believed the reports and expected an attack.[89] Many American officers, however, doubted that Leslie would approve such a measure.[90]

Parliament's prohibition of offensive action in the colonies did prevent Leslie from authorizing an attack by the Loyalists in Charleston, but those outside British lines persisted in fighting the Whigs despite the apparent hopelessness of their situation. In the vicinity of Georgetown, Loyalist activity had become such a threat by early March that Marion advised Peter Horry to remove the vessels and supplies at the town to safety at Black Mingo "and send a guard there for their protection from the Tories."[91] A few days later Marion instructed Horry to build a redoubt at Black Mingo for greater security in the event that Loyalists mounted a surprise attack.[92] In mid-May another party of Loyalists operating in the area captured Col. Hezekiah Maham, one of Marion's best officers, in his own home. Maham and his fellow prisoner, a rebel lieutenant, "expected nothing else then to be torturd in the Most Horrid Manner," but to their surprise the Loyalists paroled them.[93]

South and west of Charleston other Loyalists also challenged the Whigs. Gen. John Barnwell, commanding rebel militia in that region, told Greene in March that he could not defend the area adequately and that two of his regiments were unable to leave their home districts to do duty elsewhere "or the Torys will destroy every thing."[94]

Greene noted that Georgia and the Carolinas "are still torn to peices by little parties of disaffected who elude all search, and conceal themselves in the thickets and swamps from the most dilligent pursuit and issue forth from these hidden recesses committing the most horrid Murders and plunder and lay waste the Country." He asserted that "altho their collective force is not great yet they do a world of mischief and keep the people in perpetual alarms and render traveling very unsafe." Even so, Greene believed that the Whigs were gaining the upper hand against the Loyalist raiders.[95]

British observers also commented on the fierce nature of the fighting behind rebel lines but believed that it was growing in intensity. Robert Biddulph wrote that "the War has driven both Parties to that State of Animosity that they fight whenever they meet with't prospect of Advantage, like two Species of Animals whose Nature it is to work the Destruction of each other."[96]

Biddulph's assessment of the situation proved more accurate than Greene's, as Loyalist activity continued unabated throughout the spring. Shortly after Greene had declared that Loyalist resistance was subsiding, a raiding party captured a Whig messenger carrying military dispatches, and on April 10 a rebel officer complained that Greene's correspondence was frequently being intercepted.[97] Another Continental officer described the area around the army as "Totally abandened to the Torys, and the Roads Dayle infested by those Miscreants."[98] Near Orangeburg one party based in Dean's Swamp ambushed a Whig force that was attempting to root them out. Recovering from the unexpected assault, the Whigs counterattacked but managed only to drive the Loyalists deeper into the swamp at the cost of many casualties.[99] At the end of May, Loyalists on a foray from Charleston captured a rebel lieutenant, two other men, and several horses.[100]

Some Loyalists demonstrated a growing willingness to cooperate with blacks against the rebels. "Two hundred of those persons called Refugees including some Negroes Armed" left James Island in late April and on two successive nights "plundered all the Inhabitants on Ashly River Neck" for a considerable distance. Expecting further attacks, residents of the area begged Greene for protection.[101]

Greene's aide, Maj. Ichabod Burnet, conceded that the Whigs had proved unable to suppress Loyalist partisans. "The disaffected are numerous and their Situation so desperate," he wrote, "that they confine themselves to their private haunts and conceal themselves in the Swamps from whence they issue forth and murder and rob every person on the road." The danger was so severe that "in the greatest part of the three Southern States it is unsafe to travel without an escort of Dragoons."[102] This was made plain on May 7 when only three Loyalists succeeded in capturing and burning six wagons filled with supplies for Greene's army; the raiders also took most of the horses. The repercussions of the attack were felt long afterward. A month later a rebel officer reported that he was unable to ship provisions from North Carolina to Greene's army because after news of the incident spread, no one could be found to drive the wagons.[103] When the flow of supplies finally resumed in late May, Greene found it necessary to send Lt. William McDowell with a detachment of Continentals to the Congaree River to guard a shipment of clothing coming to the American army. McDowell reported that "the Torys was verry troublesome" in that area. After marching a mere twenty-five miles from Greene's camp, McDowell reported that he was "in the midst" of a Loyalist stronghold.[104]

Emboldened by their ability to operate with impunity virtually within musket shot of the Continental army, some Loyalists plotted to seize its commander. A woman who lived on the Ashley River concocted the bold plan of luring Greene away from his camp and arranging his capture. She invited the general and his wife to her home for dinner and then notified British officials in Charleston of the time and location of the gathering so that troops could be dispatched to capture the American commander. The scheme nearly succeeded, but a rebel in Charleston happened to witness the woman's meeting with British officers and somehow deduced its purpose. On the evening of April 29 this man managed to leave Charleston, reached the woman's house, and interrupted dinner to warn Greene, his wife, and two aides that "he was not safe in that place, for there was a plot laid for him." Greene immediately left "and had not been gone twenty minutes when the house was surrounded by a number of the British Horse." The commander of the detachment was "sadly disappointed" to learn that he had so narrowly missed his quarry.[105]

The Whigs' continuing inability to establish control of the province had an effect on both Greene's troops and the civilian population. William Peters, the general's steward, was angered by the army's lack of success and constant supply shortages and so opened a correspondence with Loyalists in Charleston. He eventually agreed to enlist other disgruntled American soldiers for British service but was caught and sentenced to death.[106] At the same time, many former Whigs who had taken British protection chose to await the outcome of the ongoing struggle before recommitting themselves to the rebels. Edward Rutledge derisively referred to such people as "protection Gentry" and complained that "not one in ten . . . will do any Duty at all. The Reason is plain; if the Enemy should again get the Country, they can do what you & I cannot, that is, they can turn back again, & live as easy under one Government as another; Curse on such Politics & such Principles!"[107]

The British too had problems with lukewarm supporters. A steady stream of disheartened Loyalists trickled out of Charleston, avoiding both the British posts intended to keep them in the town and American patrols attempting to prevent their escape. Leslie complained to Clinton that "some of the leading people of our militia" were escaping to the rebels "and persuading others to follow them."[108] In a three-day period in late April, between thirty and forty people made their way back to their homes from Charleston. Edward Rutledge thought that they would be allowed to stay "if they are peaceably inclined; if not, the People in that part of the State will soon make their Situation very uncomfortable." However, Rutledge believed that they had suffered enough misfortune to discourage them from acting in support of the British. "The Tories in general seem heartily tired of their Situation," he concluded.[109] An officer in Greene's army agreed. "The loyalists in Charles Town and upon the islands within its vicinity are very much dissatisfied with their situation," he wrote. "They complain bitterly of their ill-usage, and desert every day to the American standard."[110]

Leslie attributed the Loyalists' desertion in part to the cruel treatment that prisoners received from the Whigs, and he appealed to Greene to halt the brutality. When the Whig commander failed to send a satisfactory response, Leslie threatened retaliation. On May 18 he reminded Greene that he had received no answer to his complaint that Captain Christian House of the loyal militia was confined in irons at Orangeburg, and he pointed out that two other militiamen, Henry Johns and James Nix, were similarly confined. Greene "Having thus on principles of humanity" failed to effect their release, Leslie issued an ultimatum, stating that unless the three Loyalists were freed, "immediate orders will be given for retaliating, to the extent of its rigours, their treatment on the persons" of an equal number of rebel prisoners, "in which I shall not discriminate between civil or military characters." Such a severe response was necessary, Leslie said, to "evince to His Majestys faithful subjects in this province, that their interest and security, will be at all times, with me, a principal object of consideration."[111]

Although a Charleston merchant noted that "militia Duty is . . . severe on the inhabitants," many Loyalists continued to serve with the faithfulness Leslie had noted.[112] Hundreds helped to man the defensive lines around Charleston, and the militia provided about half of the 750 troops stationed on James Island.[113] Yet, Leslie and his subordinates understood that a factor more important than fear of Whig cruelty was working to undermine Loyalist morale. At a meeting on April 15, British officers observed that Charleston residents "are mostly of doubtful principles, many desirous by every means to make their peace" with the rebels, and thus "there is too much reason not implicitly to confide in the attachment of the Militia." The officers agreed that persistent rumors that Charleston would soon be evacuated were the principal cause of this disaffection.[114]

Given added credence by the withdrawal of two British regiments from Charleston at the end of April, reports that the evacuation of the province was imminent, combined with offers of pardon, convinced many Loyalists to cease resistance.[115] One especially dangerous band of "Out Lyers," which had killed many Whigs, including a member of the assembly, and defied all efforts to defeat them, agreed in mid-May to return to their homes after Gov. John Mathews sent them "terms of pardon & reconciliation."[116]

In the Pee Dee region, Micajah Ganey and sixty-five of his men renewed their activities in May, forcing Greene to detach Marion to quell them. Greene hoped that Marion could convince the Loyalists to submit without bloodshed. Ganey too preferred to avoid further combat and sent representatives to Marion asking what peace terms the Whigs were willing to offer. At a conference on June 7, Marion and Ganey reached an agreement. The Loyalists pledged to lay down their arms; give up all their military supplies, captured property, and prisoners; take an oath to the United States; and conduct themselves peaceably. In return, Marion promised them full protection for their persons and property. Any Loyalists who chose not to comply were given until June 25 to go into the British lines. The black Loyalist partisan Gibson and David Fanning and his troops were exempted from the treaty but managed to reach British-held territory.[117] Marion permitted some Loyalists to go to Charleston, he explained to Greene, because they "had Committed so many Enormaties that my men woud kill them tho they had been pardon'd, & they ware so Attached to the British that they woud never Comply With any terms" but instead take to the swamps and "give us a Great deal of trouble to subdue them." The effect of the treaty justified this concession. Twenty men from the Lynch's Creek area and thirty from the Cheraws promptly "came in & submitted" after learning that the agreement also applied to them. Marion believed that the treaty would finally pacify northeastern South Carolina.[118] Despite doubts as to whether most of the inhabitants in the Pee Dee region agreed with Ganey's actions, Leslie approved of the agreement because it restored "tranquility" and prevented unnecessary loss of life.[119]

By the time he learned of the treaty, Leslie knew that further Loyalist resistance was futile. On June 11 Leslie received orders from Gen. Sir Guy Carleton, who had replaced Clinton as commander in chief in America, to evacuate Charleston, Savannah, and East Florida as soon as adequate shipping was available.[120]

Leslie tried to conceal the news as long as possible but eventually published the evacuation order on August 7.[121] The announcement threw the Loyalists into a panic, and news of their consternation soon reached the American lines. Col. Tadeusz Kosciuszko heard that the evacuation orders had caused "Great terror and confusion among the Tories and the Inhabitence of the Town."[122] Lewis Morris told his father, "you cannot possibly conceive the confusion despair and distresses which prevail" in the town. Morris stated that many Loyalists "are determined to throw themselves upon the mercy and protection of their country," but those "whose crimes are too atrocious to be pardoned" intended to seek refuge in East Florida.[123]

In succeeding days "a prodigious number of refugees" left Charleston.[124] They included militiamen and civilians "of all ranks and denominations" who sought "to make their peace with the State." Lt. William McDowell of Greene's army, on guard duty at the American outposts, was "much troubled" when nearly three hundred people entered Whig lines to seek pardon from Governor Mathews.[125] Three militia deserters told John Laurens that "their Comrades do duty with reluctance & are anxious only for opportunities to escape."[126]

Mathews encouraged the exodus by offering amnesty to Loyalists; with victory certain, the Whigs' desire for vengeance began to wane. "The minds of men are growing more cool, & subsiding into calmness," Aedenus Burke observed. The governor still wished to prosecute Loyalists accused of serious crimes, but only through proper judicial proceedings. He asked Burke to convene a special court at Orangeburg to try about one hundred Loyalists.[127]

Although state officials encouraged Loyalists to flee Charleston, Greene ordered his troops to turn back the refugees in the hope that food shortages in the town would speed the British evacuation. Maj. Ebenezer Denny of the Pennsylvania Continentals, whose soldiers guarded a bridge over the Ashley River in October, disagreed with the general's policy. "Many poor devils had taken protection and followed the British in" to the town, Denny wrote, "and those people sick of their situation—they were anxious to get back to their old places of abode in the country. Some very miserable objects came out—whole families, battered and starving." Denny felt such pity for these Loyalists that he sent an appeal to headquarters, expecting that "upon my representation, leave would be given to let them pass." Greene, however, would not relent, a decision that Denny considered "an unnecessary cruelty."[128] Nevertheless, many American officers apparently ignored Greene's orders. In November a Continental officer estimated that an average of thirty people per week were leaving Charleston, and he believed that more refugees would have reached American lines had British patrols not prevented their escape.[129]

Some Loyalists who preferred to remain in Charleston sought to ingratiate themselves with the Whigs by acting as spies. One unnamed informant, an English-born "Gentleman," made his private peace with the rebels by providing them with information on such matters as the quantity of provisions in Charleston and the positions of British troops.[130] A Maryland officer wrote that he had "several capital spies in town, who furnish me . . . with every interesting intelligence," including "accurate returns" of British strength.[131] Col. Edward Fenwick of the loyal militia became one of Greene's most reliable informers. The

American commander praised Fenwick for the valuable service he had provided, and Greene promised "to use all my influence" to have Fenwick's citizenship and property restored after the war.[132]

British merchants in Charleston also decided to make their own accommodation with the Whigs. At an August 8 meeting, they appointed ten men to represent them and petitioned Leslie asking what measures had been taken to provide for their security after the army evacuated the town. If Leslie could not guarantee their safety, they asked his permission to open private negotiations with Governor Mathews. Leslie's aide replied that no provisions could be made for the merchants' security and approved their plan to negotiate. The merchants then requested permission from Mathews to remain in Charleston for eighteen months after the British evacuation to sell their stocks of merchandise and collect outstanding debts. Mathews consented to their remaining, but only for six months.[133]

Outside British lines, Loyalists continued to control some parts of South Carolina into the summer of 1782 but began to surrender after learning that the British army was to leave Charleston. In mid-July, Mathews observed that the state government still could not exert its authority in many areas and that each region outside Whig control served as "a nest for a great part of the devils in the British service."[134] Once news of the planned evacuation circulated, however, rebel officers reported that the Loyalists became "quiet and peaceable" and "are joining us very fast."[135]

As gloomy as their circumstances appeared, many Loyalists chose to continue fighting. Just two days after Ganey and Marion came to terms, Greene ordered Marion to rush his troops to the Santee region. "The Tories in that quarter are doing Great Mischief, & distressing all the good people" in that area, Greene wrote.[136] Andrew Pickens had to leave many of his militiamen behind when he marched to join Greene's army in late July, because "several parties of Tories" began raiding in the Long Canes district, requiring many men to remain to protect their crops and families.[137] After Pickens returned to Long Canes in early September, he reported that the area was again in "Allarm & Confusion" as the result of Loyalist attacks. The Whigs, however, eventually killed or drove off most of the raiders.[138]

Other Loyalist bands met a similar fate. Learning that as many as fifteen hundred Loyalists were concealed in swamps near the Edisto River, Greene, in hopes of inducing them to surrender, ordered Sumter to circulate offers of pardon along with false rumors that the Americans were to receive substantial reinforcements. These tactics led many Loyalists to submit, including numerous women and children. Others remained in their hideouts, so Sumter assigned several Catawba Indians to hunt them down; however, the Catawbas could not find all of them. In Ninety Six district the Whigs used dogs to track Loyalist partisans and succeeded in killing and capturing several men who had been raiding in the area.[139]

Angered by the Whigs' confiscation laws, some Charleston Loyalists in September "solicited Gen. Leslie for leave to go out into the Country and make reprisals of all property they could lay their hands on to compensate themselves for what they had lost." British merchants, busily trying to negotiate their own agreement with American authorities, "remonstrated with Gen. Leslie against sending expeditions to the Country and Plundering property." Leslie refused to authorize the proposed raid. When David Fanning left Charleston that same month "to endeavour to accomplish some vile Purpose," rumors circulated that he intended "to carry the Head" of Greene, Marion, or another prominent Whig back to Leslie. The report, however, proved completely false.[140]

Some Loyalists believed that with the help of armed slaves, they could retain control of Charleston after the British troops departed. On August 5 John Laurens sent Greene intelligence from Charleston indicating that a committee of diehard Loyalists planned to ask Leslie for "Arms Ammunition &c for the defence of Charlestown which they promise to undertake with the aid of Negroes." The plan, Laurens said, "resembles the desperate unavailing efforts of a drowning man."[141] Several days later Whig captain William Wilmot heard a similar report; his informant asserted that the Loyalists wished to make their appeal to Carleton in person and insisted that they could "defend themselves in the Town" with the aid of "all the Neggros now in their Lines."[142] Perhaps as an offshoot of this plan, a "party of Whites & Blacks" emerged from Charleston in September and burned houses and carried off provisions in the Goose Creek area.[143]

All of these schemes came to naught after failing to win Leslie's approval. On October 10 the first stage of the evacuation began as almost 1,100 men of the South Carolina Royalists, Florida Rangers, and Royal North Carolina Regiment embarked for St. Augustine. They were accompanied by Loyalist civilians, family members, and slaves. Later in the month another 500 Loyalists sailed for Nova Scotia. A few wealthy Loyalists chartered ships and left the province.[144] Chaos reigned in Charleston in late November as preparations were completed for the last phase of the evacuation. "It is impossible to describe, what Confusion people of all denominations, seem to be in at the thought of the Approaching evacuation," a Loyalist soldier wrote. Some people bought up all the goods they could, others tried to make sure they had a place on the transports or "went from house to house" trying to collect debts, while "the Young Ladies" were heartbroken at the thought of being left in "the power of the Merciless and Insolent" Whigs.[145] Leslie and his officers managed to restore sufficient order to get the ships loaded, and on December 14 the fleet carrying 3,794 whites and 5,333 blacks left Charleston as American troops entered the town.[146]

While the evacuees set about rebuilding their lives in England, Jamaica, Nova Scotia, or other British colonies, those Loyalists who remained behind often found that their sufferings were far from over. Upon entering Charleston, Governor Mathews appointed Daniel Stevens as sheriff of the town, giving him orders to arrest and confine anyone he found who was named in the banishment and confiscation acts. Stevens arrested a total of 126 Loyalists, who were confined until they could be put on trial.[147]

In the backcountry, groups of Whigs gathered at night to strike at those Loyalists they considered most obnoxious. "Wherever we found any Tories, we would surround the house, one party would force the doors and enter sword in hand, extinguish all the lights," and then "commence hacking the man or men that were found in the house, threatening them with instant death," James Collins recalled. While an attack took place inside, other Whigs "would mount the roof of the house and commence pulling it down; thus the dwelling house, smoke house and kitchen, if any, were dismantled and torn down." Collins noted that the attacks were meant to intimidate rather than kill: sword blows were deliberately misdirected at furniture and other objects. "There were none of the poor fellows much hurt, only they were hacked about their heads and arms enough to bleed freely." However, this was enough to extort promises from the victims that they would leave the state and never return, which was the object of these assaults. "I never knew an instance of one that failed to comply," Collins stated, "and numbers put off without any such measures."[148]

A far worse fate befell a Loyalist named Love, who had participated in William Cunningham's raid in the winter of 1781. Love had been accused of killing rebel prisoners in the Ninety Six district. When he returned to Ninety Six in 1784, he was promptly arrested for the crime. At his trial, Judge Aedenus Burke dismissed the charges on the grounds that Love was immune to prosecution under the terms of the peace treaty between Britain and the United States. Love was released, only to be immediately retaken by a party of local men, who prepared to hang him. The prisoner, "urging in vain the injustice of killing a man without a trial," was reminded by his captors that "he should have thought of that when he was slaughtering their kinsmen." The execution was duly carried out.[149]

Prominent Loyalists with ties to leading Whigs often avoided the severe punishments inflicted on their less well-connected counterparts. Philip Porcher's estate was placed on the confiscation list, but Porcher remained in South Carolina after the British evacuation. He and other Loyalists petitioned the assembly in January 1783 for permission to remain in the state and for the restoration of their property. Although some of the petitioners were "Confined in the Provost," legislators allowed Porcher to stay at the home of a relative. He "amongst others having great many Powerfull Friends," a legislative committee recommended that Porcher's estate be restored; he and about seventy other Loyalists were permitted to return to their homes on bail, and decisions concerning their estates were postponed. Porcher was eventually permitted to retain his property, but many other Loyalists lost their homes and possessions, were denied permission to return to the state, or were imprisoned when they tried to do so. One Whig asserted that the confiscation laws had made South Carolina "a very Distressed and disagreable" place.[150]

Georgia Loyalists suffered the consequences of defeat and evacuation five months earlier than their counterparts in South Carolina, despite putting up a fierce resistance of their own in the final months of the war. The first months following the Whigs' capture of Augusta had been relatively quiet as the rebels worked to consolidate their hold on the Georgia backcountry and Governor Wright labored to undo the damage to the British position in the province. Wright noted that Augusta's surrender had dampened the spirits of Georgia Loyalists and that the backcountry militia at Ebenezer could be kept at their post only with difficulty. He asked Balfour to send five hundred regulars from Charleston to assist in recapturing Augusta; otherwise, Wright warned, nearly eight thousand people in the backcountry, most of them Loyalists, would be lost to the British. When Balfour effectively shelved the proposal by referring Wright to Cornwallis, who was so distant that it might take months to receive a reply, Wright formulated his own plan. The Savannah militia and two hundred regulars from the town's garrison would advance to Ebenezer, unite with the four hundred militia there, and with the aid of another two hundred men Wright expected to join along the march, seize Augusta. Wright set about strengthening his forces for this mission, forming three new troops of cavalry while recently exchanged Thomas Brown rebuilt his depleted Rangers. Many of the recruits were refugees from the backcountry. The plan, however, was never put into effect.[151]

Several Loyalists who had escaped punishment by enlisting in Georgia's rebel forces devised their own scheme to strike at the Whigs. Twenty men led by John Goodgame and William Simmons contacted Alured Clarke in the summer of 1781, informing him that they intended to kill their commander, Col. James Jackson, and then capture Gov. Nathan Brownson and his council and carry them to Savannah. Clarke allegedly sent a small party to the vicinity of Augusta to aid the plotters, but the plan failed when a rebel soldier overheard the conspirators, insinuated himself into the conspiracy, and revealed the details to Jackson. The participants were arrested, three of the leaders hanged, and the remainder pardoned in exchange for their confessions.[152]

These men were not the only victims of Whig cruelty. In mid-September a Hessian officer noted that the rebels "do nothing but murder, plunder, lay waste by fire and the sword, and drive away the women and children within our lines; who belong to those who will not side with them."[153] Six weeks later Whig troops overwhelmed a guard of fifteen militiamen at James Butler's plantation near the Great Ogeechee River. The victors then "barbarously murdered" six Loyalists, including one man dragged from his sickbed when the Whigs set Butler's house on fire.[154] Another account put the Loyalists' death toll at eleven. A party of the Florida Rangers avoided a similarly bloody fate on November 2 after rebel captain Patrick Carr, whose penchant for murdering Loyalists had made him infamous, killed a man while the Rangers were in the process of surrendering to Whig militia. The Rangers promptly resumed the fight and withstood the rebel attack.[155]

The violence caused many Loyalists to flee the backcountry or conceal themselves. Wright informed Clinton on October 16 that "upwards of 500 Country People, have quitted their Families," gone to Savannah, "and have taken Arms in Support of Government & a great many more, have been, and still Skulking about, and hiding in the Swamps."[156] These people struck back at the Whigs whenever opportunity offered; some parties attacked rebel troops in the vicinity of Augusta during the summer. Partisans in the Ceded Lands killed eight Whigs in a skirmish on September 1. Other Loyalists on a foray from Savannah attacked a rebel force at Heard's Mill on September 10, killing three and capturing seventeen. Another raiding party succeeded in killing Myrick Davis, president of the state council, on December 7.[157]

Shortly afterward the Loyalists' situation deteriorated. After defeating Cornwallis at Yorktown, Washington had dispatched Gen. Anthony Wayne and the Pennsylvania Continentals to reinforce Greene, and Greene ordered Wayne to take his troops to Georgia and assume command there. In response, Clarke evacuated Ebenezer and concentrated his forces closer to Savannah. Most of the militia accompanied the retreating British troops.[158] So did large numbers of panic-stricken civilians. Once the rebels took control of the area, they were said to "ill-treat the male inhabitants who have remained behind in the most murderous manner almost killing them, and take their negroes away, if they will not go over to their side."[159] In January, Georgia troops under James Jackson raiding the environs of Savannah encountered a camp where the Whigs held about two hundred Loyalists, many of whom were wounded. Only Jackson's intervention prevented his men from slaughtering the helpless prisoners.[160]

Many Loyalists nevertheless left the British to take their chances with the rebels because at the same time Wayne's troops arrived, so too had details of the surrender terms that Cornwallis signed at Yorktown. On December 20 Clarke wrote Clinton that "the tenth article of the capitulation of Yorktown," in which Cornwallis had effectively abandoned the Loyalists with his army to the whims of the Whigs, "has made a very alarming impression on the minds of the people in general . . . I have just grounds of apprehension that it will amount to so *considerable a defection* of the militia—if our situation should become more critical—as to leave us but very little hopes of any material assistance from them, many having already gone off."[161] Clinton therefore instructed both Clarke and Leslie to assure the Loyalists that in all cases army officers would give them the same consideration that was given to British troops.[162]

While the British were trying to reassure their supporters, the Whigs made overtures of their own to Georgia's Loyalists. Hoping to end the bitter internecine warfare, Greene instructed Wayne to invite them to join the Americans and to protect those who accepted the offer. "Try by every means in your power to soften the malignity and deadly resentment subsisting between the Whigs and tories," Greene advised, "and put a stop as much as possible to that cruel custom of putting people to death after they have surrendered themselves prisoners."[163] Wayne relayed this advice to Gen. John Twiggs of the Georgia militia and Gov. John Martin. The general recommended to the latter the "expediency of opening a wide door for the reception of such Citizens, as have taken protection or joined the Enemy." A generous policy, Wayne predicted, would secure the gratitude of repentant Loyalists.[164] He had already found that many Georgia Loyalists had lost hope and wished to make their peace with the Whigs. In late January 1782 Wayne's troops captured "a few armed tories who Immediately inlisted for the war" with the American forces. Another fifteen loyal militiamen and their commanding officer surrendered on January 22 and also joined the Whigs.[165]

Martin pronounced Wayne's suggestion "extremely just and humane, and such as good policy at this crisis would undoubtedly dictate." Martin noted that he had made similar proposals to the assembly, "which were entirely disregarded." The governor attributed the legislators' refusal to pardon Loyalists to bitterness engendered by the war. "Owing to the repeated injuries and distresses those very characters have brought upon the virtuous citizens of this State, nature would not be nature could it immediately forget injuries like those," he wrote.[166]

Greene urged Wayne "to hold out encouragement to the Tories, to abandon the enemy's interest," regardless of the policy of Georgia's assembly. Even though Wayne had no power to issue pardons, Greene advised him to "promise to do all in your power to procure it, which will be nearly to the same amount." Greene promised to do everything possible to assist Wayne in that regard.[167]

Wayne, in turn, continued to prod Martin on the issue. On February 20 the governor relented and issued a proclamation offering Loyalists pardon in exchange for military service with the Whigs. Taking advantage of a network of Whig sympathizers in the town, Wayne had the proclamation circulated in Savannah, with immediate results.

During the following weeks many Loyalists, including prominent persons such as Sir Patrick Houstoun and Maj. David Douglass, members of the militia, and a unit of thirty-eight provincial cavalrymen, abandoned resistance and came into the rebel lines.[168] These defections irritated Clarke, who took steps to prevent deserters from leaving Savannah. "The enemy have filled the Swamps round their works with tories, Indians & armed negros to prevent desertions," Wayne observed.[169] With the incentive of a two-guinea bounty ($275) for each captured deserter, the loyal militia patrolled the area just outside British lines and by the end of April had considerably reduced the number of desertions.[170]

Governor Wright chafed as he watched loyalism in his province crumble while the military authorities refused to take action. In January, Clinton had rejected the governor's plan to retake Augusta and also denied a request for reinforcements on the grounds that Savannah was not seriously threatened.[171] The assembly pressed Wright to do something to defend Georgia, noting in a petition dated February 23 that the rebels had been "continually committing depredations, and murders upon

His Majesty's loyal Subjects . . . and have within these few days past, cruelly put to death many of our Constituents, for no other cause than their Loyalty and attachment to Government."[172] Wright had already appealed to Germain's deputy, William Knox, in the hope that the ministry might order the army to act, but to no avail.[173] "This Province has been Shamefully Neglected," Wright later complained to Carleton.[174]

If the Loyalists who clung to their cause suffered for their allegiance to George III, those who had joined the Whigs found their situation equally unpleasant. On March 8 Governor Martin was forced to send Major Douglass to Wayne for protection because "many of his Countrymen are very inveterate against him" and had threatened to kill the Loyalist officer. Martin believed that if he had not intervened, Douglass "wou'd have been Murderd." A few days earlier, the governor told Wayne, another former Loyalist "was cooly and deliberately murderd at noon day, in the streets of Augusta" by someone who claimed that the victim had been involved in the death of the murderer's father. The people had refused to comply with Martin's demand to arrest the killer.[175] Martin declared that at the present time "it is morally impossible to carry the laws fully into effect. Plundering and killing have heretofore been frequent." He expressed his determination "to crush these horrid practices in future."[176] The governor wrote that "if justice is prevented, and every man to be a judge in his own cause, there will shortly be no safety in this country."[177] He also informed Wayne that "the many daily murders committed, in which women & children are not excluded," required him to employ the militia to prevent such crimes, and thus limited the number of men Martin could send to assist the Continentals.[178]

The violence irritated Wayne, who warned Martin that if people who came to the Whigs expecting protection were "exposed to this cruelty," they "will act against us."[179] The general did not need more enemies, since his own troops were few and he was disappointed with the Loyalists who had enlisted in the Whig forces, calling them "an unprincipled banditti."[180] Wayne told a friend that of all the problems he had encountered since his arrival in Georgia, "what is yet more difficult than all" was "to make Whiggs out of tories, & with them wrest their Country out of the enemy."[181]

Not every Loyalist desired to become a Whig, and those who did not launched occasional attacks marked by retaliatory violence. In the spring of 1782 five Loyalists captured former Whig governor John Adam Treutlen at his home, "carried him some Distance into a Swamp," and "barbarously murder'd him."[182] Some Loyalists harassed the rebel army's lines of communication, and one party raided Augusta, where they captured and paroled three Whigs, although they failed to capture Governor Martin because he was away from home at the time of the raid.[183] Daniel McGirt's troops ranged across Georgia with the objective of capturing rebel property; on March 23 Martin reported that McGirt had "collected a large property belonging to this State consisting of negroes, horses, cattle, etc."[184]

The raids resulted in frequent skirmishes, with losses on both sides. As the evacuation of Georgia approached, however, many Loyalists outside the British lines surrendered to the rebels or made their way to Savannah.[185]

Some of the Loyalists who submitted to the Whigs did so in hopes of retaining their property, because the Georgia Assembly passed a confiscation law in May 1782. Whig Joseph Clay described the act as "pretty general, perhaps more so than sound Policy wou'd dictate."[186] It pronounced 277 people guilty of treason, only 61 of whom had been named in the similar act of 1778. The assembly appointed thirteen commissioners to supervise the confiscation and sales of the Loyalists' property.[187]

Wright learned of the law in early June and promptly wrote to Wayne to remonstrate against it. The governor argued that confiscation "must Raise Animosities instead of Healing & Conciliating." He also asked the general to allow an officer to carry a similar message to the rebel governor.[188] Wayne sympathetically replied that he too wished "to heal Animosities" but that the matter "being of Civil resort precludes me from interfering."[189]

Throughout the spring and early summer, Clarke ignored confiscation and other matters relating to the Loyalists and focused on carrying out his orders to evacuate Savannah. Preparations were completed in early July, and the last of the garrison and refugees boarded the transport ships on July 11. Many Loyalists who had decided to remain behind were grief-stricken. "Nothing Can Surpass The Sorrow, which many of the Inhabitants express'd at our departure," a Loyalist soldier wrote.[190] Robert Biddulph called the evacuation "an Act which of all others hurts the Pride of Loyalists all over the Continent, whilst it absolutely Ruins the Inhabitants affected to Government."[191] Altogether, between twenty-five hundred and thirty-one hundred whites, and thirty-five hundred to five thousand blacks left Georgia at the evacuation, with most going to East Florida and Jamaica. The evacuees comprised between 15 and 33 percent of the province's prewar white and black populations, respectively.[192]

To the very end Wright protested the government's policy in Georgia. From the evacuation fleet at Tybee, he informed Carleton that only the latter's lack of knowledge of the situation could have led him to insist on abandoning the province. Wright found it difficult to believe that "when a reinforcemt of 4 or 500 Men would have effectually held the country," it had been given up and the Loyalists left to suffer. The "distress and misery brought on His Majesty's Loyal Subjects here, you cannot conceive," Wright concluded.[193] Members of the assembly echoed the governor's sentiments, asserting that the loss of the province "hath not been owing to any want of attention or exertions on the part of the Civil Government or of the loyal Inhabitants." Rather, military officers in the garrison, jealous at having to share power with civil officials, had undermined the authority of the governor and assembly and ignored the province's defense. As a result, the writers declared, the rebels had gained "full possession" of Georgia, "the friends of Government either Murder'd or obliged to fly for protection within our narrow Lines & many well affected, compell'd to join the Rebels as the only means left them to save their own lives & their helpless families." The authors stated that in the previous year over two hundred Loyalists had "been cruelly murder'd in cold blood by their inhuman enemies attended with circumstances of wanton barbarity that would disgrace a savage."[194]

This barbarity did not end with the departure of the British. Learning that the evacuation of Savannah was imminent, rebels at White Bluff "embodyed & are already striking at the Tories" even before the British left.[195] Loyalists fought back, and although by mid-August many had surrendered, others were "still sculking about their homes." One band led by Sam Moore, which a rebel officer described as an "infernal set of outlaws," frequently murdered and robbed Whigs while eluding the militia.[196]

Governor Martin assured Greene on August 9 that "my endeavors shall not be wanting to soften the resentment of parties and correct the abuses which the confusion and disorders of war have given rise to."[197] In an effort to halt the raiding that had broken out along the border with East Florida, Martin sent a delegation to St. Augustine to ask Governor Tonyn for an agreement to end the warfare. Tonyn accepted the proposal, and by mid-September both governors had issued orders prohibiting cross-border incursions.[198] Gangs of bandits on both sides of the border, however, ignored these orders and continued "plundering both sides indiscriminately."[199]

Patrick Carr noted that in the backcountry, the "Tories keep dropping in every day. Their number increases up here and is very large."[200] Martin ordered Carr to capture any Loyalists he could and send them to Savannah, along with "any women that harbour those fellows." Those who could not be captured, the governor ordered, should be dealt with as Carr thought proper—an invitation to greater violence.[201]

The continuing civil war, along with wartime deaths and the flight of thousands of Loyalists, left Georgia devastated. The town of Queensborough lost so many of its inhabitants that it ceased to exist.[202] Lachlan McIntosh asserted on October 30 that plundering "has grown to such a Higth, by a Lawless, Savage and unprincipled Banditti, that no Man is Safe one Night in His House in any part of this State[,] travelling a Mile upon the Roads, or even in the Town of Savannah." He asserted that this criminal behavior had both disgraced the American cause "and nearly depopulated & ruined this fine Country."[203] In the spring of 1783 one observer reported that the town of Ebenezer was still "in a most deplorable Situation," with nearly two-thirds of the inhabitants having either left with the British or been killed during the war. Those few remaining were impoverished and the buildings damaged.[204] Noting that Georgia Whigs were still persecuting Loyalists months after the evacuation of Savannah, British general James Paterson declared that the sufferings of that state's Loyalists demonstrated that "prayers and tears cant obtain from the enemy pardon for the Crime of Loyalty."[205]

Intensive lobbying by Governor Tonyn and the assembly spared East Florida from evacuation in 1782, so that it was the only southern province in British hands at the end of the war. This must have surprised Tonyn, who since the fall of Pensacola had expected a Spanish attack on St. Augustine. The governor had worked strenuously to strengthen the province; but at the end of December 1781, he could muster only 300 militia to support the garrison of 436 regulars. Tonyn could not even arm all of the militia. He had distributed the muskets available to him earlier to Brown's Rangers, and Lt. Col. Beamsley Glazier, commander of the garrison, refused to supply the militia from the army's stores.[206]

Fortunately, the Spaniards did not attack, and the Whigs in Georgia were too preoccupied with the British forces at Savannah to concern themselves with East Florida. Affairs in the province remained relatively quiet until the arrival of Carleton's orders that East Florida be evacuated sparked a firestorm of protest.

Neither Tonyn nor the East Floridians could understand why the ministry wished to abandon a province that had been steadfastly loyal and was not menaced by the enemy. On June 14, 1782, the inhabitants composed a petition to Leslie explaining the hardships they would suffer as a result of evacuation, East Florida's economic importance to the empire, and its utility "as an Asylum for Refugees" from the other southern provinces.[207] Five days later the assembly expressed similar objections to Tonyn; on June 20 members passed a resolution declaring their intention to defend the province even if the troops were withdrawn. Tonyn, after informing the assembly that he would request arms so that the inhabitants could hold East Florida on their own, forwarded the assembly's petitions and resolutions to Carleton and Leslie, accompanied by his own letters of protest.[208]

In response to the protests, Leslie suspended the evacuation, and Carleton approved of the decision. The fate of the province had not yet been decided at the peace negotiations, and its proximity to Savannah made East Florida a convenient destination for the evacuated Georgians and South Carolinians. Thousands of refugees moved into the province, which was ceded to Spain the following year. The Spaniards permitted the British inhabitants to remain until the summer of 1785.[209]

West Florida had been under Spanish control since May 1781, although some Britons and Loyalists hoped that the province could be recovered. Robert Ross, a British merchant who had traded at Natchez and New Orleans, proposed to Lord Dunmore that a British army attack the latter town. The capture of New Orleans, Ross believed, would not only deal a serious blow to Spain but also enable the British to reestablish a presence at Natchez, where Ross believed the Loyalists could maintain control. Possession of Natchez would also enable the British to retain their ties to the Choctaws and Chickasaws.[210] Dunmore liked the idea and submitted a revised version to the ministry, proposing that the various provincial units be united to form an army capable of conquering the Mississippi valley as far north as the Ohio River. The conquered territory could then be organized into a new province where displaced Loyalists could reside.[211]

West Floridians unwilling to wait in the vain hope that the ministry would send troops to assist them instead left the province. After the fall of Pensacola, a large number of Loyalist families decided to make their way to Georgia. The seven-hundred-mile journey took them through Choctaw and Creek territory; the Indians provided the starving travelers with food once they were convinced that the bedraggled people were in fact Loyalists. Upon leaving Creek territory the group split into two parties. One passed through East Florida and reached Savannah 149 days after they had set out. Their leader, Sereno Dwight, joined the British army along with many of the other men. The second group, less fortunate, was captured by the rebels.[212]

A few other Loyalists took to the woods and occasionally harassed the Spanish along the Mississippi. John Turner, commanding a small force of ten whites and three blacks, captured a Spanish vessel on April 19, 1782, but only he and one black escaped when the crew revolted and overwhelmed their captors. Apparently this convinced Turner to abandon his efforts, although other Loyalists in the area continued to cooperate with James Colbert and the Chickasaws.[213]

Too Little, Too Late: The Indians' Final Effort

After the capture of Augusta, Whig officer Lewis Morris had predicted that the victory "will lead to the most happy consequences as it was a place from whence all orders to the western tribes issued and from whence they were supplied with goods and the implements of war." With the town in Whig hands, he wrote, the region "will enjoy peace and tranquility."[214] Unfortunately for the rebels, Morris was completely wrong.

By the summer of 1781 the Cherokees had suffered more than any other southern Indian nation; yet, they persisted in their support of the British, launching another round of attacks in the backcountry. Their offensive provided indirect assistance to the British by depriving the rebels of the services of the overmountain militia. Isaac Shelby had promised Greene that he would march to join the army in mid-July, but the outbreak of hostilities with the Cherokees led Shelby to conclude that it was "impracticable to draw any force from here" until the Indians were defeated. The Whigs won a quick victory, and a peace treaty was signed on July 29. Shelby then set out to join Greene with seven hundred men, only to turn back upon learning that the British had withdrawn from the South Carolina interior.[215]

The defeat caused another rift among the Cherokees. While Oconostota and other leaders discussed peace with the Virginians in Williamsburg, the Raven journeyed to Savannah in August to confer with Thomas Brown. Brown was in Charleston, but the Raven left a message assuring the superintendent of the

Cherokees' loyalty. Some Cherokees provided even stronger proof when they attacked a Whig party in Georgia in late August, killing several men.[216]

Another party of Cherokees and white traders was on its way to Savannah when two prorebel Creeks informed Gen. John Twiggs of the Georgia militia of its approach on December 1. Twiggs found and attacked the group, capturing nearly two hundred horses and a vast quantity of deerskins. He claimed to have killed twelve whites and twenty Indians. Seven women and two children were taken prisoner. "I am led to believe this Action will be attended with infinite good consequences to the Southern States, as it will be the means of stopping all Trade from that Nation to Savannah, or any Military Stores being sent them," Twiggs wrote.[217]

Brown was equally aware that British inability to supply the Indians might put an end to their assistance. While noting in early December that "the indians in general are steady in their attachment to His Majesty's interest" and that the Cherokees "have been warmly engaged" against the overmountain settlements, he noted that both they and the Creeks were in dire need of goods. The two nations, Brown observed, "depend solely on Government for supplies of ammunition clothing etc." Brown was busy assembling the needed items, which had to be sent "on packhorses by a circuitous route of 600 miles."[218]

Brown's troubles increased when Alexander Cameron died on December 27. Germain rejected Brown's offer to place all of the southern nations under the latter's supervision and instead appointed John Graham, the lieutenant governor of Georgia, to succeed Cameron. Graham had no experience dealing with Indians, and his appointment angered Cameron's deputy, Farquhar Bethune, who felt he deserved the promotion. Graham's unfamiliarity with Indian affairs and strained relationship with Bethune further complicated British relations with the Choctaws and Chickasaws.[219]

Most Whigs were unaware of these difficulties, and their response to the sporadic Indian raids was out of all proportion to the actual threat. Earlier, Twiggs had complained that "fear of the Indians" had kept at home many Georgians who would otherwise have been available to serve against the British.[220] On December 1 Gov. Nathan Brownson warned Greene that an Indian war would "add to our difficulties which are now almost insupportable" and expressed his fear that William Cunningham's raid into the backcountry was intended as "a diversion in favour of the Indians."[221] Greene agreed that the rebels' position in the South would be endangered if the British managed to get the Indians to act in force. "Great industry is . . . made use of to spirit up the savages," he noted, "which I fear will be but too successful, as the Enemy can furnish them with such Articles as they want, and we cannot."[222]

After taking office as governor of Georgia, John Martin took immediate steps to eliminate the threat of Indian attacks on the exhausted and almost defenseless state. Martin sent a talk to the Creeks on January 11, 1782, in which he combined veiled threats and professions of friendship with denunciations of Brown and the British. Informing the Indians that a large American army was in South Carolina and would soon drive the British from Charleston while the Spanish attacked St. Augustine, Martin insisted that the Georgians desired "to live in peace and friendship with our old friends and brothers, the Creeks." He attributed Creek hostilities against Georgians to a few "mad people and the Tories" instigated by "Brown's lying talks," thus indicating that he was not holding the whole nation responsible for past conflict. Martin advised the Creeks to prove their friendship by returning all the prisoners and livestock they had captured and by sending down "all those Tories, bad people, and King's men that are among you making mischief." The governor concluded by emphasizing that the Americans did not want Creek assistance and that once the British left, the Georgians "will then love you as friends . . . and you shall share our riches and happiness with us."[223]

Anthony Wayne assisted Martin in the effort to neutralize the Indians. On January 27 Wayne learned that a party of Creeks was en route to Savannah and so dispatched Col. James McKay to intercept them. McKay soon encountered the group of "about 30 mounted Indians & tories" with over ninety pack horses. One of the whites was Joseph Cornell, an influential Indian trader.[224] After his capture, Cornell told his Whig interrogators that about three hundred Choctaws were also on the way to Savannah but were eighty or ninety miles behind his party. He added that between two hundred and three hundred Creeks under British agent William McIntosh had left Coweta Town about a month earlier intending "to create a diversion on one of the frontiers of Georgia."[225] Wayne initially considered Cornell "a dangerous villain."[226] However, the trader's cooperation convinced the general that Cornell could be trusted, whereupon Wayne sent him and another man to the Creeks and Choctaws with a talk. Wayne declared that the Indians could avoid bringing destruction upon themselves by ceasing to support the British and explained that he had spared Cornell and the twenty-six Indian prisoners as a demonstration of his good intentions.[227]

Rather than fight the approaching Choctaws, Wayne detached Maj. John Habersham with sixty South Carolina dragoons and some Georgia militia to find the Indians. Habersham had orders, upon encountering them, "to send home the women & Children & keep their principle warriors as hostages, assuring them of the friendly disposition of the Americans, & the deception of the Enemy—who have wickedly and Wantonly endeavoured to promote a war between them and a people who never Injured them." If the Indians wished to fight, however, Habersham was to tell them that the Whigs were prepared to move against them.[228]

Habersham set out on January 30 and immediately ran into problems with the militia and its commander, the notorious Patrick Carr. After a night of heavy rain, Carr's men refused orders to march on February 1, insisting that the bad roads would kill their horses. Habersham "did not venture to expostulate with them, knowing it would not avail." He would have preferred sending Carr and his men off. "Indeed had it not been that I was certain they would plunder the Inhabitants in our rear, I should have been glad to have got free of such a disorderly set," Habersham wrote. Later that day two of Carr's men encountered a party of Indians they believed to be Chickasaws, one of whom the Georgians killed. On February 2 Carr's men captured eleven more Indians, evidently all Choctaws. Habersham then decided to deceive the Indians by pretending to be Thomas Brown, and in this guise he dispatched one of the prisoners to bring the rest of the Choctaws into the rebel camp.[229]

Habersham's ruse brought another Choctaw and a white Loyalist to the Whigs on February 3. These men assured the American commander that the rest of the Indians would come in the next day. However, on February 4 the only arrival was a single Indian envoy, who reported that one of the Choctaw leaders had become ill and that the Indians were returning home. Habersham wanted to pursue the Choctaws, "but on sounding the Militia, I found them bent on going to the Scots settlements, in the Southern part of this State, in quest of plunder." This convinced Habersham that he could no longer rely on the militia's assistance; to compound the problem, the state troops demanded to be discharged. Forced to abandon his planned pursuit, Habersham sent two Indians and an interpreter to find the Choctaws. They had instructions to bring the Indian leaders and twenty of their men to Habersham's camp the next day.[230]

Habersham marched on the evening of February 4 to find forage, bringing along the twelve Indians still with him. To maintain the pose that he was Brown, Habersham did not place the Choctaws under restraint. One of the Indians disappeared on the march and another the next day. Habersham sent men to look for this second absentee, but the Indian could not be found. That night Habersham received disturbing news that boded ill for his expedition. A report arrived that some of the Georgia militia "had met with an Indian, whom they carried into the woods, tied to a tree, shot and afterwards cut him to pieces. I was now pretty certain that the two missing Indians . . . were treated in the same way," Habersham stated.[231]

The ten Indians with Habersham clearly came to the same conclusion, because they disappeared from the camp during the night. "I could not now entertain a doubt that the Indians were apprised of our being Americans," Habersham wrote. This was confirmed when he learned that one of the Indians spoke some English and that the militiamen "had several times thrown out threats in their [Indians'] presence and abused them." Thus, the vicious behavior of the Georgians wrecked Habersham's plan to deceive the Indians into entering his camp, where they could be disarmed and captured or convinced to return home. With his strategy ruined, Habersham's only option was to pursue the Choctaws, but the militia refused to assist him. Instead, they created more trouble. Three rebels subjected a suspected Loyalist to "barbarous treatment," while others "completely plundered" the Loyalist Scottish settlement at St.

Andrew's, where they "killed eleven Men." Loyalist partisans retaliated by twice ambushing Habersham's troops on their return, wounding one man. The savagery of the militia had completely sabotaged the expedition, causing Habersham to lament his failure as well as the injury done to "my reputation as an Officer, and my feelings as a Citizen."[232]

Wayne overlooked the vicious behavior of the Georgians and instead blamed the desertion of the militia for Habersham's failure. Had the expedition succeeded, Wayne told Governor Martin, it would have secured Georgia from "an Indian Invasion." Yet, the general still hoped that "we have convinced the savages that the British can't support them & that they are now upon their return to their own Country."[233] Some Choctaws did reach Savannah at the end of February, much to Wayne's disappointment, but he still believed that the British "will not be able to derive much service" from the Indians.[234]

Wayne's prediction soon proved to have been too optimistic. In late March, Whig troops captured letters that indicated "to a Certainty that every measure is attempted to draw down the Creeks & other Indians." The Choctaws, Wayne declared, had "already commenced hostilities" by killing and scalping a rebel dragoon. The Whigs had in turn "taken a Chickasaw chief & I expect that the party he commanded are by this time either killed or Prisoners." Wayne said that he would hold this Indian "as a Victim, who together with the first British Officer that fall into our hands will *eventually* be sacrificed to the Maner of that brave unfortunate Dragoon." Wayne asserted that such retaliation was justified because the British had displayed the dragoon's body in Savannah and paraded his scalp through the town.[235] Whether the events in Savannah had actually occurred or were merely rumor, Wayne abandoned his intentions of dealing humanely with the Indians and adopted a policy of brutality instead. He determined "to prevent any more Indians getting in" to Savannah and "to strike them going out."[236]

Andrew Pickens similarly expressed frustration with his inability to halt Indian raids. Early in 1782 the Cherokees, assisted by Loyalists, renewed their attacks on the rebels; one raiding party killed several people and burned some houses in Ninety Six district.[237] Pickens countered by mounting a winter campaign against the Cherokees, which destroyed their towns east of the Appalachians. To his dismay, however, Pickens found that "the Indians had removed from their towns with their provisions." Since he had relied on capturing supplies to feed his militia, this unforeseen setback left the rebels hungry as well as physically exhausted.[238] This, along with the failure to receive expected reinforcements from North Carolina and the overmountain settlements, forced Pickens to end his incursion. "We were well nigh perishing," one participant wrote.[239] The abortive offensive also deprived Wayne of reinforcements, since Governor Martin dispatched Elijah Clarke and eighty men to assist Pickens.[240] Martin then withheld additional troops to protect the Georgia backcountry from "the frequent alarms on the frontiers, by the Indians and Tories."[241]

Pickens believed that his operations would have succeeded "had it not been for the Tories that went up under Col. Williams and others small parties that has since gon up" to Cherokee territory to cooperate with the Indians. Pickens warned that "unless some Spirited meassures are taken and Immediately Carried into Execution against the Cherokees and Tories that are harboured in the nation—this part of the Country must be Evacuated for some time." In response, Governor Rutledge approved a combined attack by militia from North and South Carolina and the overmountain settlers against the Cherokees and Loyalists.[242] Once Pickens had defeated the Cherokees, he hoped to strike the Creeks too. In a letter to Martin soliciting assistance from Georgia for his offensive, Pickens declared that he "would wish at the Same time to carry my Idear further than the Cherokees if possible, I mean to the Coweatuas."[243]

While Pickens worked to assemble his expedition, Brown ordered further Indian attacks against the Whigs. He observed that the Cherokees had demonstrated "manly, spirited perseverance," despite the "wanton bloody outrages . . . committed by the rebels" against them, and had forced "all the inhabitants over the mountains to live in blockhouses for their security." However, their efforts and those of the other nations "have not been productive of any other essential advantage other than preventing any very considerable reinforcements from the back country to Green's army."[244] To increase the pressure on the rebels, Brown in February instructed his newly appointed deputy to the Cherokees, Col. Thomas Waters, to "send out from time to time as many Indians as you can possibly collect to harrass and annoy" the enemy. Brown also ordered Waters to place his assistants in command of the raiding parties and that all "refugees . . . must be employed" in what Brown envisioned as a joint Indian-Loyalist effort.[245]

Brown's plan accomplished little. On April 2 Elijah Clarke and his militia attacked a group of Creeks and Loyalists west of the Oconee River. The outnumbered raiding party scattered. The Whigs pursued them, killed a few Indians, and captured two Loyalists, who were promptly hanged. One week later a rebel force under Maj. Francis Moore encountered about twenty Indians and a few Loyalists near the mouth of the Altamaha River. The Indians and Loyalists took refuge in a log house and repulsed their attackers, killing Moore and two of his men; another drowned trying to escape across the river. A party of Whig militia skirmished with fifteen Choctaws on May 2. Three Indians were killed before more arrived and forced the rebels to retreat. Several other Indian raiding parties launched attacks in the vicinity of Augusta later in the month and then quickly withdrew before the Whigs could mount an effective pursuit.[246]

A Creek attempt to reach Savannah resulted in the two largest battles of the campaign in May and June. Learning that Emestisiguo, the most ardent British supporter among the Creeks, was advancing to Savannah with 150 warriors, Brown sent a detachment of provincials and militia to the Ogeechee River to meet the Indians. The Loyalists drove back Whig troops in the area on May 19, and shortly afterward Brown joined them with 340 additional soldiers. Wayne also sent reinforcements and attacked the Loyalists. Brown defeated the Whigs, but seeing no sign of the Indians, he withdrew to Savannah the next day.[247]

Emestisiguo's party did not approach Savannah until late June. In the early morning of June 24, the Creeks encountered Wayne's Continentals encamped for the night at Gibbons's plantation and launched a surprise assault. According to Brown, who received his information from Creek participants, the Indians attacked the rebels twice, driving Wayne's troops from their camp, overrunning the American artillery, and destroying "a great part of their ammunition tents & baggage." The Creeks successfully resisted three charges made by the Continentals after Wayne rallied his troops. Brown reported the Indian losses as seventeen killed, wounded, or captured, compared to an estimated seven American officers and about one hundred soldiers killed or wounded. The most serious loss to the Creeks, Brown wrote, was their horses; the animals "took flight at the noise of the musketry & ran off in the night."[248] The Americans claimed to have killed eighteen Creeks and two Loyalists, while losing five killed and eight wounded. Among the dead was Emestisiguo. Most of the Creeks took advantage of the confusion to evade the rebels and were able to reach Savannah.[249]

The morning after the battle, Gen. Thomas Posey of the Virginia Continentals saw some Creeks near the rebel position. On Posey's approach, the Creeks, thinking that the troops might be British, sent forward twelve men to confer with them. The Whigs seized them, and the rest of the party fled. Posey took the captives to Wayne, who became enraged when he saw them and ordered their immediate execution. Posey protested that it was inhumane to kill them, especially considering the circumstances of their capture. However, Wayne would not relent, and the Indian prisoners were murdered.[250]

The Creeks had given their lives in vain, because preparations for the evacuation of Savannah were already well advanced. Wayne feared that either the Indians would try to fight their way out of town before the British left or the British would transport the Indians by boat to the west side of the Ogeechee River, from whence they would raid the backcountry on their way home. "I have every reason to Apprehend that they will endeavour to avenge their blood they have lost, by sheding that of the Innocent & defensless Women & Children in their route," Wayne stated. He ordered the Georgia militia to Sunbury to protect the inhabitants there.[251]

The Indians, however, decided to sail to St. Augustine in the evacuation fleet. About 200 Choctaws and 250 Creeks accompanied Brown and Graham to East Florida.[252] Brown was uncertain of what he should do with the Indians; Leslie had sent no orders other than to see that "the strictest economy may be preserved" in the Indian department.[253] Brown praised the Cherokees and Creeks for their "fidelity and attachment to His Majesty's interest," but realizing that the war was over, he asked Carleton if the general thought it worthwhile to purchase the

Indians' neutrality since their military services were no longer required.[254] Graham likewise lauded the "spirit . . . good order and regularity" that the Choctaws had displayed throughout their service with the British; however, he proposed to Carleton that they and the Chickasaws should continue "to harrass the Spanish" in West Florida.[255]

After the British evacuated Savannah, Whig leaders tried to convince the Creeks to shift their allegiance to the Americans. In a message to the leaders of both the Upper and Lower Creeks, Governor Martin pointed out that the Americans had clearly won the war and that therefore Creek interests could be best served by abandoning their alliance with the British, who had "basely deserted" the Creeks. The governor offered the Creeks peace and a generous supply of trade goods if they would "deliver up all the commissaries & traders. Likewise all our negroes, horses & cattle that are among you."[256] Wayne cooperated with Martin in the effort to make peace with the Creeks, sending Tactor of the pro-American Tallassees back to his people in late July with presents and a message of friendship.[257] A second messenger whom Wayne dispatched to the Creeks was seized by pro-British warriors, and the documents he carried were turned over to Brown.[258]

Some Creeks continued to harass the Whigs. One group of ten warriors who had been captured by Wayne's troops in August escaped and avenged an earlier wrong inflicted on their friend Thomas Brown. After escaping, these Indians "went straight to Thomas Graham's house . . . & killed him," Patrick Carr reported. Graham had been "the most active man in tarring and feathering Brown" in 1775.[259] In the fall of 1782 three thousand Creeks visited St. Augustine to consult with Brown and to express their willingness to continue the struggle. Brown gave them presents but advised them to come to an accommodation with the Americans. Some Creeks offered to leave with the British when East Florida was evacuated, but Brown suggested that they would do better to remain on their lands and turn to the Spaniards for support.[260] Meanwhile, several Creek leaders had gone to Augusta in October for talks with the Georgians, which proved inconclusive. Martin did not attend the meetings and was not optimistic about reaching an agreement, noting that the Indians "have by no means complied" with the demands he had made earlier.[261]

While the Creeks' war against the Americans petered out with a mixture of sporadic fighting and hesitant negotiations, Cherokee participation in the Revolution ended in a cataclysm of violence. In the summer of 1782 Col. Thomas Waters had led the Cherokees and Loyalists in another series of attacks in the backcountry, which spurred Whig officials to launch Pickens's long-delayed offensive against the Cherokees.[262] On September 16 an eager Pickens assembled his troops at Cherokee Ford on the Savannah River. The Cherokees, he told Greene, "are a people who only can be brought to measures by fear or Necessity," and he hoped this time to punish them severely.[263]

Pickens set out two days later with five hundred South Carolinians and Georgians, while another force advanced against the Cherokees from North Carolina. After crossing the Chattahoochee River, the Whigs captured two Indians, one of whom agreed to guide them.[264] Moving through the woods to avoid being sighted, Pickens's troops reached and attacked a Cherokee town, but they "gave a great many of the Indians an opportunity of making their escape," because the principal objective "was to get the white men that was in the *Nation* and bring about a peace with the *Indians*."[265] About fifty Cherokee women and children, plus a few men, were captured. Pickens sent three of the male captives to tell the Cherokees that he promised to halt his march and release the prisoners if the Indians released their white captives and all the slaves they had taken.[266]

One Whig participant described a much more violent battle than Pickens reported. The troops, this soldier asserted, had orders "to kill all who had the appearances of warriors, to save the old men, squaws & children." Taken by surprise, the Cherokees "ran in the greatest consternation in every direction" with the Whigs in pursuit, "cutting down the Indians with their swords." When the slaughter ended, seventy-seven Indians, a Loyalist, and a black were dead and another forty-six Indians captured. The rebels then destroyed all the crops before advancing to a smaller town, where they captured five Loyalists. A hastily organized tribunal sentenced them to death, but Elijah Clarke interceded to have four of them spared on condition that he would return them to Georgia for trial. The fifth, charged with murder and burning houses, was hanged.[267]

Pickens had sent his message to the Cherokees on September 25, threatening them with further destruction if they did not make peace. Frightened by the devastation that the Whigs had already inflicted, the first Cherokee leaders arrived for negotiations five days later. Pickens formally presented his demands on October 17. He insisted that the Cherokees return all prisoners, slaves, horses, and other captured property and that they seize any Loyalists and British agents still among them and turn them over to the Whigs. In addition, the Cherokees had to surrender all of their land claims south of the Savannah and east of the Chattahoochee rivers as the price for peace with South Carolina and Georgia. The Cherokees agreed to the terms and signed the Treaty of Long Swamp the same day. As a sign of their good intentions, they also turned over six Loyalists to Pickens. Waters and most of his men, however, escaped and made their way to East Florida.[268] For the Cherokees, their last battle ended like the first, with defeat and the loss of their land.

The Seminole Creeks fared far better than the Cherokees, not only preserving their land but also avoiding further combat. Since the surrender of Pensacola, Patrick Tonyn had understood that "the aid of Indians will be of the utmost importance to us" if the Spaniards attacked East Florida as expected, and the governor had labored to keep the Seminoles' friendship. He "employed them as scouting parties along the coast" to give advance warning of a Spanish invasion. The only battles involving the Seminoles in the last months of the war were those that Tonyn fought with the army and the ministry to secure a generous supply of presents for his Indian allies.[269]

Whereas the Seminoles never had to fight the Spaniards, the Creeks, Choctaws, and Chickasaws maintained constant pressure on the Spanish in West Florida. In December 1781 Brown informed Leslie that the "Upper Creeks carry on their operations against the Spaniards" at Pensacola and Mobile, despite Spanish officials' "many ineffectual attempts by promises & presents to detach the Indians from His Majesty's Service." Creek pressure was so severe, Brown reported, that the troops at Pensacola could "draw no subsistence from the country & are compelled to live on jerked beef . . . from Mexico."[270]

The Spanish offered the Choctaws bribes to switch their allegiance to Spain, but without success. Instead, the Indian agent Farquhar Bethune sent raiding parties to carry off the cattle around the Spanish posts. Inspired by the lack of Spanish opposition, Bethune suggested that if the Choctaws and Chickasaws received adequate ammunition, with the help of two troops of cavalry formed from Loyalist refugees, a major attack could be made along the Mississippi "and the whole country reduced to the utmost distress."[271]

The Chickasaws, under the leadership of the agent James Colbert, were already attacking the Spanish along the Mississippi. Colbert, who had lived with the Indians since his youth, began his operations in the spring of 1782 in hopes of forcing the Spanish to release eight Loyalists still imprisoned for their role in the Natchez rebellion. Colbert and the Chickasaws made travel so hazardous that few Spanish vessels dared venture upriver from New Orleans. Their most successful attack took place on May 2, when they seized vessels carrying munitions, provisions, and the wife and children of the lieutenant governor of Illinois. Colbert released his captives on parole so that they could arrange their exchange for the Loyalist prisoners. The Spaniards did release a few of the Loyalists and then launched an unsuccessful attack on the Chickasaws. Colbert's force of Indians and Loyalists continued to harass the Spaniards into 1783. Eventually, however, the Chickasaws, Choctaws, and Creeks all followed the Cherokees' example and opened peace negotiations with the Spanish and Americans.[272]

AFRICAN AMERICANS: FROM BARGAINING CHIPS TO SOLDIERS

When the British army withdrew to the environs of Charleston, many South Carolinians began trying to reclaim their slaves, who were often scattered throughout the South. Robert Heriot, a paroled American prisoner in Charleston, sought his missing slaves so that they could be sent to his plantation at Georgetown. He learned that three of them were in North Carolina, where they had been "reserved for me," and found a fourth in town. Another, Jac, had vanished, while Mingo had been employed by the British "on the public works, but I understand is run away from them."[273] On his journey south from Philadelphia, Aedenus Burke stopped at Yorktown, Virginia, and there took possession of "several Negroes" belonging to his Carolina friends, who had been with Cornwallis's army. One, however, owned by Arthur Middleton, escaped aboard a British vessel.[274]

Gen. Isaac Huger of the South Carolina Continentals took time from his duties to search for his slaves, only to learn that the British had taken most of them. Huger tried without success to find a white man to escort his remaining slaves to safety in Virginia. He also expressed concern at Sumter's seizure of 150 slaves belonging to Lt. Gov. William Bull, probably because Huger feared that Sumter's actions would provoke retaliation in kind by the British and the loss of more Whig-owned slaves.[275] Sumter, however, continued to seize slaves to distribute as bounties to his troops and quickly accumulated a surplus.[276] In December, Governor Rutledge advised Sumter to put a group of blacks that the latter had recently taken "in Charge of some person, of honest Character," to care for them and insure that "they do not escape to the Enemy," until the state government called for them.[277]

Rebel officials assigned many unclaimed and Loyalist-owned slaves to repair some of the deterioration that had resulted from years of wartime neglect. In early December a party of blacks was sent under guard to repair the road between Ferguson's Mill and Orangeburg. The captain commanding the guards received orders to "prevent the Negroes from Defecting" as well as "to repel any attack that may be made on them by the disaffected Inhabitants who may desire to interrupt them in their duty or steal them from their masters."[278]

The Whigs had good reason to fear the loss of their slaves because British and Loyalist parties had made repeated forays from Charleston to capture blacks. On September 28 Greene had informed Sumter that "the enemy . . . are collecting all the Negroes they can."[279] Six weeks later Francis Marion reported that several raiding parties took "a great number of Negroes out of St Stephens and St Johns" counties.[280] Marion initially thought that the British wanted the slaves to work on Charleston's fortifications, and he was puzzled when raiders carried off "women and children, who will be of no use to them in Charleston and will use up provisions."[281] Evidently the British intended to use some of these slaves as laborers, while Loyalists sought slaves as compensation for the property they had been forced to abandon. Depriving the Whigs of slaves also made it harder for them to raise the crops needed to feed the militia and Greene's army.

A significant percentage of the seized slaves found themselves among the increasing number of blacks working directly for the army. By October 1781 the Royal Artillery Department employed ninety blacks, eighty-five of them as laborers. King Staniard continued as sergeant, assisted by four corporals. The number peaked at ninety-five in January 1782 and then declined slightly; there were eighty-six men on the rolls in September.[282]

In addition to these laborers, the Royal Artillery relied on fifty-seven wagon drivers from the Horse Department to transport guns and supplies. Most or all of these were apparently black, since the muster roll lists first names such as Quamino, Monday, Bristol, Pompey, and Mingo. The Artillery Department also employed skilled blacks, although most of these appear to have been hired from Loyalist owners, whereas most of the laborers and teamsters were apparently fugitives who had fled to the British. A return of skilled black workers dated April 21, 1782, shows eight carpenters, a wheeler, two smiths, and ten sawyers, for a total of twenty-one men. Skilled workers who maintained the artillery train consisted of a mixed group of white and black craftsmen. Pay, however, was generally lower for blacks. White workers received three shillings per day, while blacks received only two, except in the case of sawyers, who were paid two shillings per day regardless of race. Blacks working for the army often had their families with them; one muster roll listed fifty-two women attached to the Artillery Department.[283]

British officers also turned to Loyalist masters in the fall of 1781 to procure slaves to strengthen the defenses around Charleston. The army advertised in the newspapers for slaves to perform this task, instructing masters to have them report each morning to an official from the Engineer Department for assignment. The promised pay was one shilling per day, which apparently went to the masters rather than the laborers.[284] General Leslie later established a fixed scale of payment to Loyalists whose slaves worked in the various departments. Masters received eightpence per day for laborers and eighteenpence for skilled workers; women's work was valued at half the rate of a male laborer. The slaves received clothing "made up in Uniform" along with a direct allowance of two dollars per month for artisans and one dollar for laborers, on condition that their overseers gave them a "Certificate of their deserving it."[285]

Hired, seized, and refugee slaves still did not meet the army's insatiable demand for labor, so officers turned to John Cruden, who had abandoned the sequestered properties he managed when the army withdrew to Charleston and taken his slaves within British lines. Cruden "amply supplied the Public Departments" with able-bodied males but retained responsibility for supporting the "Women, Children, and Infirm." The cost of clothing, medical care, and food for these people nearly bankrupted him, even though "provisions was purchased of the cheapest kind, and issued as sparingly as possible."[286]

While slave women and children often proved to be more burden than benefit to the British, many of the male slaves sometimes provided more assistance than simple labor. The roster of a company of fifty-four black laborers listed particular information on each man, such as his knowledge of certain roads and wooded areas.[287] This information indicates that these men may have been called upon occasionally to carry messages or procure information for the army.

Black spies and messengers comprised a key component of British intelligence operations. Henry Lee discovered in August that a Loyalist behind rebel lines was using "two of his Negroe fellows" to send a steady stream of information to Balfour in Charleston.[288] Lee also learned that one black had offered to lead the British across the Santee and through the swamps to make a surprise attack on Greene's camp.[289] Boston King thwarted a planned rebel attack on the British post at Nelson's Ferry by carrying a message through Whig lines to another British detachment at Monck's Corner, which promptly marched to the aid of the threatened position. The officer to whom he delivered the message welcomed him "with great kindness" and praised King's "courage and conduct in this dangerous business." The British paid King a three-shilling reward for his services, a sum that the former slave considered paltry in view of the risks he had taken.[290]

Angered by the harm that blacks were doing to the rebel cause, Governor Rutledge issued orders in September to punish slaves who helped the British. "Severe examples must be made of all negroes who carry any provisions of any kind, aid or assist, or carry any intelligence to or for the enemy," he wrote; "agreeably to the laws of this State all such negroes shall suffer death."[291] The governor's threats had little effect, for two months later Greene decided that kindness toward slaves might work better than threats. Greene told Henry Lee to insure that Whig troops did not abuse "the Negroes from whom the enemy get all their best intelligence and who will be either more or less useful to them as they are treated well or ill by us."[292]

Of even greater concern to Greene was the growing possibility that the British might augment their forces by arming large numbers of slaves. In August, Greene believed that "four or five hundred Negroes may be calculated upon" to fight alongside the British and Loyalists.[293] By December he learned that the British had finally begun to organize black military units. "An attempt is . . . making to Arm the Negroes and some are now in service," he reported.[294]

Balfour had been considering ways to procure more assistance from slaves since the summer, but even the limited plan he had suggested then provoked an outburst of furor among Loyalists in New York when it became known. "There is an Absurd and exasperating Promise of Freedom and a Gratuity to Slaves who will inform against their Masters Strange Defect of sound Policy!" raged William Smith when he heard Balfour's proposal. James Simpson pronounced the idea "Madness."[295]

Others, however, believed that the best means to retrieve British fortunes in America was to abandon all reservations and arm large numbers of blacks. An anonymous writer calculated the strength available to the rebels and concluded that black troops would give Britain a decisive advantage in the war. He estimated the population of the thirteen colonies at 2.4 million, of which 600,000 were "Negroes or Slaves." Assuming that one in four people was capable of bearing arms, the rebels had a potential fighting strength of 460,000 men and the blacks 150,000. However, the writer calculated that the war had already incapacitated about 50,000 whites and that the number of whites available for military service would be further reduced because many farmers and artisans made indispensable contributions as civilians, while merchants and the propertied class would not fight. Therefore, since slaves were "desirous of recovering their freedom, and are ever ready to embrace an opportunity of doing it," and because their numbers would not be diminished by merchants, artisans, and others who could not or would not serve, "more fighting Men might be raised among them upon proper Encouragement than among the Whites."[296] Although the writer did not say so explicitly, he clearly believed that armed slaves could provide the manpower needed to defeat the rebels.

Loyalists and British officers in South Carolina had come to the same conclusion. When Greene's army advanced in mid-November and forced the British to evacuate their post at Dorchester and to withdraw into the fortifications of Charleston, "the most active negroes were called to arms and enrolled" to meet the emergency.[297] The new policy was limited and almost furtive. Only a fraction of the many slaves with the army were armed, and neither Leslie nor Balfour ever mentioned the black units in correspondence with their superiors.

John Laurens saw the British decision to arm blacks as an opportunity to revive his cherished plan to enlist slaves to serve in the Whig forces. He proposed that South Carolina use the promise of freedom after the war to recruit twenty-five hundred slave soldiers. Greene, who was eager to increase the strength of his army, lent his full support.[298] Laurens intended to bring the proposal before the assembly, and Greene urged Governor Rutledge to help secure its passage. "The natural strength of this country in point of numbers, appears to me to consist much more in the blacks, than the whites," Greene observed. "Could they be incorporated, and employed for it's defence, it would afford you double security. That they would make good Soldiers I have not the least doubt."[299] After consulting with the council, Rutledge replied that the decision would be left to the legislature. He also reminded Greene that the previous proposal to arm blacks had been overwhelmingly rejected.[300]

Pressured by Laurens, who declared that "unless they are goaded upon the subject" state officials would do nothing, Greene again addressed the governor.[301] "I cannot help repeating my recommendation of raising some black regiments for the more effectual protection and security of this country," the general wrote. He conceded that this "remedy may be disagreeable"; yet, it was preferable to having the province again overrun by the British. To emphasize this danger, Greene asserted that the British "are now arming a considerable body of negroes and I am well informed that they determine to compleat them to the number of 3,000."[302]

Laurens managed to have the matter brought up for a vote in the assembly on February 4, but his proposal was overwhelmingly defeated. Only Laurens, David Ramsay, and fourteen others voted for the measure. "By all the rest it was execrated," Aedenus Burke wrote. He noted that the use of slave soldiers was becoming a divisive issue between the northern and southern states. "The northern people I have observed, regard the condition in which we hold our slaves in a light different from us. I am much deceived indeed, if they do not secretly *wish* for a general Emancipation, if the present struggle was over," Burke declared.[303]

Leading the opposition to Laurens's proposal were John and Edward Rutledge, Jacob Read, and Christopher Gadsden, and nearly one hundred other representatives supported them. Edward Rutledge described the contest over the bill as a "hard Battle" and said that although Laurens and his allies had "pushed the matter as far as it could well go," upon hearing the debate "people in general returned to their Senses" and opposed arming slaves. Rutledge confessed to being "very much alarmed on the Occasion" and expressed a hope that the issue "will rest for ever & a day."[304]

A Continental officer agreed with Rutledge's assessment, writing that the "fears of the people started an alarm, and the force of interest annihilated the scheme."[305] Another added that "prejudices against the measure are so prevailing that no consideration could induce them to adopt it."[306] In a letter to George Washington, Greene asserted that the assembly had rejected the plan "not because they objected to the expence . . . but from an apprehension of the consequences."[307] Laurens sarcastically remarked to Alexander Hamilton that he could not succeed in the face of overwhelming odds, "having only reason on my side and being opposed by a triple-headed monster . . . of Avarice, prejudice, and pusillanimity."[308]

Informing Greene that the assembly had rejected Laurens's plan, South Carolina's new governor, John Mathews, offered instead to provide the army "with a Sufficient number of Negroes, as Officers servants, Pioneers, Waggoners, Artificers &c." However, state officials wanted Greene's assurance that the Continental Congress would count those men toward the quota of troops the state had been asked to furnish. In other words, the state government refused to provide the army with black troops, but it wanted black noncombatants counted as white soldiers.[309] Greene replied that the army could use four or five hundred blacks to serve in the capacities Mathews had specified, but only if they were employed "upon such terms as will engage their fidelity . . . unless the Negroes have an interest in their servitude, I am persuaded they will be of little benefit." The general suggested that the state clothe the blacks and pay them the same amount that Continental soldiers received.[310]

In addition to providing slaves to perform noncombat duties with Greene's army, the legislators approved their own version of "Sumter's Law," the practice of distributing slaves as an enlistment bounty. Their plan called for the formation of two Continental battalions, with each recruit to receive "the enormous Bounty of 1 Negroe for each Year" served, Edward Rutledge explained. He wished, however, that Congress would send more troops to South Carolina, which would "let us save two Negroes out of three."[311]

Contrary to what Rutledge implied, Governor Mathews in March 1782 assured Sumter that an adequate supply of slaves was available to provide bounties for the recruits. The commissioners of confiscation had assumed control of

Loyalists' slaves and "wish to get rid of the Negroes as fast as possible," Mathews wrote. He instructed Sumter to assemble recruits in parties of twenty and send them to him with "an Order on me for a Negroe each."[312]

The loss of their land and slaves angered many Loyalists, who sought to reclaim the latter or at least replace them with other slaves. Some, such as James Penman of Johns Island, sought the help of Whig officers in recovering their slaves. Penman had left thirty slaves behind when British troops evacuated the island, "flattering himself that this Sort of property would not be molested." The rebels, however, carried off his slaves, and Penman appealed in vain to one of Greene's officers for their return.[313]

Most Loyalists turned to General Leslie, requesting that he seize slaves from the Whigs in retaliation for the confiscation act. On March 27 Leslie ordered Maj. Simon Fraser of the provincial cavalry to pursue a rebel party and recover slaves stolen from Loyalists as the first step in the general's plan to secure compensation for the Loyalists. Leslie's aide explained to Fraser that "the principal business to prosecute, is, the collecting of all the Slaves, who belong to those, in arms against the British government." Fraser was to circulate word throughout the country that if slaves of rebel masters came to the British, "it is the determination of the General never to return them to their masters, but to take care of them and their familys, and that they may depend upon the generosity of the English Government should they behave with fidelity during the course of the war." The aide told Fraser to send all blacks who came in response to this offer to Haddrell's Point, where they would receive Leslie's directions.[314]

Leslie informed Clinton that he had been "induced to make this movement in order to convince the loyalists of my desire . . . to counteract the effect of the sanguinary laws lately passed by the rebel assembly against them."[315] Leslie also explained his actions to Greene and offered to discuss the issue of confiscation. The British general stated that he had watched the state's proceedings regarding confiscation "with deep concern," hoping that "Humanity, as well as Policy, would have Arrested their execution." Now that the Whigs had begun to carry out their confiscation measures, Leslie believed that he had no choice but to counter them by "seizing the Negroes of your friends, that restitution may be thereby made to such of ours, as may suffer under these oppressive and ruinous resolutions." He proposed to send commissioners to meet with rebel leaders to discuss the issue.[316] Greene replied that the matter was "of civil resort" and referred Leslie to Governor Mathews.[317] Greene then ordered Marion to warn the people of "the enemies intentions."[318]

The warnings had little effect, as parties of British troops carried off large numbers of slaves. The *South Carolina Royal Gazette* announced in March that in a recent raid the troops had seized three times as many slaves from the Whigs as had recently been lost to them. "The Rebels will therefore find that *their* Estates, not those of the Loyalists have been confiscated by the Assembly at

Jacksonborough," the newspaper asserted.[319] On March 29 Marion reported that British troops were in St. James Parish, "taking all the negroes from every place."[320] Another officer noted that in early April the British had made two raids into St. Thomas Parish, from which "they carried off 150 negroes."[321] John Laurens denounced the British "excursions" as having "no other object than the stealing Negroes" and hoped that pressure from Whig civil and military officials would force Leslie to "renounce his project of kidnapping."[322]

Greene sent troops to oppose the British raiding parties, but occasionally these men engaged in the very practice they had been ordered to halt. Pennsylvania soldiers returning from a failed attempt to intercept a British force "began to plunder the negroes" along the Cooper River on April 3. They were stopped when a soldier from Henry Lee's legion shot one of the Pennsylvanians.[323]

Although British officers kept no record of how many slaves were forcibly seized and how many willingly accompanied the raiding parties, many Whigs feared that their slaves would take the opportunity to escape if British troops were in the area. In May a rebel militia officer removed the slaves from the Gaillard plantation "for the sake of Security," but John Fauchereau Grimké suggested that they be brought back, "as there is little difference in the two Situations & it would be impossible to restrain the negroes from running away from either place."[324] Slaves belonging to the planter Thomas Farr threatened to go to Charleston "whenever I cannot feed them." In turn, Farr, who owned about a hundred slaves, asked Greene to take no more provisions for the army from his plantation, which had only a two-month food supply left.[325]

While his troops collected some slaves to be used as pawns in the dispute over confiscation, Leslie at last officially proposed to arm others for the defense of Charleston. He did so in response to growing pressure from Loyalists and from the former governor of Virginia, Lord Dunmore, who had made his own attempt to arm slaves in 1775.

Dunmore, who had recently arrived in Charleston, saw the large number of blacks with the British and immediately recognized their military potential. He recommended arming ten thousand slaves as "the most efficatious, expeditious, cheapest, and certain means of reducing this Country to a proper sense of their Duty." Furthermore, he asserted, blacks "are perfectly attached to our Sovereign, and by employing them you cannot desire a means more effectual to distress your Foes." Dunmore suggested that the government pay slave recruits an enlistment bonus of one guinea and one crown (over $150) and free them when the war ended.[326] The government would also compensate Loyalist masters whose slaves were enlisted. Other slaves would labor behind the lines to provide the black soldiers with supplies. Dunmore sent this proposal to Germain on February 5, 1782, along with his plan to create a separate Loyalist army; he apparently envisioned the two forces cooperating to drive the rebels from the southern provinces. By the time the letter reached England, however, Germain was out of office. The plan ended up in the hands of Lord Shelburne, who did not reply until June 5. He stated that General Carleton had received instructions concerning black troops and would respond to Dunmore's proposal.[327]

In the interim, Dunmore had sent Loyalist Edmund Fanning to London with a request that the governor be given "Command of all the Provincials . . . and Liberty to raise several Corps of Blacks upon the Promise of Freedom." Dunmore went to New York and presented his case to Clinton. Despite Dunmore's insistence that "the King's Affairs are recoverable" if the army would adopt a policy of "more War and less Conciliation," Clinton rejected the plan.[328] Frustrated, Dunmore gave up and sailed for England. A similar proposal to train blacks in Charleston as soldiers and use them to retake some of the southern provinces was advanced by John Morison, a Loyalist who while in India had previously trained sepoys (native troops who served under British officers). The ministry ignored his suggestion.[329]

Lacking Dunmore's boldness, Leslie did not suggest the use of black soldiers to Clinton until March 12. Lt. Col. James Moncrief, the highly respected engineer officer, added his endorsement the next day. He proposed forming an entire brigade of black troops.[330] Desperate Loyalists also embraced the idea; on March 30 Leslie sent Clinton an address from the Loyalists requesting that slaves be armed and asked the commander in chief "how far the measure of arming the negroes should be carried into execution." Leslie declared his own support for such a measure: "It is an object of great importance to establish a plan upon this subject, and to determine in what manner their officers should be appointed and on what terms their freedom should be given them." He suggested Moncrief "as a very proper person to be at their head, being well acquainted with their disposition, and in the highest estimation amongst them." Leslie indicated that for the plan to be effective, he needed Clinton's immediate approval.[331] Neither Leslie nor Moncrief mentioned the unit of black cavalry that had been in the field since late 1781, perhaps because they feared that Clinton would order the unit disbanded. Leslie did ask Lt. Col. Benjamin Thompson, a New Hampshire Loyalist who was going to New York, to explain the need for black troops to Clinton. In a letter sent with Thompson, Leslie insisted that arming slaves "will soon become indispensably necessary shou'd the war continue . . . in this part of America."[332]

Thompson was an excellent choice for the mission; in addition to having served as Germain's assistant, he had commanded and trained the black troops during his stay in South Carolina. When Thompson arrived in Charleston in December 1781, Leslie placed him in command of the cavalry, which consisted of "five weak Troops" of regulars, "Two strong Troops of Mounted Militia, and a Seapoy Troop (Gens de Couleurs) that will act with us occasionally," Thompson noted.[333] He immediately began training his men to instill "order and attention to discipline." After some time spent in lengthy marches and mock charges, on January 23, 1782, Thompson took his cavalry on a sweep of the area near Dorchester, in which they scattered a rebel unit and took five prisoners. "Capt. Smarts Seapoy Troop" was placed in the rear of the column. Thompson praised the performance of his soldiers on this expedition, without distinguishing between whites and blacks.[334]

Eventually the black cavalrymen became known to Loyalists and Whigs alike as the "Black Dragoons" and were one of the most active British units in the last months of the war. Their operations showed both the advantages and disadvantages of using black soldiers. While they did a creditable job in a variety of roles, including foraging, capturing deserters, and combat, they aroused great enmity among rebel civilians and soldiers.

William Mathews, who lived a short distance from Charleston, was enraged when the Black Dragoons visited his home on the night of January 17, 1782. Guided by a runaway slave from a nearby plantation, the black troops, who were commanded by "one John Jackson," surrounded Mathews's house and demanded entry. Mathews complied and provided the soldiers with food and drink. After they had refreshed themselves, they left, telling Mathews "that had I not been an Invalid they would have fired the House & cut me in Peices."[335] In August, Charles Cotesworth Pinckney complained that the Black Dragoons "are daily committing the most horrible depredations and murder in the defenceless parts of our Country."[336] In addition, just over a week before the evacuation of Charleston, Thomas Bee wrote to Governor Mathews "at the request of several inhabitants of the Goose Creek neighborhood," soliciting protection "from the ravages of the Black Dragoons who have been out four times within the last ten days plundering & robbing between the Quarter House and this place."[337] Former lieutenant governor William Bull, a slave owner and opponent of the use of black troops, sympathized with the Whigs. He declared that the "savage nature" of blacks made it inevitable that they would commit depredations.[338]

The mere sight of armed blacks infuriated rebel soldiers as much as it did civilians, leading to several violent encounters. On April 21 an American cavalry patrol battled a British mounted force between Dorchester and the Quarter House. The British unit included white troops as well as the Black Dragoons.[339] During the fighting, some American soldiers singled out March, a former slave who had been "extremely active, & very troublesome," and "cut him" and two or three other black troops "to pieces."[340] Edward Rutledge praised the rebel soldiers' behavior. "Besides dispatching so infamous a fellow, I have my hopes that others will be prevented from following his Example, if they are not, I hope they will meet his Fate," he wrote.[341]

Marion encountered the Black Dragoons, operating with a Loyalist unit, in a late August skirmish near Biggin's Bridge. About one hundred white cavalrymen and "some Coloured Dragoons" charged the rebels, but Marion had posted some of his men to fire into the British right flank, which forced the attackers to withdraw.[342] In another skirmish some of Marion's troops "encountered a party of twenty-six of the British black dragoons, and cut them to pieces."[343] Marion fought the Black Dragoons again in October and this time captured some. He then asked Governor Mathews what he should do with his black prisoners. Mathews replied that since "the negroes you mention . . . were taken in arms, they must be tried by the negro law; and, if found guilty, executed" unless the court recommended clemency or they were pardoned by him. Such lenience, however, was unlikely. "Exemplary punishments on such notorious offenders will have a very salutary effect," Mathews declared.[344]

Animosity toward the Black Dragoons was not limited to southerners. Even northern soldiers, who were often sympathetic to the plight of slaves, expressed disgust with the Black Dragoons. Col. Lewis Morris of New York lamented the condition of "the poor unhappy blacks who, to the disgrace of human nature, are subject to every species of oppression while we are contending for the rights and liberties of mankind."[345] Yet, he wrote admiringly of the "*slicing Captain,*" a Continental officer who craved a confrontation with the black soldiers. "Fortunate for the poor black dragoons that he did not fall in with them," Morris stated.[346] Capt. Walter Finney of the Pennsylvania Line gloated that a skirmish between the rebels and "a Negroe Captn. Nam'd Smart, and some of his Affrican Banditty" had resulted in the Americans "Dissecting" Smart.[347] The Polish-born colonel Tadeusz Kosciuszko seemed to harbor a particular enmity for the black cavalrymen. He constantly tried to bring the Black Dragoons to battle, although he succeeded on only one occasion.[348]

In addition to fighting and foraging, the Black Dragoons patrolled the lines to deter or capture deserters. Low morale and inactivity among the soldiers resulted in high rates of desertion, especially among the three Hessian regiments in Charleston. During October 1782 forty-six Hessians deserted. However, desertions practically ceased after three fugitives from the von Benning regiment "were pounced upon by the Black Dragoons" in the early morning of October 31. Two of the deserters were killed, and although the third escaped, few soldiers dared make the attempt afterward. The Black Dragoons received a bounty of two guineas ($275) for each deserter, living or dead, they brought back to the British lines.[349]

Leslie apparently organized a second black unit shortly before the British left Charleston, since Kosciuszko informed Greene on November 14 that the British had formed a black corps. These troops were posted on Charleston Neck and may have been armed for the specific purpose of holding the lines while British and provincial soldiers were withdrawn to prepare for the evacuation.[350]

A few blacks carried arms as individuals attached to British units or fought as partisans alongside white Loyalists. Capt. Alexander Campbell evidently armed his servant, since the unnamed man died in battle with the rebels in April 1782 after "making a most gallant defence." The man's actions merited a flattering newspaper report, indicating that many Loyalists had come to accept, and even admire, the military service of blacks.[351] "Two White men & some Negroes" wounded Whig captain Richard Gough and a companion behind rebel lines on July 13 and escaped unscathed.[352]

Blacks had also served aboard British naval vessels since the beginning of the war and did so until the evacuation of Charleston. Most were crew members of the armed galleys that protected the inland waterways.[353] When the Whigs captured the galley *Balfour* at the end of September, they found a roster of "Blacks on Brd" that contained the names of two free men, five slaves, and "Moses a good friend."[354]

The captain of the *Balfour* was unusual in compiling such a list, since British officers rarely kept records or made reports of the black soldiers and sailors. Thus, it is impossible to say with certainty how many blacks served in combat roles. Greene's estimate, made in April 1782, that "not less than 700 are said to be armed and in Uniform at this time" in South Carolina, was undoubtedly exaggerated.[355]

The contributions that black spies and informants made to British operations often proved as valuable as those made by black soldiers. Greene worried that blacks were furnishing the British with intelligence of his army's strength and position. On January 29 he ordered his officers to carefully watch "all unknown characters coming into camp, particularly Negroes among who Spies are suspected."[356] Thomas Farr warned the general on March 13 that a "Mulato Servant" belonging to John McQueen, another of Greene's informants, was probably a spy for the British.[357]

Benjamin Thompson questioned slaves he encountered during his February 24 march to strike the rebels outside Charleston, and he received information that enabled him to mount a successful attack.[358] When Kosciuszko planned to surprise British parties operating outside Charleston in September, he had to cancel his attack when "two Negroes Coming from Town" spotted his concealed troops and "went down and told the British."[359] A slave thwarted Kosciuszko yet again on November 14, in what may have been the last combat in South Carolina. The colonel led a small force to attack a party of British troops who, according to the slave, were cutting wood on James Island. Instead of taking the British by surprise, as Kosciuszko had expected, the rebels marched unsuspectingly into a volley of musket fire that killed one man and wounded several others. The Whigs were certain that the slave who gave Kosciuszko the information had arranged the ambush.[360]

Blacks who provided information to the British ran great risks. Officially employed as a guide in the quartermaster's department, a former slave named Harry served primarily as a "very serviceable" spy for Lord Rawdon and later for Balfour. In late November, Harry set out from Monck's Corner to get intelligence of the rebel army. This would be his last assignment; captured by some of Marion's men, Harry "was beheaded & his head set upon a Stake" near Greenland Swamp.[361]

On rare occasions slaves acted as clandestine messengers for the rebels. A Whig sympathizer living behind British lines used his slave Prince to deliver intelligence reports to Kosciuszko. Prince's knowledge of the countryside around Charleston enabled him to slip past British outposts into the Whig lines. Prince was clearly a willing participant in the scheme; he could easily have escaped to the British and received a reward for the information he carried.[362]

As General Leslie observed the faithful service of thousands of blacks in many important roles, he became increasingly sympathetic toward them, which soon provoked a serious dispute with Whig officials. Initially, Leslie had hoped to use the slaves in British possession to convince state authorities to ameliorate the confiscation laws in exchange for the slaves' return, or if that failed, to compensate the Loyalists for their confiscated property. He therefore tried to prevent his officers from carrying off slaves when two regiments were sent from Charleston to the West Indies in May 1782. Having learned that "a number of Negroes the property of Persons in this Province . . . are now embarked on board the different Transports contrary to a general Order of mine," Leslie demanded that the blacks be sent ashore and turned over to Colonel Ballingall, the commissioner of claims for Negroes.[363]

Governor Mathews had ignored the overtures made in April by Leslie through Greene to negotiate the issue of slaves and confiscation. In mid-August, however, Mathews learned that the British intended to take away all of their supporters when Charleston was evacuated, and the governor correctly assumed that former slaves were included. This prompted him to dash off a letter to Leslie threatening retaliation if the British refused to return Whig-owned slaves. "It is well known that there are also a considerable number of the Negroes and other property of the Citizens of this State, that are in possession of the Officers and other persons belonging to the Army under your command," Mathews wrote, "and others that are employed in the various departments of your Army, who are lyable to be removed from the State with the Army." If these blacks were evacuated, the governor warned Leslie, state officials would "seize on the whole of the debts due to the Subjects of Great Britain, and to those whose estates are Confiscated," which, according to Mathews, far exceeded the value of the slaves who would leave with the British.[364]

Anticipating that the matter would soon come to a head, Leslie had already taken steps to resolve it. In late July he wrote Carleton asking what he should do with the slaves in the event that Charleston were evacuated. Leslie noted that "many negroes" had provided valuable services to the army and had been promised their freedom.[365] Two weeks later Leslie made an effort to distinguish between those slaves whose masters were in rebellion, and therefore were considered sequestered property, and other blacks who had come to the British voluntarily. He ordered everyone possessing sequestered slaves to submit lists of them and declared that anyone who attempted "to secret or carry out of this district any Negro that does not belong to them" would be punished.[366]

Leslie found it necessary to issue such orders because some Loyalists were pressing him for permission to sell slaves from the sequestered estates and keep the proceeds as compensation for their property that had been confiscated by the rebels. These people saw every slave who left the province as a potential financial loss. Leslie asked Carleton for directions on this subject.[367] He also reminded his commander that there were many slaves "who have voluntarily come in, under the faith of our protection." These blacks, Leslie declared, "cannot in justice be abandoned to the merciless resentment of their former masters; I shall form these under some regulation, and make an appointment of proper Officers to superintend them." They could then be sent to East Florida or the West Indies, as Carleton might direct, "where their past services will engage the grateful attention of Government to which they will continue to be useful."[368]

Carleton allowed Leslie to determine the fate of the slaves. Regarding sequestered slaves, Carleton stated that the matter "is left to Genl. Leslie's decision, to act as he judges best." Those slaves who had joined the British of their own accord and been promised freedom were to have it; "the others left to the General's decision."[369] Later, Carleton asked Leslie to recruit two hundred blacks at Charleston for military service in the West Indies, at wages of sixpence per day.[370]

After receiving Carleton's reply, Leslie considered himself authorized to open direct negotiations with the Whigs to resolve the slave issue. Mathews accepted the offer and appointed Edward Rutledge and Benjamin Guerard to represent the state. Leslie chose Alexander Wright and James Johnston to act for the Loyalists. On October 10, 1782, the negotiators came to an agreement. The treaty stipulated that all slaves with the British who belonged to citizens of South Carolina "shall be restored to their former Owners, as far as is practicable, except such Slaves as may have rendered themselves particularly obnoxious on Account of their Attachment and Services to the *British* Troops, and such as have had specifick Promises of Freedom." Slaves thus excepted would be "fairly valued by a Person to be chosen on each Side" and their owners compensated by the British government. Slaves returned under the agreement would not be punished by the state for having escaped to the British, and officials would advise slave owners to forgo punishing their slaves as well. Loyalists were permitted to take their slaves with them at the evacuation, and the state pledged to allow both Loyalists and British merchants to collect debts owed them by South Carolinians so long as the agreement remained in force.[371]

Neither side was satisfied with the agreement. Christopher Gadsden thought that it was "so particularly careful of the great negro owners" that most South Carolinians might "think their honor and safety sacrificed to that particular species of property!" He implied that throughout the war, large slaveholders had put their personal welfare ahead of the public good and were now being rewarded for doing so. "Their interest has indisputably occasioned more danger to the State than their fellow citizens, with less of that kind of property," Gadsden declared.[372] Loyalists, for their part, denounced the treaty as unfair to rebel-owned slaves who "have borne arms in our service." In an address to British officials, many Loyalists insisted that it would be inhumane to return those slaves to their owners. The Loyalists' motives were not entirely altruistic—they wanted the British government to pay those slaves' value into a fund to compensate Loyalists for their wartime losses. Leslie replied to the petition with a pledge that the number of such blacks and their families returned to the rebels would be kept "within the narrowest possible limits."[373]

The dispute over the agreement had barely begun when the treaty was repudiated. Mathews appointed commissioners to identify slaves in Charleston and send them back to their owners, but the Whig agents immediately ran into difficulties. The first group of evacuees was preparing to sail, and British naval officers refused to allow the commissioners to board their vessels and search for slaves. Instead, the captains gave their word that there were no blacks subject to the agreement on their ships. Leslie tried to resolve the controversy by sending Carleton a request to have the admiral at New York order naval officers to permit the Whigs to search the ships. However, it would take weeks to get an answer from New York, and in the meantime the commissioners searched privately owned vessels and claimed 136 slaves. British officers approved the return of only 73 and declared the rest exempt under the terms of the treaty.[374]

As Leslie explained to Carleton, "officers long in this country look on negroes as their property, and the slaves are exceeding unwilling to return to hard labour, and severe punishment from their former masters." It was difficult to press the matter because "every department, and every officer, wishes to include his slave into the number to be brought off. They pretend them spys, or guides, and of course obnoxious, or under promises of freedom from Genl. Prevost, Ld. Cornwallis, Ld. Rawdon, or some other officer of rank, or free by proclamation." Leslie feared that if the rebels were compensated for all of the slaves retained for these reasons, it would "amount to a monstrous expense."[375]

The seventy-three slaves claimed by the Whigs never left Charleston. While the commissioners searched for slaves, some of Greene's troops captured three British soldiers just outside the town's fortifications. Leslie believed that a truce was in effect to permit the transfer of slaves, accused Greene of violating it, and refused to allow any slaves to leave the British lines until the rebels returned the prisoners. When Mathews learned of Leslie's actions, he became angry and informed the general that the treaty was dissolved.[376]

Whigs blamed British greed for the collapse of the agreement. Thomas Farr had heard reports in June that British officers were taking "the first Negroes they meet with" and selling them "for whatever money they can obtain" to Spaniards who came to Charleston from Havana to purchase slaves.[377] An informant told Marion in November that the British wished to retain as many slaves as possible in order to "Gratify an Infamous avarice, which must be accompanied with a like breach of Faith, to the poor unfortunate negroes who will be carried from hence, into a Thousand times (if Possible) worse Bondage, than they Experience here."[378] William Moultrie agreed, asserting that the opportunities to profit "from the sale of plundered negroes, were too seducing to be resisted by the officers, privates and followers of the British army." He accused Moncrief of transporting over eight hundred slaves to the West Indies and selling them for personal profit, and he estimated that a total of twenty-five thousand South Carolina slaves were lost during the war.[379] The figure represents about one-fourth of the state's prewar slave population, but more conservative estimates put the number at approximately thirteen thousand.[380]

Amid all the accusations of greed and larceny, few Whigs considered that the slaves themselves might have had a preference. One rebel informant, however, did question several blacks in Charleston and found that "none Inclines to go home."[381]

Leslie did make an effort to return some slaves to Whig owners after Mathews abrogated the treaty. In November he appointed a board of officers headed by Maj. Thomas Fraser to determine which slaves had voluntarily come to the British and which had served as soldiers or in other capacities.[382] The board evidently identified a few slaves whom they decided should be returned, since on November 25 Whig officers sent a small force of troops to Charleston "to escort the Negroes from the lines."[383]

In the last months before the British left Charleston, rebel soldiers directed most of their efforts to preventing further losses of slaves. Because provisions were scarce in Charleston, Leslie sent out foraging parties, which invariably returned with considerable numbers of slaves. Greene urged his subordinates to do everything possible to thwart the British expeditions, as "the more scanty we can render their supplies of provisions the sooner [the evacuation] will take place and the fewer Negroes they will have it in their power to take with them."[384] In obedience to Greene's orders, John Laurens led an attack on one raiding party in late August. Laurens lost his life in the battle, and the British still succeeded in carrying off all the slaves from two nearby plantations.[385] A few weeks before the evacuation, Governor Mathews asked Greene to order that "all Negroes . . . not belonging to the inhabitants found in the town, be detained" when Continental troops entered Charleston, until Mathews determined what to do with them.[386] Greene complied with the request.[387]

The victorious rebels found few slaves to arrest when they marched into the town. As many as 2,000 had gone to St. Augustine in October, more than 50 had sailed for Halifax with the army's heavy artillery that same month, and 5,327 left in the December evacuation. Others made their way overland to East Florida or Indian territory. William Bull put the total number of blacks who left South Carolina with the British in the final months of the war at 9,000.[388]

Thousands of other blacks had already left Georgia after steadfastly supporting the British despite the deteriorating military situation. The small number of British regulars in Savannah led Lt. Cols. Alured Clarke and Thomas Brown to arm slaves for the defense of the town. In early January 1782 a rebel prisoner, who had enlisted in the Georgia Royalists to avoid confinement on a prison ship, deserted and informed Whig officers that Savannah's garrison included "about 150 Negroes armed & equipt as infantry, commanded by Coll: Brown."[389] These men comprised more than 10 percent of the troops under Clarke's command.[390]

By spring substantial numbers of black soldiers joined Indians and Loyalists in forays against the rebels. A Whig officer described a British raiding party that emerged from Savannah on April 2 as "a motly crew . . . consisting of British Hessians Indians and Negroes."[391] Later that month black foragers succeeded in driving a large quantity of cattle into Savannah, where there was a severe food shortage.[392] Rebel troops encountered "a strong party of Indians & Negroes" two miles from town in late May and defeated them, killing "three Indians & one Negroe." The same day a second rebel unit "broke up a Guard of Tories & Negroes at White Bluff," all of whom managed to escape.[393] On May 23 Wayne advanced his army within sight of Savannah, hoping to provoke a battle, but Clarke responded by "advancing a few Indians & negroes to the skirt of a swamp from whence they commenced a scattering and ineffective fire."[394]

Blacks who had remained outside Savannah also harassed the Whigs in company with Loyalists and Indians. "Some outlaying negroes" and a white Loyalist plundered several houses on the night of March 24 and "had the insolence to fire two Guns" at an American sentry early the next morning. Rebel troops captured the group, but all of the prisoners managed to escape.[395] A rebel scouting party searching for Indians in early April surprised the camp of "six White Men & some armd Negroes"; three whites and "a few" blacks escaped, and the rest were taken prisoner.[396]

Many Georgia Loyalists remained uncomfortable with the idea of arming blacks. In a petition to Governor Wright, they complained that Daniel McGirt's troops were plundering people without distinction and noted that McGirt, "not Content with Employing his Gange in the sole business of Robbery, had, & now has a Great number of Negroes arm'd." The petitioners alleged that McGirt had procured these blacks "from the Kings or Superintendants stores" under false pretenses.[397]

Georgia's Whigs disliked the idea of black soldiers even more than the Loyalists did. After the South Carolina Assembly had rejected John Laurens's proposal to arm slaves, Greene sent copies of his correspondence with South Carolina officials on the subject to Governor Martin in hopes that the Georgians might adopt the plan. Martin replied that he agreed in principle and promised to bring the matter before the assembly. He also warned Greene that "the raising of a body of blacks I am sure would answer every purpose intended; but, am afraid it will not go down with the people here." Nevertheless, Martin promised to do all he could to "carry it into effect."[398] Wayne also argued on behalf of the proposal, telling Martin that "this measure will become a matter of necessity if the report is true of the enemy forming a black Corps in Charlestown and Savannah."[399]

Greene made another appeal to the Georgians in June, asking them to form "a black Regiment" in order to meet the state's quota of troops. "It appears to me that you have no other resource but trying the experiment of raising a black Corps," Greene told Martin, noting that neither Georgia nor South Carolina had been able to enlist a sufficient number of white soldiers. Greene declared that he was so convinced of "the practicability success and advantage of the measure that I cannot help wishing to see it attempted."[400]

Like their counterparts in South Carolina, the members of Georgia's assembly refused to approve the use of black troops and instead opted to distribute slaves to recruits as an incentive to enlist. In May representatives voted to give every man who enlisted for three months' service "a Bounty of 20 Guins . . . to be paid in Negro's."[401] The following month the assembly decided that recruits for the state cavalry should also "be paid the bounty out of the Negroes provided for that Purpose," while Loyalists who switched their allegiance and assisted the Whigs would receive one slave each.[402]

Slaves became in effect the currency of the financially strapped state government, and officials routinely diverted manpower from military duty in order to gather slaves. To pay for horses purchased for the state legion, Martin sent troops to seize slaves from Loyalists' plantations near Savannah. All slaves thus taken were to be sent under guard to Augusta to be appraised and applied to the cost of the horses.[403] In addition, having learned that many Loyalist-owned slaves had "been feloniously carried out of this State" to South Carolina, Martin issued a proclamation on May 3 authorizing Capt. John Green to recover such slaves for the state's use. The governor ordered all civil and military officers to assist Green in this endeavor.[404] Martin also asked the governor of North Carolina, where authorities had recovered some slaves belonging to a Georgia Loyalist, to "have the said negroes disposed of as speedily as possible . . . for the benefit of this State."[405]

Martin was not without a personal interest in such matters. He had repeatedly asked the assembly to grant him some sort of financial assistance, since the state had no cash to pay salaries to its officials. The assembly eventually awarded him ten slaves from confiscated estates to support his family, and Martin promptly asked the commissioners of confiscated property "to select ten prime slaves" for him. Martin told the commissioners that if the price of slaves was not excessive, he would like to purchase six more.[406]

When Georgia's leaders discovered that the British were in the process of evacuating Savannah, they immediately tried to prevent the removal of Whig-owned slaves. The assembly demanded that Alured Clarke take steps to insure "that no negroes or other property" belonging to Americans should be taken from the state. If the British did carry off such slaves, the legislators threatened that Loyalists who remained in Georgia might suffer and that slave owners would be reimbursed for their lost property "out of debts owing to British Merchants."[407] The assembly also sent commissioners to Savannah to negotiate for the return of the slaves and asked Wayne to pressure Clarke for his cooperation.[408]

Clarke brushed aside the rebels' demands. "My intentions went no farther than to assist any of the Inhabitants of the neighbourhood of Savannah in the recovery of Such Negroes as had recently absented themselves from the service of their owner," he informed Wayne, "and this I have done in every instance within my power, though not altogether wth the Success I could have wished."[409]

Several months after the evacuation of Savannah, Governor Martin made another attempt to regain slaves claimed by Georgians. In November he appointed Col. John Eustace and Maj. Peter Deveaux as his representatives and sent them to Charleston to meet with Leslie. The pair brought Leslie a letter from Martin in which the governor stated that all reports indicated that Carleton had "directed the immediate restoration of such slaves as have eloped from the citizens of the United States, and have followed the armies and fleets of his Brittanic Majesty." Martin understood that there were many such slaves belonging to Georgians in Charleston and asked Leslie to assist Eustace and Deveaux in "that humane and generous purpose" of restoring these slaves to their owners. Leslie, however, refused to cooperate.[410]

About five thousand blacks, possibly as many as six thousand, left Savannah in the evacuation. Most went to East Florida or Jamaica; a few went to Indian territory or Spanish West Florida.[411] Nearly all slaves traveled in vessels provided by the British government and were sometimes allowed to choose their destinations.[412] David George was an exception. Because he wanted to be sure that he and his family went to Charleston, he saved money to pay for their passage on a private vessel. Unfortunately, some British soldiers robbed him. George earned more and sailed to Charleston, where he met a British major who "was very kind" to him. The officer found places for George and his family aboard a vessel bound for Halifax.[413]

Blacks who went to East Florida typically found themselves laboring to establish new plantations for Loyalist refugees. In the late autumn of 1781 Governor Tonyn and his council had engaged in a bitter dispute with the assembly over how slaves accused of crimes should be tried. Tonyn and the council advocated jury trials before provincial judges, while the assembly wished to leave such cases to local justices of the peace. Both sides, however, did agree on the role of slaves in defending the province. Officials asked the inhabitants to provide 10 percent of their slaves to work on the fortifications; when progress appeared too slow, many masters allocated 20 percent of their slaves to the project.[414]

With Spanish attack still a possibility in 1782, the assembly authorized Tonyn to arm every male in the province if an invasion occurred. Tonyn estimated that in addition to the white inhabitants, "about five hundred negroes might be trusted with arms." No invasion occurred, however; Spain acquired the province without bloodshed in the 1783 peace treaty.[415]

Through the months leading to the British evacuations of Georgia and South Carolina, the Loyalists, Indians, and slaves of the Deep South colonies had for the most part remained faithful to king and country. Neither defeat, loss of their property, nor fierce persecution swayed them from their allegiance. Even in the seemingly hopeless atmosphere that followed the disaster at Yorktown, all were willing to continue the fight; in fact, Loyalists advocated aggressive action in an effort to turn the tide against the rebels. Loyalists frequently cast aside old prejudices to make common cause with slaves and Indians against the king's enemies. Many Loyalists and some British officials believed, with considerable justification, that even in 1782 it was not too late to reverse the military situation in the South. Deprived by Parliament and the Rockingham ministry of leadership and the British army's support, however, the king's American supporters never got the chance to try. The British government had chosen to admit defeat, and Loyalists, Indians, and blacks had no alternative but to accept the outcome.

Conclusion

As THE WAR CAME TO A CLOSE, tens of thousands of the king's southern supporters struggled to establish themselves in new homes or to adjust to new conditions
in their old homes. For many, postwar life would be an endless battle fought with
few resources against circumstances they had not made and could not control.
Some would achieve a fairly comfortable new existence; a few would thrive; but
none would escape the stigma of defeat and of their association with a cause that
had become equated with tyranny. This stigma would endure and continue to
tarnish their reputations for more than two centuries after the last Loyalist, Indian,
and slave who fought alongside the British had departed this world.

The Loyalists had been slandered by their Whig neighbors as treacherous, cruel,
and self-serving even before the first shots of the Revolution had been fired in
Massachusetts; these accusations had grown more shrill and more frequent over
the course of the war. In the last years of the conflict, many Britons added their
voices to this chorus of denunciation. Members of Parliament who had opposed
the war, and some generals and politicians who had directed it, began to seek
excuses for Britain's defeat and found the Loyalists convenient scapegoats. The
Loyalists, these people charged, were liars and cowards who had encouraged the
British government to wage war in America with promises of support and then
shrank from battle, preferring to let the king's troops do the fighting for them.

Although this characterization of the Loyalists has persisted to the present
day, many British officials who were in a position to judge staunchly defended
the Loyalists from their critics. Maj. Patrick Ferguson declared repeatedly that
the Loyalists were courageous and committed and needed only confidence to
improve their effectiveness. Sir Henry Clinton argued that the Loyalists had
never been given a fair chance to prove themselves because the army had never
given them adequate support. In addition, Lord Rawdon, after serving more
than a year in South Carolina, testified to "the fidelity of the Loyalists" and
criticized the "inhuman disregard with which they have been repaid."[1]

"It has been the fashion to say," Rawdon wrote, "that the Loyalists were few
in number; & that their activity in our cause was never such as ought to have a
claim upon our gratitude." However, he asserted, his extensive experience in the
South enabled him to refute this "most unjust opinion." Rawdon pointed out

that over five thousand whites had left Charleston at the evacuation, "all of whom had sacrificed their possessions thro' attachment to us." In addition, "a very considerable number" of Loyalists chose to remain in South Carolina, "preferring the hazard of the Whig's vengeance, to the danger of the Seas, at that inclement season, in such miserable Craft" as were provided for them. "This List of Sufferers," he declared, "surely is not to be reckoned small."[2]

Concerning the accusations that the Loyalists had not exerted themselves in the king's behalf, Rawdon explained that many difficulties had arisen in employing them. "It does not seem as if Lord Cornwallis had ever thought it necessary before his Victory over Gates to embody any of the Country People; on the contrary, the Proclamations of that Date enjoin a quiet residence in their several districts," he wrote. After militia units had been organized, keeping them in the field for any length of time proved impractical. The subsistence of both Loyalists and British troops in South Carolina "depended on the cultivation of the Country, which was already grievously wasted" by the ravages of war; thus, "the most serious distress must have been entailed upon us by such a number being withheld from the tillage of their Farms." The drawback to this was that when Loyalists stayed at home to raise crops, they were vulnerable to surprise attack by rebel partisans.[3]

When embodied, Rawdon insisted, the Loyalists fought well, if not always successfully, and demonstrated remarkable persistence in the face of adversity. "If a succession of misfortunes diminished the numbers & broke the spirits of these people, the circumstance does not weaken the testimony of their attachment," he declared. Rawdon added that even in eastern South Carolina, where Loyalists were far fewer in relation to the Whigs than in the backcountry and therefore "were more exposed to powerful efforts of the Enemy: Yet on several occasions they manifested a fidelity, which in other instances would have been universally extolled. A number of them fell in unsuccessful skirmishes; & still more of them were murdered in detail." The weight of evidence, Rawdon concluded, proved "that in the Two Carolinas we had numerous Friends, who, to the hazard of their Lives, to the sacrifice of their Families, to the utter ruin of their Possessions, adhered to us under every change of Fortune."[4]

Gen. James Murray believed that the ministry may have overestimated the number of Loyalists in the colonies, but that the key problem was the army's inability to mobilize more than a fraction of the Loyalists. Murray attributed this in part to the constantly shifting military fortunes: the number of professed Loyalists increased when the army was successful and declined in times of defeat. In addition, he pointed out that "the haughtiness of our Officers," along with differing views on how the war should be conducted, impeded cooperation between the army and the Loyalists. He identified the worst problem, however, as a lack of sustained support from the king's troops. "Our Evacuation of places, & leaving" Loyalists "to the vengeance of the Rebels after they had been induced to discover themselves, have rendered many of them hitherto Cautious," Murray observed. The Loyalists could hardly be expected to make greater exertions in light of "the disgusting Experience they have had of Us."[5]

Another British officer, Frederick Mackenzie, agreed with Murray. Although he often criticized Loyalists for their failure to turn out in support of the army, Mackenzie conceded that such behavior was to be expected. On numerous occasions, he noted, the army had arrived in a region, called on the Loyalists to join them, and withdrawn shortly afterward, "abandoning the people to the fury of their bitterest Enemies." If the Loyalists became hesitant to declare themselves after such incidents, they had good reason for their reluctance.[6]

Many Loyalists held similar opinions. Pennsylvanian Joseph Galloway, an exile in London, blamed British officers for first failing to employ the Loyalists and then leaving them exposed to Whig brutality. "Instead of rejecting the loyal force of the country, and daily sacrificing it to the savage barbarity of rebellion, *enjoin our Generals to embrace it with zeal and cordiality, and to make use of its aid in suppressing the rebellion*," he suggested in a 1782 plea to continue the war. Galloway insisted that there remained "multitudes of our fellow subjects, attached to us by principle, and groaning under the horrid tyranny and cruelty of the usurpers," who stood "ready to unite in the proper measures for delivering themselves from their present slavery, and for restoring the government of your Sovereign." He asked what measures had been taken "to embody, arm, and support the loyalists," or to inspirit them, and provided his own answer: "There has been scarcely one!" Galloway singled out Cornwallis for particular criticism, asserting that the earl failed to secure South Carolina and instead raced off into North Carolina like "a winged Mercury" in futile pursuit of Greene's army.[7]

Gov. James Wright too placed much of the blame for the loss of the southern provinces on Cornwallis, while defending the efforts of Georgia's Loyalists. Georgia "was Peopling very fast the latter End of the year 1780. when great Numbers of Loyal Subjects were Flocking in, to Settle, Expecting His Majesty's Protection, and Safety, from the Tyranny & Oppression of the Rebellion.—and When the Loyal Subjects in that Province, were beginning to Raise their Drooping Spirits, & to Collect & Improve the Remains of their Scattered & almost Ruined & lost Property," Wright remarked. "But alas! . . . before the Minds of the People were Settled, & wholly Reconciled to a return of their Allegiance," most of the British troops were withdrawn from Georgia. Encouraged by the weakness of the British garrison and Cornwallis's disappearance into North Carolina, the rebels began "to Raise Commotions . . . & assassinated & Otherwise Cruelly Murdered, as Many Loyalists as they Could come at, & upwards of an Hundred Good Men, in the Space of one Month, fell Victims to their Loyalty, & the Cruelty of the Rebels." Overpowered and without aid, by June 1781 fourteen hundred people had sought refuge in Savannah. Wright noted that his pleas for troops had been ignored, even though in his opinion five hundred regulars would have been sufficient to resurrect Loyalist spirits and retake the province.[8]

Even some Whigs recognized the steadfast commitment of many southern Loyalists. William Pierce observed that large numbers of people had "been uniform in their opposition, and have favored the British measures through all the mutations of fortune. Such men appear to have a fixed principle for the governing rule of their conduct, and, although they stand confessed my enemies, yet I cannot help admiring and esteeming them."[9] Capt. Tarleton Brown of the South Carolina Whig militia likewise acknowledged, albeit in harsher terms, that the Loyalists had made significant contributions to the British cause. Had the British not been "aided and abetted by those unprincipled and bloodthirsty tools . . . the enemy would never have gained a solid foothold upon our shores," he fumed.[10]

In addition to such testimony, the very nature of the war in the South demonstrated that Loyalists there were numerous, courageous, and steadfast in the face of brutal persecution. Long before British troops established a foothold in Georgia or South Carolina, Loyalists in both provinces took up arms to oppose the rebels, turning the contest into a genuine civil war that continued long after officials in London ordered a cessation of operations against the Whigs. In dozens of small battles and untold numbers of skirmishes, Loyalists fought rebels without either British prompting or British support.

Nevertheless, the negative myths about the Loyalists became widely accepted. In Britain the views of politically influential critics such as Earl Cornwallis and Gen. Charles O'Hara gained more credence than those of lower-ranking officers or the discredited Clinton. Across the Atlantic the victorious Whigs found that the stereotype of the greedy, vicious, craven Loyalist made an ideal villain in the epic story of the glorious American cause. Loyalists could also be made to shoulder the blame for the cruelty that had marred what the Whigs considered a virtuous struggle. By portraying the Loyalists as instigators of the murders and hangings that characterized the war in the South, Americans could justify their commission of such crimes as legitimate acts of vengeance against a ruthless foe.

Eventually myth became accepted as truth. The British government's southern strategy was considered doomed from the outset, since it depended on Loyalists who were not there. According to the myth, the few Loyalists who did come forward alienated the people by murdering and plundering across South Carolina and Georgia but were too cowardly to face rebel troops in the field.

Once the myths are pruned away, however, the historical record tells a very different story. It is an account of people who remained loyal to their king and suffered greatly for their allegiance. Beginning in 1775 Loyalists were beaten, tarred and feathered, imprisoned, harassed, and sometimes murdered. Their property was seized; they were banished from their lifelong homes or fled voluntarily to escape the rebels' wrath. Yet, their loyalty to Britain remained unshaken. When British troops finally arrived in the South, some Loyalists, intimidated by five years of savage persecution, hesitated to declare themselves. However, many thousands came forward and served faithfully throughout the war. Whig partisans launched a campaign of violence more brutal than the Loyalists had previously experienced; yet, the king's supporters persevered. Their neighbors and the British officer they trusted most were slaughtered at King's Mountain, and the survivors were forced to undergo the eighteenth-century equivalent of the Bataan Death March, but the Loyalists soon returned to the field. When Nathanael Greene forced the British to abandon the Georgia and South Carolina backcountry, thousands of Loyalists left their homes and marched hundreds of miles to Savannah and Charleston rather than forsake their principles. Others remained behind and continued the fight from the woods and swamps. After Parliament ordered an end to offensive operations against the rebels, the Loyalists pleaded unsuccessfully with British officers for permission to carry the fight to the Whigs. The Loyalists' story is one of fidelity, courage, and persistence in the face of adversity, and it is every bit as heroic as the story of the Whigs' fight for independence.

Like the Loyalists, Indians also found themselves cast as villains in the Revolutionary saga. In the eyes of most Americans, this was hardly a new role; the Indians who allied themselves with the British in the Revolution merely added another chapter to a story of hostility and violence that had begun in 1607. Whether alone or in partnership with France or Britain, the Indians had long been considered bloodthirsty savages blocking Americans' path to land and wealth in the West.

Again, Britons joined Americans in denouncing the Indians. From the start of the war, members of the parliamentary opposition had assailed the ministry for employing the barbaric, murderous Indians against the rebels. Even Lord George Germain came to criticize the Indians in the latter years of the war, declaring that their feeble military contributions were out of all proportion to the expense incurred in supplying them. Rarely did anyone in Britain try to defend the Native Americans. Galloway made one of the few attempts to do so, replying to those who accused them of savagery that if the Indians had "killed *in war* a few *rebels,* who, they know, will deprive them of their country, and of their existence as a people as soon as they are independent, the rebel states have with yet more cruelty and less justice *murdered in cool blood* four times as many loyalists."[11]

To add injury to insult, the British ministry completely ignored the Indians' interests during the peace negotiations and in 1783 ceded all of the territory from the Appalachians to the Mississippi—land claimed by the Indians—to the new United States. This betrayal shocked the southern nations. Alexander McGillivray drew up a protest on behalf of the Creeks, Cherokees, and Chickasaws, asserting that since the Native Americans had not been party to the agreement, they did not consider themselves bound by it. McGillivray observed that the Indians had not given Britain any authority to dispose of their lands, "unless fighting by the side of [the king's] soldiers in the day of battle and Spilling our best blood in the Service of his Nation can be deemed so."[12]

If the Indians' wartime assistance did not meet British expectations, most of the blame lay with the ministry and the generals. True, the Cherokees had gone to war against John Stuart's orders in 1776 and suffered a defeat that made other nations reluctant to commit to the British alliance. However, the Cherokees had nevertheless waged sporadic warfare against the Whigs into 1782. The Creeks and Choctaws helped forestall one Spanish attack on Pensacola and bore the largest burden of the defense during the 1781 siege, even though Gen. John Campbell's arrogant attitude resulted in fewer Indians turning out to assist the British. The Chickasaws maintained a fairly effective blockade of the Mississippi River throughout the war, while the Seminoles were the bulwark of East Florida's defense. The Cherokees and Creeks disappointed Germain by launching few raids on the southern frontier, but in the early years of the war they realized that without British support, launching a war in the backcountry could accomplish nothing of significance. When the Cherokees and the Creeks announced their readiness to fight in 1780, Cornwallis rejected their offer. By the time the siege of Pensacola ended and the Creeks were available to assist the British elsewhere in 1781, the king's troops and Loyalists had been driven from the backcountry, making effective cooperation impossible. Yet, even when the Indians did not provide direct support, the threat of attack caused the Whigs to divert substantial numbers of militia to the frontier, complicating the Continental army's manpower shortages, although British commanders failed to take advantage of this.

Slaves too made important contributions to the royal cause but quickly became the forgotten member of the trinity of Britain's southern supporters. The Whigs, having denominated themselves as defenders of liberty, preferred not to dwell on the fact that thousands of their slaves, over whom they claimed to exercise a benevolent paternalism, had seen the British army as the real agent of freedom. These slaves had served the king as laborers, spies, messengers, and occasionally as soldiers in hopes of securing their release from bondage.

Only a small percentage of slaves who joined the British earned their freedom after the war. The Black Dragoons, for example, became the nucleus of a 264-man unit that arrived in St. Lucia in December 1782 and "became a permanent part of the British West India military establishment" the following year.[13] Other free blacks went to the West Indies, Britain, or Nova Scotia, while most of those who left Savannah and Charleston remained enslaved on West Indian plantations.[14]

Even if only a small number of blacks realized immediate gains from their service, they and their descendants benefited in the long term. American independence "helped the cause of abolitionists in both Britain and the United States: it more than halved the number of slaves in the British Empire" and divided slave owners on the mainland from those in the Caribbean, thus weakening the proslavery lobby in Parliament. In 1833 Parliament abolished slavery throughout the British Empire.[15] Those slaves who had gambled on finding freedom with the British had finally won, whereas those who remained with the liberty-loving Whigs would have to wait another thirty years and endure a bloody war.

Given the valuable contributions of Loyalists, Indians, and slaves to the British during the war in the South, why did the southern strategy fail? One reason was strategy: when Cornwallis took his army into Virginia and allowed Greene to bring the Continental troops back to South Carolina, it became impossible for the British to hold their widely scattered outposts and made withdrawal to the coast inevitable. Even then, the British could have recovered had not Cornwallis's surrender at Yorktown led Parliament to put an end to offensive operations in America. A major flaw in policy was a second reason. Although the ministry counted on support from Loyalists, Indians, and slaves from the beginning of the war, neither Germain nor anyone else devised a plan to bring the three peoples together in the king's service. As a result, these incompatible allies fought separate wars against the Whigs (and occasionally against each other), while the British army also often fought in isolation. Thus, the efforts of the British army and its supporters were diffused rather than concentrated, making the task of regaining the southern provinces much more difficult.

A third reason for the British failure to derive full support from Loyalists, slaves, and Indians lay with the Whigs. While British officers hesitated to punish rebels who had violated their parole or committed atrocities, the Whigs showed no such compunction. Anyone who challenged rebel authority was likely to suffer terribly. Loyalists were shot, hanged, beaten; rebel militia burned Indian towns and crops, killed Indians regardless of age or sex, and sold captives into slavery; slaves caught assisting the British faced whippings, hanging, even beheading. This relentless cruelty, as intended, intimidated many supporters of the British into remaining inactive.

A question is whether the large number of Loyalists, Indians, and slaves who were undaunted by Whig terrorism could have fought side by side. The answer is that they could have, and sometimes did. Since 1776 some backcountry whites had fought alongside the Cherokees, and by 1782 the two groups cooperated with considerable effectiveness. The same was true of whites and blacks. The Black Dragoons rode into battle alongside white militiamen, and parties of blacks and whites raided behind Whig lines late in the war. During the siege of Savannah, Loyalists, Indians, and slaves fought together and contributed to the successful defense of the town against a vastly larger force—an important lesson for the future had anyone in the ministry or military command bothered to heed it. If Germain and the generals had followed Lord Dunmore's advice and brought every supporter of the king, regardless of race, into action against the rebels, victory in the South was well within the British grasp. British officials needed only to explain the need for such a policy, secure cooperation, and then sort out everyone's situation after the war was won.

There remains one other intriguing possibility, which would have spared the ministers from dealing with complex racial issues and might have won the war. Had the government chosen in 1776 to strike at what it knew was the soft underbelly of the rebellion, the southern provinces, rather than to direct a blow at the heart of the Revolution in the North, it is hard to imagine how the Whigs could have succeeded.

In this hypothetical scenario, Gen. William Howe brings his massive invasion armada to Georgia and South Carolina in the summer of 1776. Five thousand British troops land at Savannah, while Howe and the remaining twenty-five thousand soldiers follow Clinton's route and attack Charleston. Both towns would have fallen within days, and powerful British columns could have advanced into the backcountry and North Carolina with little opposition. The Loyalists, emboldened by this show of force and not intimidated by five years of persecution, take control of the provincial governments. Because the Whigs have been deprived of five years to establish the civil and military machinery of government, there is little basis on which to build partisan resistance. Far to the north George Washington faces a dilemma. Does he risk marching southward to aid the rebels there or hold his ground in case the British mount a later strike in New York or Pennsylvania? If he chooses to march south, it is hard to imagine many New England soldiers agreeing to undertake the trek when British forces are nearby in Quebec and Nova Scotia. In addition, it would have been almost impossible for the poorly trained and disciplined, inadequately supplied Continentals to make such a march. Had the army not evaporated along the way, the exhausted, hungry soldiers would have offered only feeble opposition to Howe's regulars. British troops might have been at the Susquehanna River, facing almost no organized resistance, by the spring of 1777.

Such a plan, of course, would have had to originate in London, as would a policy to unite Loyalists, Indians, and slaves into an effective force to operate in conjunction with British troops. That British officials never addressed the matter was not the fault of those in the Deep South colonies who fought so valiantly for King George. Without adequate guidance from the government, and often ignored by the generals whom they were supposed to assist, Loyalists, Indians, and slaves made significant contributions that enabled the British army to come within a hairsbreadth of retaining Georgia, South Carolina, and the Floridas. Their achievements, however, have never been properly recognized; instead they were unjustly made the scapegoats for defeat.

ABBREVIATIONS

AHR	*American Historical Review*
BPL	Boston Public Library, Boston, Mass.
CGHS	*Collections of the Georgia Historical Society*
CP	Cornwallis Papers
CRG	*Colonial Records of Georgia*
DAR	*Documents of the American Revolution*
DLAR	David Library of the American Revolution, Washington Crossing, Pa.
EHR	*English Historical Review*
FHQ	*Florida Historical Quarterly*
GHQ	*Georgia Historical Quarterly*
GHS	Georgia Historical Society, Savannah
HCIL	Harriet C. Irving Library, University of New Brunswick, Fredericton
HDAR	Hessian Documents of the American Revolution
HSP	Historical Society of Pennsylvania, Philadelphia
JAH	*Journal of American History*
JSH	*Journal of Southern History*
LHQ	*Louisiana Historical Quarterly*
LOC	Library of Congress, Washington, D.C.
MAH	*Magazine of American History*
MHM	*Maryland Historical Magazine*
MHS	Maryland Historical Society, Baltimore
MVHR	*Mississippi Valley Historical Review*
NAS	National Archives of Scotland, Edinburgh
NBM	New Brunswick Museum, St. John
NCHR	*North Carolina Historical Review*
NCSA	North Carolina State Archives, Raleigh
NYHS	New-York Historical Society, New York

NYPL	New York Public Library, New York
NYSL	New York State Library, Albany
PAH	*Papers of Alexander Hamilton*
PERK	Perkins Library, Duke University, Durham, N.C.
PHL	*Papers of Henry Laurens*
PJA	*Papers of John Adams*
PMHB	*Pennsylvania Magazine of History and Biography*
PNG	*Papers of Nathanael Greene*
PRO	Public Record Office (United Kingdom)
PTJ	*Papers of Thomas Jefferson*
RAM	*Report on American Manuscripts*
SCDAH	South Carolina Department of Archives and History, Columbia
SCHGM	*South Carolina Historical and Genealogical Magazine*
SCHM	*South Carolina Historical Magazine*
SCHS	South Carolina Historical Society, Charleston
SCL	South Caroliniana Library, Columbia, S.C.
SHC	Southern Historical Collection, University of North Carolina, Chapel Hill
SLSC	Swem Library Special Collections, College of William & Mary, Williamsburg, Va.
WLCL	William L. Clements Library, Ann Arbor, Mich.
WMQ	*William & Mary Quarterly*

NOTES

INTRODUCTION

1. Don Higginbotham, "Reflections on the War of Independence, Modern Guerrilla Warfare, and the War in Vietnam," in *Arms and Independence,* ed. Hoffman and Albert, 18. See also Paul David Nelson, "British Conduct of the Revolutionary War," *JAH,* in which Nelson states that Loyalist support in the South was less than expected, "partly because loyalists were restrained from joining the British army by the activity of patriot guerrillas, but mostly because loyalist numbers had been greatly exaggerated in the first place" (628). H. T. Dickinson makes the same assertion; see Dickinson, ed., *Britain and the American Revolution,* 16. For similar assessments, see Valentine, *Lord George Germain,* 433; Calhoon, *Loyalists in Revolutionary America,* xi; Lambert, *South Carolina Loyalists,* 307; and Pancake, *This Destructive War,* 3.

2. Higginbotham, *Daniel Morgan,* 101.

3. Higginbotham, *War of American Independence,* 135.

4. Fortescue, *War of Independence,* 21–22.

5. Mackesy, *War for America,* 32.

6. Mackesy, *Could the British Have Won the War of Independence?,* 10.

7. David K. Wilson, *Southern Strategy,* xiii.

8. See Agniel, *Late Affair,* 9, 12; and Buchanan, *Road to Guilford Courthouse,* 105.

9. John Shy quoted in Paul David Nelson, "British Conduct of the Revolutionary War," 638.

10. Alden, *South in the Revolution,* 324–25. A few historians agree with Alden's assessment; see Callahan, *Royal Raiders,* 37; and Lumpkin, *From Savannah to Yorktown,* 9.

11. Weigley, *Partisan War,* 10.

12. Paul Smith, *Loyalists and Redcoats,* viii–ix.

13. Ibid., ix.

14. Ibid., 58. Piers Mackesy, departing from his opinion that British officials vastly overestimated the number of Loyalists, takes a position similar to that of Paul Smith. Mackesy writes that the British belief in Loyalist strength "was nearer the truth than was once supposed," and that "American loyalists were indeed numerous. But . . . they lacked organisation, unity of interests, and a common standard around which they could rally" (Mackesy, *War for America,* 36).

15. Wallace Brown, *Good Americans,* 65.

16. Ann Gorman Condon, "Foundations of Loyalism," in *Loyal Americans,* ed. Allen, 2.

17. Charles, Earl Cornwallis, to Alexander Leslie, November 12, 1780, in Cornwallis, *Correspondence,* 1:69.

18. Chastellux, *Travels in North America,* 2:570.

19. Ramsay, *History of the Revolution of South-Carolina*; McCrady, *History of South Carolina in the Revolution*; McCall, *History of Georgia.* A rare exception to the endless attacks on Loyalists, from an American writer, is Alexander Garden's praise for the

Loyalists' "zeal and activity in the cause in which they had engaged." Garden describes the Loyalists' efforts as being "of the highest utility to our enemies, and leads to the developement of a melancholy fact, that in almost every instance where our armies have been foiled in action, the opposition proceeded from our own countrymen." Garden, who served in the rebel forces and wrote his history forty years after the war ended, may have been influenced by the fact that his father, Dr. Benjamin Garden, was a staunch Loyalist. Yet, Garden, referring to the operations of Loyalist units such as the British Legion and the partisan bands of Daniel McGirt and David Fanning, criticizes "the deeds of horror perpetrated by this merciless banditti." See Garden, *Anecdotes of the Revolutionary War,* 258–59.

20. Joseph Johnson, *Traditions and Reminiscences,* 106.

21. M. A. Moore, *Life of Lacey,* 11.

22. Holman, "William Gilmore Simms' Picture of the Revolution," *JSH,* 460.

23. Simms, *Joscelyn,* 76, 117, 296, 298.

24. Simms, *Scout,* 109, 160.

25. Simms, *Eutaw,* e.g., 10, 233, 468.

26. Hesseltine, "Lyman Draper and the South," *JSH,* 20, 27.

27. Draper, *King's Mountain.*

28. Raddall, "Tarleton's Legion," 1, 2.

29. Royster, *Revolutionary People at War,* 3.

30. Higginbotham, "Reflections on the War of Independence," 5, 7, 11, 20–21. John Shy expressed a similar view, writing that British support for bitter, vengeful Loyalists, along with efforts to gain assistance from Indians and slaves, had "ultimately counterproductive effects." See Shy, "American Society and Its War for Independence," in *Reconsiderations on the Revolutionary War,* ed. Higginbotham, 81.

31. Kierner, *Southern Women in Revolution,* 17.

32. Edgar, *Partisans and Redcoats,* xvi, xvii, 71.

33. Fortescue, *War of Independence,* 259.

34. Searcy, *Georgia-Florida Contest,* 171.

35. Wallace Brown, *King's Friends,* 213–14. Brown writes that South Carolinians filed 328 claims, representing .47 percent of the province's prewar white population. This proportion, while slightly less than that in New York, was "much higher than in any other colony . . . except Georgia." Among Charleston residents, the percentage of inhabitants filing claims stood at 2.17, making that place "the most strongly loyal city in all America," with a proportion more than four times higher than that of New York. For the difficulty of using the Loyalist claims as a basis for statistical analysis, see Fingerhut, "Uses and Abuses of the American Loyalists' Claims," *WMQ,* 245–58.

36. The issues of Loyalist motivation and political belief are for the most part beyond the scope of this study. For information on these topics, see Wallace Brown, *Good Americans;* Calhoon, *Loyalists in Revolutionary America;* Wallace Brown, *King's Friends;* William H. Nelson, *American Tory;* Ann Gorman Condon, "Marching to a Different Drummer—The Political Philosophy of the American Loyalists," in *Red, White, and True Blue,* ed. Esmond Wright; and Condon, "Foundations of Loyalism," 2–4.

37. Morrill, *Southern Campaigns of the Revolution,* 3.

38. Hall, *Land and Allegiance,* esp. xi–xii.

39. Klein, *Unification of a Slave State,* 81–82.

40. Hessian officer quoted in Uhlendorf, ed. and trans., *Siege of Charleston,* 11.

41. O'Donnell, *Southern Indians,* ix.

42. Peter Marshall, "First Americans and Last Loyalists: An Indian Dilemma in War and Peace," in *Red, White, and True Blue,* ed. Esmond Wright, 33.

43. Edward J. Cashin, "'But Brothers, It Is Our Land We Are Talking About': Winners and Losers in the Georgia Backcountry," in *Uncivil War,* ed. Hoffman et al., 249–50.

44. Gary Nash, "The Forgotten Experience: Indians, Blacks, and the American Revolution," in *American Revolution,* ed. Fowler and Coyle, 39.

45. David Ramsay quoted in Shaffer, "Between Two Worlds," *JSH,* 190.

46. Nash, *Race and Revolution,* 57, 59–60.

47. Nash, "Forgotten Experience," 36.

48. Berlin, *Many Thousands Gone,* 219–20.

49. Peter H. Wood, "'The Dream Deferred': Black Freedom Struggles on the Eve of White Independence," in *In Resistance,* ed. Okihiro, 173. Benjamin Quarles expresses a similar opinion in "The Revolutionary War as a Black Declaration of Independence," in *Slavery and Freedom,* ed. Berlin and Hoffman, 290.

50. Ellen Wilson, *Loyal Blacks,* 21; Quarles, *Negro in the Revolution,* 37.

51. Ellen Wilson, *Loyal Blacks,* 3.

52. MacLeod, *Slavery, Race and the Revolution,* 136.

53. Jordan, *White over Black,* 112, 115.

54. Quarles, *Negro in the Revolution,* 14.

55. Berlin, *Many Thousands Gone,* 296–97, 298.

56. Ibid., 91.

57. Frey, *Water from the Rock,* 113.

58. Peter H. Wood, "'The Facts Speak Loudly Enough': Exploring Early Southern Black History," in *Devil's Lane,* ed. Clinton and Gillespie, 12.

59. Willis, "Divide and Rule," *Journal of Negro History,* 157–76, esp. 157, 168, 160.

60. J. Leitch Wright, *Only Land They Knew,* 272–73.

61. Nash, "Forgotten Experience," 32.

CHAPTER 1: REVOLUTION COMES TO THE DEEP SOUTH

1. Alden, *South in the Revolution,* 24–25; Weir, *"Most Important Epocha,"* 3–5.

2. Weir, *"Most Important Epocha,"* 15, 17, 21.

3. Ibid., 32, 34–35; Walsh, *Charleston's Sons of Liberty,* 44, 45.

4. Walsh, *Charleston's Sons of Liberty,* 48, 50.

5. Maier, *From Resistance to Revolution,* 122.

6. Weir, *"Most Important Epocha,"* 36–37.

7. Main, "Government by the People," *WMQ,* 396.

8. Klein, *Unification of a Slave State,* 47–48, 74; Main, "Government by the People," 398.

9. Walsh, *Charleston's Sons of Liberty,* 31. The 2002 value of the contribution is based on information at Economic History Services, http://eh.net/hmit, using the pound's value in 1780.

10. Greene, "Bridge to Revolution," *JSH,* 19–52, quotation, 52.

11. Weir, *"Most Important Epocha,"* 51–52; Maier, *From Resistance to Revolution,* 275–76.

12. Weir, *"Most Important Epocha,"* 52–55.

13. Ibid., 58–59, 62–64, 68.

14. Greene, "Role of the Lower Houses of Assembly," *JSH*, 455.

15. William Bull to Second Earl of Dartmouth, March 15, 1775, Second Earl of Dartmouth Papers, no. 1107.

16. Charleston Whigs quoted in Maier, *From Resistance to Revolution*, 121.

17. Klein, *Unification of a Slave State*, 9; Edgar, *Partisans and Redcoats*, xiii.

18. Jordan, *White over Black*, 85.

19. Maier, "Charleston Mob and Popular Politics," *Perspectives in American History*, 176–77.

20. Berlin, *Many Thousands Gone*, 175.

21. Morgan, "Black Life in Eighteenth-Century Charleston," *Perspectives in American History*, 208–9.

22. Olwell, *Masters, Slaves, and Subjects*, 31.

23. Remonstrance of the Regulators to the S.C. Assembly, 1767, in Woodmason, *Carolina Backcountry*, 226.

24. Olwell, *Masters, Slaves, and Subjects*, 31.

25. Woodmason, *Carolina Backcountry*, 93–94.

26. Ibid., 121.

27. Ibid., 93–94.

28. Ibid., 121.

29. Coleman, *American Revolution in Georgia*, 3, 53.

30. Abbot, *Royal Governors*, 104–5, 107, 113–15; Maier, *From Resistance to Revolution*, 84; Coleman, *American Revolution in Georgia*, 18–22.

31. James Wright quoted in Maier, *From Resistance to Revolution*, 92.

32. Abbot, *Royal Governors*, 126–27, 134, 140–43; Coleman, *American Revolution in Georgia*, 26–27.

33. Kenneth Coleman, "James Wright and the Origins of the Revolution in Georgia," in *Human Dimensions of Nation Making*, ed. James Martin; Coleman, *American Revolution in Georgia*, 28–32.

34. Abbot, *Royal Governors*, 156; Coleman, *American Revolution in Georgia*, 34–37.

35. Abbot, *Royal Governors*, 158, 162; Edward J. Cashin, "Sowing the Wind: Governor Wright and the Georgia Backcountry on the Eve of the Revolution," in *Forty Years of Diversity*, ed. Jackson and Spalding, 240–43.

36. Coleman, *American Revolution in Georgia*, 40–42.

37. Jackson, "Consensus and Conflict," *GHQ*, 389–91.

38. Coleman, *American Revolution in Georgia*, 42–43. For examples of some of the dissenting petitions, see "Dissent to the Resolutions of August 10, 1774," "St. Paul Parish Dissent to August 10 Meeting," and "Kyokee and Broad River Settlements Dissent to August 10 Resolutions," in *Georgia and the Revolution*, ed. Killion and Waller, 107–11.

39. Coleman, *American Revolution in Georgia*, 45–49.

40. Jackson, "Consensus and Conflict," 392; Coleman, *American Revolution in Georgia*, 49–50.

41. Jackson, "Consensus and Conflict," 392–94; Abbot, *Royal Governors*, 171, 173, 178–79; Coleman, *American Revolution in Georgia*, 52.

42. Coleman, *American Revolution in Georgia*, 53.

43. Alden, *South in the Revolution*, 9; Bennett and Lennon, *Quest for Glory*, 45–46.

44. J. Leitch Wright, *Florida in the Revolution*, 2–4, 6, 7, 12. Population estimates for East Florida vary. In a different essay, Wright provides a figure of two thousand

slaves, who he states outnumbered the white population by a two to one ratio; see J. Leitch Wright, "Blacks in British East Florida," *FHQ,* 427. Another estimate is that only one-third of the province's three thousand inhabitants were slaves; see Troxler, "Refuge, Resistance, and Reward," *JSH,* 566.

45. Williams, "Negro Slavery in Florida," *FHQ,* 94, 96.

46. Barrs, *East Florida,* 3.

47. Kerr, "Stamp Act in the Floridas," *MVHR,* 463; J. Leitch Wright, *Florida in the Revolution,* 17, 18.

48. Barrs, *East Florida,* 4; J. Leitch Wright, *Florida in the Revolution,* 15, 17, 19.

49. J. Leitch Wright, *Florida in the Revolution,* 22, 23–24.

50. Fabel, *Economy of West Florida,* 108–9; Fitzpatrick, *Merchant of Manchac,* 9; J. Leitch Wright, *Florida in the Revolution,* 2, 4, 9–10; Cecil Johnson, *British West Florida,* 3, 149; Howard, "Some Economic Aspects of West Florida," *JSH,* 203, 205.

51. Kerr, "Stamp Act in the Floridas," 465–68; Starr, *Tories, Dons, and Rebels,* 37–40, 42.

52. Starr, *Tories, Dons, and Rebels,* 36.

53. Ibid., 11–12, 16–17; Cecil Johnson, *British West Florida,* 60–62, 69–71, 76.

54. Cecil Johnson, *British West Florida,* 136, 138; Starr, *Tories, Dons, and Rebels,* 28.

55. Garland Taylor, "Colonial Settlement and Revolutionary Activity in West Florida," *MVHR,* 353–54; Robin F. A. Fabel, "Born of War, Killed by War: The Company of Military Adventurers in West Florida," in *Adapting to Conditions,* ed. Ultee, 109–11.

56. Starr, *Tories, Dons, and Rebels,* 45–46.

57. Cecil Johnson, *British West Florida,* 144, 147; J. Leitch Wright, *Florida in the Revolution,* 20, 22; Starr, *Tories, Dons, and Rebels,* 48–49, 230. Starr notes that even the figures for those granted lands cannot be exactly determined since many grantees listed family members who may not have accompanied them to West Florida.

58. Sosin, *Revolutionary Frontier,* 5.

59. Merrell, "Indians' New World," *WMQ,* 541, 544, 554, 555–59.

60. Merrell, *Indians' New World,* 214.

61. Hatley, *Dividing Paths,* 139–40, 217.

62. Dowd, *Spirited Resistance,* 48; Hatley, *Dividing Paths,* 217–18.

63. Lumpkin, *From Savannah to Yorktown,* 19.

64. Calloway, *American Revolution in Indian Country,* 185.

65. J. Leitch Wright, *Creeks and Seminoles,* 1, 3, 12.

66. Saunt, *New Order of Things,* 19, 22, 32.

67. J. Leitch Wright, *Creeks and Seminoles,* 113–14.

68. Boyd and Latorre, "Spanish Interest in British Florida," *FHQ,* 92–97.

69. J. Leitch Wright, *Only Land They Knew,* 145; Calloway, *American Revolution in Indian Country,* 246–47, 249, 255.

70. Saunt, *New Order of Things,* 51; Braund, "Creek Indians, Blacks, and Slavery," *JSH,* 608–9; Searcy, "Introduction of Slavery," *GHQ,* 22–23, 24.

71. White, *Roots of Dependency,* 4.

72. O'Brien, *Choctaws,* xvi, 13, 15, 16, 18, 19.

73. White, *Roots of Dependency,* 40.

74. O'Brien, *Choctaws,* 27; White, *Roots of Dependency,* 65, 70, 72; Greg O'Brien, "Protecting Trade through War: Choctaw Elites and British Occupation of the Floridas," in *Empire and Others,* ed. Daunton and Halpern, 149.

75. White, *Roots of Dependency,* 75.

76. O'Brien, *Choctaws,* 27, 83.

77. White, *Roots of Dependency,* 77–78.

78. Calloway, *American Revolution in Indian Country,* 213, 214, 216–17.

79. Gibson, *Chickasaws,* 59–60, 62, 65, 124.

80. Ibid., 65–67.

81. Ibid., 63.

82. Christie, *Crisis of Empire,* 26.

83. Alden, *John Stuart,* 159, 164–65; Snapp, *John Stuart,* 56–57.

84. Alden, *John Stuart,* 336.

85. Snapp, *John Stuart,* 2–3.

86. Ibid., 57, 59.

87. O'Donnell, *Southern Indians,* 7.

88. Snapp, *John Stuart,* 60–62, 69–71, 73, 78, 102.

89. O'Donnell, *Southern Indians,* 12–13.

90. Coleman, *American Revolution in Georgia,* 7; Cashin, "Sowing the Wind," 240–41.

91. Snapp, *John Stuart,* 121, 139–40; Hayes, *Hero of Hornet's Nest,* 24–26; Coleman, *American Revolution in Georgia,* 8.

92. Cashin, "Sowing the Wind," 241–42.

93. John Stuart to Thomas Gage, January 18, 1775, Thomas Gage Papers, vol. 125.

94. David Taitt to John Stuart, December 17, 1774, Gage Papers, vol. 125.

95. Taitt to John Stuart, December 29, 1775, Gage Papers, vol. 125.

96. Gage to John Stuart, December 28, 1774, Gage Papers, vol. 125.

97. Extract, Patrick Tonyn to John Stuart, December 18, 1774, Gage Papers, vol. 125.

98. Extract, James Wright to John Stuart, January 12, 1775, Gage Papers, vol. 125.

99. John Stuart to Gage, January 18, 1775, Gage Papers, vol. 125.

100. Gage to John Stuart, March 11, 1775, Gage Papers, vol. 126.

101. Saunt, *New Order of Things,* 51–53.

102. Braund, "Creek Indians, Blacks, and Slavery," 613.

103. O'Donnell, *Southern Indians,* 31–32.

104. John Stuart to Henry Stuart, October 24, 1775, in Davies, ed., *DAR,* 11:162–63; John Stuart to Lord George Germain, October 26, 1776, *DAR,* 12:239–40.

105. O'Donnell, *Southern Indians,* 11; J. Leitch Wright, *Only Land They Knew,* 174.

106. J. Leitch Wright, *Only Land They Knew,* 222.

107. "Indian Agents" [1775], in Dartmouth Papers. This document is not numbered but follows no. 1210B.

108. John Stuart to Gage, March 27, 1775, Gage Papers, vol. 127.

109. John Stuart to Gage, May 26, 1775, Gage Papers, vol. 129.

110. Jack M. Sosin, "The Use of Indians in the War of the American Revolution: A Re-Assessment of Responsibility," in *Race Relations in British North America,* ed. Glasrud and Smith, 284.

111. James H. O'Donnell III, "The South on the Eve of the Revolution: The Native Americans," in *Revolutionary War in the South,* ed. Higgins, 71.

112. Dowd, *Spirited Resistance,* 46.

113. Calloway, *American Revolution in Indian Country,* 19, 23. See also Sosin, *Revolutionary Frontier,* 87.

CHAPTER 2: THE BRITISH GOVERNMENT AND ITS SUPPORTERS
REACT TO THE REVOLUTION

1. Lord North quoted in Hibbert, *Redcoats and Rebels,* 18.

2. Valentine, *Lord North,* 1:383; Christie, *Wars and Revolutions,* 114, 128; Gerald Brown, *American Secretary,* 26, 30.

3. Hibbert, *George III,* 72, 76, 145, 150, 153.

4. Ira D. Gruber, "Britain's Southern Strategy," in *Revolutionary War in the South,* ed. Higgins, 206–7.

5. Alexander Innes to Lord Dartmouth, May 16, 1775, in Innes, "Charles Town Loyalism," *SCHM,* 129.

6. Innes to Dartmouth, June 10, 1775, in Innes, "Charles Town Loyalism," 132.

7. William Campbell to Dartmouth, July 19 and 20, 1775, *DAR,* 11:50.

8. William Campbell to Dartmouth, August 19, 1775, Dartmouth Papers, no. 1446.

9. Thomas Fletchall to William Campbell, August 19, 1775, Dartmouth Papers, no. 1446.

10. William Campbell to Dartmouth, September 19, 1775, *DAR,* 11:118.

11. Wright to Dartmouth, June 9, 1775, *DAR,* 9:167.

12. Wright to William Campbell, June 27, 1775, in Middleton, "Correspondence," *SCHGM,* part 4, 115.

13. Wright to Dartmouth, August 7, 1775, *DAR,* 11:68.

14. "Extract of a letter from Charles-Town, South Carolina, January 17, [1775]," in Willard, ed., *Letters on the Revolution,* 57.

15. "Copy of a letter received by a tradesman at York from his son," February 3, 1775, in Willard, ed., *Letters on the Revolution,* 61.

16. Valentine, *Lord North,* 1:375.

17. Edward J. Cashin, "'But Brothers, It Is Our Land We Are Talking About': Winners and Losers in the Georgia Backcountry," in *Uncivil War,* ed. Hoffman et al., 250.

18. O'Donnell, *Southern Indians,* 29–31.

19. Valentine, *Lord George Germain,* 185.

20. Germain to Tonyn, December 23, 1775, Germain Papers, vol. 4.

21. Bellot, *William Knox,* 153.

22. Lord Shelburne's Speech, November 10, 1775; Duke of Richmond's Speech, November 10, 1775, in Simmons and Thomas, eds., *Proceedings and Debates,* 6:227, 234.

23. Frank O'Gorman, "The Parliamentary Opposition to the Government's American Policy 1760–1782," in *Britain and the American Revolution,* ed. Dickinson, 117.

24. Jordan, *White over Black,* 208–9.

25. Christopher Brown, "Empire without Slaves," *WMQ,* 273–306, quotation, 304.

26. Frey, *Water from the Rock,* 54–55.

27. Edmund Burke's Speech, March 22, 1775, in Simmons and Thomas, eds., *Proceedings and Debates,* 5:612.

28. William Lyttelton's Speech, October 26, 1775, in Simmons and Thomas, eds., *Proceedings and Debates,* 6:96.

29. George Johnstone's Speech, October 26, 1775, in Simmons and Thomas, eds., *Proceedings and Debates,* 6:105.

30. Frey, *Water from the Rock,* 67.

31. Ralph Izard to "a friend in Bath," October 27, 1775, in Deas, ed., *Correspondence of Ralph Izard,* 1:135.

32. Frey, *Water from the Rock,* 60.

33. Brooke, *King George III,* 178.

34. Hibbert, *Redcoats and Rebels,* 57.

35. "Project for Strengthening General Howe's Operations in the North by a Diversion in the South, without taking off the Troops" [1775], Germain Papers, vol. 4.

36. "Advantages of Lord Cornwallis's Expedition going rather to Chesapeak Bay than to the Carolinas" [1775?], Germain Papers, vol. 4.

37. "Campbell" to Germain, January 16, 1776, Germain Papers, vol. 4. Frey identifies the writer of this document and the one cited below as Lt. Col. Archibald Campbell, who later commanded the expedition to Georgia; see Frey, *Water from the Rock,* 69.

38. "Campbell" to Lord North, n.d., enclosed in letter to Germain, January 16, 1776, Germain Papers, vol. 4.

39. O'Shaughnessy, *Empire Divided,* 45–46, 175.

40. Ibid., 149.

41. Hibbert, *George III,* 143–44; Egerton Leigh to Lord Gower, January 15, 1775, in Greene, "Political Authorship of Leigh," *SCHM,* 146–48; Ellen Wilson, *Loyal Blacks,* 2–3.

42. Dartmouth to Earl of Dunmore, July 12, 1775, *DAR,* 11:45.

43. Quarles, *Negro in the Revolution,* 112.

44. Frey, *Water from the Rock,* 69, 72–73.

45. Jordan, *White over Black,* 114.

46. Duke of Manchester's Speech, May 22, 1776, in Simmons and Thomas, eds., *Proceedings and Debates,* 6:565.

47. Conway, "To Subdue America," *WMQ,* 381–407.

48. Black, *War for America,* 37. See also Brooke, *King George III,* 178.

49. William Campbell quoted in Stephen Conway, "British Governments and the Conduct of the American War," in *Britain and the American Revolution,* ed. Dickinson, 160.

50. James Murray to Mrs. Smyth, November 18, 1775, in Murray, *Letters from America,* 16–17.

51. Frey, *Water from the Rock,* 45.

52. Lord North's Speech, November 20, 1775, in Simmons and Thomas, eds., *Proceedings and Debates,* 6:281.

53. Adams, *Diary and Autobiography,* September 24, 1775, 2:182–83.

54. Wright to Dartmouth, May 25, 1775, *DAR,* 9:144.

55. William Campbell to Dartmouth, August 31, 1775, *DAR,* 11:94.

56. Thomas Lynch to Izard, November 19, 1775, in Deas, ed., *Correspondence of Izard,* 1:154.

57. Henry Laurens to William Manning, February 27, 1776, *PHL,* 11:123–24.

58. Christopher Moore, *Loyalists,* 110.

59. Arthur Middleton to William Henry Drayton, April 15, 1775, in Middleton, "Correspondence," part 4, 113.

60. Simpson, "British View of the Siege of Charleston," *JSH,* 95–96.

61. Berkeley and Berkeley, *Dr. Alexander Garden,* 263.

62. Henry Laurens to John Laurens, June 8, 1775, *PHL,* 10:167–68.

63. Krawczynski, *William Drayton,* 141–42. The author gives Dealy's first name as John.

64. Lipscomb, *Carolina Lowcountry,* 14.

65. Peter Timothy to Drayton, August 13, 1775, in Middleton, "Correspondence," part 4, 129.

66. Middleton to Drayton, August 12, 1775, in Middleton, "Correspondence," part 4, 126.

67. Ibid.; Timothy to Drayton, August 13, 1775, in Middleton, "Correspondence," part 4, 129.

68. Berkeley and Berkeley, *Dr. Alexander Garden,* 265–66.

69. Middleton to Drayton, August 22, 1775, in Middleton, "Correspondence," part 4, 135.

70. Cashin, *King's Ranger,* 27–29.

71. Middleton to Drayton, August 4, 1775, in Middleton, "Correspondence," part 4, 122.

72. Stuart, "Note on James Stuart," *JSH,* 573.

73. Timothy to Drayton, August 13, 1775, in Middleton, "Correspondence," part 4, 129.

74. "Loyalists reasons for refusing to unite with the Whigs," South Carolina Box—Loyalists, NYPL. Although the document is undated, Governor Campbell stated that the proceeding took place on July 22, and he described it in some detail; see William Campbell to Dartmouth, July 23, 1775, *DAR,* 11:55. Arthur Middleton stated in a letter to William Henry Drayton dated August 12, 1775, that the investigation of the "non-subscribers" would take place on August 14, which apparently refers to a separate proceeding; see Middleton, "Correspondence," part 4, 126.

75. Drayton, *Memoirs of the Revolution,* 1:315–17.

76. William Wragg to Henry Laurens, September 5, 1775, *PHL,* 10:369–70.

77. Henry Laurens to Jonas Baird, August 16, 1776, *PHL,* 11:247.

78. Council of Safety to Stephen Bull, September 23, 1775, *PHL,* 10:418–19.

79. Krawczynski, *William Drayton,* 127–29.

80. Andrew MacKenzie Loyalist Claim, March 24, 1784, On-Line Institute for Advanced Loyalist Studies, www.royalprovincial.com/military/mems/sc/clmmckz.htm (accessed June 6, 2002).

81. William Campbell to Fletchall, August 1, 1775, Dartmouth Papers, no. 1446.

82. Henry Laurens to Fletchall, July 14, 1775, *PHL,* 10:214–17.

83. Fletchall to Council of Safety, July 24, 1775, in Gibbes, ed., *Documentary History,* 1:123–24.

84. Resolution of Loyalists on Pacolet River [1775], in Chesney, *Journal,* 144–45.

85. Cann, "Prelude to War," *SCHM,* 198.

86. William Thomson to Council of Safety, July 22, 1775, *PHL,* 10:241–42.

87. Middleton to Drayton, August 4, 1775, in Middleton, "Correspondence," part 4, 122–23.

88. Middleton to Drayton, August 12, 1775, in Middleton, "Correspondence," part 4, 126.

89. Henry Laurens to John Laurens, July 30, 1775, *PHL,* 10:257–58.

90. Moultrie, *Memoirs,* 1:82–83; Krawczynski, *William Drayton,* 160.

91. Krawczynski, *William Drayton,* 163.

92. Drayton and William Tennent to Council of Safety, August 7, 1775, *PHL,* 10:278–79.

93. Tennent, "Fragment of a Journal," 297–98.

94. Ibid.; Krawczynski, *William Drayton,* 169–70.

95. Drayton to Council of Safety, August 9, 1775, *PHL,* 10:286–87.

96. Council of Safety to Drayton, August 13, 1775, *PHL,* 10:297.

97. Oliver Hart, "Diary," August 9, 1775.

98. Ibid., August 10, 1775.

99. Ibid., August 11, 1775. Hart calls Robinson "Major Robertson."

100. Tennent, "Fragment of a Journal," 299.

101. Tennent to Henry Laurens, August 20, 1775, *PHL,* 10:337–39.

102. Krawczynski, *William Drayton,* 175–76.

103. Tennent, "Fragment of a Journal," 301–2; Krawczynski, *William Drayton,* 179–80.

104. Middleton to Drayton, August 22, 1775, in Middleton, "Correspondence," part 4, 134.

105. Thomas Brown to William Campbell, October 18, 1775, in Thomas Brown, "Loyalist View of the Drayton-Tennent-Hart Mission," *SCHM,* 17–18.

106. William Campbell to Dartmouth, August 31, 1775, abstract, Dartmouth Papers, no. 1467.

107. Drayton to Council of Safety, August 21, 1775, *PHL,* 10:344–45.

108. Moses Kirkland to Dartmouth, September 20, 1775, Dartmouth Papers, no. 1526.

109. Drayton to Council of Safety, September 11, 1775, *PHL,* 10:375–78.

110. Thomson to Henry Laurens, September 6, 1775, *PHL,* 10:371.

111. Drayton to Council of Safety, August 30, 1775, Drayton Papers.

112. Krawczynski, *William Drayton,* 184–86; Thomas Brown to William Campbell, October 18, 1775, in Thomas Brown, "Loyalist View," 19.

113. Krawczynski, *William Drayton,* 186–89.

114. Treaty of Ninety Six, September 16, 1775, in Gibbes, ed., *Documentary History,* 1:184–86.

115. Drayton to Council of Safety, September 17, 1775, *PHL,* 10:392–93.

116. Thomas Brown to William Campbell, October 18, 1775, in Thomas Brown, "Loyalist View," 20–21, 24.

117. Robert Cunningham to Drayton, October 5, 1775, in Gibbes, ed., *Documentary History,* 1:200.

118. Thomas Brown to William Campbell, October 18, 1775, in Thomas Brown, "Loyalist View," 24–25; Council of Safety to Drayton, September 15, 1775, *PHL,* 10:386–87; Moultrie, *Memoirs,* 1:69–70; John Ball to Isaac Ball, September 19, 1775, Ball Family Papers.

119. Robinson, "Memoir."

120. Innes to Tonyn, October 15, 1775, in "Papers of the First Council of Safety," *SCHGM,* 75.

121. Moultrie, *Memoirs,* 1:96; Affidavit of Moses Cotter, November 3, 1775, in Moultrie, *Memoirs,* 1:97–100; Cann, "Prelude to War," 207; Lambert, *South Carolina Loyalists,* 44–45.

122. Cann, "Prelude to War," 208–11; Lambert, *South Carolina Loyalists,* 45.

123. "Agreement for a Cessation of Arms" between Robinson and Williamson, November 22, 1775, in Gibbes, ed., *Documentary History,* 1:214–15.

124. Thomson to Council of Safety, November 28, 1775, *PHL,* 10:523.

125. Lewis Jones, *South Carolina Civil War,* 77–79.

126. Richard Richardson to Council of Safety, December 2, 1775, *PHL,* 10:529–30.

127. Richardson to Council of Safety, December 16, 1775, *PHL,* 10:567.

128. Richardson to Henry Laurens, January 2, 1776, *PHL,* 10:610–11.

129. Robinson, "Memoir."

130. Chesney, *Journal,* 6.

131. "Prisoners Sent to Charles Town by Richardson," n.d., in Gibbes, ed., *Documentary History,* 1:249–53.

132. Petition from Backcountry Prisoners, January 20, 1776, *PHL,* 11:51–52.

133. Richardson to Council of Safety, January 23, 1776, *PHL,* 11:56.

134. Richard Pearis Loyalist Claim, August 22, 1783, SCHS.

135. Isabella McLaurin Memorial, April 8, 1783, SCHS.

136. Council of Safety to Richardson, and to Thomson, December 4, 1775, *PHL,* 10:533–35.

137. Henry Laurens to Robert Deans, January 8, 1776, *PHL,* 11:11.

138. Henry Laurens to John Laurens, January 16, 1776, *PHL,* 11:35.

139. William Campbell to Dartmouth, July 19 and 20, 1775, *DAR,* 11:50.

140. William Campbell to Dartmouth, January 1, 1776, *DAR,* 12:30.

141. Piers Mackesy, "What the British Army Learned," in *Arms and Independence,* ed. Hoffman and Albert, 195.

142. Josiah Culbertson, Pension Application, in Dann, ed., *Revolution Remembered,* 175.

143. Champneys, *Account of the sufferings,* 1–2, 4–5.

144. Robertson, ed., "Georgia's Banishment and Expulsion Act," *GHQ,* 275.

145. Affidavit of William Tongue, June 7, 1775, *DAR,* 9:166–67.

146. Deposition of John Hopkins, July 25, 1775, in Crary, ed., *Price of Loyalty,* 63.

147. Wright to Dartmouth, July 29, 1775, *DAR,* 11:59.

148. Coleman, *American Revolution in Georgia,* 65.

149. Robertson, *Loyalism in Revolutionary Georgia,* 6; James Kitching Loyalist Claim, February 2, 1783, On-Line Institute for Advanced Loyalist Studies, www.royalprovincial.com/military/mems/ga/clmkit.htm (accessed June 6, 2002).

150. Peter Taarling to John Houstoun, October 24, 1775, John Houstoun Papers.

151. "Extract of a letter from Savannah," November 29, 1775, in Willard, ed., *Letters on the Revolution,* 226.

152. Thomas Taylor to Mr. Morrison, December 16, 1775, in Taylor, "Georgia Loyalist's Perspective," *GHQ,* 125.

153. Thomas Taylor to the Reverend Thomas Percy, January 13, 1776, Misc. Mss., WLCL.

154. "Extract of a letter, dated on board the Brig Allerton, Cockspur, in Georgia," March 24, 1776, in Willard, ed., *Letters on the Revolution,* 297.

155. Coulter, "Edward Telfair," *GHQ,* 107–8.

156. Lachlan McIntosh to George Washington, March 8, 1776, in McIntosh, "Papers," *GHQ,* part 1, 151.

157. Coleman, *American Revolution in Georgia,* 70.

158. Coulter, "Edward Telfair," 108–9.

159. Memorial of Sir James Wright to William Pitt, 1785, British Museum, Egerton Mss. 2135.

160. Roberts, "Losses of a Loyalist Merchant," *GHQ,* 272–73; Johnston, *Recollections of a Georgia Loyalist,* 45–46.

161. [McIntosh?] to Button Gwinnett, May 1, 1776, in McIntosh, "Papers," part 1, 154–55.

162. Robertson, ed., "Georgia's Banishment and Expulsion Act," 277; Zubly, *"Warm & Zealous Spirit,"* 20–22.

163. "Resolve of St. Andrews Parochial Committee," in McIntosh, "Papers," part 4, 58–59.

164. Norton, "Eighteenth-Century Women," *WMQ,* 398.

165. Callahan, *Royal Raiders,* 91; Troxler, "Refuge, Resistance, and Reward," 567–68.

166. Siebert, *Loyalists in East Florida,* 1:23–24.

167. Ibid., 1:48–50.

168. Troxler, "Refuge, Resistance, and Reward," 569.

169. Tonyn to Germain, August 21, 1776, On-Line Institute for Advanced Loyalist Studies, www.royalprovincial.com/military/rhist/eastflmil/eflmillet1.htm (accessed August 16, 2002).

170. Searcy, *Georgia-Florida Contest,* 34–36, 43–44, 50.

171. Ibid., 54–56.

172. Bennett and Lennon, *Quest for Glory,* 48–50; Searcy, *Georgia-Florida Contest,* 61–62.

173. Searcy, *Georgia-Florida Contest,* 37–38.

174. Ibid., 68.

175. Council of Safety to Joseph Kershaw, July 25, 1775, *PHL,* 10:247.

176. Moultrie, *Memoirs,* 1:81.

177. Quoted in Merrell, *Indians' New World,* 215.

178. Douglas Brown, *Catawba Indians,* 260–61.

179. Quoted in Merrell, *Indians' New World,* 215, 216.

180. Douglas Brown, *Catawba Indians,* 261–62.

181. Henry Laurens to Samuel Boykin, January 14, 1776, *PHL,* 11:28.

182. Douglas Brown, *Catawba Indians,* 263.

183. O'Donnell, *Southern Indians,* 18; Snapp, *John Stuart,* 160.

184. Snapp, *John Stuart,* 160.

185. Krawczynski, *William Drayton,* 132.

186. John Stuart to Gage, July 9, 1775, Gage Papers, vol. 131.

187. Committee of Intelligence to John Stuart, June 21, 1775, Gage Papers, vol. 132.

188. John Stuart to Committee of Intelligence, July 18, 1775, Gage Papers, vol. 132.

189. Moultrie, *Memoirs,* 1:123.

190. Henry Laurens to Georgia Council of Safety, February 7, 1776, *PHL,* 11:91.

191. John Stuart to Taitt, August 29, 1775, in Gibbes, ed., *Documentary History,* 1:159.

192. Moultrie, *Memoirs,* 1:123.

193. Williamson to Council of Safety, July 14, 1775, and enclosure, July 12, 1775, *PHL,* 10:222–23.

194. Moultrie, *Memoirs,* 1:76.

195. Drayton to Alexander Cameron, September 26, 1775, in Gibbes, ed., *Documentary History,* 1:194–95.

196. Cameron to Drayton, October 16, 1775, in Gibbes, ed., *Documentary History,* 1:208.

197. Thomson to Drayton, August 4, 1775, in Gibbes, ed., *Documentary History,* 1:125–27.

198. Cameron to Andrew M'Lean, August 16, 1775, in Gibbes, ed., *Documentary History,* 1:143–44.

199. Deposition of Robert Goudey, July 10, 1775, Ninety Six District Papers.

200. Tennent to Henry Laurens, August 20, 1775, in Gibbes, ed., *Documentary History,* 1:146.

201. Tennent to Council of Safety, September 1, 1775, *PHL,* 10:359.

202. Affidavit of Jonathan Clark, August 21, 1775, in Gibbes, ed., *Documentary History,* 1:147–48.

203. Henry Laurens to John Laurens, August 20, 1775, *PHL,* 10:325.

204. Middleton to Drayton, August 5, 1775, in Middleton, "Correspondence," part 4, 124; O'Donnell, *Southern Indians,* 20–21.

205. Hatley, *Dividing Paths,* 187–88.

206. Henry Laurens to John Laurens, September 26, 1775, *PHL,* 10:428–29.

207. Thomson to Council of Safety, September 29, 1775, *PHL,* 10:439.

208. O'Donnell, *Southern Indians,* 25–27.

209. John Stuart to Taitt, August 29, 1775, in Gibbes, ed., *Documentary History,* 1:158–59.

210. John Stuart's Talk to the Cherokees, August 30, 1775; John Stuart's Talk to the Creeks, August 1775, in Gibbes, ed., *Documentary History,* 1:159–62.

211. Nichols, "Alexander Cameron," *SCHM,* 106–7.

212. Gage to John Stuart, September 12, 1775, *DAR,* 11:105.

213. John Stuart to [Henry Stuart], October 24, 1775; John Stuart to Gage, October 24, 1775, *DAR,* 11:162–64.

214. Nichols, "Alexander Cameron," 107.

215. Richardson to Henry Laurens, December 16, 1775, *PHL,* 10:567.

216. Henry Laurens to John Laurens, February 22, 1776, *PHL,* 11:121.

217. Pierce Butler to unnamed, March 21, 1776, in Middleton, "Correspondence," part 4, 140.

218. Hatley, *Dividing Paths,* 218–19; Calloway, *American Revolution in Indian Country,* 191, 194–95.

219. Lumpkin, *From Savannah to Yorktown,* 20.

220. Henry Laurens to John Laurens, August 14, 1776, *PHL,* 11:229.

221. Francis Salvador to Drayton, July 18, 1776, in Gibbes, ed., *Documentary History,* 2:24.

222. James Creswell to Drayton, July 27, 1776, in Gibbes, ed., *Documentary History,* 2:31.

223. William Sharpe to Cornelius Harnett, July 27, 1776, Misc. Mss., WLCL.

224. Salvador to Drayton, July 18, 1776, and addendum of July 19, 1776, in Gibbes, ed., *Documentary History,* 2:25–26.

225. McJunkin, "Memoir," 32, 33.

226. Creswell to Drayton, July 27, 1776, in Gibbes, ed., *Documentary History,* 2:30–31.

227. Chesney, *Journal,* 7.

228. Henry Laurens to John Laurens, August 14, 1776, *PHL*, 11:231.

229. Williamson to unnamed, July 22, 1776, in Gibbes, ed., *Documentary History,* 2:27.

230. Fanning, *Narrative,* 9–10.

231. Henry Laurens to John Laurens, August 14, 1776, *PHL*, 11:229, 231.

232. Williamson to unnamed, July 22, 1776, in Gibbes, ed., *Documentary History,* 2:26.

233. Douglas Brown, *Catawba Indians,* 263.

234. Lumpkin, *From Savannah to Yorktown,* 22–23; Waring, *Fighting Elder,* 16–18.

235. Williamson to Drayton, August 22, 1776, in Gibbes, ed., *Documentary History,* 2:32.

236. Lenoir, "Revolutionary Diary," *JSH,* 254–55.

237. Ibid.

238. Lumpkin, *From Savannah to Yorktown,* 25.

239. William Moore to Griffith Rutherford, November 18, 1776, Griffith Rutherford Paper.

240. William Christian to Colonel Russell, November 12, 1776, Misc. Papers, series 1, vol. 1, NCSA.

241. O'Donnell, *Southern Indians,* 48–49.

242. Hatley, *Dividing Paths,* 189.

243. Drayton to Salvador, July 24, 1776, in Gibbes, ed., *Documentary History,* 2:28–29.

244. Henry Laurens to John Laurens, August 14, 1776, *PHL*, 11:227.

245. Creswell to Drayton, July 27, 1776, in Gibbes, ed., *Documentary History,* 2:30–31.

246. Charles Lee to Edmund Pendleton, July 21, 1776, Charles Lee Letterbook.

247. Henry Laurens to John Laurens, August 14, 1776, *PHL*, 11:230.

248. O'Donnell, *Southern Indians,* 49–50, 52.

249. South Carolina Council of Safety to Georgia Council of Safety, July 24, 1775, *PHL*, 10:243–44.

250. George Galphin to Council of Safety, October 15, 1775, *PHL*, 10:467–68.

251. South Carolina Council of Safety to Galphin, October 22, 1775, and December 18, 1775, *PHL*, 10:491, 572.

252. "Proceedings of the Georgia Council of Safety," January 8, 1776, in *CGHS*, vol. 5, part 1, 29.

253. Galphin to South Carolina Council of Safety, February 7, 1776, *PHL*, 11:93–97.

254. Henry Laurens to Galphin, February 14, 1776, *PHL*, 11:102.

255. South Carolina Council of Safety to Georgetown Committee of Safety, March 15, 1776, *PHL*, 11:165.

256. Saunt, *New Order of Things,* 50.

257. "Proceedings of the Georgia Council of Safety," May 15 and 16, 1776, in *CGHS,* vol. 5, 52–55.

258. Lachlan McIntosh to George Washington, April 28, 1776, in McIntosh, "Papers," part 1, 154.

259. Samuel Elbert to Charles Lee, May 14, 1776, in McIntosh, "Papers," part 1, 155.

260. "Proceedings of the Georgia Council of Safety," July 5, 1776, in *CGHS*, vol. 5, 72.

261. Charles Lee to [John Rutledge], August 1, 1776, Lee Letterbook.

262. "Proceedings of the Georgia Council of Safety," August 19, 1776, in *CGHS*, vol. 5, 93.

263. McIntosh to Charles Lee, July 29, 1776, in McIntosh, "Papers," part 1, 159.

264. Searcy, *Georgia-Florida Contest*, 31.

265. McIntosh to William Howe, October 22, 1776, in McIntosh, "Papers," part 1, 160.

266. Searcy, *Georgia-Florida Contest*, 73.

267. Gerald Brown, *American Secretary*, 60.

268. Tonyn to Germain, July 19, 1776, in Tonyn, "Letter," *MVHR*, 290.

269. Snapp, *John Stuart*, 168.

270. Tonyn to Germain, July 19, 1776, in Tonyn, "Letter," 291–92.

271. Germain to William Knox, October 19, 1776, Knox Papers.

272. Germain to William Howe, November 6, 1776, Germain Papers, vol. 5.

273. William Howe to John Stuart, August 25, 1776, Sir Guy Carleton Papers, 3:258.

274. Searcy, *Georgia-Florida Contest*, 68, 77–78; Lachlan McIntosh to [Robert Howe?], October 29, 1776; McIntosh to Robert Howe, October 1, 1776, October 29, 1776, in McIntosh, "Papers," part 1, 157, 159, 160.

275. Calloway, *American Revolution in Indian Country*, 258–59; Dowd, *Spirited Resistance*, 55–56; John Stuart to Germain, November 24, 1776, *DAR*, 12:253.

276. Abbey, "Peter Chester's Defense," *MVHR*, 19.

277. John Stuart quoted in Starr, *Tories, Dons, and Rebels*, 52–53.

278. Ibid., 52.

279. Gibson, *Chickasaws*, 71; Calloway, *American Revolution in Indian Country*, 222.

280. Berlin, *Many Thousands Gone*, 292.

281. Alden, "Stuart Accuses Bull," *WMQ*, 318–19.

282. Frey, *Water from the Rock*, 57.

283. Olwell, *Masters, Slaves, and Subjects*, 238.

284. Frey, *Water from the Rock*, 57.

285. "Report of the Committee for Forming a Plan of Defence," 1775, in Gibbes, ed., *Documentary History*, 1:205.

286. Henry Laurens to James Laurens, June 7, 1775, *PHL*, 10:162–63.

287. Frey, *Water from the Rock*, 56.

288. Joseph Manigault to Gabriel Manigault, June 4, 1775, Manigault Family Papers.

289. Henry Laurens to John Laurens, June 18, 1775, *PHL*, 10:184–85.

290. Henry Laurens to John Laurens, June 23, 1775, *PHL*, 10:191–92.

291. Henry Laurens to James Laurens, July 2, 1775, *PHL*, 10:202.

292. Gabriel Manigault to Gabriel Manigault Jr., July 8, 1775, in Manigault, "Papers," *SCHM*, 2.

293. Thomas Hutchinson to Council of Safety, July 5, 1775, *PHL*, 10:206–8.

294. Council of Safety to St. Bartholomew Committee, July 18, 1775, *PHL*, 10:231.

295. Henry Laurens to John Laurens, July 30, 1775, *PHL*, 10:258, 260.

296. Henry Laurens to John Laurens, August 20, 1775, *PHL*, 10:320–22.

297. William Campbell to Dartmouth, August 31, 1775, abstract, Dartmouth Papers, no. 1467.

298. William Campbell to Dartmouth, August 31, 1775, *DAR*, 11:95–96.

299. William Campbell to Henry Laurens, August 17, 1775, *PHL*, 10:328.

300. Henry Laurens to William Campbell, [August 17, 1775], *PHL*, 10:329.

301. Innes to Henry Laurens, August 18, 1775 [two letters of this date] and Laurens to Innes, August 18, 1775 [two letters of this date], *PHL*, 10:330–34.

302. Timothy to Drayton, August 22, 1775, in Middleton, "Correspondence," part 4, 132.

303. Henry Laurens to John Laurens, August 20, 1775, *PHL*, 10:320–22.

304. William Campbell to Dartmouth, August 31, 1775, *DAR*, 11:97.

305. William Campbell to Dartmouth, August 19, 1775, Dartmouth Papers, no. 1446.

306. William Campbell to Dartmouth, August 31, 1775, *DAR*, 11:96.

307. Gould, "American Independence," *Past and Present*, 115.

308. Earl of Sandwich's Speech, November 20, 1775, in Simmons and Thomas, eds., *Proceedings and Debates*, 6:365, 370.

309. John Laurens to Henry Laurens, October 4, 1775, *PHL*, 10:450.

310. Stephen Bull to Henry Laurens, September 19, 1775, *PHL*, 10:313–14.

311. Stephen Bull to Henry Laurens, August 18, 1775, *PHL*, 10:309.

312. Joseph Glover to Henry Laurens, September 22, 1775, *PHL*, 10:416.

313. Quarles, "Lord Dunmore as Liberator," *WMQ*, 495–96, 501, 506.

314. "Extract of a letter from Philadelphia," December 6, 1775, in Willard, ed., *Letters on the Revolution*, 233. Based on the writer's familiarity with the situation of slaves in the southern provinces, it is probable that he was either a southern delegate attending the Congress in Philadelphia or a northern delegate who obtained his information from a southern colleague.

315. Edward Rutledge to Izard, December 8, 1775, in Deas, ed., *Correspondence of Izard*, 1:165–66. On Rutledge's opposition to the enlistment of blacks in the rebel forces, see Alden, *South in the Revolution*, 40. Rutledge eventually succeeded in convincing Congress to stop the enlistment of blacks.

316. Peter H. Wood, "'The Facts Speak Loudly Enough': Exploring Early Southern Black History," in *Devil's Lane*, ed. Clinton and Gillespie, 7.

317. Moultrie, *Memoirs*, 1:113–14.

318. Peter H. Wood, "'The Dream Deferred': Black Freedom Struggles on the Eve of White Independence," in *In Resistance*, ed. Okihiro, 179; Wood, "Facts Speak Loudly," 8; Douglas Brown, *Catawba Indians*, 262; Lipscomb, *Carolina Lowcountry*, 20.

319. Council of Safety to Richard Richardson, December 19, 1775, *PHL*, 10:576.

320. Moultrie, *Memoirs*, 1:112.

321. Henry Laurens to James Laurens, January 6, 1776, *PHL*, 11:7.

322. Henry Laurens to John Laurens, July 14, 1775, *PHL*, 10:220,

323. Marrant, *Narrative*, 35.

324. Henry Laurens to Stephen Bull, January 20, 1776, *PHL*, 11:50.

325. Quarles, *Negro in the Revolution*, 128.

326. Richard Hutson to Isaac Hayne, May 27, 1776, in Hutson, "Letters," 315.

327. Pierce Butler to unnamed, March 21, 1776, in Middleton, "Correspondence," part 4, 140.

328. Henry Laurens to John Laurens, March 26, 1776, *PHL*, 11:191.

329. Charles Lee quoted in Quarles, *Negro in the Revolution*, 122.

330. Henry Laurens to John Laurens, August 14, 1776, *PHL*, 11:223–24, 227.

331. Henry Laurens to William Brisbane, September 6, 1776, *PHL*, 11:265.

332. Jackson, "Battle of the Riceboats," *GHQ,* 230; South Carolina Council of Safety to Georgia Council of Safety, January 19, 1776, *PHL,* 11:44.

333. McIntosh to Washington, March 8, 1776, in McIntosh, "Papers," part 1, 150.

334. Stephen Bull to Henry Laurens, March 12, 1776, *PHL,* 11:153.

335. Stephen Bull to Henry Laurens, March 12, 1776, and March 13, 1776, in Gibbes, ed., *Documentary History,* 1:266.

336. Stephen Bull to Henry Laurens, March 14, 1776, in Gibbes, ed., *Documentary History,* 1:268.

337. Stephen Bull to Henry Laurens, March 12, 1776, in Gibbes, ed., *Documentary History,* 1:266.

338. Stephen Bull to Henry Laurens, March 14, 1776, in Gibbes, ed., *Documentary History,* 1:268–69.

339. South Carolina Council of Safety to Stephen Bull, March 16, 1776, *PHL,* 11:172.

340. Searcy, "Introduction of Slavery," 27.

341. *PHL,* 11:173n.

342. "Proceedings of the Georgia Council of Safety," July 5, 1776, in *CGHS,* vol. 5, 71.

343. Lachlan McIntosh to Lachlan McIntosh Jr., August 14, 1776, in McIntosh, "Papers," part 4, 56.

344. Henry Laurens to Joseph Clay, September 2, 1777, *PHL,* 11:482.

345. J. Leitch Wright, *Florida in the Revolution,* 39.

346. Governor Tonyn quoted in Pennington, "East Florida in the Revolution," *FHQ,* 28.

347. Tonyn to Germain, August 21, 1776, On-Line Institute for Advanced Loyalist Studies, www.royalprovincial.com/military/rhist/eastflmil/eflmiller1.htm (accessed August 16, 2002).

348. J. Leitch Wright, *Florida in the Revolution,* 108.

349. J. Leitch Wright, "Blacks in East Florida," 434–35.

350. Hayes, *Hero of Hornet's Nest,* 40.

351. Diary of William Dunbar, July 12, 1776, in Dunbar, *Life, Letters and Papers,* 27.

352. Gruber, "Britain's Southern Strategy," 210; Ritcheson, *British Politics,* 199; Robson, "Expedition to the Southern Colonies," *EHR,* 538–40.

353. Dartmouth to William Howe, October 22, 1775, Carleton Papers, 1:68.

354. Robson, "Expedition to the Southern Colonies," 541–43.

355. Paul Smith, *Loyalists and Redcoats,* 22.

356. Gerald Brown, *American Secretary,* 52.

357. Willcox, *Portrait of a General,* 67–69.

358. John Pownall to William Howe, September 25, 1775, Carleton Papers, 1:52.

359. Simpson, "British View of the Siege of Charleston," *JSH,* 95. As editor of this work, Frances Reece Kepner attributes authorship of the document to James Simpson.

360. Willcox, *Portrait of a General,* 76–77.

361. Clinton, *American Rebellion,* 26.

362. Paul Smith, *Loyalists and Redcoats,* 26.

363. J. Leitch Wright, *Florida in the Revolution,* 32; Gary D. Olson, "Thomas Brown, the East Florida Rangers, and the Defense of East Florida," in *Eighteenth-Century Florida,* ed. Proctor, 16–17.

364. Tonyn to Sir Henry Clinton, April 15, 1776, Sir Henry Clinton Papers, 15:17.

365. Olson, "Thomas Brown," 18; J. Leitch Wright, *Florida in the Revolution,* 34.

366. Robson, "Expedition to the Southern Colonies," 544–45, 547–48, 553; Willcox, *Portrait of a General,* 81.

367. Willcox, *Portrait of a General,* 83.

368. Clinton, *American Rebellion,* 27.

369. Willcox, *Portrait of a General,* 84–85; Clinton, *American Rebellion,* 29; Germain to William Howe, November 8, 1775; Dartmouth to William Campbell, November 7, 1775, Carleton Papers, 1:80, 81.

370. Richard Hutson to Thomas Hutson, June 7, 1776, in Hutson, "Letters," 316.

371. Pierce Butler to unnamed, March 21, 1776, in Middleton, "Correspondence," part 4, 140.

372. Richard Hutson to Isaac Hayne, June 24, 1776, in Hutson, "Letters," 319.

373. Simpson, "British View of the Siege of Charleston," 97.

374. William Richardson to Nan, [May 19, 1776], in Richardson, "Letters," *SCHGM,* 16.

375. Chesney, *Journal,* 7.

376. Henry Laurens to Martha Laurens, August 17, 1776, *PHL,* 11:253; Willcox, *Portrait of a General,* 87–88.

377. Henry Laurens to John Laurens, August 14, 1776, *PHL,* 11:232.

378. McIntosh to George Walton, July 11, 1776, in McIntosh, "Papers," part 1, 157.

379. Bellot, *William Knox,* 145.

380. Higginbotham, *War of American Independence,* 137.

381. Excerpt of Robert Howe's letter to unnamed recipient, September 6, 1776, in Archibald MacLaine Hooper, unpublished biography of Robert Howe, Robert Howe Papers, SHC.

382. Excerpt, Robert Howe to unnamed, November 21, 1776, in Hooper biography, Howe Papers, SHC.

CHAPTER 3: WHIGS ASCENDANT

1. William Howe to Germain, November 30, 1776, Germain Papers, vol. 5.

2. Germain to William Howe, January 14, 1777, Germain Papers, vol. 5.

3. Germain to Knox, September 13, 1777, Knox Papers.

4. Paul Smith, *Loyalists and Redcoats,* 89–90; William Howe to Germain, October 22, 1777, Germain Papers, vol. 6.

5. Tonyn to Sir William Howe, April 4, 1778, in *RAM,* 1:223.

6. Henry Laurens to James Brisbane, April 24, 1777, *PHL,* 11:333.

7. Norton, *British Americans,* 34–35.

8. Royster, *Revolutionary People at War,* 105.

9. Lambert, *South Carolina Loyalists,* 60.

10. Hartley, "George Hartley's Claim," *SCHGM,* 47, 48.

11. Stuart, "Note on James Stuart," 572–73.

12. Isabella MacLaurin Memorial, April 8, 1783, SCHS; Robinson, "Memoir."

13. Richard Pearis Loyalist Claim, August 22, 1783, SCHS; John Rutledge to [South Carolina delegates in Congress], August 30, 1777, John Rutledge Papers; John Wells Jr. to Henry Laurens, September 29, 1777, *PHL,* 11:536.

14. Fanning, *Narrative,* 10–12.

15. Callahan, *Royal Raiders,* 227.

16. Fraser, "Reflections of 'Democracy,'" *SCHM,* 210.

17. Gabriel Manigault to Gabriel Manigault Jr., April 30, 1777, in Gabriel Manigault, "Papers," 6–7.

18. Gibbes, "Story of His Life," *SCHGM,* 64–65.

19. Christopher Gadsden to Thomas Mumford, February 19, 1777, in Gadsden, *Writings,* 120.

20. "Frenchman Visits Charleston," *SCHGM,* 91. The author of this account is unknown.

21. Lambert, *South Carolina Loyalists,* 62–64.

22. Edward Rutledge to John Adams, July 16, 1778, *PJA,* 6:295.

23. Louisa Wells, *Journal of a Voyage,* 23.

24. Berkeley and Berkeley, *Dr. Alexander Garden,* 274–75.

25. Lambert, *South Carolina Loyalists,* 66.

26. Harry Ward, *Between the Lines,* 195.

27. Thomas Pinckney to Harriott Pinckney, April 7, 1778, in Thomas Pinckney, "Letters," *SCHM,* 148–49.

28. Rawlins Lowndes to Henry Laurens, April 14, 1778, *PHL,* 13:114.

29. William Moultrie to Robert Howe, April 10, 1778, in Moultrie, *Memoirs,* 1:205.

30. Robert Howe to Samuel Elbert, April 6, 1778, Robert Howe Papers, GHS.

31. Robert Howe to unnamed, April 13, 1778, Robert Howe Papers, GHS.

32. Harry Ward, *Between the Lines,* 195.

33. Houstoun to Henry Laurens, April 16, 1778, *PHL,* 13:121–22.

34. Bennett and Lennon, *Quest for Glory,* 71–72; William Moultrie to Henry Laurens, April 20, 1778, *PHL,* 13:160.

35. Clay to Josiah Smith Jr. [undated, c. March–May 1778], in Clay, *Letters, CGHS,* 70.

36. Clay to Henry Laurens, May 30, 1778, in Clay, *Letters,* 76.

37. Robert Howe to Henry Laurens, April 26, 1778, *PHL,* 13:190–92.

38. William Gipson, Pension Application, in Dann, ed., *Revolution Remembered,* 187.

39. Thomas Brown to Augustine Prevost, April 10, 1778, *RAM,* 1:227–28.

40. James Whitefield to Henry Laurens, May 6, 1778, *PHL,* 13:261–62.

41. Galphin to Henry Laurens, June 25, 1778, *PHL,* 13:514.

42. John Wells Jr. to Henry Laurens, April 20, 1778, *PHL,* 13:162.

43. John Lewis Gervais to Henry Laurens, May 8, 1778, *PHL,* 13:276.

44. John Wells Jr. to Henry Laurens, June 10, 1778, *PHL,* 13:437–38.

45. Nadelhaft, *Disorders of War,* 45–46.

46. Gervais to Henry Laurens, June 26, 1778, *PHL,* 13:518–20.

47. Rawlins Lowndes to Henry Laurens, June 17, 1778, *PHL,* 13:479–80.

48. Henry Laurens to Gervais, September 15, 1778, *PHL,* 14:312–13.

49. Lowndes to Henry Laurens, September 22, 1778, *PHL,* 14:343.

50. Edgar, *Partisans and Redcoats,* 44.

51. Gervais to Henry Laurens, June 19, 1778, *PHL,* 13:491.

52. Edward Rutledge to John Adams, July 16, 1778, *PJA,* 6:295.

53. John Wells Jr. to Henry Laurens, October 14, 1778, *PHL,* 13:416.

54. Clay to Messrs. Bright and Pechin, July 2, 1777, in Clay, *Letters,* 35.

55. John Adam Treutlen to John Hancock, June 19, 1777, John Adam Treutlen Papers.

56. Robertson, ed., "Georgia's Banishment and Expulsion Act," 275, 276.

57. Ibid., 279–81.

58. Robertson, *Loyalism in Revolutionary Georgia,* 8.

59. Clay to Henry Laurens, October 21, 1777, in Clay, *Letters,* 54.

60. Lamplugh, "'To Check and Discourage the Wicked,'" *GHQ,* 297–98; Lambert, "Confiscation of Loyalist Property," *WMQ,* 80.

61. Green, "Queensborough Township," *WMQ,* 197; Zubly, *"Warm & Zealous Spirit,"* 22–23.

62. Robertson, *Loyalism in Revolutionary Georgia,* 9.

63. Troxler, "Refuge, Resistance, and Reward," 569–70, 572–75.

64. Cashin, *King's Ranger,* 49, 59, 61.

65. Searcy, *Georgia-Florida Contest,* 84–88; Cashin, *King's Ranger,* 61–62.

66. Searcy, *Georgia-Florida Contest,* 89, 94.

67. Bennett and Lennon, *Quest for Glory,* 62; Searcy, *Georgia-Florida Contest,* 89, 94–95; Charles Jones, *Life of Samuel Elbert,* 12.

68. Searcy, *Georgia-Florida Contest,* 92–96.

69. Ibid., 113.

70. Clay to Henry Laurens, September 29, 1777, in Clay, *Letters,* 40.

71. Thomas Brown to Tonyn, March 13, 1778, Carleton Papers, 9:1014.

72. Tonyn to William Howe, April 6, 1778, Carleton Papers, 10:1073.

73. Clay to Robert Howe, October 15, 1777, in Clay, *Letters,* 50.

74. Houstoun to Henry Laurens, June 9, 1778, *PHL,* 13:428.

75. Grimké, "Journal," *SCHGM,* part 1, 63–64.

76. Gadsden to Drayton, June 1, 1778, in Gadsden, *Writings,* 126–27.

77. Robert Howe to unnamed, April 13, 1778, Robert Howe Papers, GHS.

78. Robert Howe to Governor of Georgia, February 7, 1778, Robert Howe Papers, GHS.

79. Robert Howe Orderly Book, March 26 and 30, 1778, WLCL.

80. Searcy, *Georgia-Florida Contest,* 141.

81. Howe Orderly Book, May 13, 14, 18, 19, and 21, 1778, WLCL. See also Grimké, "Journal," part 1, 64.

82. Howe Orderly Book, May 22 and 23, 1778, WLCL; Thomas Pinckney to Harriott Pinckney, May 23, 1778, in Thomas Pinckney, "Letters," 149–50; Grimké, "Journal," part 1, 66–67; Bennett and Lennon, *Quest for Glory,* 75.

83. Thomas Pinckney to Harriott Pinckney, May 23, 1778, in Thomas Pinckney, "Letters," 149–50.

84. Howe Orderly Book, May 22 and 23, 1778, WLCL; Grimké, "Journal," part 1, 67.

85. Grimké, "Journal," part 2, 120, 125.

86. J. Leitch Wright, *Florida in the Revolution,* 57.

87. Grimké," Journal," part 3, 198.

88. Ibid., part 1, 65.

89. Ibid., part 2, 130.

90. Thomas Brown to Tonyn, June 30, 1778, Carleton Papers, 11:1247; Cashin, *King's Ranger,* 77–78; Thomas Pinckney to Harriott Pinckney, July 1, 1778, in Thomas Pinckney, "Letters," 157.

91. Augustine Prevost to William Howe, June 13, 1778, Carleton Papers, 11:1236.

92. Searcy, *Georgia-Florida Contest,* 142, 144, 145–47; Grimké, "Journal," part 3, 191.

93. Robert Howe to Congress, September 22, 1778, Howe Papers, GHS.

94. Robert Howe to unnamed, August 18, 1778, Howe Papers, GHS.

95. Robert Howe to Henry Laurens, October 12, 1778, Howe Papers, GHS.

96. Searcy, *Georgia-Florida Contest,* 157.

97. Clay to Henry Laurens, September 9, 1778; Clay to Gervais, September 25, 1778, in Clay, *Letters,* 106, 109.

98. Starr, *Tories, Dons, and Rebels,* 58.

99. Henry Laurens to John Rutledge, August 12, 1777, *PHL,* 11:444–45.

100. Starr, *Tories, Dons, and Rebels,* 86, 88.

101. Dunbar, Diary, May 1, 1778, in Dunbar, *Life, Letters and Papers,* 62.

102. Phelps, *Memoirs and Adventures,* 112.

103. John Fitzpatrick to McGillivray, Struthers, & Co., April 10, 1778, in Fitzpatrick, *Merchant of Manchac,* 289.

104. Abbey, "Peter Chester's Defense," 24.

105. Starr, *Tories, Dons, and Rebels,* 106.

106. Abbey, "Peter Chester's Defense," 27–29.

107. Anthony Hutchins to Germain, May 21, 1778, in Abbey, ed., "Intrigue of a British Refugee," *WMQ,* 400–401.

108. Caughey, "Willing's Expedition," *LHQ,* 27; Hutchins to Germain, May 21, 1778, in Abbey, ed., "Intrigue of a British Refugee," 401–3; Starr, *Tories, Dons, and Rebels,* 111; Abbey, "Peter Chester's Defense," 29–30; Dunbar, Diary, May 1, 1778, in Dunbar, *Life, Letters and Papers,* 63.

109. Phelps, *Memoirs and Adventures,* 119.

110. Starr, *Tories, Dons, and Rebels,* 120.

111. John Stuart to Clinton, November 22, 1778, Clinton Papers, 46:25.

112. Calloway, *American Revolution in Indian Country,* 200; Henry Laurens to John Laurens, February 3, 1777, *PHL,* 11:294–95.

113. Calloway, *American Revolution in Indian Country,* 200; O'Donnell, *Southern Indians,* 57–58.

114. "Articles of the definite Treaty of Peace . . . between the States of So. Carolina and Georgia and the Cherokee Indians," May 20, 1777, in "Treaty of Long Island," *NCHR,* 76–78.

115. Patrick Henry to Virginia Commissioners, June 26, 1777, in "Treaty of Long Island," 58–59.

116. "Proceedings at a Treaty with the Overhill Cherokee Indians," in "Treaty of Long Island," 62–63.

117. Ibid., 78–86.

118. Ibid., 87–91.

119. "Articles of a Treaty of peace made and concluded at Fort Henry," July 20, 1777, in "Treaty of Long Island," 107–8; Calloway, *American Revolution in Indian Country,* 200.

120. Gervais to Henry Laurens, November 3, 1777; Drayton to Henry Laurens, November 1, 1777, *PHL,* 12:2, 16.

121. Talk of Dragging Canoe, June 8, 1777, in "Treaty of Long Island," 64.

122. Dowd, *Spirited Resistance,* 54–55.

123. Samuel Riggs, Pension Application, in Dann, ed., *Revolution Remembered,* 306.

124. John Stuart to Germain, January 23, 1777, *DAR*, 14:34–35.

125. John Stuart to Germain, March 10, 1777, *DAR*, 14:49.

126. John Stuart to Germain, June 14, 1777, *DAR*, 14:114.

127. William Howe to Stuart, January 13, 1777, On-Line Institute for Advanced Loyalist Studies, www.royalprovincial.com/military.rhist/wflrlet1.htm (accessed August 16, 2002).

128. John Stuart to Cameron, July 11, 1777, Carleton Papers, 6:602.

129. "Talk Sent by Tom Gray," December 23, 1776, in McIntosh, "Papers," part 4, 61–62.

130. McIntosh to Robert Howe, December 30, 1776; McIntosh to William McIntosh, January 2, 1777; McIntosh to Howe, January 7, 1777, in McIntosh, "Papers," part 2, 261–62, 264; McIntosh to Hall, Brownson, and Walton, January 23, 1777, in McIntosh, "Papers," part 3, 357–58.

131. O'Donnell, *Southern Indians,* 60; Galphin to Henry Laurens, July 20, 1777; John Wells Jr. to Henry Laurens, June 23, 1777, *PHL,* 11:388, 402.

132. Galphin to Henry Laurens, July 20, 1777, *PHL,* 11:402–3.

133. Galphin to Henry Laurens, December 22, 1777, *PHL,* 12:175–76.

134. William Howe to Lt. Col. Alexander Dickson, May 6, 1777; Augustine Prevost to John Stuart, June 14, 1777, Carleton Papers, 5:516, 585.

135. Elias Durnford to [William Howe], June 10, 1777, Carleton Papers, 5:574.

136. John Stuart to William Howe, August 23, 1777, Carleton Papers, 6:649.

137. Alexander McGillivray to John Stuart, September 25, 1777, Carleton Papers, 6:677.

138. McGillivray to John Stuart, September 25, 1777; John Stuart to William Howe, October 6, 1777; Copy of a Talk from the Lower Creek Nation to John Stuart, October 19, 1777, Carleton Papers, 6:677, 695, 707; O'Donnell, *Southern Indians,* 66.

139. John Stuart to Germain, March 10, 1777, and August 22, 1777, *DAR,* 14:49, 168.

140. Germain to William Howe, September 3, 1777, Germain Papers, vol. 6.

141. Boyd and Latorre, "Spanish Interest in Florida," 97.

142. McIntosh to Robert Howe, April 2, 1777, in McIntosh, "Papers," part 3, 365.

143. McIntosh to Button Gwinnett, April 13, 1777, in McIntosh, "Papers," part 3, 367.

144. Searcy, *Georgia-Florida Contest,* 112–13.

145. John Rutledge to [South Carolina delegates in Congress], August 30, 1777, John Rutledge Papers; Gervais to Henry Laurens, August 16, 1777, *PHL,* 11:461.

146. Gervais to Henry Laurens, August 16, 1777, *PHL,* 11:461.

147. John Rutledge to [South Carolina delegates], August 30, 1777, John Rutledge Papers.

148. Gervais to Henry Laurens, November 13, 1777, *PHL,* 12:16.

149. Galphin to Henry Laurens, October 13, 1777, *PHL,* 11:552–53.

150. Lennon, "'Graveyard of American Commanders,'" *NCHR,* 154.

151. Clay to Robert Howe, October 15, 1777, in Clay, *Letters,* 51.

152. Clay to Henry Laurens, October 21, 1777, in Clay, *Letters,* 54.

153. John Stuart to William Howe, February 4, 1778, *RAM,* 1:189.

154. John Stuart to William Howe, March 22, 1778, Clinton Papers, 32:29.

155. John Stuart to Germain, May 2, 1778, *DAR,* 15:113–14.

156. Tonyn to William Howe, February 24, 1778, *RAM,* 1:197.

157. Kennett, ed. and trans., "French Report on St. Augustine," *FHQ,* 135.

158. Tonyn to William Howe, April 6, 1778, *RAM,* 1:225.

159. Tonyn to William Howe, May 15, 1778, *RAM,* 1:251–52.

160. John Stuart to William Howe, February 4, 1778, *RAM,* 1:190.

161. John Stuart to Germain, August 10, 1778, *DAR,* 15:181–82.

162. Thomas Pinckney to Harriott Pinckney, June 4, 1778, in Thomas Pinckney, "Letters," 154; Grimké, "Journal," part 2, 119.

163. Thomas Pinckney to Harriott Pinckney, May 23, 1778, in Thomas Pinckney, "Letters," 149.

164. Augustine Prevost to Clinton, September 16, 1778, *RAM,* 1:293–94.

165. Williamson to John Bowie, August 9, 1778, John Bowie Papers.

166. Lowndes to Henry Laurens, August 16, 1778, *PHL,* 14:169.

167. Houstoun to Henry Laurens, August 20, 1778, *PHL,* 14:192.

168. John Wells Jr. to Henry Laurens, August 23, 1778, *PHL,* 14:213.

169. Wells to Henry Laurens, August 28, 1778, *PHL,* 14:242–43.

170. Williamson to Bowie, October 14, 1778, and October 18, 1778, Bowie Papers; Lowndes to Henry Laurens, October 18, 1778, *PHL,* 13:425.

171. Galphin to Henry Laurens, October 26, 1778, *PHL,* 13:452–54.

172. Report of Committee, November 10, 1778, Edward Telfair Papers, PERK.

173. Augustine Prevost to Jeffery Amherst, January 18, 1779, Jeffery Amherst Papers, War Office 34/112/3.

174. John Stuart to William Howe, June 16, 1777, Carleton Papers, 5:586; Calloway, *American Revolution in Indian Country,* 222–23.

175. James H. O'Donnell III, "The Southern Indians in the War for American Independence, 1775–1783," in *Race Relations in British North America,* ed. Glasrud and Smith, 315–16.

176. Snapp, *John Stuart,* 193.

177. John Stuart to William Howe, February 4, 1778, *RAM,* 1:190.

178. Osborn, "Relations with the Indians in West Florida," *FHQ,* 260.

179. Caughey, "Panis Mission to Pensacola," *Hispanic-American Historical Review,* 483–84.

180. John Stuart to William Howe, March 22, 1778, Clinton Papers, 32:29.

181. John Stuart to William Howe, March 22, 1778, Clinton Papers, 32:29.

182. Hutchins to Germain, May 21, 1778, in Abbey, ed., "Intrigue of a British Refugee," 401.

183. John Stuart to William Howe, March 22, 1778, Clinton Papers, 32:29.

184. Gibson, *Chickasaws,* 72.

185. O'Brien, *Choctaws,* 40–41.

186. Chester quoted in Abbey, "Peter Chester's Defense," 24.

187. Germain quoted in Starr, *Tories, Dons, and Rebels,* 84.

188. Gould, *Persistence of Empire,* 185.

189. Valentine, *Lord North,* 1:470, 502.

190. Germain quoted in Gerald Brown, *American Secretary,* 62.

191. Valentine, *Lord North,* 1:470, 502.

192. Henry Laurens to Izard, June 9, 1777, *PHL,* 11:350.

193. Gervais to Henry Laurens, August 2, 1777, *PHL,* 11:414.

194. Gervais to Henry Laurens, July 26, 1777, *PHL,* 11:405.

195. Clay to Robert Howe, October 15, 1777, in Clay, *Letters,* 50.

196. Watson, *Men and Times of the Revolution,* 25, 43.

197. Hazard, "View of Coastal Carolina," *SCHM,* 187.

198. Gervais to Henry Laurens, June 19, 1778, *PHL,* 13:494.

199. Gervais to Henry Laurens, July 26, 1777, *PHL,* 11:407–8.

200. Drayton to Henry Laurens, November 1, 1777, *PHL,* 12:1.

201. Grimké, "Journal," part 1, 67.

202. Bennett and Lennon, *Quest for Glory,* 75–76, 79. Concerning the man's death, the authors assert "that black Americans apparently were serving in a combat capacity during the expedition" (79). No evidence exists to support this claim, however. It is more likely that the man was a pioneer or an officer's servant.

203. John Laurens to Henry Laurens, January 14, 1778, *PHL,* 12:305. For an account of John Laurens's efforts during the Revolution to arm slaves for American service, see Massey, "Limits of Antislavery Thought," *JSH,* 495–530.

204. Henry Laurens to John Laurens, January 22, 1778, *PHL,* 12:328.

205. Henry Laurens to John Laurens, January 28, 1778, *PHL,* 12:368.

206. John Laurens to Henry Laurens, February 2, 1778, *PHL,* 12:390–92.

207. Henry Laurens to John Laurens, February 6, 1778, *PHL,* 12:412–13.

208. John Laurens to Henry Laurens, February 15, 1778, *PHL,* 12:446.

209. Louisa Wells, *Journal of a Voyage,* 2, 4.

210. Fabel, *Economy of West Florida,* 38.

Chapter 4: The British Return

1. Willcox, "British Strategy in America," *Journal of Modern History,* 97–121, esp. 102. See also Mackesy, "British Strategy in the War of American Independence," *Yale Review,* 539–57; Ira D. Gruber, "British Strategy: The Theory and Practice of Eighteenth-Century Warfare," in *Reconsiderations on the Revolutionary War,* ed. Higginbotham, 14–31; Ira D. Gruber, "Britain's Southern Strategy," in *Revolutionary War in the South,* ed. Higgins, 205–38; and John Shy, "British Strategy for Pacifying the Southern Colonies, 1778–1781," in Shy, *People Numerous & Armed,* 193–212.

2. K. G. Davies, "The Restoration of Civil Government by the British in the War of Independence," in *Red, White, and True Blue,* ed. Edmond Wright, 115–16; Paul Smith, *Loyalists and Redcoats,* 82–94.

3. Willcox, *Portrait of a General,* 208, 222; Mackesy, *War for America,* 159; Davies, "Restoration of Civil Government," 116.

4. Smith, *Loyalists and Redcoats,* 83–84.

5. Germain to Clinton, August 5, 1778, Clinton Papers, 38:42.

6. Bellot, *William Knox,* 164, 167.

7. Memorial of Lord William Campbell and Others to Germain, [August 1777], *DAR,* 14:182–84.

8. Simpson to Germain, [September 1, 1778], Germain Papers, vol. 20.

9. Moses Kirkland to Clinton, October 13, 1778, in Kirkland, "Backcountry Loyalist Plan," *SCHM,* 209–12.

10. Kirkland to His Majesty's Commissioners, October 21, 1778, in Kirkland, "Backcountry Loyalist Plan," 212–14.

11. Tonyn to Amherst, November 11, 1778, Amherst Papers, War Office 34/111/184.

12. William Smith, *Historical Memoirs,* 23.

13. Proceedings of Peace Commissioners, December 12, 1778, William Eden Auckland Papers, no. 125.

14. Carlisle, Clinton, and Eden to Germain, October 16, 1778, Auckland Papers, no. 60.

15. Bellot, *William Knox,* 146.

16. Ibid., 163–64.

17. Germain to Clinton, March 8, 1778, Germain Papers, vol. 18.

18. Higginbotham, *War of American Independence,* 354; Hibbert, *George III,* 161.

19. "Remarks on some Improvements Proposed by an Officer to be made in the Plan of the American War," 1778, Amherst Papers, War Office 34/110/144.

20. Charles Stuart to the Earl of Bute, February 4, 1777, in Stuart, *Prime Minister and His Son,* 97.

21. Mackenzie, *Diary,* 1:299.

22. William Smith, *Historical Memoirs,* 110.

23. Innes quoted in Paul Smith, *Loyalists and Redcoats,* 71.

24. Quarles, *Negro in the Revolution,* 113.

25. Edmund Burke quoted in Frey, *Water from the Rock,* 76.

26. O'Shaughnessy, *Empire Divided,* 175–81.

27. Stephen Conway, "British Governments and the Conduct of the American War," in *Britain and the American Revolution,* ed. Dickinson, 164; Germain to Clinton, August 5, 1778, Clinton Papers, 38:42.

28. Valentine, *Lord George Germain,* 366.

29. Borick, *Gallant Defense,* 5; "Observations on the Trade of America & its Effects in the present Rebellion," May 1779, Germain Papers, vol. 9.

30. Higginbotham, *War of American Independence,* 353.

31. Hibbert, *Redcoats and Rebels,* 239; Carlisle, Clinton, and Eden to Germain, October 16, 1778, Auckland Papers, no. 60; Carlisle, Clinton, and Eden to Archibald Campbell, November 3, 1778, in Campbell, *Journal,* 6.

32. Germain to Clinton, December 3, 1778, Clinton Papers, 47:32.

33. Charles Inglis to Joseph Galloway, December 12, 1778, in "Letters to Galloway," *Historical Magazine* 5 (October 1861): 300.

34. Daniel Coxe to Galloway, December 17, 1778, in "Letters to Galloway," *Historical Magazine* 5 (December 1861): 358.

35. William Franklin to Galloway, February 6, 1779, in "More Galloway Letters," *Historical Magazine* 6 (June 1862): 177.

36. Clinton to Germain, November 8, 1778, Clinton Papers, 45:30.

37. Christie, *End of North's Ministry,* 10.

38. Valentine, *Lord North,* 2:87.

39. Lutnick, *American Revolution and the British Press,* 118, 130.

40. Germain to Clinton, August 5, 1779, in Clinton, *American Rebellion,* 415–16.

41. Germain to Clinton, September 27, 1779, in Clinton, *American Rebellion,* 423.

42. "General Observations, Relative to . . . the War," August 8, 1779, Richard Oswald Papers.

43. "Supplement to the Papers of August 1779 Relative to . . . the War," September 1779, Oswald Papers.

44. Henry Laurens to William Read, February 9, 1779, *PHL,* 15: 55–56.

45. Clinton to Eden, February 14, 1779, Auckland Papers, no. 271.

46. Clinton to Germain, April 4, 1779, Germain Papers, vol. 9.

47. Germain to Clinton, March [31], 1779, Clinton Papers, 54:32.

48. Simpson to Germain, August 28, 1779, in Simpson, "Simpson's Reports," *JSH,* 515–17.

49. Coleman, *American Revolution in Georgia,* 119, 120.

50. Campbell, *Journal,* 7.

51. Archibald Campbell to Tonyn, December 5, 1778; Archibald Campbell to A. Prevost, December 5, 1778, in Campbell, *Journal,* 11–13.

52. Campbell, *Journal,* 20–21. Campbell calls the plantation "Sheridoe's" in his account.

53. Campbell, *Journal,* 22–26, quotation, 26.

54. Ibid., 27–28, 110n58. Alexander A. Lawrence states that the slave agreed to guide the British for "a small reward"; see Lawrence, "General Robert Howe and the Capture of Savannah," *GHQ,* 317. There is no mention of this in the British accounts, although it is possible that Campbell later compensated the slave for his services. See Coleman, *American Revolution in Georgia,* 121.

55. Coleman, *American Revolution in Georgia,* 121.

56. Houstoun to Henry Laurens, November 25, 1778, *PHL,* 13:534–35.

57. Lowndes to Henry Laurens, December 3, 1778, *PHL,* 13:554–55.

58. Houstoun to Henry Laurens, November 25, 1778, *PHL,* 13:534–35.

59. James Fergus, Pension Application, in Dann, ed., *Revolution Remembered,* 177–78.

60. Campbell, *Journal,* 34.

61. Jenkin Davis to Henry Muhlenberg, March 18, 1783, in Muhlenberg, "Muhlenberg's Georgia Correspondence," *GHQ,* 435; Campbell, *Journal,* 34–36.

62. Proclamation by Hyde Parker and Archibald Campbell, January 4, 1779, Auckland Papers, no. 235.

63. Proclamation of Archibald Campbell, January 8, 1779, in Campbell, *Journal,* 38–39. One British guinea in 1780 was worth the equivalent of 137.87 American dollars in 2002, based on information at Economic History Services, http://eh.net/hmit.

64. Campbell, *Journal,* 39.

65. Col. Archibald Lytle to Benjamin Lincoln, January 22, 1779, Benjamin Lincoln Papers; Campbell, *Journal,* 51.

66. Memorial of Thomas Manson, On-Line Institute for Advanced Loyalist Studies, www.royalprovincial.com/military/mems/ga/clmman.htm (accessed June 6, 2002).

67. "Examn. Deserter," January 12, 1779, Lincoln Papers.

68. "Copy of a letter from Quarter-Master-Sergeant Kitz . . . to one of his friends in New York," January 17, 1779, "Correspondence of General von Knyphausen, HDAR, item G.

69. Thomas Taylor to unnamed, January 18, 1779, in Taylor, "Georgia Loyalist's Perspective," 131.

70. Thomas Robinson to Galloway, January 19, 1779, in "More Galloway Letters," *Historical Magazine* 6 (June 1862): 177. For a discussion of this outpouring of Loyalist support, see Norton, *British Americans,* 35.

71. S. D. H. to unnamed, January 16, 1779, in Murray, *Letters from America,* 204.

72. Archibald Campbell to Germain, January 19, 1779, in Campbell, *Journal,* 43.

73. Archibald Campbell to Eden, January 19, 1779, Auckland Papers, no. 246.

74. Germain to Archibald Campbell, March 13, 1779, in Campbell, *Journal,* 80.

75. Norton, *British Americans,* 112.

76. S. H. Jenkins to John Inglis, June 26, 1779, John Inglis Papers, GHS.

77. Isaac Ogden to Galloway, February 6, 1779, in "More Galloway Letters," *Historical Magazine* 6 (June 1862): 178–79; William Smith, *Historical Memoirs,* 69.

78. Galphin to Henry Laurens, December 29, 1778, *PHL,* 15:20.

79. William Stafford to Lincoln, January 7, 1779, Lincoln Papers.

80. Stephen Bull to Lincoln, January 10, 1779, Lincoln Papers.

81. Bennett and Lennon, *Quest for Glory,* 100.

82. Williamson to Lincoln, February 1, 1779, Lincoln Papers.

83. Moultrie to Lincoln, February 8, 1779, Lincoln Papers.

84. Clay to Bright and Pechin, March 23, 1779, in Clay, *Letters,* 130.

85. Clinton quoted in Valentine, *Lord George Germain,* 435.

86. Germain to Clinton, March [31], 1779, Clinton Papers, 54:32.

87. "Journal of the Hessian Regiment von Knoblauch," HDAR, item W.

88. "Minute Book, Savannah Board of Police," *GHQ,* 245.

89. Davis and Thomas, *Kettle Creek,* 31.

90. Campbell, *Journal,* 39, quotation, 45.

91. John Wilson, *Encounters,* 19.

92. Ibid.

93. Campbell, *Journal,* 48.

94. Ibid., 48–50.

95. Lincoln to Lowndes, January 6, 1779, Lincoln Papers.

96. Lincoln to Elbert, February 4, 1779, Lincoln Papers.

97. Lincoln to Lowndes, February 4, 1779, Lincoln Papers.

98. Lincoln to Lowndes, February 10, 1779, Lincoln Papers.

99. Joseph Kershaw to Lincoln, February 18, 1779, Lincoln Papers.

100. John Wilson, *Encounters,* 42.

101. Campbell, *Journal,* 54–56, 58–60.

102. John Wilson, *Encounters,* 42.

103. Archibald Campbell to Clinton, March 4, 1779, *DAR,* 17:74, 75.

104. "State of the Enemy in Georgia," March [15], 1779, Misc. Papers, series 1, vol. 1, no. 53, NCSA.

105. Campbell, *Journal,* 54–56, 58–60.

106. John Wilson, *Encounters,* 42.

107. Davis and Thomas, *Kettle Creek,* 21; Harry Ward, *Between the Lines,* 204; Cashin, *King's Ranger,* 85, 88.

108. Campbell, *Journal,* 64.

109. Lincoln to Williamson, February 16, 1779, Lincoln Papers.

110. Augustine Prevost to Archibald Campbell, February 17, 1779, Misc. Mss., WLCL.

111. Augustine Prevost to Clinton, March 1, 1779, *DAR,* 17:69.

112. Davis and Thomas, *Kettle Creek,* 33–34, 36–39, 43.

113. Campbell, *Journal,* 66.

114. Don Higginbotham, "The American Militia: A Traditional Institution with Revolutionary Responsibilities," in Higginbotham, *War and Society in Revolutionary America,* 121.

115. Williamson to Lincoln, February 20, 1779, Lincoln Papers.

116. Lincoln to John Rutledge, February 28, 1779, Lincoln Papers.

117. Lincoln to John Rutledge, March 3, 1779, Lincoln Papers.

118. Williamson to John Ashe, undated, enclosed in Ashe to Lincoln, February 16, 1779, Lincoln Papers.

119. Hayes, *Hero of Hornet's Nest,* 59.

120. "Extract of a letter from Augusta," February 6, 1779, *Royal Georgia Gazette,* February 11, 1779.

121. Heidler, "American Defeat at Briar Creek," *GHQ,* 318.

122. John Dooly to Samuel Elbert, February 16, 1779, Misc. Mss.—John Dooly, LOC.

123. Cashin, "George Walton and the Forged Letter," *GHQ,* 136–37.

124. Proceedings of a Council of War, January 14, 1779, in Davis, ed., *Georgia Citizens and Soldiers,* 64.

125. Thomas Bee to Lincoln, April 9, 1779, Lincoln Papers.

126. Court of Inquiry Proceedings, April 10–12, 1779, Matthew Singleton Papers.

127. Augustine Prevost to Lincoln, March 28, 1779, Thomas Addis Emmet Manuscript Collection, no. 7404.

128. "John Rutledge to Lincoln," February 28, 1779, *SCHGM,* 133–34.

129. Lambert, *South Carolina Loyalists,* 83.

130. "John Rutledge to Lincoln," 133–34.

131. Davis, "Loyalist Trials," *SCHM,* 174–75.

132. John Christian Senf to Lincoln, April 19, 1779, Lincoln Papers.

133. Senf to Lincoln, April 24, 1779, Lincoln Papers.

134. Davis, "Loyalist Trials," 175–76, 178–79.

135. Ann Manigault, "Extracts from the Journal," *SCHGM,* 117, 117n.

136. Heidler, "American Defeat at Briar Creek," 322–30.

137. Leonard Marbury to Lincoln, March 6, 1779, Emmet Collection, no. 6665.

138. Williamson to [Samuel Elbert?], April 1, 1779, Sol Feinstone Manuscript Collection, no. 1680.

139. John Smith to Lincoln, March 26, 1779, Lincoln Papers.

140. Thomas Pinckney to Harriott Pinckney, April 19, 1779, in Thomas Pinckney, "Letters," part 4, 232.

141. Lincoln to James Lovell, April 12, 1779, Lincoln Papers.

142. Lincoln to Drayton, April 17, 1779, Lincoln Papers.

143. Davis, "Lord Montagu's Mission," *SCHM,* 92, 94; Archibald Campbell to A. Prevost, March 2, 1779, in Campbell, *Journal,* 72.

144. Archibald Campbell to J. M. Prevost, March 4, 1779, in Campbell, *Journal,* 75; Coleman, "Restored Colonial Georgia," *GHQ,* 9.

145. Furlong, "Civilian-Military Conflict," *JSH,* 422–23.

146. Bellot, *William Knox,* 168; Coleman, "Restored Colonial Georgia," 10; Norton, *British Americans,* 107–8; Wright to Germain, "Points on Matters which it Seems Necessary to have Some Directions about," c. Spring 1779, Germain Papers, vol. 16; Germain to Knox, March 12, 1779, Knox Papers.

147. Wright to Germain, March 24–28, 1780, *DAR,* 18:67.

148. Coleman, *American Revolution in Georgia,* 126.

149. "Account from Bowman," May 13, 1779, Lincoln Papers.

150. Moultrie to John Rutledge, May 3, 1779, in Moultrie, *Memoirs,* 1:397.

151. Eliza Wilkinson to Miss M. P., 1782, in Wilkinson, *Letters,* 36–37.

152. Memorial of Robert Ballingall, March 13, 1786, Misc. Mss. SC7003/AT7003, box 2, no. 154, NYSL.

153. Berkeley and Berkeley, *Dr. Alexander Garden,* 299; Edgar, *Partisans and Redcoats,* 46; Lambert, *South Carolina Loyalists,* 87.

154. A. Prevost to Germain, June 10, 1779, *DAR,* 17:143.

155. Lambert, *South Carolina Loyalists,* 86.

156. Benjamin Few to Lincoln, June 2, 1779, Benjamin Few Papers.

157. Harry Ward, *Between the Lines,* 205; Lachlan McIntosh to Lincoln, September 6, 1779, Feinstone Collection, no. 855.

158. John Wereat to Lincoln, August 18, 1779, Lincoln Papers, PERK.

159. Ibid.

160. Lincoln to Lachlan McIntosh, July 15, 1779, Lincoln Papers.

161. Andrew Cumming Loyalist Claim, On-Line Institute for Advanced Loyalist Studies, www.royalprovincial.com/military/mems/sc/clmcumm.htm (accessed June 6, 2002).

162. John Cone to Benjamin Garden, June 26, 1779, Pringle-Garden Family Papers.

163. Anthony Stokes to Mrs. Stokes, November 9, 1779, in Kennedy, ed. and trans., *Muskets, Cannon Balls, and Bombs,* 116.

164. Ibid., 108, 116.

165. John Glen quoted in Lawrence, *Storm over Savannah,* 40.

166. Stokes to Mrs. Stokes, November 9, 1779, in Kennedy, ed. and trans., *Muskets, Cannon Balls, and Bombs,* 115; Augustine Prevost to Germain, November 1, 1779, in "Papers Relating to the Attack on Savannah," *Historical Magazine,* 291.

167. Lawrence, *Storm over Savannah,* 98.

168. John Baker to Lincoln, October 1779, Emmet Collection, no. 6696.

169. Lambert, *South Carolina Loyalists,* 86–87.

170. Lawrence, *Storm over Savannah,* 44.

171. "Case of Sir James Wright," 1784, Sir James Wright Papers, GHS.

172. A. Prevost to Germain, November 1, 1779; and "Return of Casualties," October 18, 1779, in "Papers Relating to the Attack on Savannah," 293, 296.

173. Charles Henri, Comte D'Estaing, "Journal of the Siege of Savannah," in Kennedy, ed. and trans., *Muskets, Cannon Balls, and Bombs,* 75.

174. Moses Buffington to Peter Buffington, Sr., December 8, 1779, Moses Buffington Paper; Proceedings of a Court Martial held at Sheldon, November 6, 1779; Benjamin Garden to Lincoln, January 5, 1780; Francis Marion to Lincoln, January 9, 1780, Lincoln Papers.

175. Lachlan McIntosh to Lincoln, December 11, 1779, Lincoln Papers, PERK.

176. Richard Parker Jr. to Lincoln, December 11, 1779, Lincoln Papers.

177. George Walton to Lincoln, December 25, 1779, Lincoln Papers.

178. Fitzpatrick to John Miller, July 10, 1779, in Fitzpatrick, *Merchant of Manchac,* 329.

179. Haarmann, "Spanish Conquest of West Florida," *FHQ,* 112, 114; Starr, *Tories, Dons, and Rebels,* 142, 144, 156.

180. Starr, *Tories, Dons, and Rebels,* 147.

181. John Campbell to Clinton, November 7, 1779, in Clinton, *American Rebellion,* 436.

182. Alan Gantzhorn, "The British in Pensacola," in *Siege!,* ed. Parks, 20; Starr, *Tories, Dons, and Rebels,* 147, 161.

183. Germain to John Stuart, December 2, 1778, *DAR,* 15:277.

184. John Stuart to Germain, January 11, 1779, *DAR,* 17:29.

185. Robert Howe to President of Congress, November 24, 1778, Howe Papers, GHS.

186. Lincoln to Williamson, January 12, 1779, Lincoln Papers.

187. Campbell, *Journal,* 52–53, 56.

188. "Heads of Campbell's Talk to . . . the Creek Nation," c. March 1779, Clinton Papers, 53:40.

189. Campbell, *Journal,* 87.

190. O'Donnell, *Southern Indians,* 81; Campbell, *Journal,* 88–90; "Heads of Mr. Taitt's Letter," June 11, 1779, Clinton Papers, 60:39; Few, "Autobiography," *MAH,* 349.

191. Campbell, *Journal,* 88–90; "Heads of Mr. Taitt's Letter," June 11, 1779, Clinton Papers, 60:39; Few, "Autobiography," 349; Williamson to [Elbert?], April 1, 1779, Feinstone Collection, no. 1680; Cashin, *King's Ranger,* 93.

192. Joseph Habersham to Isabel Habersham, March 5, 1778 [misdated, should be 1779], in Joseph Habersham, "Some Letters," *GHQ,* 146–47.

193. "Heads of Prevost to Taitt," March 14, 1779, Clinton Papers, 60:40.

194. Lawrence, *Storm over Savannah,* 6.

195. Germain to A. Prevost, March 13, 1779, *DAR,* 17:85.

196. Germain to John Stuart, March 31, 1779, Carleton Papers, 15:1871.

197. John Campbell to Clinton, February 10, 1779, *DAR,* 17:62.

198. O'Donnell, *Southern Indians,* 82.

199. Germain to Clinton, June 25, 1779, Germain Papers, vol. 9.

200. Lincoln to Williamson, January 25, 1779, Lincoln Papers.

201. Lincoln to Lowndes, January 28, 1779; Lincoln to Galphin, January 30, 1779, Lincoln Papers.

202. Williamson to Lincoln, February 1, 1779, Lincoln Papers.

203. Lincoln to Galphin, April 4, 1779, Lincoln Papers.

204. Dowd, *Spirited Resistance,* 55, 56.

205. James Fergus, Pension Application, in Dann, ed., *Revolution Remembered,* 181.

206. Moultrie to Lincoln, April 24, 1779, Lincoln Papers.

207. Moultrie to John Rutledge, April 23, 1779, in Moultrie, *Memoirs,* 1:379.

208. Joseph Kershaw, Diary, April 15, 1779.

209. Lincoln to Galphin, March 29, 1779, Lincoln Papers.

210. Lincoln to Williamson, March 29, 1779, Lincoln Papers.

211. E. Skelly, "Demonstration against Charleston," *MAH,* 152, 153. Skelly's initial is incorrectly given as "F." See "Journal of the Hessian Regiment von Knoblauch," HDAR, item W; and "Account from Bowman," May 13, 1779, Lincoln Papers.

212. Garden, *Anecdotes of the Revolutionary War,* 49.

213. Williamson to Lincoln, May 8, 1779, Lincoln Papers.

214. John Rutledge to Lincoln, May 5, 1779, Lincoln Papers.

215. Moultrie to Lincoln, May 21, 1779, Lincoln Papers.

216. Saunt, *New Order of Things,* 55, 58; Searcy, "Introduction of Slavery," 29.

217. "Heads of Mr. Taitt's Letter," June 11, 1779, Clinton Papers, 60:39.

218. Moultrie to John Rutledge, July 3, 1779, in Moultrie, *Memoirs,* 2:7.

219. Lincoln to John Rutledge, May 28, 1779, Lincoln Papers.

220. Lachlan McIntosh to Lincoln, August 4, 1779, Misc. Mss., WLCL.

221. Barnard Beekman to Lincoln, August 7, 1779, Lincoln Papers.

222. Beekman to Lincoln, August 19, 1779, Lincoln Papers.

223. Lt. James Moore to Beekman, August 18, 1779, Lincoln Papers. The Loyalist Cowper was a different individual than the Whig Cowper mentioned earlier in this chapter.

224. Committee of Congress to John Jay, September 1, 1779, Lincoln Papers.

225. John Wereat to Lincoln, August 18, 1779, Lincoln Papers, PERK.

226. Lincoln to John Rutledge, August 8, 1779; Lincoln to Georgia Council, August 14, 1779, Lincoln Papers, BPL.

227. Fenn, *Pox Americana,* 114–15.

228. Henry Laurens to George Washington, October 24, 1779, *PHL,* 15:196–97.

229. Williamson to Lincoln, September 22, 1779, Lincoln Papers.

230. [James Wright] to [Alexander McGillivray], August 5, 1779, Revolutionary War Papers, folder 1, SHC.

231. Wright to Clinton, August 9, 1779, Carleton Papers, 18:2177.

232. A. Prevost to Germain, August 4, 1779, *DAR,* 17:176.

233. Taitt to Germain, August 6, 1779, *DAR,* 17:178–83. Taitt was in Savannah at the time Prevost sent his letter and was evidently aware of the general's comments.

234. A. Prevost to Germain, November 1, 1779, *DAR,* 17:241.

235. Lawrence, *Storm over Savannah,* 81, 157.

236. Henry Laurens to Jonathan Trumbull, September 25, 1779, Misc. Mss., WLCL.

237. Richard Parker to Lincoln, January 13, 1780; Williamson to Lincoln, January 25, 1780, Lincoln Papers.

238. Talk for the six Towns Indians to Captain Colbert, November 19, 1779, Carleton Papers, 20:2436; White, *Roots of Dependency,* 81, 87–88.

239. Germain to John Campbell, June 25, 1779, Germain Papers, vol. 18.

240. Haarmann, "Spanish Conquest of West Florida," 110.

241. Waldeck, *Eighteenth Century America,* 127–28.

242. Ibid., 129.

243. Ibid., 132.

244. Ibid., 134.

245. O'Brien, *Choctaws,* 10.

246. William Lee, *True and Interesting Travels,* 28, 37, 39–40.

247. O'Donnell, *Southern Indians,* 92.

248. Lewis Fuser to Clinton, postscript of October 24 to letter dated September 25, 1779, *RAM,* 2:39.

249. Gervais to Henry Laurens, December 26, 1778, *PHL,* 15:17.

250. Galphin to Henry Laurens, December 29, 1778, *PHL,* 15:20.

251. Nathaniel Hall to Lincoln, January 20, 1779, Lincoln Papers.

252. Mr. Wright to Lincoln, February 5, 1779, Lincoln Papers.

253. Samuel Stiles to William Telfair, February 21, 1779, Telfair Papers.

254. Oliver Hart to Joseph Hart, February 16, 1779, Oliver Hart Papers, SCL.

255. Quarles, *Negro in the Revolution,* 127.

256. Campbell, *Journal,* 33–34.

257. Lincoln to John Rutledge, February 11, 1779, Lincoln Papers.

258. Lincoln to Galphin, February 19, 1779, Lincoln Papers.

259. Undated, unsigned letter to "Sir," [1779], Lincoln Papers.

260. Stephen Delancey to Mrs. Delancey, January 14, 1779, in Crary, ed., *Price of Loyalty,* 273.

261. Wright to Assistant Commissary Gernon, May 13, 1779, Lincoln Papers.

262. Wright to Michie, May 13, 1779, Lincoln Papers. This and the previous letter were evidently intercepted by the Americans. Wright may have listed an eighth slave in this letter, but the name was either crossed out or obscured by an ink blot.

263. "An Account of the Life of Mr. David George from S.L.A. given by himself," Canada's Digital Collections, http://collections.ic.gc.ca/blackloyalists/documents (accessed July 30, 2001).

264. Edward Rutledge to [Thomas Rutledge?], February 17, 1779, Edward Rutledge Letters.

265. Moultrie to Charles Pinckney, April 6, 1779, in Moultrie, *Memoirs,* 1:364–65.

266. Quarles, *Negro in the Revolution,* 154.

267. Hart, Diary, March 4, 1779.

268. Stephen Bull to Moultrie, February 12, 1779, in Moultrie, *Memoirs,* 1:313.

269. Harry Ward, *Between the Lines,* 205.

270. Williamson to Lincoln, March 11, 1779, Lincoln Papers. In his reply, Williamson gives the captain's name as McKay.

271. Campbell, *Journal,* 63–64.

272. "Instructions to the Commissioners of Claims," March 5, 1779, Germain Papers, vol. 9.

273. "Commissioners of Claims Office," March 15, 1779, Germain Papers, vol. 9.

274. Searcy, "1779," *GHQ,* 178–79.

275. "Minute Book, Savannah Board of Police," February 17, 18, and 19, 1779, 251–53; Betty Wood, "'Until He Shall Be Dead,'" *GHQ,* 384–86.

276. "Minute Book, Savannah Board of Police," 245–57.

277. John Ashe to Lincoln, February 22, 1779, Lincoln Papers.

278. This information is compiled from advertisements for runaway slaves in the *Royal Georgia Gazette* from March 11, 1779, to March 14, 1782. The advertisement quoted was published in the June 28, 1781, edition.

279. John Laurens to Henry Laurens, February 17, 1779, *PHL,* 15:59–60.

280. Henry Laurens to George Washington, March 16, 1779, *PHL,* 15:66.

281. Alexander Hamilton to John Jay, March 14, 1779, in Hamilton, *PAH,* 2:17–19.

282. Committee Report to Congress, [March 25, 1779], *PHL,* 15:72–73.

283. Lincoln to John Rutledge, July 24, 1779, Lincoln Papers.

284. Henry Laurens to John Laurens, September 21, 1779, *PHL,* 15:169, 172.

285. Shaffer, "Between Two Worlds," *JSH,* 181–82.

286. Gadsden to Samuel Adams, July 6, 1779, in Gadsden, *Writings,* 166.

287. John Laurens to Hamilton, July 14, 1779, *PAH,* 2:102–3; Shaffer, "Between Two Worlds," 181; Charles Cotesworth Pinckney to Lincoln, June 28, 1779, Lincoln Papers.

288. Hamilton to John Laurens, September 11, 1779, *PAH,* 2:166–67.

289. Edward Telfair to Lincoln, June 1, 1779, Telfair Papers; Skelly, "Demonstration against Charleston," 153.

290. Eliza Lucas Pinckney to Thomas Pinckney, May 17, 1779, in Eliza Pinckney, "Letters," *SCHM,* 158–59.

291. Thomas Tudor Tucker to St. George Tucker, July 10, 1779, Tucker-Coleman Papers.

292. Moultrie to [Lincoln], May 15, 1779, in "Revolutionary Letters," *SCHGM,* part 1, 3.

293. Eliza Wilkinson to Miss M. P., 1782, in Wilkinson, *Letters,* 25, 26, 29.

294. Barnwell, "Rutledge," *JSH,* 218.

295. James Fergus, Pension Application, in Dann, ed., *Revolution Remembered,* 183.

296. Dillon to Col. John [Bourganin?], undated, April 1779, Lincoln Papers.

297. Moultrie to Lincoln, May 15, 1779, Lincoln Papers.

298. Morton Wilkinson to Lincoln, May 26, 1779, Lincoln Papers.

299. Lincoln to Moultrie, May 17, 1779, Lincoln Papers.

300. Capt. Philip Smith to Lincoln, June 25, 1779, Lincoln Papers.

301. James Hall Jr. to Lincoln, June 25, 1779, Lincoln Papers.

302. Eliza Wilkinson to Miss M. P., 1782, in Wilkinson, *Letters,* 62, 67–68, 70.

303. Moultrie to Lincoln, July 7, 1779, Lincoln Papers.

304. Joseph Barnwell to Lincoln, September 14, 1779, Lincoln Papers.

305. Lincoln to Lachlan McIntosh, August 2, 1779, Lincoln Papers.

306. Memorial of Sir James Wright . . . and several other Gentlemen, n.d., Carleton Papers, 16:1962; Searcy, "1779," 176–77.

307. "Case of Sir James Wright," 1784, Wright Papers, GHS.

308. Petition of James Graham and Basil Cowper, July 23, 1779, in *Proceedings and Minutes of the Governor and Council,* vol. 12, *CRG,* ed. Candler, 441–42.

309. Proceedings of the Georgia Council, July 26, 1779, *CRG,* 12:443–49.

310. Ibid., 12:444–45.

311. Frey, *Water from the Rock,* 96.

312. Meyronnet, "Journal of the Operations of the French Army," *New York Historical Society Quarterly,* 272; Lawrence, *Storm over Savannah,* 5.

313. John Jones to Polly Jones, October 3, 1779, Seaborn Jones Papers.

314. Timothy to Lincoln, September 25, 1779, Lincoln Papers.

315. John Rutledge to Lincoln, [September 26, 1779], Lincoln Papers.

316. John Rutledge to Lincoln, October 10, 1779, Lincoln Papers.

317. Petition of William Hanscomb to Augustine Prevost, March 30, 1780, 90:29; Return of Loyal Refugees who have come into Georgia, April 15, 1780, Clinton Papers, 92:44.

318. John J. Zubly to unnamed, November 30, 1779, John J. Zubly Papers.

319. Petition of Scipio Handley, On-Line Institute for Advanced Loyalist Studies, www.royalprovincial.com/military/mems.sc/clmhandley (accessed December 17, 2002).

320. Lawrence, *Storm over Savannah,* 81–82.

321. "English Journal of the Siege of Savannah," *Historical Magazine,* 13; Johnston, *Recollections of a Georgia Loyalist,* 58.

322. Lawrence, *Storm over Savannah,* 29, 49.

323. "Account of the attack upon Savannah," by a French artillery officer, in Kennedy, ed. and trans., *Muskets, Cannon Balls, and Bombs,* 30; Francis Rush Clark to John Strutt, October 27, 1779, Francis Rush Clark Papers, Feinstone Collection, no. 2338.

324. Lawrence, *Storm over Savannah,* 77–78; Francis Rush Clark to John Strutt, October 27, 1779, Clark Papers, Feinstone Collection, no. 2338.

325. Stokes to Mrs. Stokes, November 9, 1779, in Kennedy, ed. and trans., *Muskets, Cannon Balls, and Bombs,* 110, 111–12, 116n.

326. "English Journal of the Siege of Savannah," 15.

327. "Account of the Siege of Savannah," in *CGHS,* vol. 5, part 1, 138.

328. "English Journal of the Siege," 16.

329. Lawrence, *Storm over Savannah,* 129; Account Book, 1770–1800, typescript pp. 96–97, Philip Porcher Papers.

330. Petition of sundry Inhabitants of Savannah and . . . Christ Church, October 23, 1779, in *CRG,* 12:451–52.

331. Young, *Domesticating Slavery,* 78.

332. Marion to Lincoln, December 23, 1779, Lincoln Papers.

333. Marion to Lincoln, January 31, 1780, Lincoln Papers, PERK.

334. Daniel Horry to Lincoln, February 16, 1780, Lincoln Papers.

335. Augustine Prevost to Clinton, November 22, 1779, *RAM,* 2:64.

336. J. Leitch Wright, "Blacks in East Florida," 435.

337. Tonyn to Germain, July 3, 1779, *DAR,* 17:156–57.

338. Osborn, "Major-General John Campbell," *FHQ,* 319.

339. J. Leitch Wright, *Florida in the Revolution,* 108.

340. James Campbell to Alexander Dickson, September 9, 1779, Carleton Papers, 18:2264.

341. James Campbell to Captain Forster, September 9, 1779, Carleton Papers, 18:2265; Haarmann, "Spanish Conquest of West Florida," 110, 112.

342. Charles Grey quoted in Paul David Nelson, *Sir Charles Grey,* 93.

Chapter 5: The Reconquest of South Carolina

1. Germain to Clinton, September 27, 1779, Germain Papers, vol. 18.

2. Clinton, *American Rebellion,* 151; Clinton to Germain, August 21, 1779, and September 26, 1779, Clinton Papers, 66:13, 69:14; Clinton to unnamed, c. October 26, 1779, Clinton Papers, 73:17; Clinton to Germain, November 10, 1779, Clinton Papers, 74:35; Pancake, *This Destructive War,* 57, 60, 66.

3. "John Rutledge to Lincoln," February 28, 1779, 134.

4. Committee of Congress to Lincoln, March 19, 1780, Lincoln Papers.

5. David Ramsay quoted in Mattern, *Benjamin Lincoln,* 88.

6. Paul David Nelson, *General Horatio Gates,* 218, 220, 222.

7. Clinton, *American Rebellion,* 174.

8. "Handbill Issued after the Surrender of Charles Town," in Tarleton, *History of the Campaigns,* 68.

9. Returns of Arms and Ammunition, March 27, 1780; April 28, 1780; May 9, 1780; Request of Joseph Robinson, June 6, 1780, George Wray Papers, vol. 4, WLCL.

10. Harry Ward, *Between the Lines,* 174; John Hamilton's request for arms, May 23, 1780, and Donald Campbell's request for arms, June 21, 1780, Wray Papers, vol. 4.

11. Russell, "Siege of Charleston," *AHR,* 484, 485–86; "List of Inhabitants of Edisto who came on board the John to solicit Protection," February 14, 1780, Clinton Papers, 85:23.

12. Thomas Harvy and Moses Eastan to Clinton, March 18, 1780, Clinton Papers, 89:9.

13. Josiah Culbertson, Pension Application, in Dann, ed., *Revolution Remembered,* 175–76.

14. Moultrie to Lincoln, February 26, 1780, Lincoln Papers.

15. Borick, *Gallant Defense,* 58.

16. Kershaw to Lincoln, March 8, 1780, Lincoln Papers.

17. "Diary kept by Ensign Hartung," "Hessian Military Reports and Accounts," HDAR, item Z.

18. Ewald, *Diary of the American War,* 216–17; Borick, *Gallant Defense,* 58; Tarleton, *History of the Campaigns,* 19–20.

19. Clinton, *American Rebellion,* 161–62; Wright to Clinton, March 18, 1780, *RAM,* 2:104.

20. Wright to Clinton, April 6, 1780, *RAM,* 2:111.

21. James Simpson to Richard Pearis, May 3, 1780, On-Line Institute for Advanced Loyalist Studies, www.royalprovincial.com/military/rhist/scmil/scmlet1.htm (accessed August 16, 2002).

22. Borick, *Gallant Defense,* 231.

23. Tarleton, *History of the Campaigns,* 24.

24. "Handbill Issued after the Surrender of Charles Town," in Tarleton, *History of the Campaigns,* 69–70.

25. Clinton, Proclamation of May 22, 1780, in Tarleton, *History of the Campaigns,* 71–72.

26. Clinton and Marriot Arbuthnot, Proclamation of June 1, 1780, in Tarleton, *History of the Campaigns,* 75.

27. Paul Smith, *Loyalists and Redcoats,* 131.

28. Tarleton, *History of the Campaigns,* 25.

29. Letter from Charleston, May 14, 1780, no addressee or signature, in "Sundry Journals of Brunswick Troops," HDAR, item HZ.

30. "Diary kept by Ensign Hartung," "Hessian Military Reports and Accounts," HDAR, item Z. Ewald said that the group numbered sixty men and that they wanted officers as well as arms and ammunition to "take revenge on their neighbors, who had oppressed them very much up to now"; see Ewald, *Diary of the American War,* 242.

31. Peebles, *John Peebles' American War,* 377.

32. Borick, *Gallant Defense,* 231–32.

33. Clinton to Cornwallis, May 29, 1780, CP, PRO 30/11/2, 54.

34. Clinton to Germain, June 4, 1780, in Miller, ed., *American Revolution,* 14.

35. Wilhelm von Wilmowsky to Baron von Jungkenn, June 4, 1780, in Uhlendorf, ed. and trans., *Siege of Charleston,* 419.

36. Lambert, *South Carolina Loyalists,* 96; K. G. Davies, "The Restoration of Civil Government by the British in the War of Independence," in *Red, White, and True Blue,* ed. Esmond Wright, 125–26.

37. Simpson to Clinton, May 15, 1780, in Simpson, "Simpson's Reports," 518–19.

38. Simpson to Clinton, July 1, 1780, *RAM,* 2:149; Gibbes, "Story of His Life," 65; Stevens, "Autobiography," *SCHM,* 10. Gibbes put the number of those arrested at 100, Stevens at 150.

39. Patrick Ferguson to Cornwallis, May 30, 1780, CP, PRO 30/11/2, 58.

40. Nisbet Balfour to Cornwallis, June [3 or 4], 1780; Memorial of the Companies of Militia of Orangeburgh, June 12, 1780; Ferguson to Cornwallis, June 14, 1780, CP, PRO 30/11/2, 81, 129, 145.

41. Balfour to Cornwallis, June 6, 1780, CP, PRO 30/11/2, 96.

42. Innes to Cornwallis, June 8, 1780, CP, PRO 30/11/2, 114.

43. Fanning, *Narrative,* 14; Terms of Capitulation, June 10, 1780, CP, PRO 30/11/2, 133.

44. Joseph Robinson to his Friends, on the Frontiers of South Carolina, June 27, 1780, Carleton Papers, 24:2842.

45. Gray, "Colonel Robert Gray's Observations," *SCHGM,* 140, 148.

46. Cornwallis to Clinton, June 2, 1780, CP, PRO 30/11/72, 16.

47. Griffith Rutherford to Richard Caswell, June 29, 1780, Misc. Papers, series 1, vol. 1, NCSA.

48. Lutnick, *American Revolution and the British Press,* 156–58.

49. Robert Biddulph to [parents], March 24, 1780, in Biddulph, "Letters," *AHR,* 93.

50. Kathleen Wilson, *Sense of the People,* 259, 265.

51. Quoted in Hibbert, *Redcoats and Rebels,* 321.

52. Germain to Clinton, July 4, 1780, Germain Papers, vol. 18.

53. Norton, *British Americans,* 112. See, for example, Thomas Digges to Benjamin Franklin, July 12, 1780, and to John Adams, August 22, 1780, in Digges, *Letters,* 239, 252–53.

54. John Rutledge to S.C. Delegates in Congress, May 24, 1780, in Rutledge, "Letters," *SCHGM,* part 1, 133–34.

55. Seymour, "Journal of the Southern Expedition," in *Papers of the Delaware Historical Society,* 15:3–4.

56. Collins, *Autobiography,* 24.

57. Tarleton Brown, *Memoirs,* 9–10.

58. Abner Nash to Thomas Jefferson, June 25, 1780, in Jefferson, *PTJ,* 3:462.

59. Johann Hinrichs, "Diary," in *Siege of Charleston,* ed. and trans. Uhlendorf, 321–23.

60. Biddulph to [parents], August 26, 1780, in Biddulph, "Letters," 94.

61. Treacy, *Prelude to Yorktown,* 14.

62. Moultrie, *Memoirs,* 2:209–10.

63. Collins, *Autobiography,* 23.

64. Clinton, *American Rebellion,* 181–82.

65. Clinton, Proclamation of June 3, 1780, in Tarleton, *History of the Campaigns,* 73.

66. Clinton, Proclamation of May 22, 1780, in Tarleton, *History of the Campaigns,* 72; Stumpf, *Josiah Martin,* 185–87; William Smith, *Historical Memoirs,* 198–99.

67. Willcox, *Portrait of a General,* 313; Clinton, *American Rebellion,* 182.

68. Arbuthnot to Germain, May 2, 1780, Germain Papers, vol. 12.

69. Norton, *British Americans,* 108–9.

70. Germain to Clinton, July 4, 1780, Germain Papers, vol. 18.

71. Alexander Hamilton to Francois Marbois, September 13, 1780, Vandenberg Papers, Misc. Coll., WLCL.

72. William Smith, *Historical Memoirs,* 284, 296–97.

73. McCowen, *British Occupation,* 13–14, 16, 18–19; Balfour to Germain, February 18, 1781, Alexander Leslie Letterbook.

74. William Bull to unnamed, February 18, 1782, Earl of Shelburne Papers, 68:127.

75. Simpson to Clinton, July 16, 1780, *RAM,* 2:158.

76. Clinton, *American Rebellion,* 186.

77. Tarleton, *History of the Campaigns,* 89.

78. Proclamation of Charles, Earl Cornwallis, July 25, 1780, in Tarleton, *History of the Campaigns,* 125.

79. Bowler, *Logistics,* 27.

80. Tarleton, *History of the Campaigns,* 90.

81. Cornwallis to James Paterson, June 10, 1780, in Cornwallis, *Correspondence,* 1:46. Charles Ross, the editor, spells the recipient's name as "Pattison."

82. Cornwallis to Balfour, June 11, 1781, in Cornwallis, *Correspondence,* 46–47.

83. Samuel Carne to Christopher Rolleston, October 12, 1780, Samuel Carne Papers.

84. Tarleton, *History of the Campaigns,* 90.

85. "Instructions to Major Ferguson Inspector of Militia," May 22, 1780, CP, PRO 30/11/2, 44.

86. Cornwallis to Clinton, August 29, 1780, in Cornwallis, *Correspondence,* 58.

87. Paul Smith, *Loyalists and Redcoats,* 137.

88. Wickwire and Wickwire, *Cornwallis,* 128.

89. Clinton, "Journal of the Siege of Charleston," *SCHM,* 172.

90. Wickwire and Wickwire, *Cornwallis,* 171.

91. Ferguson to Cornwallis, June 6, 1780, CP, PRO 30/11/2, 92.

92. Balfour to Cornwallis, June 6, 1780, CP, PRO 30/11/2, 96.

93. Lambert, "Loyalist Odyssey," *SCHM,* 168–71.

94. Memorial of Robert Ballingall, March 13, 1786; Balfour to Ballingall, September 18, 1780; Affidavit of Cornwallis, March 14, 1786; Affidavit of Leslie, January 30, 1784, Misc. Mss. SC7003/AT7003, box 2, 154, 154a, NYSL.

95. Tarleton, *History of the Campaigns,* 90–91.

96. Cornwallis to Clinton, July 14, 1780, in Tarleton, *History of the Campaigns,* 118.

97. Memorial of Sundry Loyal Inhabitants of Charlestown, August 13, 1780, *Royal South Carolina Gazette,* August 23, 1780.

98. Anthony Allaire, Diary, June 5, 6, 10, 1780, Robinson Family Papers, NBM.

99. Uzal Johnson, Diary, June 22, 1780.

100. Bowler, *Logistics,* 151–53.

101. Balfour to Clinton, January 31, 1781, Leslie Letterbook.

102. Balfour to Clinton, April 7, 1781, Leslie Letterbook.

103. Orders, October 7, October 11, October 14, October 29, November 19, November 22, December 13, December 30, 1780, Wray Papers, vol. 5.

104. Major C. Fraser to Major Peter Traille, December 30, 1780, Wray Papers, vol. 5.

105. Evan McLaurin to Balfour, August 7, 1780, Emmet Collection, no. 6589.

106. Gray, "Colonel Robert Gray's Observations," 141, 144.

107. Cornwallis to Ferguson, June 16, 1780, CP, PRO 30/11/77, 14.

108. Wickwire and Wickwire, *Cornwallis,* 203–4.

109. Balfour to Cornwallis, June 27, 1780, CP, PRO 30/11/2, 200.

110. Uzal Johnson, Diary, June 23, 1780.

111. Lord Rawdon to Cornwallis, July 7, 1780, CP, PRO 30/11/2, 252.

112. Cornwallis to Paterson, June 10, 1780, CP, PRO 30/11/77, 3.

113. Cornwallis to Clinton, June 30, 1780, Germain Papers, vol. 12.

114. James, *Life of Marion,* 64; Winn, "General Winn's Notes," *SCHGM,* part 1, 202.

115. Flood, *Rise and Fight Again,* 271, 273; M. A. Moore, *Life of Lacey,* 3–4, 7.

116. Banastre Tarleton to Cornwallis, August 5, 1780, CP, PRO 30/11/63, 19.

117. Tarleton, *History of the Campaigns,* 91.

118. Ibid., 93. See also Lambert, *South Carolina Loyalists,* 128.

119. Tarleton, *History of the Campaigns,* 98; Bass, *Swamp Fox,* 35; Lambert, *South Carolina Loyalists,* 128–29.

120. Cornwallis to Nash, August 17, 1780, CP, PRO 30/11/79, 23. Nash denied the accusations, although he admitted that he had been unable to obtain information regarding Gray and Cassells. See Nash to Cornwallis, August 27, 1780, CP, PRO 30/11/63, 70.

121. Cornwallis to Clinton, August 6, 1780, in Tarleton, *History of the Campaigns,* 127.

122. Tarleton, *History of the Campaigns,* 98.

123. Cornwallis to Clinton, July 14, 1780, in Cornwallis, *Correspondence,* 51–52.

124. Gray, "Colonel Robert Gray's Observations," 141.

125. Rawdon to Cornwallis, July 7, 1780, CP, PRO 30/11/2, 252; Lambert, *South Carolina Loyalists,* 127–28.

126. Tarleton, *History of the Campaigns,* 91.

127. Cornwallis to Clinton, July 15, 1780, CP, PRO 30/11/72, 30.

128. Cornwallis to Clinton, August 6, 1780, in Clinton, *American Rebellion,* 448.

129. Balfour to [Henry Strachey?], August 30, [1780], Sir Henry Strachey Papers, vol. 1.

130. Horatio Gates to Colonels Hicks and Giles, Circular, July 29, 1780; "Copy of a Proclamation issued by General Gates, at Pedee," August 4, 1780, Horatio Gates Papers.

131. Thomas Sumter to Thomas Pinckney, August 12, 1780, Gates Papers.

132. Quoted in Flood, *Rise and Fight Again,* 302.

133. John Lloyd to [Mark Harford Jr.], January 20, 1781, John Lloyd Letters, photocopies provided by Gloucestershire Record Office.

134. Seymour, "Journal of the Southern Expedition," 4.

135. Charles Porterfield to Gates, August 3, 1780, Gates Papers.

136. Richard Caswell to Gates, August 4, 1780, Gates Papers.

137. Flood, *Rise and Fight Again,* 292.

138. Caswell to Gates, August 5, 1780, Gates Papers.

139. Matthew Ramsey to Gates, August 9, 1780, Gates Papers.

140. Flood, *Rise and Fight Again,* 311, 313.

141. Bass, *Green Dragoon,* 92–93; Christopher Ward, *Delaware Continentals,* 355; Sumter to Gates, August 15, 1780, in Tarleton, *History of the Campaigns,* 147–48.

142. Tarleton, *History of the Campaigns,* 104; Flood, *Rise and Fight Again,* 313, 325, 331. The actual numbers of Loyalist militia who served in the battle of Camden were fourteen officers, eight sergeants, and three hundred rank and file. Their proportion of casualties was the smallest of the units engaged, totaling only two wounded and three missing, which indicates that they must have been committed late in the action and then in a peripheral role. See Field Return of Cornwallis's Army, August 15, 1780, and Return of Casualties, August 16, 1780, Amherst Papers, War Office 34/126/73.

143. Seymour, "Journal of the Southern Expedition," 7; Christopher Ward, *Delaware Continentals,* 352; Edward Stevens to Jefferson, August 20, 1780, *PTJ,* 3:558.

144. Otho Williams to Hamilton, August 30, 1780, *PAH,* 2:385.

145. Flood, *Rise and Fight Again,* 336–37.

146. Otho Williams to Hamilton, August 30, 1780, *PAH,* 2:385.

147. Treacy, *Prelude to Yorktown,* 43, 46; Cornwallis to Germain, August 20, 1780, *DAR,* 18:145.

148. Cornwallis to Germain, August 21, 1780, in Tarleton, *History of the Campaigns,* 135.

149. Robert Gray to Cornwallis, September 30, 1780, CP, PRO 30/11/64, 130.

150. Innes to Cornwallis, September 5, 1780, CP, PRO 30/11/64, 29.

151. Tarleton, *History of the Campaigns,* 98.

152. George Turnbull to Cornwallis, June 14, 1780, CP, PRO 30/11/2, 147.

153. Cornwallis to Clinton, September 22, 1780, CP, PRO 30/11/72, 53.

154. Cornwallis to Clinton, June 30, 1780, in Tarleton, *History of the Campaigns,* 117.

155. Cornwallis to Germain, September 21, 1780, *DAR,* 18:173.

156. Cornwallis to Balfour, October 7, 1780, CP, PRO 30/11/81, 25; John Harris Cruger to Balfour, October 24, 1780, CP, PRO 30/11/3, 311.

157. James Dunlap to Balfour, July 15, 1780, CP, PRO 30/11/2, 315.

158. Ferguson to Cornwallis, July 24, 1780, CP, PRO 30/11/2, 360.

159. Ferguson to Rawdon, [August 14, 1780]; Resolution of Militia, August 13, 1780, CP, PRO 30/11/63, 95, 97.

160. Ferguson to Cornwallis, August 29, 1780, CP, PRO 30/11/63, 81.

161. Marion to Gates, September 15, 1780, Gates Papers; Bass, *Swamp Fox,* 48–51.

162. Bass, *Swamp Fox,* 68–69.

163. Cornwallis to Rawdon, August 4, 1780, CP, PRO 30/11/79, 8.

164. Marion to Gates, October 4, 1780, Gates Papers.

165. Robert England to Cornwallis, September 14, 1780, CP, PRO 30/11/64, 57.

166. James Wemyss to Cornwallis, July 28, 1780, CP, PRO 30/11/2, 377.

167. Wemyss to Cornwallis, July 31, 1780, CP, PRO 30/11/2, 395.

168. Wemyss to Cornwallis, September 20, 1780, and October 4, 1780, CP, PRO 30/11/3, 80, 184.

169. Turnbull to Cornwallis, October 4, 1780, CP, PRO 30/11/3, 178.

170. Balfour to Rawdon, October 26, 1780, CP, PRO 30/11/3, 289.

171. Report of James Williams, September 5, 1780, Gates Papers.

172. Flood, *Rise and Fight Again,* 351–52.

173. Allaire, Diary, September 7, 9, 12, 14, 1780.

174. Col. J. Phillips to Cornwallis, September 13, 1780, CP, PRO 30/11/64, 54.

175. Barnwell, "Rutledge," 221–22.

176. John Rutledge to Sumter, October 6, 1780, Thomas Sumter Papers, vol. 1.

177. John Rutledge to S.C. Delegates in Congress, September 20, 1780, in Rutledge, "Letters," part 1, 137–38.

178. Cornwallis to Balfour, September 13, 1780, CP, PRO 30/11/80, 20; Pancake, *This Destructive War,* 109, 112.

179. Examination of William Allman, September 20, 1780, Gates Papers.

180. William Davidson to Gates, September 24, 1780; Jethro Sumner to Gates, September 24, 1780, Gates Papers.

181. Cornwallis to Clinton, August 29, 1780, in Cornwallis, *Correspondence,* 58–59.

182. Cornwallis to Balfour, August 29, 1780. See also Cornwallis to Cruger, August 27, 1780, CP, PRO 30/11/79, 45, 39.

183. Ferguson to Cornwallis, September 14, 1780, CP, PRO 30/11/64, 60.

184. Allaire, Diary, September 15, 20, 23, 24, 30, 1780; Davidson to Gates, September 24, 1780; Sumner to Gates, September 24, 1780, Gates Papers.

185. Collins, *Autobiography,* 50.

186. Pancake, *This Destructive War,* 117–18, 120.

187. Ferguson to Cornwallis, October 1, 1780, CP, PRO 30/11/3, 160.

188. Flood, *Rise and Fight Again,* 356–57.

189. Collins, *Autobiography,* 52–53.

190. Calhoon, *Loyalists in Revolutionary America,* 496; Fanning, *Narrative,* 14.

191. Rawdon to Clinton, October 29, 1780, in Cornwallis, *Correspondence,* 63.

192. Allaire, Diary, October 14, 1780.

193. Quoted in Hibbert, *Redcoats and Rebels,* 284.

194. Allaire, Diary, October 15, 17, and 18, 1780.

195. Lts. John Taylor and William Stevenson to Cornwallis, November 30, 1780, CP, PRO 30/11/4, 254.

196. Uzal Johnson, Diary, November 1, 1780.

197. Treacy, *Prelude to Yorktown,* 74.

198. Allaire, Diary, November 5–22, 1780.

199. Chesney, *Journal,* 10, 19–21.

200. Wickwire and Wickwire, *Cornwallis,* 219.

201. *Royal Georgia Gazette,* January 4, 1781.

202. Tarleton, *History of the Campaigns,* 166.

203. William Smallwood to Gates, October 27, 1780, Gates Papers.

204. Cornwallis to Smallwood, November 10, 1780, Gates Papers.

205. Cornwallis to Gates, December 1, 1780, Gates Papers.

206. Gates to President of Congress, November 26, 1780, Gates Letterbook, Gates Papers. Smallwood, in his reply to Cornwallis, said that while it was his duty "to discountenance Acts of Inhumanity," those who had abused the prisoners were volunteers and thus fell outside the Continental army's jurisdiction; see Smallwood to Cornwallis, December 8, 1780, CP, PRO 30/11/91, 19.

207. John Rutledge to S.C. Delegates in Congress, November 20, 1780, in Rutledge, "Letters," part 1, 143–44.

208. Gray, "Colonel Robert Gray's Observations," 144–45.

209. Lamb, *Original and Authentic Journal,* 308.

210. Gray, "Colonel Robert Gray's Observations," 144.

211. Wickwire and Wickwire, *Cornwallis,* 221.

212. Gray, "Colonel Robert Gray's Observations," 143; Collins, *Autobiography,* 54.

213. Wright to Clinton, February 3, 1780, *DAR,* 18:45.

214. Return of Georgia Loyalists, February 1780, Clinton Papers, 87:25; A. Prevost to Clinton, April 7, 1780, Carleton Papers, 22:2680.

215. Wright to Germain, May 20, 1780, *DAR,* 18:98.

216. Coleman, "Restored Colonial Georgia," 13; Wright's Speech to the Assembly, May 9, 1780, and Disqualifying Act of 1780, in Killion and Waller, eds., *Georgia and the Revolution,* 212–13, 213–20; Furlong, "Civilian-Military Conflict," 428.

217. Robertson, "Second Occupation of Augusta," *GHQ,* 424–25; Cashin, *King's Ranger,* 108.

218. Robertson, "Second Occupation of Augusta," 428, 431.

219. Brown to Cruger, August 6, 1780, CP, PRO 30/11/62, 6.

220. Robertson, "Second Occupation of Augusta," 432–36; Cashin, *King's Ranger,* 114–15, 118.

221. Cruger to Cornwallis, October 2, 1780, CP, PRO 30/11/3, 170.

222. Robertson, *Loyalism in Revolutionary Georgia,* 13.

223. Alured Clarke to Cornwallis, August 20, 1780, CP, PRO 30/11/63, 50.

224. John Campbell to Clinton, February 10, 1780, Carleton Papers, 21:2565; Starr, *Tories, Dons, and Rebels,* 169–74; Haarmann, "Spanish Conquest of West Florida," 116–17, 119; Elias Durnford to John Campbell, March 2, 1780, Carleton Papers, 22:2604.

225. Lincoln to Galphin, January 18, 1780, Lincoln Papers, BPL.

226. Williamson to Lincoln, March 7, 1780, Lincoln Papers, PERK.

227. Maj. Gen. Johann Christoph von Huyn to Gen. Wilhelm Knyphausen, March 8, 1780, "Correspondence of Knyphausen," part 2, HDAR, item GG.

228. Russell, "Siege of Charleston," 483; Johann Hinrichs, "Diary," in *Siege of Charleston,* ed. and trans. Uhlendorf, 157, 221.

229. Uzal Johnson, Diary, March 7, 1780.

230. Lt. Christian Friedrich Bartholomai, "Extracts from the Diary Covering the Expedition to the Southern Part of North America," in Bartholomai and von Feilitzsch, *Diaries of Two Anspach Jaegers,* 106.

231. Hinrichs, "Diary," in *Siege of Charleston,* ed. and trans. Uhlendorf, 157, 159.

232. Augustine Prevost to Clinton, March 2, 1780, *RAM,* 2:96.

233. Clinton to Augustine Prevost, March 8, 1780, *RAM,* 2:99.

234. Augustine Prevost to Clinton, March 19, 1780, *RAM,* 2:104.

235. Augustine Prevost to Clinton, March 30, 1780, *RAM,* 2:108.

236. Wright to Clinton, March 18, 1780, *RAM,* 2:104.

237. Clinton to Wright, March 25, 1780, *RAM,* 2:106.

238. Thomas Brown to Germain, March 10, 1780, *DAR,* 18:55.

239. Clinton to [Alexander Innes], February 19, 1780, *RAM,* 2:93.

240. Ewald, *Diary of the American War,* 231–32.

241. Bartholomai, "Extracts from the Diary," in Bartholomai and von Feilitzsch, *Diaries of Two Anspach Jaegers,* 135.

242. Clinton, "Journal of the Siege of Charleston," 164.

243. Cashin, *King's Ranger,* 105, 106.

244. Thomas Brown to Cornwallis, June 18, 1780, CP, PRO 30/11/2, 166.

245. Ibid.

246. Balfour to Cornwallis, June 24, 1780, CP, PRO 30/11/2, 191.

247. Thomas Brown to Cornwallis, June 28, 1780, CP, PRO 30/11/2, 208.

248. Cornwallis to Balfour, July 3, 1780, CP, PRO 30/11/78, 3.

249. Cornwallis to Brown, July 17, 1780, CP, PRO 30/11/78, 22.

250. Isaac Shelby to the Public, April 1823, in "Battle of King's Mountain," *MAH,* 353.

251. Valentine, *Lord North,* 2:213; O'Donnell, *Southern Indians,* 102.

252. William Smith, *Historical Memoirs,* 155.

253. Declaration of Amnesty to Rebels, September 9, 1780, CP, PRO 30/11/64, 62.

254. Rawdon to Cornwallis, June 11, 1780, CP, PRO 30/11/2, no. 123.

255. Douglas Brown, *Catawba Indians,* 266–67, 270; Bass, *Gamecock,* 55.

256. Evan McLaurin to Balfour, August 7, 1780, Emmet Collection, no. 6589.

257. Cashin, *King's Ranger,* 114–18; O'Donnell, *Southern Indians,* 103–4; Cruger to Cornwallis, September 19, 1780, CP, PRO 30/11/64, 77.

258. Balfour to Cornwallis, September 20, 1780, CP, PRO 30/11/64, 83.

259. Calloway, *American Revolution in Indian Country,* 262; Germain to Thomas Brown, July 5, 1780, *DAR,* 18:116.

260. O'Donnell, *Southern Indians,* 96.

261. John Campbell to Clinton, February 10, 1780, Carleton Papers, 21:2565.

262. Cameron to Clinton, July 18, 1780, *RAM,* 2:159; Cameron to Germain, July 18, 1780, *DAR,* 18:124; O'Donnell, *Southern Indians,* 96–97.

263. Waldeck, *Eighteenth Century America,* 149, 152–53.

264. Cameron to Clinton, July 18, 1780, *RAM,* 2:159.

265. John Campbell to Germain, May 15, 1780, *DAR,* 18:93; O'Donnell, *Southern Indians,* 98; Osborn, "Major-General John Campbell," 329.

266. Waldeck, *Eighteenth Century America,* 154–56.

267. Ibid., 160–66.

268. Cameron to Germain, July 18, 1780, *DAR,* 18:120–21.

269. Osborn, "Major-General John Campbell," 332–34.

270. Bernardo de Galvez to John Campbell, April 9, 1780, Carleton Papers, 22:2681; John Campbell to Galvez, April 20, 1780, Carleton Papers, 22:2692.

271. Cameron quoted in Starr, *Tories, Dons, and Rebels,* 177.

272. Osborn, "Major-General John Campbell," 334.

273. Cameron to Clinton, July 18, 1780, *RAM,* 2:159, 160; O'Donnell, *Southern Indians,* 99, 101.

274. Charles Shaw to Germain, June 19, 1780, Germain Papers, vol. 12.

275. John Campbell quoted in Rush, *Spain's Final Triumph,* 21.

276. Waldeck, *Eighteenth Century America,* 168.

277. O'Brien, *Choctaws,* 45–46, Waldeck, *Eighteenth Century America,* 169–71.

278. Cameron to Germain, July 18, 1780, *DAR,* 18:120.

279. Gibson, *Chickasaws,* 72; Calloway, *American Revolution in Indian Country,* 227.

280. Lincoln to John Rutledge, January 30, 1780, and February 14, 1780, Lincoln Papers, BPL; Mattern, *Benjamin Lincoln,* 92; Borick, *Gallant Defense,* 40, 43.

281. Lincoln to John Rutledge, February 28, 1780, Lincoln Papers, BPL.

282. Mattern, *Benjamin Lincoln,* 105.

283. Charles Cotesworth Pinckney to Isaac Harleston, January 20, 1780, Isaac Harleston Papers; Bartholomai, "Extracts from the Diary," in Bartholomai and von Feilitzsch, *Diaries of Two Anspach Jaegers,* 115; Sayen, "Oared Fighting Ships," *SCHM,* 233. Permission to recruit blacks was granted on January 27, 1780, when the British invasion was imminent.

284. Bartholomai, "Extracts from the Diary," in Bartholomai and von Feilitzsch, *Diaries of Two Anspach Jaegers,* 124.

285. Frey, *Water from the Rock,* 118.

286. Bartholomai, "Extracts from the Diary," in Bartholomai and von Feilitzsch, *Diaries of Two Anspach Jaegers,* 116.

287. Bauer, "1780 Siege of Charleston," part 2, *SCHM,* 70.

288. Borick, *Gallant Defense,* 100.

289. Mary Beth Norton, "'What an Alarming Crisis Is This': Southern Women and the American Revolution," in *Southern Experience in the American Revolution,* ed. Crow and Tise, 213.

290. Wemyss to John André, February 27 and 29, 1780, Clinton Papers, 87:9, 87:21.

291. Clinton, "Journal of the Siege of Charleston," 168; Maj. James Habersham's Journal of the Siege of Charleston, Joseph V. Bevan Collection.

292. Hinrichs, "Diary," in *Siege of Charleston,* ed. and trans. Uhlendorf, 189, 199; Johann Christoph von Huyn, "Diary of Major General Johann Christoph von Huyn," in *Siege of Charleston,* ed. and trans. Uhlendorf, 371; "Diary kept by Ensign Hartung," "Hessian Military Reports and Accounts," HDAR, item Z.

293. Ewald, *Diary of the American War,* 202. Additional descriptions of slave-gathering excursions are found on pp. 199 and 214.

294. Borick, *Gallant Defense,* 100.

295. Frey, *Water from the Rock,* 119.

296. Unnamed to Captain Russell, December 22, 1779, CP, PRO 30/11/1, 33. The probable author was Andrew Elliott, who wrote several documents concerning military government, civil regulations, and proclamations that were included in a packet with the letter to Russell.

297. Ferguson to Clinton, February 20, 1780, in Hugh F. Rankin, ed., "An Officer Out of His Time: Correspondence of Major Patrick Ferguson, 1779–1780," in *Sources of American Independence,* ed. Peckham, 356.

298. Clinton's Commission to Moncrief, Hay, and Fraser, February 13, 1780, Clinton Papers, 85:16.

299. Commissarys of Captures Return of Negroes Horses &ca, March 17, 1780, Clinton Papers, 89:1.

300. Abraham Depeyster, Orderly Book.

301. Return of Negroes employ'd in the Service of the Royal Artillery, April 28, 1780, Clinton Papers, 95:27.

302. Bauer, "1780 Siege of Charleston," part 2, 28; John Wilson, "Journal of the Siege of Charleston," *SCHM,* 176.

303. Bartholomai, "Extracts from the Diary," in Bartholomai and von Feilitzsch, *Diaries of Two Anspach Jaegers,* 127.

304. Ewald, *Diary of the American War,* 203, 221, 225; Bauer, "1780 Siege of Charleston," part 2, 64, 70; Von der Malsburg to General Knyphausen, June 3, 1780, "Hessian Military Reports and Accounts," HDAR, item Z; Hinrichs, "Diary," in *Siege of Charleston,* ed. and trans. Uhlendorf, 301.

305. Uzal Johnson, Diary, March 25, 1780.

306. Allaire, Orderly Book, March 8, 1780, Robinson Family Papers, NBM.

307. Depeyster, Orderly Book.

308. Bartholomai, "Extracts from the Diary," in Bartholomai and von Feilitzsch, *Diaries of Two Anspach Jaegers,* 111, 113; Quarles, *Negro in the Revolution,* 143; Russell, "Siege of Charleston," *AHR,* 494–95; Peebles, *John Peebles' American War,* 356, 357, 369.

309. Von Huyn, "Diary," in *Siege of Charleston,* ed. and trans. Uhlendorf, 379.

310. Tarleton, *History of the Campaigns,* 15–17.

311. Uzal Johnson, Diary, April 14, 1780.

312. Hinrichs, "Diary," in *Siege of Charleston,* ed. and trans. Uhlendorf, 207.

313. Proceedings of Court Martial, March 24, 1780, Clinton Papers, 89:34.

314. Hinrichs, "Diary," in *Siege of Charleston,* ed. and trans. Uhlendorf, 185.

315. Ewald, *Diary of the American War,* 197, 199, 202.

316. John Rutledge to Benjamin Garden, March 2, 1780, Pringle-Garden Family Papers.

317. Lamb, *Original and Authentic Journal,* 294–95.

318. Bauer, "1780 Siege of Charleston," part 2, 71–73.

319. Bartholomai, "Extracts from the Diary," in Bartholomai and von Feilitzsch, *Diaries of Two Anspach Jaegers,* 112.

320. George Jones, "Black Hessians," *SCHM,* 292, 294–95, 300.

321. Stephen Jarvis, "Narrative of Colonel Stephen Jarvis," in *Loyalist Narratives,* ed. Talman, 185, 186, 189–90.

322. Clinton to Cornwallis, May 20, 1780, CP, PRO 30/11/2, 38.

323. Proclamation of Sir Henry Clinton, June 30, 1779, Clinton Papers, 62:28.

324. George Wray Orderly Book, June 1, 1780, Wray Papers; Frey, *Water from the Rock,* 124.

325. Clinton, Proclamation of May 27, 1780, Carleton Papers, 23:2767.

326. Clinton to Commandant of Charlestown and Cornwallis, June 3, 1780, Carleton Papers, 23:2800.

327. "Answers to Several Queries and Memorandums relative to the Command in Carolina," June 3, 1780, CP, PRO 30/11/61, 7.

328. Tarleton, *History of the Campaigns,* 89–90.

329. McCowen, *British Occupation,* 100–101; Frey, *Water from the Rock,* 121.

330. Tarleton, *History of the Campaigns,* 89–90.

331. McCowen, *British Occupation,* 101, 103.

332. Crow, "What Price Loyalism?," *NCHR,* 219, 220, 222–23.

333. Olwell, *Masters, Slaves, and Subjects,* 253.

334. Frey, *Water from the Rock,* 127.

335. Borick, *Gallant Defense,* 101.

336. James Custer to Henry Laurens, June 1780, *PHL,* 15:303–4.

337. Samuel Massey to Henry Laurens, June 12, 1780, *PHL,* 15:305.

338. Turnbull to Cornwallis, September 22, 1780, CP, PRO 30/11/64, 102.

339. This information is compiled from advertisements for runaway slaves that appeared in the *South Carolina Royal Gazette, South Carolina and American General Gazette,* and *Royal South Carolina Gazette* from June 1780 to March 1782. The advertisement quoted appears in the *South Carolina and American General Gazette,* December 13, 1780.

340. Proclamation of Nisbet Balfour, February 9, 1781, *Royal South Carolina Gazette,* February 14, 1781.

341. McCowen, *British Occupation,* 101, 103, 105.

342. Gervais to Henry Laurens, July 6, 1780, *PHL,* 15:311–12.

343. William Ancrum to James Edward Colleton, July 14, 1780, Margaret Colleton Papers.

344. Simpson to Clinton, July 16, 1780, Carleton Papers, 24:915.

345. McLaurin to Balfour, August 7, 1780, Emmet Collection, no. 6589.

346. Lloyd to [Mark Harford Jr.], August 8, 1780, Lloyd Letters.

347. Lloyd to [Mark Harford Jr.], January 20, 1781, Lloyd Letters.

348. Peter Bounetheau to Cornwallis, August 3, 1780, Peter Bounetheau Papers.

349. Rawdon to Cornwallis, July 27, 1780, CP, PRO 30/11/2, 369.

350. King, *Memoirs,* http://collections.ic.gc.ca/blackloyalists/documents (accessed July 30, 2001).

351. Fenn, *Pox Americana,* 127–28, 274.

352. King, *Memoirs.*

353. Ibid.

354. James, *Life of Marion,* 68.
355. Balfour to Cornwallis, September 22, 1780, CP, PRO 30/11/64, 96.
356. Cornwallis to Balfour, September 27, 1780, CP, PRO 30/11/80, 48A.
357. "Lord Cornwallis's Orders 27th. Septr. 1780," in Newsome, ed., "British Orderly Book," part 3, *NCHR,* 280.
358. Augustine Prevost to Clinton, March 30, 1780, *RAM,* 2:107–8.
359. Gervais to Henry Laurens, April 28, 1780, *PHL,* 15:287.
360. Wright to Germain, October 27, 1780, *DAR,* 18:211.
361. Alured Clarke to Cornwallis, July 10, 1780, CP, PRO 30/11/2, 258.
362. Haarmann, "Spanish Conquest of West Florida," 119.

CHAPTER 6: PRECIPICE

1. Balfour to Blucke, October 25, 1780, John Saunders Papers.
2. Balfour to Blucke, October 31, 1780, Saunders Papers.
3. Marion to Gates, October 15, 1780, Gates Papers.
4. Marion to Gates, October 15, 1780, and November 4, 1780, Gates Papers.
5. Marion to Gates, November 4, 1780, Gates Papers; Bass, *Swamp Fox,* 75–77.
6. Balfour to Blucke, October 31, 1780, Saunders Papers.
7. Cornwallis to Clinton, December 3, 1780, in Tarleton, *History of the Campaigns,* 200.
8. Marion to Gates, November 9, 1780, Gates Papers.
9. Tarleton, *History of the Campaigns,* 174.
10. Tarleton to Cornwallis, November 11, 1781, CP, PRO 30/11/4, 96; Tarleton, *History of the Campaigns,* 174; Marion to Gates, December 6, 1780, Gates Papers.
11. Bass, *Swamp Fox,* 89–90.
12. Marion to Gates, November 21, 1780, Gates Papers.
13. M. Coffin to Cornwallis, November 23, 1780; Balfour to Cornwallis, November 24, 1780, CP, PRO 30/11/4, 183, 193.
14. Rawdon to Cornwallis, November 27, 1780, CP, PRO 30/11/4, 215.
15. Cornwallis to Balfour, November 4, 1780, CP, PRO 30/11/82, 6.
16. Cornwallis to Balfour, November 1, 1780; Cornwallis to Cruger, November 4, 1780; Cornwallis to Balfour, November 16, 1780, CP, PRO 30/11/82, 1, 8, 48.
17. Cornwallis to Tarleton, November 8, 1780, in Cornwallis, *Correspondence,* 65.
18. Kirkland to Cornwallis, November 8, 1780, CP, PRO 30/11/4, 67.
19. Kirkland to Cornwallis, November 10, 1780, CP, PRO 30/11/4, 82.
20. Balfour to Cornwallis, November 5, 1780, CP, PRO 30/11/4, 27.
21. Bass, *Gamecock,* 102.
22. Cornwallis to Balfour, November 17, 1780, CP, PRO 30/11/82, 55.
23. Daniel Wallace, "Incidents of the Revolution in Union York & Spartanburgh Districts," undated manuscript, South Carolina box, NYPL.
24. Cornwallis to Cruger, November 11, 1780, CP, PRO 30/11/82, 24.
25. Cornwallis to Leslie, November 12, 1780, in Cornwallis, *Correspondence,* 69.
26. Cornwallis to Balfour, November 16, 1780, CP, PRO 30/11/82, 46.
27. Pancake, *This Destructive War,* 126; Cornwallis to Kirkland, November 11, 1780, CP, PRO 30/11/82, 28.
28. Cornwallis to Rawdon, November 13, 1780, CP, PRO 30/11/82, 38.
29. Cruger to Cornwallis, November 23, 1780, CP, PRO 30/11/4, 181.

30. Pancake, *This Destructive War,* 126–27; Cornwallis to Balfour, November 22, 1780, CP, PRO 30/11/82, 81.

31. Cornwallis to Rawdon, November 20, 1780, CP, PRO 30/11/82, 71.

32. Cornwallis to Balfour, November 22, 1780, CP, PRO 30/11/82, 81.

33. Cornwallis to Clinton, December 3, 1780, in Clinton, *American Rebellion,* 476.

34. Cruger to Cornwallis, November 27, 1780, and December 3, 1780; Cunningham to Cornwallis, December 3, 1780, CP, PRO 30/11/4, 217, 173, 275; Chesney, *Journal,* 113–14; Sumter to Gates, December 1, 1780, Gates Papers; Kirkland to Cornwallis, February 22, 1781, CP, PRO 30/11/67, 83.

35. Tarleton, *History of the Campaigns,* 181.

36. Cornwallis to Cruger, November 25, 1780, CP, PRO 30/11/82, 101.

37. Thomas Brandon to Sumter, December 4, 1780, Sumter Papers, vol. 1.

38. Turnbull to Cornwallis, November 5, 1780, CP, PRO 30/11/4, 25; Smallwood to Morgan, November 3, 1780, Theodorus Bailey Myers Manuscript Collection, no. 1022, DLAR.

39. Rawdon to Cornwallis, November 19, 1780, CP, PRO 30/11/4, 234.

40. Rawdon to Cornwallis, December 8, 1780, CP, PRO 30/11/4, 291.

41. Plan for a Corps of Volunteers, [December 8, 1780]; Rawdon to Cornwallis, December 9 and 18, 1780, CP, PRO 30/11/4, 294, 298, 355.

42. Smallwood to Greene, December 6, 1780, *PNG,* 6:538–39.

43. Kirkwood, "Journal and Order Book," 12–13; Haller, *William Washington,* 68; Cornwallis to Rawdon, December 2, 1780, CP, PRO 30/11/83, 3; Rawdon to Cornwallis, December 1, 1780, CP, PRO 30/11/4, 261.

44. Seymour, "Journal of the Southern Expedition," 10.

45. John Marshel to Greene, December 22, 1780; Greene to Marshel, December 25, 1780, *PNG,* 6:606, 612.

46. Tarleton, *History of the Campaigns,* 184.

47. Rawdon to Cornwallis, December 3, 1780; David George to Cornwallis, December 11, 1780, CP, PRO 30/11/66, 25, 33.

48. Wickwire and Wickwire, *Cornwallis,* 233.

49. Cornwallis to Tarleton, December 18, 1780, CP, PRO 30/11/83, 55.

50. George to Cornwallis, December 30, 1780, CP, PRO 30/11/66, 44. For a sampling of additional intelligence provided by Loyalists, see also Rawdon to Cornwallis, January 1 and 5, 1781, CP, PRO 30/11/67, 3, 12; and Rawdon to Cornwallis, November 22, 1780, CP, PRO 30/11/4, 175. These are only a fraction of the references to Loyalists' intelligence reports in the collection.

51. Cornwallis to Cruger, December 7, 1780, CP, PRO 30/11/83, 25.

52. H. Barry to Robert Ballingall, January 18, 1781, Misc. Mss. SC7003/AT7003, box 2, 154a, NYSL.

53. Cornwallis to Rawdon, December 19, 1780, CP, PRO 30/11/83, 57; Account of British and American forces, enclosed in John Rutledge to S.C. Delegates in Congress, December 8, 1780, in Rutledge, "Letters," *SCHGM,* part 3, 59–60.

54. John Rutledge to [S.C. Delegates in Congress], January 10, 1781, in Rutledge, "Letters," part 3, 67.

55. Thomas Jefferson to Thomas Sim Lee, January 15, 1781, in Thomas Sim Lee, "Revolutionary Mail Bag," *MHM,* 223.

56. Mackenzie, *Diary,* 2:447.

57. Valentine, *Lord North,* 2:238.
58. Pancake, *This Destructive War,* 128, 130–31.
59. Thayer, *Nathanael Greene,* 290.
60. Ichabod Burnet to unnamed, January 23, 1781, Ichabod Burnet Letter.
61. Greene to John Cox, January 9, 1781, *PNG,* 7:82.
62. Greene to Hamilton, January 10, 1781, *PAH,* 2:529.
63. Greene to Catharine Greene, December 29, 1780; William Pendergast to Greene, January 23, 1781, *PNG,* 7:16, 179; Babits, *Devil of a Whipping,* 8.
64. Rawdon to Cornwallis, January 11, 1781, CP, PRO 30/11/67, 14.
65. Gray, "Colonel Robert Gray's Observations," 148–49.
66. Cruger to Cornwallis, December 9 and 16, 1780, CP, PRO 30/11/4, 300, 335.
67. Isaac Allen to Cornwallis, December 19, 1780, CP, PRO 30/11/4, 359.
68. Ichabod Burnet to unnamed, January 23, 1781, Burnet Letter.
69. Frederick Kimball to Greene, January 16, 1781, *PNG,* 7:135; Rawdon to Cornwallis, December 29, 1780, CP, PRO 30/11/4, 419; State of the Troops . . . at Camden, January 1, 1781, CP, PRO 30/11/103, 3.
70. Edward Giles to Otho Williams, December 29, 1780, Robert Gilmor Jr. Papers.
71. Christopher Ward, *Delaware Continentals,* 367.
72. Greene to unnamed, January 1–23, 1781, *PNG,* 7:176.
73. Greene to Marion, December 24, 1780, *PNG,* 6:607.
74. Greene to Morgan, undated, Myers Collection, no. 867.
75. Greene to Morgan, January 8, 1781, Myers Collection, no. 869.
76. Rawdon to Cornwallis, December 8, 1780, CP, PRO 30/11/4, 291.
77. Archibald McArthur to Cornwallis, December 16, 1780, CP, PRO 30/11/4, 339.
78. Lewis Morris Jr. to Lewis Morris, December 29, 1780, in Morris, "Letters to General Morris," in *Collections of the New York Historical Society,* 8:475.
79. Charles O'Hara to the Duke of Grafton, January 6, 1781, in O'Hara, "Letters," *SCHM,* 171.
80. Lloyd to [Mark Harford Jr.], January 20, 1781, Lloyd Letters.
81. Rawdon to Cornwallis, December 5, 1780, CP, PRO 30/11/4, 281.
82. Cornwallis to Rawdon, December 7, 1780, CP, PRO 30/11/83, 27.
83. Cornwallis to Clinton, December 4, 1780, CP, PRO 30/11/72, 65.
84. Gray to Cornwallis, November 5, 1780, CP, PRO 30/11/4, 98.
85. Cornwallis to Greene, December 27, 1780, *PNG,* 7:5–6.
86. Greene to Hamilton, January 10, 1781, *PAH,* 2:529.
87. Greene to Samuel Huntington, December 28, 1780, *PNG,* 7:9.
88. Higginbotham, *Daniel Morgan,* 124.
89. Giles to Otho Williams, December 29, 1780, Gilmor Papers.
90. Haller, *William Washington,* 80–81.
91. Higginbotham, *Daniel Morgan,* 124.
92. Morgan to Greene, December 31, 1780, *PNG,* 7:30.
93. John Davidson to Mordecai Gist, January 10, 1781, Mordecai Gist Papers, MHS.
94. Seymour, "Journal of the Southern Expedition," 12–13.
95. Christopher Ward, *Delaware Continentals,* 370; Treacy, *Prelude to Yorktown,* 77. Ward mistakenly calls the stream "Fairfort Creek."
96. Morgan to Greene, January 15, 1781, *PNG,* 7:127.
97. Greene to Morgan, January 8, 1781, Myers Collection, no. 869.

98. Morgan to Greene, January 4, 1781, Myers Collection, no. 944.

99. Higginbotham, *Daniel Morgan,* 129.

100. Pancake, *This Destructive War,* 132–33; Cornwallis to Tarleton, January 3, 1781, CP, PRO 30/11/84, 39.

101. Babits, *Devil of a Whipping,* 51; Chesney, *Journal,* 21; Tarleton, *History of the Campaigns,* 214.

102. Tarleton, *History of the Campaigns,* 214.

103. Landrum, *Colonial and Revolutionary History of Upper South Carolina,* 289; Treacy, *Prelude to Yorktown,* 99; Babits, *Devil of a Whipping,* 53, 81; Higginbotham, *Daniel Morgan,* 135.

104. Pancake, *This Destructive War,* 135–38.

105. Cornwallis to Tarleton, January 7, 1781, CP, PRO 30/11/84, 29.

106. Cornwallis to Leslie, January 14, 1781, CP, PRO 30/11/84, 61; Babits, *Devil of a Whipping,* 133.

107. Pancake, *This Destructive War,* 157–61.

108. Balfour to Jeffery Amherst, March 28, 1781, Jeffery Amherst Correspondence and Papers, DLAR.

109. Chesney, *Journal,* 22.

110. Balfour to Cornwallis, February 2, 1781, CP, PRO 30/11/70, no. 26.

111. O'Hara to the Duke of Grafton, April 20, 1781, in O'Hara, "Letters," 173.

112. Babits, *Devil of a Whipping,* 138, 141.

113. John Rutledge to S.C. Delegates in Congress, December 8, 1780, in Rutledge, "Letters," *SCHGM,* part 2, 44–45.

114. Balfour to Germain, January 16, 1781, Leslie Letterbook.

115. South Carolina Loyalists Oath of Allegiance, 1781, South Carolina Box—Loyalists, NYPL.

116. Rawdon to Cornwallis, January 14, 1781, CP, PRO 30/11/67, 20.

117. William Charles Wells to James Currie, March 18, 1781, in William Charles Wells, "Letter from Wells to Currie," *SCHGM,* 43.

118. Cornwallis to Balfour, January 12, 1781, CP, PRO 30/11/84, 51; "Narrative of Colonel Jarvis," in Talman, ed., *Loyalist Narratives,* 196, 201; Bass, *Gamecock,* 153.

119. Cornwallis to Rawdon, February 4, 1781, CP, PRO 30/11/85, 1.

120. Kirkland to Cornwallis, February 22, 1781, CP, PRO 30/11/67, 83.

121. Rawdon to Cornwallis, March 7, 1781, CP, PRO 30/11/69, 7.

122. John Watson to Marion, March 9, 1781, in Gibbes, ed., *Documentary History,* 3:34.

123. Bass, *Gamecock,* 130–31; Bass, *Swamp Fox,* 156–57; Rawdon to Cornwallis, March 7 and 24, 1781, CP, PRO 30/11/69, 7, 21.

124. Balfour to Marion, March 2, 1781, in Gibbes, ed., *Documentary History,* 3:27.

125. Marion to Balfour, March 7, 1781, Emmet Collection, no. 6625.

126. Watson to Marion, March 15, 1781, in Gibbes, ed., *Documentary History,* 3:39.

127. Moultrie to Marion, April 16, 1781, in Gibbes, ed., *Documentary History,* 3:52.

128. Sumter to Marion, March 28, 1781, in Gibbes, ed., *Documentary History,* 3:45.

129. Benjamin Ford to Gist, April 15, 1781, Gist Papers; Pickens to Greene, April 4, 1781, in "Letters to General Greene and Others," *SCHGM,* part 1, 102.

130. Pickens to Greene, April 4, 1781, in "Letters to General Greene and Others," part 1, 102.

131. Pancake, *This Destructive War,* 190; State of the Troops left in South Carolina under . . . Lord Rawdon, January 15, 1781, CP, PRO 30/11/103, 15. Most secondary sources give a total British strength of 8,000, but this detailed return gives a total of 5,240 officers and men, including sick and wounded, in the southern district.

132. Cornwallis to Balfour, April 24, 1781, CP, PRO 30/11/85, 49.

133. Ewald, *Diary of the American War,* 299.

134. Thayer, *Nathanael Greene,* 342.

135. Rawdon to Cornwallis, April 26, 1781, CP, PRO 30/11/5, 262.

136. Kyte, "Victory in the South," *NCHR,* 338.

137. Thayer, *Nathanael Greene,* 348.

138. Greene to Samuel Huntington, April 22, 1781, *PNG,* 8:130.

139. Bass, *Swamp Fox,* 183; Marion to Greene, April 21, 1781; Thomas Wade to Greene, April 29, 1781, *PNG,* 8:129, 175.

140. Bass, *Gamecock,* 150–51.

141. Henry Nase, Diary, April 14, 1781, Nase Family Papers.

142. Pancake, *This Destructive War,* 191–92.

143. Henry Lee to Greene, April 19, 1781, *PNG,* 8:120–21.

144. Pickens to Greene, April 8, 1781, *PNG,* 8:71.

145. Pickens to Greene, May 3 and 8, 1781, *PNG,* 8:197, 223.

146. Sumter to Greene, April 25, 1781, *PNG,* 8:150.

147. Sumter to Greene, April 27, 1781, *PNG,* 8:164.

148. Balfour to Cornwallis, April 20, 1780, CP, PRO 30/11/5, 231.

149. Balfour to McArthur, April 10, 1781, Leslie Letterbook; William Harden to Marion, April 18, 1781, in Gibbes, ed., *Documentary History,* 3:53–55.

150. Davie, *Revolutionary War Sketches,* 40.

151. Von der Malsburg to Knyphausen, April 29, 1781, "Hessian Military Reports and Accounts," HDAR, item Z.

152. Balfour to Cornwallis, April 26, 1781, CP, PRO 30/11/6, 29.

153. Balfour to Cornwallis, April 20, 1781, CP, PRO 30/11/5, 231; Pancake, *This Destructive War,* 195–200; Christopher Ward, *Delaware Continentals,* 432.

154. Rawdon to Cornwallis, May 24, 1781, CP, PRO 30/11/6, 106.

155. Moultrie, *Memoirs,* 2:279.

156. Sumter to Greene, May 2, 1781, *PNG,* 8:193.

157. Sumter to Greene, May 4, 1781, *PNG,* 8:204.

158. Pickens to Greene, May 20, 1781, *PNG,* 8:286.

159. Marion to Greene, May 19, 1781, *PNG,* 8:285.

160. Marion to Greene, May 29, 1781, *PNG,* 8:329.

161. Marion to Greene, June 16, 1781, *PNG,* 8:394.

162. Sumter to Greene, May 12, 1781; Greene to Nash, May 14, 1781; Ichabod Burnet to Robert Lawson, May 17, 1781, *PNG,* 8:248, 255, 275; Henry Lee, *Revolutionary War Memoirs,* 352; Balfour to Cornwallis, May 21, 1781, CP, PRO 30/11/6, 93; Pancake, *This Destructive War,* 200–201.

163. Greene to William Davie, May 23, 1781, *PNG,* 8:298.

164. Major General Carl von Bose to Knyphausen, May 4, 1781, "Correspondence of Knyphausen," HDAR, item GG.

165. Balfour to Cornwallis, May 21, 1781, CP, PRO 30/11/6, 93.

166. Cornwallis to Rawdon, May 20, 1781, in Cornwallis, *Correspondence,* 98.

167. Cornwallis to Balfour, May 3, 1781, CP, PRO 30/11/86, 1.

168. Proclamation of Rawdon and Balfour, May 24, 1781, *South Carolina Royal Gazette,* May 30–June 2, 1781.

169. Rawdon to Cornwallis, June 5, 1781, CP, PRO 30/11/6, 174; Chesney, *Journal,* 23–24, 27; Nase, Diary, May 19, 1781; Balfour to Alexander Stewart, June 2, 1781, Misc. Mss. SC7003/AT7003, box 2, 125, NYSL.

170. "State of the Troops Embarked under . . . Coll. Gould," March 18, 1781; Rawdon to Cornwallis, June 5, 1781; Balfour to Cornwallis, June 10, 1781, CP, PRO 30/11/6, 155, 174, 208.

171. Otho Williams to Mercy Stull, May 4, 1781, Otho Holland Williams Papers.

172. Seymour, "Journal of the Southern Expedition," 27–28.

173. Kirkwood, "Journal and Order Book," 18.

174. Otho Williams to Elie Williams, June 12, 1781, Williams Papers.

175. Greene to Samuel Huntington, June 20, 1781, *PNG,* 8:422.

176. Thayer, *Nathanael Greene,* 357.

177. Otho Williams to Elie Williams, June 12, 1781, Williams Papers.

178. Cann, "War in the Backcountry," *SCHM,* 10–11; Cruger to Rawdon, June 3, 1781, CP, PRO 30/11/6, 213.

179. Henry Lee to Greene, June 22, 1781, *PNG,* 8:442.

180. John Rudulph to Greene, June 18, 1781, *PNG,* 8:412.

181. Bass, *Gamecock,* 184, 187.

182. Cann, "War in the Backcountry," 10–11; Rawdon to Cornwallis, August 2, 1781, CP, PRO 30/11/6, 347; Pancake, *This Destructive War,* 213–14.

183. Rawdon to Cornwallis, August 2, 1781, CP, PRO 30/11/6, 347.

184. Lambert, *South Carolina Loyalists,* 173–74.

185. Pickens to Greene, July 10, 1781, *PNG,* 8:518–19.

186. Otho Williams to Greene, July 5, 1781, *PNG,* 8:500.

187. William Henderson to Greene, July 6, 1781; Greene to Thomas McKean, July 17, 1781, *PNG,* 8:501, 9:30.

188. Seymour, "Journal of the Southern Expedition," 28.

189. Joseph Johnson, *Traditions and Reminiscences,* 101–2, 583; Harry Ward, *Between the Lines,* 225; Lambert, *South Carolina Loyalists,* 200–203.

190. Janice Potter and Robert M. Calhoon, "The Character and Coherence of the Loyalist Press," in *Press and the Revolution,* ed. Bailyn and Hench, 263–64.

191. Rawdon to Cornwallis, June 6, 1781, in Tarleton, *History of the Campaigns,* 481.

192. Balfour to the Militia Prisoners of War, May 17, 1781, Feinstone Collection, no. 74.

193. Stephen Moore and John Barnwell to Balfour, May 18, 1781, Feinstone Collection, no. 954; Stephen Moore, Barnwell, et al. to Balfour, May 19, 1781, Stephen Moore Papers.

194. Potter and Calhoon, "Character and Coherence of the Loyalist Press," 262.

195. Greene to the Inhabitants upon the Saluda, June 5, 1781, *PNG,* 8:349.

196. Greene to Pickens, June 5, 1781, *PNG,* 8:350.

197. Royster, *Light-Horse Harry Lee,* 35–38.

198. Address of Council of Georgia to Governor Wright, November 21, 1780, *DAR,* 18:231.

199. Wright to Cornwallis, November 20, 1780, CP, PRO 30/11/4, 166; Alured Clarke to Cornwallis, January 26, 1781, CP, PRO 30/11/5, 64.

200. Cashin, *King's Ranger,* 126; Robertson, "Second Occupation of Augusta," 437–38; Brown to [Cruger?], January 23, 1781 [misdated 1780], CP, PRO 30/11/62, 2.

201. Brown to [Cruger?], January 23, 1781 [misdated 1780], CP, PRO 30/11/62, 2.

202. Cashin, *King's Ranger,* 127; Balfour to Brown, February 9, 1781 [misdated 1782], Leslie Letterbook.

203. Brown to [Cruger?], January 23, 1781 [misdated 1780], CP, PRO 30/11/62, 2.

204. Wright to Germain, March 5, 1781, *DAR,* 20:73.

205. Cashin, *King's Ranger,* 127–28.

206. Cashin, "Nathanael Greene's Campaign for Georgia," *GHQ,* 48.

207. Scott, "Quaker Settlement of Wrightsborough," *GHQ,* 220.

208. Wright to Cornwallis, April 23, 1781, CP, PRO 30/11/5, 247.

209. Address to Governor Wright, May 4, 1781, Wright Papers, PERK.

210. Cashin, *King's Ranger,* 131–37.

211. Pickens to Greene, June 7, 1781, *PNG,* 8:359.

212. Taylor to John Wesley, February 28, 1782, in Taylor, "Georgia Loyalist's Perspective," 136–38.

213. Richard Pearis Loyalist Claim, August 22, 1783, SCHS.

214. Proclamation of Greene, June 9, 1781, *PNG,* 8:370.

215. Wright to Germain, June 14, 1781, *DAR,* 20:161; Coleman, *American Revolution in Georgia,* 135–36.

216. Elijah Clarke to Greene, June 19, 1781, *PNG,* 8:414.

217. William Lee, *True and Interesting Travels,* 28–30.

218. Tonyn to Germain, December 9, 1780, *DAR,* 18:253.

219. John Campbell to Germain, November 26, 1780, *DAR,* 18:232–34.

220. Haarmann, "Spanish Conquest of West Florida," 120.

221. Haynes, *Natchez District,* 134–35; John Campbell to Germain, May 7, 1781, *DAR,* 20:136; Caughey, "Natchez Rebellion," *LHQ,* 57–59.

222. Haynes, *Natchez District,* 136–37; Caughey, "Natchez Rebellion," 59–60.

223. Starr, *Tories, Dons, and Rebels,* 190–91.

224. Haynes, *Natchez District,* 137, 140; Caughey, "Natchez Rebellion," 60, 63–68.

225. Gibson, *Chickasaws,* 73; Starr, *Tories, Dons, and Rebels,* 217–18.

226. Starr, ed., "Case and Petition of His Majesty's Loyal Subjects," *FHQ,* 205.

227. John Rutledge to Morgan, December 22, 1780, Myers Collection, no. 1017.

228. Thomas Brown to Cornwallis, December 17, 1780, CP, PRO 30/11/4, 345.

229. Cornwallis to Balfour, December 29, 1780, in Cornwallis, *Correspondence,* 75–76.

230. Cornwallis to Clinton, December 29, 1780, in Cornwallis, *Correspondence,* 76.

231. Cornwallis to Rawdon, December 28, 1780, CP, PRO 30/11/83, 89.

232. Greene to Samuel Huntington, December 28, 1780, *PNG,* 7:9.

233. John Rutledge to S.C. Delegates in Congress, December 30, 1780, in Rutledge, "Letters," part 3, 63. See also Greene to Jefferson, December 31, 1780, in Jefferson, *PTJ,* 4:254.

234. Calloway, *American Revolution in Indian Country,* 204; Samuel Riggs, Pension Application, in Dann, ed., *Revolution Remembered,* 307–9; Arthur Campbell to Jefferson, January 15, 1781, *PTJ,* 4:362; O'Donnell, *Southern Indians,* 106–8.

235. Arthur Campbell to Greene, February 8, 1781, *PNG,* 7:258.

236. Greene to Arthur Campbell, February 26, 1781, *PNG,* 7:351.

237. Appointment of a Commission to Deal with the Cherokee and Chickasaw Nations, February 26, 1781, *PNG,* 7:351–52.

238. Benjamin Ford to Gist, March 10, 1781, Gist Papers.

239. Thayer, *Nathanael Greene,* 339.

240. Arthur Campbell to Nathaniel Pendleton, April 23, 1781, *PNG,* 8:136–37.

241. Robert Anderson to Greene, May 24, 1781, *PNG,* 8:307.

242. Calloway, *American Revolution in Indian Country,* 205.

243. Robert Lanier to Greene, May 27, 1781, *PNG,* 8:317.

244. Cashin, *King's Ranger,* 125.

245. Ibid., 130, 133, 136.

246. Gates to Greene, December 10, 1780, and note, *PNG,* 6:560; Douglas Brown, *Catawba Indians,* 266–67, 270; Merrell, *Indians' New World,* 216.

247. Tonyn to Cornwallis, January 29, 1781, CP, PRO 30/11/67, 35.

248. Tonyn to Alured Clarke, January 29, 1781, CP, PRO 30/11/67, 44.

249. Tonyn to Alured Clarke, April 30, 1781, CP, PRO 30/11/5, 274.

250. Alured Clarke to Tonyn, May 1, 1781; Tonyn to Clarke, May 4, 1781, CP, PRO 30/11/6, 17, 43.

251. Clinton to John Campbell, October 21, 1780, Carleton Papers, 26:3079.

252. Cameron to Germain, October 31, 1780, *DAR,* 18:220–22.

253. Ibid., 18:219–20.

254. Starr, *Tories, Dons, and Rebels,* 182; O'Donnell, *Southern Indians,* 104.

255. John Campbell to Thomas Brown, November 15, 1780, Carleton Papers, 26:3149.

256. Starr, *Tories, Dons, and Rebels,* 178–79; O'Donnell, *Southern Indians,* 105.

257. Haarmann, "Spanish Conquest of West Florida," 120–21; Starr, *Tories, Dons, and Rebels,* 183; O'Donnell, *Southern Indians,* 112; Cameron to Germain, February 10, 1781, *DAR,* 20:58–59.

258. O'Donnell, *Southern Indians,* 113; O'Brien, *Choctaws,* 10; Miranda, "Diary of the Siege of Pensacola," *FHQ,* 176.

259. James Bruce to Clarke & Milligan, September 19, 1780, in Bruce, "Ordeal by Siege," *FHQ,* 293.

260. Bruce to Clarke & Milligan, April 26, 1781, in Bruce, "Ordeal by Siege," 296.

261. Farmar, "Bernardo de Galvez's Siege of Pensacola," *LHQ,* 316.

262. Galvez, "Combat Diary," *FHQ,* 181.

263. Farmar, "Bernardo de Galvez's Siege of Pensacola," 317; Galvez, "Combat Diary," 182.

264. Galvez, "Combat Diary," 182.

265. Ibid., 183; Farmar, "Bernardo de Galvez's Siege of Pensacola," 318; O'Brien, *Choctaws,* 49.

266. Galvez, "Combat Diary," 183.

267. Miranda, "Diary of the Siege of Pensacola," 177.

268. Galvez, "Combat Diary," 184.

269. Farmar, "Bernardo de Galvez's Siege of Pensacola," 319, 320–22; Galvez, "Combat Diary," 187, 188, 189–93; Miranda, "Diary of the Siege of Pensacola," 177–84.

270. Farmar, "Bernardo de Galvez's Siege of Pensacola," 323.

271. Ibid., 326.

272. Ibid., 326; Miranda, "Diary of the Siege of Pensacola," 190–91; John Campbell to Germain, May 12, 1781, *DAR,* 20:138–39.

273. John Campbell to Clinton, April 9, 1781, in Rush, *Spain's Final Triumph,* 94–96.

274. John Campbell to Clinton, May 7 and 12, 1781, in Rush, *Spain's Final Triumph,* 97, 101.

275. Michael D. Green, "The Creek Confederacy in the American Revolution: Cautious Participants," in *Anglo-Spanish Confrontation,* ed. Coker and Rea, 71–72.

276. Cameron to Germain, May 27, 1781, *DAR,* 20:150.

277. Miranda, "Diary of the Siege of Pensacola," 194.

278. O'Donnell, *Southern Indians,* 114, 116.

279. Cameron to Germain, May 27, 1781, *DAR,* 20:150.

280. For examples, see Cornwallis to Tarleton, November 14, 1780, CP, PRO 30/11/82, 45A; Tarleton to [Turnbull?], November 5, 1780; Rawdon to Cornwallis, November 13, 1780; Rawdon to Cornwallis, December 1, 1780, CP, PRO 30/11/4, 63, 110, 236; Bass, *Green Dragoon,* 110; Kyte, "Francis Marion as an Intelligence Officer," *SCHM,* 224; Bass, *Swamp Fox,* 129.

281. Otho Williams to Morgan, January 25, 1781, Myers Collection, no. 1072.

282. Allen to Henry Haldane, December 29, 1780, CP, PRO 30/11/4, 426.

283. Christopher Ward, *Delaware Continentals,* 447.

284. Ibid., 447–48; Bass, *Ninety Six,* 398; Cann, "War in the Backcountry," *SCHM,* 4, 6, 8.

285. Balfour to Blucke, October 25, 1780; G. Benson to Saunders, February 26, 1781; [Saunders?] to [Balfour?], February 26, 1781, Saunders Papers.

286. Alured Clarke to Cornwallis, November 29, 1780, CP, PRO 30/11/4, 236.

287. Thomas Brown to John Douglass, April 12, 1781; Certification of Douglass's Slaves Captured at Fort Cornwallis, June 5, 1781, On-Line Institute for Advanced Loyalist Studies, www.royalprovincial.com/military/black/blkord.htm and www.royalprovincial.com/military/black/blkpris1.htm (accessed February 2, 2004); Pearis Loyalist Claim, August 22, 1783, SCHS.

288. Turnbull to Cornwallis, November 3, 1780, CP, PRO 30/11/4, 14.

289. William Burrows to unnamed, February 27, 1781, CP, PRO 30/11/105, 4.

290. Robert Muncreef to Allen Swainston, February 17, 1781, Colleton Papers.

291. Sampson Neyle to John Sandford Dart, March 3, 1781, CP, PRO 30/11/105, 5.

292. William Bull to Germain, June 28, 1781, *DAR,* 20:165; John Cruden to Col. Alexander Stewart, October 28, 1781, CP, PRO 30/11/7, 10.

293. Olwell, *Masters, Slaves, and Subjects,* 149–50.

294. William Bull to Germain, March 22, 1781, *DAR,* 20:94–95.

295. Simpson to Germain, December 31, 1780, *DAR,* 18:264.

296. William Bull to Germain, March 22, 1781, *DAR,* 20:94; Cruden to Capt. McMahon, February 2, 1781, CP, PRO 30/11/7, 8.

297. Deposition of Ephraim Harrison, November 21, 1780, Emmet Collection, no. 6820.

298. Balfour to Cornwallis, November 17, 1780, CP, PRO 30/11/4, 149.

299. William Mills to Cornwallis, November 28, 1780, CP, PRO 30/11/4, 229.

300. Cornwallis to Balfour, December 11, 1780, CP, PRO 30/11/83, 36.

301. Cornwallis to Tarleton, December 15, 1780, in Tarleton, *History of the Campaigns,* 206.

302. Newsome, ed., "British Orderly Book," part 3, *NCHR,* 276, 277, 280, 287.

303. Ibid., part 2, 177, 183.

304. Olwell, *Masters, Slaves, and Subjects,* 254; General List of Negores [*sic*] Employed in the Royal Artillery Department, Returns of April, May, and June 1781, Wray Papers, vol. 6.

305. Greene to George Washington, February 28, 1781, *PNG,* 7:370.

306. Woodward B. Skinner, "Ethnic Groups Influence the History of Pensacola," in *Siege!,* ed. Parks, 69.

307. Articles of Capitulation, May 9, 1781, in Rush, *Spain's Final Triumph,* 89, 90.

308. Samuel Mathis to William Davie, June 26, 1819, Samuel Mathis Papers; Coleman, *American Revolution in Georgia,* 139.

309. Troxler, "Refuge, Resistance, and Reward," 591; J. Leitch Wright, "Blacks in East Florida," 436–38; Siebert, *Loyalists in East Florida,* 1:96–100.

310. Tonyn to Germain, July 30, 1781, *DAR,* 20:204; J. Leitch Wright, "Blacks in East Florida," 435; Siebert, *Loyalists in East Florida,* 1:93.

311. John Rutledge to Morgan, December 22, 1780, Myers Collection, no. 1017.

312. John Rutledge to Morgan, January 25, 1781, Myers Collection, no. 1019.

313. Higginbotham, *Daniel Morgan,* 142; Receipts given by Andrew Pickens as agent for the American troops, January 24, 1780 (misdated, should be 1781), Andrew Pickens Papers.

314. Babits, *Devil of a Whipping,* 134, 135.

315. Bass, *Gamecock,* 144.

316. Greene to Marion, May 17, 1781, *PNG,* 8:276–77.

317. Greene to Sumter, May 17, 1781, *PNG,* 8:278.

318. Bass, *Gamecock,* 145.

CHAPTER 7: BRITISH COLLAPSE

1. Balfour to [Wright?], July 20, 1781, Carleton Papers, 31:3633.

2. Narrative and Observations of John Cruden, June 1, 1781, Misc. Mss. SC7003/AT7003, box 2, NYSL.

3. Simpson to Knox, July 28, 1781, *DAR,* 20:199–200.

4. William Bull to Germain, July 2, 1781, *DAR,* 20:168–69.

5. *South Carolina Royal Gazette,* July 7–11, 1781.

6. Pickens to Greene, July 19, 1781, *PNG,* 9:49.

7. Pickens to Greene, July 25, 1781, *PNG,* 9:77.

8. Isaac Huger to Lewis Morris Jr., July 26, 1781, *PNG,* 9:86.

9. Henry Lee to Greene, July 29, 1781; Greene to Lee, July 29, 1781; Greene to Pickens, July 30, 1781, *PNG,* 9:102, 103, 109.

10. William Pierce to St. George Tucker, July 20, 1781, in Pierce, "Southern Campaign of Greene," *MAH,* 434.

11. Balfour to Clinton, July 21, 1781, Leslie Letterbook; Lambert, *South Carolina Loyalists,* 204–5.

12. William Pierce to St. George Tucker, August 26, 1781, in Pierce, "Southern Campaign of Greene," 436.

13. Lambert, *South Carolina Loyalists,* 205.

14. Balfour to Greene, September 3, 1781, *PNG,* 9:284–85.

15. Fletchall et al. to King George III, April 19, 1782, South Carolina Loyalists and Rebels, http://sc_tories.tripod.com/list_of_murdered_loyalists.htm (accessed July 11, 2002).

16. John Rutledge to [S.C. Delegates in Congress], September 18, 1781, in Rutledge, "Letters," *SCHGM,* part 5, 156–57, 158.

17. Henry Lee to Greene, August 8, 1781; Thomas Wade to Greene, August 9, 1781, *PNG,* 9:150–51, 156.

18. Greene to Joseph Reed, August 6, 1781, *PNG,* 9:136.

19. Greene to Washington, August 6, 1781, *PNG,* 9:139, 140.

20. Greene to Washington, December 12, 1782, *PNG,* 12:281.

21. Alexander Stewart to Cornwallis, September 9, 1781, *DAR,* 20:227; Pancake, *This Destructive War,* 216–17, 220–21.

22. John Rutledge to Marion, September 2, 1781, in Gibbes, ed., *Documentary History,* 3:131.

23. John Rutledge to Marion, September 3, 1781, in Gibbes, ed., *Documentary History,* 3:134.

24. Gadsden to S.C. Delegates in Congress, September 17, 1781, in Gadsden, *Writings,* 176.

25. John Rutledge to Marion, September 15, 1781, in Gibbes, ed., *Documentary History,* 3:162.

26. Proclamation of John Rutledge, September 27, 1781, in Gibbes, ed., *Documentary History,* 3:175–78.

27. John Rutledge to Sumter, October 9, 1781, Sumter Papers, vol. 2.

28. Henry Lee to unnamed, October 2, 1781, in Lee, "Henry Lee on the Southern Campaign," *Virginia Magazine of History and Biography,* 147.

29. John James to Marion, September 20, 1781, in Gibbes, ed., *Documentary History,* 3:171.

30. Peter Horry to Greene, September 20, 1781, *PNG,* 9:379.

31. Marion to Greene, September 23, 1781, *PNG,* 9:386.

32. Marion to Greene, September 27, 1781, *PNG,* 9:403.

33. Peter Horry to Greene, September 27, 1781, *PNG,* 9:406.

34. Pancake, *This Destructive War,* 233–35.

35. Ibid., 237; Henry Lee, *Revolutionary War Memoirs,* 523; Leslie to Clinton, December 1, 1781, *DAR,* 20:267–68.

36. Greene to John Rutledge, December 3, 1781, *PNG,* 10:3–4.

37. William Bull to Germain, November 11, 1781, *DAR,* 20:259.

38. Derrill Hart to Richard Hampton, November 1, 1781, in Gibbes, ed., *Documentary History,* 3:205.

39. Gray, "Colonel Robert Gray's Observations," 154–55.

40. Bass, *Gamecock,* 212–13.

41. Greene to Sumter, November 2, 1781, *PNG,* 9:517–18.

42. Greene to William Parsons, November 3, 1781, *PNG,* 9:524.

43. Sumter to Greene, November 14 and 23, 1781, *PNG,* 9:575, 615; Sumter to Greene, December 7 and 9, 1781, *PNG,* 10:15, 24; Lambert, *South Carolina Loyalists,* 207.

44. LeRoy Hammond to Greene, December 2, 1781, *PNG,* 9:651; Lambert, *South Carolina Loyalists,* 208–9; Waring, *Fighting Elder,* 103–4; Bass, *Gamecock,* 212–13.

45. Sumter to Greene, November 23, 1781, *PNG,* 9:615.

46. Sumter to Greene, November 24, 1781, *PNG,* 9:623–24.

47. Greene to Otho Williams, December 2, 1781, *PNG,* 9:650.

48. Sumter to Greene, November 23 and 27, 1781; Greene to Sumter, November 25 and 28, 1781, *PNG,* 9:615, 627, 633–34; Sumter to Greene, December 7, 1781, *PNG,* 10:15.

49. Gray, "Colonel Robert Gray's Observations," 154–55.

50. Sumter to Greene, December 9, 1781, *PNG,* 10:24.

51. Sumter to Greene, December 19, 1781, *PNG,* 10:80–81.

52. Leslie to Earl of Leven, November 29, 1781, Alexander Leslie Papers, NAS.

53. Leslie to Earl of Leven, December 14, 1781, Leslie Papers, NAS.

54. Leslie to Clinton, December 4, 1781, Carleton Papers, 34:3927.

55. Lambert, *South Carolina Loyalists,* 220.

56. Leslie to Clinton, December 4, 1781, Carleton Papers, 34:3926.

57. Proclamation of Leslie, December 15, 1781, Alexander Leslie Paper, NCSA.

58. Leslie to Clinton, December 27, 1781, *DAR,* 20:287.

59. Aedenus Burke to Middleton, January 25, 1782, in Middleton, "Correspondence," *SCHGM,* part 1, 191.

60. Edward Rutledge to Middleton, February 26, 1782, in Middleton, "Correspondence," part 2, 7.

61. Nadelhaft, *Disorders of War,* 77.

62. Edward Rutledge to Middleton, February 8, 1782, in Middleton, "Correspondence," part 2, 2–3.

63. Edward Rutledge to Middleton, February 14, 1782, in Middleton, "Correspondence," part 2, 5.

64. Burke to Middleton, January 25, 1782, in Middleton, "Correspondence," part 1, 192–93.

65. Middleton to Burke, April 7, 1782, in Middleton, "Correspondence," part 2, 29.

66. *South Carolina Royal Gazette,* March 16–20, 1782.

67. Edward Rutledge to Middleton, February 14, 1782, in Middleton, "Correspondence," part 2, 5–6.

68. Burke to Middleton, May 14, 1782, in Middleton, "Correspondence," part 1, 197.

69. William Pierce to St. George Tucker, April 6, 1782, in Pierce, "Southern Campaign of Greene," 441.

70. "A Suffering Loyalist," July 12, 1782, *South Carolina Royal Gazette,* July 10–13, 1782.

71. William Bull to Germain, March 25, 1782, *DAR,* 21:50.

72. Frey, *Water from the Rock,* 137.

73. Leslie to Clinton, January 29, 1782, *RAM,* 2:388.

74. Memorial of Robert Ballingall, March 13, 1786; Affidavit of Balfour, March 10, 1783; Affidavit of Leslie, January 30, 1784, Misc. Mss. SC7003/AT7003, 154, 154a, NYSL.

75. Tilden, "Extracts from the Journal," *PMHB,* 217.

76. McDowell, "Journal," *Pennsylvania Archives,* 310.

77. Burke to Middleton, January 25, 1782, in Middleton, "Correspondence," part 1, 192.

78. Greene to Joseph Vince, January 3, 1782, *PNG,* 10:155.

79. Burke to Middleton, January 25, 1782, in Middleton, "Correspondence," part 1, 192.

80. Burke to Middleton, May 14, 1782, in Middleton, "Correspondence," part 1, 200, 201.

81. Lambert, *South Carolina Loyalists,* 221.

82. Benjamin Thompson to Leslie, February 25, 1782, *RAM,* 2:404–5.

83. Narrative of John Cruden, [1782], South Carolina Box—Loyalists.

84. Cruden to Clinton, February 19, 1782, in Crary, ed., *Price of Loyalty,* 292.

85. Dunmore to Germain, February 5, 1782, *DAR,* 21:36–37.

86. Selby, *Dunmore,* 65.

87. Gray, "Colonel Robert Gray's Observations," 158.

88. Unnamed to Greene, April 1, 1782, in Gibbes, ed., *Documentary History,* 3:288.

89. Greene to Marion, April 12, 1782, *PNG,* 11:36.

90. Josiah Harmar to Otho Williams, April 10, 1782, Williams Papers.

91. Marion to Peter Horry, March 7, 1782, in Gibbes, ed., *Documentary History,* 3:264.

92. Marion to Peter Horry, March 13, 1782, in Gibbes, ed., *Documentary History,* 3:271.

93. Hezekiah Maham to Greene, May 20, 1782, *PNG,* 11:225–26.

94. John Barnwell to Greene, March 6, 1782, *PNG,* 10:458.

95. Greene to Robert Morris, March 9, 1782, *PNG,* 10:469.

96. Biddulph to [parents], March 12, 1782, in Biddulph, "Letters," 106.

97. John Wallace to Greene, March 26, 1782, *PNG,* 10:542; Gist to John Sterett, April 10, 1782, Gist Papers.

98. Finney, "Revolutionary War Diaries," April 6, 1782, *SCHM,* 134.

99. Joseph Johnson, *Traditions and Reminiscences,* 548–49.

100. Marion to Greene, June 1, 1782, *PNG,* 11:278.

101. Thomas Farr to Greene, April 27, 1782, *PNG,* 11:127.

102. Ichabod Burnet to Charles Pettit, April 12, 1782, *PNG,* 11:38.

103. William Pierce Jr. to Officer Commanding at Orangeburg, May 8, 1782; Abner Crump to Greene, May 8, 1782; Thomas Wade to Greene, June 11, 1782, *PNG,* 11:172, 173, 321.

104. McDowell, "Journal," 323.

105. Seymour, "Journal of the Southern Expedition," 36–37.

106. Ibid., 36.

107. Edward Rutledge to Middleton, April 14, 1782, Edward Rutledge Letters.

108. Leslie to Clinton, March 12, 1782, *RAM,* 2:418.

109. Edward Rutledge to Middleton, April 23, 1782, in Middleton, "Correspondence," part 2, 14.

110. William Pierce to St. George Tucker, April 6, 1782, in Pierce, "Southern Campaign of Greene," 441.

111. Leslie to Greene, May 18, 1782, Leslie Letterbook.

112. John Hicks to Thomas Dickson Jr., May 27, 1782, in Mills and Hicks, "Letter-Book of Mills & Hicks," *NCHR,* 62.

113. Farr to John Laurens, May 17, 1782, in "Revolutionary Letters," part 1, 7–8.

114. Meeting of a Board of Field Officers, April 15, 1782, Leslie Letterbook.

115. Embarkation Return of the 19th and 30th Regiments, April 28, 1782, Carleton Papers, 39:4496.

116. Burke to Middleton, May 14, 1782, in Middleton, "Correspondence," part 1, 201.

117. Marion to Greene, May 21, 1782; William Pierce Jr. to Marion, May 24, 1782, *PNG,* 11:232, 238; Articles of a Treaty between General Marion . . . and Major Ganey,

June 7, 1782, in Moultrie, *Memoirs,* 2:419–21; Bass, *Swamp Fox,* 236–37; Lambert, *South Carolina Loyalists,* 205–6; James, *Life of Marion,* 166–67. The treaty is misdated 1781 in Moultrie, and Lambert also uses that date, although the Greene Papers clearly indicate that this occurred in 1782.

118. Marion to Greene, June 9, 1782, *PNG,* 11:313–14.

119. Leslie to Greene, June 30, 1782, *PNG,* 11:383.

120. Leslie to Carleton, June 11, 1782 (two letters of this date), Carleton Papers, 42:4771, 4772.

121. Lambert, *South Carolina Loyalists,* 250.

122. Tadeusz Kosciuszko to Otho Williams, [1782], Williams Papers.

123. Lewis Morris Jr. to Lewis Morris, August 13, 1782, in Morris, "Letters to General Morris," 504.

124. Charles Cotesworth Pinckney to Middleton, August 13, 1782, in Middleton, "Correspondence," part 3, 65.

125. McDowell, "Journal," 327.

126. John Laurens to Major Burnet, August 10, 1782, John Laurens Papers.

127. Burke to Middleton, July 6, 1782, in Middleton, "Correspondence," part 1, 205.

128. Denny, "Military Journal," *Pennsylvania Historical Society Memoirs,* 252–53.

129. Seymour, "Journal of the Southern Expedition," 41.

130. Farr to John Laurens, May 17, 1782, in "Revolutionary Letters," part 1, 7–8.

131. William Wilmot to Smallwood, September 26, 1782, in Culver, "Last Bloodshed," *MHM,* 336.

132. Greene to unnamed, August 14, 1782, *PNG,* 11:545.

133. Proceedings of the Merchants & Citizens of Charlestown, August 8, 1782; Wemyss to the Merchants and Citizens, August 10, 1782; Memorial and Petition of the Committee representing the Merchts. . . . to Governor Mathews, [August 11, 1782]; Mathews' Answers to Proposals, August 14, 1782, George Chalmers Manuscript Collection.

134. John Mathews to Marion, July 18, 1782, in Gibbes, ed., *Documentary History,* 2:200.

135. William Davis to Marion, August 24, 1782, in Gibbes, ed., *Documentary History,* 2:212.

136. Greene to Marion, June 9, 1782, *PNG,* 11:311.

137. Pickens to Greene, July 23, 1782, *PNG,* 11:452.

138. Pickens to Greene, September 7, 1782, *PNG,* 11:633–34.

139. Thayer, *Nathanael Greene,* 388–89; Harry Ward, *Between the Lines,* 176.

140. Farr to [Greene], September 9, 1782 [misdated 1783], in "Revolutionary Letters," part 1, 9–10.

141. John Laurens to Greene, [August 5, 1782], *PNG,* 11:490.

142. Wilmot to Ichabod Burnet, August 8, 1782, *PNG,* 11:507.

143. Sarah Detollenare to Greene, September 10, 1782, *PNG,* 11:641.

144. Embarkation Return . . . to East Florida, October 10, 1782, Carleton Papers, 51:5836; Lambert, *South Carolina Loyalists,* 254–55, 256.

145. Nase, Diary, November 27, 1782.

146. McCowen, *British Occupation,* 149n; Lambert, *South Carolina Loyalists,* 255.

147. Stevens, "Autobiography," 16; Gibbes, "Story of His Life," 66.

148. Collins, *Autobiography,* 66–67.

149. Burke to Governor Guerard, December 14, 1784, Burke Papers.

150. "Stephon Mazyck to Philip Porcher," June 14, 1783, *SCHGM,* 12–13.

151. Wright to Balfour, July 27, 1781, and August 16, 1781, *RAM,* 2:306, 315; Cashin, *King's Ranger,* 142, 144.

152. Foster, *James Jackson,* 17–18; *Royal Georgia Gazette,* September 20, 1781.

153. Friedrich von Porbeck to Sovereign, September 18, 1781, in "Matters Concerning the Garrison Regiment von Wissenbach in America, 1780–1783," HDAR, item BZ21.

154. *Royal Georgia Gazette,* November 8, 1781.

155. James Jackson to Nathan Brownson, November 7, 1781, in Jackson, "Miscellaneous Papers," *GHQ,* 56; Cashin, *King's Ranger,* 144.

156. Wright to Clinton, October 16, 1781, Carleton Papers, 33:3829.

157. *Royal Georgia Gazette,* September 20 and 27, 1781; Nathan Brownson to Greene, December 15, 1781, *PNG,* 10:59.

158. Coleman, *American Revolution in Georgia,* 141; Nase, Diary, December 8, 1781.

159. Von Porbeck to Sovereign, January 1, 1782, in "Matters Concerning the Garrison Regiment von Wissenbach," HDAR, BZ30.

160. Foster, *James Jackson,* 21.

161. Alured Clarke to Clinton, December 20, 1781, in Clinton, *American Rebellion,* 591.

162. Extract of the minutes of a council of war held at New York, January 17, 1782, in Clinton, *American Rebellion,* 592–93.

163. Greene to Anthony Wayne, January 9, 1782, Anthony Wayne Manuscripts, vol. 14, HSP.

164. Wayne to John Twiggs, January 14, 1782; Wayne to John Martin, January 14, 1782, Wayne Manuscripts, vol. 14.

165. Wayne to Greene, January 23, 1782, Wayne Manuscripts, vol. 15.

166. John Martin to Wayne, January 19, 1782, in Martin, "Official Letters of Governor Martin," *GHQ,* 286.

167. Greene to Wayne, February 4, 1782, Wayne Manuscripts, vol. 15.

168. Wayne to John Martin, February 19, 1782; Wayne to Greene, February 22, 1782, Wayne Manuscripts, vol. 15; Paul David Nelson, *Anthony Wayne,* 167.

169. Wayne to Greene, March 11, 1782, Wayne Manuscripts, vol. 15.

170. Von Porbeck to Sovereign, March 1, March 27, and May 1, 1782, in "Matters Concerning the Garrison Regiment von Wissenbach," HDAR, BZ36, BZ39, BZ52.

171. Clinton to Wright, January 6, 1782, Carleton Papers, 35:4042.

172. Georgia Assembly to Wright, February 23, 1782, Carleton Papers, 36:4145.

173. Wright to Knox, February 16, 1782, *DAR,* 21:41.

174. Wright to Carleton, June 1, 1782, Carleton Papers, 42:4716.

175. John Martin to Wayne, March 8, 1782, Wayne Manuscripts, vol. 15.

176. John Martin to GA Delegates in Congress, March 14, 1782, in Martin, "Official Letters," 295.

177. John Martin to Wayne, March 14, 1782, in Martin, "Official Letters," 295–96.

178. John Martin to Wayne, March 14, 1782 (second letter of this date), in Martin, "Official Letters," 298.

179. Wayne to John Martin, March 15, 1782, Wayne Manuscripts, vol. 15.

180. Wayne to Greene, February 28, 1782, Wayne Manuscripts, vol. 15.

181. Wayne to Walter Stewart, February 25, 1782, Wayne Manuscripts, vol. 15.

182. Jenkin Davis to Muhlenberg, March 18, 1783, in Muhlenberg, "Muhlenberg's Georgia Correspondence," 435.

183. John Martin to Wayne, May 3, 1782, in Martin, "Official Letters," 309; Cashin, *King's Ranger,* 149.

184. John Martin to Wayne, March 23, 1782, in Martin, "Official Letters," 302.

185. James Jackson to Wayne, May 10, 1782, Wayne Manuscripts, vol. 16; Wayne to Jackson, April 27, 1782, James S. Schoff Collection, Misc. Mss., WLCL.

186. Clay to Greene, May 13, 1782, *PNG,* 11:189.

187. Lambert, "Confiscation of Loyalist Property," 82–83.

188. Wright to Wayne, June 5, 1782, Wayne Papers, WLCL.

189. Wayne to Wright, June 7, 1782, Wayne Papers, WLCL.

190. Nase, Diary, July 11, 1782.

191. Biddulph to [parents], [July 10, 1782?,] in Biddulph, "Letters," 108.

192. Robertson, *Loyalism in Revolutionary Georgia,* 15; Coleman, *American Revolution in Georgia,* 145. Robertson gives figures of twenty-five hundred whites and forty-nine hundred blacks; Coleman gives thirty-one hundred whites and over thirty-five hundred blacks but also cites a contemporary estimate of five to six thousand black evacuees.

193. Wright to Carleton, July 6, 1782, *RAM,* 3:11.

194. [Georgia Assembly] to unnamed, [1782], Loyalist Papers, GHS. This letter is unfinished. It appears to have been composed shortly before the evacuation of Savannah, and when the authors realized it would not accomplish its purpose, they did not complete it. The salutation indicates that it was to be sent to a prominent British official.

195. James Jackson to Wayne, June 1782, Wayne Manuscripts, vol. 17.

196. Patrick Carr to Martin, August 11, 1782, in Carr, "Letters," *GHQ,* 337–38.

197. John Martin to Greene, August 8, 1782, in Martin, "Official Letters," 316.

198. John Martin to Tonyn, August 15, 1782; Martin to Colonel Cooper, September 17, 1782, in Martin, "Official Letters," 320, 328.

199. John Martin to Colonel Cooper, September 17, 1782, in Martin, "Official Letters," 328.

200. Carr to John Martin, August 22, 1782, in Carr, "Letters," 339.

201. John Martin to Carr, August 28, 1782, in Martin, "Official Letters," 323.

202. Green, "Queensborough Township," 197.

203. McIntosh to Greene, October 30, 1782, in "Letters to General Greene and Others," part 2, 148–49.

204. Jenkin Davis to Muhlenberg, March 18, 1783, in Muhlenberg, "Muhlenberg's Georgia Correspondence," 434.

205. James Paterson to Amherst, September 13, 1782, Amherst Correspondence and Papers.

206. Tonyn to Germain, December 31, 1781, *DAR,* 20:290, 291.

207. East Florida Proprietors to Leslie, June 14, 1782, Carleton Papers, 42:4793.

208. East Florida Assembly to Tonyn, Tonyn to East Florida Assembly, June 19, 1782; East Florida Resolution . . . and His Excellency's Answer, Tonyn to Carleton, Tonyn to Leslie, June 20, 1782, Carleton Papers, 42:4809, 4810, 4816, 4818, 4819.

209. Carleton to Leslie, July 15, 1782, Carleton Papers, 44:5071; Siebert, *Loyalists in East Florida,* 1:131; Cashin, *King's Ranger,* 169.

210. Holmes, "Robert Ross' Plan," *Louisiana History,* 175.

211. Dunmore to Viscount Sydney, August 24, 1782, Thomas Townshend Papers.

212. Robin F. A. Fabel, "Born of War, Killed by War: The Company of Military Adventurers in West Florida," in *Adapting to Conditions,* ed. Ultee, 112–13.

213. Gilbert C. Din, "Loyalist Resistance after Pensacola: The Case of James Colbert," in *Anglo-Spanish Confrontation,* ed. Coker and Rea, 161.

214. Lewis Morris Jr. to Lewis Morris, June 7, 1781, in Morris, "Letters to General Morris," 487.

215. Isaac Shelby to Greene, August 3, 1781, in "Letters to General Greene and Others," part 1, 104.

216. O'Donnell, *Southern Indians,* 118–19; Cashin, *King's Ranger,* 141; Jonathan Bryan to Greene, August 27, 1781, *PNG,* 9:261.

217. Twiggs to Greene, December 16, 1781, *PNG,* 10:66.

218. Thomas Brown to Leslie, December 5, 1781, Carleton Papers, 34:3930.

219. Clinton to Germain, March 24, 1782, Shelburne Papers, 68:205; O'Donnell, *Southern Indians,* 120–21.

220. Twiggs to Greene, October 30, 1781, *PNG,* 9:500.

221. Nathan Brownson to Greene, December 1, 1781, *PNG,* 9:644–45.

222. Greene to Thomas McKean, December 9, 1781, *PNG,* 10:18.

223. John Martin's Talk to the Creeks, January 11, 1782, in Martin, "Official Letters," 282–85.

224. Wayne to Greene, February 1, 1782, Wayne Manuscripts, vol. 15.

225. Examination of Joseph Cornell, n.d., Wayne Manuscripts, vol. 15.

226. Wayne to Greene, February 1, 1782, Wayne Manuscripts, vol. 15.

227. Wayne to Mr. Anderson, February 25, 1782; Wayne to Mr. Cornell, February 25, 1782, Anthony Wayne Letters, Chester County Historical Society.

228. Wayne to Greene, February 1, 1782, Wayne Manuscripts, vol. 15.

229. John Habersham to Wayne, February 8, 1782, Wayne Papers, PERK.

230. Ibid.

231. Ibid.

232. Ibid.

233. Wayne to John Martin, February 13, 1782, Wayne Manuscripts, vol. 15.

234. Wayne to Greene, February 28, 1782, Wayne Manuscripts, vol. 15.

235. Wayne to Greene, March 25, 1782, Wayne Manuscripts, vol. 15.

236. Wayne to Major [Francis?] Moore, March 30, 1782, Wayne Manuscripts, vol. 16.

237. Moultrie, *Memoirs,* 2:320.

238. Andrew Pickens letter, n.d., in Hayes, *Hero of Hornet's Nest,* 327n, 328n.

239. Hayes, *Hero of Hornet's Nest,* 149.

240. John Martin to Wayne, February 3, 1782, in Martin, "Official Letters," 288–89.

241. John Martin to Greene, February 9, 1782, in Martin, "Official Letters," 291.

242. Pickens to Elijah Clarke, January 25, 1782, Emmet Collection, no. 6670.

243. Pickens to John Martin, June 22, 1782, Pickens Papers.

244. Thomas Brown to Germain, April 6, 1782, *DAR,* 21:55.

245. Thomas Brown to Thomas Waters [February 1782], On-Line Institute for Advanced Loyalist Studies, www.royalprovincial.com/military/rhist/dian (accessed December 17, 2002).

246. Waring, *Fighting Elder,* 107; Hayes, *Hero of Hornet's Nest,* 151–52; Jno. Lyon to Wayne, April 13, 1782, and James Jackson to Wayne, May 3, 1782, Wayne Manuscripts, vol. 16; Elijah Clarke to John Martin, May 29, 1782, in Hayes, *Hero of Hornet's Nest,* 156.

247. Cashin, *King's Ranger,* 151.

248. Thomas Brown to Leslie, July 1, 1782, Emmet Collection, no. 6673.

249. Wayne to Greene, June 24, 1782, Wayne Manuscripts, vol. 17; Paul David Nelson, *Anthony Wayne,* 175–76; Cashin, *King's Ranger,* 152; O'Donnell, *Southern Indians,* 123.

250. Posey, *General Thomas Posey,* 96–97; Paul David Nelson, *Anthony Wayne,* 175–76.

251. Wayne to Carr, June 26, 1782, Feinstone Collection, no. 1650.

252. "Journal of the Hessian Regiment von Knoblauch," HDAR, item W; Beamsley Glazier to Leslie, August 25, 1782, Emmet Collection, no. 6733.

253. Leslie to Thomas Brown, August 4, 1782, Leslie Letterbook.

254. Thomas Brown to Carleton, October 9, 1782, *RAM,* 3:157.

255. John Graham to Carleton, July 20, 1782, *RAM,* 3:30.

256. John Martin to the . . . Upper and Lower Creek Nation, July 19, 1782, in Martin, "Official Letters," 313–15.

257. Wayne to Greene, July 28, 1782, *PNG,* 11:471.

258. Ibid.; Thomas Brown to Leslie, July 1, 1782, Emmet Collection, no. 6673.

259. Carr to John Martin, August 22, 1782, in Carr, "Letters," 339.

260. Cashin, *King's Ranger,* 157, 160–61.

261. John Martin to Colonel McMurphy, October 4, 1782, in Martin, "Official Letters," 330.

262. Cashin, *King's Ranger,* 155.

263. Pickens to Greene, September 7, 1782, *PNG,* 11:634.

264. Pickens to John Martin, October 26, 1782, Bevan Collection; Pickens to Clarke, September 2, 1782, and Pickens to Henry Lee, August 28, 1811, Sumter Papers, Draper Manuscripts, microfilm reel 1VV.

265. Pickens to John Martin, October 26, 1782, Bevan Collection.

266. Pickens to Elijah Clarke, September 2, 1782; Pickens to Henry Lee, August 28, 1811, Sumter Papers, Draper Manuscripts, microfilm reel 1VV.

267. "Pickens's Campaign of '81," Sumter Papers, Draper Manuscripts, microfilm reel 3VV. Although the memoir is dated 1781, other documentary evidence indicates that it is actually an account of the 1782 campaign.

268. "A message sent . . . by Charles Beaman," September 25, 1782, and "A Talk delivered by General Pickens," October 17, 1782, Bevan Collection; Hayes, *Hero of Hornet's Nest,* 162; Pickens to Clarke, September 2, 1782, and Pickens to Lee, August 28, 1811, Sumter Papers, Draper Manuscripts, microfilm reel 1VV.

269. Tonyn to Germain, December 31, 1781, *DAR,* 20:290.

270. Thomas Brown to Leslie, December 5, 1781, Carleton Papers, 34:3930.

271. Farquhar Bethune to Leslie, January 19, 1782, *DAR,* 21:28–29.

272. Caughey, "Natchez Rebellion," 70; Gibson, *Chickasaws,* 73–74; Haynes, *Natchez District,* 143–44, 146, 148, 151; John Graham to Carleton, October 20, 1782, Carleton Papers, 52:5936; O'Donnell, *Southern Indians,* 131–32.

273. Robert Heriot to Polly Heriot, June 9, 1781, Robert Heriot Correspondence.

274. Burke to Middleton, November 18, 1781, in Middleton, "Correspondence," part 1, 190.

275. Isaac Huger to Lewis Morris, May 22, 1781, in "Revolutionary Letters," part 2, 78.

276. For examples of slaves seized by Sumter and distributed as bounties to his troops, see Petition of Anne Lord, February 5, 1783; Petition of Joannah Boylstone and

George Boylstone, December 12, 1793; Petition of Ann Summerall, January 29, 1791; and Petition of Sarah Armstrong, November 30, 1792, in Kierner, *Southern Women in Revolution,* 32, 44, 78, 83.

277. John Rutledge to Sumter, December 25, 1781, Sumter Papers, vol. 2.

278. "Warrant to Repair the Road to Orangeburgh," December 7, 1781, Williams Papers.

279. Greene to Sumter, September 28, 1781, *PNG,* 9:404.

280. Marion to Greene, November 10, 1781, *PNG,* 9:557.

281. Marion to Greene, November 14, 1781, *PNG,* 9:573.

282. General List of Negores [*sic*] Employed in the Royal Artillery Department, Returns of October, November, and December 1781, Wray Papers, vol. 7; General List of Negroes Employed in the Royal Artillery Department, Returns of January, February, March, and April 1782, Wray Papers, vol. 8; Returns of May, June, July, and August 1782, Wray Papers, vol. 9; Return of September 1782, Wray Papers, vol. 10.

283. Muster Roll of the Horse Department attending His Majesty's Field Train, October 1, 1782, Wray Papers, Muster Rolls; Return of Negroes, April 21, 1782, Wray Papers, vol. 8; Muster Roll of the Civil Branch attending His Majesty's Field Train of Artillery in Charlestown, August 8, 1782, Wray Papers, vol. 9; September 28, 1782, and undated, Wray Papers, vol. 10; Muster Roll of Civil Branch, October 1, 1782, Wray Papers, Muster Rolls; Return of Negroe Wenches and their Children belonging to the Artillery Dept., November 5, 1782, Wray Papers, Muster Rolls. There are only fifty-two names on the list, although the last is numbered 53; there is no name listed at no. 15, nor are any children listed on this return.

284. Olwell, *Masters, Slaves, and Subjects,* 254.

285. Instructions for the Office Established to receive the Pay of Negroes Employed in the different Departments, n.d., Leslie Letterbook.

286. Narrative of Cruden, [1782], South Carolina Box—Loyalists.

287. Quarles, *Negro in the Revolution,* 144.

288. Henry Lee to Greene, August 18, 1781, *PNG,* 9:203.

289. Thayer, *Nathanael Greene,* 374.

290. King, *Memoirs.*

291. John Rutledge to Marion, September 2, 1781, in Gibbes, ed., *Documentary History,* 3:131.

292. Greene to Henry Lee, December 7, 1781, *PNG,* 10:13.

293. Greene to Washington, August 6, 1781, *PNG,* 9:139.

294. Greene to Otho Williams, December 2, 1781, *PNG,* 9:650.

295. William Smith, *Historical Memoirs,* 443.

296. "A View of the present Strength of America in respect to Her Number of Fighting Men," 1781, British Museum, Egerton Mss. 2135.

297. Christopher Ward, *Delaware Continentals,* 476.

298. Greene to Robert Livingston, April 12, 1782, *PNG,* 11:35.

299. Greene to John Rutledge, December 9, 1781, *PNG,* 10:22.

300. John Rutledge to Greene, December 24, 1781, *PNG,* 10:101.

301. John Laurens to Greene, December 28, 1781, *PNG,* 10:130–31.

302. Greene to John Rutledge, January 21, 1782, Myers Collection, no. 1209.

303. Burke to Middleton, January 25, 1782, addition dated February 5, in Middleton, "Correspondence," part 1, 194.

304. Edward Rutledge to Middleton, February 8, 1782, in Middleton, "Correspondence," part 2, 4.

305. William Pierce to St. George Tucker, February 6, 1782, in Pierce, "Southern Campaign of Greene," 439.

306. Lewis Morris Jr. to Jacob Morris, February 7, 1782, in Morris, "Letters to General Morris," 499.

307. Greene to Washington, March 9, 1782, *PNG,* 10:472.

308. John Laurens to Hamilton, [July 1782], *PAH,* 3:121.

309. John Mathews to Greene, February 6, 1782, *PNG,* 10:325.

310. Greene to Mathews, February 11, 1782, *PNG,* 10:355–56.

311. Edward Rutledge to Middleton, February 14, 1782, in Middleton, "Correspondence," part 2, 5.

312. John Mathews to Sumter, March 4, 1782, Sumter Papers, vol. 2.

313. Maj. Augustine Prevost to Arthur St. Clair, March 15, 1782, Arthur St. Clair Papers, box 1, folder 11, DLAR.

314. Edward Scott to Simon Fraser, March 27, 1782, Leslie Letterbook.

315. Leslie to Clinton, March 30, 1782, *RAM,* 2:435.

316. Leslie to Greene, April 4, 1782, *PNG,* 10:582–84.

317. Greene to Leslie, April 4, 1782, *PNG,* 10:585.

318. Greene to Marion, April 6, 1782, *PNG,* 10:589.

319. Frey, *Water from the Rock,* 137.

320. Marion to Greene, March 29, 1782, *PNG,* 10:561.

321. Gist to Smallwood, April 5, 1782, Gist Papers.

322. John Laurens to Thomas Bee, April 14, 1782, Thomas Bee Papers, LOC.

323. McDowell, "Journal," 315.

324. John Grimké to Col. [John?] Starke, May 2, 1782, Grimké Family Papers.

325. Farr to Greene, June 14, 1782, *PNG,* 11:329.

326. Ellen Wilson, *Loyal Blacks,* 27.

327. Selby, *Dunmore,* 65–66; Quarles, *Negro in the Revolution,* 151.

328. William Smith, *Historical Memoirs,* 497–98.

329. Quarles, *Negro in the Revolution,* 151; J. Leitch Wright, *Florida in the Revolution,* 120.

330. Leslie to Clinton, March 12, 1782; James Moncrief to Clinton, March 13, 1782, *RAM,* 2:417, 419.

331. Leslie to Clinton, March 30, 1782, *RAM,* 2:435.

332. Leslie to Clinton, March 1782, *RAM,* 2:438.

333. Benjamin Thompson to Germain, January 11, 1782, Germain Papers, vol. 15.

334. Thompson to Germain, January 24, 1782, Germain Papers, vol. 15.

335. William Mathews to Gideon White, April 26, 1782, Gideon White Collection.

336. Charles Cotesworth Pinckney to Middleton, August 13, 1782, in Middleton, "Correspondence," part 3, 65.

337. Bee to John Mathews, December 9, 1782, Bee Papers, SCL.

338. Quarles, *Negro in the Revolution,* 149.

339. Seymour, "Journal of the Southern Expedition," 35; E. Rutledge to Middleton, April 23, 1782, in Middleton, "Correspondence," part 2, 14; Tilden, "Extracts from the Journal," 225. Tilden's account states that the initial American encounter was with "one of ye British negro Captains and his Troop," who were attacked and fled, and that the encounter with the larger British force came afterward.

340. E. Rutledge to Middleton, April 23, 1782, in Middleton, "Correspondence," part 2, 14. Rutledge stated that March was once "the Governor's Man," apparently the slave of John Mathews. The encounter took place "near Mrs. Izard's Gate."

341. E. Rutledge to Middleton, April 23, 1782, in Middleton, "Correspondence," part 2, 14.

342. Marion to John Mathews, August 30, 1782, in "Marion's Report of the Affair at Wadboo," *SCHGM,* 176–77.

343. James, *Life of Marion,* 168–69.

344. John Mathews to Marion, October 6, 1782, in Gibbes, ed., *Documentary History,* 2:232–33.

345. Lewis Morris Jr. to Jacob Morris, December 10, 1781, in Morris, "Letters to General Morris," 496.

346. Lewis Morris to Ann Elliott, October 29, 1782, in "Letters from Col. Morris," *SCHGM,* part 2, 5.

347. Finney, "Revolutionary War Diaries," 137. Finney's entry is dated April 21, 1782, but refers to several encounters between British and American parties during the two previous weeks.

348. Kosciuszko to Greene, September 20, 1782, *PNG,* 11:680; Seymour, "Journal of the Southern Expedition," 40–41.

349. Lt. General von Bose to Lt. General Friedrich Wilhelm von Lossberg, November 18, 1782, in "Reports of the War under General von Lossberg, 1782–1784," HDAR, band V, lage 15.

350. Kosciuszko to Greene, November 14, 1782, *PNG,* 12:181.

351. Olwell, *Masters, Slaves, and Subjects,* 257.

352. Marion to Greene, July 16, 1782, *PNG,* 11:447.

353. Kosciuszko to Greene, December 26, 1781, Feinstone Collection, no. 710.

354. "Papers taken in the Galley *Balfour,*" September 31 [*sic*], 1782, Gist Papers.

355. Greene to Washington, April 15, 1782, *PNG,* 11:65.

356. Greene's Orders, January 29, 1782, *PNG,* 10:277.

357. Farr to Greene, March 13, 1782, *PNG,* 10:495.

358. Thompson to Leslie, February 24, 1782, *RAM,* 2:403.

359. Kosciuszko to Greene, October 1, 1782, *PNG,* 12:7.

360. Culver, "Last Bloodshed," 334.

361. John Doyle to Jno. McKinnon, November 27, 1782, On-Line Institute for Advanced Loyalist Studies, www.royalprovincial.com/military/black/blkharry.htm (accessed March 1, 2000).

362. Kyte, "Thaddeus Kosciuszko at the Liberation of Charleston," *SCHM,* 18, 20.

363. Leslie to O'Hara, May 3, 1782, Leslie Letterbook.

364. John Mathews to Leslie, August 17, 1782, Emmet Collection, no. 6829.

365. Leslie to Carleton, July 27, 1782, *RAM,* 2:544.

366. Leslie's Orders, August 13, 1782, in Middleton, "Correspondence," part 3, 69.

367. Leslie to Carleton, August 10, 1782, Leslie Letterbook.

368. Leslie to Carleton, August 10, 1782 (second letter of this date), Leslie Letterbook.

369. "Answers to General Leslie's queries," [July 1782?], Carleton Papers, 45:5180.

370. Carleton to Leslie, September 10, 1782, Carleton Papers, 49:5575.

371. "Articles of a Treaty, Respecting Slaves," October 10, 1782, Chalmers Collection.

372. Gadsden to Mathews, October 16, 1782, in Gadsden, *Writings,* 182.

373. Leslie to Carleton, October 18, 1782, Leslie Letterbook.

374. Leslie to Carleton, October 18, 1782, *RAM*, 3:175; Moultrie, *Memoirs*, 2:346–47.

375. Leslie to Carleton, October 18, 1782, *RAM*, 3:175–76.

376. Moultrie, *Memoirs*, 2:346–51.

377. Farr to Greene, June 21, 1782, *PNG*, 11:355.

378. "97" to Marion, November 4, 1782, Horry's War Letters, Peter Force Manuscript Collection, series 7E.

379. Moultrie, *Memoirs*, 2:350–51.

380. Philip D. Morgan, "Black Society in the Lowcountry, 1760–1810," in *Slavery and Freedom in the Age of the American Revolution*, ed. Berlin and Hoffman, 111; Allan Kulikoff, "Uprooted Peoples: Black Migrants in the Age of the American Revolution, 1790–1820," in *Slavery and Freedom*, ed. Berlin and Hoffman, 144.

381. "100" to unnamed, November 8, 1782, Horry's War Letters, Force Collection.

382. Leslie to Carleton, November 18, 1782; Commission for the Examination of Negroes, n.d., Leslie Letterbook.

383. Major Swan to Gist, November 25, 1782, Gist Papers.

384. Greene to Marion, [August 9, 1782], *PNG*, 11:510.

385. John Mathews to Arthur Middleton Jr., August 25, 1782, in Middleton, "Correspondence," part 3, 71.

386. John Mathews to Greene, November 17, 1782, *PNG*, 12:198.

387. Greene to John Mathews, November 18, 1782, *PNG*, 12:205.

388. Lambert, *South Carolina Loyalists*, 254–56; Quarles, *Negro in the Revolution*, 167.

389. Deposition of Mark King, January 5, 1782, GHS.

390. Quarles, *Negro in the Revolution*, 149.

391. James Jackson to Wayne, April 3, 1782, Wayne Manuscripts, removed box.

392. Rebecca Read to Wayne, April 29, 1782; James Jackson to Wayne, April 16, 1782, Wayne Manuscripts, vol. 16.

393. Jackson to Wayne, May 20, 1782, Wayne Manuscripts, vol. 17.

394. Wayne to Greene, May 24, 1781, Wayne Manuscripts, vol. 17.

395. Jackson to Wayne, March 25, 1782, Wayne Manuscripts, vol. 15.

396. Jno. Lyon to Wayne, April 13, 1782, Wayne Manuscripts, vol. 16.

397. Memorial of Cols. Simon Munro & Roger Kelsall, September 6, 1781, in Davis, ed., *Georgia Citizens and Soldiers*, 177–78.

398. John Martin to Greene, March 15, 1782, *PNG*, 10:506–7.

399. Wayne to John Martin, February 19, 1782, Wayne Manuscripts, vol. 15.

400. Greene to John Martin, June 8, 1782, *PNG*, 11:308.

401. Clay to Greene, May 13, 1782, *PNG*, 11:189.

402. Foster, *James Jackson*, 17.

403. John Martin to Colonel James Jackson, April 29, 1782, in Martin, "Official Letters," 307.

404. Proclamation, May 3, 1782, in Martin, "Official Letters," 310.

405. John Martin to Governor Alexander Martin of North Carolina, March 6, 1782, in Martin, "Official Letters," 292–93.

406. John Martin to Washington and Odingsell, August 13, 1782, in Martin, "Official Letters," 318.

407. Resolve of Georgia Assembly, n.d., Wayne Manuscripts, vol. 17.

408. Richard Howley to Wayne, July 4, 1782, Wayne Manuscripts, vol. 17.

409. Alured Clarke to Wayne, July 21, 1782, Wayne Manuscripts, vol. 18.

410. Martin to Leslie, November 6, 1782, Emmet Collection, no. 6743.

411. Frey, *Water from the Rock,* 106; Quarles, *Negro in the Revolution,* 163; Carr to Martin, August 22, 1782, in Carr, "Letters," 339.

412. Ellen Wilson, *Loyal Blacks,* 42.

413. George, "Life of David George."

414. Tonyn to Germain, November 30, 1781, and December 31, 1781, *DAR,* 20:266, 291–92.

415. Tonyn to Carleton, October 11, 1782, Carleton Papers, 51:5850.

CONCLUSION

1. "The attitude of the Loyalists in America and particularly in the south" [after 1782]; authorship attributed to Lord Rawdon, Alexander Wedderburn Papers, 1:46.

2. "Attitude of the Loyalists," Wedderburn Papers.

3. Ibid.

4. Ibid.

5. James Murray to George Townshend, September 1, 1782, Feinstone Collection, no. 992.

6. Mackenzie, *Diary,* 2:581–82.

7. Galloway, *Fabricius,* 1044, 1057, 1059, 1073.

8. James Wright, "A Concise View of the Situation of . . . Georgia," n.d., Shelburne Papers, 66:669.

9. William Pierce to St. George Tucker, February 6, 1782, in Pierce, "Southern Campaign of Greene," 438–39.

10. Tarleton Brown, *Memoirs,* 9–10.

11. Galloway, *Fabricius,* 1094.

12. Dowd, *Spirited Resistance,* 93.

13. Tyson, "Carolina Black Corps," *Review Interamericana,* 648–64, esp. 649, 650–51, 656.

14. O'Shaughnessy, *Empire Divided,* 244; Frey, *Water from the Rock,* 192.

15. O'Shaughnessy, *Empire Divided,* xii.

BIBLIOGRAPHY

PRIMARY SOURCES

Manuscripts

Allaire, Anthony. Diary and Orderly Book. Robinson Family Papers. NBM.

Amherst, Jeffery. Correspondence and Papers. Microfilm, DLAR.

———. Papers, War Office 34. Microfilm, DLAR.

Auckland, William Eden, First Baron. Papers. Microfilm, DLAR.

Ball Family. Papers. SCHS.

Ballingall, Robert. Memorial and Related Correspondence. Miscellaneous Manuscripts SC7003/AT7003, Box 2, No. 154. NYSL.

Bee, Thomas. Papers. LOC.

———. Papers, SCL.

Bevan, Joseph V. Manuscript Collection. LOC.

Bounetheau, Peter. Papers. LOC.

Bowie, John. Papers. SCDAH.

British Museum, Egerton Mss. 2135. Transcript, LOC.

Brown, Thomas, to John Douglass, April 12, 1781, and Certification of Douglass's Slaves Captured at Fort Cornwallis, June 5, 1781. www.royalprovincial.com/military/black/blkords.htm and www.royalprovincial.com/military/black/blkpris1.htm (accessed February 2, 2004).

Brown, Thomas, to Thomas Waters, [February 1782]. www.royalprovincial.com/military/rhist/dian/dianlet5.htm (accessed December 17, 2002).

Buffington, Moses. Paper. GHS.

Burke, Aedanus. Papers. SCL.

Burnet, Ichabod. Letter. SCL.

Carleton, Sir Guy. Papers (Headquarters Papers of the British Army in America). Microfilm, various repositories.

Carne, Samuel. Papers. SCL.

Chalmers, George. Manuscript Collection. LOC.

Clinton, Sir Henry. Papers. WLCL.

Colleton, Margaret. Papers. SCL.

Cornwallis, Charles, Earl. CP, PRO 30/11. Microfilm, various repositories.

Cruden, John. Narrative and Observations. Misc. Mss. SC7003/AT7003. NYSL.

Cumming, Andrew. Loyalist Claim. www.royalprovincial.com/military/mems/sc/clmcumm.htm (accessed June 6, 2002).

Dartmouth, Second Earl of. American Papers. Microfilm, DLAR.

Depeyster, Abraham. Orderly Book. NYHS.

Doyle, Major John., to Jno. McKinnon, November 27, 1782. www.royalprovincial.com/military/black/blkharry.htm (accessed March 1, 2000).

Draper, Lyman C. Manuscript Collection. Microfilm, LOC.

Drayton, William Henry. Papers. SCL.

Emmet, Thomas Addis. Manuscript Collection. NYPL.

Feinstone, Sol. Manuscript Collection. DLAR.

Few, William. Papers. PERK.

Fletchall, Thomas, et al. Letter to King George III, April 19, 1782. http://sc_tories.tri-pod.com/list_of_murdered_loyalists.htm (accessed July 11, 2002).

Force, Peter. Manuscript Collection. Microfilm, DLAR.

Gage, Thomas. Papers, American Series. WLCL.

Gates, Horatio. Papers. Microfilm, DLAR.

Germain, Lord George. Papers. WLCL.

Gilmor, Robert, Jr. Papers. MHS.

Gist, Mordecai. Papers. MHS.

Grimké Family. Papers. SCHS.

Habersham, James. Journal of the Siege of Charleston. Joseph V. Bevan Collection, LOC.

Handley, Scipio. Petition. www.royalprovincial.com/military/mems.sc/clmhandley.htm (accessed December 17, 2002).

Harleston, Isaac. Papers. SCHS.

Hart, Oliver. Diary. SCL.

———. "Diary of Oliver Hart written during his Journey to the Back-Country, 31 July–6 September 1775." SCL.

———. Papers. SCL.

Heriot, Robert. Correspondence. SCHS.

Hessian Documents of the American Revolution. Microfiche, DLAR.

Houstoun, John. Papers. GHS.

Howe, Robert. Orderly Book. WLCL.

———. Papers. GHS.

———. Papers. SHC.

Howe, William, to John Stuart, January 13, 1777. www.royalprovincial.com/military.rhist/wflr/wflrlet1.htm (accessed August 16, 2002).

Inglis, John. Papers. GHS.

Johnson, Uzal. Diary. Typescript, SCDAH.

Jones, Seaborn. Papers. PERK.

Kershaw, Joseph. Diary. SCL.

King, Mark. Deposition. GHS.

Kitching, James. Loyalist Claim. www.royalprovincial.com/military/mems/ga/clmkit.htm (accessed June 6, 2002).

Knox, William. Papers. WLCL.

Laurens, John. Papers. SCL.

Lee, Charles. Letterbook. SCL.

Leslie, Alexander. Letterbook. Microfilm, SCDAH.

———. Paper. NCSA.

———. Papers. NAS, GD 26/9/512.

Lincoln, Benjamin. Papers. BPL.

———. Papers. Microfilm, various repositories.

———. Papers. PERK.

Lloyd, John. Letters. Photocopies provided by Gloucestershire Record Office.

Loyalist Papers. GHS.

MacKenzie, Andrew. Loyalist Claim. www.royalprovincial.com/military/mems/sc/clmmckz.htm (accessed June 6, 2002).

Manigault Family. Papers. SCL.

Manson, Thomas. Memorial. www.royalprovincial.com/military/mems/ga/clmman.htm (accessed June 6, 2002).

Mathis, Samuel. Papers. SCL.

McLaurin, Isabella. Loyalist Claim. SCHS.

Miscellaneous Manuscripts. SC7003/AT7003. NYSL.

Miscellaneous Manuscripts. WLCL.

Miscellaneous Manuscripts—John Dooly. LOC.

Miscellaneous Papers, Series 1, Vol. 1. NCSA.

Moore, Stephen. Papers. SCL.

Myers, Theodorus Bailey. Manuscript Collection. Microfilm, DLAR.

Nase, Henry. Diary. Nase Family Papers. NBM.

Ninety Six District Papers. SCL.

Oswald, Richard. Papers. WLCL.

Pearis, Richard. Loyalist Claim. SCHS.

Pickens, Andrew. Papers. SCL.

Porcher, Philip. Papers. SCL.

Pringle-Garden Family. Papers. SCHS.

Revolutionary War Papers. SHC.

Robinson, Joseph. "Memoir of Lt. Col. Joseph Robinson, 1797." McGill University Library, Montreal.

Rutherford, Griffith. Paper. SHC.

Rutledge, Edward. Letters. SCHS.

Rutledge, John. Papers. SCL.

St. Clair, Arthur. Papers. Microfilm, DLAR.

Saunders, John. Papers. HCIL.

Shelburne, Earl of. Papers. WLCL.

Simpson, James, to Richard Pearis, May 3, 1780. www.royalprovincial.com/military/rhist/scmil/scmlet1.htm (accessed August 16, 2002).

Singleton, Matthew. Papers. SCL.

South Carolina Box—Loyalists. NYPL.

Strachey, Sir Henry. Papers. LOC.

Sumter, Thomas. Papers. LOC.

Telfair, Edward. Papers. PERK.

Tonyn, Patrick, to Lord George Germain, August 21, 1776. www.royalprovincial.com/military/rhist/eastflmil/eflmillet1.htm (accessed August 16, 2002).

Townshend, Thomas (Viscount Sydney). Papers. WLCL.

Treutlen, John Adam. Papers. GHS.

Tucker-Coleman Family. Papers. SLSC.

Wallace, Daniel. "Incidents of the Revolution in Union York & Spartanburgh Districts." South Carolina Box, NYPL.

Wayne, Anthony. Letters. Chester County Historical Society, Chester, Pa.
———. Manuscripts. HSP.
———. Papers. PERK.
———. Papers. WLCL.
Wedderburn, Alexander. Papers. WLCL.
White, Gideon. Manuscript Collection. HCIL.
Williams, Otho Holland. Papers. MHS.
Wray, George. Papers. WLCL.
Wright, Sir James. Papers. GHS.
———. Papers. PERK.
Zubly, John J. Papers. GHS.

Published Sources

Abbey, Kathryn Trimmer, ed. "The Intrigue of a British Refugee against the Willing Raid, 1778." *WMQ* 1 (October 1944): 397–404.
"Account of the Siege of Savannah, from a British Source." In *CGHS*, 5:129–39. Savannah: Braid & Hutton, 1901.
Adams, John. *Diary and Autobiography of John Adams.* Vol. 2. Edited by L. H. Butterfield. Cambridge, Mass.: Belknap Press, 1961.
———. *Papers of John Adams.* Vol. 6. Edited by Robert J. Taylor. Cambridge, Mass.: Belknap Press, 1983.
Bartholomai, Christian Friedrich, and Heinrich Carl Philipp von Feilitzsch. *Diaries of Two Anspach Jaegers.* Translated and edited by Bruce E. Burgoyne. Bowie, Md.: Heritage Books, 1997.
"Battle of King's Mountain October 7, 1780." *MAH* 4 (November 1880): 351–62.
Bauer, Carl. "The 1780 Siege of Charleston as Experienced by a Hessian Officer." 2 parts. Edited by George Fenwick Jones. *SCHM* 88 (January and April 1987): 23–33, 63–75.
Biddulph, Robert. "Letters of Robert Biddulph." Edited by Violet Biddulph. *AHR* 29 (October 1923): 87–109.
Brown, Tarleton. *Memoirs of Tarleton Brown, a Captain in the Revolutionary Army.* New York: privately printed, 1862. Reprint, Barnwell, S.C.: Barnwell County Museum and Historical Board, 1999.
Brown, Thomas. "A Loyalist View of the Drayton-Tennent-Hart Mission to the Upcountry." Edited by James H. O'Donnell. *SCHM* 67 (January 1966): 15–28.
Bruce, James. "Ordeal by Siege: James Bruce in Pensacola." Edited by Robin F. A. Fabel. *FHQ* 66 (January 1988): 280–97.
Campbell, Archibald. *Journal of an Expedition against the Rebels of Georgia in North America under the Orders of Archibald Campbell Esquire Lieut. Colol. of His Majesty's 71st Regimt. 1778.* Edited by Colin Campbell. Darien, Ga.: Ashantilly Press, 1981.
Candler, Alan D., ed. *Proceedings and Minutes of the Governor and Council: From August 6, 1771 to February 13, 1782.* Vol. 12, *The Colonial Records of the State of Georgia.* Atlanta: Franklin-Turner Co., 1907.
Carr, Patrick. "Letters of Patrick Carr, Terror to British Loyalists, to Governors John Martin and Lyman Hall, 1782 and 1783." *GHQ* 1 (December 1917): 337–43.

Champneys, John. *An account of the sufferings and persecution of John Champneys, a native of Charles-town, South-Carolina: Inflicted by order of Congress, for his refusal to take up arms in defence of the arbitrary proceedings carried on by the rulers of said place; Together with his protest, &c.* London, 1778.

Chastellux, Marquis de. *Travels in North America in the Years 1780, 1781, and 1782.* Vol. 2. Translated by Howard C. Rice. Chapel Hill: University of North Carolina Press, 1963.

Chesney, Alexander. *The Journal of Alexander Chesney, a South Carolina Loyalist in the Revolution and After.* Edited by E. Alfred Jones. *Ohio State University Bulletin* 26 (October 30, 1921).

Clay, Joseph. *Letters of Joseph Clay, Merchant of Savannah, 1776–1793.* In *CGHS,* vol. 8. Savannah: Georgia Historical Society, 1913.

Clinton, Sir Henry. *The American Rebellion, Sir Henry Clinton's Narrative of His Campaigns, 1775–1782, with an Appendix of Original Documents.* Edited by William B. Willcox. New Haven, Conn.: Yale University Press, 1954.

———. "Sir Henry Clinton's 'Journal of the Siege of Charleston, 1780.'" Edited by William T. Bulger. *SCHM* 66 (July 1965): 147–74.

Collins, James P. *Autobiography of a Revolutionary Soldier.* Edited by John M. Roberts. Clinton, La.: Feliciana Democrat, 1859. Reprint, Stratford, N.H.: Ayer Company, 1989.

Cornwallis, Charles, First Marquis. *Correspondence of Charles, First Marquis Cornwallis.* Vol. 1. Edited by Charles Ross. London: J. Murray, 1859.

Crary, Catherine S., ed. *The Price of Loyalty: Tory Writings from the Revolutionary Era.* New York: McGraw-Hill, 1973.

Dann, John C., ed. *The Revolution Remembered: Eyewitness Accounts of the War for Independence.* Chicago: University of Chicago Press, 1980.

Davie, William R. *The Revolutionary War Sketches of William R. Davie.* Edited by Blackwell P. Robinson. Raleigh: North Carolina Department of Cultural Resources, Division of Archives and History, 1976.

Davies, K. G., ed. *Documents of the American Revolution, 1770–1783 (Colonial Office Series).* Vols. 9–21. Dublin: Irish University Press, 1976–81.

Davis, Robert S., ed. *Georgia Citizens and Soldiers of the American Revolution.* Easley, S.C.: Southern Historical Press, 1979.

Deas, Anne Izard, ed. *Correspondence of Mr. Ralph Izard of South Carolina, from the Year 1774 to 1804; with a Short Memoir.* Vol. 1. New York: Charles S. Francis and Co., 1844.

Denny, Ebenezer. "Military Journal of Major Ebenezer Denny." *Pennsylvania Historical Society Memoirs* 7 (1860): 237–409.

Digges, Thomas Attwood. *Letters of Thomas Attwood Digges (1742–1821).* Edited by Robert H. Elias and Eugene D. Finch. Columbia: University of South Carolina Press, 1982.

Drayton, John. *Memoirs of the American Revolution as Relating to the State of South Carolina.* 2 vols. Charleston, S.C.: A. E. Miller, 1821. Reprint, New York: New York Times, 1969.

Dunbar, William. *Life, Letters and Papers of William Dunbar of Elgin, Morayshire, Scotland, and Natchez, Mississippi: Pioneer Scientist of the Southern United States.* Jackson: Press of the Mississippi Historical Society, 1930.

"An English Journal of the Siege of Savannah in 1779." *Historical Magazine* 8 (January 1864): 12–16.

Ewald, Johann. *Diary of the American War: A Hessian Journal.* Translated and edited by Joseph P. Tustin. New Haven, Conn.: Yale University Press, 1979.

Fanning, David. *Col. David Fanning's Narrative of His Exploits and Adventures as a Loyalist of North Carolina in the American Revolution.* Edited by A. W. Savary. Toronto: Reprinted from the *Canadian Magazine,* 1908.

Farmar, Robert. "Bernardo de Galvez's Siege of Pensacola in 1781 (As Related in Robert Farmar's Journal)." Edited by James A. Padgett. *LHQ* 26 (April 1943): 311–29.

Few, William. "Autobiography of Col. William Few of Georgia." *MAH* 7 (November 1881): 343–58.

Finney, Walter. "The Revolutionary War Diaries of Captain Walter Finney." Edited by Joseph Lee Boyle. *SCHM* 98 (April 1997): 126–52.

Fitzpatrick, John. *The Merchant of Manchac: The Letterbooks of John Fitzpatrick, 1768–1790.* Edited by Margaret Fisher Dalrymple. Baton Rouge: Louisiana State University Press, 1978.

"A Frenchman Visits Charleston in 1777." Translated by Elmer Douglas Johnson. *SCHGM* 52 (April 1951): 88–92.

Gadsden, Christopher. *The Writings of Christopher Gadsden.* Edited by Richard Walsh. Columbia: University of South Carolina Press, 1966.

Galloway, Joseph. *Fabricius: Or, Letters to the People of Great Britain; On the Absurdity and Mischiefs of Defensive Operations* only *in the American War; and on the Causes of the Failure in the Southern Operations.* London: G. Wilkie, 1782. Reprinted in Joseph Galloway. *Selected Tracts.* Vol. 3. New York: Da Capo Press, 1974.

Galvez, Bernardo de. "Bernardo de Galvez's Combat Diary for the Battle of Pensacola, 1781." Edited by Maury Baker and Margaret Bissler Haas. *FHQ* 56 (October 1977): 176–99.

Garden, Alexander. *Anecdotes of the Revolutionary War in America, with Sketches of Character of Persons the Most Distinguished, in the Southern States, for Civil and Military Service.* Charleston, S.C.: A. E. Miller, 1822. Reprint, Spartanburg, S.C.: Reprint Co., 1972.

George, David. "An Account of the Life of Mr. David George from S.L.A. Given by Himself." http://collections.ic.gc.ca/blackloyalists/documents (accessed July 30, 2001).

Gibbes, Robert W., ed. *Documentary History of the American Revolution, Consisting of Letters and Papers Relating to the Contest for Liberty Chiefly in South Carolina, from Originals in the Possession of Gen. Francis Marion, by Gen. Peter Horry, of Marion's Brigade: Together with Others from the Collection of the Editor.* 3 vols. New York: D. Appleton & Co., 1853–57.

Gibbes, William Hasell. "William Hasell Gibbes' Story of His Life." Edited by Arney R. Childs. *SCHGM* 50 (April 1949): 59–67.

Gray, Robert. "Colonel Robert Gray's Observations on the War in Carolina." *SCHGM* 11 (July 1910): 139–59.

Greene, Nathanael. *The Papers of General Nathanael Greene.* Vol. 6. Edited by Richard K. Showman. Vol. 7. Edited by Richard K. Showman and Dennis M. Conrad. Vols. 8–12. Edited by Dennis M. Conrad. Chapel Hill: University of North Carolina Press, 1991, 1994, 1995–2002.

Grimké, John Faucherau. "Journal of a Campaign to the Southward: May 9th to July 14th, 1778." *SCHGM* 12 (April, July, and October 1911): 60–69, 118–34, 190–206.

Habersham, Joseph. "Some Letters of Joseph Habersham." Edited by Ulrich B. Phillips. *GHQ* 10 (June 1926): 144–63.

Hamilton, Alexander. *The Papers of Alexander Hamilton.* Vol. 2. Edited by Harold C. Syrett. New York: Columbia University Press, 1961.

Hartley, George Harland. "George Harland Hartley's Claim for Losses as a Loyalist." *SCHGM* 51 (January 1950): 45–50.

Hazard, Ebenezer. "A View of Coastal South Carolina in 1778: The Journal of Ebenezer Hazard." Edited by H. Roy Merrens. *SCHM* 73 (October 1972): 177–93.

Hutson, Richard. "Letters of the Hon. Richard Hutson." In *Year Book, City of Charleston, South Carolina,* 313–25. Charleston: News and Courier Book Press, 1895.

Innes, Alexander. "Charles Town Loyalism in 1775: The Secret Reports of Alexander Innes." Edited by B. D. Bargar. *SCHM* 63 (July 1962): 125–36.

Jackson, James. "Miscellaneous Papers of James Jackson, 1781–1798." Edited by Lilla Mills Hawes. *GHQ* 37 (March 1953): 54–80.

James, William Dobein. *A Sketch of the Life of Brig. Gen. Francis Marion and a History of His Brigade from Its Rise in June 1780 until Disbanded in December, 1782.* Charleston, S.C.: Gould and Riley, 1821. Reprint, Marietta, Ga: Continental Book Co., 1948.

Jefferson, Thomas. *The Papers of Thomas Jefferson.* Vols. 3 and 4. Edited by Julian P. Boyd. Princeton, N.J.: Princeton University Press, 1951.

Johnston, Elizabeth Lichtenstein. *Recollections of a Georgia Loyalist.* Edited by Rev. Arthur Wentworth Eaton. New York: M. F. Mansfield and Company, 1901. Reprint, Spartanburg, S.C.: Reprint Co., 1974.

Kennedy, Benjamin, ed. and trans. *Muskets, Cannon Balls, and Bombs: Nine Narratives of the Siege of Savannah in 1779.* Savannah: Beehive Press, 1974.

Kennett, Lee, ed. and trans. "A French Report on St. Augustine in the 1770's." *FHQ* 44 (July and October 1965): 133–35.

Killion, Ronald G., and Charles T. Waller, eds. *Georgia and the Revolution.* Atlanta: Cherokee, 1975.

King, Boston. *Memoirs of Boston King.* http://collections.ic.gc.ca/blackloyalists/documents (accessed July 30, 2001).

Kirkland, Moses. "A Backcountry Loyalist Plan to Retake Georgia and the Carolinas, 1778." Edited by Randall M. Miller. *SCHM* 75 (October 1974): 207–14.

Kirkwood, Robert. "The Journal and Order Book of Captain Robert Kirkwood of the Delaware Regiment of the Continental Line." In *Papers of the Historical Society of Delaware,* vol. 56. Wilmington: Historical Society of Delaware, 1910.

Lamb, Roger. *An Original and Authentic Journal of Occurrences during the Late American War, from Its Commencement to the Year 1783.* Dublin: Wilkinson & Courtney, 1809. Reprint, New York: Arno Press, 1968.

Laurens, Henry. *The Papers of Henry Laurens.* Vols. 10–14. Edited by David R. Chesnutt. Vol. 15. Edited by David R. Chesnutt and C. James Taylor. Columbia: University of South Carolina Press, 1985–94, 2000.

Lee, Henry. "Henry Lee on the Southern Campaign." Edited by George F. Scheer Jr. *Virginia Magazine of History and Biography* 51 (April 1943): 141–50.

————. *The Revolutionary War Memoirs of General Henry Lee.* Edited by R. E. Lee. New York: Da Capo Press, 1998. Originally published as *Memoirs of the War in the Southern Department of the United States.* Washington, D.C.: P. Force, 1827.

Lee, Thomas Sim. "Revolutionary Mail Bag: Governor Thomas Sim Lee's Correspondence." Edited by Helen Lee Peabody. *MHM* 49 (September 1954): 223–37.

Lee, William. *The True and Interesting Travels of William Lee.* London: Franklin Press, 1808.

Lenoir, William. "Revolutionary Diary of William Lenoir." Edited by J. G. De Roulhac Hamilton. *JSH* 6 (May 1940): 247–59.

Letters from America, 1775–1779, Being Letters of Brunswick, Hessian, and Waldeck Officers with the British Armies during the Revolution. Translated by Ray W. Pettengill. Boston: Houghton Mifflin, 1924. Reprint, Port Washington, N.Y.: Kennikat Press, 1964.

"Letters to General Greene and Others." *SCHGM* 16 (July and October 1915): 97–108, 139–49; 17 (January and April 1916): 3–13, 53–57.

"Letters to Joseph Galloway, from Leading Tories in America." *Historical Magazine* 5 (October and December 1861): 295–301, 356–64; 6 (June 1862): 177–82.

Mackenzie, Frederick. *Diary of Frederick Mackenzie, Giving a Daily Narrative of His Military Service as an Officer of the Regiment of Royal Welch Fusiliers during the Years 1775–1781 in Massachusetts, Rhode Island, and New York.* 2 vols. Edited by Allen French. Cambridge, Mass.: Harvard University Press, 1926. Reprint, 1930.

Manigault, Ann. "Extracts from the Journal of Mrs. Ann Manigault, 1754–1781." Edited by Mabel L. Webber. *SCHGM* 21 (July 1920): 112–20.

Manigault, Gabriel. "Papers of Gabriel Manigault." Edited by Maurice A. Crouse. *SCHM* 64 (January 1963): 1–12.

Marion, Francis. "Genl. Marion's Report of the Affair at Wadboo." *SCHGM* 17 (October 1916): 176–77.

Marrant, John. *A Narrative of the Lord's Wonderful Dealings with John Marrant, a Black.* London: Gilbert and Plummer, 1785. Reprinted in *The Garland Library of Narratives of North American Indian Captivities.* Vol. 17. New York: Garland, 1978.

Martin, John. "Official Letters of Governor John Martin, 1782–1783." *GHQ* 1 (December 1917): 281–335.

Mazyck, Stephon. "Stephon Mazyck to Philip Porcher." *SCHGM* 38 (January 1937): 11–15.

McDowell, William. "Journal of Lieut. William McDowell, of the First Penn'a Regiment, in the Southern Campaign. 1781–1782." *Pennsylvania Archives* 15 (1890): 295–340.

McIntosh, Lachlan. "The Papers of Lachlan McIntosh, 1774–1779." Edited by Lilla M. Hawes. *GHQ* 38 (June, September, and December 1954): 148–69, 253–67, 356–68; 39 (March, June, September, and December 1955): 52–68, 172–86, 253–68, 356–75.

McJunkin, Joseph. "Memoir of Joseph McJunkin, of Union." *The Magnolia; or Southern Appalachian,* new series, 2 (January–June 1843): 30–40.

Meyronnet de Saint-Marc, Philippe-Auguste de. "Meyronnet de Saint-Marc's Journal of the Operations of the French Army under D'Estaing at the Siege of Savannah, September 1779." Edited by Roberta Leighton. *New York Historical Society Quarterly* 36 (July 1952): 255–87.

Middleton, Arthur. "Correspondence of Hon. Arthur Middleton, Signer of the Declaration of Independence." Edited by Joseph W. Barnwell. *SCHGM* 26 (October 1925): 183–213; 27 (January, April, and July 1926): 1–29, 51–80, 107–55.

Miller, Elizabeth R., ed. *The American Revolution, as Described by British Writers and the Morning Chronicle and London Advertiser.* Bowie, Md.: Heritage Books, 1991.

Mills, Nathaniel, and John Hicks. "The Letter-Book of Mills & Hicks (Nathaniel Mills and John Hicks), August 13th, 1781, to August 22nd, 1784, at Charles Town (South Carolina), Saint Augustine (East Florida), New York (New York), and Granville (Nova Scotia)." Edited by Robert Earle Moody and Charles Christopher Crittenden. *NCHR* 14 (January 1937): 39–83.

"Minute Book, Savannah Board of Police, 1779." Edited by Lilla Mills Hawes. *GHQ* 45 (September 1961): 245–57.

Miranda, Francisco de. "Miranda's Diary of the Siege of Pensacola." Translated by Donald E. Worcester. *FHQ* 29 (January 1951): 163–96.

Morris, Lewis, Jr. "Letters from Col. Lewis Morris to Miss Ann Elliott." *SCHGM* 40 (October 1939): 122–36; 41 (January 1940): 1–14.

———. "Letters to General Lewis Morris." In *Collections of the New York Historical Society for the Year 1875.* Vol. 8, 433–512. New York: New-York Historical Society, 1876.

Moultrie, William. *Memoirs of the American Revolution, So Far as It Related to the States of North and South-Carolina, and Georgia.* 2 vols. New York: David Longworth, 1802.

Muhlenberg, Henry. "Henry Muhlenberg's Georgia Correspondence." Edited by Andrew W. Lewis. *GHQ* 49 (December 1965): 424–54.

Murray, Sir James. *Letters from America, 1773–1780: Being the Letters of a Scots Officer, Sir James Murray, to His Home during the War of American Independence.* Edited by Eric Robson. New York: Barnes & Noble, 1950.

Newsome, A. R., ed. "A British Orderly Book, 1780–1781." *NCHR* 9 (January, April, and July 1932): 57–78, 163–86, 273–98.

O'Hara, Charles. "Letters of Charles O'Hara to the Duke of Grafton." Edited by George C. Rogers Jr. *SCHM* 65 (July 1964): 158–80.

"Papers of the First Council of Safety of the Revolutionary Party in South Carolina, June–November, 1775." *SCHGM* 3 (April 1902): 69–85.

"Papers Relating to the Allied Attack on Savannah in 1779." *Historical Magazine* 8 (September 1864): 290–97.

Peckham, Howard H., ed. *Sources of American Independence. Selected Manuscripts from the Collections of the William L. Clements Library.* Chicago: University of Chicago Press, 1978.

Peebles, John. *John Peebles' American War: The Diary of a Scottish Grenadier, 1776–1782.* Edited by Ira D. Gruber. Mechanicsburg, Pa.: Stackpole Books, 1998.

Phelps, Matthew. *Memoirs and Adventures of Captain Matthew Phelps; Formerly of Harwington in Connecticut, Now Resident in Newhaven in Vermont: Particularly in Two Voyages, from Connecticut to the River Mississippi, from December 1773 to October 1780.* Bennington, Vt.: Haswell's Press, 1802.

Pierce, William. "Southern Campaign of General Greene 1781–2, Letters of Major William Pierce to St. George Tucker." *MAH* 7 (December 1881): 431–45.

Pinckney, Eliza Lucas. "Letters of Eliza Lucas Pinckney, 1768–1782." Edited by Elise Pinckney. *SCHM* 76 (July 1975): 143–70.

Pinckney, Thomas. "Letters of Thomas Pinckney, 1775–1780." Edited by Jack L. Cross. *SCHM* 58 (July 1957): 19–33.

"Proceedings of the Georgia Council of Safety." In *CGHS,* vol. 5, part 1. Savannah: Braid & Hutton, 1901.

Ramsay, David. *The History of the Revolution of South-Carolina, from a British Province to an Independent State.* Trenton, N.J.: Isaac Collins, 1785.

Report on American Manuscripts in the Royal Institutions of Great Britain. Vol. 1. London: Mackie & Co. for His Majesty's Stationery Office, 1904. Vol. 2. Dublin: John Falconer for His Majesty's Stationery Office, 1906. Vol. 3. Hereford: Anthony Brothers for His Majesty's Stationery Office, 1907.

"Revolutionary Letters." *SCHGM* 38 (January and July 1937): 1–10, 75–80.

Richardson, William. "Letters of William Richardson, 1765–1784." Edited by Emma B. Richardson. *SCHGM* 47 (January 1946): 1–20.

Robertson, Heard, ed. "Georgia's Banishment and Expulsion Act of September 16, 1777." *GHQ* 55 (Summer 1971): 274–82.

Russell, Peter. "The Siege of Charleston: Journal of Captain Peter Russell, December 25, 1779, to May 2, 1780." Edited by James Bain Jr. *AHR* 4 (April 1899): 478–501.

Rutledge, John. "John Rutledge to Benjamin Lincoln." *SCHGM* 25 (July 1924): 133–35.

———. "Letters of John Rutledge." Edited by Joseph W. Barnwell. *SCHGM* 17 (October 1916): 131–46; 18 (January and April 1917): 42–69, 131–67.

Seymour, William. "A Journal of the Southern Expedition, 1780–1783." In *Papers of the Delaware Historical Society,* vol. 15. Wilmington: Historical Society of Delaware, 1896.

Simmons, R. C., and P. D. G. Thomas, eds. *Proceedings and Debates of the British Parliaments Respecting North America, 1754–1783.* Vols. 5 and 6. White Plains, N.Y.: Kraus International Publications, 1986.

Simpson, James. "A British View of the Siege of Charleston, 1776." Edited by Frances Reece Kepner. *JSH* 11 (February 1945): 93–103.

———. "James Simpson's Reports on the Carolina Loyalists, 1779–1780." Edited by Alan S. Brown. *JSH* 21 (November 1955): 513–19.

Skelly, E. "Demonstration against Charleston, South Carolina, in 1779: Journal of Brigade Major F. Skelly." *MAH* 26 (August and November 1891): 152–54, 392–93.

Smith, William. *Historical Memoirs from 26 August 1778 to 12 November 1783 of William Smith Historian of the Province of New York: Member of the Governor's Council, and Last Chief Justice of That Province under the Crown; Chief Justice of Quebec.* Edited by William H. W. Sabine. New York: Arno Press, 1971.

Starr, J. Barton, ed. "The Case and Petition of His Majesty's Loyal Subjects, Late of West Florida." *FHQ* 59 (October 1980): 199–212.

Stevens, Daniel. "Autobiography of Daniel Stevens, 1746–1835." *SCHM* 58 (January 1957): 1–18.

Stuart, Charles. *A Prime Minister and His Son: From the Correspondence of the 3rd Earl of Bute and of Lt.-General The Hon. Sir Charles Stuart, K.B.* Edited by Mrs. E. Stuart Wortley. London: John Murray, 1925.

Stuart, James. "A Note on James Stuart, Loyalist Clergyman in South Carolina." Edited by Henry D. Bull. *JSH* 12 (November 1946): 570–75.

Talman, James J., ed. *Loyalist Narratives from Upper Canada*. Toronto: Champlain Society, 1946.

Tarleton, Banastre. *A History of the Campaigns of 1780 and 1781, in the Southern Provinces of North America*. London: T. Cadell, 1787. Reprint, Spartanburg, S.C.: Reprint Co., 1967.

Taylor, Thomas. "A Georgia Loyalist's Perspective on the American Revolution: The Letters of Dr. Thomas Taylor." Edited by Robert Scott Davis. *GHQ* 81 (Spring 1997): 118–38.

Tennent, William. "Fragment of a Journal kept by the Rev. William Tennent Describing his Journey, in 1775, to Upper South Carolina at the request of the Council of Safety, To induce the Tories to sign an Association to support the cause of the Colonists." In *City Year Book of Charleston*, 295–312. Charleston: News and Courier Book Press, 1894.

Tilden, John Bell. "Extracts from the Journal of Lieutenant John Bell Tilden, Second Pennsylvania Line, 1781–1782." *PMHB* 19 (1895): 51–63.

Tonyn, Patrick. "Letter from Governor Patrick Tonyn of East Florida to Lord George Germain, Secretary of State for the Colonies, 1776." Edited by Edward M. Coleman. *MVHR* 33 (September 1946): 289–92.

"The Treaty of Long Island of Holston, July, 1777." Edited by Archibald Henderson. *NCHR* 8 (January 1931): 55–116.

Uhlendorf, Bernard A., ed. and trans. *The Siege of Charleston, with an Account of the Province of South Carolina: Diaries and Letters of Hessian Officers from the von Jungkenn Papers in the William L. Clements Library*. Ann Arbor: University of Michigan Press, 1938.

Waldeck, Philipp. *Eighteenth Century America: A Hessian Report on the People, the Land, the War as Noted in the Diary of Chaplain Philipp Waldeck (1776–1780)*. Translated by Bruce E. Burgoyne. Bowie, Md.: Heritage Books, 1995.

Watson, Elkanah. *Men and Times of the Revolution; or, Memoirs of Elkanah Watson, Including Journals of Travels in Europe and America, from 1777 to 1842*. Edited by Winslow C. Watson. New York: Dana and Company, 1856.

Wells, Louisa Susannah. *The Journal of a Voyage from Charleston, South Carolina, to London Undertaken during the American Revolution by the Daughter of an Eminent American Loyalist in the Year 1778 and Written from Memory Only in 1779*. New York: Printed for the New-York Historical Society, 1906. Reprint, New York: New York Times and Arno Press, 1968.

Wells, William Charles. "Letter from Wm. Charles Wells to Dr. James Currie." *SCHGM* 26 (January 1925): 41–44.

Wilkinson, Eliza. *Letters of Eliza Wilkinson*. Edited by Caroline Gilman. New York: S. Colman, 1839. Reprint, New York: New York Times and Arno Press, 1969.

Willard, Margaret Wheeler, ed. *Letters on the American Revolution, 1774–1776*. Boston: Houghton Mifflin, 1925.

Wilson, John. *Encounters on a March through Georgia in 1779: The Maps and Memorandums of John Wilson, Engineer, 71st Highland Regiment*. Edited by Robert Scott Davis Jr. Sylvania, Ga.: Partridge Pond Press, 1986.

―――. "Lieutenant John Wilson's 'Journal of the Siege of Charleston.'" Edited by Joseph I. Waring. *SCHM* 66 (July 1965): 176–82.

Winn, Richard. "General Richard Winn's Notes—1780." Edited by Samuel C. Williams. *SCHGM* 43 (October 1942): 201–12; 44 (January 1943): 1–10.

Woodmason, Charles. *The Carolina Backcountry on the Eve of the Revolution.* Edited by Richard J. Hooker. Chapel Hill: University of North Carolina Press, 1953.

Zubly, John J. *"A Warm & Zealous Spirit": John J. Zubly and the American Revolution; a Selection of His Writings.* Edited by Randall M. Miller. Macon, Ga.: Mercer University Press, 1982.

Newspapers

Royal Georgia Gazette (Savannah). 1779–82.

Royal South Carolina Gazette (Charleston). 1780–82.

South Carolina and American General Gazette (Charleston). 1780–82.

South Carolina Royal Gazette (Charleston). 1780–82.

SECONDARY SOURCES

Articles

Abbey, Kathryn T. "Peter Chester's Defense of the Mississippi after the Willing Raid." *MVHR* 22 (June 1935): 17–32.

Alden, John Richard. "John Stuart Accuses William Bull." *WMQ* 2 (July 1945): 315–20.

Barnwell, Robert W., Jr. "Rutledge: The Dictator." *JSH* 7 (May 1941): 215–24.

Boyd, Mark F., and Jose Navarro Latorre. "Spanish Interest in British Florida, and in the Progress of the American Revolution." *FHQ* 32 (October 1953): 92–130.

Braund, Kathryn E. Holland. "The Creek Indians, Blacks, and Slavery." *JSH* 57 (November 1991): 601–36.

Brown, Christopher L. "Empire without Slaves: British Concepts of Emancipation in the Age of the American Revolution." *WMQ* 56 (April 1999): 273–306.

Cann, Marvin L. "Prelude to War: The First Battle of Ninety Six, November 19–21, 1775." *SCHM* 76 (October 1975): 197–214.

―――. "War in the Backcountry: The Siege of Ninety Six, May 22–June 19, 1781." *SCHM* 72 (January 1971): 1–14.

Cashin, Edward J., Jr. "George Walton and the Forged Letter." *GHQ* 62 (Summer 1978): 133–45.

―――. "Nathanael Greene's Campaign for Georgia in 1781." *GHQ* 61 (Spring 1977): 43–58.

Caughey, John. "The Natchez Rebellion of 1781 and Its Aftermath." *LHQ* 16 (January 1933): 57–83.

―――. "The Panis Mission to Pensacola, 1778." *Hispanic-American Historical Review* 10 (November 1930): 480–89.

―――. "Willing's Expedition down the Mississippi, 1778." *LHQ* 15 (January 1932): 5–36.

Coleman, Kenneth. "Restored Colonial Georgia, 1779–1782." *GHQ* 40 (March 1956): 1–20.

Conway, Stephen. "To Subdue America: British Army Officers and the Conduct of the Revolutionary War." *WMQ* 43 (July 1986): 381–407.

Coulter, E. Merton. "Edward Telfair." *GHQ* 20 (June 1936): 99–124.

Crow, Jeffrey J. "What Price Loyalism? The Case of John Cruden, Commissioner of Sequestered Estates." *NCHR* 58 (July 1981): 215–33.

Culver, Francis B. "The Last Bloodshed of the Revolution: Death of Captain Wilmot of the Maryland Line." *MHM* 5 (December 1910): 329–38.

Davis, Robert Scott, Jr. "Lord Montagu's Mission to South Carolina in 1781: American POWs for the King's Service in Jamaica." *SCHM* 84 (April 1983): 89–109.

———. "The Loyalist Trials at Ninety Six in 1779." *SCHM* 80 (April 1979): 172–81.

Fingerhut, Eugene R. "Uses and Abuses of the American Loyalists' Claims." *WMQ* 25 (April 1968): 245–58.

Fraser, Walter J., Jr. "Reflections of 'Democracy' in Revolutionary South Carolina?: The Composition of Military Organizations and the Attitudes and Relationships of the Officers and Men, 1775–1780." *SCHM* 78 (July 1977): 202–12.

Furlong, Patrick S. "Civilian-Military Conflict and the Restoration of the Royal Province of Georgia, 1778–1782." *JSH* 38 (August 1972): 415–42.

Gould, Eliga H. "American Independence and Britain's Counter-Revolution." *Past and Present,* no. 154 (February 1997): 107–41.

Green, E. R. R. "Queensborough Township: Scotch-Irish Emigration and the Expansion of Georgia, 1763–1776." *WMQ* 17 (April 1960): 183–99.

Greene, Jack P. "Bridge to Revolution: The Wilkes Fund Controversy in South Carolina." *JSH* 29 (February 1963): 19–52.

———. "The Political Authorship of Sir Egerton Leigh." *SCHM* (July 1975): 143–52.

———. "The Role of the Lower Houses of Assembly in Eighteenth-Century Politics." *JSH* 27 (November 1961): 451–74.

Haarmann, Albert W. "The Spanish Conquest of West Florida, 1779–1781." *FHQ* 39 (October 1960): 107–34.

Heidler, David S. "The American Defeat at Briar Creek, 3 March 1779." *GHQ* 66 (Fall 1982): 317–31.

Hesseltine, William B. "Lyman Draper and the South." *JSH* 19 (February 1953): 20–31.

Holman, C. Hugh. "William Gilmore Simms' Picture of the Revolution as a Civil Conflict." *JSH* 15 (November 1949): 441–62.

Holmes, Jack D. L. "Robert Ross' Plan for an English Invasion of Louisiana in 1782." *Louisiana History* 5 (Spring 1964): 161–77.

Howard, C. N. "Some Economic Aspects of British West Florida, 1763–1768." *JSH* 6 (May 1940): 201–21.

Jackson, Harvey H. "The Battle of the Riceboats: Georgia Joins the Revolution." *GHQ* 58 (Summer 1974): 229–43.

———. "Consensus and Conflict: Factional Politics in Revolutionary Georgia, 1774–1777." *GHQ* 59 (Winter 1975): 388–401.

Jones, George Fenwick. "The Black Hessians: Negroes Recruited by the Hessians in South Carolina and Other Colonies." *SCHM* 83 (October 1982): 287–302.

Kerr, Wilfred B. "The Stamp Act in the Floridas." *MVHR* 21 (March 1935): 463–70.

Kyte, George W. "Francis Marion as an Intelligence Officer." *SCHM* 77 (October 1976): 215–26.

———. "Thaddeus Kosciuszko at the Liberation of Charleston, 1782." *SCHM* 84 (January 1983): 11–21.

———. "Victory in the South: An Appraisal of General Greene's Strategy in the Carolinas." *NCHR* 37 (July 1960): 321–47.

Lambert, Robert S. "The Confiscation of Loyalist Property in Georgia, 1782–1786." *WMQ* 20 (January 1963): 80–94.

———. "A Loyalist Odyssey: James and Mary Cary in Exile, 1783–1804." *SCHM* 79 (July 1978): 167–81.

Lamplugh, George R. "'To Check and Discourage the Wicked and Designing': John Wereat and the Revolution in Georgia." *GHQ* 61 (Winter 1977): 295–307.

Lawrence, Alexander A. "General Robert Howe and the British Capture of Savannah in 1778." *GHQ* 36 (December 1952): 303–27.

Lennon, Donald R. "'The Graveyard of American Commanders': The Continental Army's Southern Department, 1776–1778." *NCHR* 67 (April 1990): 133–58.

Mackesy, Piers. "British Strategy in the War of American Independence." *Yale Review* 52 (Summer 1963): 539–57.

Maier, Pauline. "The Charleston Mob and the Evolution of Popular Politics in Revolutionary South Carolina, 1765–1784." *Perspectives in American History* 4 (1970): 173–96.

Main, Jackson Turner. "Government by the People: The American Revolution and the Democratization of the Legislatures." *WMQ* 23 (July 1966): 391–407.

Massey, Gregory D. "The Limits of Antislavery Thought in the Revolutionary Lower South: John Laurens and Henry Laurens." *JSH* 63 (August 1997): 495–530.

Merrell, James H. "The Indians' New World: The Catawba Experience." *WMQ* 41 (October 1984): 537–65.

Morgan, Philip D. "Black Life in Eighteenth-Century Charleston." *Perspectives in American History,* new series, 1 (1984): 187–232.

Nelson, Paul David. "British Conduct of the Revolutionary War: A Review of Interpretations." *JAH* 65 (December 1978): 623–53.

Nichols, John L. "Alexander Cameron: British Agent among the Cherokee, 1764–1781." *SCHM* 97 (April 1996): 94–114.

Norton, Mary Beth. "Eighteenth-Century Women in Peace and War: The Case of the Loyalists." *WMQ* 33 (July 1976): 386–409.

Osborn, George C. "Major-General John Campbell in British West Florida." *FHQ* 27 (April 1949): 317–39.

———. "Relations with the Indians in West Florida during the Administration of Governor Peter Chester, 1770–1781." *FHQ* 31 (April 1953): 239–72.

Pennington, Edgar Legare. "East Florida in the American Revolution, 1775–1778." *FHQ* 9 (July 1930): 24–46.

Quarles, Benjamin. "Lord Dunmore as Liberator." *WMQ* 15 (October 1958): 494–507.

Raddall, Thomas H. "Tarleton's Legion." *Collections of the Nova Scotia Historical Society* 28 (1947): 1–50.

Roberts, William I., III. "The Losses of a Loyalist Merchant in Georgia during the Revolution." *GHQ* 52 (September 1968): 270–76.

Robertson, Heard. "The Second British Occupation of Augusta, 1780–1781." *GHQ* 58 (Winter 1974): 422–46.

Robson, Eric. "The Expedition to the Southern Colonies, 1775–1776." *EHR* 67 (October 1951): 535–60.

Sayen, John J., Jr. "Oared Fighting Ships of the South Carolina Navy, 1776–1780." *SCHM* 87 (October 1986): 213–37.

Scott, Ralph C., Jr. "The Quaker Settlement of Wrightsborough, Georgia." *GHQ* 56 (Summer 1972): 210–23.

Searcy, Martha Condray. "1779: The First Year of the British Occupation of Georgia." *GHQ* 67 (Summer 1983): 168–88.

———. "The Introduction of African Slavery into the Creek Indian Nation." *GHQ* 66 (Spring 1982): 21–32.

Shaffer, Arthur H. "Between Two Worlds: David Ramsay and the Politics of Slavery." *JSH* 50 (May 1984): 175–96.

Taylor, Garland. "Colonial Settlement and Early Revolutionary Activity in West Florida up to 1779." *MVHR* 22 (December 1935): 351–60.

Troxler, Carole Watterson. "Refuge, Resistance, and Reward: The Southern Loyalists' Claim on East Florida." *JSH* 55 (November 1989): 563–96.

Tyson, George F., Jr. "The Carolina Black Corps: Legacy of Revolution (1782–1798)." *Review Interamericana* 5 (Winter 1975/76): 648–64.

Willcox, William B. "British Strategy in America, 1778." *Journal of Modern History* 19 (June 1947): 97–121.

Williams, Edwin L., Jr. "Negro Slavery in Florida." *FHQ* 28 (October 1949): 93–110.

Willis, William S. "Divide and Rule: Red, White, and Black in the Southeast." *Journal of Negro History* 48 (July 1963): 157–76.

Wood, Betty. "'Until He Shall Be Dead, Dead, Dead': The Judicial Treatment of Slaves in Eighteenth-Century Georgia." *GHQ* 71 (Fall 1987): 377–98.

Wright, J. Leitch. "Blacks in British East Florida." *FHQ* 54 (April 1976): 425–42.

Books

Abbot, W. W. *The Royal Governors of Georgia, 1754–1775.* Chapel Hill: University of North Carolina Press, 1959.

Agniel, Lucien. *The Late Affair Has Almost Broke My Heart: The American Revolution in the South, 1780–1781.* Riverside, Conn.: Chatham Press, 1972.

Alden, John Richard. *John Stuart and the Southern Colonial Frontier: A Study of Indian Relations, War, Trade, and Land Problems in the Southern Wilderness, 1754–1775.* Ann Arbor: University of Michigan Press, 1944.

———. *The South in the Revolution, 1763–1789.* Baton Rouge: Louisiana State University Press, 1957.

Allen, Robert S., ed. *The Loyal Americans: The Military Role of the Loyalist Provincial Corps and Their Settlement in British North America, 1775–1784.* Ottawa: National Museums of Canada, 1983.

Babits, Lawrence E. *A Devil of a Whipping: The Battle of Cowpens.* Chapel Hill: University of North Carolina Press, 1998.

Bailyn, Bernard, and John B. Hench, eds. *The Press and the American Revolution.* Boston: Northeastern University Press, 1981.

Barrs, Burton. *East Florida in the American Revolution.* Jacksonville, Fla.: Guild Press, 1932.

Bass, Robert D. *Gamecock: The Life and Campaigns of General Thomas Sumter.* New York: Holt, Rinehart and Winston, 1961.

———. *The Green Dragoon: The Lives of Banastre Tarleton and Mary Robinson.* New York: Henry Holt & Co., 1957.

———. *Ninety Six: The Struggle for the South Carolina Back Country.* Lexington, S.C.: Sandlapper Store, 1978.

———. *Swamp Fox: The Life and Campaigns of Francis Marion.* Orangeburg, S.C.: Sandlapper Publishing Co., 1974.

Bellot, Leland J. *William Knox: The Life & Thought of an Eighteenth-Century Imperialist.* Austin: University of Texas Press, 1977.

Bennett, Charles E., and Donald R. Lennon. *A Quest for Glory: Major General Robert Howe and the American Revolution.* Chapel Hill: University of North Carolina Press, 1991.

Berkeley, Edmund, and Dorothy Smith Berkeley. *Dr. Alexander Garden of Charles Town.* Chapel Hill: University of North Carolina Press, 1969.

Berlin, Ira. *Many Thousands Gone: The First Two Centuries of Slavery in North America.* Cambridge, Mass.: Belknap Press of Harvard University Press, 1998.

Berlin, Ira, and Ronald Hoffman, eds. *Slavery and Freedom in the Age of the American Revolution.* Urbana: University of Illinois Press, 1986.

Black, Jeremy. *War for America: The Fight for Independence, 1775–1783.* Bridgend: Sutton Publishing Ltd., 1991.

Borick, Carl P. *A Gallant Defense: The Siege of Charleston, 1780.* Columbia: University of South Carolina Press, 2003.

Bowler, R. Arthur. *Logistics and the Failure of the British Army in America, 1775–1783.* Princeton, N.J.: Princeton University Press, 1975.

Brooke, John. *King George III.* New York: McGraw-Hill, 1972.

Brown, Douglas Summers. *The Catawba Indians: The People of the River.* Columbia: University of South Carolina Press, 1966.

Brown, Gerald Saxon. *The American Secretary: The Colonial Policy of Lord George Germain, 1775–1778.* Ann Arbor: University of Michigan Press, 1963.

Brown, Wallace. *The Good Americans: The Loyalists in the American Revolution.* New York: Morrow, 1969.

———. *The King's Friends: The Composition and Motives of the American Loyalist Claimants.* Providence, R.I.: Brown University Press, 1965.

Buchanan, John. *The Road to Guilford Courthouse: The American Revolution in the Carolinas.* New York: John Wiley & Sons, 1997.

Calhoon, Robert McCluer. *The Loyalists in Revolutionary America, 1760–1781.* New York: Harcourt Brace Jovanovich, 1973.

Callahan, North. *Royal Raiders: The Tories of the American Revolution.* Indianapolis: Bobbs-Merrill, 1963.

Calloway, Colin G. *The American Revolution in Indian Country: Crisis and Diversity in Native American Communities.* Cambridge: Cambridge University Press, 1995.

Cashin, Edward J. *The King's Ranger: Thomas Brown and the American Revolution on the Southern Frontier*. New York: Fordham University Press, 1999.

Christie, Ian R. *Crisis of Empire: Great Britain and the American Colonies, 1754–1783*. New York: W. W. Norton, 1966.

———. *The End of North's Ministry, 1780–1782*. London: Macmillan, 1958.

———. *Wars and Revolutions: Britain, 1760–1815*. Cambridge, Mass.: Harvard University Press, 1982.

Clinton, Catherine, and Michele Gillespie, eds. *The Devil's Lane: Sex and Race in the Early South*. New York: Oxford University Press, 1997.

Coker, William S., and Robert R. Rea, eds. *Anglo-Spanish Confrontation on the Gulf Coast during the American Revolution*. Pensacola, Fla.: Gulf Coast History and Humanities Conference, 1982.

Coleman, Kenneth. *The American Revolution in Georgia, 1763–1789*. Athens: University of Georgia Press, 1958.

Crow, Jeffrey J., and Larry E. Tise, eds. *The Southern Experience in the American Revolution*. Chapel Hill: University of North Carolina Press, 1978.

Daunton, Martin, and Rick Halpern, eds. *Empire and Others: British Encounters with Indigenous Peoples, 1600–1850*. Philadelphia: University of Pennsylvania Press, 1999.

Davis, Robert S., Jr., and Kenneth H. Thomas, Jr. *Kettle Creek: The Battle of the Cane Brakes; Wilkes County, Georgia*. [Atlanta]: Georgia Department of Natural Resources, 1975.

Dickinson, H. T., ed. *Britain and the American Revolution*. New York: Addison Wesley Longman, 1998.

Dowd, Gregory Evans. *A Spirited Resistance: The North American Indian Struggle for Unity, 1745–1815*. Baltimore: Johns Hopkins University Press, 1992.

Draper, Lyman C. *King's Mountain and Its Heroes: History of the Battle of King's Mountain, October 7th, 1780, and the Events Which Led to It*. Cincinnati: P. G. Thomson, 1881. Reprint, Bowie, Md.: Heritage Books, 2002.

Edgar, Walter. *Partisans and Redcoats: The Southern Conflict That Turned the Tide of the American Revolution*. New York: Morrow, 2001.

Fabel, Robin F. A. *The Economy of British West Florida, 1763–1783*. Tuscaloosa: University of Alabama Press, 1988.

Fenn, Elizabeth A. *Pox Americana: The Great Smallpox Epidemic of 1775–1782*. New York: Hill and Wang, 2001.

Flood, Charles Bracelen. *Rise and Fight Again: Perilous Times on the Road to Independence*. New York: Dodd, Mead, and Company, 1976.

Fortescue, Sir John. *The War of Independence: The British Army in North America*. Mechanicsburg, Pa.: Stackpole Books, 2001.

Foster, William Omer, Sr. *James Jackson, Duelist and Militant Statesman, 1757–1806*. Athens: University of Georgia Press, 1960.

Fowler, William M., Jr., and Wallace Coyle, eds. *The American Revolution: Changing Perspectives*. Boston: Northeastern University Press, 1979.

Frey, Sylvia R. *Water from the Rock: Black Resistance in a Revolutionary Age*. Princeton, N.J.: Princeton University Press, 1991.

Gibson, Arrell M. *The Chickasaws*. Norman: University of Oklahoma Press, 1971.

Glasrud, Bruce A., and Alan M. Smith, eds. *Race Relations in British North America, 1607–1783*. Chicago: Nelson-Hall, 1982.

Gould, Eliga H. *The Persistence of Empire: British Political Culture in the Age of the American Revolution*. Chapel Hill: University of North Carolina Press, 2000.

Hall, Leslie. *Land and Allegiance in Revolutionary Georgia*. Athens: University of Georgia Press, 2001.

Haller, Stephen E. *William Washington, Cavalryman of the Revolution*. Bowie, Md.: Heritage Books, 2001.

Hatley, Tom. *The Dividing Paths: Cherokees and South Carolinians through the Revolutionary Era*. New York: Oxford University Press, 1995.

Hayes, Louise Frederick. *Hero of Hornet's Nest: A Biography of Elijah Clark, 1733 to 1799*. New York: Stratford House, 1946.

Haynes, Robert V. *The Natchez District and the American Revolution*. Jackson: University Press of Mississippi, 1976.

Hibbert, Christopher. *George III: A Personal History*. New York: Basic Books, 1998.

———. *Redcoats and Rebels: The American Revolution through British Eyes*. New York: Avon Books, 1990.

Higginbotham, Don. *Daniel Morgan: Revolutionary Rifleman*. Chapel Hill: University of North Carolina Press, 1961.

———. *War and Society in Revolutionary America: The Wider Dimensions of Conflict*. Columbia: University of South Carolina Press, 1988.

———. *The War of American Independence: Military Attitudes, Policies, and Practice, 1763–1789*. Boston: Northeastern University Press, 1983.

———, ed. *Reconsiderations on the Revolutionary War: Selected Essays*. Westport, Conn.: Greenwood Press, 1978.

Higgins, W. Robert, ed. *The Revolutionary War in the South: Power, Conflict, and Leadership*. Durham, N.C.: Duke University Press, 1979.

Hoffman, Ronald, and Peter J. Albert, eds. *Arms and Independence: The Military Character of the American Revolution*. Charlottesville: University Press of Virginia, 1984.

Hoffman, Ronald, Thad W. Tate, and Peter J. Albert, eds. *An Uncivil War: The Southern Backcountry in the American Revolution*. Charlottesville: University Press of Virginia, 1985.

Jackson, Harvey H., and Phinizy Spalding, eds. *Forty Years of Diversity: Essays on Colonial Georgia*. Athens: University of Georgia Press, 1984.

Johnson, Cecil. *British West Florida, 1763–1783*. New Haven, Conn.: Yale University Press, 1943. Reprint, [Hamden, Conn.:] Archon Books, 1971.

Johnson, Joseph. *Traditions and Reminiscences Chiefly of the American Revolution in the South: Including Biographical Sketches, Incidents and Anecdotes, Few of Which Have Been Published, Particularly of Residents in the Upper Country*. Charleston, S.C.: Walker and James, 1851. Reprint, Spartanburg, S.C.: Reprint Co., 1972.

Jones, Charles C., Jr. *The Life and Services of the Honorable Maj. Gen. Samuel Elbert of Georgia*. Cambridge: Riverside Press, 1887.

Jones, Lewis Pinckney. *The South Carolina Civil War of 1775*. Lexington, S.C.: Sandlapper Store, 1975.

Jordan, Winthrop D. *White over Black: American Attitudes toward the Negro, 1550–1812*. Chapel Hill: University of North Carolina Press, 1968.

Kierner, Cynthia. *Southern Women in Revolution, 1776–1800: Personal and Political Narratives*. Columbia: University of South Carolina Press, 1998.

Klein, Rachel. *Unification of a Slave State: The Rise of the Planter Class in the South Carolina Backcountry, 1760–1808*. Chapel Hill: University of North Carolina Press, 1990.

Krawczynski, Keith. *William Henry Drayton: South Carolina Revolutionary Patriot*. Baton Rouge: Louisiana State University Press, 2001.

Lambert, Robert Stansbury. *South Carolina Loyalists in the American Revolution*. Columbia: University of South Carolina Press, 1987.

Landrum, J. B. O. *Colonial and Revolutionary History of Upper South Carolina: Embracing for the most part the primitive and colonial history of the territory comprising the original county of Spartanburg*. Greenville, S.C.: Shannon Printers, 1897.

Lawrence, Alexander A. *Storm over Savannah: The Story of Count d'Estaing and the Siege of the Town in 1779*. Athens: University of Georgia Press, 1951.

Lipscomb, Terry W. *The Carolina Lowcountry, April 1775–June 1776, and the Battle of Fort Moultrie*. Columbia: South Carolina Department of Archives and History, 1994.

Lossing, Benson J. *The Pictorial Field-book of the Revolution; or, Illustrations, by Pen and Pencil, of the History, Biography, Scenery, Relics, and Traditions of the War for Independence*. 2 vols. New York: Harper, 1851, 1852.

Lumpkin, Henry. *From Savannah to Yorktown: The American Revolution in the South*. New York: Paragon House, 1981.

Lutnick, Solomon. *The American Revolution and the British Press, 1775–1783*. Columbia: University of Missouri Press, 1967.

Mackesy, Piers. *Could the British Have Won the War of Independence?* Worcester, Mass.: Clark University Press, 1976.

———— *The War for America, 1775–1783*. Lincoln: University of Nebraska Press, 1993.

MacLeod, Duncan J. *Slavery, Race and the American Revolution*. Cambridge: Cambridge University Press, 1974.

Maier, Pauline. *From Resistance to Revolution: Colonial Radicals and the Development of American Opposition to Britain, 1765–1776*. New York: W. W. Norton, 1991.

Martin, James Kirby, ed. *The Human Dimensions of Nation Making: Essays on Colonial and Revolutionary America*. Madison: State Historical Society of Wisconsin, 1976.

Mattern, David B. *Benjamin Lincoln and the American Revolution*. Columbia: University of South Carolina Press, 1995.

McCall, Hugh. *The History of Georgia Containing Brief Sketches of the Most Remarkable Events, up to the Present Day*. Savannah: Seymour & Williams, 1811–16.

McCowen, George Smith, Jr. *The British Occupation of Charleston, 1780–1782*. Columbia: University of South Carolina Press, 1972.

McCrady, Edward. *The History of South Carolina in the Revolution, 1775–1780*. New York: Macmillan, 1901. Reprint, New York: Russell & Russell, 1969.

Merrell, James H. *The Indians' New World: Catawbas and Their Neighbors from European Contact through the Era of Removal*. Chapel Hill: University of North Carolina Press, 1989.

Moore, Christopher. *The Loyalists: Revolution, Exile, Settlement.* Toronto: McClelland & Stuart, 1994.

Moore, M. A., Sr. *Life of General Edward Lacey.* Spartanburg, S.C.: Douglass, Evins & Co., 1859. Reprint, Greenville, S.C.: A Press, 1981.

Morrill, Dan. *Southern Campaigns of the American Revolution.* Baltimore: Nautical and Aviation Publishing Company of America, 1993.

Nadelhaft, Jerome J. *The Disorders of War: The Revolution in South Carolina.* Orono: University of Maine at Orono Press, 1981.

Nash, Gary. *Race and Revolution.* Madison, Wis.: Madison House, 1990.

Nelson, Paul David. *Anthony Wayne, Soldier of the Early Republic.* Bloomington: Indiana University Press, 1985.

———. *General Horatio Gates: A Biography.* Baton Rouge: Louisiana State University Press, 1976.

———. *Sir Charles Grey, First Earl Grey: Royal Soldier, Family Patriarch.* Madison/Teaneck, N.J.: Fairleigh Dickinson University Press, 1996.

Nelson, William H. *The American Tory.* London: Oxford University Press, 1961.

Norton, Mary Beth. *The British Americans: The Loyalist Exiles in England, 1774–1789.* Boston: Little, Brown, & Co., 1972.

O'Brien, Greg. *Choctaws in a Revolutionary Age, 1750–1830.* Lincoln: University of Nebraska Press, 2002.

O'Donnell, James H., III. *Southern Indians in the American Revolution.* Knoxville: University of Tennessee Press, 1973.

Okihiro, Gary Y., ed. *In Resistance: Studies in African, Caribbean, and Afro-American History.* Amherst: University of Massachusetts Press, 1986.

Olwell, Robert. *Masters, Slaves, and Subjects: The Culture of Power in the South Carolina Lowcountry, 1740–1790.* Ithaca, N.Y.: Cornell University Press, 1998.

O'Shaughnessy, Andrew Jackson. *An Empire Divided: The American Revolution and the British Caribbean.* Philadelphia: University of Pennsylvania Press, 2000.

Pancake, John S. *This Destructive War: The British Campaign in the Carolinas, 1780–1782.* University: University of Alabama Press, 1985.

Parks, Virginia, ed. *Siege! Spain and Britain: Battle of Pensacola, March 9–May 8, 1781.* Pensacola, Fla.: Pensacola Historical Society, 1981.

Posey, John Thornton. *General Thomas Posey: Son of the American Revolution.* East Lansing: Michigan State University Press, 1992.

Proctor, Samuel, ed. *Eighteenth-Century Florida and the Revolutionary South.* Gainesville: University Presses of Florida, 1978.

Quarles, Benjamin. *The Negro in the American Revolution.* Chapel Hill: University of North Carolina Press, 1996.

Ritcheson, Charles R. *British Politics and the American Revolution.* Norman: University of Oklahoma Press, 1954.

Robertson, Heard. *Loyalism in Revolutionary Georgia.* [Atlanta]: Georgia Commission for the National Bicentennial Celebration and Georgia Department of Education, 1978.

Royster, Charles. *Light-Horse Harry Lee & the Legacy of the American Revolution.* Cambridge: Cambridge University Press, 1982.

———. *A Revolutionary People at War: The Continental Army and American Character, 1775–1783*. New York: W. W. Norton, 1979.

Rush, N. Orwin. *Spain's Final Triumph over Great Britain in the Gulf of Mexico: The Battle of Pensacola, March 9 to May 8, 1781*. Tallahassee: Rose Printing Co., 1966.

Saunt, Claudio. *A New Order of Things: Property, Power, and the Transformation of the Creek Indians, 1733–1816*. Cambridge: Cambridge University Press, 1999.

Searcy, Martha Condray. *The Georgia-Florida Contest in the American Revolution, 1776–1778*. University: University of Alabama Press, 1985.

Selby, John. *Dunmore*. Williamsburg: Virginia Independence Bicentennial Commission, 1977.

Shy, John. *A People Numerous & Armed: Reflections on the Military Struggle for Independence*. Ann Arbor: University of Michigan Press, 1990.

Siebert, Wilbur H. *Loyalists in East Florida, 1774 to 1785: The Most Important Documents Pertaining Thereto Edited with an Accompanying Narrative*. 2 vols. Deland: Florida State Historical Society, 1929.

Smith, Paul H. *Loyalists and Redcoats: A Study in British Revolutionary Policy*. Chapel Hill: University of North Carolina Press, 1964.

Snapp, J. Russell. *John Stuart and the Struggle for Empire on the Southern Frontier*. Baton Rouge: Louisiana State University Press, 1996.

Sosin, Jack M. *The Revolutionary Frontier, 1763–1783*. New York: Holt, Rinehart and Winston, 1967.

Starr, J. Barton. *Tories, Dons, and Rebels: The American Revolution in British West Florida*. Gainesville: University Presses of Florida, 1976.

Stumpf, Vernon O. *Josiah Martin: The Last Royal Governor of North Carolina*. Durham, N.C.: Carolina Academic Press, 1986.

Thayer, Theodore. *Nathanael Greene: Strategist of the Revolution*. New York: Twayne, 1960.

Treacy, M. F. *Prelude to Yorktown: The Southern Campaign of Nathanael Greene, 1780–1781*. Chapel Hill: University of North Carolina Press, 1963.

Ultee, Maarten, ed. *Adapting to Conditions: War and Society in the Eighteenth Century*. University: University of Alabama Press, 1986.

Valentine, Alan. *Lord George Germain*. Oxford: Oxford University Press, 1962.

———. *Lord North*. 2 vols. Norman: University of Oklahoma Press, 1967.

Walsh, Richard. *Charleston's Sons of Liberty: A Study of the Artisans, 1763–1789*. Columbia: University of South Carolina Press, 1959.

Ward, Christopher. *The Delaware Continentals, 1776–1783*. Wilmington: Historical Society of Delaware, 1941.

Ward, Harry M. *Between the Lines: Banditti of the American Revolution*. Westport, Conn.: Praeger, 2002.

Waring, Alice Noble. *The Fighting Elder: Andrew Pickens (1739–1817)*. Columbia: University of South Carolina Press, 1962.

Weigley, Russell F. *The Partisan War: The South Carolina Campaign of 1780–1782*. Columbia: University of South Carolina Press, 1970.

Weir, Robert M. *"A Most Important Epocha": The Coming of the Revolution in South Carolina*. Columbia: University of South Carolina Press, 1970.

White, Richard. *The Roots of Dependency: Subsistence, Environment, and Social Change among the Choctaws, Pawnees, and Navajos.* Lincoln: University of Nebraska Press, 1983.

Wickwire, Franklin, and Mary Wickwire. *Cornwallis: The American Adventure.* Boston: Houghton Mifflin, 1970.

Willcox, William B. *Portrait of a General: Sir Henry Clinton in the War of Independence.* New York: Alfred A. Knopf, 1964.

Wilson, David K. *The Southern Strategy: Britain's Conquest of South Carolina and Georgia, 1775–1780.* Columbia: University of South Carolina Press, 2005.

Wilson, Ellen Gibson. *The Loyal Blacks.* New York: Capricorn Books, 1976.

Wilson, Kathleen. *The Sense of the People: Politics, Culture and Imperialism in England, 1715–1785.* Cambridge: Cambridge University Press, 1995.

Wright, Esmond, ed. *Red, White, and True Blue: The Loyalists in the Revolution.* New York: AMS Press, 1976.

Wright, J. Leitch. *Creeks and Seminoles: The Destruction and Regeneration of the Muscogulge People.* Lincoln: University of Nebraska Press, 1986.

———. *Florida in the American Revolution.* Gainesville: University Presses of Florida, 1975.

———. *The Only Land They Knew: American Indians in the Old South.* Lincoln: University of Nebraska Press, 1999.

Young, Jeffrey Robert. *Domesticating Slavery: The Master Class in Georgia and South Carolina, 1670–1837.* Chapel Hill: University of North Carolina Press, 1999.

Miscellaneous

Simms, William Gilmore. *Eutaw, A Sequel to The Forayers, or the Raid of the Dog-Days: A Tale of the Revolution.* New York: Redfield Co., 1856.

———. *Joscelyn.* Published serially in the *Old Guard*, January–December 1867. Reprint, Spartanburg, S.C.: Reprint Co., 1976.

———. *The Scout; or, the Black Riders of Congaree.* New York: Redfield Co., 1854. Reprint, Atlanta: Martin & Hoyt Co., n.d.

INDEX

Man Killer of Keowee, 66
Manchester, Duke of, 42
Manigault, Gabriel, 78, 95, 241
Manson, Thomas, 134
March (Black Dragoon officer), 317
March (slave), 121
Margate, David, 18
Marion, Francis, 171, 175, 189, 196, 197,
    229–31, 236, 237, 243, 245, 247, 252, 265,
    270, 277, 282, 283–84, 287, 289, 309,
    314, 315, 317–18
Marion, Gabriel, 231
Marrant, John, 82–83
Martin, John, 294, 295, 297, 300–301, 303,
    306, 324, 325, 326
Martin, Joseph, 259
Martin, Josiah, 32, 183
Martin, Laughlin, 45–46
Massey, Samuel, 222
Mathew, Edward, 128
Mathews, John, 287, 288, 289, 290, 313–14,
    318, 320, 321, 322, 323
Mathews, William, 317
May (slave), 218
Mayson, James, 49
McArthur, Archibald, 162, 190
McDowell, Joseph, 197
McDowell, William, 285, 288
McGillivray, Alexander, 112, 114, 156, 212,
    332
McGillivray, John, 107
McGirt, Daniel, 138, 139, 144, 145, 149,
    159, 161–62, 165, 202, 295, 324
McIntosh, John, 262
McIntosh, Lachlan, 60, 74, 91, 111, 113,
    146, 155, 167, 297
McIntosh, William (British Indian agent),
    112, 113, 301
McIntosh, William (Loyalist), 206
McIntosh, William (Whig officer), 62
McKay, James, 301
McLaurin, Evan, 50, 56, 94, 188, 194, 209,
    223, 232
McNeil, Hector, 277
McQueen, John, 319
Middleton, Arthur, 45, 46, 49, 241, 281, 309
Middleton, Henry, 178

Milligen, George, 46
Mills, Ambrose, 187, 190, 199, 201
Mills, William, 267–68
Mingo Pouscouche (Choctaw leader), 213
Moncrief, James, 164–65, 216, 316, 323
Moore, Colonel (Loyalist), 176
Moore, Francis, 304
Moore, Isham, 234
Moore, James (Loyalist officer), 105
Moore, James (Whig officer), 155
Moore, William, 72
Moore's Creek Bridge, North Carolina,
    Battle of, 88
Morgan, Daniel, 228, 234, 236, 237, 239,
    240, 241, 258, 269–70
Morison, John, 316
Morris, Lewis, 237, 287–88, 299, 318
Mortar (Creek leader), 25
Moses (African American Loyalist), 319
Moss, William, 60
Moultrie, John, 23, 62
Moultrie, William, 82, 83, 97, 136, 144,
    153, 154, 161, 165, 166, 176, 182, 243, 323
Mulkey, Rev. Philip, 50
Muncreef, Robert, 266
Murphy, John, 97, 98
Murphy, Maurice, 196
Murray, Sir James, 43, 329–30

Nash, Abner, 181
New River (Catawba leader), 260–61
Neyle, Sampson, 266
Ninety Six, South Carolina: British
    evacuation of (1781), 251–52; Loyalist siege
    of (1775), 54–55; Treaty of (1775), 53; Whig
    siege of (1781), 229, 248, 250–51, 266
Nix, James, 286
nonimportation. See Continental
    Association
North, Frederick, Lord, 36–37, 41, 43, 87,
    181, 278

Oates, Captain, 238
Oath of Allegiance: Georgia, 100; South
    Carolina, 94, 96, 98–99, 100
Oconostota, 69, 109, 299
O'Hara, Charles, 238, 331

ABOUT THE AUTHOR

JIM PIECUCH is an assistant professor of history at Kennesaw State University in Georgia and the author of *The Battle of Camden: A Documentary History.* A former firefighter and newspaper journalist, he earned his M.A. in history from the University of New Hampshire and his Ph.D. degree from the College of William and Mary.